# The Complete Walt Disney World® 2010

Julie and Mike Neal

coconut
press

COCONUT PRESS
Sanibel Florida

# Contents

3 6109 00388 3037

Mickey Mouse and
Donald Duck star in
Mickey's PhilharMagic
at Magic Kingdom

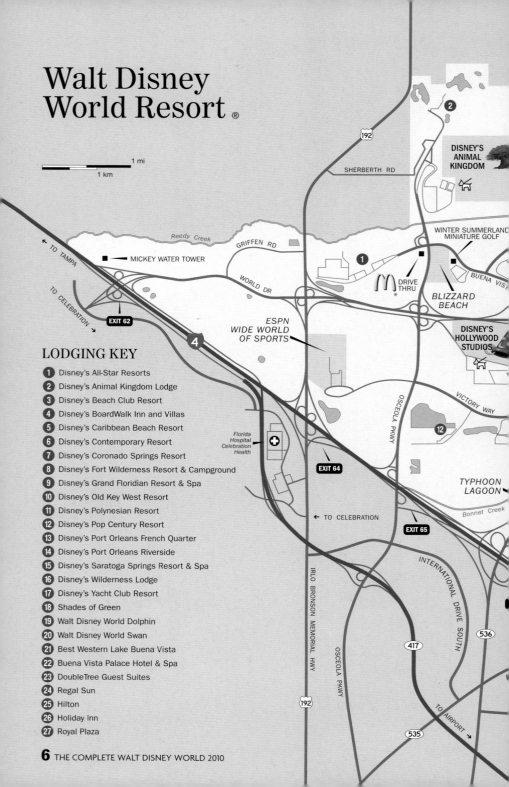

# Walt Disney World Resort ®

1 mi
1 km

MICKEY WATER TOWER

TO TAMPA
TO CELEBRATION
EXIT 62

Reedy Creek
GRIFFEN RD
WORLD DR

192
SHERBERTH RD

DISNEY'S ANIMAL KINGDOM

WINTER SUMMERLAND MINIATURE GOLF

DRIVE THRU

BUENA VIST

BLIZZARD BEACH

DISNEY'S HOLLYWOOD STUDIOS

ESPN WIDE WORLD OF SPORTS

Florida Hospital Celebration Health

VICTORY WAY

OSCEOLA PKWY

TYPHOON LAGOON

Bonnet Creek

EXIT 64

EXIT 65

← TO CELEBRATION

INTERNATIONAL DRIVE SOUTH

IRLO BRONSON MEMORIAL HWY

OSCEOLA PKWY

417

536

535

TO AIRPORT

192

## LODGING KEY

1. Disney's All-Star Resorts
2. Disney's Animal Kingdom Lodge
3. Disney's Beach Club Resort
4. Disney's BoardWalk Inn and Villas
5. Disney's Caribbean Beach Resort
6. Disney's Contemporary Resort
7. Disney's Coronado Springs Resort
8. Disney's Fort Wilderness Resort & Campground
9. Disney's Grand Floridian Resort & Spa
10. Disney's Old Key West Resort
11. Disney's Polynesian Resort
12. Disney's Pop Century Resort
13. Disney's Port Orleans French Quarter
14. Disney's Port Orleans Riverside
15. Disney's Saratoga Springs Resort & Spa
16. Disney's Wilderness Lodge
17. Disney's Yacht Club Resort
18. Shades of Green
19. Walt Disney World Dolphin
20. Walt Disney World Swan
21. Best Western Lake Buena Vista
22. Buena Vista Palace Hotel & Spa
23. DoubleTree Guest Suites
24. Regal Sun
25. Hilton
26. Holiday Inn
27. Royal Plaza

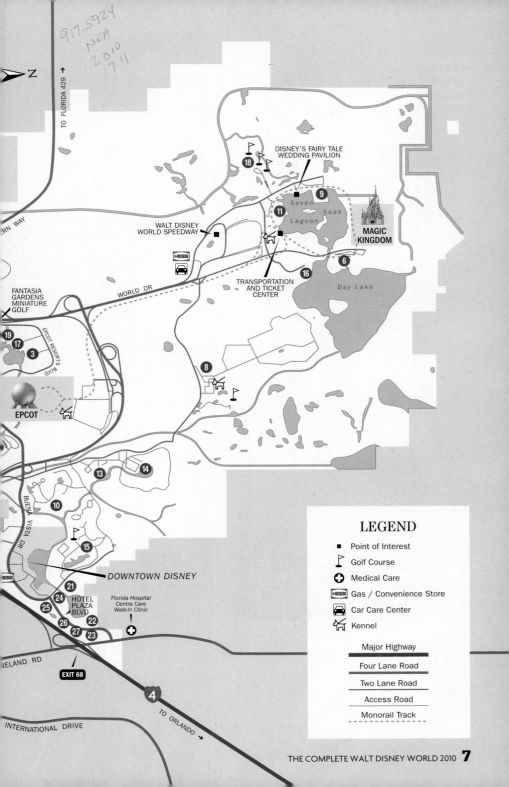

917.5924
NEA
2010
7.11

N

King Louie and Baloo appear in Magic Kingdom's Move It! Shake It! Celebrate It! street party

# What's new

## Here's everything that's different at Disney for 2010

**Have you heard? A new Fantasyland** is coming to Walt Disney World's Magic Kingdom. In the largest expansion in the history of the park, it will include two Dumbo the Flying Elephant rides, a journey under the sea with Ariel, the Little Mermaid, and opportunities to dance with Cinderella and celebrate Sleeping Beauty's birthday with the Good Fairies.

It will be finished in 2013.

In the meantime, there's a lot of new stuff for 2010.

Magic Kingdom has spruced up its iconic Space Mountain, added a robotic President Obama into an all-new Hall of Presidents, debuted a new street party and introduced two new major meet-and-greet characters—Tinker Bell and Princess Tiana. Disney's Hollywood Studios has a new "American Idol" talent show. A tethered balloon, some new shops and restaurants and, unfortunately, some closings have changed the look of Downtown Disney.

A new promotion gives you a free theme-park ticket if you volunteer in your community.

As for accommodations, many hotel rooms have been remodeled, and there are new timeshare complexes.

In the next few pages we will chart all of the World's changes for the new year.

## Magic Kingdom

Yes they did! A robotic Barack Obama has joined **The Hall of Presidents**. In fact, the attraction has been completely redone with a new movie, new narrator (Morgan Freeman) and all-new staging for its Audio-Animatronics presidents. George Washington, Abraham Lincoln and Obama speak... **Tinker Bell** and her fairy friends now pose for pix and sign autographs at the Toontown Hall of Fame... A seven-month, $12 million refurbishment for **Space Mountain** has made the ride more exciting, with a darker, quieter track; faster swoops and drops; a more colorful view of space; and an optional souvenir photo. A portion of the standby queue is lined

with 1970s-style video games... The **Tomorrowland Transit Authority** has new audio narration—no more cheesy "intergalactic spaceport" blather—and lighting... Donald Duck is among the Disney characters who shake their tail feathers at the **Move It! Shake It! Celebrate It! Street Party**. Guests dance with the characters around the hub in front of Cinderella Castle... Dozens of characters now walk with the **Celebrate a Dream Come True Parade**, which recycles floats from former processions... Disney's first African-American princess, **Tiana** of the 2009 movie "The Princess and the Frog," greets guests and signs autographs with **Prince Naveen** in a Mardi Gras-themed area in Liberty Square. It's near the bridge from Cinderella Castle, next to the Christmas shop... The new **Pirates League** makeover salon transforms adults and children into cosmetic swashbucklers. The shop is at the exit to Pirates of the Caribbean... Say goodbye to the long-empty **Tomorrowland Skyway Station**. It was demolished and removed in 2009. The restrooms beneath it have been remodeled.

## Epcot

You use a cell-phone-like "Kimmunicator" to get clues and manipulate items in the World Showcase in the unique high-tech scavenger hunt **Kim Possible World Showcase Adventure**... New **Innoventions** corporate exhibits include The Great Piggy Bank Adventure (financial planning from T. Rowe Price); IBM's Runtime, which lets families record videos of themselves and use them

The American Idol Experience, Disney's Hollywood Studios

The Hall of Presidents, Magic Kingdom

in a video game; and Raytheon's The Sum of All Thrills, an ambitious math-based exhibit which lets you create your own attraction and then ride it on a robotic arm simulator... The **Living with the Land** boat ride reopened in late 2009 after a refurbishment... At Test Track, the post-show area now displays a **Chevy Volt** Extended Range Electric Vehicle, in particular the modified "Jolt" car that appeared in the 2009 movie "Transformers: Revenge of the Fallen"... Gourmand rat **Remy,** star of the 2007 Disney-Pixar film "Ratatouille," appears as a small Audio-Animatronics creature at Chefs de France... At the Japan pavilion, the Tin Toy exhibit has been replaced by **Timeless Beauty: World Heritage Sites of Japan**... Mexico's new **La Cava del Tequila** bar offers 70 varieties and a "tequila ambassador" to teach guests the history of the drink... The **Kidcot** children's arts-and-crafts stations in Future World have been removed. They remain in World Showcase.

## Disney's Hollywood Studios

The **American Idol Experience** talent contest lets guests compete on a set modeled after the one used on the "American Idol" television series... A street show, **High School Musical 3: Right Here! Right Now!** features songs from the third High School Musical movie... **Luxo Jr.**, Pixar's hopping desk-lamp mascot, meets guests and performs in Pixar Place... Nighttime extravaganza **Fantasmic** is now performed only a few nights a week... The indoor **ABC Commissary** no longer serves breakfast. Instead, it's offered at the outdoor **Fairfax Fare** food court on Sunset Blvd.... The **Sounds Dangerous** sound-effects show is now open only seasonally... The ambient sound inside the **Once Upon a Time** gift shop is now the actual radio broadcast of the 1937 premiere of Disney's "Snow White and the Seven Dwarfs." The event was held at the store's

**Magic Kingdom's refurbished Space Mountain includes new ceilings in the loading areas that keep the ride itself dark**

architectural inspiration, Hollywood's Carthay Circle theater... Kids can draw and color at a **new arts and craft area** near the exit of Rock 'n' Roller Coaster Starring Aerosmith... The colorful chicken coop featured in the 2009 film "Hannah Montana: The Movie" is now a prop on the **Studio Backlot Tour**... That tour's **AFI Villains exhibit** now features a creature costume from 1986's "Aliens" and clothing from 2007's "Enchanted"... That huge **Coca-Cola bottle** in front of the Studio Backlot Tour has been replaced. It opens to spray mist... Newly painted: the hot air balloon outside **MuppetVision 3-D** and **Mickey's Sorcerer's Hat**, the icon of the park.

## Disney's Animal Kingdom

You don't need cash anymore to play the **Fossil Fun Games** in Dino-Rama. Instead, you buy vouchers (with cash or plastic) at the Shop Till You're Dizzy cart. The price for each game has increased from $2 to $2.50... At **Festival of the Lion King,** host Timon's eyes now blink and move... Two male giraffes—Bolo and Bruehler—were born at Animal Kingdom in October, 2009. They were the 13th and 14th giraffes born at the park... Amphibian windows at **Conservation Station** now display unusual frogs, newts, salamanders and toads... **Primeval Whirl** has been repainted... Families can order a **Picnic in the Park** packaged lunch for three to six people. It's packed in an "Every Tree Has Character" reusable bag... There's finally a sign for the **Asian catfish.** Located on Discovery Island near the bridge to Africa, this huge paroon shark-catfish had been lurking in obscurity for years.

## Water parks

Summer guests can now meet **Goofy** at Blizzard Beach, **Lilo and Stitch** at Typhoon Lagoon... For $250 a day guests can rent shady cabana-style areas with lounge chairs and tables, all-day drink mugs, bottled water, private lockers, towels and an attendant. Blizzard Beach has four **Polar Patios**; Typhoon Lagoon four **Beachcomber Shacks.** (Who would do that?)

## Downtown Disney

**Characters in Flight**, a tethered helium-filled balloon, takes guests on rides 400 feet above the West Side... The **Virgin Megastore** and **Starabilias** memorabilia shop closed in 2009... New Pleasure Island restaurant and bar **Paradiso 37** features "street cuisine" from North, South and Central America and nightly entertainment... All Pleasure Island **nightclubs** were closed in 2008... Elaborately themed Marketplace restaurant **T-Rex: A Prehistoric Family Adventure** opened in late 2008. It's from the Rainforest Cafe folks... Stocking fashionable junior apparel, **Tren-D** has replaced Summer Sands.

## Sports and rec

The **ESPN Wide World of Sports** complex is installing large video screens at many of its venues, to give parents and other spectators close-up views of its youth sporting events... Disney has introduced two new **tours.** Epcot's Nature-Inspired Design includes a trip backstage on a Segway. Holiday DeLites includes a viewing of Epcot's Candlelight Processional... **Surfing lessons** have resumed at Typhoon Lagoon... The **Richard Petty Driving Experience** has lowered the minimum age for its ride-along program to 14; previously it was 16... The **Pirates & Pals Fireworks Voyage**, formerly the Magical Fireworks Voyage, is now open to all guests, not just those booking Disney's Grand Gatherings... Two foot races are no more: **Disney's Race for the Taste** during the Epcot International Food and Wine Festival, and the **Twilight Zone Tower of Terror 13K** through Disney's Hollywood Studios... A new race, the **Wine & Dine Half Marathon,** will pass through multiple theme parks and end at Epcot's Food & Wine Festival. It will be held Oct. 1 and 2.

**Tinker Bell now greets guests at Magic Kingdom**

TINKER BELL PHOTO: MICAELA NEAL

Kidani Village Grand Villa,
Disney's Animal Kingdom Lodge

## Accommodations

Rooms at **Disney's Coronado Springs Resort** have undergone an extensive renovation that includes flat-screen TVs and all-new furnishings and carpet... **Disney's Caribbean Beach Resort** has redone some rooms in a pirate theme; all others now have subtle "Finding Nemo" decor... **Fort Wilderness Resort and Campground** has added archery lessons, as well as bicycle and surrey rentals... The **Downtown Disney Holiday Inn** is scheduled to reopen this year, just as it was the past two years. The resort was heavily damaged during the 2004 hurricane season and has been closed since... Three new Disney Vacation Club (timeshare) properties opened in 2009: **Bay Lake Tower** at Disney's Contemporary Resort, **Kidani Village** at Disney's Animal Kingdom Lodge and **Treehouse Villas** at Disney's Saratoga Springs Resort... A **Four Seasons** hotel, golf course and vacation-home complex is being built on the site of the former Eagle Pines golf course... First announced for 2009, a **luxury pet resort** is now promised for 2010-2011. To be located on Bonnet Creek Parkway, it will offer luxury suites with televisions, raised bedding, nature walks, ice cream treats and bedtime stories.

## Restaurants

New resort restaurants include **Kouzzina,** with recipes from Iron Chef Cat Cora, at the BoardWalk Resort (replacing Spoodles); **The Wave** at the Contemporary Resort (replacing Concourse Steakhouse); and East African/Indian **Sanaa** at the new Kidani Village at Animal Kingdom Lodge... **Dining reservations** can now be made online at disneyworld.disney.go.com/dining... Effective Feb. 7, 2010, all meals at **Cinderella's Royal Table** (in Magic Kingdom's Cinderella Castle) will feature Cinderella in the lobby and other Disney princesses mingling with guests in the dining room. The experience is now Fairytale Dining...

The basic **Disney Dining Plan** has increased from $42 to $47 per adult per day... The **Tables in Wonderland discount card**, which saves its holders 20 percent on most Disney restaurant meals, now costs $100 a year for Florida residents, up from $85... Walt Disney World no longer sells **all-beef hot dogs.** The World's weiners are now a mixture of beef and chicken... **Candlelight Processional Dinner Packages**, which include a meal at an Epcot restaurant and guaranteed seating for that show, now require two Disney Dining Plan credits instead of one.

## Practical matters

A one-day "base" **theme-park ticket** now costs $79 for adults, up from $75... Other price increases include theme-park **parking** (now $14 per day) and hotel valet parking ($12)... Introduced late in 2009, **Mobile Magic** is the first Disney-developed mobile application. It lets guests easily navigate Disney parks and access an array of park features on their Verizon Wireless phones. The application costs $9.99 for a 180-day subscription... A new mobile web site, **mdisneyworld.com**, offers a handy overview of the resort... Disney is experimenting with a centralized **Fastpass distribution system** where guests can pick up multiple Fastpasses at one location... A new handheld device delivers **audio description** of visual images at 33 attractions for use by the blind; the same device has captions for hearing-impaired guests... You can now order over 500 theme-park merchandise items online at **DisneyStore.com**.

A baby giraffe, Disney's Animal Kingdom

## New promotion

**"Give a Day, Get a Disney Day"** hopes to inspire families to volunteer in their communities. One million volunteers will receive a free one-day ticket to a Walt Disney World theme park. Starting Jan. 1, 2010, Disneyparks.com will list opportunities and include registration forms. An entire family can volunteer, but participants must be at least 6 years of age.

## Special events

Magic Kingdom's **Totally Tomorrowland Christmas** show has replaced **Twas the Night Before Christmas.** At Epcot, **Lights of Winter** has been removed; gospel choir **D'Vine Voices** has been added.

**Headin' to Walt Disney World? With this book, the Internet and a cell phone, it's easy to plan your trip.**

VA 4053366    VA 6576257

SEP   **VIRGINIA**   09

# HDN2 WDW

# Planning YourTrip

## With just a little bit of preparation, it's easy to put together a terrific Walt Disney World vacation

**Planning your Walt Disney World trip** takes some thought, but it isn't brain surgery. All it takes is this book, access to the Internet, a cell phone and a few hours of your time. You can do it at Starbucks. Ideally you should put your plan together seven months early. Here's how to do it:

## 1. Decide when to go

You can have a good time at Walt Disney World any day of the year, but if you've got the flexibility, the first two weeks of December is the **best time to go.** It's not crowded, and there's more to see and do than any other time of the year, thanks to the holiday decor and entertainment. Crowds are also light, and hotel rooms often less expensive, from mid-January to Valentine's Day, late April to late May and the weeks between Labor Day and mid-November (but it's not all good: some attractions shut down during these periods and Magic Kingdom often closes at 6 p.m.). The least crowded week of the year is the one that starts the day after Labor Day.

The **worst times to visit?** July and early August, when crowds are thick and the air even thicker, and between Christmas and New Year's, when the crowds are incredible. In general, the parks can be packed any time schools are not in session. In fact, many families take their kids out of school to visit Disney World in a less-crowded period. If you come during a peak time, you do get the benefit of the parks being open late into the evening.

For detailed **weather data** log on to weather.com, type in the ZIP code 32830 and then scroll down to the tab "Averages."

**Cinderella Castle, Magic Kingdom**

## 2. Plan how long to stay

Want to see the best of everything Disney World has to offer? You'll need at least a week. Each theme park takes at least a day to fully enjoy, and you can easily spend a day at both water parks. Diversions such as golf and horseback riding add variety to your trip.

If you can't stay that long, three days is enough to get a fun dose of Disney if you have a good plan. You'll find "Magical Day" itineraries in every theme-park chapter in this book.

## 3. Decide where to stay

You have hundreds of choices. Disney itself operates 19 resorts, and nearly every hotel chain known to man has at least one property within 10 miles. This book's Accommodations chapter (page 282) reviews every Disney resort and every hotel of at least 3-star quality within 10 miles.

## 4. Buy airline tickets

The Orlando International Airport (airport code MCO) is about 20 miles (30 minutes) from Walt Disney World. It's served by 33 airlines, including American, Delta, Frontier, Southwest, United, U.S. Airways and Air Canada. (Driving? Walt Disney World is 15 miles south of downtown Orlando on Interstate 4. See complete driving directions on page 35.)

## 5. Decide what to do

Take a few minutes to thumb through this book's chapters on Walt Disney World theme parks (pages 40, 116, 162, and 206), water parks (page 256) and Downtown Disney (page 266) and Sports and Recreation (page 274). If you have children, have them look over this book and pick out their favorites.

## 6. Choose park tickets

A review of Disney's unusual Magic Your Way ticketing system starts on page 22.

## 7. Book it!

Book your park tickets and, if you decide to stay at a Disney resort, your room at **disneyworld.com**, or call Disney at 407-934-7639 between 7 a.m. and 10 p.m. Eastern time.

## 8. Plan your days

First, determine what days to go to what theme parks. If you're staying at a Disney resort, you'll want to take advantage of Extra Magic Hours, which offer additional time in the parks when crowds are relatively light. Log on to **disneyworld.disney.go.com/calendars** and click "Calendar" to find the hours, Extra Magic Hours, special events and parade and fireworks schedules for the theme parks during the days of your stay (available six months in advance).

CASTLE PHOTO © DISNEY

Wacky Star Wars
Weekends storm
Disney's Hollywood
Studios each spring

## 9. Make reservations

You will find restaurant reviews in our chapters on theme parks, Downtown Disney and accommodations. Disney restaurant reservations (407-939-3463 or online at **disneyworld.disney.go.com/ dining**) can be made 180 days in advance, or 190 days early if you're staying at a Disney owned-and-operated resort hotel. Dinner shows take reservations a year in advance.

In general, character meals and dinner shows book the quickest. For recreation, you can book fishing and surfing a year out, tours and stock car driving six months in advance, boat cruises and golf tee times 30 days early (90 days for Disney resort guests) and water sports 30 days early. Other reservations to consider: Birthday parties, florist services, special events, and Cirque du Soleil's La Nouba. For telephone numbers for these spots and more see the directory on the last page of this book.

## 10. Need to rent a car?

If you stay at a Disney resort hotel, the complimentary Disney transportation system makes it possible to avoid renting a car. Its speed and efficiency varies by resort, however; those Disney hotels offering only bus service are often more quickly served by automobile. You can rent a car at the airport, or from many places on Disney property including the Car Care Center, the Walt Disney World Dolphin Resort and the Downtown Disney Hilton.

When making your plan, keep in mind the five most common mistakes guests make when they visit Disney World:
▶ **They don't get to a theme park** first thing in the morning, before it opens.
▶ **They don't use Fastpass.**
▶ **They underestimate** how long it takes to travel on Disney transportation.
▶ **They don't make reservations** at restaurants before they leave home.
▶ **They wear themselves out.**

# A world of its own

Twice the size of Manhattan, the 47-square-mile Walt Disney World is the No. 1 vacation destination on the planet. It includes four theme parks, two water parks, a sports complex, a shopping and entertainment district and 19 resort hotels. A visit here is not just an escape from day-to-day doldrums, it's a reawakening of that free-spirited, good-natured soul who lives deep inside you—the one your spouse married, the one you want your children to emulate. No other man-made vacation-land so embraces creativity, optimism or a sense of wonder about the world.

## Magic Kingdom

It's only 122 acres, just 0.5 percent of Walt Disney World, but to many folks the Magic Kingdom simply *is* Walt Disney World. The most popular theme park in the (real) world, this family favorite has more than 40 attractions, many based on classic Disney animated films and characters. Best bets include household names such as it's a small world, Pirates of the Caribbean and Space Mountain. Iconic lands include Main Street U.S.A.

## Epcot

Sort of a permanent World's Fair, this 300-acre park showcases nature and science in its Future World and celebrates the cultures of 11 nations in its World Showcase. Future World attractions include simulators that offer realistic sensations of hang gliding (Soarin') and astronaut training (Mission Space). Staffed by natives of the countries it represents, World Showcase is highlighted by unique shopping, dining and entertainment.

## Disney's Hollywood Studios

This intimate park celebrates show biz with stage musicals, stunt performances and thrill rides. Fans of Pixar films will enjoy the ride-through 3-D video game Toy Story Mania as well as a street party themed to that studio, Block Party Bash. Other top attractions include two thrill rides, the Twilight Zone Tower of Terror and the Rock 'n' Roller Coaster Starring Aerosmith. The front half of the 135-acre park is a tribute to Old Hollywood.

## Disney's Animal Kingdom

Themed to the world's conservation movement, this lushly landscaped park combines exotic live animals with high-quality attractions that focus on the natural world, in particular that of Asia and Africa. The park contains many subtle references to Disney's 1994 movie "The Lion King." A separate tongue-in-cheek area is devoted to dinosaurs. Top stops include Expedition Everest, a roller coaster that travels backward into a mountain cave.

## Water parks

On a summer morning it's hard to beat the family fun at Disney's two themed water parks. Thrilling body and tube slides—including Teamboat Springs, the world's longest family tube ride and the terrifying Summit Plummet—highlight the melting-ski-resort theme of Blizzard Beach. Set in a tropical landscape, storm-ravaged Typhoon Lagoon includes a surf pool, Crush 'n' Gusher water coaster, lush Castaway Creek lazy river and saltwater snorkeling.

## Downtown Disney

This 120-acre dining, entertainment and shopping district sits on the eastern edge of Walt Disney World. The West Side area includes Cirque du Soleil's La Nouba musical circus and a House of Blues. Pleasure Island was until 2008 a nightclub hot spot; today it contains only shops and restaurants. The Downtown Disney Marketplace is a 1970s-vintage open-air shopping mall. It has 25 shops, including the World of Disney, Disney World's largest gift shop.

## Sports and recreation

Disney World has four championship 18-hole golf courses as well as a walking 9-hole and two miniature-golf centers. Other recreation options include fishing, tennis, horseback and pony rides, Segway tours, the Richard Petty Driving Experience and various water sports. The 220-acre ESPN Wide World of Sports complex hosts amateur and professional competitions. It includes a baseball stadium, two fieldhouses and many outdoor fields.

## Disney characters

A hug from Snow White. A kiss from Minnie Mouse. A dance with Goofy. Stars of Disney (and Pixar) movies and cartoons interact with guests throughout Walt Disney World, in greeting lines, character meals, parades and street parties. Characters include vintage stars, obscure oddballs (hello, Mr. Smee!) and modern celebrities such as Princess Tiana from "The Princess and the Frog." The most popular is Tinker Bell, who appears only at Magic Kingdom.

## Cast members

The world's largest single-site employer, Walt Disney World employs more than 54,000 people, all of which Disney calls cast members. Its workforce wardrobe consists of 2,500 different "costumes" (there are no "uniforms") comprised of 1.8 million separate pieces. New hires learn the Disney Way, which includes a strict code of behavior. Among the lessons: always point with two fingers, as not to offend international guests.

# Tickets Walt Disney World's unconventional 'Magic Your Way' ticketing concept offers a variety of options. Here's a guide through it.

Though Walt Disney World's Magic Your Way ticket plan is promoted as a way to let guests create tickets that match their particular needs, it's also so complicated that, at first glance, it can seem impossible to understand. In this article, we hope to explain it in a simple, easy-to-understand manner.

In a nutshell, Disney's plan lets you tailor tickets to include from one to 10 days of theme park visits, and then add options such as the ability to visit more than one park a day or spend time at Disney's water parks. You can also add a prepaid dining plan, itself with various options, some of which include recreation activities.

To buy tickets from the Disney company go to **disneyworld.disney.go.com/tickets-passes** or call 407-W-DISNEY (934-7639) from 7 a.m. to 10 p.m. Eastern time. Orlando Fun Tickets sells discounted park passes at **orlandofuntickets.com** or 866-225-4712.

## Base tickets

Let's start with the basic theme-park ticket, which Disney calls the Base Ticket. It provides admission to one Disney World theme park per day, and is good for up to 10 days. The more days it includes, the cheaper the per-day expense becomes. This difference is substantial. For example, the difference between a three-day ticket and a seven-day ticket is just $15. The days the ticket is used for admission do not need to be consecutive, but it expires 14 days after its first use. Base Tickets have three options:

▶ **Park Hopper** lets you visit more than one Walt Disney World theme park a day. Its price ($52) is the same regardless of the number of days the ticket is good for. Some potential benefits of the Park Hopper option include the ability to ❶ go to one park during the day, then another at night to see its fireworks show, ❷ sample a variety of theme parks during a short visit and ❸ easily revisit favorite individual attractions.

▶ **Water Park Fun & More** adds visits to Disney's water parks, DisneyQuest, ESPN Wide World of Sports complex and/or rounds of golf at Disney's 9-hole Oak Trail walking golf course, in any combination. Like the Park Hopper option, the price of

this option ($52) is fixed, but the number of admissions it provides varies by the number of days the ticket is good for. Regardless, if you use this option at least twice during your visit it pays for itself.

▶ **No Expiration** ($18–$209, depending on how many days your ticket includes) means unused days never expire. You can add it anytime within 14 days of your first use. The cost of this option varies based on the number of days the ticket was originally good for.

Disney offers discounts for Florida residents and members of the U.S. military. For other discounts see the article a few pages forward titled "Saving Money." Once you buy your tickets, you can always upgrade them but can't downgrade them.

## Annual passes

Plan on visiting Disney more than once this year? An **annual pass** gives you 365 consecutive days of admission to the four theme parks, plus perks such as theme-park parking and discounts on dining, entertainment and merchandise. A Premium option adds admission to water parks, DisneyQuest and ESPN Wide World of Sports. Discounts are available for Florida residents, members of the U.S. military, Disney Vacation Club members and charter annual passholders.

## The Disney Dining Plan

Disney resort guests and Disney Vacation Club members can add a prepaid Disney Dining Plan to their ticket purchase, which can include a variety of dining and even recreation options. Over a hundred Disney restaurants participate. There are five packages available.

▶ **The Basic Plan** (Per day: $42 A, $12 C Jan. 1–Feb 11, April 11–June 3, Aug. 18–Dec 16; $47 A, $13 C other dates) includes one table-service meal, one fast food ("quick-service") meal and one snack per person, per night of your Disney stay.

▶ **The Deluxe Plan** (Per day: $72 A, $21 C) gives you three daily meals at table-service restaurants and comes with two snacks and a refillable drink mug for use at your resort.

▶ **The Quick-Service Plan** (Per day: $32 A, $10 C) includes two counter-service meals and two snacks per day, plus a refillable mug.

# WALT DISNEY WORLD TICKET PRICES

This table shows Walt Disney World ticket prices as of January 1, 2010. Other annual and seasonal options are available for Florida residents and military members. For more information go to **disneyworld.disney.go.com/tickets-passes** or call Disney at 407-934-7639.

| GENERAL PUBLIC | 1-Day | 2-Day | 3-Day | 4-Day | 5-Day | 6-Day | 7-Day | 8-Day | 9-Day | 10-Day |
|---|---|---|---|---|---|---|---|---|---|---|
| Base ticket ages 10+ | $79 | $156 | $219 | $225 | $228 | $231 | $234 | $237 | $240 | $243 |
| Base ticket ages 3–9 | $68 | $133 | $187 | $192 | $195 | $198 | $201 | $204 | $207 | $210 |
| Park Hopper option | $52 | $52 | $52 | $52 | $52 | $52 | $52 | $52 | $52 | $52 |
| Water Park Fun & More | $52 | $52 | $52 | $52 | $52 | $52 | $52 | $52 | $52 | $52 |
| No expiration | N/A | $18 | $24 | $52 | $73 | $84 | $115 | $152 | $178 | $209 |

Tickets expire 14 days from date of first use unless No Expiration option is purchased. Tax not included.

| FLORIDA RESIDENTS | 1-Day | 2-Day | 3-Day | 4-Day | 5-Day | 6-Day | 7-Day | 8-Day | 9-Day | 10-Day |
|---|---|---|---|---|---|---|---|---|---|---|
| Base ticket ages 10+ | $71.10 | N/A | $134 | $164 | $201 | $216 | $219 | N/A | N/A | N/A |
| Base ticket ages 3–9 | $57.50 | N/A | $139 | $139 | $172 | $184 | $187 | N/A | N/A | N/A |
| Park Hopper option | $26 | N/A | $26 | $26 | $26 | $26 | $26 | N/A | N/A | N/A |
| Water Park Fun & More | $26 | N/A | $26 | $26 | $26 | $26 | $26 | N/A | N/A | N/A |
| No expiration | N/A | N/A | $24 | $36 | $46 | $76 | $112 | N/A | N/A | N/A |

Tickets expire 6 months from activation date unless No Expiration option is purchased. Tax not included.

| U.S. MILITARY | 1-Day | 2-Day | 3-Day | 4-Day | 5-Day | 6-Day | 7-Day | 8-Day | 9-Day | 10-Day |
|---|---|---|---|---|---|---|---|---|---|---|
| Base ticket ages 10+ | $77 | $152 | $202 | $208 | $210 | $213 | $216 | $219 | $221 | $223 |
| Base ticket ages 3–9 | $66 | $130 | $172 | $177 | $179 | $182 | $185 | $188 | $191 | $193 |
| Park Hopper option | $52 | $52 | $52 | $52 | $52 | $52 | $52 | $52 | $52 | $52 |
| Water Park Fun & More | $52 | $52 | $52 | $52 | $52 | $52 | $52 | $52 | $52 | $52 |
| No expiration | N/A | $18 | $24 | $52 | $73 | $84 | $115 | $152 | $178 | $209 |
| Stars & Stripes ages 10+ | N/A | $243 | $299 | $305 | $308 | $310 | $313 | $316 | $319 | $322 |
| Stars & Stripes ages 3–9 | N/A | $221 | $270 | $274 | $277 | $280 | $283 | $285 | $288 | $291 |

Standard tickets expire 14 days from date of first use unless No Expiration option is purchased. Tax not included. **Stars & Stripes ticket** entitles military guest staying at Shades of Green or Disney-owned resort to unlimited admission to all Walt Disney World theme and water parks, DisneyQuest and Disney's ESPN Wide World of Sports complex as well as complimentary parking, except activities and events separately priced. Expires one day longer than the number of days on the ticket. Tax not included.

| ANNUAL PASSES | 10+ | 3–9 | 10+ R | 3–9 R | 10+ D | 3–9 D | 10+ DR | 3–9 DR | 10+ C | 3–9 C |
|---|---|---|---|---|---|---|---|---|---|---|
| Regular | $489 | $432 | $449 | $397 | $389 | $344 | $344 | $304 | $391 | $346 |
| Premium | $619 | $546 | $569 | $502 | $494 | $436 | $454 | $401 | $494 | $438 |
| Fla. Resident Regular | $369 | $325 | $334 | $295 | $364 | $322 | $295 | $261 | $295 | $261 |
| Fla. Resident Premium | $489 | $431 | $444 | $392 | $463 | $406 | $391 | $345 | $391 | $345 |
| U.S. Military Regular | $480 | $424 | | | | | | | | |
| U.S. Military Premium | $607 | $536 | | | | | | | | |
| Military/FL Res. Reg. | $362 | $319 | | | | | | | | |
| Military/FL Res. Prem. | $480 | $424 | | | | | | | | |

**R: Renewal. D: DVC member. DR: DVC member renewal. C: Charter.** Annual Pass entitles guest to unlimited admission for 365 days from the activation date (except activities/events separately priced) to all Walt Disney World theme parks and free parking. Premium passes add admission to water parks, Disney's Oak Trail golf course, DisneyQuest and Disney's ESPN Wide World of Sports complex. No block-out dates. Tax not included.

▶ **The Premium Plan** If you want an active vacation but don't need much time in the parks, this plan (Per day: $164 A, $114 C) can actually be a great deal. It gives you unlimited use of many recreation options, including golf and water sports. Like the Deluxe plan, you get three meals a day and all can be in table-service restaurants. The package also adds vouchers to La Nouba, unlimited use of child-care facilities and unlimited theme-park tours. You need to buy at least a one-day park ticket. Book the plan six months early to cherry-pick recreation times.

▶ **The Platinum Plan** (Per day: $220 A, $155 C, available to guests of Disney Deluxe and Vacation Club resorts) includes everything in the Premium Plan and adds extras such as an itinerary planning service, a spa treatment and a fireworks cruise.

Available with any plan, a **Wine and Dine** option (about $40 A) adds a bottle of wine each evening of your stay, redeemable at a range of restaurants and merchandise locations.

### How the Dining Plan works

You can use Disney Dining Plan meals and snack credits in any combination during your stay. For example, you can eat all table-service meals one day, all fast-food meals the next, and nothing but snacks the day after that. If one person in your party uses up his or her plan, others can continue to use theirs. Disney defines a breakfast meal as one single-serving of juice, one entree and one beverage; or a combo meal and a beverage or juice. Lunch and dinner are defined as one entree, one dessert and one beverage; or a combo meal, dessert and beverage. Plans have four key conditions:

▶ **They are sold per party,** not per person. If one person in your party buys a Dining Plan, everyone else must, too. The only exception: children under age 3. They can eat from an adult's plate at no extra charge.

▶ **Children 3–9 must order from a kid's menu** when one is available. Likewise, those over 10 can't do so.

▶ **Some restaurants charge two credits for one meal,** including Disney Signature restaurants, dinner shows and Cinderella's Royal Table at Magic Kingdom. Room-service meals at Disney Deluxe Resorts ("in-room dining") charge two credits, too.

▶ **You can't take it with you.** Apparently inspired by Cinderella's magical accoutrements, unused meals and snacks expire at midnight on your checkout date.

To use the Dining Plan, you present your Key to the World card (room key) to your cashier or server. Your food usage is tracked electronically; your receipt will show your balance of that particular meal type. Summaries of your balances are available from your hotel concierge.

Nearly every Disney-owned restaurant participates in the Dining Plan, as do snack locations such as food carts and sweet shops. Tips are not included; neither are alcoholic beverages, some bottled drinks, souvenir or refillable drink mugs (except in the Deluxe and Quick-Service plans) or snacks and beverages from recreation rental counters. In this book, participating Dining Plan restaurants are indicated by one of three symbols:

**DP** Accepts table-service credits
**DP2** Requires 2 table-service credits
**DPQ** Accepts quick-service credits

### How to use it wisely

If you take advantage of it, the Dining Plan will give you great food and memorable meals. Handle it poorly, however, and your magical vacation can include a frustrating waste of time and money. Here are four keys to getting the most for your money:

▶ **Don't overestimate your hunger** When determining which plan to purchase, keep in mind that it's tough to eat enough food to justify having three table-service meals a day. It's also hard to dine at more than *one* Signature Restaurant a day, as each takes hours to fully experience.

▶ **Use your credits efficiently** Except for those at Signature Restaurants, nearly all table-service meals are considered equal. In most cases, dining with Cinderella or Lilo and Stitch at an all-you-can-eat feast uses no more credits than getting a hamburger at Magic Kingdom's Plaza or a fish sandwich at Cap'n Jack's at Downtown Disney.

▶ **Know where the deals are** Though the Dining Plan charges you the same amount—one credit—for most meals, some restaurants offer better values. Great breakfast buffets include Boma at Animal Kingdom Lodge and the 1900 Park Fare character meal at the Grand Floridian Resort. For lunch, you'll get a great value at Coral Reef and Le Cellier in Epcot and Sanaa at Disney's Animal Kingdom Lodge. For dinner, consider Boma, 1900 Park Fare or Kouzzina at the BoardWalk Resort. Good quick-service choices include Earl of Sandwich at Downtown Disney, Flame Tree Barbecue and Pizzafari at Animal Kingdom and Sunshine Seasons at The Land pavilion at Epcot.

▶ **Make reservations far in advance** so you can dine at places that best suit your needs.

© DISNEY

Guests meet
Mickey Mouse
at the Chef
Mickey's
character meal

A stilt walker dances in Mickey's Jammin' Jungle Parade at Disney's Animal Kingdom

Guests at the Contemporary, Grand Floridian and Polynesian resorts are whisked to Magic Kingdom and Epcot on elevated monorail trains

# Saving time You *could* spend your Disney vacation waiting in long lines, but you don't have to. Here's how to control your time.

## Use Fastpasses

▶ **What it is** You'll skip the line at Disney's top attractions by using this *free* automated reservation system. It allows you to use an express line, at a window of time later in the day, at particular rides that you select. To get a Fastpass, you insert your park ticket into an attraction's Fastpass machine, which is located at its entrance. The machine returns your ticket with your Fastpass.

▶ **How it works** When you insert your park ticket into a Fastpass machine, you get back a small card that shows your reservation time, which is a one-hour window. When you return, you show that card and enter the ride or show through a separate entrance that has little or no wait. You can't pick your return time, but displays at each Fastpass-machine bank show you what it will be before you insert your ticket. You can get additional Fastpasses throughout a day, but not more than once every hour or two. The Fastpass service is not well understood, so only about half of all visitors use it.

▶ **How to take advantage of it** Follow this four-step plan and you'll save literally hours waiting in line: ❶ Designate someone in your group as your Fastpass manager. This person will hold everyone's park tickets, head off now and then to get Fastpasses, and keep track of when each pass is valid and when to get more. This information is shown on each Fastpass. ❷ Always hold at least one Fastpass, so you're always on the clock for at least one attraction. Pick one up first thing when you arrive at a park, then get others throughout the day. ❸ Don't sweat it if you miss your return time. Disney doesn't enforce the end time. ❹ Use the service for every Fastpass attraction except those you'll be riding before 10 a.m.

## Use Single Rider lines

▶ **What they are** Single Rider lines are for those who don't mind experiencing a ride without their family or friends. Four Disney rides have one: Mission Space and Test Track at Epcot, Rock 'n' Roller Coaster Starring Aerosmith at Disney's Hollywood Studios and Expedition Everest at Disney's Animal Kingdom. There's also a Single Rider line at the Blizzard Beach chair lift, which offers a speedy way up to that water park's main body and mat slides.

▶ **How it works** When ride operators can't fill a vehicle from guests in a regular line without breaking up a group, they take a guest from a Single Rider line. During peak periods, using this line can cut your wait time by at least 30 minutes.

## Use Extra Magic Hours
▶ **What they are** Each day at least one Disney theme park or water park opens an hour early or stays open three hours later exclusively for the use of guests staying at Disney-owned resorts or the Walt Disney World Swan and Dolphin, Shades of Green or Downtown Disney Hilton. Most major attractions are open. *On a day when a park offers an Extra Magic Hour morning, it will be more crowded during its regular hours.*

## Use Child Swap
▶ **What it is** This unpublicized policy lets parents with young children stand in the line for a ride only once, even if they both want to go on it but have to attend to a child who doesn't want to go, or is too short.
▶ **How it works** First, find a cast member at the ride entrance and let him know your situation. You'll need his consent to bring in your too-short child, which he'll give if he understands what you're doing. You'll also need to clue in the loading-area cast member. After that, you go on the ride alone while your spouse waits behind with your boy or girl. When you return, your spouse goes.

## Have a touring plan
Having a daily plan will save you hours of time at any park, whether you want to do as much as possible or just have a good time.
▶ **This book's 'Magical Days'** There are four touring plans in this book, one at the beginning of each theme-park chapter. Each is a relaxed schedule that includes all of its park's best attractions.
▶ **Tour Guide Mike (tourguidemike.com)** creates custom Disney itineraries based on your preferences. Use of its Automated Vacation Planner starts at $22.
▶ **Making your own** Even if you've never been to Disney before, it's easy to make your own itinerary: ❶ First, skim through this book's park chapters and determine which attractions you want to see. ❷ Compare your list to our Magical Day plans, which appear at the front of each chapter. ❸ Make a custom plan by exchanging attractions evenly, based on their location, wait times and Fastpass return times. If you can take advantage of Extra Magic Hours, do.

## Avoid morning delays
If you come to Disney during spring break, early summer or between Christmas and New Year's, you can run into huge delays long before you even get to a theme park:
▶ **Breakfast blues** For peak periods many Disney restaurants get fully booked months in advance, making the wait for walk-up patrons up to two hours. Often an eatery will be so busy it will *refuse* all walk-up business. Even fast food spots can get packed; sometimes at food courts it can take 30 minutes just to get through a checkout line. To avoid these problems book your meals in advance. If you eat breakfast at a food court, get there at 7 a.m. The crowds don't show up until 8.
▶ **'Been waitin' on the bus all day'** Another way to ruin your Disney day during a peak season is to rely on the company's free bus service to get you around. During peak mornings the wait for a Disney bus may take 60 minutes or more. Then, even though your destination is just a few miles away, your bus may take up to another hour to get there, as it may stop at other resort hotels or water parks along the way.

The easiest way around the bus problem is to stay at a resort that is within walking distance to the park you most want to visit. For Magic Kingdom that's the Contemporary; for Epcot it's the Yacht and Beach Club Resort; for Hollywood Studios it's the BoardWalk or the Swan and Dolphin. Alas, Disney's Animal Kingdom isn't within walking distance of any hotel. If you stay at Disney's Contemporary, Grand Floridian or Polynesian resorts, Magic Kingdom and Epcot are easily reached via the monorail system, which usually runs smoothly.

Other solutions to the bus problem include renting a car (Alamo/National has a facility on Disney property with a free shuttle: 407-824-3470), using taxis (Mears, 407-922-2222) or simply getting up so early that you're first in line for the day's first bus.
▶ **Getting to Magic Kingdom** Visitors often underestimate how much time it takes to get to this theme park. If you're driving, you have to park (in the world's second largest parking lot), walk to and wait for a tram, take it to a monorail station or boat dock, then ride to the park. The process takes at least 30 minutes from the time you park your car. Staying at a monorail hotel? Allow 25 minutes from the Contemporary Resort, 15 minutes from the Polynesian, 5 minutes from the Grand Floridian. If you're staying at any other Disney resort and taking a bus to Magic Kingdom, give yourself an hour.

**FASTPASS®**
eturn Anytime Between

**11:55 AM**
**AND**
**12:55 PM**

Riders must be at
least 40"(102cm)
to experience
Big Thunder Mountain

Another FASTPASS® ticket
will be available
after 11:55am

**SUN JUN 22**

WMK:CAS009 06/05/2008 T 12
TD2-H4

06/22/2008                                    11:17

**A Fastpass reserves a window of time for you to
experience an attraction later in the day. It also
states the time you can get another Fastpass.**

Not all Disney resorts are expensive. Rates at the Pop Century complex start at $82 a night.

# Saving money An average Disney World vacation costs over $3,000, but you can control your expenses. Here are 31 ways to do it.

**Theme parks**

▶ **Week-long tickets** It's not exactly *saving* money, but you get the best value on park tickets by buying passes good for at least a week. They cost far less per day. The difference between a three-day Base Ticket and a seven-day Base Ticket is just $15.

▶ **Orlando Fun Tickets** sells discounted park passes. The savings are substantial on multiple-day tickets. You can pick up your tickets at the company's office near Downtown Disney or have them delivered. Contact the company at 866-225-4712, or online at **orlandofuntickets.com**.

▶ **Disneyworld.com** often has deals. Check the "Special Offers" link on the home page.

▶ **Other deals** exist for Florida residents, American Automobile Association members (407-934-7639) and members of the U.S. military (Shades of Green, 888-593-2242).

▶ **Corporate sponsors** of Disney World such as Coca-Cola and Kodak often get employee discounts. Ask your benefits office.

▶ **Convention attendees** often can buy discounted park tickets that are good only after 2 or 4 p.m. or on non-convention days. Family discounts are sometimes available.

▶ **Old tickets** with unused days may be used for admission or as credits toward new passes. Learn their value at a theme-park or Downtown Disney Guest Relations office.

**Lodging**

▶ **Disney's Value Resorts** The budget-style All-Star and Pop Century resorts offer rack rates as low as $82 a night.

▶ **Value Season** The lowest rates of the year are during Disney's Value Season, which for 2010 is Jan. 3–Feb. 11, Aug. 15–Sept. 30, Nov. 28–Dec. 16. Rooms start at $82–$410 per night. Other pricing seasons: **New Year** (Jan. 1–2, room rates start at $145–$650 per night); **Regular** (Apr. 11–June 3, Oct. 1–Nov. 23; rooms $105–$465); **Summer** (Value and Moderate resorts only, June 4–Aug. 14; $119–$185); **Peak** (Feb. 15–March 27; $125–$555); and **Holiday** (Dec. 17–Dec. 31; $139–$655).

▶ **Disneyworld.com** often has deals. Check the "Special Offers" link on the home page.

▶ **Unpublished discounts** Ask a Disney reservations agent (407-934-7639) if there are any discounts for the dates, or resorts, you prefer. There often are, especially for Florida residents and annual passholders.

▶ **E-mail discounts** Sign up for a complimentary Disney World trip-planning DVD at **disneyvacations.com**. You'll get on the list for Disney's marketing e-mails, which include special room rates and other deals.
▶ **Trade group, association deals** Some trade groups and associations offer Disney World discounts to members. These include **airlines** (call Disney reservations for a list at 407-934-7639), **AAA** (800-222-1134, members typically save 10–20 percent on Disney rates except during the Holiday Season; AAA Escapes has significant package savings), **AARP** (members can save 10 percent or more on Disney hotel rooms), **CAA** (the Canadian Automobile Assoc. has deals similar to AAA), and **nurses, teachers** and **civil employees** (at the Starwood-owned Walt Disney World Swan and Dolphin Resorts).
▶ **Members of the U.S. military** get great rates at the Shades of Green AFRC (888-593-2242). If Shades of Green is full, members get "overflow" rates (not tied to rank) discounted up to 40 percent at Disney resorts. Discounts are also offered at the Walt Disney World Swan and Dolphin Resorts.

### Transportation
▶ **Disney transportation** Disney offers a complimentary Magical Express airport shuttle and free monorail, bus and boat shuttles within its property.

### Food
▶ **Bring your own snacks** into a theme park. Granola bars fit easily in a fanny pack or the side pocket of a pair of cargo pants. Disney allows food, but not alcohol.
▶ **Order free ice water** instead of soft drinks. It's available at every snack stand or restaurant that serves fountain drinks.
▶ **Eat at fast-food spots** instead of full-service restaurants. Good theme-park choices include Columbia Harbour House at Magic Kingdom, Sunshine Seasons at Epcot, Starring Rolls at Disney's Hollywood Studios and Pizzafari at Disney's Animal Kingdom.
▶ **Have lunch instead of dinner** at table-service restaurants. Portions will be slightly smaller; the check significantly less. This strategy works well in theme parks and at Downtown Disney.
▶ **Get a refrigerator** for your room. They rent for $5–$10 daily at Disney Value resorts, and are complimentary at all other Disney-owned resorts. Eating breakfast in your room can save time and money.
▶ **Refillable soft-drink mugs** ($13), available at most Disney resorts, are good for free refills throughout your stay. If you spend a lot of time at your resort they can be a good deal.
▶ **A Quick-Service option** in the Disney Dining Plan ($32 per day per adult, $10 per child) gives you two fast-food meals and two snacks a day and a refillable soft-drink mug good for the length of your stay.
▶ **Use unused Dining Plan snack credits** to buy treats for your trip back home.
▶ **Shop the Hess stations** The best prices on snacks and soft drinks on Disney property are at its three Hess convenience stores, located at the exits of Magic Kingdom, Hollywood Studios and Downtown Disney.

### Cheap thrills
▶ **Disney resorts** offer many complimentary or low-cost activities, such as arcades, basketball courts, board games, fitness centers, hot tubs, ping-pong tables, playgrounds, tennis and volleyball courts and walking trails. Many rent bikes for $9 an hour or four-person surreys for $20 a half hour.
▶ **Fishing poles** and rods rent at the Ft. Wilderness and Port Orleans Riverside resorts for less than $10 each. The resorts sell small quantities of bait.
▶ **For inexpensive nightlife** consider Disney's BoardWalk Resort. Jellyrolls, a dueling-pianos bar, has a $10 cover; the Atlantic Dance nightclub has none. A short walk away is Kimonos, a cover-free karaoke sushi bar at the Walt Disney World Swan.

### Free stuff
▶ **A monorail ride** can be more fun for children than many theme-park attractions. The longest monorail route runs from Epcot to the Transportation and Ticket Center.
▶ **Free boat rides** shuttle guests between select resorts and theme parks. The most enjoyable are on boats with outdoor seats, such as the small launches that run between Magic Kingdom and the Grand Floridian and Polynesian resorts.
▶ **A dip into a swimming pool** is a great way to have fun and relax. Many Disney World resort pools have fountains, slides, splash pads, waterfalls and other extras, as do pools at some hotels off property (see the Accommodations chapter for details).

### General savings
▶ **MouseSavers.com** has over 300 pages of Disney deals, including codes and coupons to save on hotels, rental cars and Disney merchandise. Other good web sites include **laughingplace.com**. and **miceage.com**.

**Vehicles stream into** one of the five entrances to Walt Disney World, which covers an area almost twice the size of Manhattan

## Birthdays

▶ **Buttons** Free at theme-park Guest Relations offices, "It's My Birthday" buttons cue cast members to recognize the celebrating family member.

▶ **Cakes** Many table-service restaurants can provide a 6-inch birthday cake ($21, personalized with 48 hours notice at 407-827-2253).

▶ **Cruises** Epcot offers a birthday fireworks cruise (407-WDW-BDAY (939-2329)).

▶ **Goofy will call your Disney hotel room** with a free birthday greeting. To arrange it call 407-824-2222.

▶ **Parties** can be held at the Winter Summerland miniature golf course, Blizzard Beach water park and Downtown Disney's Goofy's Candy Co. ($25 per person. Includes cake, either hot dogs or pizza).

## Characters

Though some fantasy-free parents may not appreciate it, the Disney characters are real. That's not a sweaty young woman in a fur suit, it's Pluto (just ask your kids).

▶ **Face or fur?** Disney has two types of characters. "Face" characters such as Cinderella show the performer's actual face. "Fur" characters such as Winnie the Pooh are fully costumed. Though face characters rarely intimidate, the odd, huge heads of the fur family sometimes do. To help your child feel comfortable, talk with her beforehand so she knows what to expect. For meet-and-greet lines, buy her an autograph book to give her something to focus on besides the face-to-fur encounter. Don't push her; the characters are super patient.

▶ **Finding characters** Besides getting a hand slap at a parade, there are two ways to meet Disney

characters: at meet-and-greet lines and character meals. Each theme park chapter of this book has a list of character locations in its overview. At the parks, a free Times Guide has a general overview of character locations. In addition, cast members can track down the schedule of any particular character.

## Childcare

▶ **Disney resort hotels** Five Disney-owned resort hotels include an evening childcare center. Disney's Animal Kingdom Lodge, Beach Club, Grand Floridian, Polynesian and Wilderness Lodge resorts each have a secure room staffed with childcare professionals and filled with arts and crafts, books, games, toys and videos. Rates are $11.50 per hour per child with a 2-hour minimum charge, and include dinner from 6 to 8 p.m. Children must be toilet trained (no pull-ups) and 4 to 12 years old. Hours are 4 or 4:30 p.m. to midnight daily. For details or reservations call 407-WDW-DINE.

▶ **In-room care** Walt Disney World works with two in-room childcare services. Kids Nite Out (800-696-8105, 407-828-0920, kidsniteout.com) provides baby-sitting and childcare for kids ages 6 weeks to 12 years, including those with special needs. Caregivers arrive prepared with age-appropriate toys, activities, books, games, and arts and crafts. Rates start at $16 per hour with a 4-hour minimum charge, plus a $10 transportation fee. All About Kids (800-728-6506, 407-812-9300, all-about-kids.com) offers child-sitting services; services for adults, those with special needs and pets; and rents car seats, high chairs, playpens,

toys and other baby and children's equipment. Childcare rates start at $13 per hour with a 4-hour minimum charge, plus a $12 transportation fee.

## Disability, hearing

▶ **Assistive Listening** systems use Disney's Handheld Device to receive a signal from overhead transmitters to amplify sound. Devices with headphones or induction loops are available through Guest Relations offices. $100 deposit.

▶ **Handheld captioning** This portable captioning system uses a wireless handheld receiver to display text on moving attractions. Devices are available through Guest Relations. $100 deposit.

▶ **Reflective captioning** is available at many theater-type attractions. This technology uses an LED display to project captions onto an acrylic panel positioned in front of the guest. To use this system contact a cast member at the attraction.

▶ **Sign language interpretation** Disney World Resort provides sign language interpretation at specific live shows typically at Magic Kingdom on Mondays and Thursdays, Epcot on Tuesdays and Fridays, Disney's Hollywood Studios on Sundays and Wednesdays and Disney's Animal Kingdom on Saturdays. Check the current schedule at (407) 824-4321 [voice] or (407) 827-5141 [TTY]. Sign Language interpretation can be requested for other special events and shows, including the Hoop-Dee-Doo Revue and Disney's Spirit of Aloha dinner shows, with 14 days notice at the above phone numbers. Cast members with sign language abilities wear an identifying pin.

▶ **TTY telephones** Pay phones equipped with amplified handsets and Text Typewriters are available throughout Walt Disney World.

▶ **Video captioning** Many Walt Disney World attractions have caption-ready video monitors, designated with a "CC" symbol and activated by remote control. Single-button activators are available through Guest Relations. $25 deposit. Video Captioning can also be activated using Disney's Handheld Device (see Assistive Listening, above).

▶ **Written aids** Guest Assistance Packets containing dialogue, flashlights, a pen and paper are available at or near the performance areas or entrances for most Disney World shows and attractions. Contact a cast member to request one. Cast members use pads of paper and pens or pencils when needed to communicate with guests.

## Disability, mobility

▶ **Guest Assistance Cards** Each Walt Disney World Guest Relations office has complimentary Guest Assistance Cards for visitors with non-apparent

**From the top:** Special viewing areas for disabled guests are available for Mickey's Jammin' Jungle Parade and Block Party Bash. Disney offers sign-language interpretation for High School Musical 3: Senior Year—Right Here! Right Now!

assistance needs (i.e., autism, heart condition). About the size of a Pop Tart, the card provides privileges such as waiting in shaded areas or entering through auxillary entrances. At Magic Kingdom's It's a Small World these guests board through the wheelchair entrance. Card holders at Animal Kingdom's Kilimanjaro Safaris are put in the Fastpass line. Each card is good for a party of up to six people.

▶ **Wheelchairs** You can bring your own wheelchair or rent one ($12/day) at any Walt Disney World theme park. Wheelchairs are available on a first-come, first-served basis. Rental wheelchairs may not be transferred from park to park, but the deposit ticket from your first rental will let you rent a second wheelchair on the same day, if available, at another Disney park at no additional charge. Complimentary wheelchairs are available for guests with limited mobility to travel to and from disability parking and the nearest wheelchair rental location. These wheelchairs can be identified by their blue seats, backrests and blue flags. They are not permitted inside Disney theme parks. Wheelchairs are also available at Walt Disney World resort hotels ($315 deposit). At the ESPN Wide World of Sports complex, a limited number of complimentary wheelchairs are available at the turnstiles. The best way to guarantee the use of a wheelchair throughout your stay is to contact local area rental companies such as Apria Health Care (407-291-2229), Care Medical Equipment (407-856-2273) or Walker Mobility (407-518-6000).

▶ **Electric Convenience Vehicles** A limited number of Electric Convenience Vehicles (four-wheeled powered scooters, $50/day, $20 deposit) are also available on a first-come, first-served basis. Guests must be 18 years of age or older to rent ECVs, and quantities are limited. Arrive early. ECVs are available only on a same-day basis and may only be used in the theme park where they are rented, but, like wheelchairs, the deposit ticket from your first rental will let you rent a second ECV on the same day, if available, at another Disney park at no additional charge. ECVs will be held if guests wish to leave and return to the same park.

▶ **Designated viewing areas** Parade routes and some attractions have designated viewing areas for disabled guests, filled on a first-come, first-served basis for parties up to six people.

### Disability, visual

▶ **Handheld braille guides** are available at theme-park Guest Relations offices. $25 deposit.

**From the top:** Pinocchio greets guests at Magic Kingdom. Outside the Epcot kennel. The Hess convenience store at the Magic Kingdom Car Care Center. Disney's only drive-through restaurant, the McDonald's at Osceola Parkway and Buena Vista Drive (in front of the All-Star Resorts, near Disney's Animal Kingdom and Blizzard Beach water park) is open 24 hours a day.

▶ **Stationary braille maps** are located in each Disney World theme park (near the Guest Relations lobby and near the tip board) and at Downtown Disney. These maps use large print with a clear Braille overlay and some additional raised graphics to highlight key landmarks and attractions.

▶ **Audiotape guides and tours** are available at each Disney World theme park. Audio Guides provide a brief summary of the services available at Walt Disney World, as well as an orientation to the layout of its theme park. The Audio Tour offers a detailed guided tour of the park, with a specific route to follow, distances between attractions and key stopping locations. Tape players are available at Guest Relations offices. $25 deposit.

▶ **Audio description** uses Disney's Handheld Device to provide supplemental attraction audio. Devices are available at theme-park Guest Relations offices. $100 deposit. (Identified in this book by the symbol *AuDe*.)

## Getting here

▶ **By automobile** Two major highways border Walt Disney World. Interstate 4 runs along the southern edge of the property, connecting it to Orlando (18 miles northeast) and Tampa (53 miles southwest). An interstate-like toll road opened in 2007, Florida 429 runs along the western edge of Disney World, creating a shortcut for travelers coming from the north on Florida's Turnpike. It saves about a half-hour in travel time compared to taking the turnpike all the way into Orlando, and instead of congested urbania offers a pleasant, almost traffic-free drive past farms and orange groves. To use it, take the turnpike south to Exit 267A, then head southeast on Florida 429 11 miles to Exit 8, which brings you to Disney's new Western Way entrance. The toll for 429 is $1. As you travel it, after about 4 miles you can see, way off to your left, Cinderella Castle, Space Mountain, the Contemporary Resort, Spaceship Earth and the Walt Disney World Dolphin Resort.

▶ **From the Orlando airport** Walt Disney World is 19 miles southwest of the Orlando International Airport. You can get to Disney by taxi ($50–$60, Yellow Cab: 407-699-9999), town car ($70–$90, Mears: 407-423-5566), bus or van ($20 per person, Mears: 407-423-5566) or by renting a car (Hertz: 800-654-3131. Avis: 800-331-1212. National: 800-227-7368.). The simplest route (25 min): take the airport's South Exit road 4 miles to Florida 417 ($2 toll), go west on 417 13 miles to Osceola Parkway (Exit 3), then west again 2 miles. Guests staying at a Disney-owned resort can take a free Magical Express bus.

## Lost and found

▶ **Theme parks** Located at the Magic Kingdom kennel adjacent to the Transportation and Ticket Center, Disney's Theme Park Lost and Found office stores items found at theme parks, water parks, Downtown Disney and the ESPN Wide World of Sports complex. Guests can retrieve items from its walk-up window or via telephone (407-824-4245, shipping at no charge). It keeps most items 30 days. Cameras, prescription eyeglasses and purses are kept 90 days; hats, strollers and sunglasses only 7 days.

▶ **Disney resort hotels** Each has its own lost and found office. Contact particular hotels for policies.

## Money matters

▶ **ATMs** There's at least one ATM at every theme park and resort. $2–$2.50 fee per transaction.

▶ **Cash advances** Across from the Downtown Disney Marketplace, SunTrust Bank handles cash advances (Discover, MasterCard or Visa). Open 9a–4p weekdays, until 5:30p Thursdays. 407-828-6103.

▶ **Credit cards** All Disney charge locations accept these credit cards: American Express, Diner's Club, Discover, JCB, MasterCard and Visa.

▶ **Disney Dollars** Character-faced Disney Dollars are accepted as currency at the theme parks and Disney-owned resorts and gift shops. They're sold at Guest Relations centers, Disney concierge desks and the World of Disney store at Downtown Disney.

▶ **Foreign currency** Guest Relations centers will exchange foreign currency up to $100.

▶ **Traveler's checks** Nearly any Disney purchase can be paid for with a traveler's check. SunTrust Bank sells AmEx traveler's checks.

▶ **Wire transfers** SunTrust handles wire transfers. Gooding's Supermarket (in the nearby CrossRoads shopping center, 8a–10p daily, 407-827-1200) handles Western Union transfers.

## Packing

Let's see. You're going to the hottest state in the country and planning to spend most of the day outside walking on pavement. Sounds like fun! Actually, it doesn't have to be bad. Just be prepared, and dress light and comfortably.

▶ **For all ages** Fundamental are T-shirts, loose-fitting cotton tops, capris and shorts with large pockets, baseball caps and swimsuits, and broken-in walking shoes (pack two pair of shoes per person, so if it rains everyone stills has a dry pair). In the winter you'll need clothes you can layer, such as jackets, sweaters and sweatshirts, as days start off cool but warm quickly. January mornings can be below freezing at 9 a.m. but 60 degrees by noon. Temperatures at 7 p.m. will be in the 50s through March. Other essentials include an umbrella, sunglasses and sunscreen (sweat-proof, SPF rating at least 30). Instead of a purse, try a waist pack to keep your hands free. Don't forget your tickets and various confirmations.

▶ **For children** Dress your kids like you dress yourself, casually and comfortably, but protect them more from the sun. Wide-brimmed hats help. Bring snacks (granola bars, raisin boxes) and, for autographs, a Sharpie pen.

## Theme park closures

During peak periods Walt Disney World theme parks and water parks can fill to capacity and close to additional guests. To learn if a park is currently closed call Disney at 407-939-4636.

## Pets

▶ **At Disney Resorts** Fort Wilderness campers may keep their pet with them for $5 per day at select locations. Except for Fort Wilderness, only service animals are allowed in Disney resorts, theme parks, water parks or Downtown Disney.

▶ **Kennels** Five small kennels—at Magic Kingdom (407-824-6568), Epcot (407-560-6229), Disney's Hollywood Studios (407-560-4282), Disney's Animal Kingdom (407-938-2100) and Fort Wilderness Resort & Campground (407-824-2735)—offer daytime and overnight caged boarding for dogs, cats, rabbits and other small creatures. At Magic Kingdom, Epcot and Fort Wilderness rates include two walks and two feedings. Day boarding: $18 day. Overnight: $23 ($21 Disney resort guests). Reservations rec. Vaccinations req. 24-hr access. Cats, dogs must be 8 wks. At Hollywood Studios and Animal Kingdom kennels, guests are required to walk their pets two times a day; three times for puppies. Day boarding: $13 day. Overnight: $18 ($16 Disney resort guests).

## Photos and video

Besides letting you photograph landmarks and characters, a camera lets you capture spontaneous moments that create treasured memories. Whatever shots you snap, take turns being the photographer (if dad takes all of the pictures, none of them will include dad). Also, consider separate cameras for your kids, and waterproof cameras for the water parks. The results are sure to add to your memories.

▶ **Camera supplies** Every theme park has a Camera Center which sells disposable cameras, batteries, memory cards and other supplies. Each is located just inside its park in the first building on the right. At Magic Kingdom it's in Exposition Hall on Main Street U.S.A.; at Epcot the Camera Center under Spaceship Earth; at Disney's Hollywood Studios the Darkroom on Hollywood Blvd.; at Animal Kingdom it's inside Garden Gate Gifts. At the water parks, camera supplies are sold at the main gift shops. If you have your charger with you, Guest Relations offices will charge your batteries at no charge.

▶ **Digital imaging** The Magic Kingdom and Hollywood Studios Camera Centers and the Epcot Imageworks area (at the Imagination pavilion) have Kodak PictureMaker kiosks. Simplified versions of machines in drug and grocery stores, these touch-screen devices create CDs of digital files (120 images for $16.99) as well as 4-by-6-inch prints (19 cents). They accept nearly every type of storage device.

▶ **Photopass** With this service Disney photographers take shots of you and your group, but you pay for only those you choose. Photographers are stationed in front of each theme-park icon, at most character locations and at many other key spots. Each gives away free credit-card-like PhotoPasses, which you carry with you as an ID. Disney applies no sales pressure. You view the images at theme-park Camera Centers or at disneyphotopass.com, and decide which, if any, you want to buy. PhotoPass is not a replacement for your own camera, as photographers shoot only posed shots at particular locations. If you use it, write down your Photopass ID number. That way if you lose your card you won't lose your images.

▶ **Souvenir ride photos** At some rides an automated camera takes your picture then an exitway gift shop offers to sell you the shot. This happens at Buzz Lightyear's Space Ranger Spin, Space Mountain and Splash Mountain at Magic Kingdom, Test Track at Epcot, Rock 'n' Roller Coaster Starring Aerosmith and The Twilight Zone Tower of Terror at Disney's Hollywood Studios and Dinosaur and Expedition Everest at Animal Kingdom.

# Everything Mickey...

**Mickey-shoe slippers.** Various adult sizes. Polyester. The Emporium, Magic Kingdom. $22.95.

**Retro salt and pepper shakers.** With car holder. Celebrity 5 and 10, Disney's Hollywood Studios. $12.95.

**Mickey's "Really Swell" Coffee.** Medium roast. 12 oz. Mickey's Pantry, Downtown Disney. $8.95

**Round Mickey.** 10-inch Spandex plush. Mickey's of Hollywood, Disney's Hollywood Studios. $18.

**Salad plate.** Glass. 8-inch diameter. Mickey's Pantry, Downtown Disney. $8.

## Restaurants

▶ **Reservations** At Disney World, having a dining reservation is often a must. The best restaurants often book to capacity far in advance, especially for the most popular dining times. During peak periods many don't accept walk-up diners, regardless of how long you're willing to wait. Reservations can be made up to 180 days in advance (190 for Disney resort guests) at 407-WDW-DINE (407-939-3463) or at disneyworld.disney.go.com/dining as well as most restaurant check-in counters and resort concierge desks. Reservations are required for dinner shows and Grand Gathering Experiences. Some locations require a credit-card guarantee, while others charge a cancellation fee. Reservations for parties of 13 or more always need a credit card. Most restaurants will hold your reservation for 15 minutes beyond its stated time. The toughest reservation is Cinderella's Royal Table inside Cinderella Castle. It often books in full on the first day of availability. Its meals are charged at the time you book them. Other hot spots include California Grill and Chef Mickey's (at the Contemporary Resort), Le Cellier (Canada pavilion, Epcot) and Victoria and Albert's (Grand Floridian Resort). The toughest reservation time is 7 to 8 p.m. To eat at that hour make a reservation at least a few days early, especially for a party of six or more. All Disney restaurants are nonsmoking and add an automatic 18 percent gratuity to parties of 8 or more. *Note: At Disney, making a reservation does not mean Disney holds a table for you. Instead, it books you into its system, and gives your party the next available table for its size after you arrive.*

▶ **Kids meals** At theme parks, Disney's Kids Picks meals include many nutritious entrees. Each comes with unsweetened applesauce, baby carrots or fresh fruit (your choice of two) and a beverage of low-fat milk, juice or water. Less than 35 percent of a Kids Picks meal's calories come from fat, and of those, no more than 10 percent come from saturated fat and sugar. Fries and soft drinks can be substituted. Kids meals are also available at most resort restaurants.

▶ **Dress codes** All Disney Signature Restaurants except Cinderella's Royal Table and the Hollywood Brown Derby have a business casual dress code. For men, that means dress slacks, jeans, trousers or dress shorts; and a shirt with a collar or T-shirt underneath. Women are required to wear dress shorts, jeans or a skirt with a blouse or sweater, or a dress. Not permitted: Cut-offs, men's caps or hats, swimsuits, swimsuit cover-ups, tank tops or torn clothing. Victoria & Albert's (Grand Floridian) requires jackets for men and dresses or dressy pants suits for women.

▶ **Special diets** No-sugar, low-fat, low-sodium, vegetarian or vegan diets can be met at table-service restaurants by telling a reservation clerk, host or server. Dinner shows need 24 hours notice. With three days notice, these restaurants accommodate needs such as allergies to gluten or wheat, shellfish, soy, lactose or milk, peanuts, tree nuts, fish or eggs. At buffet restaurants, guests who have had gastric-bypass surgery pay the kids price for an adult meal. Many counter-service restaurants offer low-fat or vegetarian options. No Disney restaurant serves food with added trans fats or partially hydrogenated oils.

▶ **Kosher meals** Glatt kosher meals are available at most full-service Disney restaurants with 24 hours notice at 407-WDW-DINE (939-3463). Food is prepared in Miami. Kosher quick-service meals are always available at Cosmic Ray's Starlight Cafe (Magic Kingdom), Liberty Inn (Epcot), ABC Commissary (Hollywood Studios), Pizzafari (Animal Kingdom) and the food courts at the All-Star, Caribbean Beach, Pop Century and Port Orleans Riverside resorts.

▶ **Tables in Wonderland card** Formerly called the Disney Dining Experience, this discount card ($75–$100 annually, available to annual passholders and Florida residents only, 407-566-5858, weekdays 9 a.m. to 5 p.m.) saves its holder and up to nine guests 20 percent off food and beverages during non-

**Comic reverse purse.** Vinyl and plastic. Zippered top. The Emporium, Magic Kingdom. $24.95.

**Cookie jar.** Glass. Celebrity 5 and 10, Disney's Hollywood Studios. $28.

**Ladies hipster panties.** Cotton and spandex. The Emporium, Magic Kingdom. Various prints. 3-pack, $15.

**Peace-and-love Juniors T-shirt.** 100-percent cotton. The Emporium, Magic Kingdom. $28.

**"Gallopin' Gaucho" ornament.** 4-inch. Resin. Disney's Days of Christmas, Downtown Disney. 7-piece set, $29.50.

holiday periods at most Disney table-service restaurants and a handful of other spots, including food courts at Value Resorts. An 18 percent gratuity is automatically added.

## Shopping

Walt Disney World has hundreds of stores, selling everything from kiddie souvenirs to hand-rolled cigars. It stocks exclusive perfumes, serious fine art and—to no one's surprise—the largest selection of Mickey Mouse merchandise in the world.

▶ **Return policy** Walt Disney World will accept returns on merchandise with a receipt within 90 days of date of purchase. Items that cannot be returned include those marked "as is" or "all sales final," original artwork, fine jewelry and special orders. A guest returning an item without a receipt receives credit based on its current selling price. Some stores on Disney property are not run by Disney; return policies at these shops vary.

▶ **Disney Store returns** In most cases, Disney Stores in shopping malls accept returns of items bought at Disney-owned Disney World stores with a receipt.

▶ **Unusual items** Men's dress shirts: Ralph Lauren styles are at the Commander's Porter shop at Disney's Grand Floridian Resort (9a–10p). XXXL shirts: Typically at World of Disney (Downtown Disney), the Emporium (Magic Kingdom) and MouseGear (Epcot).

▶ **Non-Disney apparel** is sold at Downtown Disney, in gift shops at Disney Deluxe resorts, at Epcot's World Showcase and at water parks. Some theme-park shops sell World Wildlife Fund T-shirts.

▶ **Outlet Mall** The Orlando Premium Outlet Mall (8200 Vineland Ave. at I-4 Exit 68; 407-238-7787; Mon.–Sat. 10a–10p (11p in summer), Sun. 10a–9p). is 5 minutes away from Walt Disney World.

## Transportation

You get around Disney's 47-square-mile property via a network of two- and four-lane roads or by using Disney's complimentary transportation system.

▶ **A bus system** connects Disney resorts with all theme and water parks and Downtown Disney, and also travel between some parks. Some buses run to character breakfasts. *Despite its benefits Disney's bus system has a few flaws: 1. Though they run from theme park to theme park, and from any theme park to Blizzard Beach, the buses do not go from any theme park to Downtown Disney or Typhoon Lagoon. 2. There is no direct service between resorts. You can, however, take a bus from a resort to a theme park or Downtown Disney, and then transfer to a different bus that goes to a second resort. (Downtown Disney buses often aren't as crowded, and run until after 1 a.m.) 3. Buses do not run from*

**From the top:** Cat Cora at her new Disney-operated Kouzzina restaurant. Chef Kevin Dundon at Raglan Road. Sandwiches at Sanaa and Earl of Sandwich.

KEVIN DUNDON PHOTO © GREAT IRISH PUBS FLORIDA. EARL OF SANDWICH PHOTO © EARL OF SANDWICH USA.

the Epcot resorts (BoardWalk, Yacht and Beach Club, Walt Disney World Swan and Dolphin) to Epcot or to Disney's Hollywood Studios. Guests at those resorts get to those parks via ferry boat or on foot. They enter Epcot through its rear International Gateway entrance. (During thunderstorms, when the boats can't run, the buses do.) 4. Disney buses do not serve the ESPN Wide World of Sports except from (but of course!) Disney's Hollywood Studios (8a–8p).

▶ **Monorail trains** connect the Transportation and Ticket Center (TTC) with Magic Kingdom and with the Contemporary, Grand Floridian and Polynesian resorts. A separate line connects the TTC to Epcot.

▶ **Ferry boats** connect Magic Kingdom with the TTC and resorts on Seven Seas Lagoon and Bay Lake, Epcot and Hollywood Studios with resorts between those parks, and Downtown Disney with the Port Orleans, Old Key West and Saratoga Springs resorts.

▶ **Hess gasoline stations** sit outside the parking lot exits of Magic Kingdom, Disney's Hollywood Studios and Downtown Disney.

▶ **Renting a car** The most convenient way to rent a car on Disney property may be from Disney's Car Care Center (adjacent to the Magic Kingdom parking lot), which provides a shuttle bus to pick you up from any Disney resort hotel to pick up your vehicle. Many Disney resorts have on-site car rental counters of their own: Alamo/National at the Walt Disney World Dolphin (407) 934-4930, Alamo/National at the Buena Vista Palace (407) 827-6363, Avis at the Downtown Disney Hilton (407) 827-2847, Budget at the Doubletree Guest Suites (407) 827-6089, Dollar at the Regal Sun Resort (407) 583-8000 and Hertz at the Shades of Green Resort (407) 938-0600. You also can rent a car at the Orlando International Airport, where the major in-terminal agencies are Alamo, Avis, Budget, Dollar, Enterprise, National and Thrifty (Hertz is off-site). Car rental rates in Orlando tend to run from $20 to $30 a day plus fees. You'll find car-rental discount codes at mousesavers.com.

## Weddings and honeymoons

▶ **Weddings** Up to a dozen couples tie the knot at Disney World every day. And no wonder—it has unrivaled facilities for a family gathering, great year-round weather and a one-stop Fairy Tale Weddings division. The average wedding costs $26,000 and includes 100 people. Prices start at $4,750.

▶ **Honeymoon** packages include an online registry, which lets couples create a wish list for the trip and have family and friends contribute toward particulars.

▶ **For details** on weddings and honeymoons call 877-566-0969 or go online to disneyweddings.com or disneyhoneymoons.com.

**From the top:** A Walt Disney World monorail train. A Disney bus. Cars at the Alamo/National rental car center. The Hess station at the corner of Buena Vista Dr. and Epcot Resorts Blvd., across from the exit to Disney's Hollywood Studios.

One of the world's most famous landmarks, Cinderella Castle sits at the end of Magic Kingdom's Main Street U.S.A.

# Magic Kingdom

## The world's most popular theme park

**A realm that, if real, you would love to escape to,** Magic Kingdom is a place straight out of your imagination, filled with barbershop quartets and hoop skirts, small towns and clean streets, charming pirates and cute dolls, an empire where everyone is always glad to see you. The definitive theme park, Magic Kingdom has a universal appeal. For newcomers it's like a postcard come to life. For Disney veterans it's like seeing an old friend.

### Lay of the land

The park is laid out like a spoked wheel. You enter under a train station, where a colorful American avenue leads to a stately European castle. From there walkways lead to six separate lands.

It all begins with a stroll through a 1900s-era county seat. The past made perfect, **Main Street U.S.A.** is a world of Victorian buildings, homemade fudge, horse-drawn streetcars and horseless carriages. A central Town Square green is surrounded by the town's key civic buildings—its courthouse (or city hall), firehouse, train station and exhibition hall. In the center is a statue of the town's founding father, in this case Walt Disney's brother, Roy, who supervised the creation of Disney World after his brother's death.

Next is Main Street itself. Fronted with flowers and trees, building facades use the motion-picture technique of forced perspective to appear larger than they are—first floors are at full scale, second floors are at 80 percent of full size, third floors 80 percent of that. Upper-story windows appear to mark the offices of the street's business people, though in reality they identify key Disney alumni who have contributed to the park's success.

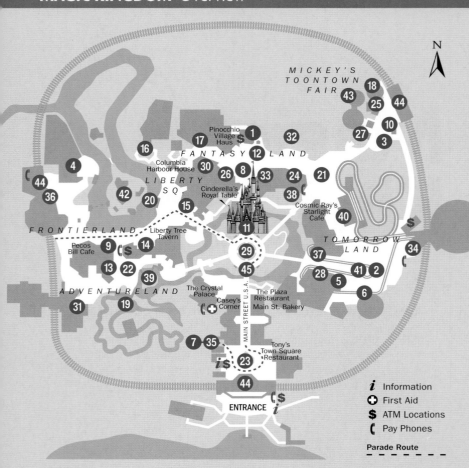

N

MICKEY'S TOONTOWN FAIR

Pinocchio Village Haus

FANTASY LAND

Columbia Harbour House

LIBERTY SQ.

Cinderella's Royal Table

Cosmic Ray's Starlight Cafe

TOMORROW LAND

FRONTIERLAND

Liberty Tree Tavern

Pecos Bill Cafe

ADVENTURELAND

The Crystal Palace

Casey's Corner

The Plaza Restaurant

Main St. Bakery

MAIN STREET U.S.A.

Tony's Town Square Restaurant

ENTRANCE

*i* Information
✚ First Aid
$ ATM Locations
( Pay Phones

Parade Route

## ATTRACTIONS

1. Ariel's Grotto
2. Astro Orbiter
3. The Barnstormer
4. Big Thunder Mountain RR
5. Buzz Lightyear's Space Ranger Spin
6. Carousel of Progress
7. Celebrate a Dream Come True Parade (step-off)
8. Cinderella's Golden Carrousel
9. Country Bear Jamboree
10. Donald's Boat
11. Dream Along with Mickey
12. Dumbo the Flying Elephant
13. Enchanted Tiki Room
14. Frontierl'd Shootin' Arcade

15. The Hall of Presidents
16. The Haunted Mansion
17. it's a small world
18. Judge's Tent
19. Jungle Cruise
20. Liberty Square Riverboat
21. Mad Tea Party
22. Magic Carpets of Aladdin
23. Main Street Vehicles
24. The Many Adventures of Winnie the Pooh
25. Mickey's Country House
26. Mickey's PhilharMagic
27. Minnie's Country House
28. Monsters Inc. Laugh Floor
29. Move It! Shake It! Celebrate It!
30. Peter Pan's Flight

31. Pirates of the Caribbean
32. Pooh's Playful Spot
33. Snow White's Scary Adventures
34. Space Mountain
35. SpectroMagic (step-off)
36. Splash Mountain
37. Stitch's Great Escape!
38. Storytime with Belle
39. Swiss Family Treehouse
40. Tomorrowland Indy Speedway
41. Tomorrowland Transit Authority
42. Tom Sawyer Island
43. Toontown Hall of Fame
44. WDW Railroad
45. Wishes (best viewing spot)

Many of the 51 Main Street U.S.A. facades use Cape Cod clapboarding and gingerbread trim. Some include prefabricated metalwork, an Industrial Age invention. Each has its own window framing, frieze work and cornice. Interiors include tin ceilings, brick floors and huge chandeliers.

Main Street U.S.A. represents a town in transition. Horse hitches are giving way to bus stops. Streetlights are changing from gas to electricity.

The sound of beating drums introduces you to **Adventureland,** a mix of African jungles, Arabian nights, Caribbean architecture and South Seas landscaping. **Liberty Square's** Federal and Georgian architecture brings back the time of the Revolutionary War. **Frontierland** looks to be a 19th-century American rural settlement, with raised wooden sidewalks, rocking chairs and lots of banjo and fiddle music twangin' from trees.

Set within the walls of Cinderella's castle estate, **Fantasyland** resembles a royal courtyard during a Renaissance fair. Some buildings are designed as tournament tents; others blend styles from Great Britain and Germany.

Themed to be a rural farming exhibition, the two-acre **Mickey's Toontown Fair** also has the country homes of Mickey and Minnie Mouse.

The theme of **Tomorrowland?** An intergalactic spaceport, a nostalgic trip back to the future as envisioned by 1930s comic books and sci-fi films. It's best seen at night, when the brushed-metal curves of the buildings are lit by colorful beacons, lasers and neon.

# Attractions at a glance

## CARNIVAL GAME
🄔 **Frontierland Shootin' Arcade** ★★★ Allow 10 min. Extra charge. Frontierland. Old-fashioned arcade has infrared rifles.

## CHARACTER-GREETING ATTRACTIONS
❶ **Ariel's Grotto** ★★ Avg wait 45 min. Outdoor line. Fantasyland. The Little Mermaid.
🄮 **Judge's Tent** ★★★★ Avg wait 20 min. Air-

conditioned queue. Mickey's Toontown Fair. Meet Mickey Mouse, Minnie Mouse.
🄴 **Toontown Hall of Fame** ★★★★ Avg wait 60 min. Air-conditioned queue. Mickey's Toontown Fair. One line leads to princesses Aurora, Belle, Cinderella; second to Tinker Bell, fairy friends.

## EXHIBITS
🄯 **Mickey's Country House** ★★★ Allow 15 min. No wait. Mickey's Toontown Fair. AuDe Walk-through; leads to Judge's Tent (see above).
🄬 **Minnie's Country House** ★★★ Allow 15 min. No wait. Mickey's Toontown Fair. AuDe Walk-through; has hands-on activities.
🄳 **Swiss Family Treehouse** ★★ Allow 15 min. No wait. Adventureland. Climb-through "Swiss Family Robinson" home.

## FIREWORKS
🄵 **Wishes** ★★★★★ ✔ 12 min. Loud explosions. Creative explosions sync with dialogue, music; life lesson.

## PARADES
❼ **Celebrate a Dream Come True Parade** ★★★ 30 min. 3p. Travels Main Street U.S.A., then Liberty Square, Adventureland. Half-hearted floats and music, but many Disney characters.
🄵 **SpectroMagic** ★★★★★ ✔ 20 min. Travels Main Street U.S.A., then Liberty Square, Adventureland. Evening light parade based on vintage animation.

## PLAYGROUNDS
🄖 **Donald's Boat** ★★★ Allow 15 min. No wait. Mickey's Toontown Fair. Kiddie water-play area has cartoon tugboat.
🄲 **Pooh's Playful Spot** ★★★ Allow 15–20 min. No wait. Fantasyland. Small area has toddler-sized slides, tunnels, splash-pad "pond," tiny walk-in version of Mr. Sanders tree house.
🄶 **Tom Sawyer Island** ★★★ Allow 45 min. Avg wait 15 min. Frontierland. Two wooded islands connected by bridge have cave, mine, calvary fort, other adventures.

## RIDES
❷ **Astro Orbiter** ★★★ 2 min. Avg wait 25 min. Steep tilt. Tomorrowland. Elevated rockets circle at 45-degree angle.

it's a small world,
Fantasyland

**❸ The Barnstormer** ★★★★ ✔ 1 min. Avg wait 20 min. Height restriction 35 in. Intense for some preschoolers. Mickey's Toontown Fair. Kiddie roller coaster has brief thrills.

**❹ Big Thunder Mountain Railroad** ★★★★★ ✔ 4 min. Avg wait 35 min. Height restriction 40 in. No steep drops. Frontierland. *FastPass* Coaster twists, turns through mountain landscapes, mining town.

**❺ Buzz Lightyear's Space Ranger Spin** ★★★★ ✔ 5 min. Avg wait 30 min. Tomorrowland. *FastPass AuDe* Ride-through shooting gallery uses lasers.

**❽ Cinderella's Golden Carrousel** ★★★★ 2 min. Avg wait 8 min. Fantasyland. Canopy-covered antique merry-go-round.

**⑫ Dumbo the Flying Elephant** ★★★★ ✔ 2 min. Avg wait 30 min. Fantasyland. Gentle hub-and-spoke ride.

**⑯ The Haunted Mansion** ★★★★ ✔ 11 min. Avg wait 15 min. Dark, ominous atmosphere, some screams, pop-up heads. Liberty Square. *AuDe* Classic dark ride tours ghostly retirement home.

**⑰ it's a small world** ★★★★★ ✔ 11 min. Avg wait 15 min. Fantasyland. *AuDe* Dark indoor boat ride tours world cultures. Many singing dolls and whimsical animals front colorful abstract settings.

**⑲ Jungle Cruise** ★★★ ✔ 10 min. Avg wait 30 min. Adventureland. *FastPass* Shady outdoor boat ride now played for puns, laughs.

**⑳ Liberty Square Riverboat** ★★★ 15 min. Avg wait 20 min. Liberty Square. Paddle wheeler circles Tom Sawyer Island.

**㉑ Mad Tea Party** ★★★ 2 min. Avg wait 15 min. You'll get dizzy. Fantasyland. Canopy-covered spinning teacups.

**㉒ Magic Carpets of Aladdin** ★★★ 2 min. Avg wait 10 min. Adventureland. Four-seat hub-and-spoke ride.

**㉓ Main Street Vehicles** ★★★★ ✔ 3 min. No wait. Mornings only. Main Street U.S.A. Horse trolleys, antique-style vehicles shuttle passengers between Town Square and Cinderella Castle.

**㉔ The Many Adventures of Winnie the Pooh** ★★★★ ✔ 4 min. Avg wait 30 min. Fantasyland. *FastPass AuDe* Charming storybook ride recalls the Blustery Day. Many modern special effects.

**㉚ Peter Pan's Flight** ★★★ 3 min. Avg wait 45 min. Fantasyland. *FastPass AuDe* Vintage dark ride offers classic aerial views of London and Never Land.

**㉛ Pirates of the Caribbean** ★★★★★ ✓
9 min. Avg wait 10 min. Short dark drop, realistic cannon fire. Adventureland. *AuDe* Indoor dark boat ride travels through elaborate settings with robotic pirates.

**㉝ Snow White's Scary Adventures** ★★★ 3 min. Avg wait 20 min. Threatening scenes, loud screams. Fantasyland. *AuDe* Spook-house ride recalls scary moments of "Snow White and the Seven Dwarfs."

**㉞ Space Mountain** ★★★★★ ✓ 3 min. Avg wait 45 min. Height restriction 44 in. Dark drops, turns. Tomorrowland. *FastPass* Dark indoor roller coaster simulates space trip.

**㊱ Splash Mountain** ★★★★★ ✓ 12 min. Avg wait 50 min. Height restriction 40 in. Steep drop, most riders get wet. Frontierland. *FastPass* Soggy flume ride travels through robotic indoor scenes, drops 52 feet. Tells tale of Brer Rabbit (from 1946 film "Song of the South").

**㊵ Tomorrowland Indy Speedway** ★★ 5 min. Avg wait 30 min. Height restriction 32 in. to ride; 54 in. to take car out alone. Tomorrowland. Old-fashioned freewheeling race cars for children top out at 7 mph.

**㊶ Tomorrowland Transit Authority** ★★★ ✓ 10 min. No wait. Tomorrowland. *AuDe* Elevated tour of Tomorrowland.

**㊹ Walt Disney World Railroad** ★★★ 20 min (round trip). Avg wait 5 min. Main Street U.S.A., Frontierland, Mickey's Toontown Fair. Steam trains circle park. Wooded route.

**STREET PARTY**

**㉙ Move It! Shake It! Celebrate It!** ★★★★ ✓ 20 min. Cinderella Castle hub. Interactive parade-like show stars Disney and Pixar characters, dancers, stilt-walkers; invites guests to come into street and dance with performers.

**THEATRICAL SHOWS**

**⑥ Carousel of Progress** ★★★★ ✓ 21 min. Avg wait 13 min. Tomorrowland. Robotic family shows how electricity has improved family life. Rotating theater.

**⑨ Country Bear Jamboree** ★★ 16 min. Avg wait 10 min. Frontierland. Lowbrow musical revue stars robotic bears.

**⑪ Dream Along with Mickey** ★★★ 20 min. No seats, no shade. Fireworks burst. Cinderella Castle

forecourt, Fantasyland. With Mickey, Minnie Mouse; Donald Duck; Goofy; princesses; "Peter Pan" stars.

**⑬ The Enchanted Tiki Room—Under New Management** ★★ 9 min. Avg wait 5 min. Scary Tiki goddess, realistic thunderstorm. Adventureland. *AuDe* Iago ("Aladdin"), Zazu ("The Lion King") take over, make fun of, Disney's vintage robotic-bird revue.

**⑮ The Hall of Presidents** ★★★★★ ✓ 20 min. Avg wait 12 min. Liberty Square. Widescreen film followed by robotic presentation of every U.S. president, including speaking Washington, Obama. All-new show debuted 2009.

**㉘ Monsters Inc. Laugh Floor** ★★★ 15–20 min. Avg wait 15 min. Tomorrowland. Live comedy show has animated characters interact with audience.

**㊲ Stitch's Great Escape!** ★ 18 min. Avg wait 15 min. Height restriction 40 in. Restrictive harness, dark periods. Tomorrowland. *FastPass* Dark show creates illusion of Experiment 626 skittering around you.

**㊳ Storytime with Belle** ★★★ 15 min. Arrive 15 min early. Fantasyland. "Beauty and the Beast" heroine bring kids onstage to help tell her story. Intimate, cute.

**3-D MOVIE**

**㉖ Mickey's PhilharMagic** ★★★★★ ✓ 12 min. Avg wait 15 min. Some sudden images. Briefly totally dark. Fantasyland. *FastPass* Donald Duck travels through Disney's best animated musicals. Delightful.

# Restaurants and food

Magic Kingdom has four table-service restaurants, one character-meal buffet and seven indoor fast-food spots. Make **reservations** (available 180 days in advance; 190 days for Disney resort guests) as early as possible at 407-WDW-DINE (407-939-3463) or online at **disneyworld.disney.go.com/dining**. If you will be using the **Disney Dining Plan,** note that Cinderella's Royal Table (below) takes two credits.

**TABLE SERVICE**

Cinderella's Royal Table ★ *DP2 Disney Signature* Character meals $$$$$ Cinderella in lobby,

Fantasyland crowds are
light early in the morning

other princesses in dining room. B: $47 (children $31), 8–11:15a. L: $51 (children $32), Noon–3p. D: $57 (children $35), 4p–park close. Seats 184. Cinderella Castle, Fantasyland. With princesses at every meal starting Feb. 7, 2010, these Fairytale Dining pre-plated meals can still disappoint. Like before, you meet Cinderella only in the lobby, and are usually subtly rushed through your expensive meal. Prices do include a cheap toy and a nice souvenir photo with Cinderella. Meals are fully booked far in advance; reservations must be guaranteed. The Gothic hall overlooks Fantasyland. Much better princess meals can be found at 1900 Park Fare at Disney's Grand Floridian Resort (dinner with Cinderella and friends), and the Akershus Royal Banquet Hall at Epcot's Norway pavilion (assorted princesses, other female Disney stars).

**Liberty Tree Tavern** ★ ★ ★ ★ ✔ *DP* American $$$$ L: $11–$19; 11:30a–2:45p. D: $30 (children $15), 4p–park close. Seats 250. Liberty Square. Not a bar, this New England-themed restaurant serves a hearty menu in six dining rooms themed to Colonial American figures. At lunch, the crab cakes are smooth, the pot roast tender. Dinner is a fixed-price, family-style Thanksgiving feast. Window-side tables in the Paul Revere and John Paul Jones rooms offer views of evening parades. The smaller Betsy Ross room is quiet and cozy.

**The Plaza** ★ ★ ★ ★ ✔ *DP* American $$ L,D: $9–$13; 11a–park close. Seats 94. Main Street U.S.A. The crowd is calm, the salads and sandwiches good at this small Victorian cafe. Desserts from the adjacent ice cream parlor include hand-dipped shakes, splits and sundaes. A pleasant decor features marble-like tabletops, a carpeted floor and wrought iron chairs with padded seats. Restrooms are next door.

**Tony's Town Square** ★ ★ ★ ★ ✔ *DP* Italian $$$$ L: $11–$17; 11:30a–2:45p. D: $17–$28; 4:30p–park close. Seats 286. Main Street U.S.A. Overlooked by Disney neophytes, this comfortable cafe at the front of the park often has tables available, especially at 11:30 a.m. Lunch offers flatbreads, pasta, salads,

sandwiches; dinner has chicken, fish, pasta, seafood, steak. Marble tables, a tile floor and central fountain keep things cool. Many booths. Lightly themed as the restaurant in 1955's "Lady and the Tramp." A window in the back looks into that movie's alley.

### CHARACTER BUFFET

**Crystal Palace** ★ ★ *DP* American $$$$ Winnie the Pooh, Tigger, Eeyore, Piglet. B: $19 (children $11), 8–10:30a. L: $21 (children $12), 11:30a–2:45p. D: $29 (children $14), 3:45p–park close. Seats 400. Main Street U.S.A. During peak times it's hard to hear yourself think at this mediocre, crowded cafeteria. The characters are irresistible, but have so many tables to visit they hardly have time for you. Food is uneven—decent meats, fair eggs and seafood, salty soups and vegetables. The pretty dining room has marble tabletops, wrought iron chairs and cathedral windows, though a raised wood ceiling amplifies every sound. For the best experience, make your reservation at 8:05 a.m. (the first breakfast seating), 10:30 a.m. (the last) or 3:45 p.m. (the first dinner seating).

### INDOOR FAST FOOD

**Casey's Corner** *DPQ* Hot dogs. 11a–park close. Seats 123 inc. 43 inside. Main Street U.S.A. Good dogs, worn atmosphere, usually crowded. Large screen shows montage of Goofy sports cartoons. Named for the baseball poem "Casey at the Bat," the basis for a 1946 Disney cartoon.

**Columbia Harbour House** ✔ *DPQ* Sandwiches, fish, chicken, veggie chili. 10:30a–park close. Seats 593. Liberty Sq. Noisy downstairs, peaceful upstairs.

**Cosmic Ray's Starlight Cafe** *DPQ* Chicken, burgers, ribs, kosher. 10:30a–park close. Seats 1,162. Tomorrowland. Robotic lounge singer; different lines for different foods. Loud crowd.

**Diamond Horseshoe** *DPQ* Sandwiches. Open seasonally. Seats 300. Frontierland.

**Main Street Bakery** ✔ *DPQ* Bagels, pastry, yogurt parfaits, quiche. Park open–park close. Seats 29. Main Street U.S.A. Mornings are crowded.

**Pecos Bill Cafe** *DPQ* Burgers, wraps, salads. 10a–park close. Seats 1,107. Frontierland. Right rooms stay quiet.

**Pinocchio Village Haus** *DPQ* Pizza, chicken, salads. 10:30a–park close. Seats 400. Fantasyland. Very crowded, loud by noon.

## OUTDOOR FAST FOOD

**Aunt Polly's Dockside Inn** Desserts. Seats 44. Tom Sawyer Island, Frontierland.

**Auntie Gravity's Galactic Goodies** Soft-serve ice cream, smoothies. Seats 12. Tomorrowland.

**Enchanted Grove** Swirls, slushes, orange juice. Seats 28. Fantasyland.

**El Pirata y el Perico Restaurante** ✓ *DPQ* Tacos, taco salads. Open seasonally. Shares 1,107 seats with Pecos Bill Cafe. Adventureland.

**Friars Nook** Hot dogs, chicken sandwiches, salads, fries. Shares 53 seats with Mrs. Potts. Formerly Village Fry Shoppe. Fantasyland.

**Liberty Square Market** ✓ Corn on the cob, baked potatoes, fresh fruit. Seats 22. Liberty Square.

**The Lunching Pad** *DPQ* Turkey legs, pretzels, frozen drinks. Seats 83. Tomorrowland.

**Mrs. Potts' Cupboard** Soft-serve ice cream. Seats 53. (You, too, can look like a teapot!) Fantasyland.

**Plaza Ice Cream Parlor** ✓ Hand-dipped ice cream treats. Seats 40. Main Street U.S.A.

**Scuttle's Landing** Muffins, pretzels, coffee. Seats 80 under covered pavilion. Fantasyland.

**Sleepy Hollow** Funnel cakes, caramel corn, soft-serve ice cream. Seats 51. Liberty Square.

**Sunshine Tree Terrace** Frozen orange juice swirled with vanilla soft serve, slushes, floats. Seats 46. Adventureland.

**Tomorrowland Terrace Noodle Station** *DPQ* Menu varies. Seasonal. Seats 500. Tomorrowland.

## NOTABLE SNACK STANDS

Legendary 'Dole Whip' pineapple/vanilla soft-serve (also juice, pineapple spears, floats) is served at Adventureland's **Aloha Isle,** across from Swiss Family Treehouse. At Mickey's Toontown Fair, the **Toontown Farmer's Market** has yogurt, fresh fruit.

# Shopping

## MAIN STREET U.S.A.

**The Art of Disney** Fine art. Lithographs, oils, porcelain, 2-ft. character figurines, Disney books. 'Main Street Cinema' facade.

**The Chapeau** Caps, novelty hats. Custom monogrammed Mickey Mouse ears.

**Crystal Arts** Crystal, glass. Ceramics, decorative swords. Craftsmen work in view of guests.

**Disney Clothiers** Apparel. Fashion, sportswear.

**The Emporium** Main souvenir store. T-shirts, other apparel, toys. Infant wear. Caps, novelty hats.

Princess, Tinker Bell costumes. Housewares, books, costume jewelry, pet items, sandals.

**Firehouse Gift Station** Firefighter, police-themed items. Pet products. Engine Co. 71. Decor includes authentic fire-fighting paraphernalia.

**Harmony Barber Shop** Haircuts. 9a–4:30p. daily. No reservations. The tiny shop has authentic 1920s barber chairs and an 1870s shoeshine chair.

**Main Street Confectionery** Candy store. Fudge; candy, caramel, chocolate apples; cotton candy; peanut brittle all made within guest view.

**Newsstand** Souvenirs. Inside park turnstiles.

**Town Square Exposition Hall** Photo shop. PhotoPass counter, collectible pins. Kodak camera history exhibit. Exterior replicates the look of the 1877 Adelphi Hotel in Saratoga, N.Y.

**Uptown Jewelers** Fine jewelry, watches. China figurines, clocks, collectible pins.

## ADVENTURELAND

**Agrabah Bazaar / Zanzibar Trading Co.** Apparel. African woodcarvings, musical instruments. Next to Magic Carpets of Aladdin.

**Bwana Bob's cart** Costume jewelry. Accessories. Adventureland entrance.

**Island Supply** Fashion apparel. Brands include Roxy, Quiksilver. Costume jewelry, sandals. Opposite Swiss Family Treehouse.

**La Princesa de Cristal** Crystal. Ceramics, glass art. Caribbean Plaza.

**Pirate's Bazaar** Pirate-themed items. T-shirts, apparel, costumes, toys. Costume jewelry. Includes new **Pirates League** makeover salon for all ages (reservations req.). Pirates of the Caribbean exit.

## FANTASYLAND

**Bibbidi Bobbidi Boutique** Children's hair, makeover salon. Girls made up to be princesses, Hannah Montana; boys "cool dudes." Cinderella Castle. Reservations req.

**Fantasy Faire** Disney sundries. Children's wear, books, Donald Duck items. Mickey's PhilharMagic.

**Pooh's Thotful Shop** Winnie the Pooh items. Books, DVDs, toys; children's wear, infant wear. Exit to The Many Adventures of Winnie the Pooh.

**Seven Dwarfs Mine** "Snow White and the Seven Dwarfs" merchandise. Character costumes, T-shirts. At exit to Snow White's Scary Adventures.

**Sir Mickey's** Disney sundries. Monogrammed Mickey Mouse ears; sandals. Next to Cinderella Castle. Themed to two cartoons: 1938's "The Brave

▲ **Park music**
Fireworks, parade and attraction soundtracks. Emporium. $12.98–$19.98

▼ **Dumbo plush** 14-inch, Emporium. $19.95

▶ **Cinderella figurine**
Disney Traditions "Princess of Dreams," from Walt Disney Showcase Collection. Uptown Jewelers. $35

▲ **Haunted Mansion license plate**
Reflective metal. Emporium. $8

◀ **Roo bean bag**
9-inch. Pooh's Thotful Shop. $11.95

▶ **Remote control Space Cruiser** from Buzz Lightyear's Space Ranger Spin. Includes cordless remote control. Emporium. $16

▲ **Magic Kingdom retro T-shirts** Juniors, various styles. $21.95. **Retro caps,** one size. $19.95. Both at Emporium.

▼ **Walt Disney World Railroad** With engine, tender, two passenger cars, track, characters. Emporium. $74.95

Little Tailor" (Mickey Mouse defeats a giant to win Princess Minnie's hand) and 1947's "Mickey and the Beanstalk" (with the famous quick-growing vine). **Tinker Bell's Treasures** Princess, Tinker Bell merchandise. Character costumes, accessories; costume jewelry. Next to Cinderella Castle.

## FRONTIERLAND
**Briar Patch** Disney sundries. Splash Mountain, Big Thunder Mountain T-shirts. Splash Mountain.
**Frontier Trading Post** Pin central.
**Prairie Outpost & Supply** Candy, coffee, treats. Replicates old general store.

## LIBERTY SQUARE
**Heritage House** Americana. History books; presidential merchandise; family-name history, family-crest items. Hall of Presidents.
**Madame Leota's cart** Haunted Mansion merchandise. Pins, toys. Haunted Mansion.
**Yankee Trader** Housewares. Front porch has rocking chairs.
**Ye Olde Christmas Shoppe** Christmas items.

## MICKEY'S TOONTOWN FAIR
**County Bounty** General merchandise. T-shirts, caps and novelty hats, children's wear, infant's wear. Princess, Tinker Bell costumes. Books, housewares, pet items, sandals, toys. Candy from Main Street Confectionery. Looks like a fair tent.

## TOMORROWLAND
**Buzz Star Command** "Toy Story" items. Buzz Lightyear's Space Ranger Spin T-shirts, R/C vehicles. At Buzz Lightyear's Space Ranger Spin.
**Merchant of Venus** "Star Wars," Stitch merchandise. Adjacent to Stitch's Great Escape.
**Mickey's Star Traders** General merchandise. Disney souvenirs, T-shirts.
**Space Mountain shop** Disney items. Space Mountain T-shirts. Space Mountain.

# Character locations

### MICKEY MOUSE AND FRIENDS
**Mickey Mouse, Minnie Mouse** Optimistic everyman; girlfriend ❊ Judge's Tent, Mickey's Country House, Mickey's Toontown Fair.
**Donald Duck** Foul-tempered fowl Across from Frontierland Shootin' Gallery.
**Goofy** Good-natured, dim-witted dog-man Left of Splash Mountain, Frontierland.
**Pluto** Mickey's pet Town Square, Main Street U.S.A.

**Characters at Magic Kingdom include Alice and the Mad Hatter (top) from 1951's "Alice in Wonderland" and Tinker Bell (above)**

## PRINCESSES

**Ariel** Star of 1989's "The Little Mermaid" Ariel's Grotto, Fantasyland.

**Aurora** Star of 1959's "Sleeping Beauty" ❊ Toontown Hall of Fame, Mickey's Toontown Fair; ❊ Cinderella's Royal Table (B,L; often), Cinderella Castle.

**Belle** Star of 1991's "Beauty and the Beast" ❊ Toontown Hall of Fame, Mickey's Toontown Fair; after "Storytime with Belle," Fairytale Garden, Fantasyland; ❊ Cinderella's Royal Table (B,L; often), Cinderella Castle.

**Cinderella** Star of 1950's "Cinderella" ❊ Toontown Hall of Fame, Mickey's Toontown Fair; ❊ Cinderella's Royal Table (B,L), Cinderella Castle.

**Jasmine** Co-star of 1992's "Aladdin" Magic Carpets of Aladdin, Adventureland; ❊ Cinderella's Royal Table (B,L; often), Cinderella Castle.

**Snow White** Star of 1937's "Snow White and the Seven Dwarfs" Town Square outside Expo Hall*, Main Street U.S.A.; ❊ Toontown Hall of Fame, Mickey's Toontown Fair; ❊ Cinderella's Royal Table (B,L; often), Cinderella Castle.

**Tiana, Prince Naveen** Stars of 2009's "The Princess and the Frog" Behind Ye Olde Christmas Shoppe, Liberty Square.

## OTHER CHARACTERS

**Aladdin** Star of 1992's "Aladdin" Magic Carpets of Aladdin, Adventureland.

**Alice, Mad Hatter** Stars of 1951's "Alice in Wonderland" Mad Tea Party, Fantasyland.

**Buzz Lightyear** "Toy Story" space ranger Carousel of Progress, Tomorrowland.

**Captain Hook, Mr. Smee** Head pirate, comical first mate in 1953's "Peter Pan" Pirates of the Caribbean, Adventureland.

**Chip 'n Dale** 1940s–50s cartoon chipmunks Town Square, Main Street U.S.A.

**Daisy Duck** Donald Duck's girlfriend Town Square, Main Street U.S.A.

**Dopey** Dimwit dwarf in 1937's "Snow White and the Seven Dwarfs" Town Square, Main Street U.S.A.

**Fairy Godmother** From 1950's "Cinderella" Cinderella Castle (back left corner), Fantasyland; ❊ Cinderella's Royal Table (D), Cinderella Castle.

**Gus, Jacques** Lead mice in 1950's "Cinderella" ❊ Cinderella's Royal Table (D), Cinderella Castle.

\* Moves inside Exposition Hall in inclement weather.
❊ Air-conditioned meeting area.

Appearance times vary. For weekly updated schedules of Walt Disney World characters and street performers log on to pages.prodigy.net/stevesoares.

**Top: Lady Tremaine from 1950's "Cinderella."**
**Above: Citizen of Main Street Inga DaPointe channels Dolly Levi of 1969's "Hello Dolly."**

**Lady Tremaine, Anastasia, Drizella** Evil stepmother, stepsisters in 1950's "Cinderella" Fairytale Garden, Fantasyland.

**Mary Poppins** Star of 1964's "Mary Poppins" Town Square, Main Street U.S.A.

**Penguins** Waiters in 1964's "Mary Poppins" Town Square, Main Street U.S.A. (often with Mary).

**Peter Pan, Wendy** Stars of 1953's "Peter Pan" Pirates of the Caribbean, Adventureland.

**Pinocchio** Star of 1940's "Pinocchio" Town Square*, Main Street U.S.A.

**Pooh, Tigger, Eeyore, Piglet** Bear, tiger, donkey, piglet from 1977's "The Many Adventures of Winnie the Pooh" Pooh's Playful Spot, Fantasyland; ❋ Crystal Palace, Main Street U.S.A.

**Rafiki, Timon** Baboon, meerkat of 1994's "The Lion King" Adventureland front entrance veranda.

**Stitch** Mischievous alien of 2002's "Lilo & Stitch" Carousel of Progress, Tomorrowland.

**Tinker Bell, Fawn, Iridessa, Rosetta, Silvermist, Terence** Fairies (Tinker Bell from 1953's "Peter Pan," other from modern books, movies; Terence is a sparrow man). ❋ Toontown Hall of Fame, Mickey's Toontown Fair.

**Woody, Jessie** Stars of "Toy Story" movies Splash Mountain, Frontierland.

# Street performers

## MUSICIANS AND SINGERS

**Casey's Corner Pianist** 20 min. Casey's Corner patio, Main Street U.S.A. Entertainer bangs out honky tonk, rag, requests.

**Dapper Dans** 20 min. Main Street U.S.A. Barbershop quartet mixes harmonically perfect repertoire with chimes, tap dancing and corny humor. Sings "Happy Birthday" on request.

**Fantasyland Woodwind Society** 20 min. Fantasyland. Sax quartet plays whimsical Disney tunes. Appears in mornings as Main Street Saxophone Four, Main Street U.S.A.

**Main Street Philharmonic** 20 min. Main Street U.S.A. Americana revue with 12-piece comedic brass band. Finale "volunteers" park guest to honk horn as band plays "Hold That Tiger."

**Main Street Saxophone Four** 20 min. Main Street U.S.A. Sax quartet harmonizes deftly on ragtime, jazz, Disney tunes. Same group appears in afternoon as Fantasyland Woodwind Society.

**The Notorious Banjo Brothers and Bob** 20 min. Frontierland. Two banjo pickers, tuba player perform Disney tunes, bluegrass, cowboy melodies such as "Back in the Saddle Again."

## STREET SHOWS

**Captain Jack Sparrow's Pirate Tutorial** 20 min. On left side of Pirates of the Caribbean entrance, Adventureland. Comical Capt. Jack, first mate Mack teach kids how to be rescued from deserted island, use swordplay trick to flee enemy, sing Disney tune "Yo Ho (A Pirate's Life for Me)."

**Frontierland Hoedown** 20 min. 4:45p. Some days have add'l later shows. In front of Prairie Outpost and Supply Shop, Frontierland. Seven friendly country couples teach guests to square dance, do hokey pokey. Country Bears characters play washboard, spoons. Brer Rabbit greets guests.

**Magic Kingdom Welcome Show** 8 min. Park entrance, inside turnstiles. Stage is train station. A Citizen of Main Street (below) welcomes Mickey Mouse, other characters and a selected guest family who arrive on Walt Disney World show train to open the park. Trolley Parade couples (see below) lip-sync a medley of "Good Morning" (from 1952's "Singin' in the Rain"), "Casey Junior" (from 1941's "Dumbo") and "Zip-A-Dee-Doo-Dah" (from 1946's "Song of the South").

**Main Street Trolley Parade** Three 5 min. shows per parade. Mornings only. Main Street U.S.A. Gay '90s couples hop off horse trolley to perform soft-shoe pantomime; lip-sync "The Trolley Song" (from 1944's "Meet Me in St. Louis"), service number that exalts Magic Kingdom (*"The place was made with a magical plan! And just around the corner is a Fantasyland!"*). So strange, yet so very Disney.

## IMPROVISATIONAL TROUPE

**Citizens of Main Street** 20 min. In streets, shops, restaurants of Main Street U.S.A. Portrays boulevard's living, breathing townsfolk. Characters include town mayor, councilman, fire chief, news reporter, voice teacher, assorted socialites. Characters chat, dance, joke, sing and pose for pictures with guests.

## PERFORMANCE ARTIST

**PUSH, The Talking Trashcan** 20 min, on walkway between Indy Speedway and Auntie Gravity's Galactic Goodies, Tomorrowland. Roving trash can jokes with guests.

## FLAG-LOWERING CEREMONY

**Flag Retreat** 20 min. 5p daily. Town Square, Main Street U.S.A. Park Security Color Guard lowers U.S. flag, often with guest military veteran. Includes Main Street Philharmonic, Dapper Dans.

Capt. Jack Sparrow trains new crew members at his Pirate Tutorial, held outside the Pirates of the Caribbean ride

# Planning Your Day

**For most families,** the key to a successful Magic Kingdom plan is simple: Do Fantasyland first thing in the morning. In the afternoon these short, classic rides have impossible lines. After that, however, you'll still need a good plan. With long lines often the rule rather than the exception, it's not possible to simply wing it and see everything you want.

## 1. Choose a day to go

Before deciding what day to visit Magic Kingdom, check what time the park closes on each day of your vacation. Choose a day with late hours, that includes a SpectroMagic parade and Wishes fireworks show. Operating hours are posted six months in advance at the "Calendar" link at **disneyworld. disney.go.com/parks/magic-kingdom**.

▶ **'Extra Magic Hours'** The park usually opens an hour early on Thursdays for guests staying at Disney resorts, and stays open late for these guests on Sundays. The extra hours makes it easier for those guests to see the most popular attractions, but, conversely, create a larger crowd during the regular morning and afternoon.

## 2. Decide what to do

There is something for everyone at Magic Kingdom. The trick is picking the right mix of attractions to see, because, with over 40 attractions at the park, it's impossible to experience them all in just one day. You'll find an "Attractions At a Glance" summary of everything there is to do earlier in this chapter, while further back are detailed descriptions. If you are traveling with

# HOUR-BY-HOUR WAIT TIMES

This table shows the average **wait time** (in min) for each Magic Kingdom ride or show that has one. *Live shows are shown with the early arrival time needed to get a good seat.

| ATTRACTION | 9A | 10A | 11A | Noon | 1P | 2P | 3P | 4P | 5P | 6P | 7P | 8P | 9P |
|---|---|---|---|---|---|---|---|---|---|---|---|---|---|
| Astro Orbiter | 5 | 10 | 30 | 30 | 25 | 35 | 25 | 40 | 40 | 40 | 20 | 20 | 10 |
| Barnstormer | CLSD | 0 | 10 | 10 | 20 | 25 | 30 | 20 | 15 | 20 | 30 | 20 | 10 |
| Big Thunder Mountain | 0 | 25 | 40 | 35 | 45 | 45 | 50 | 40 | 45 | 45 | 45 | 35 | 30 |
| Buzz Lightyear | 0 | 10 | 15 | 25 | 45 | 40 | 30 | 35 | 35 | 25 | 30 | 35 | 30 |
| Carousel of Progress | 5 | 5 | 5 | 5 | 5 | 5 | 5 | 5 | 5 | 5 | 5 | 5 | 5 |
| Cinderella Carrousel | 0 | 5 | 5 | 5 | 10 | 10 | 10 | 10 | 10 | 10 | 5 | 5 | 5 |
| Country Bears | CLSD | 0 | 10 | 10 | 10 | 10 | 10 | 10 | 10 | 10 | 10 | 10 | 10 |
| Dumbo | 0 | 25 | 25 | 25 | 25 | 35 | 35 | 45 | 40 | 30 | 30 | 30 | 20 |
| Enchant. Tiki Room | CLSD | 5 | 5 | 5 | 5 | 5 | 5 | 5 | 5 | 5 | 5 | 5 | 5 |
| Hall of Presidents | CLSD | 15 | 15 | 15 | 15 | 15 | 15 | 15 | 15 | 15 | 15 | 15 | 15 |
| Haunted Mansion | 0 | 10 | 10 | 20 | 20 | 25 | 25 | 15 | 15 | 10 | 10 | 5 | 5 |
| It's a Small World | 0 | 5 | 10 | 15 | 20 | 20 | 30 | 25 | 20 | 15 | 15 | 5 | 5 |
| Jungle Cruise | 0 | 15 | 30 | 30 | 40 | 45 | 45 | 40 | 30 | 30 | 20 | 20 | 10 |
| Liberty Sq Riverboat | CLSD | 15 | 15 | 15 | 15 | 15 | 15 | 15 | 15 | 15 | CLSD | CLSD | CLSD |
| Mad Tea Party | 0 | 5 | 10 | 10 | 15 | 15 | 15 | 15 | 15 | 15 | 10 | 10 | 10 |
| Magic Carpets | 0 | 5 | 10 | 15 | 15 | 10 | 5 | 5 | 5 | 5 | 10 | 10 | 0 |
| Mickey's House | CLSD | 0 | 15 | 15 | 15 | 20 | 25 | 25 | 20 | 20 | 15 | 15 | 10 |
| Mickey's PhilharMagic | 0 | 10 | 10 | 10 | 15 | 15 | 15 | 20 | 20 | 10 | 15 | 10 | 10 |
| Monsters Inc. | 0 | 15 | 20 | 15 | 15 | 20 | 15 | 15 | 15 | 15 | 10 | 10 | 10 |
| Peter Pan's Flight | 0 | 15 | 30 | 40 | 60 | 55 | 45 | 55 | 60 | 45 | 45 | 60 | 60 |
| Pirates of Caribbean | 0 | 5 | 15 | 15 | 20 | 20 | 15 | 10 | 5 | 5 | 5 | 5 | 5 |
| Snow White's Adv. | 0 | 15 | 15 | 15 | 20 | 25 | 30 | 25 | 25 | 25 | 30 | 25 | 25 |
| Space Mountain | 0 | 20 | 40 | 50 | 60 | 60 | 50 | 50 | 60 | 70 | 60 | 60 | 45 |
| Splash Mountain | 0 | 30 | 30 | 50 | 70 | 80 | 70 | 60 | 70 | 60 | 70 | 45 | 30 |
| Stitch's Great Escape | 0 | 5 | 10 | 20 | 20 | 15 | 15 | 10 | 20 | 10 | 15 | 5 | 5 |
| Storytime w/Belle* | CLSD | CLSD | 15 | 15 | 15 | 15 | 15 | 15 | 15 | CLSD | CLSD | CLSD | CLSD |
| Tom'land Speedway | 0 | 20 | 20 | 30 | 30 | 35 | 30 | 35 | 30 | 30 | 30 | 30 | 20 |
| Tom Sawyer Island | 0 | 5 | 5 | 15 | 20 | 20 | 20 | 15 | 5 | 5 | 5 | CLSD | CLSD |
| Toont'n Hall of Fame | CLSD | 0 | 40 | 50 | 70 | 65 | 60 | 70 | 70 | 75 | 70 | 70 | 70 |
| WDW Railroad | 5 | 5 | 5 | 5 | 5 | 5 | CLSD | 5 | 5 | 5 | 5 | 5 | CLSD |
| Winnie the Pooh | 0 | 15 | 30 | 35 | 40 | 45 | 35 | 30 | 35 | 35 | 45 | 30 | 30 |

Data based on surveys taken on random days during the summers of 2008 and 2009.

children, give them this book and have them point out the rides and shows they would like to see.

Hearing-impaired guests can take advantage of sign-language interpreted performances on Mondays and Thursdays: Move It! Shake It! Celebrate It! Street Party (5:40 p.m.), Dream Along with Mickey (10:35 a.m.), Storytime with Belle (noon), Celebrate a Dream Come True Parade (3 p.m.). The Jungle Cruise, Liberty Square

Riverboat and Monsters Inc. Laugh Floor also hold signed performances on these days; Guest Relations has times.

## 3. Family matters

Magic Kingdom is the most child-focused Walt Disney World theme park. It has the most rides, the most parades, and the most characters and places to meet them. And it's relatively condensed, with rides and shows placed closely together.

▶ **Height restrictions** exist at The Barnstormer (35 in.), Big Thunder Mountain Railroad (40 in.), Space Mountain (44 in.), Splash Mountain (40 in.), Stitch's Great Escape (40 in.) and Tomorrowland Indy Speedway (54 in. to take car out alone, 32 in. to ride in car as passenger).

▶ **Fear factors** Except Indy Speedway, all rides with height restrictions also have scary elements. Others that might scare young children include Astro Orbiter (fast, high, tilted flight), The Haunted Mansion (dark, with ominous atmosphere, some screams, pop-up heads), Pirates of the Caribbean (short, dark drop; realistic cannon battle; simulated fire) and, especially, Snow White's Scary Adventures (dark, threatening scenes).

▶ **Kids meals** Every park restaurant offers a children's menu. Magic Kingdom has two restaurants with character meals: Cinderella's Royal Table in Cinderella Castle and Crystal Palace off Main Street U.S.A.

▶ **Baby care** A Baby Care Center is next to the Crystal Palace restaurant, off Main Street U.S.A. It provides changing rooms, nursing areas, a microwave and a playroom. Diapers, formula, pacifiers and over-the-counter medications are available for purchase. Moms can nurse their babies anywhere; good spots include the tiny theater showing cartoons in the back of Exposition Hall and upstairs at Columbia Harbour House in Liberty Square.

▶ **Lost children** Report them to Guest Relations or any cast member.

## PARK RESOURCES

**ATMs** Lockers, City Hall, Adventure-land–Frontierland breezeway, near restrooms of Pinocchio Village Haus, Tomorrowland arcade.

**First Aid center** For minor emergencies. Registered nurses. Next to the Crystal Palace, Main Street U.S.A.

**Guest Relations** General questions, dining reservations, currency exchange. Maps, Times Guides for all WDW theme parks. Stores items found in the park that day. Multilingual. Walk-up window outside gate; City Hall on Main Street U.S.A.

**Lockers** $7 a day plus $5 deposit. Entrance plaza, on the right.

**Mobile app** (Verizon) $10, at m.disneyworld.com. "Mobile Magic" covers all WDW theme parks.

**Package pickup** Up to 3 hours before you leave, anything you buy in the park can be sent to Package Pickup for you to pick up on your way out free of charge. Packages can also be delivered the next day to your Disney hotel or shipped to your home. Left of City Hall, Main Street U.S.A.

**Parking** $14 per day. Free for Disney resort guests, annual passholders.

**Strollers** Singles $15/day, $13/day length of stay. Doubles $31, $27. Stroller Shop, just inside entrance.

**Tip Board** Shows attraction wait times. Main Street U.S.A.

**Transportation** Monorails to Epcot; Contemporary, Grand Fla., Polynesian resorts. Boats to Ft. Wilderness, Grand Fla., Polynesian, Wilderness Lodge resorts. Walkway to Contemporary. Buses to Animal Kingdom, Blizzard Beach, Hollywood Studios, all other Disney hotels. No direct service to Downtown Disney, Typhoon Lagoon.

**Wheelchairs, Scooters** Wheelchairs $12/day, $10/day length of stay. Electric Convenience Vehicles (4-wheeled scooters) $50/day w/$20 deposit. Stroller Shop, just inside entrance.

Even though most park attractions are indoors, rain drives guests away. Most gift shops sell plastic rain ponchos.

## 4. Decide where to eat

Flip back a few pages to find listings of every Magic Kingdom restaurant.

## 5. Make a plan

As you create your plan, keep in mind the average wait times and typical Fastpass return times for the rides and shows you want to see. You can find weekly schedules for parades and fireworks at the "Calendar" link at **disneyworld.disney.go.com/parks/magic-kingdom.** Schedules of characters and street performers are online at **pages.prodigy.net/stevesoares.** Assume you need to arrive 15 minutes early for a table-service reservation. For a road-tested ready-made plan, see our "A Magical Day" schedule below.

## A MAGICAL DAY

| | |
|---|---|
| **8:30a** | Arrive at the entrance turnstiles. Be sure to allow time for your boat, bus or monorail trip. |
| **8:55a** | Rush to Fantasyland. The crowd will be light, so you'll be able to see every major attraction in one hour. Do them in this order: Dumbo the Flying Elephant, Peter Pan's Flight, It's a Small World, Mickey's PhilharMagic. |
| **9:55a** | Get Fastpasses for The Many Adventures of Winnie the Pooh. |

| | |
|---|---|
| **10:00a** | Mickey's Toontown Fair. Meet Tinker Bell and her pixie friends at the Toontown Hall of Fame. Then meet Mickey and Minnie Mouse in the Judge's Tent behind Mickey's Country House. |
| **11:15a** | Use your Fastpasses at The Many Adventures of Winnie the Pooh. |
| **11:45a** | Get Space Mountain Fastpasses. |
| **Noon** | Lunch at Liberty Tree Tavern, Liberty Square. Make your reservations ahead of time. |

# FASTPASS RETURN TIMES

Nine park attractions offer Disney's Fastpass system, a free service which reserves a time for you to return later in the day to experience that ride or show without standing in the regular line. This table shows the average **return times** for Fastpasses dispensed at those attractions for each hour of a typical park day. Note that Peter Pan's Flight and Space Mountain typically run out of Fastpasses by late afternoon.

| ATTRACTION | 9A | 10A | 11A | Noon | 1P | 2P | 3P | 4P | 5P | 6P | 7P | 8P | 9P |
|---|---|---|---|---|---|---|---|---|---|---|---|---|---|
| Big Thunder Mount. | 10:05 | 10:35 | 11:45 | 12:35 | 1:50 | 2:45 | 3:40 | 4:40 | 5:40 | 6:40 | 7:40 | 8:50 | 9:35 |
| Buzz Lightyear | 10:20 | 10:45 | 11:50 | 12:40 | 2:15 | 3:10 | 4:00 | 5:15 | 5:45 | 6:50 | 7:50 | 8:45 | 9:35 |
| Jungle Cruise | 9:40 | 10:30 | 11:40 | 12:35 | 2:10 | 2:35 | 3:35 | 4:35 | 5:35 | 6:40 | 7:35 | 8:35 | 9:30 |
| Mickey's PhilharMagic | 10:05 | 10:40 | 11:40 | 12:40 | 1:40 | 2:40 | 3:40 | 4:40 | 5:40 | 6:40 | 7:40 | OUT | OUT |
| Peter Pan's Flight | 10:10 | 10:40 | 11:50 | 1:15 | 4:10 | 4:45 | 6:40 | 8:30 | 9:25 | OUT | OUT | OUT | OUT |
| Space Mountain | 10:10 | 11:10 | 12:25 | 3:30 | 5:25 | 6:40 | 7:40 | 9:00 | OUT | OUT | OUT | OUT | OUT |
| Splash Mountain | 10:05 | 10:35 | 11:45 | 12:45 | 2:40 | 4:00 | 5:25 | 6:15 | 7:10 | 8:05 | 8:45 | 9:35 | OUT |
| Stitch's Great Escape | 10:10 | 10:40 | 11:45 | 12:40 | 1:40 | 2:50 | 3:45 | 4:40 | 6:00 | 6:50 | 7:50 | 8:40 | OUT |
| Winnie the Pooh | 10:10 | 10:40 | 11:40 | 12:40 | 1:50 | 3:10 | 4:20 | 5:50 | 6:40 | 7:20 | 8:05 | 9:10 | 9:40 |

Data based on surveys taken on random days during the summers of 2008 and 2009.

## 6. Beating the heat

A good trick to staying cool is to walk through the stores instead of walking outside on the streets and walkways. You have the chance to get wet on Splash Mountain. A good spot to sit and cool off is the back of Exposition Hall, which has a tiny theater showing classic Disney cartoons.

## 7. What if it rains?

There are lots of places to duck out of the rain at Magic Kingdom, mostly stores and counter-service restaurants. The Barnstormer and Big Thunder Mountain Railroad roller coasters close when it rains, and the parades, street party, outdoor performances and fireworks can get cancelled. Astro Orbiter, Donald's Boat, Dumbo the Flying Elephant, Jungle Cruise, Liberty Square Riverboat, Magic Carpets of Aladdin, Main Street Vehicles, Splash Mountain, Swiss Family Treehouse, Tomorrowland Indy Speedway and Tom Sawyer Island close when lightning is in the area, as does the Walt Disney World Railroad.

| | | | |
|---|---|---|---|
| 1:00p | Get Fastpasses for Buzz Lightyear's Space Ranger Spin. | 5:15p | Leave Magic Kingdom. Take the monorail to the Grand Floridian |
| 1:10p | Ride Pirates of the Caribbean. | | Resort to have dinner with |
| 1:45p | Get Splash Mountain Fastpasses. | | Cinderella at 1900 Park Fare. |
| 2:05p | Use your Fastpasses to ride Buzz Lightyear's Space Ranger Spin. | | Make reservations ahead of time. |
| | | 7:30p | Return to Magic Kingdom to |
| 2:45p | Use your Fastpasses to ride Space Mountain. | | watch the SpectroMagic parade. |
| | | 9:00p | Watch the Wishes fireworks |
| 3:45p | Get Fastpasses for Big Thunder Mountain Railroad. | | show from Main Street U.S.A., near the castle hub. |
| 4:45p | Use your Fastpasses to ride Splash Mountain. | 9:30p | Use your Fastpasses to ride the Big Thunder Mountain Railroad. |

**Built in 1925,** the 10-wheel Roger E. Broggie steam locomotive is one of four in Disney's fleet

# Walt Disney World Railroad

★ ★ ★ 20 min round trip (1.5 mi). Capacity: 360. Outdoor covered queue. Fear factor: None. No eating, drinking, smoking. Idle during parades, fireworks, thunderstorms. Folding strollers OK, no Disney rental strollers. Access: Must be ambulatory. Handheld captioning available. Debuted: 1971.

Chugging around the outside of the park, these full-size trains stop at Main Street U.S.A., Frontierland and Mickey's Toontown Fair. Pulled by authentic steam locomotives, the open passenger cars look like Industrial Age street trolleys. Though a folksy narrator warns "Be on the lookout!" there are no surprises. Ironically, the ride does not show much of the park. You only glimpse three attractions—Splash Mountain, Big Thunder Mountain Railroad and the Tomorrowland Indy Speedway. You do pass two small Indian encampments and some wildlife figures, including two "snapping" alligators. Most of the trip is heavily wooded.

| Average Wait | |
| --- | --- |
| 9am | 5 min |
| 10am | 5 |
| 11am | 5 |
| Noon | 5 |
| 1pm | 5 |
| 2pm | 5 |
| 3pm | closed |
| 4pm | 5 |
| 5pm | 5 |
| 6pm | 5 |
| 7pm | 5 |
| 8pm | 5 |
| 9pm | closed |

Disney acquired the four steam engines from the United Railway of the Yucatan. Built by Philadelphia's Baldwin Locomotive Works between 1916 and 1928, they hauled passengers, jute, sisal and sugar cane through Mexico for decades. Disney had the engines restored at the Tampa Shipbuilding and Dry Dock Co. in 1971.

The Main Street station replicates an bygone small-town depot. Its lobby has working mutoscopes and other antique amusements (bring pennies to play). The lower level has vintage railway maps and placards that detail the engines' histories.

**Fun facts ❶** The trains travel at a speed between 10 and 12 mph. **❷** The steel bridge just past Frontierland is half of an original two-track bridge from the Florida Flagler route. **❸** Some trees past the Indian village have charred trunks, the result of falling Wishes fireworks. **❹** The engines take on water every third time they stop at the Mickey's Toontown Fair station. **❺** Every few hours, each engine gets a quick service from a Toontown Fair "pit crew." **❻** There are four sets of passenger cars—red, yellow, blue and green. **❼** The green passenger cars—known internally as the "show train" cars—appear only during the park's opening ceremony. In order for performers to exit that train's left side, those cars are missing their left safety rails.

▶ The best views are on the right, though live alligators sometimes swim in a canal on the left.

# Main Street Vehicles

★★★★ ✓ Apx 3 min, depending on traffic (and, with trolleys, the horse). No horse petting. Fear factor: None. Access: Must be ambulatory. Debuted: 1971.

These old-fashioned vehicles shuttle passengers between Town Square and Cinderella Castle. The rides are free, and there's never a line. The vehicles are only out in the mornings. The fleet consists of:

■ **Horse trolleys.** There are four of these open-air vehicles, which run on a track embedded in the center of the street. Passengers are often joined by the Dapper Dans barbershop quartet. Each trolley seats 22.

■ **A double-decker bus.** A replica of buses used in New York City in the 1920s, this International Harvester-built vehicle has a loud "ah-ooo-gah" horn to keep pedestrians out of its way. The 6-cylinder engine gives the bus the ability to top out at 50 mph, though around guests it never gets out of first gear. It seats 40.

■ **A miniature fire truck.** Complete with a giant spotlight and a ladder and fire hose strapped to its sides, this bright red vehicle seats eight.

■ **Horseless carriages.** Each literally a "surrey with the fringe on the top," these self-powered canopied carriages are based on luxury Franklin-brand automobiles built between 1903 and 1907. There are three vehicles, one blue, one red and one yellow. Each has two benches and seats six.

■ **Jitneys.** These two topless paddy wagons look like the small buses that once shuttled tourists along the Atlantic City, N.J., boardwalk. Each seats eight.

The trolley horses are all former workhorses. The

team is made up of three Percherons (Charlie, Dave and Lucky), two Belgians (Fritz and Drummer) and one flashy Clydesdale (Qes, nicknamed, for phonetic reasons only, "Queasy.") Formerly a lawnmower horse in Amish country, laid-back Fritz has been pulling the trolley for 11 years. All geldings, the horses are stabled at Fort Wilderness. An infant Clydesdale, Jacob, is being groomed to join the group in a few years.

Built specifically for the Disney company, the motorized vehicles are the same ones that debuted at Magic Kingdom when it opened in 1971. They run on natural gas.

**Fun fact** The motorized vehicles' license plates are dated "1915" to commemorate the first year the state of Florida issued automobile license plates.

**A Main Street trolley** pulled by the Clydesdale known among Disney cast members as "Queasy"

| Average Wait | |
|---|---|
| 9am | 0 min |
| 10am | 0 |
| 11am | 0 |
| Noon | 0 |
| 1pm | n/a |
| 2pm | n/a |
| 3pm | n/a |
| 4pm | n/a |
| 5pm | n/a |
| 6pm | n/a |
| 7pm | n/a |
| 8pm | n/a |
| 9pm | n/a |

▶ The horse trolleys stay on the street until 11:30 a.m. The other vehicles go in about noon.

Surrounded by tropical vegetation, the Swiss Family Treehouse is 60 feet tall and 90 feet wide

The bouncy, low-sided Magic Carpets can be a fun diversion for all ages, even teenagers

# Swiss Family Treehouse

★★ Allow 15 min. Capacity: 300. Shaded queue. Fear factor: None. Access: Must be ambulatory. Debuted: 1971 (Disneyland 1962).

Based on the 1960 movie "Swiss Family Robinson," this climb-through treehouse re-creates the makeshift home of a shipwrecked family. A narrow stairway leads past a dining room, kitchen and two bedrooms. The house is filled with ideas on how to live in the wild, from vine handrails to an ingenious water system that uses pulleys and bamboo buckets. The dining room's pull-stop organ is a real antique.

Unfortunately, the tree shows its age. Designed in 1962, it has no interactive elements, and its 62-step climb can exhaust guests who aren't that fit. The house seems the most realistic at night.

| Average Wait | |
| --- | --- |
| 9am | 0 min |
| 10am | 0 |
| 11am | 0 |
| Noon | 0 |
| 1pm | 0 |
| 2pm | 0 |
| 3pm | 0 |
| 4pm | 0 |
| 5pm | 0 |
| 6pm | 0 |
| 7pm | 0 |
| 8pm | 0 |
| 9pm | 0 |

# Magic Carpets of Aladdin

★★★ 90 sec. Capacity: 64. Shaded queue. Fear factor: None. Closed during thunderstorms. Access: ECV users must transfer to a wheelchair. Debuted: 2001.

This breezy hub-and-spoke ride can be more fun than Dumbo the Flying Elephant. The line is shorter, each low-sided vehicle seats four instead of two. Riders control their height and pitch, and can be "spit on" by a golden statue of a camel. (Want to get hit? Fly about halfway high.)

The ride is based on the 1992 movie "Aladdin." You fly on Prince Ali's carpet, circle Genie's bottle and hear instrumental versions of songs from the film.

**Hidden Mickey** Set in pavement behind the camel facing the ride, as a design on two yellow stones of a four-piece bracelet.

| Average Wait | |
| --- | --- |
| 9am | 0 min |
| 10am | 5 |
| 11am | 10 |
| Noon | 15 |
| 1pm | 15 |
| 2pm | 10 |
| 3pm | 5 |
| 4pm | 5 |
| 5pm | 5 |
| 6pm | 5 |
| 7pm | 10 |
| 8pm | 10 |
| 9pm | 0 |

▶ Rafiki, Timon, Aladdin and Jasmine often greet guests along the Adventureland walkway.

## The Enchanted Tiki Room — Under New Management

★★ 9 min. Capacity: 250. Opens 10a. Covered outdoor queue. Fear factor: A threatening goddess, thunderstorm effects. Access: Guests may remain in wheelchairs, ECVs. Assistive listening; handheld captioning. *AuDe* Debuted: 1998; original version 1971 (Disneyland 1963).

When Iago (from 1992's "Aladdin") and Zazu (1994's "The Lion King") take over this creaky musical revue of robotic birds and flowers, Iago wants to toss it for something more current. But when he insults the Tiki gods he learns that "you cannot toy with the Enchanted Tiki Room." Songs include "Hot Hot Hot," "Conga," and, from the mouths of Tiki poles, "In the Still of the Night."

It's an acquired taste.

An outdoor preshow has two talent-agent parrots trade bird-themed barbs over which one's client is the attractions' new owner.

**Average Wait**

| | |
|---|---|
| 9am | closed |
| 10am | 5 min |
| 11am | 5 |
| Noon | 5 |
| 1pm | 5 |
| 2pm | 5 |
| 3pm | 5 |
| 4pm | 5 |
| 5pm | 5 |
| 6pm | 5 |
| 7pm | 5 |
| 8pm | 5 |
| 9pm | 5 |

**Originally known as the Tropical Serenade,** the Tiki Room was redone with a new story in 1998

**Fun finds ❶** As the cockatoos start to sing "Conga," José says "I wonder what happened to Rosita," an original tiki bird no longer in the show. **❷** "Boy, I'm tired," Iago says just before the exit doors close. "I think I'll head over to the Hall of Presidents and take a nap."

**Fun facts ❶** Originally conceived as a restaurant, the Disneyland Tiki Room debuted in 1963 as Disney's first Audio-Animatronics attraction. After a barker bird out front enticed guests to "Come to the Tiki Room," everyone would sing along to 18 minutes of tunes such as "Let's All Sing Like the Birdies Sing." **❷** Unchanged over the years, the show's bird calls and whistles were all voiced by one man. A. Purvis Pullen was also the voice of Cheetah in the 1930s Johnny Weissmuller Tarzan films and Bonzo the chimp in the 1951 Ronald Reagan flick "Bedtime for Bonzo." **❸** Does Pierre sound like Lumiere, the candelabrum in 1991's "Beauty and the Beast"? Both are the late Jerry Orbach, Det. Lenny Briscoe on TV's "Law & Order." **❹** Don Rickles and the late Phil Hartman voice the preshow birds. **❺** The upside-down wall masks depict Negendei, the Earth Balancer, who is always portrayed standing on his head.

**Hidden Mickeys ❶** On the entrance doors, as 2-inch berries on a stem underneath a bird's tail, 4 feet off the ground. **❷** On the bottom of Iago's perch, where a small carved face is wearing Mickey ears.

▶ Sit on the left side of the theater and you'll face the Tiki goddess.

# Jungle Cruise

**Lush tropical vegetation** forms a canopy over the Jungle Cruise waterway

★★★ ✓ 10 min. Capacity: 310. *FastPass* Covered outdoor queue. Fear factor: A trip through a dark temple gets close to some unrealistic snakes. Closed during thunderstorms. Access: Guests may remain in wheelchairs, ECVs. Assistive listening; handheld captioning available. Debuted: 1971 (Disneyland 1955).

This tongue-in-cheek boat ride takes you through the jungles of the world. Your skipper tells corny jokes and puns as your canopied craft passes scenes that, though originally designed to be serious, are now played for laughs. Exploring the Amazon, Congo, Nile and Mekong rivers (all so narrow!) you learn such facts as "the Nile River goes for Niles and Niles and Niles. If you don't believe me, then you're in de-Nile."

Sights include dancing headhunters, a crashed plane and, inside a flooded temple, a monkey shrine guarded by pythons.

To a child the ride offers a lot. Its cartoonish scenes include one of gorillas sacking a camp that was re-created in 1999's "Tarzan." Rising hippo heads and squirting elephant trunks create some kid-friendly thrills.

Designed in the 1950s, the attraction isn't exactly modern. Many of its animals don't move, and the ones that do never change expression. The cultural stuff is often mixed up (the designs on the Congo canoes are Polynesian) and the colonialistic theme of it all is, if taken seriously, implicitly racist.

The ride makes more sense if you look at it from the personal perspective of Walt Disney: a Missouri farm boy's wide-eyed interpretation of the mysterious Third World. Disney wasn't looking down on these people and places, he—like most of 1950s America—just didn't know much about them. In fact, the ride's only buffoons are the British—the colonialists themselves. Portrayed as hapless boobs who never know what they're doing, they end up forced up a tree by a rhino.

Premiering at Disneyland shortly after that park's opening in 1955, the Jungle Cruise was originally a serious attraction, an educational tour of regions most Americans had never seen, even in pictures. The humor began in the 1960s, with the addition of the playful bathing elephant grotto (1962) and the treed safari party (1964). By the time the Florida version opened the entire thing was meant to be a joke. In 1994 the ride's

**Average Wait**

| | |
|---|---|
| 9am | 0 min |
| 10am | 15 |
| 11am | 30 |
| Noon | 30 |
| 1pm | 40 |
| 2pm | 45 |
| 3pm | 45 |
| 4pm | 40 |
| 5pm | 30 |
| 6pm | 30 |
| 7pm | 20 |
| 8pm | 20 |
| 9pm | 10 |

▶Ask nicely and your child may be able to join the real pilot in the wheelhouse.

queue area got its radio broadcast and some new props. In 1998 its boats were redone in their current vintage design, a look that includes cooking gear hanging from a roof net.

With all that in mind, the trip can be a jolly good time. Its best quips usually come at the end. "After five years of college you too can become a Jungle Cruise skipper!" a guide often tells guests. "My parents are so proud."

**Fun finds ❶** A sign along the queue honors the cruise company's latest Employee of the Month: E.L. O'Fevre. **❷** Toward the end of the queue, a cage holds a giant tarantula. It jerks and rears up. Next to it are crates labeled "arachnid sedative." **❸** A chalkboard on the dock lists the crew's weekly lunch menu as fricassee of giant stag beetle, BBQ'd 3-toed skink, consomme of river basin slug and fillet of rock python. **❹** The headhunters include the line "I love disco!" in their chant. It's often drowned out by the skipper's spiel. **❺** Next to the exit, a list of missing persons includes "Ilene Dover" followed by "Ann Fellen." **❻** Two crates just outside the exit were once part of the Swiss Family Treehouse landscape. One is addressed to "Thomas Kirk Esq." and "M. Jones" on the island of "Bora Danno," references to Tommy Kirk (a star of the 1960 film "Swiss Family Robinson" and the title character of the 1964's "The Misadventures of Merlin Jones") and James MacArthur (a "Swiss" star who went on to play "Danno" Williams in the 1968–1980 television series "Hawaii Five-O"). The other is addressed to "Swiss" director Kenneth Annakin.

**Fun facts ❶** The river is only 3 feet deep. **❷** The water is dyed its dark, murky color. **❸** Walt Disney wanted the trip to have live animals. The robotic versions were Plan B. **❹** The boats are on a track. Skippers control their speed, but not their course.

**Hidden Mickeys ❶** The queue-area radio plays Cole Porter's 1935 hit "You're the Top," including the lyrics "you're a Bendel bonnet, a Shakespeare sonnet, you're Mickey Mouse!" **❷** On the side of

**Smiling elephants** bathe beside a waterfall along the Jungle Cruise

the crashed plane, between and below the windows. **❸** As yellow spots on the back of a giant spider in the temple, on your right just past the snakes. **❹** In the framing of the temple, directly above each of the statues on your left (nearly impossible to see because of the darkness). Some of these are said to be Hidden Minnies, as they have what can look like bows (three smaller circles) on their heads.

**SHRUNKEN NED'S JUNIOR JUNGLE BOATS**
You steer a miniature Jungle Cruise boat through obstacles at this diversion at the ride entrance. The boats are hard to control. If you play, pick one that's already in a fun spot and not stuck behind something. Rely on your forward gear. $2 for 2 minutes.

▶ **Consider a night cruise. The line will be short and the boat's spotlight adds to the fun.**

LYRICS © WONDERLAND MUSIC COMPANY INC.

**The Pirates of the Caribbean** facade resembles the 16th-century El Morro fortress of Puerto Rico

# Pirates of the Caribbean

★★★★★ ✓ 9 min. Capacity: 330 (15 per boat). Indoor, air-conditioned queue. Fear factor: Darkness, cannon fire may scare toddlers. Access: ECV and wheelchair users must transfer. Handheld captioning available. *AuDe* Debuted: 1973, revised 2006 (Disneyland 1967).

A rowdy, rum-soaked version of It's a Small World, this dark indoor boat ride takes you on a slow-moving cruise through stage sets filled with robotic characters. But instead of clean, cute little dolls singing a clean, cute little song, here you get hairy, scruffy, drunken life-size pirates who, as the attraction's jaunty theme "Yo Ho (A Pirate's Life For Me)" says, *"pillage and plunder... rifle and loot... kidnap and ravage and don't give a hoot."*

The inspiration for the series of "Pirates of the Caribbean" motion pictures, the ride keeps a lightweight tone. Audio-Animatronics villains have such carica-tured features they seem straight out of a cartoon. Updated in 2006 to include characters from the movies, the ride features Davy Jones, Capt. Hector Barbossa and Capt. Jack Sparrow. The Sparrow robot looks just like Johnny Depp. Special effects simulate fire, lightning, wind and splashing cannon fire. There's one fall, but it's short.

### Aye, a Story There Be!
The attraction has a storyline, though it's tough to grasp without repeat visits. After the 2006 revision, it now tells the tale of Capt. Barbossa's sacking of a Spanish port in the Caribbean as he searches for Capt. Jack. Barbossa's men loot the village, cap-ture its women and set fire to its buildings. Meanwhile, the sneaky Sparrow nabs the town's treasure.

The ride tells its story in flashback form. It begins with the present—a watery grotto lined with the skeletons of dead pirates— then takes you back to the past, to the golden age of piracy. You take the time trip despite the warnings of Davy Jones, the octopus-faced ocean ruler who appears in the fog.

Literally falling into the waters of an old Caribbean port, you sail between the guns of Barbossa's ship and those of a Spanish fortress. As shots splash close to your boat, Barbossa yells "It's Capt. Jack we're after,

| Average Wait | |
|---|---|
| 9am | 0 min |
| 10am | 5 |
| 11am | 15 |
| Noon | 15 |
| 1pm | 20 |
| 2pm | 20 |
| 3pm | 15 |
| 4pm | 10 |
| 5pm | 5 |
| 6pm | 5 |
| 7pm | 5 |
| 8pm | 5 |
| 9pm | 5 |

▶ The right queue has the most fun detail, including some chess-playing skeletons.

and a fortune in gold!" Attempting to literally shiver Barbossa's timbers, the Spanish respond with "¡Apenten! ¡Disparen! ¡Fuego!" ("Ready! Aim! Fire!")

Rounding a bend, you come upon more of Barbossa's crew in a courtyard, interrogating the mayor by dunking him in a well. "Where be Capt. Jack Sparrow and the treasure, ya bilge rat?" one demands. Actually Jack is just a few feet away, peering out from behind some dressmaker forms.

Next you sail through a bridal auction, where a band of buccaneers are selling off the town's maidens to raucous, drunken hecklers.

Another turn sends you deeper into the village. As an old pirate with a treasure map rambles on ("What I wouldn't give to see the look on Capt. Jack Sparrow's face when he hears tell 'tis only me that gots the goods…"), Sparrow himself pops up out of a barrel, sneaking a peek at the old salt's map before ducking back out of sight. Behind those two, a few Spanish matrons chase looting pirates in endless circles.

Other scenes show pirates setting fire to the town and trying to escape from its jail by luring a dog that holds keys. In the finale a giddy Sparrow has found the village treasure room. Lolling on an ornate rocking chair, leg draped over an arm, he sings, slurs, and chats with a parrot.

### Historic It Be

The last ride developed by Walt Disney, Pirates of the Caribbean combines a Missouri farm boy's view of high-seas adventure with a Hollywood showman's use of theatrics. "Walt came from a world of movies," explains Imagineer Jason Surrell. "He wanted rides that use lighting and backdrops, establishing shots and lots of characters—up-close ones who are most important, and far-away characters who are less so."

Premiering at California's Disneyland in the 1960s, the attraction was not part of

**Bone daddy.** A skeleton sailor greets guests outside the entrance to Pirates of the Caribbean

Walt Disney World when it opened in 1971. Disney officials figured the ride wouldn't be popular in Florida since the actual Caribbean is close by. They changed their minds almost immediately, and debuted this version in 1973, just two years later.

Additional 2006 improvements include a revamped soundtrack featuring the new films' rousing instrumental theme, a new sound system that adds a "whumph" to each cannon shot, and remastered vintage tracks that make it easier to understand what the pirates are saying. An upgraded lighting system makes everything easier to see.

### PC It Be Not

The attraction's story is all in good fun, but even the most carefree parent may wonder

▶ Captain Hook and Mr. Smee often greet guests across from the ride entrance.

**Two pirates loot and set fire to a Spanish port** in a scene from Pirates of the Caribbean

if scenes showing torture, heavy drinking and the selling of women are sending the best messages to a wide-eyed child. "There is nothing politically correct about Pirates of the Caribbean," admits Imagineer Eric Jacobson. "Much of it is patently offensive."

In fairness, the ride does imply the results of such behavior. As the first scene illustrates, the pirates end up murdered, their skeletons left behind in a deserted cave.

It *is* more sensitive than it used to be. That barrel that now holds Capt. Jack? Originally it hid an embarrassed young woman, nearly naked. As the pirate in front held her slip in his hand, he spoke of his desire to "hoist me colors on the likes of that shy little wench." Then, believe it or not, this Disney character added: "I be willin' to share, I be!"

To most, the ride is a hoot. As we heard some college girls sing as they waited in line (to the tune of "It's a Small World"):

*"It's a world of fog and a world of caves.*
*It's a world of torture and of sex slaves.*
*But there's gold, and there's rum!*
*Johnny Depp? He's no bum!*
*It's the Disney pirates ride!"*

**Fun finds Entrance:** ❶ Along the right entrance queue, visible through some right windows, two chess-playing pirates in a dungeon apparently reached a stalemate some time ago. Their skeletons still stare at the board. **Caverns:** ❷ A crab on your left rears up as it moves its eyes, claws and pinchers. **Harbor attack:** ❸ A sign on the ship's stern reveals its name: the Wicked Wench. ❹ Capt. Barbossa orders his men to "Strike yer colors, ye bloomin' cockroaches!" **Interrogation:** ❺ The captain has a hook for a hand. ❻ When the pirates ask the mayor where Jack is, his wife calls from the window "Don't tell him Carlos! Don't be chicken!" Carlos responds "I am no chicken! I will not talk!" ❼ Jack's hands rest on the derrieres of the female forms around him. **Bridal auction:** ❽ A crate on your left is filled with bobbing, clucking chickens. ❾ The first woman in line is beaming, happy to be sold. ❿ The auctioneer refers to her portly body as "stout-hearted and cornfed" and asks her to "shift yer cargo, dearie. Show 'em yer larboard side." ⓫ Impatient to be next, a buxom redhead pulls up her skirt to show her leg. ⓬ The auctioneer instructs her to "Strike yer colors you brazen wench! No need to expose yer superstructure!" ⓭ The second-to-last woman is crying. **Chasing scene:** ⓮ A drunken pirate to your right invites two gray cats to join him in "a little ol' tot of rum." **Burning town:** ⓯ On your left, a dog barks along to the cantina band. ⓰ On the right a snoring pirate lolls in the mud with three intoxicated pigs. His chest heaves. ⓱ As you leave that scene, the hairy leg of a pirate above dangles toward your face. ⓲ A parrot with him squawks "A parrot's life for me!" **Dungeon:** ⓳ Frustrated the dog in front of the jail won't respond, a prisoner demands "Hit him with the soup bone!" ⓴ As the dog looks at you, another captive says "Rover, it's us what needs yer ruddy help, not them blasted lubbers." **Treasure room:** ㉑ Jack says the loot is "my reward for a life of villainy, larceny, skullduggery and persnickety." ㉒ After Jack sings the "Yo, Ho" lyric "maraud and embezzle and even hijack" his parrot interrupts with "Hi Jack! Hi Jack!" ㉓ Jack refers to the colorful bird as "my chromatic winged beast." **Exit area:** ㉔ Painted on the exit ramp's moving walkway, "shoeprints" that indicate where to step consist of a normal right shoe and peg-leg left mark.

**Fun facts** ❶ The Davy Jones fog screen is made of water droplets so small that you stay dry as you pass through them. The droplets are held in place by columns of air. ❷ The fall drops 14 feet. ❸ The voices of Davy Jones and Capts. Barbossa and Sparrow are those of Bill Nighey, Geoffrey Rush and Johnny Depp. ❹ The auctioneer is Paul Frees, the Haunted Mansion's ghost host. ❺ In reality, the redhead is little more than a pole from the waist down. ❻ The ride has 125 Audio-Animatronics characters: 65 people and 60 animals. ❼ The exterior facade, the "Castillo del Morro," is based on the 16th-century El Morro fortress in San Juan, P.R.

▶ Peter Pan and Wendy are often across from the ride exit, ready to greet fans.

© DISNEY

**Barack Obama speaks** at the Hall of Presidents

# The Hall of Presidents

★★★★★ ✔ 20 min. Capacity: 740. Open 10a–park close. Every 30 min. on hr, half hr. Indoor queue. Fear factor: None. Access: Guests may stay in wheelchairs, ECVs. Assistive listening, reflective captioning. Debuted: 1971, updated 2009.

"The American Dream is as old as our founding, but as timeless as our hopes. It is reborn every day in the heart of every child who wakes up in a land of limitless possibilities, in a country where 'we the people' means 'all the people.'"

Those are the words of President Barack Obama, as spoken by his robotic counterpart at this totally revamped patriotic theatrical show. It combines an inspiring short film with a unique Audio-Animatronics stage show.

Fans of American history, parents wanting to inspire their children with the American dream, or perhaps just anyone longing for a return to civility in American civics, should love every minute.

Children of nearly any age can enjoy it, as the show is always visual and focuses more on an inspirational message than any dry set of facts or figures. It plays in a comfortable, air-conditioned theater near the center of the park. Actor Morgan Freeman narrates the presentation, which now has the formal title "The Hall of Presidents: A Celebration of Liberty's Leaders."

As it always has, the show begins with a large-format film. Starting with George Washington's struggle to build a new nation, the movie scans U.S. history through the start of the 21st century, highlighting presidents who have reached out to the American people during times of strife. Those featured include Franklin Roosevelt during the Great Depression, Lyndon Johnson after the assassination of John F. Kennedy, Bill Clinton in the aftermath of the Oklahoma City bombing and George W. Bush encouraging citizens at Ground Zero after 9-11.

Working with historian Doris Kearns Goodwin, Disney writer Pam Fisher developed what she calls "a very human story" designed in part to illustrate how anyone can grow up to become our nation's leader.

Midway through the film, a screen rises to reveal Abraham Lincoln sitting alone on the stage. He stands, then delivers his full (ten-sentence) Gettysburg Address.

When the film ends, a curtain rises to show every U.S. president appearing on

| Average Wait | |
| --- | --- |
| 9am | closed |
| 10am | 15 min |
| 11am | 15 |
| Noon | 15 |
| 1pm | 15 |
| 2pm | 15 |
| 3pm | 15 |
| 4pm | 15 |
| 5pm | 15 |
| 6pm | 15 |
| 7pm | 15 |
| 8pm | 15 |
| 9pm | 15 |

▶ Arrive early for a good seat. The new show plays to larger crowds than previous versions.

stage simultaneously—43 life-sized animated figures, stretching out three-deep across the 100-foot-wide podium. They are introduced one by one.

As before, the robotic presidents display many human traits, though now a little more smoothly. Each nods at the audience as he is introduced, and fidgets, shifts his weight, looks around or even whispers to counterparts as the roll call continues. Warren G. Harding nervously bounces his foot. (Longtime Hall of Presidents fans will note that the roll call is slower than before, and that the presidents have been regrouped into common eras.)

Once everyone is accounted for, George Washington stands. Using portions of his second inauguration speech, he explains the importance of the presidential oath of office. Standing nearby, Obama recites that oath and then offers his thoughts about the American dream.

Disney says its Obama figure is the most dynamic Audio-Animatronics figure the company has ever created. It has an array of subtle movements and facial expressions, such as pursing its lips to pronounce the sounds of b's and p's. Like the President himself, Disney's Obama makes a point by raising its hands open-palmed while shrugging its shoulders. After reciting the oath, it checks its notes before continuing.

Disney officials traveled to the White House to record Obama (in the Map Room) and film him for reference, and worked with White House staff to create the clothing and accessories worn by the Obama figure, including an appropriate lapel pin, watch and braided wedding band.

A refurnished lobby has many new artifacts. Large display cases exhibit personal presidential belongings such as George Washington's tea caddy and George W. Bush's inaugural cowboy boots. Other cases hold dresses and objects worn by several first ladies, including Edith Roosevelt (Teddy's wife), Elizabeth Monroe and Nancy Reagan, as well as painted Easter eggs from a White House egg hunt.

The brainchild of Walt Disney himself, the Hall of Presidents exists only in Walt Disney World. Its widescreen projection system was invented by Ub Iwerks, the original animator of Mickey Mouse. Though Iwerks' 70mm film system has been replaced, his three side-by-side screens still exist, each 18 feet tall and 30 feet wide.

## Cronkite's confusion

A Walt Disney World publicist used to tell visiting reporters that some of the presidents were real people—that since there were always a few robots out for repairs, each show had at least one human stand-in. When he once asked the late Walter Cronkite to spot the live actor, the veteran newsman just laughed. A minute later he turned back and said, "Jefferson?"

## Lincoln 2.0

The Lincoln figure is a simplified remake of Disney's original problematic Honest Abe that debuted at the State of Illinois exhibit at the 1964 New York World's Fair, "Great Moments with Mr. Lincoln." With any spike in current, Disney's first Lincoln would flail its arms, hit itself repeatedly in the head and then slam itself back down in its chair. The malfunction inspired a scene in a 1993 episode of "The Simpsons." In "Selma's Choice," Aunt Selma takes Bart and Lisa to the Walt Disney World-like Duff Gardens, where every attraction is themed to Duff Beer. At the Duff Hall of Presidents, Lincoln holds up a Duff can and takes a swig, then mindlessly smashes it onto his head.

Though today's Lincoln is far more reliable, it recites the Gettysburg address using the same recording, from a 1963 session with the late character actor Royal Dano. The taping was directed by Walt Disney.

## Previous speeches

For more than two decades, Lincoln was the only Disney president to talk. Disney added a second speaking role for Bill Clinton, who starting in 1993 repeated his inauguration sentiment that "there is nothing wrong with America that can't be fixed with what is right with America." George W. Bush followed eight years later, with a speech extolling that "perhaps it falls to us, to this first generation of 21st century Americans, to say, once and for all, that no child, no race, no creed, no ethnic community will ever again be left out of the American dream." The current show is the first with a speaking George Washington.

**Fun facts ❶** George Washington is voiced by actor David Morse, who played Washington in the 2008 HBO miniseries "John Adams." ❷ Disney combed through the National Archives, Library of Congress, museums and private collections to acquire more than 130 historical images that appear in the film.

▶ Providing lots of time out of the sun, the Hall of Presidents is a great way to beat the heat.

**A large paddle wheel** drives Walt Disney World's Liberty Square Riverboat

# Liberty Square Riverboat

★★★ 13 min. Capacity: 400. Open 10a–dusk, with rides every half hour on the half hour. Outdoor covered queue. Fear factor: None. Access: Guests may remain in wheelchairs, ECVs. Debuted: 1971, updated 2007.

You relive the glory days of riverboats on this cruise around Tom Sawyer Island. Riding on a real steamboat, you pass scenes that recall life on the Mississippi and other American rivers during the time of Mark Twain. The boat's pilot, Sam Clemens himself, narrates the journey. You also hear Capt. Horace Bixby, who in real life was the boat pilot who mentored Clemens. "Steady as she goes!" he commands.

Though the sights along the riverbank aren't that special—a burning cabin, an old fisherman, an Indian village, a sacred burial ground and a few remarkably stoic animals—the boat is pretty cool. A three-tiered vessel, it has a functioning boiler room, steam

### Average Wait
| | |
|---|---|
| 9am | closed |
| 10am | 15 min |
| 11am | 15 |
| Noon | 15 |
| 1pm | 15 |
| 2pm | 15 |
| 3pm | 15 |
| 4pm | 15 |
| 5pm | 15 |
| 6pm | 15 |
| 7pm | closed |
| 8pm | closed |
| 9pm | closed |

engine and paddle wheel on its lower deck. The second floor has a small stateroom. Up on top there's a working smokestack and a steam whistle.

On hot days the best places to stand are on the shady second-floor bow. The best views, of course, are from the top deck.

Now known as the Liberty Belle, the boat was named the Richard F. Irvine until 1996. It once had a twin, the Admiral Joe Fowler, until that vessel was dropped by a crane during a 1980 refurbishment. Irvine helped design Magic Kingdom. Fowler was in charge of the original Walt Disney World construction. Today, the names Irvine and Fowler are used by ferrys in the Seven Seas Lagoon, the man-made lake in front of the park.

The boat was built by Disney at a backstage shop; its boiler and steam engine were purchased at a Tampa shipyard. It rides on a rail.

**Fun facts** ❶ River water is pumped into the boiler before each trip. ❷ The boiler is kept at 700 degrees. It uses diesel fuel. ❸ The steam engine powers everything on the boat, including its lights and sound system. ❹ The leadsman is exaggerating a little when he calls out "Mark Twain!" indicating the water is two fathoms (12 feet) deep. These "Rivers of America" are only 9 feet deep.

▶ Don't miss seeing the engine. It's on the lower deck, just in front of the paddle wheel.

The Haunted Mansion facade recalls 19th-century homes in New York's Hudson River valley

# The Haunted Mansion

★★★★ ✓ 11 min. Capacity: 320. Covered queue. Fear factor: Dark, some screams. A few ghosts are scary. Access: Must be ambulatory. Handheld captioning. *AuDe* Debuted: 1971, revised 2007.

Loaded with detail and special effects but never truly scary, this dark indoor tour of a ghostly retirement home is a spooky treat for any age. Refurbished in 2007, it now includes a room of converging staircases that's based on the work of artist M.C. Escher, a floating crystal ball and a completely new attic. Disney World veterans will notice new paintings in the portrait corridor, more movement in a suit of armor and a lot of new moving, blinking eyes in the bat-eyed wallpaper.

| Average Wait | |
|---|---|
| 9am | 0 min |
| 10am | 10 |
| 11am | 10 |
| Noon | 20 |
| 1pm | 20 |
| 2pm | 25 |
| 3pm | 25 |
| 4pm | 15 |
| 5pm | 15 |
| 6pm | 10 |
| 7pm | 10 |
| 8pm | 5 |
| 9pm | 5 |

### 'Any volunteers?'

The show starts outside. As you near the mansion, its grounds are unkempt. An old hearse is parked out in front but its horse is gone. A distant wolf howls.

A walkway leads to a side foyer. Once you're let in, a spooky voice—your "ghost host"—informs you that spirits are present, "practicing their terror with ghoulish delight." Their first trick: transforming the portrait above the room's mantelpiece from a young man to a corpse.

Next up: a portrait chamber, where again the ghosts pull pranks. The door disappears, the walls stretch, the lights go out and the ceiling suddenly reveals a hanging body above your head. Once you escape, you board a bench-seat "doom buggy" for the rest of your tour.

Soon you learn the spirits' true purpose: they want you to join them. "We have 999 happy haunts here," your host tells you as you move through the mansion, "but there's room for a thousand. Any volunteers?" In the library, busts look you over.

You pass some of the ghosts' earlier attempts to land a new resident. A man is trapped in a casket in a conservatory; locked door handles in a hallway twist and turn as knocks behind them grow desperate. One of the doors flexes so much it seems to breathe. The hall leads to a seance, where a spiritualist—a disembodied head in a floating ball—beckons the ghosts to materialize.

Then, they do. As your doom buggy rounds another corner, you look down upon the mansion's residents in the grand din-

▶ Is the Haunted Mansion scary? Only to some children. The ride is spooky, but not threatening.

**Transforming before your eyes,** a portrait in the foyer depicts a young man aging into a corpse

ing hall, where they've gathered for a rollicking "death-day" party. You pass many more ghosts as you tour takes you "outside," through a backyard graveyard and finally a crypt. One ghost appears to join you in your vehicle.

Near the ride exit a tiny bride urges you to come visit the mansion again. "Hurry back... hurry back..." she coos, standing on a ledge above you, a dead bouquet in her arms, her veil blowing in the breeze.

As you leave the building, the ghosts promote the benefits of joining them one last time. *"Mortals pay a token fee,"* the spirits sing, so faintly most guests don't hear them. *"Rest in peace, the haunting's free. So hurry back, we would like your company."*

Your tour also includes a trip through the mansion's attic, a room with its own storyline, of a woman who spent her life marrying wealthy men then chopping off their heads to collect their fortunes. Each of her wedding portraits transforms to show its groom losing his head. Holding an ax, the bride (a video projection on a three-dimensional figure) stands at the end of the room, sarcastically reciting wedding vows. "In sickness and in health" becomes "in sickness and in wealth."

**Fun finds** Entrance: ❶ Horseshoe and wheel tracks lead from a barn to the hearse. ❷ Dead roses lie inside it. ❸ Madame Leota's eyes open on her tombstone face, which tilts. **Foyer:** ❹ The fireplace grate forms a cross-eyed, arrow-tongued face. **Stretching Room:** ❺ Grates along the floor form monstrous faces. **Loading Area:** ❻ Chain stanchions are toothy brass bats. **Portrait Corridor:** ❼ A woman in a painting transforms into Medusa. **Library:** ❽ The paneling between the busts has carved bat faces. **Music Room:** ❾ The window frame has coffin trim. **Endless hallway:** ❿ Fang-baring serpents extend from the frame molding. **Conservatory:** ⓫ Coffin

handles are bats. **Corridor of Doors:** ⓬ The grandfather clock is a demon. The casing forms hair and eyes; the clockface a mouth, the pendulum a tail. **Grand Dining Hall:** ⓭ On the mantle, a ghost in a top hat has his arm around a bust. ⓮ The fireplace grate includes two black-cat silhouettes. ⓯ In front of the fireplace, an old woman knits in a rocking chair. ⓰ Five ghosts float in from a coffin, which has fallen out of a hearse that has pulled up outside. ⓱ Mr. Pickwick (from the 1836 Dickens novel "The Pickwick Papers") swings from the chandelier. ⓲ Marc Antony and Cleopatra sit next to him. ⓳ Julius Caesar sits at the left end of the table. ⓴ The sheet-music stand is a leering bat. **Graveyard:** ㉑ A medieval minstrel band has a flutist emerging from his tomb, ㉒ a drummer playing bones lying on the flutist's crypt cover, ㉓ a kilt-wearing bagpiper, ㉔ a soldier playing a small harp ㉕ and a stocking-capped, pajama-wearing trumpeter. ㉖ When the trumpeter rears, so do two owls above him. ㉗ Five tomb-sitting cats yowl and hiss to the beat. ㉘ A skeletal dog howls on a hill. ㉙ A king and queen ride a board balanced on a tombstone. ㉚ Swinging from a tree branch, a princess sips tea behind them. ㉛ A duke and duchess toast at a candlelit table. ㉜ Four ghosts circle on bicycles behind them. ㉝ A hoop-earringed pirate raises his teacup, sometimes his head, from behind a grave. ㉞ A floating teapot pours tea into a cup. ㉟ Tracks from a hearse veer off from your path. ㊱ The hearse driver chats with a duchess, who sits atop the hearse sipping tea. ㊲ A ghost sits up from the hearse coffin, which has fallen out of the back. ㊳ He's chatting with a sea captain. ㊴ A dog sniffs an Egyptian sarcophagus. ㊵ Its mummy is sitting up, stirring his tea and mumbling. ㊶ "What's that? Louder! I can't hear you! Eh?" says an old bearded man to the mummy, holding a horn to his ear. ㊷ The Grim Reaper floats inside a crypt to your extreme far right. His beady eyes stare from inside his hood. ㊸ Dressed in Viking gear, a male and female opera singer belt out exaggerated solos. ㊹ Holding his severed head, a knight cheerfully sings a duet with his executioner. ㊺ Shackled with a ball and chain, a

▶ **For the shortest wait, take your Haunted Mansion tour before noon or after dark.**

**Grave concerns.** Left to right: Each of the 20 occupants of the Haunted Mansion exitway mausoleum has a pun for a name. Rhyming tombstones line the attraction's entranceway. A pet cemetery sits on a hillside to the right of the mansion courtyard.

pint-sized prisoner harmonizes with them. **46** Sensing the party's over, an arm of a ghost trowels itself back into a crypt. **Crypt: 47** Human arms hold up wall sconces in the crypt (and in the unload area). **Outside the exit: 48** Each of 20 mausoleum occupants has a pun for a name. **49** Dogs and snakes appear in the side frames of benches in front of a hillside pet cemetery. **50** Mr. Toad is buried in the cemetery.

**Fun facts** Many Mansion moments are inspired by classic films and literature: **1** A tapping, thumping corridor of doors, including one that breathes, appears in the 1963 movie "The Haunting." **2** Human statues follow guests with their gazes and wall sconces are held by human arms in the 1946 French film "La Belle et la Bete," a version of the Beauty and the Beast fairy tale. **3** Oscar Wilde's 1890 novel "The Picture of Dorian Gray" includes a transforming portrait in which a young man becomes old and disfigured. **4** Edgar Allen Poe fans will find allusions to the 1845 poem "The Raven" and the 1846 novel "The Cask of Amontillado," in which a live man is entombed in a brick crypt. **Voice talents: 5** The ghost host is Paul Frees, who voiced Boris Badenov in the 1959–1964 TV series "The Adventures of Rocky and Bullwinkle." At the Pirates of the Caribbean he's the auctioneer, Carlos, the concertina player, nearby dog and the bridge parrot. **6** The spiritualist is voiced by Eleanor Audley, the voice of Lady Tremaine in the 1950 movie "Cinderella" as well as Maleficent in 1959's "Sleeping Beauty." Audley also played Eunice, the mother of Oliver Douglas, in the 1960s television series "Green Acres." **7** The Mellomen quartet sings "Grim Grinning Ghosts." The group sang on Rosemary Clooney's 1954 "Mambo Italiano" and were Elvis Presley's backup singers in the movies "It Happened

at the World's Fair" (1963), "Roustabout" (1964) and "Paradise Hawaiian Style" (1966). **8** The singing busts feature Mellomen lead singer Thurl Ravenscroft (second from left). The voice of Country Bear Jamboree buffalo head Buff and Enchanted Tiki Room bird Fritz the parrot, he sang "You're A Mean One, Mr. Grinch" in the 1966 TV special "How the Grinch Stole Christmas!" and was the voice of Tony the Tiger for Kellogg's Frosted Flakes cereal. **9** The graveyard's singing executioner is Candy Candido. He played the angry apple tree in 1939's "The Wizard of Oz" ("Are you hinting my apples aren't what they ought to be?"), the Indian chief in 1953's "Peter Pan" and a goon in 1959's "Sleeping Beauty." **Other fun facts: 10** A Civil War antique, the hearse appeared in the 1965 John Wayne film "The Sons of Katie Elder." **11** The mansion's interior design comes from the 1874 Harry Packer home in Jim Thorpe, Penn. **12** "Grim Grinning Ghosts" is performed in eight styles, including a dirge that plays as you enter. **13** The "dust" is made from fuller's earth, an ingredient in kitty litter. **14** Except for a few books, the library bookcase is a flat painted backdrop. **15** So is the back ballroom wall. **16** The spiritualist is known as "Madame Leota" in honor of a Disney modelmaker Leota Toombs, whose face she shares. Toombs also appears as, and voices, the crypt bride. **17** You never go in the home. The entire 960-foot ride takes place in a building behind the facade.

**Hidden Mickeys 1** The foyer and two stretching rooms form the three-circle shape. **2** As the left-most place setting on the near side of the dining hall table. **3** As a silhouette in the final graveyard scene, at the end of the uplifted arm of the Grim Reaper. **4** On the right side of the souvenir cart, on the index finger of a painted hand beneath the word "Parlour."

▶ Each Haunted Mansion 'doom buggy' seats two comfortably. Three children can ride together.

**Big Al** performs an off-key version of the Tex Ritter classic "Blood on the Saddle" during the Country Bear Jamboree

# Country Bear Jamboree

★★ 16 min. Capacity: 380. Opens 10a. Indoor, air-conditioned queue. Fear factor: None. Access: Guests may remain in wheelchairs, ECVs. Assistive listening; reflective captioning. Debuted: 1971.

Goofy-faced mechanical bears perform in this cornpone musical revue. Set in an 1880s lumber-camp union hall, it features 18 life-sized performers singing snippets of 14 country and cowboy songs. Unfortunately, however, the show is way past its prime. It suffers from lousy pacing, poor sound and jokes that only generously can be described as funny.

Tutu-clad Trixie warbles the 1966 Wanda Jackson hit, "Tears Will Be the Chaser for my Wine." Temptress Teddi Barra sings "Heart, We Did All That We Could," a 1967 Jean Shepard tune. "Ya'll come up and see me sometime!" she coos at the end, channeling Mae West. Replies the emcee: "As soon as I can find a ladder!" The best bear is sad-eyed, tone-deaf Big Al. He butchers the 1960 Tex Ritter dirge "Blood on the Saddle." Ritter himself provides the voice.

Mounted up on the side wall, talking trophy heads Buff (a buffalo), Max (a deer) and Melvin (a moose) bicker and banter.

The exaggerated faces are full of personality, as are some song titles (Tex Ritter's 1950 "My Woman Ain't Pretty (But She Don't Swear None)," Homer & Jethro's 1964 "Mama Don't Whip Little Buford (I Think You Should Shoot Him Instead)"). But unless you're already a fan, the concept is thin. Worse, the show's sound system is poor.

Designed in the 1960s, the Country Bear Jamboree was intended for the Disney company's Mineral King Ski Resort, a development planned for a historic valley in California's High Sierra mountains. Instead, the land became part of the Sequoia National Forest. Though he never saw it in finished form, the show was said to be one of Walt Disney's personal favorites.

**Fun facts ❶** Henry's phrase "'cause we've got a lot to give" refers to the 1970s slogan of the show's first sponsor: "You've got a lot to live, and Pepsi's got a lot to give." ❷ Sung here by The Five Bear Rugs, "Devilish Mary" was the first country song recorded by a woman. Roba Stanley sang it in 1924.

**Average Wait**

| | |
|---|---|
| 9am | closed |
| 10am | 0 min |
| 11am | 10 |
| Noon | 10 |
| 1pm | 10 |
| 2pm | 10 |
| 3pm | 10 |
| 4pm | 10 |
| 5pm | 10 |
| 6pm | 10 |
| 7pm | 10 |
| 8pm | 10 |
| 9pm | 10 |

▶ Sit in the front of the theater. Guests in back rows have a hard time hearing the show.

# Splash Mountain

★★★★★ ✔ 12 min. Capacity: 440. *FastPass*
Covered queue. Fear factor: One small drop is
completely dark. The big drop can scare adults.
Closed during thunderstorms. Access: Must be
ambulatory. Height restriction: 40 in. Debuted:
1992 (Disneyland 1989).

This flume ride in, out, around and down a
mountain is the most "satisfactual," but
least understood, ride in Magic Kingdom.
Lined with 68 robotic creatures in cartoon-
like musical scenes, the half-mile trip takes
you through bayous, swamps, a cave and a
flooded mine shaft. The ride includes five
short drops and a five-story plummet.

Based on scenes from Disney's 1946 film
"Song of the South," themselves based on a
series of folk tales popular with slaves in the
antebellum South, Splash Mountain has a
story that's impossible to follow if you don't
already know it, but fascinating if you do.

You're in it from the start. Climbing
through some barns in rural Georgia, you
come upon a secret passageway that leads
to Critter Cave, the home of wise old storyteller Brer Frog. "Mark my words," he tells
two grandkids, in a shadow diorama on
your left. "Brer Rabbit gonna put his foot
in Brer Fox's mouth one of these days."

Once in your log (hollowed out by bea-
vers, the story goes), you travel past the
crafty rabbit's briar patch playground and
up Chick-A-Pin Hill, home to the tenacious
but gullible Brer Fox and strong but stupid
Brer Bear. You float into the mountain and
down a magnolia bayou, where you come
upon Brer Rabbit packing to leave. *"I've had
enough of this old briar patch,"* he sings.
*"I'm lookin' for a little more adventure."*

Overhearing, Brer Fox
and Brer Bear scheme to
catch the hare and cook him
for dinner. First the fox
traps the rabbit with a rope,
but then the hare tricks the
bear into switching places.
(In the film the rabbit tells
the bear he's a scarecrow
making $1 a minute. "You'd
make a mighty fine scare-
crow, Brer Bear. How'd you
like to have this job?")

| Average Wait | |
| --- | --- |
| 9am | 0 min |
| 10am | 30 |
| 11am | 30 |
| Noon | 50 |
| 1pm | 70 |
| 2pm | 80 |
| 3pm | 70 |
| 4pm | 60 |
| 5pm | 70 |
| 6pm | 60 |
| 7pm | 70 |
| 8pm | 45 |
| 9pm | 30 |

**Left:** Splash Mountain includes
a 52-foot drop into a briar patch

▶ For the driest drop, duck down before the splash and stay down until after the slosh.

Then, saying he's headed to a "laughin' place," the rabbit leads the others into a hollow, fallen tree, which leads to a flooded mine filled with bees. "I don't see no laughin' place, just bees," the bear says. "I didn't say it was *your* laughin' place," laughs the rabbit. "I said it was *my* laughin' place!"

Brer Fox slams a beehive over the rabbit and ties him up at a cooking pot. "Well Brer Rabbit, it looks like I'm gonna have to cook ya!\*" the fox says. "Do what you will," Brer Rabbit responds, "but whatever you do, please don't fling me in that briar patch!"

Of course, that's what Brer Bear does.

A singing showboat welcomes the bunny back home, but Brer Bear and Brer Fox are in the patch, too. Stuck in the thorns, the dim-witted bear sings "Zip-A-Dee-Doo-Dah" with the rabbit's friends. "This is all your fault Brer Bear!" Brer Fox says, trying to pull the bear free while fighting off an alligator. "You flung us here. So stop that singing!"

The moral? On the surface: there's no place like home. On a subversive level: that if they're crafty, the weak can do "pretty good sure as you're born" against the strong.

**Fun finds ❶** "Fleas, flat feet and furballs" are all cured by the "Critter Elixir" trumpeted on a wagon past the second lift hill. **❷** Around a corner, Brer Bear snores in his house. **❸** Just before the drop, vultures above you warn "Time to be turning around... if only you could. If you've finally found your laughing place, how come you aren't laughing?"

**Fun facts ❶** The logs reach 40 mph on the final drop, making it the fastest Magic Kingdom moment. **❷** The ride uses 956,000 gallons of water. It's recycled every four minutes. **❸** In 1993, Great Britain's princes William and Harry, then ages 11 and 8, visited Disney World with their mother, Princess Diana. Splash Mountain was William's favorite ride, so they rode it three times. **❹** Because of the film's racial overtones, Disney does not market "Song of the South" on DVD. **❺** "Brer" is slang for "Brother."

**Hidden Mickeys ❶** As stacked barrels on your right along the second lift. **❷** As a fishing bobber on your left (inside the mountain just past Brer Frog toe-fishing on top of Brer Gator, left of a picnic basket). **❸** As a hanging rope in the flooded cavern (on your right, behind a lantern, just past a turtle on a geyser). **❹** After the big drop, reclining as a full figure in the sky to the right of the riverboat, as the upper outline of a cloud. Mickey's head is to the right.

\* Alternates with "hang ya!" "roast ya!" and "skin ya!"

**Brer Fox captures Brer Rabbit** with a beehive in a mine-shaft scene in Splash Mountain

**PUBLISHED IN** "The Complete Tales of Uncle Remus," an 1895 compilation of 185 African-American folk tales by Joel Chandler Harris, a columnist for the Atlanta Journal-Constitution, the stories "How Mr. Rabbit Was Too Sharp For Mr. Fox," "Mr. Rabbit and Mr. Bear" and "Brother Rabbit's Laughing-Place" rival the best European folk tales for charm and hidden meaning. Walt Disney loved "their rich and tolerant humor; their homely philosophy and cheerfulness." Harris, though, has been scorned. In his forward, the white Harris described his narrator, a fictional freed slave named Uncle Remus, as having "nothing but pleasant memories of the discipline of slavery." At the time, the term "uncle" was a patronizing, familiar and often racist title often reserved by whites for elderly black men in the South. Disney's film ignored those issues but was still associated with them. The 1987 book "The Tales of Uncle Remus" by Julius Lester offers most of the folk tales—which, by themselves, are wonderful—in a more unadulterated state.

▶ **The front seat gets the wettest. The back seat usually stays relatively dry.**

**All curves all the time,** Big Thunder Mountain Railroad is fun for all ages

# Big Thunder Mountain Railroad

★★★★★ ✓ 4 min. Capacity: 150. *FastPass* Outdoor covered queue. Fear factor: Jerky, violent turns toss you around in your seat. Many sharp hills and sudden dips. Closed during thunderstorms. Access: Must be ambulatory. Height restriction: 40 in. Debuted: 1980 (Disneyland 1979).

All curves all of the time, this roller coaster is exciting but never scary. Meant to be a trip through Utah's Monument Valley, the track takes you around and through a realistic mountain that's filled with detail.

Sights include swarming bats inside a watery cave, hot springs, a flooded town, a collapsing mine shaft, even some dinosaur bones.

Scattered around the attraction are hundreds of pieces of authentic mining gear, which the Disney company scoured from Old West ghost towns during the 1970s. The rusty relics include buckets, cogwheels and ore carts.

There are also nearly 20 fairly realistic animals, including big-horned sheep, bobcats and javelinas. Live cactus dots the landscape.

Technically, this "wildest ride in the wilderness" consists of three lift hills and three series of hairpin turns. There are many small hills and sudden dips, but no big drops and you never go upside down. Top speed is 36 mph.

Like vehicles of most conventional coasters, the trains run faster late in the day, after the track grease melts.

## Gods and Greed
Unlike most roller coasters, Big Thunder Mountain Railroad actually tells a story, a tale of a frontier mining town whose citizens' relentless pursuit of riches upset the spirits of nature. Here's the storyline:

During the height of the Gold Rush, men in the desert town of Tumbleweed were searching for the precious metal on a nearby mountain, which was also a Native American burial ground.

Though the ridge rumbled whenever any mining took place—Native Americans called the peak Big Thunder Mountain—the gold diggers were persistent. Determined to strike it rich, they took their ore trains deep into the mountain's cavern, and continually dynamited new shafts.

| Average Wait | |
|---|---|
| 9am | 0 min |
| 10am | 25 |
| 11am | 40 |
| Noon | 35 |
| 1pm | 45 |
| 2pm | 45 |
| 3pm | 50 |
| 4pm | 40 |
| 5pm | 45 |
| 6pm | 45 |
| 7pm | 45 |
| 8pm | 35 |
| 9pm | 30 |

▶ For the wildest ride ask for the back seat. It's faster on the drop and turns.

Adding insult to injury, the miners partied hearty at night. They entertained themselves with poker games, parlor girls and crates of whiskey.

Eventually, the spirits had enough. One day an engineer noticed that bats in the cave seemed spooked. Then his train spun out of control, flying around the mountain like a bat out of hell. Moments later a flash flood hit the town, then an earthquake. Some miners were too drunk to notice.

No gold was ever found.

In reality, the mountain is a painted cement and wire-mesh skin over a concrete-and-steel frame. Inside are the attraction's computers, electronics and water pumps.

**Fun finds ❶** The queue lights continuously flicker and dim. **❷** A box to the right of the entrance walkway reads "Lytum & Hyde Explosives Co." **❸** Melodies heard in the queue include "Oh, My Darling Clementine," "Home on the Range," "Little Brown Jug," "Red River Valley" and "Turkey in the Straw." **❹** As you enter the boarding area a crate above you holds whiskey. **❺** On the ride, as you arrive in Tumbleweed a prospector on your right has washed into town still in his bathtub. **❻** On your left rainmaker Professor Cumulus Isobar bails himself out. **❼** The proprietors of the dry goods store are D. Hydrate and U. Wither. **❽** Inside the Gold Dust Saloon, a whiskey-fueled game of poker has been flooded out. **❾** After the (actual) sun sets, drunks and dance-hall dames party on the saloon's second floor. **❿** Around a bend on your left, a "Flood-ometer" reads "Flooded Out." **⓫** If you exit the ride from the left track, you walk alongside the office of the railroad's telegraph manager, Morris Code. **⓬** The right exitway has a canary in a cage (he's not moving!) and, above a "Blasting in Progress" sign, a plunger. It's pushed in.

**Fun facts ❶** The train names are I.B. Hearty, I.M. Brave, I.M. Fearless, U.B. Bold, U.R. Courageous and U.R. Daring. **❷** The "Howdy partners!" announcer is Dallas McKennon, the voice of Ben Franklin at Epcot's American Adventure. A longtime Hollywood voice talent, he also voiced the 1960s television versions of

**The landscape** of Big Thunder Mountain Railroad is based on Utah's Monument Valley

Gumby and Archie Andrews, and the Rice Krispies characters Snap, Crackle and Pop. **❷** Big Thunder was the first Disney attraction designed with computers.

**Hidden Mickey** The three-circle shape appears toward the end of the ride as three rusty gears laying on the ground on your right, after you go under the dinosaur rib cage.

**DURING THE MID-1800s,** a discovery of gold in a remote mountain area would often bring in a feverish migration of prospectors, who would search stream beds and canyon walls hoping to instantly find their fortune. Later a commercial company often arrived to mine for gold ore, chunks of rock with deposits of the precious metal.

▶ **The ride is especially fun at night, when the landscape is lit but the track is not.**

# Tom Sawyer Island

★★★ Allow 45 min. Capacity: 400. Closes at dusk. Outdoor covered queue. Fear factor: The cave has side niches where young children can get temporarily lost. No rafts during thunderstorms. Access: Must be ambulatory. Debuted: 1973.

Accessible only by a powered raft, this large, wooded and hilly island playground sits within the waterway used by the Liberty Square Riverboat. Lined with a few paved trails, it offers a variety of small adventures.

Cranny-filled Injun Joe's Cave has a hidden scary face. Old Scratch's Mystery Mine is a creepy, twisting shaft with wailing winds and glowing crystals. Other fun spots include a climb-through grist mill, barrel bridge and windmill. Atop a hill is a brook, duck pond, a playground with a tiny rope swing and two picnic tables. Along the shore is Aunt Polly's Place, a shady snack bar (open seasonally).

A suspension footbridge leads to a second island. It's home to Fort Langhorne, a calvary outpost with a snoring sentry, robotic horses and a clearly marked "secret" escape tunnel along the back wall. Watchtowers have electronic rifles kids can shoot free of charge.

**Fun finds ❶** Games of checkers are often set up on a landing down the left trail from the dock. ❷ The mill's various creaks and groans subtly create the tune "Down By The Old Mill Stream." ❸ The bird trapped in the mill's cogs re-creates a scene from the landmark 1937 cartoon "The Old Mill." ❹ The women's restroom at Fort Langhorne is labeled "Powder Room."

| Average Wait | |
|---|---|
| 9am | 0 min |
| 10am | 5 |
| 11am | 5 |
| Noon | 15 |
| 1pm | 20 |
| 2pm | 20 |
| 3pm | 20 |
| 4pm | 15 |
| 5pm | 5 |
| 6pm | 5 |
| 7pm | 5 |
| 8pm | closed |
| 9pm | closed |

**Barrels of fun.** A bouncy bridge extends over the water on Tom Sawyer Island.

# Frontierland Shootin' Arcade

★★★ Allow 5 min. Capacity: 16. Fear factor: None. Access: Guests may remain in wheelchairs, ECVs. Debuted: 1971. $1 for 25 shots.

Surprisingly fun, this old-fashioned arcade is filled with more than 50 silly targets. Direct hits trigger sight and sound gags—a prisoner escapes from a jail, an ore car comes out of its mine, a grave-digging skeleton pops out of a hole.

Ideal for children, the targets are easy to hit and the infrared rifles easy to hold. Guns mounted in the center of the arcade have the best view of the most targets.

▶ The guns of the Shootin' Arcade are each loaded with a secret free round each morning.

# Cinderella Castle

One of the world's most photographed buildings, Cinderella Castle has its picture taken 30,000 times a day. And no wonder. It's not only a world-famous landmark, but also quite a piece of fantasy architecture.

Its design combines the looks of a medieval fortress and Renaissance castle. Heavy lower walls have saw-toothed battlements like those that hid artillery atop 11th-century stone forts. The top has the turrets, spires and Gothic trim of French castles of the 14th, 15th and 16th centuries. Accents include 13 winged gargoyles and a portcullis. An iron grate over the entrance appears ready to drop at a moment's notice.

Though the castle appears to be a 300-foot-tall stone fortress, it is actually a 189-foot steel frame covered in fiberglass. The building was designed to be seen from a mile away, so guests arriving on ferries and monorails can spot it with anticipation.

The interior includes a restaurant and gift shop, security rooms, three elevators and a fourth-floor apartment. Though planned for the use of the Disney family, the apartment space was left unfinished for decades. It was used as a radio room, switchboard center and dressing room until 2006, when it was finished off as the Cinderella Castle Suite.*

### War and Pieces

Also inside is a terrific piece of art. Created out of 500,000 bits of glass in 500 colors, the five-panel mosaic tells the Cinderella story. The 15- by 10-foot arches were crafted by a

*Occasionally offered to guests, the suite includes a foyer, salon, bedroom and bath. The bedchamber includes a 17th-century desk with inlaid computer hookups. Bath sinks resemble wash basins; faucets look like hand pumps. A cut-stone floor recalls the castle mosaic. Guests access the suite through a door in the breezeway. An elevator leads to a foyer decorated with original "Cinderella" concept art by artist Mary Blair and a display case holding a glass slipper.

**Cinderella Castle** combines the looks of a medieval fortress and a Renaissance castle

team led by Hanns-Joachim Scharff, based on a design by Disney's Dorothea Redmond.

The mosaic took two years to create. First, Redmond's paintings were redrawn to larger proportions on heavyweight brown craft paper. These images were cut up into 50 or so jigsaw-puzzle-like pieces. Scharff used both smooth and uneven glass. Many pieces were hand-cut and shaped with a power grindstone; a third were fused with silver and gold. Thin glass strips outlined hands and faces. Multihued rods were chopped crosswise for other effects.

Scharff was a fascinating man in his own right. Born in Germany in 1907, he became a Luftwaffe interrogator of captured U.S. Air Force fighter pilots during World War II. One of the best interrogators in the history

▶ Cinderella's Fairy Godmother often greets guests across from Tinker Bell's Treasures gift shop.

of armed combat, he treated his prisoners with kindness and respect, which led them to unwittingly reveal pieces of information which fit into a bigger strategic picture. Scharff even saved six Americans from execution by proving their innocence to the Gestapo. He himself was investigated by the Gestapo for collaboration with the enemy because of his unusual technique.

After the war Scharff befriended many of his former prisoners in the United States. He moved to New York, where out of a pre-war hobby he started a mosaic studio. A Neiman Marcus order of 5,000 tables gave the artist the funds to move to California and set up a new mosaic studio, where he was credited with introducing the smooth-surface Venetian glass form of mosaic art to this country in 1952. Scharff died in 1992, but his studio continues under the stewardship of his daughter-in-law, Monika. She started her mosaic apprenticeship by working on these five Cinderella murals, and later led the team that created the mosaics at The Land pavilion at Epcot.

Hanns-Joachim Scharff is widely respected today, especially by U.S. military veterans who argue against the torture of terrorist suspects.

**Top:** The castle mosaic. **Above:** In a family snapshot from 1971, mosaic artist Hanns Scharff compares a reference painting to his working art at his California studio.

**Fun finds ❶** In the castle mosaic, stepsister Drusilla's face is green with envy, while Anastasia's is red with anger. **❷** Two of the faces in the mosaic are those of Disney Imagineers. The page holding Cinderella's slipper has the profile of castle designer Herb Ryman. His assistant is Walt Disney World master planner John Hench. **❸** The columns alongside the mosaic are topped with molded sculptures of Cinderella's animal friends. **❹** Her wishing well sits to the right of the castle, along the walkway that connects the back of Fantasyland to Tomorrowland. **❺** Her fountain is behind the castle to the left. Thanks to a wall sketch behind it, toddlers who stand in front of the fountain see the princess wearing her crown.

▶ Cinderella's stepmother and stepsisters often greet guests at the Fairytale Garden theater.

Cinderella is among many princesses who appear in the stage show Dream Along with Mickey

**"Marry me, Belle!"** orders a young Gaston in Storytime with Belle

# Dream Along with Mickey

★★★ 20 min. No seats, no shade. Cancelled during rain or threatening weather. Fear factor: None. Access: Guests may stay in wheelchairs, ECVs. Best ages: 3–10. Debuted: 2006.

When Mickey and Minnie Mouse throw a party to celebrate the power of dreams, the guests include Cinderella, Snow White, Sleeping Beauty and nearly the entire cast of "Peter Pan" in this song-and-dance revue, held on the castle forecourt stage. Trouble brews when Donald Duck says he doesn't believe in dreams, then Maleficent (the evil fairy from the 1959 movie "Sleeping Beauty") shows up with a dream of her own: to turn the Magic Kingdom into a place where nightmares come true. With help from the audience, that doesn't happen.

Flame pots, fireworks and other special effects add extra spark.

The eyes and mouths of the fur characters move. Songs include "A Dream is a Wish Your Heart Makes," "So This is Love," "Some Day My Prince Will Come" and "A Pirate's Life." All vocals are prerecorded.

# Storytime with Belle

★★★★ 15 min. Capacity: Apx. 75 seats, plus standing room. Fear factor: None. Cancelled during rain. Access: Guests may stay in wheelchairs, ECVs. Debuted: 1999.

The heroine from 1991's "Beauty and the Beast" is just a few feet from you in this cozy show. Tucked into the tiny Fairytale Garden theater, a shady alcove next to Cinderella Castle, her stage sits just off the ground, in front of only four rows of benches. Six children and one dad join Belle onstage to act out her story.

To help your child be selected, sit to the left, in front of the stage steps, and have your child shout out the answers when Belle asks some early questions ("Who did I live with in my quiet little village?"). Sit at the far right to be among the first in line for an autograph when the show ends.

To get the best seats arrive 30 minutes early. To get a good seat, 15.

| Average Wait | |
| --- | --- |
| 9am | n/a |
| 10am | n/a |
| 11am | 15 min |
| Noon | 15 |
| 1pm | 15 |
| 2pm | 15 |
| 3pm | 15 |
| 4pm | 15 |
| 5pm | 15 |
| 6pm | n/a |
| 7pm | n/a |
| 8pm | n/a |
| 9pm | n/a |

▶ **"Dream Along with Mickey" is best after dark, when spotlights add a theatrical flair.**

# Cinderella's Golden Carrousel

★★★★ 2 min (4 revolutions). Capacity: 91 (87 horses, four-seat chariot). Shaded queue. Fear factor: None. All horses have safety belts. Access: Must be ambulatory. Debuted: 1971.

Every horse gallops on this large, antique merry-go-round. Designed to fit every member of the family, five sizes of ponies move to calliope-style Disney music.

The carrousel has an interesting history. It was built in 1917 by the Philadelphia Toboggan Co., a roller coaster manufacturer that also sold hand-carved merry-go-rounds. (The use of the word "toboggan" in the name comes from the fact that roller coasters evolved from actual toboggan rides down the mountains of Russia.) One of only four five-row units the shop ever built, this patriotic "Liberty" model originally had 77 maple horses as well as a cresting and six chariots adorned with Miss Liberty, a regal blonde in a robe and sandals.

**Top:** Toronto's Elise Meiers, 2, rides with her mom, Terri. **Above:** Miss Liberty decorates the chariot.

The ride debuted at Michigan's Detroit Palace Garden Park. It later moved to Olympic Park in Maplewood, N.J. In 1967 the Disney company bought it to install at Walt Disney World, which had just broken ground. To fulfill Walt Disney's belief that every carrousel rider should feel like a hero, workers repainted the horses white, repositioned their legs so they cantered instead of pranced, and removed the chariots to add more horses. To give the ride a feminine Cinderella theme, Disney painted its trim pieces blue, gold, pink and purple—even Miss Liberty's red-white-and-blue duds.

Today's horses are fiberglass replicas, but one original wooden chariot has returned. Reinstalled in 1997, it offers the carrousel's only truly antique seats.

Because of the ride's wide diameter, its outside horses move twice as fast (7 mph) as those on its inner rim (3.5 mph).

| Average Wait | |
|---|---|
| 9am | 0 min |
| 10am | 5 |
| 11am | 5 |
| Noon | 5 |
| 1pm | 10 |
| 2pm | 10 |
| 3pm | 10 |
| 4pm | 10 |
| 5pm | 10 |
| 6pm | 10 |
| 7pm | 5 |
| 8pm | 5 |
| 9pm | 5 |

▶ Accented by hundreds of tiny white light bulbs, the carrousel is most beautiful at night.

Donald Duck searches for the Sorcerer's Hat in the "Beauty and the Beast" dining hall

© DISNEY

# Mickey's PhilharMagic

★★★★★ ✓ 12 min. Capacity: 450. *FastPass*
Indoor, air-conditioned queue. Fear factor: Sudden images, briefly totally dark. Access: Viewers may stay in wheelchairs, ECVs. Assistive listening, reflective captioning. Debuted: 2003.

This 3-D film uses a panoramic screen and surprising in-theater effects to immerse you into signature moments from some of Disney's best animated musicals. Action-packed yet never scary, it's great for any age. You don 3-D glasses to watch it.

The plot? When maestro Mickey runs late for a performance of his wily musician-free orchestra, Donald Duck attempts to replace him. But when the duck loses the secret to controlling the ensemble—Mickey's magical Sorcerer's Hat—the result is a madcap adventure everyone can enjoy, as Donald gets swept into the worlds of "Beauty and the Beast," "Fantasia," "The Little Mermaid," "The Lion King," "Peter Pan" and "Aladdin."

Hidden odorizers, air guns and misters let you smell a fresh-baked pie, feel popping champagne corks and get spritzed with water. The sound system includes nine hidden speaker clusters that wrap around the audience. An innovative lighting system is synchronized with the show. Positioned above the audience, it includes miniature spotlights and strobes that emphasize the film's 3-D effects. Smoke effects make the beams of the lights visible. Everything unfolds on a 150-foot-wide screen.

Some of the 3-D objects, such as Ariel's collection of "thingamabobs," appear to leave the screen and hang in front of you. Others, like Donald himself, seem to fly right over your head. The sequence for "The Lion King" song "I Just Can't Wait to be King" features the film's kaleidoscope of flat 2-D cutouts, but here they twist and turn over the audience.

Actor John Corbett has high praise for the show. "I have never experienced anything like it," he says. "I love the Tower of Terror. I did it three times in a row, but I didn't think about it the next day. But I've been thinking about that 3-D movie and the things that are in there a lot. The special effects, like the water and the wind, and the smells, they are really fantastic."

Created by Walt Disney Feature Animation—the company's feature film division

### Average Wait

| | |
|---|---|
| 9am | 0 min |
| 10am | 10 |
| 11am | 10 |
| Noon | 10 |
| 1pm | 15 |
| 2pm | 15 |
| 3pm | 15 |
| 4pm | 20 |
| 5pm | 20 |
| 6pm | 10 |
| 7pm | 15 |
| 8pm | 10 |
| 9pm | 10 |

▶ The best seats are in the middle rear of the theater, in front of the main projector.

that rarely gets involved in park attractions—the basic animation is delightful. The best parts are the scene transitions. The "Be Our Guest" feast falls into "The Sorcerer's Apprentice" workshop; that room's water washes into Ariel's "Part of Your World" grotto; the shimmer of sunlight above that underwater cave turns into the African sun of "The Lion King."

**Fun finds** ❶ There's a murmur in the theater crowd even when there's no one there. Faint audience noise plays from the loudspeakers. ❷ As Goofy walks behind the crowd, he hums the "Mickey Mouse March" and steps on a cat ("Sorry little feller!"). ❸ The instruments gasp when Donald grabs the flute, they watch as he throws it into the audience and they laugh when it whops him on the head. ❹ When Lumiere rolls out toward you he's on a tomato that wasn't there a moment earlier. It arrived when Donald briefly blocked your view to ask, "Where's my hat?" ❺ Ariel giggles as she swims onscreen. ❻ Strobes in the ceiling flash when Donald kisses the eel. ❼ When a crocodile sends Donald flying during "I Just Can't Wait to be King" (on the line "Everybody look right!") you hear the duck circle behind you before he returns to the spotlight. ❽ When Simba sings that he's "in the spotlight," so

are some members of the audience. ❾ When a pull chain then falls into view, Zazu pulls it to turn Simba's light off and respond, "Not yet!" ❿ Jasmine waves to an audience guest as she starts to sing "A Whole New World." ⓫ When she and Aladdin wave goodbye to Donald, so does their carpet. ⓬ Once Mickey regains control of his orchestra, the flute wakes up the tuba and then trips Donald into the tuba. ⓭ As you leave the theater and exit past the gift shop, Goofy says goodbye to you in five languages ("Sigh-a-NAIR-ee!").

**Hidden Mickeys** ❶ In the lobby mural, as seven 1-inch-wide white paint splotches. From the right, they appear between the third and fourth bass violin, between the second and third clarinet, above the second trumpet, below the second trumpet, to the left of the fourth trumpet, and twice to the left of the sixth clarinet (one's a stretch). ❷ On the theater's right stage column, in the tubing of the French horn. ❸ In the film's "Be Our Guest" scene, as brief shadows on the dining table, visible as Lumiere sings the word "it's" in "Try the gray stuff, it's delicious!" Lumiere's hands cast Mickey's ears; his base Mickey's face. ❹ As a hole made in a cloud as Aladdin's carpet flies through it. ❺ When the carpets dive toward Agrabah, as three domes atop a left tower. ❻ In the gift shop, as music stands along the top of the walls.

## Déjà Donald

With just a few exceptions (such as the humming of the song "Be Our Guest"), Donald Duck's lines in Mickey's PhilharMagic come from cartoons of the 1930s and 1940s, as recorded by the original voice of Donald, Clarence "Ducky" Nash.

| DONALD'S LINE... | COMES FROM... |
|---|---|
| **"OH BOY OH BOY!,"** said when he realizes Mickey has left the Sorcerer's Hat unattended... | **1942'S "SKY TROOPER,"** said when he realizes he can train to be a pilot if he peels some potatoes. |
| **"ATTEN... TION!,"** said to the PhilharMagic Orchestra as he begins to conduct it... | **1940'S "FIRE CHIEF,"** said to nephews Huey, Dewey and Louie as he teaches them to be firemen. |
| **"I'LL SHOW YOU WHO'S BOSS!,"** shouted at an unruly flute before he tosses it into the audience... | **1941'S "EARLY TO BED,"** shouted at a noisy alarm clock before he tosses it across his bedroom. |
| **"WHO DID THAT?,"** said after the flute returns from its flight and hits Donald on the head... | **1941'S "ORPHAN'S BENEFIT,"** said after a boy blows his nose during Donald's recitation of "Little Boy Blue." |
| **"BLIBA-BLIBA-BLIBA,"** blubbered after the Sorcerer's brooms throw buckets of water on him... | **1937'S "DON DONALD,"** blubbered after early girlfriend Donna Duck pushes him into a fountain. |
| **"YOO-HOO!,"** yelled up to Ariel so the mermaid will slow down and wait up for him... | **1940'S "WINDOW CLEANERS,"** yelled down to Pluto so the dog will wake up and help him wash windows. |
| **"NOTHIN' TO IT!,"** said after Peter Pan sprinkles Tinker Bell's pixie dust on him, allowing him to fly... | **1944'S "COMMANDO DUCK,"** said after Donald learns to bend his knees when he lands, so he can parachute. |
| **"FASTER! FASTER!,"** said to his magic carpet while flying it through the narrow streets of Agrabah... | **1937'S "DON DONALD,"** said by Donna Duck (later known as Daisy) to Donald while riding in his car. |
| **"AH, PHOOEY!,"** said at the end of the show, after he falls through the back wall of the theater... | **1942'S "DONALD GETS DRAFTED,"** said at the draft board, after he learns he has to pass a physical. |

▶ The Fantasy Faire gift shop offers a wide range of Donald Duck merchandise.

# Peter Pan's Flight

**Peter Pan's Flight** guests fly miniature pirate galleons over London and off to Never Land

★★★ 3 min. Capacity: 60. *FastPass* Covered outdoor queue. Fear factor: None. Access: Must be ambulatory. Handheld captioning. *AuDe* Debuted: 1971 (Disneyland 1955).

Suspended from a ceiling-mounted track, a two-person pirate ship takes you above and through the story of Disney's 1953 movie "Peter Pan" in this old-fashioned dark ride. You feel like you're flying as you get a bird's-eye view of nighttime London and swoop and sway through Never Land.

You start off in the Darling home nursery, where Peter beckons the children (and you) to fly off with him to Never Land. You soar over London, where the roads are filled with moving automobiles. Arriving at Never Land, you pass the Lost Boys, mermaids, the Indian Encampment and, finally, Skull Rock. (One mermaid is a dead ringer for Ariel, star of 1989's "The Little Mermaid.")

Next you sail to Capt. Hook's ship, where the pirate has kidnapped the kids. As Peter duels Hook

on the mainsail, Hook's crew has Wendy walk the plank. A ticking crocodile hints that Hook's time is up, and soon Peter stands triumphantly at the helm with Wendy and her brothers. Hook, meanwhile, is in the water. "Help me Mr. Smee! Help me!" he calls, straddling the croc's jaws.

The ride's technology is way past its prime. The glow from a volcano comes from clearly visible sheets of aluminum foil.

**Hidden Mickey** As scars on the fourth painted tree trunk on your left as you face the turnstile, 4 feet off the ground.

---

**FLIGHTS, FIGHTS AND TIGHTS** Based on a 1904 play by English author James Matthew Barrie, Disney's 1953 movie "Peter Pan" follows the adventures of a boy who refuses to grow up. One night he arrives at the London home of the Darling family and convinces daughter Wendy and her brothers John (who wears a top hat) and Michael to fly off with him to Never Land, a remote island where children don't age. Sprinkled with magic dust from moody pixie Tinker Bell, the kids join Peter's gang of Lost Boys (each lost by his parents when he fell out of his pram) for a series of adventures.

| Average Wait | |
| --- | --- |
| 9am | 0 min |
| 10am | 15 |
| 11am | 30 |
| Noon | 40 |
| 1pm | 60 |
| 2pm | 55 |
| 3pm | 45 |
| 4pm | 55 |
| 5pm | 60 |
| 6pm | 45 |
| 7pm | 45 |
| 8pm | 60 |
| 9pm | 60 |

▶ **Go first thing in the morning or use a Fastpass. The afternoon wait can be more than an hour.**

**So much that we share.** It's a Small World dolls wear different costumes but have identical faces.

# it's a small world

★★★★★ ✓ 11 min. Capacity: 600. Indoor queue. Fear factor: None. Access: ECV users must transfer to a wheelchair; handheld captioning. *AuDe* Debuted: 1971, renovated 2006 (New York World's Fair 1964, Disneyland 1966).

This indoor boat ride promotes international brotherhood as it takes you on a colorful trip around the world. Singing dolls, whimsical animals and abstract settings fill your field of vision as you float through six huge dioramas, each representing the cultural history of a particular area. Though there's too much to see with just one visit, the ride can be appreciated on at least three levels:

**Average Wait**

| | |
|---|---|
| 9am | 0 min |
| 10am | 5 |
| 11am | 10 |
| Noon | 15 |
| 1pm | 20 |
| 2pm | 20 |
| 3pm | 30 |
| 4pm | 25 |
| 5pm | 20 |
| 6pm | 15 |
| 7pm | 15 |
| 8pm | 5 |
| 9pm | 5 |

**As a children's ride.** To infants It's a Small World is the cruise of their dreams, a wide-eyed journey filled with happy faces, funny animals, gentle music and the largest crib mobiles they've ever seen. To preschoolers it's a place to bond with their parents, as there's no narration and lots of time to chat ("Where are we now, mom?" "Hawaii!").

**As a political statement.** It's a Small World argues that you can honor diversity while still celebrating the commonality of mankind—or, as the dolls sing, that "it's time we're aware there's so much that we share." Though each doll wears a costume unique to its culture and has skin tone unique to its race, the doll's faces are nearly identical. And though they speak different languages, they sing the same song.

"It's a Small World portrays the world as we would like it to be," explains Disney Imagineer Jason Surrell. "It's a childlike view, yes, one which is pure and innocent and optimistic."

**As a piece of art.** Just like a painting in an art museum, the attraction has a sophisticated sensibility that is often overlooked. As created by illustrator Mary Blair—she did the backgrounds of the Disney movies "Cinderella" (1950) and "Alice in Wonderland" (1951)—the modernist sets form a stylized pop-art collage, and have a conceptual playfulness that is remarkably pleasing to the eye. They use both organic and geometric shapes, and are finished in ways that combine the impulsiveness of childhood with the classic motifs of various cultures. As for color, Blair left no hue unused and

▶ Ask to sit in the front row of a boat. You'll see more details and have more legroom.

used no shading within one, yet managed to have everything blend together.

Each doll costume is a mix of embroidery, feathers, lace, satin, sequins and ribbons. There's nearly every type of hat and shoe known to man.

**Where You Sail**
Though the ride is billed as "the happiest cruise that ever sailed," it never clearly states where you go. Here's a guide:

You start off in **Europe,** a two-minute sensory overload of dozens of dancing, marching, singing, swinging, unicycling, even yodeling dolls and creatures. Then you cross **Asia,** an orange and yellow land of belly dancers, lute players and snake charmers. Above you are flying carpets and kites. Cool blues and greens surround you in **Africa,** a hip jungle of wild animals diggin' a Dixieland band. Chilean penguins lead you to an orange **Latin America.** Rio's Carnivale is on your left; Mexico's Day of the Dead on your right. A bluegreen Brazilian rainforest is a world of twirly-headed birds. As the rain falls (as the plastic strips hang), a crocodile and jaguar bring out umbrellas.

Polynesian percussion welcomes you to a green and purple **South Pacific,** then you're back in Europe, at Copenhagen's **Tivoli Gardens,** where all the world's children come together to celebrate the "world that we share" by dressing in white and singing in unison. The world's oldest amusement park, Tivoli Gardens was Walt Disney's inspiration for the look of California's Disneyland.

**Blame It on Rio**
The history of It's a Small World dates back to 1941. Working in Brazil, illustrator Blair created dozens of collage-style paintings, which had a vibrancy unseen in commercial art at the time. "Brazil is really a very colorful country," she said. "The jungle... the costumes and native folk art are really bright and happy." Her ideas would be used in the 1944 film "The Three Caballeros."

**Pixie dusted.** Tinker Bell animator Marc Davis also designed the animals in It's a Small World.

Though she had left Disney in 1953, Blair returned a decade later, when Walt Disney asked her to help design the ride the Disney company was creating for the UNICEF pavilion at the 1964 New York World's Fair. For

**SECOND VERSE, SAME AS THE FIRST**
Yep, it's mighty repetitive, but on the ride the song "It's a Small World" isn't nearly as annoying as its reputation suggests. Though the roundelay plays constantly, it's usually as an instrumental, and sometimes just a rhythm track. When the dolls do sing, half the time they're doing so in Italian, Japanese, Spanish or Swedish. In fact, on average you hear the words "small world" only about once every 30 seconds.

▶ The ride includes 289 human dolls and 210 anthropomorphic animals and toys.

**Organic and geometric** shapes mix together in the settings of It's a Small World

background ideas, she created collages of wallpaper cuttings, cellophane and acrylic paint. For the dolls, she made three-dimensional versions of the "Mary Blair kid," a child with a large head and simple, smiling

face that she had used in the 1942 "Caballeros" prequel "Saludos Amigos" and in 1950s advertising and package art for Meadow Gold Ice Cream and Dutch Boy Paint.

To move guests through the scenes, Disney developed a first-of-its-kind flume system. It used tiny water jets to propel free-floating, open-topped boats.

The ride was a smash hit. Though the Fair had more than 50 pavilions that charged a fee, It's a Small World accounted for 20 percent of paid admissions. It also inspired some political merchandise: The Women's International League for Peace and Freedom sold It's a Small World dolls, with proceeds funding protests against the Vietnam War.

**Fun finds** ❶ In the loading area, a giant clock comes to life every 15 minutes. ❷ In the European area, a pink poodle ogles the cancan girls. ❸ A bespectacled Mary Blair doll is under the Eiffel Tower. ❹ A Bobby guards the Tower of London with a cork gun. ❺ Crazy-eyed Don Quixote tilts at a windmill while Sancho Panza looks on. ❻ One flying carpet has a steering wheel. ❼ Cleopatra winks at you from a barge. ❽ The eyes of three tongue-wagging African frogs spring out of their sockets. ❾ Singers include an ax-wielding yodeler (Europe); a horse, cow and three basket people (Mexico); and a ball-necked yellow, orange and turquoise ostrich (Brazil). ❿ Musicians include a bagpiper (Europe) and guitar-playing saguaro cactus (Mexico).

**Hidden Mickey** The three circles appear as 6-inch purple flower petals in Africa, on a vine between the giraffes on your left.

## 'Anything But That!'

Since it debuted, It's a Small World has been a popular subject for parody. In "Selma's Choice," a 1993 episode of **"The Simpsons,"** Aunt Selma takes Bart and Lisa to Duff Gardens, a theme park where every attraction is themed to Duff Beer. On the boat ride Little Land of Duff, they find hundreds of dolls singing a one-verse song: *"Duff Beer for me, Duff Beer for you, I'll have a Duff, You have one, too!"* "I want to get off!" Bart yells. "You can't," says Selma. "We have five more continents to visit!" After Lisa takes a drink of the water, she hallucinates that the dolls are coming after her. "They're all around me!" she screams. "There's no way out!"

Even Disney cracks jokes. Here at Walt Disney World, some **Jungle Cruise** skippers tell guests that any children left on board will be taken to It's a Small World, have their feet glued to the floor and be forced to sing the theme song "over and over for the rest of their lives." At Disney's Hollywood Studios, Small World dolls help destroy the theater in the finale of **Jim Henson's MuppetVision 3-D.** The song is also dissed in the 1994 film **"The Lion King."** After evil lion Scar becomes king, hornbill Zazu begins to sing "Nobody Knows the Trouble I've Seen." When Scar demands something more upbeat, the bird chirps *"It's a small world after all; It's a small world after all..."* "No, no, no!" cries Scar. "Anything but that!"

▶ The U.S. is represented by cowboy, Hawaiian, Inuit and Native American dolls.

**Above:** All ages enjoy Dumbo the Flying Elephant. **Below:** A puzzle post along the queue.

# Dumbo the Flying Elephant

★★★★ ✓ 2 min. Capacity: 32. Shaded queue. Fear factor: None. Closed during thunderstorms. Access: Must be ambulatory. Debuted: 1971, revised 1993 (Disneyland 1955).

This gentle hub-and-spoke ride features vehicles in the shape of baby pachyderms. Offering a gentle way for toddlers to fly, its 16 elephants stay level as they climb and circle. Riders control height with a lever.

Cynics who dismiss it as just a carnival ride need to wake up and smell the elephant. As anyone with an inner child knows, *this is Dumbo,* the sympathetic star of the 1941 Disney classic. His story is so sweet, his face so cute, he transforms the ride into something special.

Flying around with your child, gazing down upon Fantasyland, you realize that you're finally here, on vacation, at the epicenter of the Disney experience.

The ride itself looks like a giant windup toy. Topped with a spinning key, its hub is decorated in gilt and pinwheels. Swinging picture frames re-create the film's opening sequence of a stork delivering the baby to a Central Florida circus. Timothy Mouse stands on top on his hot-air balloon, holding Dumbo's magic feather.

A 1993 replacement for Disney World's original 1971 Dumbo ride, the Jules Verne-style contraption was initially intended for Disneyland Paris. Disney's new expanded Fantasyland will feature two side-by-side Dumbo rides, which those familar with the Universal Studios theme park are labeling "Dueling Dumbos."

**JUMBO JR.** When a stork delivers a baby to circus elephant Mrs. Jumbo in 1941's "Dumbo," she names him Jumbo Jr., but his huge ears soon earn him the nickname Dumbo. At first he fails as a performer, but when a mouse convinces him that holding a feather will let him fly, Dumbo becomes a star. Later he discovers he can fly whenever he wants, magic feather or not.

### Average Wait

| | |
|---|---|
| 9am | 0 min |
| 10am | 25 |
| 11am | 25 |
| Noon | 25 |
| 1pm | 25 |
| 2pm | 35 |
| 3pm | 35 |
| 4pm | 45 |
| 5pm | 40 |
| 6pm | 30 |
| 7pm | 30 |
| 8pm | 30 |
| 9pm | 20 |

▶ Bring a camera with you to ride Dumbo. The attraction has no PhotoPass photographers.

**Figures of Snow White** were added to Snow White's Scary Adventures in 1994

# Snow White's Scary Adventures

★★★ 2 min, 30 sec. Capacity: 66. Shaded queue. Fear factor: Scares many young children. Many threatening scenes; some with loud screams. Access: Must be ambulatory. Handheld captioning. AuDe Debuted: 1971, revised 1994 (Disneyland 1955).

Designed in 1954, this classic dark ride is a Disney take on a carnival spook house. Guided by a rail, a wheeled vehicle twists and turns through a series of scenes that depict a vain old woman trying to kill her stepdaughter, the fairytale story of Disney's 1937 movie "Snow White and the Seven Dwarfs."

Though the creepy vibe scares many toddlers and preschoolers, older riders can find a lot to like.

The attraction's creative depth is often under-appreciated. In its forest scene, Snow White's emotions are brought to life visually, from her point of view. The young girl's terror at being left alone turns the trees into predators with scowling faces and limbs that reach out to grab her, logs into alligators that chase after her, and every glint of moonlight into a glaring eye. As she calms down the forest gets friendly, and its eyes become those of small happy creatures.

The ride has an attention to detail few Disney attractions have ever matched. For example, the list of ingredients in the poisoned-apple potion include Black of Night, Old Hag's Cackle, Scream of Fright and Mummy Dust. In the dwarfs' cottage, animals are carved into the woodwork in so many places—such as candlestick bases and organ pipes—you can't possibly notice them all. As Snow White takes the poisoned apple, the water pipe to her side fears for her.

Though much of its technology is way past its prime—the mouths of the "talking" characters don't even move—one illusion, an ingenious transformation of the Queen into the old witch, still seems real.

The ride begins outside the castle, as Snow White scrubs steps while her stepmother spies on her from a window. The next scene is the throne room, where the Magic Mirror declares that Snow White is the fairest of them all. As the Queen yells "Never!" she turns herself into a witch.

Entering the castle dungeon, you pass a skeleton then see the witch mixing a potion

### Average Wait

| Time | Wait |
|---|---|
| 9am | 0 min |
| 10am | 15 |
| 11am | 15 |
| Noon | 15 |
| 1pm | 20 |
| 2pm | 25 |
| 3pm | 30 |
| 4pm | 25 |
| 5pm | 25 |
| 6pm | 25 |
| 7pm | 30 |
| 8pm | 25 |
| 9pm | 25 |

▶ Ask to sit in the front seat. Many scenes take place directly in front of you.

**Hidden Mickeys** ❶ A mischievous mural painter has converted hearts on a pair of boxer shorts (right) in the loading area to the three-circle shape. ❷ The silhouette appears on the cottage chimney directly under two flowers (above) and ❸ in the ride's first dark scene, on top of the magic mirror. ❹ On the lower right of the entrance to the dwarfs' mine, a full-figure dwarf-nosed Mickey wears dwarf clothes and has a shovel.

to make a poisoned apple. After you travel through the woods you come upon the seven dwarfs' cottage, where model figures portray the witch giving her apple to Snow White ("That's right dearie, take a bite…").

A trip through the dwarfs' mine cumulates with the seven short guys chasing the witch before she falls to her death.

The final scene shows Snow White apparently dead, lying on a funeral bier, about to be kissed by the prince. Just before the exit, a painted mural shows the smiling couple riding off to live happily ever after.

Originally the attraction had guests playing the role of Snow White throughout the ride. The princess didn't appear until the last scene, lying on the casket. Oddly, the ride didn't tell its guests they were Snow White, so children unfamiliar with the story thought it ended with the young girl dead. Disney redid things in 1994, adding in images of Snow White as well as the figure of the prince.

**ONE BITE, LONG NIGHT** When a young girl's father dies, she's forced to contend with her evil stepmother, the Queen, and is relegated to doing menial chores such as scrubbing steps in Disney's 1937 film, "Snow White and the Seven Dwarfs." Obsessed with her looks, the Queen gets jealous when a magic mirror says her stepdaughter has become "the fairest one of all." The Queen orders a huntsman to take Snow White to a forest and kill her, but he has a change of heart and lets her escape. The girl takes refuge in the cottage of the Seven Dwarfs, a group of men who work in a diamond mine. Meanwhile, the Queen transforms herself into a witch, tracks down Snow White and gives her a poisoned apple, which makes the girl faint and appear to be dead. After the witch falls to her death while trying to crush the dwarfs with a boulder, the heartbroken men plan to bury the girl. Just in time, a prince arrives and gives Snow White "love's first kiss," breaking the spell.

▶ T-shirts at a stand at the ride exit feature sayings such as "I'm Grumpy Because You're Dopey."

**Tigger warns Pooh** of heffalumps and woozles just before the bear falls asleep during The Many Adventures of Winnie the Pooh

# The Many Adventures of Winnie the Pooh

★★★★ ✓ 3 min, 30 sec. Capacity: 48. *FastPass* Shaded queue. Fear factor: Some sudden, though mild, effects. The nightmare scene can be disorienting for toddlers. Access: ECV users must transfer to a wheelchair. *AuDe* Debuted: 1999.

Retelling the story of "Winnie the Pooh and the Blustery Day," this storybook-style adventure combines the cute style of the Pooh films with imaginative visuals and effects. Riding in a four-person Hunny Pot, you travel through the pages of a book to witness the tale's windstorm, thunderstorm and flood. Hidden behind swinging doors, each scene comes as a surprise. Your vehicle travels through each scene by itself, which makes the experience more personal.

A liberal dose of special effects adds to the fun. Shaky walls and beams make it appear that Owl's treehouse is falling in as you travel through it. A simple light trick allows the dreaming Pooh to float in the air, while fiber-optic rain ripples in the Floody Place. Your vehicle jerks through the treehouse, bounces with Tigger and sways as you float through the flood. There are also mild wind, smoke and temperature effects.

Across the walkway from the attraction, **Pooh's Playful Spot** is a shady, soft-floored playground designed for children ages 2–5. It includes slides, tunnels and a splash-pad pond. It's anchored by a toddler-sized, walk-in version of Mr. Sanders house.

### Mr. Toad's Wild Fans

You get drunk, steal a car, mouth off to a cop... then go to hell! Believe it or not, that was the story told by this building's former attraction, Mr. Toad's Wild Ride, a ride based on Disney's 1949 compilation movie, "The Adventures of Ichabod and Mr. Toad." The loud, action-packed dark roadtrip had ardent fans. In 1997, when Disney announced plans to convert the ride into a Winnie the Pooh attraction, fans picketed next to its entrance while an Internet protest garnered 30,000 signatures. Disney did not respond. On the Wild Ride's last day, about 100 fans gathered outside as it closed, one with a sign reading "Here lies dear old J.T. Toad, he hit some Pooh upon the road."

| Average Wait | |
| --- | --- |
| 9am | 0 min |
| 10am | 15 |
| 11am | 30 |
| Noon | 35 |
| 1pm | 40 |
| 2pm | 45 |
| 3pm | 35 |
| 4pm | 30 |
| 5pm | 35 |
| 6pm | 35 |
| 7pm | 45 |
| 8pm | 30 |
| 9pm | 30 |

▶ Pooh, Tigger, Eeyore and Piglet often greet guests in front of Pooh's Playful Spot.

**Fun finds ❶** A boarding-area mirror makes the Hunny Pots "disappear" into the storybook. **❷** The words blow off the first storybook page on the ride. **❸** Along the side of the first diorama, Pooh grips a balloon string to float up to a beehive, a scene from the 1966 featurette "Winnie the Pooh and the Honey Tree." **❹** Perched on a rafter, Owl drones on about the big wind of '67 (or was it '76?) **❺** A framed photo of Mr. Toad handing Owl the deed to the space hangs on the left wall of Owl's house. **❻** A picture of Toad's friend Mole bowing to Pooh lays on the right floor. **❼** The air chills at the Floody Place. **❽** Words wash off the Floody Place storybook. **❾** On the treehouse of Pooh's Playful Spot, above the main door's indoor frame, is an indentation of a submarine, a reference to the former attraction on that spot, 20,000 Leagues Under the Sea: Submarine Voyage.

**Hidden Mickeys ❶** On the radish marker in Rabbit's garden. **❷** At Pooh's Playful Spot treehouse, on the transom of the front door.

**Raise your arms in the air** on the Mad Tea Party and you'll slide right into each other

**BACK TO THE DAYS...** The childhood of Christopher Robin Milne inspired his father, A.A. Milne, to create a series of books and poems featuring the boy's toys. Born in England in 1920, Christopher spent much of his young life at his family's country home in Ashdown Forest, Sussex, which was surrounded by a 500-acre wood. He received a toy stuffed bear for his first birthday. At the London Zoo, Christopher's favorite animal was Winnipeg, a black bear presented to the zoo by World War I troops from Winnipeg, Canada. Near the country home was a lake with a swan called Pooh. The boy eventually named his bear Winnie the Pooh after those animals. Christopher Robin Milne died in 1996, at age 75.

The 1968 Disney featurette "Winnie the Pooh and the Blustery Day" tells of the toys' thunderstorm adventure. Pooh's pals include excavation expert Gopher (a Disney invention), timid Piglet, fastidious gardener Rabbit, motherly Kanga and adventurous son Roo, gloomy donkey Eeyore, self-important Owl and ebullient tiger Tigger, who loves to bounce. Pooh's enemies, so he thinks, are heffalumps and woozles, the elephants and weasels who Tigger claims steal honey. Pooh has never seen one, but in his nightmares the crazy beasts blow smoke rings and morph into hot-air balloons and watering cans. The video was included in the 1977 feature film "The Many Adventures of Winnie the Pooh."

# Mad Tea Party

★ ★ ★ 2 min. Capacity: 72 (18 4-seat cups). Shaded queue. Fear factor: None. Access: Must be ambulatory. Debuted: 1971 (Disneyland 1955).

You spin around in a giant teacup on this old-fashioned carnival ride. Covered by a huge canopy, it's one of the few outdoor Disney attractions that runs in any weather.

Though kids and teens usually love it, the ride makes most guests dizzy, some nauseous. Your spinning cup sits on a spinning disk, which circles around a hub. You control your cup's spinning by turning a central wheel. (To avoid getting dizzy, stare at the wheel.)

The ride is themed to 1951's "Alice in Wonderland," in which a prim and proper Alice attends an Unbirthday Party, a nonsensical tea time that leaves her dazed and confused. The party's Japanese tea lanterns hang overhead; the hub has the film's soused mouse and teapot.

| Average Wait | |
|---|---|
| 9am | 0 min |
| 10am | 5 |
| 11am | 10 |
| Noon | 10 |
| 1pm | 15 |
| 2pm | 15 |
| 3pm | 15 |
| 4pm | 15 |
| 5pm | 15 |
| 6pm | 15 |
| 7pm | 10 |
| 8pm | 10 |
| 9pm | 10 |

▶ **Alice and the Mad Hatter often greet guests alongside the Mad Tea Party.**

**Rounded and out of proportion,** Minnie's house (and Mickey's, right) looks drawn by hand

# Minnie's Country House

★ ★ ★ Allow 15 min. Capacity: 125. Open 10a. Fear factor: None. Access: Guests may remain in wheelchairs, ECVs. *AuDe* Debuted: 1996.

Minnie Mouse lives in this walk-through bungalow. It's filled with everything from her furniture to her family heirlooms. Areas include Minnie's living room, hobby room, kitchen and flower-filled sun porch.

There's a lot for kids to do. A button on the answering machine plays messages from Mickey Mouse and other characters. In the kitchen, kids can open the refrigerator to see what Minnie eats (lots of cheese), pretend to bake a cake or microwave some popcorn, or try to grab an illusory cookie.

With no straight lines, the house looks like it was drawn by hand, like something right out of a cartoon. In fact, nearly every visual element—the walls, windows, roof, even the chimney—bulges. It's an architectural style Disney calls "squash and stretch." The home is painted pink and purple instead of Minnie's trademark red and white.

Enjoy Minnie's Country House while you can. Along with most of Mickey's Toontown Fair, it is scheduled to be demolished soon, to help make way for Magic Kingdom's soon-to-be-expanded Fantasyland.

**Fun finds ❶** The book "Famous Mice in History" sits on the living room coffee table. Subjects include Attila the Mouse, a misunderstood invader who "merely came to taste the local cheeses," and Leonardo da Moussi, the inventor of the microwave cheese pizza. Minnie wrote it. ❷ A photo on the wall is of her great-grandparents, Milo and Mabeline. ❸ In the hobby room sits her half-finished painting of Wiseacre Farm, the scene that is visible out her window. ❹ Earlier Minnie completed her take on Norman Rockwell's "Triple Self Portrait." ❺ The answering machine plays a series of messages from Goofy, who each time has called only to say he forgot why he called. ❻ The kitchen spice rack holds Thyme, Good Thyme, Bad Thyme and Out of Thyme. ❼ Sun-porch "Pun Plants" include buttercups (teacups, each with a pat of butter) and palms (with hands for fronds). ❽ "Clarabelle's Big Book of Pun Plants" sits on the room's wicker table.

**Fun fact** The house has no bedroom.

**Hidden Mickey** The three-circle shape appears as a hanging kitchen skillet and pots.

| Average Wait | |
|---|---|
| 9am | 0 min |
| 10am | 0 |
| 11am | 0 |
| Noon | 0 |
| 1pm | 0 |
| 2pm | 0 |
| 3pm | 0 |
| 4pm | 0 |
| 5pm | 0 |
| 6pm | 0 |
| 7pm | 0 |
| 8pm | 0 |
| 9pm | 0 |

▶ The loveseat and chairs in the house are the only indoor spots to sit in all of Toontown.

# Mickey's Country House

★★★ Capacity: 125. Open 10a. Fear factor: None.
Indoor air-conditioned queue. Access: Guests may
stay in wheelchairs, ECVs. *AuDe* Debuted: 1988.

This walk-through attraction is also the best
place to meet Mickey Mouse (and Minnie,
too). First you tour his cartoon home. Out
back you inspect his collection of appropri-
ately shaped produce. Finally you meet him,
in his Judge's Tent.

The house offers many details about
Mickey's life. The television is on in the living room, where he, Donald Duck and Goofy
have been watching foot-
ball. In the bedroom hang
copies of Mickey's red-and-
black tuxedo. The den has
just seen him beat his pals
in ping pong. The kitchen is
in the middle of a messy
Donald-and-Goofy renova-
tion. You view each area
from a central hall.

In the tent you watch
cartoon clips as you wait in
line, then enter a small
room with about 15 or so
other guests, where you
meet the mice. A Photopass
photographer is on hand.

| Average Wait to meet Mickey | |
|---|---|
| 9am | closed |
| 10am | 0 min |
| 11am | 15 |
| Noon | 15 |
| 1pm | 15 |
| 2pm | 20 |
| 3pm | 25 |
| 4pm | 25 |
| 5pm | 20 |
| 6pm | 20 |
| 7pm | 15 |
| 8pm | 15 |
| 9pm | 10 |

**With its picket fence,** workshop garage and
wooded yard, Mickey's Country House is an
archetypical 1940s American home

Like most of Mickey's Toontown Fair, the
house is scheduled to close soon, as it sits
in the way of the upcoming expanded
Fantasyland. The new area, sadly, will not
include a Mickey Mouse attraction.

**Fun finds ❶** A foyer photo shows Donald, Goofy
and Mickey building the home. **❷** The bedroom has
photos of Mickey as a baby, a Boy Scout and with
Santa. **❸** The room reveals that Mickey wears glasses.
**❹** Mail includes letters from Buzz Lightyear and
Ariel. **❺** The new kitchen blueprints are from the
"Chinny Chin Chin Construction Co.; General
Contractor Practical Pig," a reference to the 1933 short
"The Three Little Pigs." They include a garbage
disposal that is simply a pig under the sink. Scales
read "16 parts = 8.9 parcels," "7 pinches = 2 dollops"
and "1 smidgen = 4 oodges." **❻** A birdhouse version
of the home sits on a garage workbench. **❼** Garage
books include "The Auto Biography of Susie the Blue
Coupe," the star of an eponymous 1952 short.

**Fun fact** The queue lines for Mickey (as well as
those for the princesses next door) move faster than
those at any other character location. How? A hint:
Notice all the doors in the final hall.

**Hidden Mickeys** In the garage, as **❶** hubcaps,
**❷** paint stains on an apron and **❸** a tiny bale of hay.

▶ If you don't have time to meet Mickey, you can tour the home and leave through the garage.

**Goofy's Barnstormer** crashes through a barn

# The Barnstormer

★★★★ ✔ 1 min. Capacity: 32. Open 10a. Outdoor queue. Fear factor: Intense for some preschoolers. Access: Must be ambulatory. Height restriction: 35 in. Debuted: 1996.

With a short steep drop and a tiny tight spiral, this child-friendly roller coaster offers real thrills, but they're condensed into 19 seconds of high-speed action. (Though the total ride time is about a minute, most of that is spent leaving the boarding area and climbing the lift hill.) Taking off in Goofy's handbuilt and cleverly named Multiflex Octoplane cropduster (each coaster has eight independent sections) you immediately veer off course and eventually crash through a barn. It's a great way to introduce your kids to the fun of, in the words of Cameo's 1986 hit "Word Up," putting "your hands in the air like you don't care."

The roller coaster is the only attraction in Mickey's Toontown Fair that is not being torn down as part of the new Fantasyland expansion. It will, however, be redone with a circus theme.

| Average Wait | |
| --- | --- |
| 9am | closed |
| 10am | 0 min |
| 11am | 10 |
| Noon | 10 |
| 1pm | 20 |
| 2pm | 25 |
| 3pm | 30 |
| 4pm | 20 |
| 5pm | 15 |
| 6pm | 20 |
| 7pm | 30 |
| 8pm | 20 |
| 9pm | 10 |

**Fun finds ❶** Goofy's pants fly like a flag above the silo. **❷** The chickens in the barn squawk after each plane passes. **❸** Behind them is a "chicken exit," the slang term for the special exits at Disney's thrill rides for those who "chicken out." **❹** Plans on Goofy's drafting table (located in the barn and the boarding area) indicate that the plane is powered by Dale running on a hamster wheel. **❺** Just outside the barn, a closet door labeled "Electrical Main" has been altered to read "Electrical Main Street Parade," a reference to the park's former evening procession, the Main Street Electrical Parade. **❻** A Goofy scarecrow mans a queue garden. **❼** Real crops often include beets, cabbage, corn, kohlrabi, squash and tomatoes. **❽** Cartoon crops include "bell" peppers, popcorn, and squash that's been squashed by Goofy's feet. **❾** Cartoon-style jelly-jar lamps line the queue.

**Fun facts ❶** The coaster was built by Vekoma, the company that created the Rock 'n' Roller Coaster Starring Aerosmith. **❷** The storyline resembles a segment of the 1940 Disney cartoon "Goofy's Glider," in which the dippy dog's plane flies through a barn. **❸** The chickens originally roosted inside Epcot's World of Motion (1982–1996). **❹** The first Toontown attraction on this site was Grandma Duck's Farm (1988–1995) a petting zoo with live pigs as well as Minnie Moo, a cow with Mickey-shaped spots.

**Hidden Mickey** In the barn, on a helicopter seatback above Goofy's drafting table.

▶ **For the wildest ride ask for the back seat. It's faster on the drop and turns.**

Belle of **"Beauty of the Beast"** poses with Sara Feitz, age 8, of Huntington Beach, Calif.

**Anchoring a water-play area,** Donald's Boat looks like it came straight out of a cartoon

# Toontown Hall of Fame

★★★★ 5 min. Capacity: 45. Open 10a. 1Indoor air-conditioned queue. Fear factor: None. Access: Guests may remain in wheelchairs, ECVs. Debuted: 1996.

A variety of characters await you at this meet-and-greet center, which is located inside the County Bounty gift shop. One line leads to Disney princesses Aurora (Sleeping Beauty), Belle and Cinderella; the other goes to Tinker Bell and a rotating group of Fairy Friends who include Fawn, Iridessa, Rosetta and Silvermist.

All of the girls can be quite chatty, especially if there's not a big crowd waiting behind you.

Waits can be more than an hour, especially for the fairies. There are no lines right at 10 a.m., when this section of Magic Kingdom opens. Lines are usually shorter on Sundays.

The tent will close soon, though the princesses will have new greeting spots in the Fantasyland expansion.

**Average Wait**

| | |
|---|---|
| 9am | closed |
| 10am | 0 min |
| 11am | 40 |
| Noon | 50 |
| 1pm | 70 |
| 2pm | 65 |
| 3pm | 60 |
| 4pm | 70 |
| 5pm | 70 |
| 6pm | 75 |
| 7pm | 70 |
| 8pm | 70 |
| 9pm | 70 |

# Donald's Boat

★★★ Unlimited. Capacity: 60. Open 10a. Fear factor: None. Access: Guests may remain in wheelchairs, ECVs. Debuted: 1996. Note: The water is often turned off.

This water-play area is anchored by the S.S. Miss Daisy, a huge cartoon tugboat. The leaky vessel features a walk-in control room where pint-sized seafarers can clang a loud bell or secretly squirt water on others who have just gone out the back door.

The ship sits in a spongy duck pond, an elaborate splash pad where lily pads spout streams and spray. Bring a swimsuit, or perhaps a change of clothes, so your child can drench himself with abandon.

The boat's look and color scheme mimics Donald's sailor uniform and bill. The roof of the boat's bridge resembles the duck's signature blue cap.

The boat will not be part of the new Fantasyland.

**Average Wait**

| | |
|---|---|
| 9am | closed |
| 10am | 0 min |
| 11am | 0 |
| Noon | 0 |
| 1pm | 0 |
| 2pm | 0 |
| 3pm | 0 |
| 4pm | 0 |
| 5pm | 0 |
| 6pm | 0 |
| 7pm | 0 |
| 8pm | 0 |
| 9pm | 0 |

▶ The nearby Pete's Garage restroom makes a good changing spot for Donald's Boat.

# Stitch's Great Escape!

**Stitch's Great Escape** sits within Disney World's whimsical Buck Rogers-style Tomorrowland

★ 18 min. Capacity: 240 (2 120-seat theaters). *FastPass* Indoor air-conditioned queue. Fear factor: Restrictive harnesses, dark periods scare some children. Access: ECV users must transfer. Handheld captions, assistive listening. Height restriction: 40 in. Debuted: 2004.

A low-budget makeover of the attraction that preceded it (The ExtraTERRORestrial Alien Encounter), this in-the-round theatrical show is geared to those familiar with the early moments of the 2002 movie "Lilo & Stitch." It includes a cool Experiment 626 robot, but spends most of its time showing uninspired animated videos. Sit in the back for the best view. The character sits high off the floor.

The story takes place before the film. When 626 is held at a Planet Turo jail, he's guarded by cannons that track genetic signatures. Then the creature spits on the floor, the power shorts out and he escapes. Thanks to some hidden devices in your seat harness, it sounds, feels and smells as if 626 lingers near you.

Eventually making his way to Earth, the monster attempts to hook up with a very famous Florida female. He's rejected.

The Audio-Animatronics technology is impressive. A preshow sergeant shifts his weight from foot to foot and counts down on his fingers. The 39-inch 626 has 48 functions. His ears have multiple, simultaneous movements just like those of a dog, and his eyes, arms, fingers and spine move fluidly.

**CREATURE FEATURE** In "Lilo & Stitch," a mad scientist on Planet Turo uses the genes of ferocious beasts to create a tiny Experiment 626. Programmed to destroy everything it touches, the six-limbed monster can think faster than a supercomputer and see in the dark. When the Grand Councilwoman asks it to "show us there is something inside you that is good," it defiantly responds "Meega, nala kweesta!" As it licks its holding glass, 626 is exiled to an asteroid, then guarded by robotic cannons that track genetic signatures. When the ingenious creature coughs on the floor, the guns stalk the spit and 626 breaks loose, knocking out the jail's power grid in the process. Escaping to Earth, 626 lands in Hawaii, where it is adopted and named "Stitch" by Lilo, a 7-year-old misfit.

| Average Wait | |
| --- | --- |
| 9am | 0 min |
| 10am | 5 |
| 11am | 10 |
| Noon | 20 |
| 1pm | 20 |
| 2pm | 15 |
| 3pm | 15 |
| 4pm | 10 |
| 5pm | 20 |
| 6pm | 10 |
| 7pm | 15 |
| 8pm | 5 |
| 9pm | 5 |

▶ Stitch often appears next to the Carousel of Progress to greet guests and sign autographs.

# Monsters, Inc. Laugh Floor

★★★ 15–20 min. Capacity: 400. Indoor air-conditioned queue. Fear factor: None. Access: Guests may stay in wheelchairs, ECVs. Reflective captioning, assistive listening. Debuted: 2007.

Projected animated characters interact with the audience at this improvisational comedy show. Three large video screens front a comedy-club-style theater, where characters from the world of the 2001 film "Monsters, Inc." chat with, tease and joke with the audience just like real people. The show pulls off its magic thanks to hidden cameras, real-time animation technology and backstage actors using video-game-style control equipment.

As you wait, you can text-message jokes to the comedians to use during the show. The attraction is hosted by Mike Wazowski, a prerecorded character who is trying to generate electricity for the Monsters Inc. utility company by gathering laughter in bulk.

| Average Wait | |
| --- | --- |
| 9am | 0 min |
| 10am | 15 |
| 11am | 20 |
| Noon | 15 |
| 1pm | 15 |
| 2pm | 20 |
| 3pm | 15 |
| 4pm | 15 |
| 5pm | 15 |
| 6pm | 15 |
| 7pm | 10 |
| 8pm | 10 |
| 9pm | 10 |

**Lines for Monsters, Inc. Laugh Floor** rarely extend outside the theater

Every performance is different, as the characters base some of their jokes on guests in the audience. The best shows are those with a full house, which are typically in the middle of the day. Early morning shows can be stale, as the jokes seem to fall flat when they play to a near-empty theater.

**Fun finds ❶** In the second queue room, a vending machine immediately to your left offers such treats as Same Old Raccoon Bar as well as a Polyvinyl Chloride candy bar, which small print on its wrapper notes is artificially flavored. ❷ In the video shown in the second queue room, the first child Mike makes laugh has a poster on his bedroom wall of Tomorrowland. ❸ The newspaper Roz is reading in that video—a tabloid called The Daily Glob with the headline "Baby Born With Five Heads; Parents Thrilled"—also appeared in the "Monsters, Inc." film.

**IN THE 2001 PIXAR FILM,** the Monsters, Inc. utility company generates energy from the screams of human children. Its "scare floor" employs monsters, including eyeball-on-legs Mike Wazowski, to frighten kids and collect their reactions. As the film ends, the company learns that laughter is ten times more powerful than screams. Other characters include Roz, a surly secretary.

▶ To increase your odds of having a character speak to you, wear a colorful shirt or a big hat.

**Evil Emperor Zurg** controls his secret weapon with stolen "crystallic fusion power cells"

# Buzz Lightyear's Space Ranger Spin

★★★★ ✔ 5 min. Capacity: 201. *FastPass* Indoor air-conditioned queue. Fear factor: None. Access: ECV users must transfer to a wheelchair. Handheld captioning. *AuDe* Debuted: 1998.

This interactive indoor ride turns the idea of a shooting gallery inside out: here the targets stay in one place while you move on a track. Traveling in an egg-shaped "space cruiser," you fire a laser gun at more than a hundred targets, many of which move, make noise or light up as you rack up points. You can rotate your vehicle to access more targets. A dashboard display tracks your score. At the end of the ride you get rated based on how you did.

### Buzz vs. Zurg
Themed to the two "Toy Story" films, the attraction is presented as a battle between Buzz Lightyear and the Evil Emperor Zurg.

The queue area is Star Command Headquarters, where Buzz mistakes you

| Average Wait | |
|---|---|
| 9am | 0 min |
| 10am | 10 |
| 11am | 15 |
| Noon | 25 |
| 1pm | 45 |
| 2pm | 40 |
| 3pm | 30 |
| 4pm | 35 |
| 5pm | 35 |
| 6pm | 25 |
| 7pm | 30 |
| 8pm | 35 |
| 9pm | 30 |

for a new recruit in his Galactic Alliance. And you're just in time. In order to power his new secret-weapon space scooter, Zurg's robotic henchmen are stealing all "crystallic fusion power cells" (batteries, in Buzz-speak) from the world's toys. To fight back, Buzz orders the Little Green Men to recapture the batteries, and you to destroy the robots.

Flying into space in your XP-37 space cruiser, you and a partner first battle past two huge guards (room 1). Landing on Zurg's volcanic home of Planet Z (room 2), you fight off his monsters, then sneak into his ship (room 3) and face him head-on. Fortunately his weapon won't fire; his inept aides have knocked the batteries loose.

You chase Zurg out into space (room 4), where he and his scooter reappear, this time as a video image. "Prepare for total destruction!" he roars, darting in front of you. You fire (whether you pull the trigger or not) and send Zurg spinning right to the Little Green Men (room 5). They capture him and leave him hanging—from a claw.

The entire ride takes place in a world of toys. Buzz gets his information from a Viewmaster; Zurg's lead henchman looks like a Rock 'Em Sock 'Em Robot. Your space cruiser gets its power from a backpack of

▶ Buzz Lightyear often greets guests in front of the entrance to the Carousel of Progress.

batteries; its remote control sits to your right as you cruise in to the exit area.

The Buzz Lightyear figure in the queue is remarkably lifelike. It combines Disney's Audio-Animatronics technology with a rear-projection video system for Buzz's face.

**How to Get a High Score**
The maximum points possible on the ride is 999,999. Here's how your score can get close to that: ❶ Call dibs on the joystick, so you can keep your vehicle facing the right targets. ❷ Sit on the right side of your vehicle. That side has two-thirds of the targets. ❸ Once your gun is activated, pull the trigger and hold it in for the entire ride. The flashing laser beam will help you track your aim. It will fire about once a second. ❹ Aim only at targets with big payoffs: As you enter Room 1, aim for the left arm of the left robot (each hit is 100,000 points). As you pass the robot, turn your vehicle to the left and hit the other side of that same arm (25,000). As you leave the first room, turn backwards and aim at the overhead claw of the other robot (100,000). As you enter Room 2, aim at the top and bottom targets of the large volcano (25,000). As soon as you see Zurg, hit the bottom target of his space scooter (100,000) by firing early and late; you can't aim low enough to hit it straight on. As you go into Room 3, aim about six feet to either side of the top of the exit to hit a target in the middle of a rectangular plate (25,000). ❺ If the ride stops, keep your blaster fixed on a high-value target and keep firing. You'll rack up points.

**'If You Had Wings'**
Disney veterans will note that the track layout is unchanged from the ride's days as If You Had Wings. A 1970s Eastern Airlines attraction, it took passengers through a series of sets, each with video screens that portrayed Caribbean or Latin American destinations. One area (room 4) created the sensation of speed by combining a slight breeze

**Zurg's lead henchman** confronts you on Buzz Lightyear's Space Ranger Spin

with wraparound clips of high-speed sports shown from the participants' point of view.

**Hidden Mickeys** ❶ In the queue room, a Mickey Mouse profile appears on a poster as a green land mass on the planet Pollost Prime. The planet and its mass also appear three more times—to the left of the Viewmaster in the queue, on the right as you battle the video Zurg and in the final battle scene (room 5) on the left. ❷ Another Mickey profile appears on your left as you enter Zurg's spaceship, behind the battery-delivering robot and under the words "Initiate Battery Unload." ❸ The three-circle shape appears across from the souvenir-photo monitors as an image on a painted video monitor on a mural. ❹ Also in that room, on a painted window to the left of the full-size pink character Booster, as a cluster of three stars at the top center of a star field. ❺ As a second star cluster at the bottom right of that field.

▶ Souvenir space cruisers are sold at the gift kiosk in front of the attraction.

# Astro Orbiter

★★★ 2 min. Capacity: 32. Runs during light rains; grounded by downpours, lightning. Partially shaded queue. Fear factor: Height and steep angle bother even some adults. Access: Must be ambulatory. Debuted: 1971, updated 1994 (Disneyland 1955).

The most thrilling of Disney World's four hub-and-spoke rides, Astro Orbiter is fast, high and a little scary. With its loading area three stories off the ground, the attraction lifts its one-person-wide rockets 55 feet off the ground. It's located atop the boarding station of the Tomorrowland Transit Authority, which itself is the roof of a large snack stand. You ride an elevator to reach it.

But there's more to this ride than just height. Your tandem-seat rocket flies in a banked circle, tilted at 45 degrees. Top speed is 20 mph—plenty zippy when you're circling, especially when you feel like you're about to fall out.

There's a lot to look at. You circle within a few feet of a huge kinetic model of rings, planets and moons. One moon even has its own

**Retro rockets.** Astro Orbiter's Art Deco vehicles soar within a ring of twirling planets and moons.

moon. In the distance you can see everything from the Enchanted Tiki Room in Adventureland to the various tents and houses of Mickey's Toontown Fair. You can even spot the Twilight Zone Tower of Terror, five miles away at Disney's Hollywood Studios.

A typical trip makes about 20 revolutions. That's a mile of sky-high orbits.

Restyled in 1994 as part of a retro retheming of Tomorrowland, Astro Orbiter's highly stylized look recalls a 1920s machine-age view of the future. The look works best at night. While neon circles of blue, red and then pink pulse on the huge central antenna, the rockets glow green from their nose cones and red from their exhaust fires.

Unchanged from the ride's original incarnation as space-age Star Jets, the ride's green, steel-mesh elevator recalls the rocket gantries that were used in early launches at nearby Cape Canaveral, Fla.

Unfortunately, the waiting line for Astro Orbiter is usually awful. The ride loads as slowly as Dumbo, and the elevator delay just makes things worse. First thing in the morning, however, there's usually no one here. In fact, if you rush here immediately when the park opens you can often ride twice, maybe three times in a row without getting off.

| Average Wait | |
| --- | --- |
| 9am | 5 min |
| 10am | 10 |
| 11am | 30 |
| Noon | 30 |
| 1pm | 25 |
| 2pm | 35 |
| 3pm | 25 |
| 4pm | 40 |
| 5pm | 40 |
| 6pm | 40 |
| 7pm | 20 |
| 8pm | 20 |
| 9pm | 15 |

▶ Time it right and Astro Orbiter offers a unique way to view the Wishes fireworks display.

"**TTA**" offers an elevated tour of Tomorrowland

# Tomorrowland Transit Authority

★★★ ✔ 10 min. Capacity: 900. Covered queue. Fear factor: None. Access: Must be ambulatory. Handheld captioning available. *AuDe* Debuted: 1975, revised 1996, 2009.

A nice way to get off your feet, this elevated tour of Tomorrowland takes you alongside and through the area's four buildings. A new narration offers details about the attractions you pass, and highlights a real piece of Disney future past: the centerpiece of Walt Disney's model of his proposed EPCOT city. Also recently added, color-changing LEDs (especially cool at night) line the route.

### Train in Vain

The concept of the ride began life as a sketch drawn by Walt Disney in the 1960s. While planning EPCOT, he thought a system of small electric trains would give residents an efficient way to run errands or get to work. It would snake alongside, and sometimes circle over, convenience stores, offices and mass-transit stations without creating pollution or traffic problems.

Clean, efficient and easy to maintain, the power system has no moving parts except for its wheels. Every six feet or so a coil embedded in a shoebox-size rectangle in the track pulses with electricity in a carefully timed rhythm. The coil turns on to pull a car to it, then turns off to let the car roll over (each car has a steel plate in its floor). These bursts combine to move the trains in a near-silent glide of linear induction. Loading is fast, as each train slows but never stops. The idea won a design achievement award from the National Endowment for the Arts and the U.S. Dept. of Transportation.

The Disney Co. believed in the concept so much it formed a separate division, Community Transportation Services, to sell it to cities. Originally called the WEDway People Mover, this ride was the demonstrator.

But without Walt, the dream died. EPCOT the city was shelved, and CTS sold only one train—in 1981, to what is today known as the George Bush Intercontinental Airport in Houston. That train is still running, under that airport's main terminal.

**Hidden Mickey** On a belt buckle in a beauty salon, on your right just after you enter the building that holds Buzz Lightyear's Space Ranger Spin.

## Average Wait

| | |
|---|---|
| 9am | 0 min |
| 10am | 0 |
| 11am | 0 |
| Noon | 0 |
| 1pm | 0 |
| 2pm | 0 |
| 3pm | 0 |
| 4pm | 0 |
| 5pm | 0 |
| 6pm | 0 |
| 7pm | 0 |
| 8pm | 0 |
| 9pm | 0 |

▶ When Space Mountain is closed, hop on TTA to see that dark ride with its work lights on.

# Walt Disney's Carousel of Progress

★★★★ ✓ 21 min. Capacity: 1,440. Outdoor queue. Fear factor: None. Access: Guests may remain in wheelchairs, ECVs. Assistive listening; handheld and activated video captioning. Debuted at Walt Disney World: 1975, revised 1994 (same unit: NY World's Fair 1964, Disneyland 1967).

A robotic family demonstrates how electricity has made life better in this vintage theatrical show. Guests sit in a rotating theater to follow a dad, mom, son and daughter through four scenes depicting life in the 1900s, 1920s, 1940s and 1990s. Personally developed by Walt Disney, the show still has a wide-eyed charm, though cynics will find plenty to ridicule. Regardless of their reasons, most guests walk out with a smile.

**'Don't Bark at Him, Rover'**
Carousel of Progress debuted at the 1964 New York World's Fair, as part of a General Electric pavilion called Progressland. Starring Disney's first Audio-Animatronics humans, the show was hosted by the father of a typical American family. Four acts demonstrated how electricity—and specifically GE appliances—had improved family life. The sponsor's name was woven throughout the script. "Don't bark at him, Rover," the dad told the family dog when it barked at a stranger. "He might be a good customer of General Electric."

Walt Disney wrote much of the dialogue, and insisted his characters perform not only basic movements but also "business"–small supplemental actions that made them more real. For a 1920s scene, for example, Walt decided that visiting Cousin Orville should not only relax in a bathtub, but also wiggle his toes.

Set in a 1960s all-electric home, a Christmastime finale included "a GE push-button kitchen that all but runs itself."

To bridge the acts, songwriters Robert and Richard Sherman (best known for "It's a Small World") wrote "There's a Great Big Beautiful Tomorrow." The tune's lyrics perfectly captured the fair's blind optimism: *"There's a great big beautiful tomorrow, shining at the end of every day. There's a great big beautiful tomorrow, just a dream away!"*

After the fair closed Disney relocated the theater to California's Disneyland, where it opened in 1967. A revamped finale featured a home videocassette recorder, a product that wouldn't appear in stores for more than a decade.

**That '70s Show**
When the show moved to Walt Disney World in 1975, a new script tied it into the then-timely women's movement. Though her father warned "It's a man's world out there," the 1920s daughter searched Help Wanted ads. The 1940s wife demanded "equal pay" for wallpapering the rumpus room, rhetorically asking her husband "If you hired a man to do this, wouldn't you pay him?" (After the husband responded "Well, we might negotiate something later on, dear," a bird in a nearby cuckoo clock popped out and chirped "Now is the time! Now is the best time!")

A new finale made dad the cook.

To meet GE's demand that the show focus on the present, the Sherman Brothers wrote a new theme song, "Now is the Time." Dissing the future as *"still but a dream,"* it proclaimed *"Now is the time! Now is the best time! Now is the best time of your life!"*

Though the show had rotated clockwise, it switched directions in its new Florida theater. The 1975 show also returned to using human-hair wigs. Nylon versions had been used at Disneyland, but over time klieg lights above the father had melted his hair into a sticky pile of goo.

**Today's Carousel**
Disney created the current version of the show in 1994. Embracing the past even more than its predecessors, it's peppered with old-fashioned sayings. The wife "gets to the core of the apple." The husband knows it won't rain because "my lumbago isn't acting up." Peering into his dad's stereoscope, the son exclaims "Ooh la la! So that's Little Egypt doing the hoochie-koochie!" a reference to a scandalous exotic dancer at the 1893 Chicago World's Fair.

Today's finale takes place in the great big beautiful tomorrow of, well, 1994. While Grandma enjoys the thrills of a virtual reality helmet, mom's programming of a

LYRICS © WONDERLAND MUSIC COMPANY INC.

| Average Wait | |
| --- | --- |
| 9am | 5 min |
| 10am | 5 |
| 11am | 5 |
| Noon | 5 |
| 1pm | 5 |
| 2pm | 5 |
| 3pm | 5 |
| 4pm | 5 |
| 5pm | 5 |
| 6pm | 5 |
| 7pm | 5 |
| 8pm | 5 |
| 9pm | 5 |

▶ Kids will enjoy watching the family dog, who often glances at the audience.

"voice activation system" ends up burning the turkey. Early scenes take place on specific holidays—Valentine's Day, 1904; Independence Day, 1927; and Halloween, 1949.

Voices include Jean Shepherd (the narrator of the 1983 movie "A Christmas Story") as the father, Debi Derryberry (the voice of Nickelodeon's Jimmy Neutron) as the daughter, Mel Blanc (the longtime voice of Bugs Bunny and other Warner Bros. cartoon characters) as Cousin Orville, Rex Allen (1950s singing cowboy) as the Christmas Grandpa, and Janet Waldo (daughter Judy in the 1960s cartoon series "The Jetsons" and Josie in the 1970s "Josie and the Pussycats") as the Christmas grandma.

No longer sponsored by General Electric, today's Carousel doesn't mention the company, though antique GE appliances still appear.

### 'Bigger than Toad!'

In the fall of 2001, ironically less than a month after Walt Disney World started a 15-month celebration of Walt Disney's 100th birthday, it closed his beloved Carousel of Progress and took it off park maps. The reason: dwindling attendance, caused in part by the Sept. 11 attacks. Within days, fans of the show organized an Internet protest. "Let's make this bigger than Toad!" wrote one blogger, referring to an earlier, failed attempt to save the Walt Disney World Fantasyland attraction Mr. Toad's Wild Ride. This time, however, the protest worked. Disney reopened the Carousel a few months later.

Still, it cries out for a major refurbishment. As time has passed it by, the show now ignores the entire second half of the 20th century—the only time most of us have lived through. Imagine how fun it would be to see the daughter as a 1960s hippie chick with a stack of LPs, a 1970s 'droid daddy playing Pong, or a 1984 son writing "Hello" on his newfangled Macintosh. As for the future scene, it's just a Steve Jobs dream away.

**I, Robot.** Built in 1964, the Carousel of Progress dad was Disney's first Audio-Animatronics human.

**Fun facts** ❶ The show's first grandma also rocks in front of the fireplace in the Haunted Mansion ballroom. ❷ The six auditoriums rotate at 2 feet per second on large steel wheels and tracks, just like a train car on a railroad. Altogether the auditoriums weigh 375 tons.

**Hidden Mickeys** ❶ In Act 3, the hat Mickey Mouse wore in the Sorcerer's Apprentice sequence of the 1940 movie "Fantasia" sits on a stool to the right of the exercise machine. Mickey items in the finale scene include ❷ a nutcracker on the mantel, ❸ a plushie under the Christmas tree, ❹ a white salt shaker on the bar ❺ and an abstract painting of the Sorcerer's Apprentice on the wall to the right of the dining table. ❻ During the first moments of the virtual-reality video game, the three circles appear on the television as engines of a spaceship.

▶ **Nicely air-conditioned, Carousel of Progress offers a good way to beat the heat.**

# Space Mountain

★★★★★ ✔ 2 min, 30 sec. Capacity: 180. *FastPass*
Indoor, air-conditioned queue. Fear factor: Dark
drops and turns, but you don't go upside down.
Access: Must be ambulatory. Height restriction: 44
in. Debuted: 1975, revised 2009.

If you liked Space Mountain before, you'll
love it now. Disney's months-long refurbishment in 2009 did not alter the essence of the
indoor dark coaster, but instead simply
made it better—darker, smoother and seemingly faster. The sensation of hurtling
through deep space is still front and center.

The world's first indoor roller coaster,
this rocket ride in the dark
is still a series of constant
surprises. You never know
where you are going, and
rarely know where you are.

Projected onto the un-
derside of a smooth dome,
twinkling stars and shooting comets have no begin-
ning and no end. In fact, you
have no reference points at
all, not even the sides of
your rocket. It's all sensation, no thought required.

Half the fun is the ve-
hicle itself. Only slightly

| Average Wait | |
| --- | --- |
| 9am | 0 min |
| 10am | 20 |
| 11am | 40 |
| Noon | 50 |
| 1pm | 60 |
| 2pm | 60 |
| 3pm | 50 |
| 4pm | 50 |
| 5pm | 60 |
| 6pm | 70 |
| 7pm | 60 |
| 8pm | 60 |
| 9pm | 45 |

**Space Mountain** gets its shape from Japan's Mt.
Fuji. Inside is a roller coaster in the dark.

wider than you are, your rocket sits only
waist-high, thigh-high for taller folks.

### A futuristic space flight
The ride's story begins as you walk into the
building, a futuristic spaceport and repair
center that's orbiting above the earth. Passing the departure board, you walk to the
launching platform, an open-air loading
zone with its own control tower.

Soon after you climb into your rocket, a
sign flashes "Have a Nice Flight." This acti-
vates the rocket transporter, which takes
you through the energizing portal, a flashing blue tunnel that powers your machine
and ignites your engine. Climbing the
launch tower (the chain lift), you pass under robotic arms that secure a ship that has
come in for service. As two mechanics work
on its engines, two control-room operators
monitor their progress.

Then you blast off, on a journey through,
according to an early press release, "the
void of the universe." Zooming through
space, "you become engulfed in a spectacular spiral nebula with flashing comets and a
whirling galaxy." Apparently you lose your
bearings, as you also fly back through the
launch bay. When you return you trigger a
sonic boom in a red de-energizing tunnel.

▶ Hang on to your hat! The new ride is faster on its drops and turns.

## Changes for 2010

The ride went through a seven-month refurbishment in 2009.

Video games now appear in the last few windows along the standby queue, where 86 push-button control pads are embedded in the side handrail. The four games are based on jobs performed onboard a sci-fi spaceship: shooting asteroids, sorting lost-and-found items, moving cargo through traffic and building a starport with "expandobots." Each game lasts 90 seconds with a 90-second interval between games. Before the refurbishment the screens simulated windows looking onto 3-D images of space.

The final switchback area no longer views the coaster area above; instead an enclosed dark ceiling is dominated by dramatic blue neon-like lighting and a projected planet, nebula and space station with an occasional rocket.

The ride itself has a number of differences, all of them for the better. As the ride begins, the blue energizing tunnel no longer ends in disco-ball-like mirrored reflections.

Though the track layout hasn't changed, the track itself has; its new smooth rails let the rockets whoosh a little faster through the turns and drops. Visually the ride is much darker, with more moving stars and a more colorful spiraling nebulae projected on the domed ceiling. To help keep light out, designers have covered the loading area with its own ceiling and removed the glow-in-the-dark side stripes from the rockets.

The rockets have been upgraded with new fully padded seats and sturdier arms.

Unlike Disneyland's redone Space Mountain, this one is still all about sensation, with no tacked-on theming. The vehicles are still only one person wide, and thankfully do not blare music, letting you fully immerse yourself in a dark, breezy trip of unexpected turns and drops

One dud: a new souvenir-photo system. Like the automated cameras on Splash Mountain, Test Track and other Disney thrill rides, it takes a photo of you as you are riding the attraction, which you can then purchase as a souvenir. In this case, however, your photo is taken before you've experienced any thrills, as your vehicle approaches the chain lift.

**Top to bottom:** Video games along the standby queue. The loading area is now lit with neon-like blue lighting. The initial "energizing" tunnel. A exitway robotic control panel. The redone store.

▶ **Ask for the front row. You'll fly through the air with a breeze on your knees.**

Much of the attraction is a subtle tribute to the 1968 film, "2001: A Space Odyssey." The queue's eerie music recalls the movie's early scenes of a moon transport shuttle. The hall's angled plastic clapboard walls duplicate those of the movie's transport interior.

The movie's Discovery One spacecraft shows up three times. In the ride's boarding area, the spool-like corners the rockets pass by look just like the axle of Discovery One's rotating living quarters. The blue strobe tunnel recalls its hexagonal corridor that leads to its EVA pods. On the lift hill, the docked ship has the craft's unique head-spine-and-hip shape. The docked ship also appears in an entranceway window.

### 'Where's Mr. Smee?'
With its first passengers NASA astronauts Scott Carpenter, Gordon Cooper and Jim Irwin, Space Mountain opened with an elaborate ceremony on January 15, 1975. Disney officials declared it "the nation's most breathtaking thrill ride." But not everyone got the message. As park guests walked in, many expected something along the lines of Peter Pan's Flight, since at the time Disney didn't do roller coasters.

A few seconds later, up came their lunches and out flew their hats, purses, eyeglasses and, on more than one occasion, false teeth. Disney's response included posing two of the rockets in a dive up on an entrance tower, putting a video in the queue in which Cooper told guests it was A-OK with him if they would rather head for the exit ramp, and discreetly ironing out some of the ride's most violent jerks and jolts.

Though it opened during a recession, Space Mountain was an instant smash. When summer came, families with teenagers, many of whom would have never considered a Disney vacation before, began crowding Magic Kingdom turnstiles early each morning, running straight to Space Mountain as soon as the park opened.

### The Home of Future Living
For more than three decades the only real difference in the attraction was its postshow along the exit ramp. Originally it was the elaborate RCA Home of Future Living, as dioramas showed a dad teleconferencing from a patio chair while kids inside watched videodiscs. In 1985 the area became the RYCA-1 Dream of a New World, as robots built a pod city on a "hostile planet."

A silly Federal Express FX-1 Teleport took over the postshow from 1993 to 1998, as "teleportation units" digitized and transported alien fossils back to earth. Today, these dioramas show travel destinations such as Crater Caverns and the Coral Moons of Pisces 7. Guests see themselves placed into these scenes a few moments later.

The FedEx years also had a preshow. Monitors in the boarding area aired the futuristically wacky "SMTV" network. Commercials featured Crazy Larry selling used spaceships, while a space newscast featured ditzy weather girl Wendy Beryllium: "Our extended forecast: giant comet. Wow, scary!"

The robotic boy and dog have been around since the beginning. Known as Billy, the then-human boy used to film guests for their TV appearances on the Speedramp.

**Fun finds** ❶ The Space Mountain logo has a new color. Its lettering is now green instead of FedEx orange. ❷ Panels inside the mountain refer to it as "Star Port Seven-Five," a nod to the attraction's opening year. ❸ Intergalactic route maps along the queue contain references to the Little Mermaid, Mickey's pet dog and the 1937 movie "Snow White and the Seven Dwarfs." ❹ The chain-lift spaceship is now named MK-1 (Magic Kingdom 1). This Space Mountain is the original ride. Similar versions have since been built in California, China, France and Japan. ❺ The spaceship is marked "H-NCH 1975," a reference to the ride's designer, Disney Legend John Hench, as well as the year the ride opened.

**Fun facts** ❶ The left track has a longer first drop and covers a bit greater distance: 3,196 feet compared to the right track's 3,186. The final drop of both is 35 feet. ❷ The blue energizing portal has a practical function: its strobes shrink your pupils, so your space flight seem darker than it really is. ❸ Why do the docked ship's engine nozzles look like plastic caps of spray-paint cans? Because they are! Used by an artist on a pre-production model, real spray-paint caps were accidentally reproduced perfectly on the full-scale prop. ❹ The sonic boom heard in the red re-entry tunnel is actualy the reversed sound of a jet engine starting up. ❺ The ride has 30 rockets, numbered 1 through 31. There is no rocket 13. ❻ The building is 183 feet tall and 300 feet wide. It covers about two acres. ❼ Each of its 72 exterior concrete ribs weighs 74 tons, is 117 feet long and narrows from 13 feet wide at its base to 4 feet at the top. ❽ The building gets its sweeping-pillar look from Israel's Kennedy Memorial. Its shape comes from Japan's Mt. Fuji. ❾ Space Mountain is the oldest operating roller coaster in Florida.

▶ **For the wildest ride ask for a back seat. It's faster on the drops and turns.**

**Completing a lap** around the track, Jeff Turner of Fort Myers, Fla., cheers on his son, Andrew

# Tomorrowland Indy Speedway

★★ 5 min. Capacity: 292 (146 2-seat vehicles). Covered queue. Fear factor: None. Closed during thunderstorms. Access: Must be ambulatory. Height restriction: 54 in to take a car out alone. 32 in to ride. Debuted: 1971 (Disneyland 1955). Revised 1996.

This winding, wooded "race" track puts your little boy or girl at the controls of a 5-year-old's dream machine—a small-scale race car with a rough ride and a rumbly, smelly engine. The half-mile course takes you around five turns, down one short straightaway and over a bridge.

For what you get, the waiting line is one of the worst in the park. There's shade but no air conditioning, and on peak days wait times can exceed an hour. There's no wait first thing in the morning, or sometimes late at night.

There's never much of a race, as top speed is only 7.5 mph and you can't pass—a rail underneath your car keeps it in its lane. If your family takes up more than one car, however, you should know that the heaviest car is always the slowest. Once when my daughter, Micaela, got a car of her own and I (Mike) squeezed into a second one, she left me behind while cars behind me continuously smacked my bumper! Micaela thought it was funnier than I did.

Why is the ride in Tomorrowland? For a reason that could only make sense to Disney: When it opened in 1971, the track was an update of the Disneyland attraction Autopia, which, when that ride premiered in 1955, was a simulation of the limited-access highways destined for that era's future.

A year-2000 sponsorship by the Indianapolis Motor Speedway and a 1994 re-theming of Tomorrowland as an alien world confused the theme further. Though its cars still have their 1970s bodies, signs along the ride's queue area now present it as a wacky outer-space race, with a history that parallels that of the real Indy 500.

**Fun finds ❶** Speakers around the track feature famed Indy announcer Tom Carnegie calling your "race." **❷** A brick from the 1909 pavement of the Indianapolis Motor Speedway is embedded in the "starting line" between lanes 2 and 3, close to the elevated exit walkway.

| Average Wait | |
| --- | --- |
| 9am | 0 min |
| 10am | 20 |
| 11am | 20 |
| Noon | 30 |
| 1pm | 30 |
| 2pm | 35 |
| 3pm | 30 |
| 4pm | 35 |
| 5pm | 30 |
| 6pm | 30 |
| 7pm | 30 |
| 8pm | 30 |
| 9pm | 20 |

▶ **Take your spin early in the morning or late at night to avoid a long wait.**

**Alice** greets parade guests on Main Street U.S.A.

# Celebrate a Dream Come True Parade

★★★ 30 min. 3p daily. Travels Main Street U.S.A., then Liberty Square, Frontierland. Cancelled during rain. Arrive 20 min early for good spot. Fear factor: None. Access: Special viewing areas for those in wheelchairs, ECVs. Debuted: 2009.

Want to see characters? Don't care that much about lame, cheap floats? Then this parade is for you. It uses cheaply recycled floats from many past Magic Kingdom parades, but does feature dozens of Disney's classic animated stars. Some wave to the crowd from floats while others dance on the street and slap hands with guests.

The procession makes three stops—on Main Street U.S.A., in front of Cinderella Castle and at the junction of Liberty Square and Frontierland. Not much happens, though the dancers perform and characters mingle with the crowd.

Riding the floats are Mickey and Minnie Mouse, nearly every Disney princess and the stars of "Aladdin" (1992), "Alice in Wonderland" (1951), "The Jungle Book" (1967), "Lilo & Stitch" (2002), "Mary Poppins" (1964), "Peter Pan" (1953), "Pinocchio" (1940), and "Snow White and the Seven Dwarfs" (1937). Also on hand, Donald Duck,

Goofy, Pluto and Chip 'n Dale. As the floats pass by, you hear snippets of music to match the characters you see. "Whistle While You Work" plays from the Snow White float, "You Can Fly" comes out of hidden speakers on the Peter Pan float, and "Supercalifragilisticexpialidocious" fills the air when you see Mary Poppins.

The parade will seem familiar to park veterans, as it recycles Magic Kingdom floats that have been used for ages. The procession is a halfhearted update of the Disney Dreams Come True Parade (2006–2008), which itself was a budget-grade makeover of the Share a Dream Come True Parade (2001–2006), a rolling tribute to Walt Disney. The floats, which at one time were topped with giant snowglobes, have been redone with party-favor confetti and balloon decorations to go along with the current Disney World "Celebration" marketing theme.

The best viewing spot is anywhere along the shady western side of Main Street U.S.A. Curb seats get taken about 2:30 p.m. As guests wait for the parade, cast members keep children entertained with hula hoops, jump ropes and street games such as Red Light Green Light.

**Hidden Mickey** On the Snow White float as a dark mark on the organ, above the middle keys.

▶ The best viewing spot: On the curb on the shady western side of Main Street U.S.A.

# SpectroMagic

★★★★★ ✓ 20 min. Arrive 30 min early for a good seat, an hour early for the best spots. Route: Starts on Main Street U.S.A. between the Town Square firehouse and car barn. Continues to the castle hub, through Liberty Square and Frontierland. Fear factor: The Chernabog float has spooky music and a 30-foot-tall animated monster. Cancelled during rain. Access: Special viewing areas for guests in wheelchairs and ECVs. Debuted: 1991. Revised: 2001, 2008.

Viewing this evening light parade is like gazing at a Christmas tree in a dark living room: just the sight of it makes you feel good. A cavalcade of colorful floats and costumes, SpectroMagic is a moving gallery of synchronized light patterns. And though everything is lit, it's all against a pitch-black backdrop. Nearly all the light is emitted internally, from rope lights and fiber optics. Disney turns out its park lights just before the parade begins.

Set to a symphonic score and filled with things that normally would be figments of your imagination (twirling butterfly girls, spinning fish, dancing ostriches), the parade is also like a hallucinatory dream: you can't understand it, but it sure is interesting.

Based for the most part on heritage Disney animation, SpectroMagic features

**Cinderella's pumpkin** transforms into a white carriage as part of the finale of SpectroMagic

more than 80 characters, 90 percent of them from cartoons and animated musicals released before 1960.

### Float segments
**SpectroMen.** The procession is led through the park by this exuberant group of trumpeters, whirlyball riders and other odd fellows who, according to Disney, are keepers of light and just a little bit shy. They come from a land where everything is filled with bursts of color, and are here to share their mystical rays with you.

**Mickey Mouse.** Wearing a grand magician's cape that extends 17 feet above his head, the Mouse stands majestically on a float all his own. Powering the parade through his Electro-ball, he controls the light of the SpectroMen, altering the colors, effects and luminosity of floats near him. A confetti of light sparkles around Mickey, created by reflections from mirror balls.

**Vintage cartoons.** This three-float symphony includes the bass violins from the 1935 Silly Symphony short "Music Land," the Golden Harp from 1947's "Mickey and the Beanstalk" (a cartoon seen in that year's Disney movie "Fun and Fancy Free"), Goofy on the timpani and, dressed in Liberace capes, Chip 'n Dale on a grand pi-

▶ Running late? Good seats are often still available in front of the Town Square firehouse.

ano. The conductor is—incongruently—Genie, of the 1992 movie musical "Aladdin."

**Sleeping Beauty.** Shimmering lights create a giant peacock at the front of this three-float caravan, based on Disney's 1959 princess movie. Fairies Fauna (in green), Flora (blue) and Merriweather (pink) ride within a flower garden that changes from a multicolor day to a blue-and-green night. Dancing around them are human butterfly and dragonfly girls, their wings electroluminescent panels.

**The Little Mermaid.** This 10-piece unit combines twirling giant fish with a float that hosts the stars of Disney's 1989 musical. On board are Ariel, Sebastian and King Triton. A freewheeling Ursula spins past, stopping occasionally to shine her light, and speak with, selected parade watchers.

**Fantasia.** Six floats are themed to Disney's 1940 experiment in animating classical music. First up, a tribute to the film's "Dance of the Hours" operetta, as dancing ostriches entertain Bacchus, the god of wine. From the film's take on "The Pastoral Symphony," flying horse Pegasus and his family ride by on three floats above some dry-ice clouds. Then Chernobog, the monstrous bat-winged demon from the movie's "A Night on Bald Mountain" segment arrives, unfurling his wings dramatically to create a 38-foot span.

**Finale.** A seven-float convoy features the stars of the 1932 Silly Symphony short "The Little Pigs," 1937's "Snow White," 1940's "Pinocchio," 1950's "Cinderella," 1951's "Alice in Wonderland" and 1953's "Peter Pan." It includes Cinderella's coach, Captain Hook's ship and a full-size rotating merry-go-round. Poised in front is Practical Pig, who flicks a paint brush to change the lights behind him—on every float and every costume—from white to a rainbow of hues.

The parade was updated in late 2007. The most obvious change: the SpectroMen. Previously covered by giant plastic heads, these performers' faces are now visible, accented by silver makeup and blue and purple eye shadow and topped with LED wigs and whimsical straw hats. The butterfly and dragonfly girls also have new costumes.

### Where to sit

A good viewing spot for SpectroMagic is in front of Tony's Town Square Restaurant along Main Street U.S.A. You'll get a good view of the front and side of every float, and be right next to the park exit.

**Fun finds ❶** The SpectroMen's horns light up when they're played. **❷** When he touches it, Mickey's Electro-ball sizzles and adds rays to his cape. **❸** Other cape lights are synchronized to the soundtrack. **❹** The bass violins pluck themselves. **❺** Notes project on the ground around the violins. **❻** A sun changes to a moon on the first "Sleeping Beauty" float. **❼** A waterfall cascades down the back of the last garden float. **❽** The butterfly and dragonfly girls have painted faces. **❾** Each pair of eyes in "The Little Mermaid" fish school moves in a different way. **❿** Bubbles come from three of the freewheeling fish in that unit. **⓫** Ursula stops to chat with some guests ("Hello handsome!"). **⓬** Ariel does the breast stroke. **⓭** The spinning fish wink. **⓮** The ostriches wear heavy eyeliner and tuxedo jackets. **⓯** They often peck, kick and slap each other. **⓰** Lightning strikes under the horses and on Bald Mountain. **⓱** The pink-lined Bald Mountain turns into a red-lit Chernabog. **⓲** Two buzzards guard him. **⓳** The Three Little Pigs taunt the Big Bad Wolf, who walks in front of them. **⓴** A crown spins above Cinderella. **㉑** Her coach transforms from a pumpkin to a carriage. **㉒** An image of Tinker Bell appears in Cinderella's castle windows and flies out of them. **㉓** Two mechanical "Alice in Wonderland" playing cards paint their roses red. **㉔** An image of Cheshire Cat disappears except for his mouth and eyes. **㉕** Mary Poppins' umbrella lights up with her jacket. **㉖** Dumbo is a carrousel animal. **㉗** The stars of the 1945 movie "The Three Caballeros" appear on the carrousel's top rear panel. **㉘** Capt. Hook's hook lights up. **㉙** His cannons fire dry-ice smoke in time to the music. **㉚** Capt. Hook's Jolly Roger flag has glowing red eyes. **㉛** Riding with the captain, Snow White's Evil Queen has her magic mirror. **㉛** Peter Pan has been known to sneak up and kick Mr. Smee. **㉜** Tinker Bell appears again inside the Evil Queen's castle. **㉝** Pinocchio's teapot steams. **㉞** Lights circle the ground around Minnie Mouse and Donald Duck, who ride on the final float. **㉟** Facing backward, Jiminy Cricket appears on the last float, waving as he says "So long! See ya later!"

**Fun facts ❶** The floats are covered in scrim, a transparent black gauze. **❷** The drivers' faces hide behind mesh screens. **❸** The parade uses 2,000 car batteries. Walking performers wear battery packs. **❹** There are 600,000 miniature lights; 100 miles of fiber-optic cable. **❺** Soundtrack composer John Debney created the scores for the movies "Elf," "Bruce Almighty," "The Passion of the Christ" and "Swing Vote." **❻** SpectroMagic is the only Disney parade theme ever recorded in 3/4 time, which means it's the only one guests have ever been able to waltz to. **❼** Roger Rabbit was the parade's symphony conductor during its original run.

▶ A bad spot to sit: In Frontierland, facing the Rivers of America. A spotlight shines in your face.

# Move It! Shake It! Celebrate It!

★★★★ ✔ 20 min. Floats travel Main Street U.S.A., stop at Cinderella Castle hub for show, then travel back down Main Street U.S.A. Canceled during rain. Fear factor: None. Access: Special viewing areas for those in wheelchairs, ECVs. Debuted: 2009.

Want to dance with a Disney character? Here's your chance. Held a few times a day in front of Cinderella Castle, this colorful, high-energy street party lets guests shake their tail feathers with Sheriff Woody, Mr. Incredible, King Louie and other Disney stars. If you (or your children) aren't shy about dancing in public, it's an easy way to have a unique character experience and snap some memorable photos.

Beginning at Town Square as a five-float parade, the procession turns into an interactive party when it reaches the Cinderella Castle hub, where guests are invited to share space with characters, stilt-walkers and dance leaders.

An emcee rides in the first float along with Mickey and Minnie Mouse, Donald Duck and Goofy. Four other floats resemble gift packages, which eventually pop open to reveal characters on top—Sebastian the crab (from 1989's "The Little Mermaid"),

**'Toy Story' cowgirl Jessie** is one of eight Disney characters who get off their floats and dance with park guests during the "Move It! Shake It! Celebrate It!" street party

Lumiere (1991's "Beauty and the Beast"), the Mad Hatter (1951's "Alice in Wonderland") and Genie (1992's "Aladdin").

Eight characters dance with guests. King Louie and Baloo (from 1967's "The Jungle Book") appear near the Adventureland entrance. Woody and Jessie (the "Toy Story" movies) get down near the Liberty Square walkway. Chip 'n Dale boogie by the walkway to the right of the castle. Mr. Incredible and Frozone (2004's "The Incredibles") dance near the entrance to Tomorrowland.

Songs include the Baha Men's "Move It Like This (Shake It Like That)," Peaches & Herb's disco ditty "Shake Your Groove Thing" and the Ray Charles classic "Twist It ( Shake Your Tail Feather)." A conga line forms to Buster Poindexter's "Hot, Hot, Hot."

After 12 minutes the floats head back down Main Street to "High School Musical" star Corbin Bleu's "Celebrate You." The parade rolls out to a reworked Hannah Montana tune "Pumpin' Up the Party."

The street party takes place in direct sunlight, and the asphalt really reflects the heat (privately, some performers refer to the show as "Shake It Bake It"). During the hottest days Disney usually cuts the conga line.

▶ There's usually no need to find a viewing spot early. Crowds arrive at the last minute.

Dozens of rockets and nearly 700 explosions light up the sky during the Wishes fireworks show

# Wishes

★★★★★ ✓ 12 min. Fear factor: Loud explosions. Cancelled during thunderstorms. Access: Special viewing areas for wheelchair and ECV guests. Debuted: 2003.

Every! Other! Fire! Works! Show! Emphasizes! Every! Explosion!

Not this one. Disney's signature fireworks show is artistic, even subtle. Though it explodes 683 different pieces of pyro in just 12 minutes, Wishes paints delicate strokes as well as bold. Sometimes the sky sparkles, sometimes it flashes. Some explosions form stars, hearts, even a face. Some bursts dribble away, others disappear. Comets shoot off by themselves and by the dozen.

But that's just the half of it. Synchronizing its visuals to a symphonic score, Wishes

---

**IN 1940'S "PINOCCHIO,"** the Blue Fairy, a symbol of patient wisdom, appoints Jiminy Cricket to serve as the boy's conscience. **"STARLIGHT, STAR BRIGHT"** is a 19th-century American nursery rhyme. It's based on the notion that if you see the first star of the night sky before any others have appeared, any wish you make will come true. In reality, an evening's first visible "star" is often the planet Venus.

packs an emotional punch. Narrated by Jiminy Cricket with help from the Blue Fairy (both from the classic 1940 Disney movie "Pinocchio"), it teaches a heart-tugging lesson about believing in yourself.

The show starts without fanfare, as a quiet chord grows louder and the castle begins to glow and sparkle. "When stars are born they possess a gift or two," the Blue Fairy says. "They have the power to make a wish come true." A lone star arcs across the sky. *"Starlight, star bright, first star I see tonight,"* a chorus of little girls sings. *"I wish I may I wish I might, have the wish I wish tonight…"* Five-pointed stars explode above Cinderella Castle.

"I'll bet a lot of you folks don't believe that, about a wish coming true, do ya?" Jiminy asks. "Well I didn't either. But lemme tell you: the most fantastic, magical things can happen, and it all starts with a wish!"

And with that, the spectacle begins.

First Tinker Bell (a real person) steps off the top turret of Cinderella Castle and glides (on a wire) to Tomorrowland. Explosions fill the air as the voices of Cinderella, Ariel, Pinocchio and other Disney stars recall their wishes, then medleys of fireworks (each in its own color palette) express courage and love.

▶ Watch the show from in front of the castle. Main Street doesn't fill until showtime.

*"Fate is kind,"* a choir sings, as the tune switches to the bridge of "When You Wish Upon a Star," the "Pinocchio" theme song. *"She brings to those who love... the sweet fulfillment of... their secret longing."*

A fan of comets wipes the sky clean, then Roman candles dance to "The Sorcerer's Apprentice." A villains segment has crackling bursts, some as bright as strobes.

"Wishes *can* come true," the cricket says. "And the best part is, you'll never run out. They're shining deep down inside of you."

### Where to watch it

With fireworks that launch directly behind Cinderella Castle as well as symmetrically alongside, **Wishes is best seen from directly in front of the castle,** anywhere on Main Street U.S.A. The perfect spot is right on the crest of the Main Street bridge, between the Tip Board and the castle hub. From there you'll be close enough to see all the castle effects, but still far enough away to see all the pyrotechnics. There's always room to stand in this area, as cast members don't let guests out onto the street until just minutes before showtime.

For decades, many guests have preferred to watch the Magic Kingdom fireworks from the outdoor patio of a fast food stand that today is known as the Tomorrowland Noodle Station. Though the spot isn't the best for the symmetrical Wishes show, Disney now charges guest to stand there, reserving it for an $18 Wishes "dessert party." Other spots to avoid: Town Square (the lights stay on) and especially the Main Street U.S.A. train station balcony (there's no audio).

Want to dash out of the park as soon as the show ends? Stand in front of the Emporium, the closest dark spot to the exit.

But why fight the crowd? Instead, why not embrace the magical mood you'll be in to get an ice cream and relax. Your kids will be happy; why not talk with them? Ask about their dreams and wishes. Tell them yours.

**Fun finds ❶** Blue stars appear above Cinderella Castle three times during the opening verse, just after the lines "When you wish upon a star..." "makes no difference who you are..." and "anything your heart desires will come to you..." **❷** Tinker Bell starts her flight just after Jiminy Cricket says "...and it all starts with a wish!" **❸** As each Disney character says their wish, the accompanying fireworks are the color of his or her signature wardrobe. Those during Cinderella's line are blue; those when Ariel speaks are

© DISNEY

**Disney presents special fireworks displays** for its 4th of July, Halloween and Christmas events

green. **❹** Another blue star explodes after Aladdin tells Genie "I wish for your freedom!" and the chorus shouts "Wishes!" **❺** Red hearts appear at the end of the "Beauty and the Beast" music. **❻** More blue stars explode as Jiminy sings "...when you wish upon a star, your dreams... come true!" **❼** "Whoa!" Genie says as his fireworks appear. "Ten thousand years can give ya such a crick in the neck!" **❽** During the "Sorcerer's Apprentice" sequence, the castle is lit to resemble the blue hat Mickey Mouse wore in that segment from 1940's "Fantasia," with its white stars and moons. **❾** A massive red explosion introduces Disney villains. **❿** Images of the Evil Queen's mirror appear on the castle as she commands "Slaves in the magic mirror, come from the farthest space..." **⓫** Fireworks form a frowning face, and the castle mirror images become faces, when the queen commands "Let me see thy face!" **⓬** Meanwhile the castle glows in dark greens, oranges and purples and is flashed by lightning. **⓭** It turns blue again as the Blue Fairy returns.

**Fun facts ❶** The fireworks launch from 11 locations. **❷** Tinker Bell is sometimes a man. The role's physical requirements are only that the performer weigh no more than 105 pounds and be no taller than 5 ft 3 in. **❸** Wishes replaced the Fantasy in the Sky fireworks show, which ran from 1976 to 1993. Though only five minutes longer, Wishes has almost three times as many explosions as its predecessor.

"WHEN YOU WISH UPON A STAR" LYRICS © WONDERLAND MUSIC COMPANY INC.

▶ **Keep an eye on the castle. It sparkles, flashes and changes colors as part of the show.**

The symbol of Epcot,
Spaceship Earth is
a 180-foot-tall
geodesic sphere

# Epcot

## A permanent world's fair

**Where can you talk with a sea turtle,** crash through test barriers, soar over California, take a rocket ride to Mars, buy exclusive French perfume and feast at a German Oktoberfest? At Epcot, a unique theme park that puts a Disney spin on the science expositions and international pavilions of a classic world's fair. Nearly two dozen pavilions are spread out over 260 acres.

### Two parks in one

The front of the park is Future World, a science-and-technology zone themed to subjects such as agriculture, automotive safety and geography. Rides include a greenhouse boat cruise (Living with the Land), a spin around a General Motors proving ground (Test Track) and a hang-gliding flight over California (Soarin'). Other highlights: the interactive "Turtle Talk with Crush" and the realistic Mission Space.

You'll travel around the world when you take the 1.3-mile trek around Epcot's World Showcase. Circling a 40-acre lagoon, 11 pavilions are filled with native entertainment, food and merchandise. Most offer an attraction or small museum. Each is staffed by young natives of its country. Located throughout World Showcase, a series of Kidcot activity tables lets children create custom cardboard masks using markers, stamps and hanging paper cutouts representing the host pavilion.

The two areas keep separate hours. Future World opens at 9 a.m. and closes at 7 p.m. except for its major attractions; World Showcase opens at 11 a.m. and closes at 9 p.m.

Originally an acronym, the word "Epcot" comes from the Experimental Prototype Community of Tomorrow, an actual city Walt Disney planned to be centered on this site. After his death the Disney company took two of Walt's EPCOT ideas—a science center that would show ways to improve future communities and an international cultural expo—and reworked them into a theme park.

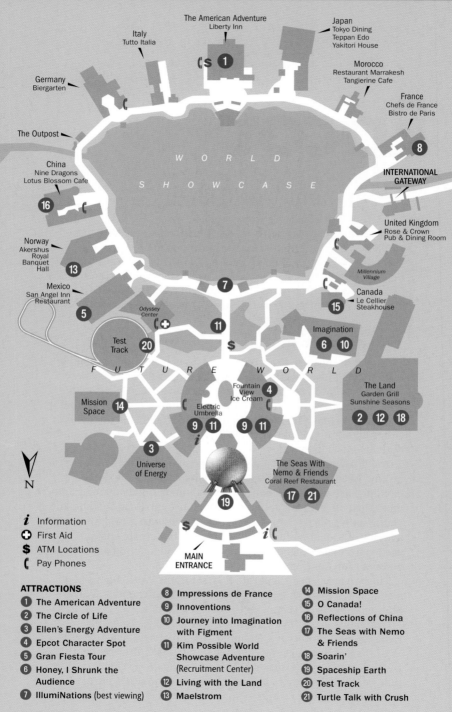

# EPCOT Overview

**The American Adventure**
Liberty Inn

**Italy**
Tutto Italia

**Japan**
Tokyo Dining
Teppan Edo
Yakitori House

**Germany**
Biergarten

**Morocco**
Restaurant Marrakesh
Tangierine Cafe

**France**
Chefs de France
Bistro de Paris

**The Outpost**

**China**
Nine Dragons
Lotus Blossom Cafe

**INTERNATIONAL GATEWAY**

*W O R L D*

*S H O W C A S E*

**United Kingdom**
Rose & Crown
Pub & Dining Room

**Norway**
Akershus
Royal
Banquet
Hall

*Millennium Village*

**Mexico**
San Angel Inn
Restaurant

Odyssey Center

**Canada**
Le Cellier
Steakhouse

**Test Track**

**Imagination**

*F U T U R E  W O R L D*

**Mission Space**

Fountain View Ice Cream

Electric Umbrella

**The Land**
Garden Grill
Sunshine Seasons

**Universe of Energy**

**The Seas With Nemo & Friends**
Coral Reef Restaurant

**N**

*i* Information
✚ First Aid
$ ATM Locations
( Pay Phones

**MAIN ENTRANCE**

## ATTRACTIONS

1. The American Adventure
2. The Circle of Life
3. Ellen's Energy Adventure
4. Epcot Character Spot
5. Gran Fiesta Tour
6. Honey, I Shrunk the Audience
7. IllumiNations (best viewing)
8. Impressions de France
9. Innoventions
10. Journey into Imagination with Figment
11. Kim Possible World Showcase Adventure (Recruitment Center)
12. Living with the Land
13. Maelstrom
14. Mission Space
15. O Canada!
16. Reflections of China
17. The Seas with Nemo & Friends
18. Soarin'
19. Spaceship Earth
20. Test Track
21. Turtle Talk with Crush

# Attractions at a glance

## CHARACTER-GREETING ATTRACTION
**④ Epcot Character Spot ★★★** Avg wait 15 min. Innoventions Plaza, Future World. Meet Goofy, Mickey and Minnie Mouse, Pluto.

## EXHIBITS
**⑨ Innoventions ★★★★ ✔** Unlimited. Wait times vary. Height restriction for Sum of All Thrills 48 in. Innoventions Plaza, Future World. Interactive corporate exhibits include new Sum of All Thrills, a design-your-own ride using a robotic arm.

## FIREWORKS
**⑦ IllumiNations: Reflections of Earth ★★★★ ✔** 15 min. 9p. Loud explosions, fire. World Showcase lagoon. Fireworks, laser, music show portray abstract world history.

## MOVIES
**② The Circle of Life ★★★** 13 min. Avg wait 7 min. The Land, Future World. Ecology lesson with stars of 1994's "The Lion King."
**⑧ Impressions de France ★★★★** 18 min. Avg wait 10 min. France, World Showcase. AuDe Honors French art, landscape, music.
**⑮ O Canada! ★★★** 14 min. Avg wait 10 min. Canada, World Showcase. AuDe Martin Short hosts CircleVision 360 travelogue.
**⑯ Reflections of China ★★★★** 15 min. Avg wait 10 min. China, World Showcase. AuDe CircleVision 360 movie celebrates Chinese culture, geography, history.

## RIDES
**③ Ellen's Energy Adventure ★★★** 45 min. Avg wait 10 min. Loud Big Bang. Universe of Energy, Future World. AuDe Dated oil-company view of energy exploration stars Ellen DeGeneres; includes wide-screen films, slow-moving ride past dinosaurs.
**⑤ Gran Fiesta Tour ★★★** 8 min. No wait. Mexico, World Showcase. AuDe Donald Duck and friends from 1944's "The Three Caballeros" cheapen a dark, indoor boat tour of Mexican cultural history.
**⑩ Journey Into Imagination with Figment ★★** 6 min. No wait. Loud noises, skunk smell, sudden flash. Imagination, Future World. AuDe Mischievous dragon wrecks Eric Idle's tour of Imagination Institute.

**⑫ Living with the Land ★★★** 14 min. Avg wait 40 min. The Land, Future World. FastPass AuDe Indoor boat ride through greenhouses of unusual plants, farming techniques.
**⑬ Maelstrom ★★★** 15 min. Avg wait 25 min. Scary faces. Short steep drop. Norway, World Showcase. FastPass Indoor boat ride, optional 5-min. Norwegian travelogue.
**⑭ Mission Space ★★★★ ✔** 6 min. Avg wait 30 min. Height restriction 44 in. Original version is seriously intense. Future World. FastPass Centrifuge simulates trip to Mars; alternate version doesn't spin.
**⑰ The Seas with Nemo & Friends ★★★★ ✔** Allow 60 min. Avg wait 10 min. Future World. Calm dark ride retells "Finding Nemo"; leads to aquariums, exhibits, Turtle Talk with Crush (below).
**⑱ Soarin' ★★★★★ ✔** 5 min. Avg wait 65 min. Height restriction 40 in. The Land, Future World. FastPass Delightful simulated hang-glider tour of California.
**⑲ Spaceship Earth ★★★★ ✔** 14 min. Avg wait 20 min. Future World. AuDe Slow-moving dark ride teaches communications history via Audio-Animatronics scenes.
**⑳ Test Track ★★★★★ ✔** 5 min. Avg wait 70 min. Height restriction 40 in. High speeds, sharp turns. Future World. FastPass Vehicles travel indoor-outdoor proving ground.

## SCAVENGER HUNT
**⑪ Kim Possible World Showcase Adventure ★★★★ ✔** Allow 45–60 min. World Showcase. Interactive scavenger hunt with cell-phone-like device.

## THEATRICAL SHOWS
**❶ The American Adventure ★★★★★ ✔** 30 min. Avg wait 20 min. World Showcase. AuDe Film, Audio-Animatronics cast tell U.S. story.
**㉑ Turtle Talk with Crush ★★★★★ ✔** 12 min. Avg wait 15 min. The Seas with Nemo & Friends pavilion, Future World. AuDe Interactive real-time conversations with animated sea turtle from 2003's "Finding Nemo."

## 3-D MOVIE
**❻ Honey, I Shrunk the Audience ★★★** 15 min. Avg wait 10 min. Some children may be terrified. Imagination pavilion, Future World. FastPass AuDe 3-D film based on 1989's "Honey, I Shrunk the Kids."

**Coral Reef restaurant, Future World**

# Restaurants and food

Epcot has 11 table-service restaurants, one buffet, two character meals and seven indoor fast-food spots. Those in the China, Italy, Japan and Mexico pavilions are not run by Disney. Make **reservations** (available 180 days in advance; 190 days for Disney resort guests) as early as possible at 407-WDW-DINE (407-939-3463) or online at **disneyworld.disney.go.com/dining**. If you will be using the **Disney Dining Plan**, note that many Epcot restaurants do not accept it (those that do are indicated below by the marks *DP* or *DPQ*).

### TABLE SERVICE

**Bistro de Paris** ★★★★★ ✔ **Gourmet French** $$$$$ D: $30–$53, 5–9p. No children's menu. Seats 120. France. Close to the quality of a top Parisian restaurant, this intimate second-floor dining room overlooks the World Showcase promenade. An ever-changing gourmet menu typically offers top-notch shellfish and seafood dishes, as well as venison and other meats. The escargot is always good. A six-course, prix-fixe meal is $75 without wine, $120 with wine pairings. A refined decor features white linens and tuxedoed servers. Like the lower-level Chefs de France, Bistro de Paris is owned by legendary French chefs Paul Bocuse (who visits often), Gaston LeNotre and Roger Verge. Bocuse's son, Jerome, is the manager.

**Chefs de France** ★★★★ ✔ French $$$$ L: $12–$20; Noon–3p. D: $19–$34; 5–9p. Seats 266. France. Generous with cream and cheese, this sophisticated spot offers everything from sandwiches to seafood. Good appetizers include lobster bisque. Big kids will love the adult menu's mac and cheese (lunch only), made with cream and gruyere. Tile floors and tin ceilings are nice but noisy.

**Coral Reef** ★★★★★ ✔ *DP* Seafood $$$$ L: $12–$26; 11:30a–3:30p. D: $17–$32; 4–8:50p. Seats 275. The Seas with Nemo & Friends pavilion. You eat fish while you watch fish at this dimly lit hidden treasure, which looks into

The Seas with Nemo & Friends aquarium. The signature appetizer is creamy lobster soup. Like spicy food? Try the blackened catfish—my husband's favorite Disney fish dish. Brushed-metal tables are trimmed in light woods. Arrive at 11:30 a.m. and you may walk right in; otherwise book lunch two weeks early, dinner 60 to 90 days out. Ask for an aquarium-front table or a booth near the tank.

**Le Cellier** ★★★★★ ✔ **DP Steakhouse $$$$** L: $13–$30; 11:30a–3p. D: $21–$37; 4–9p. Seats 156. Canada. The toughest World Showcase reservation, this low-ceilinged, stone-walled eatery resembles a chateau wine cellar. Alberta-beef steaks are aged 28 days. Other entrees include fish, seafood, chicken and sandwiches. Made with Moosehead beer, a cheddar-cheese soup makes a nice makeshift dip for complimentary soft breadsticks. The young staff is friendly.

**Nine Dragons** ★★★★ ✔ **Chinese $$$$** L: $14–$21; Noon–3:45p. D: $16–$27; 4–9p. Seats 300. China. A 2008 refurbishment at this China Company eatery has brightened its decor and livened up its menu with modern dishes. New entrees are light and savory; holdovers include honey-sesame and stir-fried Kung Pao chicken. Direct from China's National Guest House, a small cucumber stack appetizer is an indulgence. Greens, yellows and blues highlight the serene decor. Servers are helpful and humble. Window tables make for good people-watching. Good teas.

**Restaurant Marrakesh** ★★★★ ✔ **Moroccan $$$$** L: $15–$22; Noon–3:30p. D: $21–$28; 3:30–8:45p. Seats 255. Morocco. Though it sounds exotic, there is nothing scary about Moroccan cuisine. Ingredients are the same as those in American cooking, and flavors are mild. The lamb shank couscous is like your mom's pot roast, complete with roasted carrots and meat that falls off the bone, but tossed in light fluffy wheat instead of potatoes. Lunch includes beef and fish dishes; dinner adds sampler platters. Of course, mom's meals probably didn't include a belly dancer. Here, one shimmies in front of a small band (on the hour 1–8p except at 4p), her moves more graceful than sexy. Children can join in. Ceilings are intricately decorated; walls are covered in tiles. Since Moroccan food is unfamiliar to many Americans, this is the least crowded Epcot eatery. Ask to sit by the dance floor.

**Rose & Crown Dining Room** ★★★★ ✔ **DP British $$$$** L: $13–$19; Noon–3:30p. D: $13–$25; 4–9p. Seats 242, inc 40 on covered porch. U.K. It's not the fanciest food in Epcot and probably a little too hearty, but every time we eat here we want to come back. Maybe it's the menu, which includes some of the most deliciously creamy potato soup we've ever had. Maybe it's the servers, a young bunch who exude British charm. Maybe it's the little covered patio, which on a nice day is one of Disney's best outdoor dining spots. The menu includes British entrees such as bangers and mash (good) and shepherd's pie (better) and a good selection of British beers.

**San Angel Inn** ★★★★ ✔ **Mexican $$$$** L: $15–$22; 11:30a–4p. D: $24–$34; 4:30–9p. Seats 156. Mexico. *¡Aye carumba!* Prices have skyrocketed lately at this relaxing spot, though the food is as flavorful as ever. Good choices include signature tortilla soup and a steak that tastes like it's straight off a backyard grill. Sitting on padded chairs and benches around a lantern-lit table, you dine in a faux moonlit courtyard. In the distance is a rumbling volcano that, depending on your margarita intake, may appear to be the most realistic effect Disney has ever created. The restaurant is run by the Debler family, the proprietors of the namesake Mexico City restaurant.

**Teppan Edo** ★★★★ ✔ **Teppanyaki (Hibachi) $$$$** L,D: $16–$30 (children $12); noon–9p. Seats 192. Japan. An entertaining tableside chef may juggle knives or make a "smoking Mickey train" out of onion stacks in these stunning red-and-black dining rooms. Using a grill set into your table, the chef's hands fly fast as they slice, dice and stir-fry your choice of beef, seafood or chicken. You share your table with other guests.

Cinderella greets guests in line at Norway's Akershus restaurant

PHOTO © DISNEY

**Tokyo Dining** ★★★★ ✔ Japanese, sushi $$$$ L,D: $15–$28; noon–9p. Seats 116. Japan. With good food, nice atmosphere and obsessive service, this is what a World Showcase restaurant is supposed to be—a non-threatening way to experience a foreign cuisine. Traditional entrees include a tender beef teriyaki and light shrimp tempura. The sushi and sashimi menu has 49 selections. For dessert, the green tea pudding melts in your mouth. Diffused lighting, dark tables and a tile floor create a peaceful decor. Greeters, hostesses and servers bow often.

**Tutto Italia** ★★★★★ Italian $$$$$ L: $15–$30; 11:30a–3:30p. D: $24–$36; 3:30–8:45p. Seats 300. Italy. Pricey yes, but this is the best Italian spot on Disney property, thanks to its imported pastas and delicate sauces. Meat and fish entrees are good too, though sides are $10. Entree salads use ingredients like asparagus, curly endive and fava beans. As you arrive, don't let the formal maître'd fool you; the young Italian wait staff is friendly. An elegant decor has dark woods.

**BUFFET**

**Biergarten** ★★★★ ✔ DP German, with live band $$$$ L: $20 (children $11), 11a–3:45p. D: $27 (children $13), 4–9p (last show 8:05p). Seats 400. Germany. A live band rolls out a barrel full of polkas and waltzes at this Oktoberfest buffet, stopping occasionally to lead toasts or demonstrate some strange instrument. Unless you're a party of eight you'll share your table with others, toast your new friends at least once or twice, and, since the tables are small, share conversations whether you want to or not. Best bets on the buffet include potato leek soup, beef rouladen and pork schnitzel (the last two at dinner only). Skip the seafood. Beer choices include a light and dark Spaten, Becks and Franziskaner Hefe-Weisse. The dining room simulates an evening in a medieval Rothenburg courtyard. Wrapped by three-dimensional building facades, the three-tiered eating area is lit by a moon in the sky. The band plays a 20- to 25-minute set about once an hour. Young waiters wear traditional Bavarian tracht wear—green lederhosen shorts, white shirts, green suspenders, little black hats and teeny weeny little ties.

### CHARACTER MEALS

**Akershus Royal Banquet Hall** ★★★ *DP* American breakfast, Norwegian lunch and dinner. $$$$ Five characters rotate among Alice ("Alice in Wonderland"), Ariel, Aurora ("Sleeping Beauty"), Belle, Cinderella, Esmerelda, Jasmine, Mary Poppins, Mulan. B: $23 (children $13), 8:30–10:45a. L: $25 (children $14), 11:10a–4p. D $30 (children $15), 4:15–8:40p. Seats 255. Norway. Five female characters come to your table at this bustling "Princess Storybook Dining experience." Breakfast is American, served family style: all-you-can-eat but brought to your table. Lunch and dinner are three-course Norwegian buffets. Appetizers such as sliced peppered mackerel (fish jerky) are acquired tastes, but the lamb stew and kjottkake will be familiar to anyone raised on hearty American fare. Kids can choose from hot dogs, pasta, pizza and grilled chicken. The room is noisy. The last lunch and dinner seatings often have walk-up tables available. Pose for the optional photo package to endure a tableside sales pitch.

**Garden Grill** ★★★★ ✔ *DP* Character buffet $$$$ Farmer Mickey Mouse, Pluto, Chip 'n Dale. D: $29 (children $14), 4:30–8p. Seats 150. The Land pavilion. This family-style country-themed dinner includes grilled steak, turkey and fish. Some food comes from the pavilion's own greenhouses. As you dine, characters mosey up to say hi and sometimes sit a spell. Thanks to the restaurant's small size you see the characters often, at least three times each if you stay an hour. The circular dining area is built like a merry-go-round: the seating area rotates around the kitchen, circling completely every two hours. An open balcony, the outside rim overlooks the Living with the Land dioramas. Ask to sit on the outside of the ring and your booth's high-backed seats will block your family's view of the rest of the restaurant, making every character visit a delightful

surprise. If you pose for the optional photo package, you'll get a tableside sales pitch.

### INDOOR FAST FOOD

**Electric Umbrella** *DPQ* Burgers, salads, sandwiches. 11a–9p. Seats 426. Innoventions Plaza.

**Fountainview Ice Cream Shop** ✔ Hand-dipped ice cream. 10:30a–9p. Seats 108, inc. 68 outside. Made-to-order ice-cream sandwiches are especially good. Innoventions Plaza.

**Liberty Inn** *DPQ* Burgers, chicken, salads, kosher meal. 11:30a–9p. Seats 710. American Adventure.

**Lotus Blossom Cafe** Egg rolls, chicken, stir-fry, specialty drinks. 11a–9p. Seats 100. China.

**Sunshine Seasons** ✔ *DPQ* Quality salads, soups, sandwiches, noodle dishes, grilled meats, bakery. Breakfast egg dishes, oatmeal, cereals. B: 9–11a. L,D: 11a–9p. Seats 707. The Land.

**Tangierine Cafe** ✔ Chicken, lamb platters. Pastries, tea, liqueur coffees, beer. 11:30a–9p. Seats 101. Morocco.

**Yakitori House** ✔ Beef, chicken, noodles, packaged sushi. Miso soup. Salads. Beer, wine. Garden setting. 11:30a–9p. Seats 94 inc. 36 outside. Japan.

### OUTDOOR FAST FOOD

**Boulangerie Patisserie** ✔ Pastries, quiche, cheese plates. Seats 24. France.

**Cantina de San Angel** Tacos, churros, margaritas, beer. Seats 150. Mexico.

**Fife & Drum** *DPQ* Turkey legs, hot dogs, smoothies, beer. American Adventure.

**Kringla Bakeri Og Kafe** ✔ *DPQ* Sandwiches, pastries. Seats 51. Norway.

**Lotus Blossom Cafe** Chinese. Seats 107. China.

**Promenade Refreshments** *DPQ* Turkey legs, hot dogs, smoothies, beer. World Showcase Plaza.

**Sommerfest** ✔ *DPQ* Bratwurst, frankfurters, pretzels, beer. Seats 24 under a covered patio. Germany.

**Yorkshire County Fish Shop** *DPQ* Fish and chips, Bass ale. Seats 31. United Kingdom.

### BARS

**La Cava del Tequila** ✔ 70 varieties of tequila; margaritas, appetizers. Seminars. Seats 46.

**Rose & Crown Pub** ✔ Beer, cocktails, appetizers, sandwiches. Evening entertainment. Seats 20.

### NOTABLE SNACK STANDS

Tasty snow-cone-like Japanese shaved ice is served at the Japan pavilion's **Kaki Gori**. Just down the walkway, the American Adventure's **Funnel Cake Kiosk** offers a variety of funnel cakes.

**Blink and you'll miss it.**
Tough to find with no sign,
the Marketplace in the
Medina sits in the middle
of the Morocco pavilion.

PHOTO: MICAELA NEAL

# Shopping

## Future World

**The Art of Disney** Fine art. Lithographs, oils, porcelain, 2-ft. character figurines. Delicate sculptures by Giuseppe Armani. Some works use Swarovski crystals. Just past the west side of Spaceship Earth.

**Camera Center** Disposable cameras, accessories. Underneath west side of Spaceship Earth.

**Cargo Bay** Space-themed merchandise. T-shirts, toys, books, DVDs. Freeze-dried astronaut food. "Star Wars"-themed Disney character plushies, Mission Space X2 spacecraft. Mission Space exit.

**Club Cool** Coca-Cola merchandise. Free samples of soft drinks from other countries. China's watermelon-flavored Smart, Mexico's fruity Lift are good; Italy's bitter Beverly is awful. Loud pop music. West side of Innoventions Plaza.

**Gateway Gifts** Disney souvenirs. Underneath east side of Spaceship Earth.

**ImageWorks gift shop** Photo shop. Disposable cameras, camera supplies, frames, photo albums, scrapbooks. Photos can be turned into puzzles, posters, applied to mugs, etched into crystal cubes. Picture Yourself booths offer prints, stickers. Figment plushies, T-shirts. At Journey into Imagination with Figment exit, Imagination pavilion.

**Innoventions Plaza Pin Stand** Pin central. Outdoor stand. Behind Spaceship Earth.

**Inside Track** Automobile merchandise. Toys, T-shirts. Test Track souvenirs. Photo booth lets you create a Test Track "driver's license." Test Track exit.

**Kiosk East** Beach towels, sandals. East side of walkway between Future World, World Showcase.

**Kiosk West** Bags, totes; caps, hats. West side of walkway between Future World, World Showcase.

**MouseGear** Main souvenir store. T-shirts, Disney souvenirs, toys. Men's, women's, children's, infant wear. Caps, novelty hats. Princess, Tinker Bell costumes. Housewares, books, costume jewelry, pet items, sandals. Largest Walt Disney World theme-park store. East side of Innoventions Plaza.

**The Seas gift shop** "Finding Nemo" merchandise. Plushies, toys, T-shirts, books, coffee mugs, costume jewelry. At exit of The Seas with Nemo & Friends pavilion.

**Soarin' counter** Gardening supplies, Soarin' T-shirts. Also here: Tiny Mickey's Mini-Gardens plants and flowers packaged in nutrient gel in sterile tubes. Stand in front of Soarin', The Land pavilion.

# World Showcase

## WORLD SHOWCASE PLAZA
**Showcase Station East Port** Upscale youth merchandise. Children's wear, infant wear, Minnie Mouse costumes, candy, plushies, toys.
**Showcase Station West Port** Upscale adult merchandise. Apparel, hats, housewares.

## INTERNATIONAL GATEWAY
**World Traveler** Upscale merchandise. Collectible pins, housewares, toys, watches.

## CANADA
**Northwest Mercantile / Trading Post** Canadian merchandise Apparel, NHL jerseys. Pure maple syrup, maple candy, cookies; dreamcatchers; plushies of Canadian animals such as huskies, bear, beaver and moose. Hatley boutique with amusing cartoon bear and moose aprons, shirts, sleepwear.
**Wood cart** Various. Personalized leather, Off Kilter CDs, Goofy lumberjack beanbag. Promenade.

## UNITED KINGDOM
**The Crown & Crest** Family name, coat of arms merchandise. Beatles, Rolling Stones items.
**The Magic of Wales** Tartan apparel. Fine silver.
**The Queen's Table** Perfume. Lotions, toiletries. Brands such as Bronnley, Burberry, Miller Harris, Taylor of London. Heavenly aroma.
**Sportsman's Shoppe** Sporting goods. Sports apparel; tennis shoes; rugby and soccer shoes, balls, books. Authentic pub coasters. Treats include Cadbury dairy milk caramel candy bars.
**Tea Caddy** Tea, china, teapots. Fine bone china by Dunoon, Royal Albert. Many varieties of Twinings tea (loose and in bags). Biscuits, candy.
**The Toy Soldier** Toys. Alice in Wonderland, Peter Pan, Thomas the Tank Engine and Winnie the Pooh items. Kids' books. Alice costumes.
**Wood cart** Various. T-shirts, U.K. souvenirs. Outdoor stand, promenade.

## FRANCE
**Guerlain Paris** Perfume, cosmetics. Classy shop offers limited-edition and exclusive Guerlain fragrances, including some in the company's classic sculpted bee bottles. Guerlain cosmetics applied on the spot. Formerly La Signature.
**L' Esprit de la Provence** Kitchen supplies. Cookware, cookbooks, kitchen items; many from the Provençal region of France. Cozy store channels a homey kitchen in a small French village.
**Les Vins de France** Wine. By bottle or glass.
**Plume et Palette** Perfume. Brands include Annick Goutal, Chanel, Dior, Givenchy. Each year the store has one perfume exclusive in the United States. For 2010 it's Dior's Escale à Pondichéry.
**Souvenirs de France** Souvenirs. Berets have "Made in China" tags. Formerly Galerie des Halles.
**Promenade stands** Custom parasols, portraits.

## MOROCCO
**The Brass Bazaar** Housewares, cookware, food. Handmade brass plates, platters; packaged couscous, spices; ceramic, wooden cookware; rosewater bottles. Aromatic bowls, boxes made of thuya, a burled-root wood grown only in Morocco.
**Casablanca Carpets** Furnishings. Moroccan carpets, rugs. Lamps that filter light through henna-dyed lamb skin, incense holders, leather pouf chairs, colorful sequined pillows.
**Marketplace in the Medina** Various. Open-air alley with belly-dancer kits, seagrass baskets, ceramic-topped furniture, scarves. Two strange drums: ceramic tam-tams covered in camel skin; open-top darboukas with flounder-skin bottoms.
**Medina Arts** Ceramics, pottery. Tiny shop connected to The Brass Bazaar.
**Souk-Al-Magreb** Various. Mix of merchandise from the other shops. Open-air promenade stand. Name means "The Flea Market of Northern Africa."
**Tangier Traders** Apparel, footwear, jewelry. Traditional caftans, gandouras and other robes and wraps, handmade leather slippers.

## JAPAN
**Mitsukoshi** Department store. 10,000 sq ft. Largest area, **Interest** has a Pick-A-Pearl (from oyster) bar, Lucky Cats, transforming Rhythm and Seiko clocks, Hello Kitty items, quirky toys. **Harmony** zone bridges Japanese, Western cultures with handbags, glass-bead jewelry, sandals, shirts, silver. Mikimoto pearl jewelry. **Silence** area has household items: bonsai trees, drapes, lanterns, rice paper, small tables, tatami mats. Apparel includes embossed jackets, tenugui head coverings and silk kimonos. **Festivity** stocks chopsticks, cooking gear, porcelain dishes, teas, sweets. Sake tasting bar has five microbrews.
**Mitsukoshi kiosk** Various. Candy, snacks, inexpensive souvenirs. Outdoor walk-in stand.

## THE AMERICAN ADVENTURE
**Heritage Manor Gifts** Americana. Patriotic apparel. Good book section, otherwise uninspired, many items made in China.

**Wood cart** Various. Patriotic T-shirts, CDs, collectible pins. On the promenade.

### ITALY
**Il Bel Cristallo** Various. Fontanini creches, Murano glass, jewelry, Christmas ornaments, Bulgari and Ferragamo perfumes, Puma sportswear, soccer books.
**La Bottega** Wine, housewares. Wine by bottle, glass; Perugina candy; books. Artisan creates papier-mâché, fabric Carnivale masks. Cozy shop.

### GERMANY
**Das Kaufhaus** Sporting goods. Apparel, backpacks, balls, sandals.
**Der Teddybar** Children's items. Steiff bears, Schleich toys, Playmobil sets, plushies, Snow White costumes, customized Engle-Puppen dolls.
**Die Weihnachts Ecke** Christmas shop. Pickle ornaments, handmade Steinbach nutcrackers.
**Glas und Porzellan** Hummel glass, porcelain figurines. Beer steins. Goebel-sponsored, with Goebel artist often onsite painting and finishing.
**Glaskunst** Personalized glass. Glassware, steins, frames, figures. Promenade stand.
**Kunstarbeit in Kristall** Jewelry, glassware. Swarovski crystal pins. Arribas Brothers collectibles. Glassware can be personalized.
**Sussigkeiten** Sweets. Candy; cookbooks; cookies; fresh baked pastries, fudge. Imported packaged candy includes Haribo gummies.
**Volkskunst** Housewares, watches. Beer steins, Schneider cuckoo clocks, glassware, pewter, Troika watches. Egg artist Jutta Levasseur often works in the corner; a $1200 ostrich egg is on display.
**Weinkeller** Wine. Hundreds of varieties of wines and schnapps offered by the bottle or glass.

### THE OUTPOST
**Village Traders** Carved, sculpted art. Art, hats, costume jewelry, sandals. Wood and soapstone sculptor Andrew Mutiso creates exquisite unified families and friends with intertwined arms, lovely animals, busts, canes, masks. Guests can commission items. Outdoor covered stand between Germany and China.

### CHINA
**Yong Feng Shangdian** Department store. Antiques, apparel, silk fans, food, fountains, furniture, housewares, jewelry, prints, silk rugs, tea sets and jade sculptures. Prices range from a dollar or so for trinkets to thousands of dollars for intricately carved furniture and jade antiques.

**Yong Feng Shangdian stand** Various. Diabolo games, parasols, souvenirs. Outdoor stand along the walkway inside the pavilion.
**Wood cart** Various. Elaborate marionettes, personalized parasols. Along the promenade.

### NORWAY
**The Puffin's Roost** Apparel, perfume, toys. Stylish, pricey Helly Hansen items, thick woolen Dale of Norway sweaters. Christmas ornaments, Geir Ness perfume, puffin plushies, toys, plastic trolls. Viking Donald Duck plushie. Silly plastic Viking helmets, all with horns, some with braids.

### MEXICO
**Animals Fantasticos: Spirits in Wood** Folk art. Animals, humans and mythical creatures carved from copal wood with machetes and pocketknives, then painted in vivid colors with brushes, cactus spines and syringes. Artisans work on the spot. Just inside the pyramid.
**El Ranchito del Norte** Various. Sampling of merchandise from other shops. Along promenade.
**La Princesa Cristal** Crystal, figurines, jewelry. Arribas Brothers shop. Off Plaza de los Amigos.
**La Tienda Encantada** Various. Accessories, fashion apparel, fine jewelry, leather, fleece ponchos, throws. Off Plaza de los Amigos.
**Plaza de los Amigos** Various. Blankets, books, candy, glassware, musical instruments, paper flowers, piggy banks, piñatas, ponchos, salsa, sombreros, tequila, toys. Day of the Dead items. Many inexpensive choices. Scene suggests bustling Mexican market. Ceiling looks like night sky.

## Character locations
**Aladdin, Genie, Jasmine** Stars of 1992's "Aladdin" Morocco pavilion. Jasmine often at ✳ Akershus Royal Banquet Hall, Norway pavilion.
**Alice** Star of 1951's "Alice in Wonderland" The Toy Soldier, U.K. pavilion; often at ✳ Akershus Royal Banquet Hall, Norway pavilion.
**Ariel** Star of 1989's "The Little Mermaid" Often at ✳ Akershus Royal Banquet Hall, Norway pavilion.
**Aurora** Star of 1959's "Sleeping Beauty" France pavilion (location varies); often at ✳ Akershus Royal Banquet Hall, Norway pavilion.

✳ Air-conditioned meeting area.

Appearance times vary. For weekly updated schedules of Walt Disney World characters and street performers log on to pages.prodigy.net/stevesoares.

► **Authentic beer coasters** from Britain and Ireland. Box of 100. U.K. pavilion. $23.95

▲ **Yixing Purple Clay teapot** with matching cups. 16 ounce pot. China pavilion. $95

▼ **Piggy bank** Handmade ceramic, by artist Calocho. Various designs. Mexico pavilion. $22

▲ **Pure maple syrup** Turkey Hill brand, from Quebec. 8.45 oz. Canada pavilion. $16.95

► **Dior Escale à Pondichéry perfume** Epcot exclusive. 8 oz. spray bottle. France pavilion. $62.50

◄ **Limoncello** From Italy, 750 ml. 56 proof. Italy pavilion. $26.95

▲ **Nemo pajama pillow** with rear pouch. The Seas Gift Shop at The Seas with Nemo & Friends pavilion. $24.95

► **Lambskin lamp** Henna-adorned, metal frame. Morocco pavilion. $69.75

► **Miss Liberty Minnie Mouse bobblehead** Light-up torch. Inc. batteries. American Adventure pavilion. $15

◄ **Beer stein** Handmade ceramic, .75 liters. Germany pavilion. $114.95

**Belle** Star of 1991's "Beauty and the Beast" France (often with Beast); often at ✷ Akershus Royal Banquet Hall, Norway pavilion.

**Chip 'n Dale** 1940s–50s cartoon chipmunks ✷ Garden Grill character meal, The Land pavilion.

**Cinderella** Star of 1950's "Cinderella" Often at ✷ Akershus Royal Banquet Hall, Norway pavilion.

**Donald Duck** Foul-tempered fowl Mexico pavilion (dressed in garb from 1944's "The Three Caballeros").

**Esmerelda** Gypsy in 1996's "The Hunchback of Notre Dame" Often at ✷ Akershus Royal Banquet Hall, Norway pavilion.

**Goofy** Good-natured, dim-witted dog-man ✷ Epcot Character Spot.

**Mary Poppins** Star of 1964's "Mary Poppins" The Toy Soldier, U.K. pavilion.

**Mickey Mouse** Optimistic everyman ✷ Epcot Character Spot; ✷ Garden Grill, The Land pavilion.

**Minnie Mouse** Mickey's girlfriend ✷ Epcot Character Spot.

**Mulan, Mushu** Co-stars of 1998's "Mulan" China pavilion; Mulan also often at ✷ Akershus Royal Banquet Hall, Norway pavilion.

**Pluto** Mickey's pet ✷ Epcot Character Spot; ✷ Garden Grill, The Land pavilion.

**Snow White, Dopey** Star, dimwit dwarf of 1937's "Snow White and the Seven Dwarfs" Germany pavilion; Snow White also often at ✷ Akershus Royal Banquet Hall, Norway pavilion.

**Winnie the Pooh, Tigger** Stuffed toy bear, tiger from 1977's "The Many Adventures of Winnie the Pooh" ✷ Inside The Toy Soldier shop, U.K. pavilion.

## Street performers

### ACROBATS

**Dragon Legend Acrobats** 20 min. China pavilion, entrance gate. Inside during inclement weather. Impressive troupe of Chinese teenagers performs individual and group balancing acts. Shows typically include three of 10 routines; performances in calm winds feature more challenging numbers.

**Serveur Amusant** 20 min. France pavilion, in front of Chefs de France. "Amusing server" and chef mime balancing act. Tray balancing, handstands lead to finale with table, five chairs, five bottles.

### CANDY ARTIST

**Miyuki** 20 min. Japan pavilion at dept. store entrance. Arrive early to be in front. Candy artist creates animal-shaped lollipops, made-to-order for lucky children in audience. Manipulating taffy-like rice dough, the Tokyo native snips out detailed, edible creations.

**Top: Snow White meets an admirer outside Epcot's Germany pavilion. Above: Aladdin at the Morocco pavilion.**

## IMPROVISATIONAL TROUPE
World Showcase Players 20 min. U.K. pavilion promenade, Tudor Street. Also Italy pavilion central plaza. Street skits star audience volunteers as hilarious group butchers classic literature.

## JUGGLER
Sergio 20 min. Italy pavilion. Humorous mime.

## MUSICIANS
American Gardens concerts American Adventure Amphitheater. Sporadically throughout year.
The British Invasion 20 min. U.K. pavilion back green. Tribute band does spot-on Beatles hits. Each set of the day features a different Beatles era.
'Hat Lady' Carol Stein 20 min. Rose & Crown Pub, U.K. pavilion. 12 seats have direct view. Piano entertainer sings Irish anthems, Cockney show tunes.
Jammitors 20 min. Innoventions Plaza, Future World. Roving janitor trio transforms into percussion group, uses trash cans as drums.
Mariachi Cobre 20 min. Mexico pavilion. Led by trumpets, violins and confident vocals, backed by harmonizing guitars, 11-piece group is Epcot's best live band. Has played with Linda Ronstadt.
Matsuriza Taiko Drummers 20 min. Japan pavilion, base of pagoda. Intense trio creates propulsive beats on hand-made instruments.
Mo'Rockin 20 min. Morocco pavilion promenade bandstand. Hypnotic band blends Moroccan rhythms with world melodies. With violin, Zendrum, passionate vocals. Fronted by robed belly dancer.
Off Kilter 20 min. Canada pavilion promenade stage. Quirky kilt-wearing Celtic rock band combines electric guitars, bagpipe, humor ("Sweet Home Alabama"). Some guests twirl with Deadhead joy.
Si Xian 20 min. China pavilion, inside Hall. Qin zitherist (instrument is rectangular sound box with curved surface, tight strings) plays silk-music folk tunes. Multiple echoing sounds.
Spirit of America Fife & Drum Corps 10 min. American Adventure promenade. Led by town crier, dramatic group does patriotic tunes. Children join to recite Pledge of Allegiance.
The Voices of Liberty 20 min. American Adventure pavilion rotunda. Spirited a cappella group harmonizes on Americana tunes such as "Amazing Grace," "Ol' Man River," "This Land Is Your Land."

## STORYTELLER
Honobono Minwa 20 min. Japan courtyard. Geared to children, enthusiastic woman tells Japanese folk tales, teaches basic Japanese.

**Top: Juggler Sergio puts children into his act at Epcot's Italy pavilion. Above: A Dragon Legend Acrobat at the China pavilion.**

World Showcase consists of
11 international pavilions.
They circle a 40-acre lagoon.

# Planning Your Day

**It's best to take two days** to tour Epcot—one day for Future World, one for World Showcase. The key to a good Future World day is to get a Fastpass for Soarin' early in the morning. The ride is great, but the standby lines for it are miserable and Fastpasses run out early. Except for the American Adventure, the attractions are not, ironically, the attraction of World Showcase. That section of Epcot (which doesn't open until 11 a.m.) gets its appeal from its street entertainment, food, drink and shopping.

## 1. Choose when to go

Consider planning your World Showcase day so you see the most live entertainment. Most performances are only on select days. Weekly schedules are at **pages.prodigy.net/stevesoares.**

▶ **'Extra Magic Hours'** Epcot usually opens an hour early on Tuesdays for guests staying at Disney resorts, and stays open late for these guests on Fridays. Schedules are posted six months in advance at the "Calendar" link at **disneyworld.disney.go.com/ parks/epcot.**

## 2. Decide what to do

You'll find an "Attractions At a Glance" summary of everything there is to do earlier in this chapter; further back are detailed descriptions. If you are traveling with children, give them this book and have them point out what they would like to see.

Epcot is a big park, with lots of ground to cover. Guests in wheelchairs or ECVs should plan extra time to simply get from pavilion to pavilion.

Hearing-impaired guests can catch sign-language interpreted shows on Tuesdays and Fridays: Turtle Talk with Crush (11:40 a.m.), World Showcase Players United Kingdom (Friday, 1:30 p.m.), World Showcase Players Italy (Tuesday, Friday, 3 p.m.).

## 3. Family matters

Epcot is the least child-focused Disney World theme park. Guests walk a long way to get around it, and it is the only Disney park without a parade or street party. On the plus side, most attractions are geared at least in part to kids, and World Showcase pavilions offer Kidcot mask-making activities.

▶ **Height restrictions** exist at four rides: Mission Space (44 in.), Soarin' (40 in.), Test Track (40 in.) and Sum of All Thrills at Innoventions (48 in.).

▶ **Fear factors** All rides with height restrictions (see above) also have scary elements. Others that might scare children include Ellen's Energy Adventure (loud noises, bright flashes, darkened dinosaur habitat); Honey, I Shrunk the Audience (some terrifying 3-D effects); IllumiNations (loud explosions, fire); Journey Into Imagination… with Figment (loud noises, a sudden flash) and Maelstrom (dark, with scary faces).

▶ **Kids meals** You'll find them at every Epcot restaurant except Bistro de Paris in the France pavilion. Epcot has two character meals: Akershus Royal Banquet Hall in Norway and Garden Grill in The Land pavilion. Dining spots with kid-friendly extras include Coral Reef at the Seas with Nemo & Friends pavilion, which has a floor-to-ceiling aquarium full of exotic sea life and Japan's Teppan Edo, which has entertaining tableside hibachi chefs.

▶ **Baby care** Epcot's Baby Care Center is inside Future World's Odyssey Center. It provides changing rooms, nursing areas, a microwave and a playroom. Diapers, formula, pacifiers and over-the-counter medications are available for purchase. Moms can

## PARK RESOURCES

**ATMs** Entrance near kennel, on World Showcase–Future World bridge, American Adventure near restrooms.

**First Aid center** Minor emergencies. Registered nurses. Odyssey Center.

**Guest Relations** General questions, dining reservations, currency exchange. Maps, Times Guides for all WDW parks. Stores items found in park that day. Multilingual. Far right of entrance; also left of Spaceship Earth.

**Lockers** $7 a day plus $5 deposit. Lockers rent at the Camera Center under Spaceship Earth. The lockers are to the right of Spaceship Earth.

**Mobile app** (Verizon) $10, at m.disneyworld.com. "Mobile Magic" covers all WDW theme parks.

**Package pickup** Up to 3 hours before you leave, anything you buy in the park can be sent to the front of the park free of charge. Packages can be delivered the next day to your Disney hotel or shipped to your home. At far right of park entrance; also at International Gateway.

**Parking** $14 per day. Free for Disney resort guests, annual passholders.

**Strollers** Singles $15/day, $13/day length of stay. Doubles $31, $27. Entrance plaza; International Gateway.

**Tip Board** Shows attraction wait times. Innoventions Plaza.

**Transportation** Boats, walkways to Hollywood Studios; BoardWalk, Yacht and Beach Club, Swan and Dolphin resorts. Monorail to Contemporary, Grand Fla., Polynesian resorts; Magic Kingdom. Buses to all other Disney resorts, Animal Kingdom, Blizzard Beach, Hollywood Studios. No direct service to Downtown Disney, Typhoon Lagoon.

**Wheelchairs, Scooters** Wheelchairs $12/day, $10/day length of stay. Electric Convenience Vehicles (4-wheeled scooters) $50/day, $20 deposit. Entrance plaza; International Gateway.

# HOUR-BY-HOUR WAIT TIMES

This table shows the average **wait time** (in min) for each park ride or show at Epcot that has one. Gran Fiesta Tour, Innoventions, Journey Into Imagination with Figment and Kim Possible World Showcase Adventure have no waits. *A live show, Turtle Talk with Crush is shown with the early arrival time needed to get a good seat.

| ATTRACTION | 9A | 10A | 11A | Noon | 1P | 2P | 3P | 4P | 5P | 6P | 7P | 8P | 9P |
|---|---|---|---|---|---|---|---|---|---|---|---|---|---|
| American Adventure | CLSD | CLSD | 20 | 20 | 20 | 20 | 20 | 20 | 20 | 20 | 20 | 20 | CLSD |
| Circle of Life | 0 | 7 | 7 | 7 | 7 | 7 | 7 | 7 | 7 | 7 | 7 | 7 | CLSD |
| Ellen's Energy Adv. | 0 | 10 | 10 | 10 | 10 | 10 | 10 | 10 | 10 | 10 | CLSD | CLSD | CLSD |
| Honey I Shrunk... | 0 | 10 | 10 | 10 | 10 | 10 | 10 | 10 | 10 | 10 | CLSD | CLSD | CLSD |
| Impressions France | CLSD | CLSD | 10 | 10 | 10 | 10 | 10 | 10 | 10 | 10 | 10 | 10 | CLSD |
| Living with the Land | 0 | 10 | 20 | 30 | 50 | 60 | 50 | 50 | 60 | 50 | 50 | 30 | CLSD |
| Maelstrom | CLSD | CLSD | 5 | 10 | 15 | 20 | 25 | 30 | 40 | 30 | 35 | 25 | CLSD |
| Mission Space | 0 | 25 | 40 | 45 | 50 | 50 | 20 | 25 | 40 | 30 | 25 | 15 | CLSD |
| O Canada | CLSD | CLSD | 10 | 10 | 10 | 10 | 10 | 10 | 10 | 10 | 10 | 10 | CLSD |
| Reflections of China | CLSD | CLSD | 15 | 15 | 15 | 15 | 15 | 15 | 15 | 15 | 15 | 15 | CLSD |
| The Seas w/Nemo | 0 | 10 | 15 | 20 | 20 | 20 | 10 | 10 | 5 | 5 | 0 | 0 | CLSD |
| Soarin' | 0 | 30 | 60 | 65 | 70 | 80 | 75 | 80 | 90 | 80 | 70 | 60 | CLSD |
| Spaceship Earth | 10 | 20 | 25 | 20 | 30 | 25 | 25 | 20 | 15 | 15 | 10 | 5 | CLSD |
| Test Track | 0 | 30 | 60 | 60 | 110 | 90 | 95 | 110 | 95 | 70 | 70 | 60 | CLSD |
| Turtle Talk w/Crush* | N/A | 15 | 15 | 15 | 15 | 15 | 15 | 15 | 15 | 15 | 15 | 15 | CLSD |

Data based on surveys taken on random days during the summers of 2008 and 2009.

nurse babies anywhere; good spots include the back gardens at the United Kingdom, corner booths at Sunshine Seasons and in the dark theater of the American Adventure attraction.

▶ **Lost children** Report them to Guest Relations or any cast member.

## 4. Decide where to eat

Epcot has the most restaurants of any Disney World theme park. Many are very good, one is gourmet, all are expensive. Flip back a few pages to find listings of every place to eat, with ratings, reviews and prices.

## TWO MAGICAL DAYS

| Day 1 | Future World |
|---|---|
| 8:30a | Arrive at the park. As you wait for the gates to open (typically at 8:50 a.m.), pick up a Times Guide from the Guest Relations window at your far right. |
| 9:00a | Test Track and post-show exhibits. |
| 9:40a | Get Fastpasses for Soarin'. |
| 9:50a | The Seas with Nemo & Friends. See Turtle Talk with Crush, then the aquarium's 10:45 a.m. dolphin training presentation. |

| | |
|---|---|
| Noon | Visit The Land pavilion. Buy tickets to the 2 p.m. Behind the Seeds tour, then use your Fastpasses to ride Soarin', then have lunch at the Sunshine Seasons food court. |
| 2:00p | Behind the Seeds tour. |
| 3:00p | Mission Space. |
| 4:30p | Innoventions exhibits. |
| 6:00p | Ride Spaceship Earth and do the post-show activities. |
| 7:00p | Dinner at Coral Reef. |

# FASTPASS RETURN TIMES

Six Epcot attractions offer Disney's Fastpass system, a free service which reserves a time for you to return later in the day without standing in the regular line. The table below shows the average return times for Fastpasses dispensed at each participating Epcot attraction for each hour of the park day. Note that an entire day's worth of Fastpasses for Soarin' and Test Track typically run out by mid-afternoon.

| ATTRACTION | 9A | 10A | 11A | Noon | 1P | 2P | 3P | 4P | 5P | 6P | 7P | 8P | 9P |
|---|---|---|---|---|---|---|---|---|---|---|---|---|---|
| Honey I Shrunk... | 10:00 | 11:00 | 12:00 | 1:00 | 2:00 | 3:00 | 4:00 | 5:00 | 6:00 | CLSD | CLSD | CLSD | CLSD |
| Living with the Land | 9:45 | 10:30 | 11:40 | 12:40 | 1:40 | 2:40 | 3:40 | 4:40 | 5:40 | 6:40 | CLSD | CLSD | CLSD |
| Maelstrom | CLSD | CLSD | 11:50 | 1:05 | 1:40 | 2:45 | 3:50 | 5:00 | 5:55 | 6:55 | 7:45 | 8:50 | CLSD |
| Mission Space | 9:50 | 10:50 | 11:50 | 12:55 | 2:30 | 3:55 | 5:10 | 6:05 | 7:15 | 8:05 | 8:35 | OUT | CLSD |
| Soarin' | | 11:05 | 12:40 | 3:35 | 5:20 | 7:05 | OUT | OUT | OUT | OUT | OUT | OUT | CLSD |
| Test Track | 10:00 | 11:45 | 1:50 | 4:15 | 6:50 | 8:25 | OUT | OUT | OUT | OUT | OUT | OUT | OUT |

Data based on surveys taken on random days during the summers of 2008 and 2009.

# 5. Make a plan

As you do, note the average wait times and typical Fastpass return times for the attractions you want to see. Assume you need to arrive 15 minutes early for a table-service reservation. Live entertainment and character-greeting schedules are online at **pages.prodigy.net/stevesoares**. For a road-tested ready-made plan, see our "Two Magical Days" schedule below.

# 6. Other issues

▶ **Beating the heat** Nearly all Epcot attractions are indoors, in pavilions with other exhibits and activities. Play fountains throughout Future World let kids get splashed. A good indoor spot to sit down is the Sunshine Seasons food court in the Land pavilion.

▶ **What if it rains?** Epcot is a mixed blessing on rainy days. Though the park is comprised of pavilions with multiple activities, the pavilions are spread out. IllumiNations can get cancelled due to rain. Test Track closes when lightning is nearby.

▶ **What if it's really crowded?** Get Soarin' and Test Track Fastpasses early. While you wait, watch the sea life at The Seas at Nemo & Friends pavilion, hang out at Innoventions, or walk the World Showcase promenade and explore the shops and exhibits.

| Day 2 | World Showcase | | |
|---|---|---|---|
| 10:30a | Arrive at the park. Pick up a Times Guide as you enter. | 12:40p | Lunch at the Japan pavilion's Tokyo Dining. See Miyuki. |
| 10:45a | Stop at Innoventions to sign up for the Kim Possible World Showcase Adventure. Reserve a time, then alter the following plan to accommodate it (allow 1 hour). | 2:30p | See the American Adventure. |
| | | 3:15p | Germany pavilion. See the miniature train village. |
| | | 3:45p | China pavilion. See the Tomb Warriors exhibit, then the Dragon Legend Acrobats. |
| 11:00a | U.K. pavilion. See the first World Showcase Players show. | 5:30p | Norway pavilion. Ride Maelstrom. |
| Noon | France pavilion. Watch Impressions de France. | 6:30p | Dinner at either China's Nine Dragon's or Canada's Le Cellier. |
| | | 8:30p | See IllumiNations. |

**You enter the Spaceship Earth attraction** from underneath the giant sphere

# Spaceship Earth

★ ★ ★ ★ ✔ 14 min. Allow up to 45 min. for postshow activities. Capacity: 308. Open 9a–9p. Partially covered queue. Fear factor: None. Access: Must be ambulatory. The ride stops intermittently to load mobility impaired guests. Vehicles offer a choice of narration languages: English, French, German, Japanese, Portuguese and Spanish. *AuDe* Debuted: 1982, revised 1994, 2008.

For years ridiculed as one of Disney's more boring experiences, Future World's onetime showcase attraction is once again one of its most entertaining. Though the ride is still a Smithsonian-serious trip through a 56-robot history of communications, a 2008 refurbishment has made it much more fun. New scenes depict a 1960s IBM computer room where two programmers tend to a gigantic reel-to-reel mainframe and a 1977 California garage where a young man creates the first PC.

The ride's 19 other dioramas depict communication advances from the days of cave dwellers. They include new costumes, lighting and set pieces. A new narration by Dame Judi Dench emphasizes the roots of technology, while a new score features a 62-piece orchestra and 24-voice choir.

As the ride nears its finish, a new touchscreen in your ride vehicle lights up with a series of questions, asking how you'd like to live or work in the future. Then you're treated to a cartoon view of yourself a few decades from now. Your face is superimposed onto an animated character.

When you get off the ride you head into Project Tomorrow: Inventing the World of Tomorrow, a new post-show area that features four interactive video exhibits, all of which subtly showcase the attraction's new sponsor, Siemens. You learn about automotive accident-avoidance systems on a driving simulator; urban energy management by playing a group shuffleboard game; remote surgery technologies on a digital human body; and home medical diagnostic systems through a series of memory, hand-eye coordination and reflex exercises.

A giant globe in the room pinpoints the hometowns of all of that day's Spaceship Earth passengers, while video screens include your face as it appeared in your video. You can e-mail the image free of charge.

On one of our recent visits the exitway was filled with smiling faces. A preschooler

| Average Wait | |
|---|---|
| 9am | 10 min |
| 10am | 20 |
| 11am | 25 |
| Noon | 20 |
| 1pm | 30 |
| 2pm | 25 |
| 3pm | 25 |
| 4pm | 20 |
| 5pm | 15 |
| 6pm | 15 |
| 7pm | 10 |
| 8pm | 5 |
| 9pm | closed |

▶ Hop on after 5 p.m. when the line is short. After dark there's often no wait at all.

refused to get off, demanding to go again. Jumping out of his ride vehicle, a school-age boy shouted "That was awesome, dad! Let's go again!" Entering the post-show, a group of teenaged girls giggled as one glanced up at the ceiling and yelled "There I am!" If only school was this much fun.

### Building the ball

A 180-foot-high geodesic sphere, Spaceship Earth took 26 months to build, from August 1980 to September 1982. It was created without scaffolding or temporary supports.

First, a foundation team pounded over 100 steel pilings into the ground, to depths of 150 feet. Three pairs of angled legs were placed on top, themselves topped with a six-sided platform about 45 feet off the ground. Secured on that platform, adjustable cranes built a circular frame around themselves, using hundreds of metal-strut triangles.

After an outside crane hoisted the pre-constructed, 50-foot-wide dome, workers built the bottom, a separate piece that is not load-bearing. Rubber-coated panels were secured onto the triangles, creating a giant waterproof black ball. A separate, decorative outer sphere was then added, set off 2 feet from the core by 4-inch aluminum pipes.

The outer sphere is made up of 11,324 triangles of Alucobond, a rustproof material made of polyethylene plastic bonded to two layers of anodized aluminum. First used in 1978, it today covers more than 50,000 buildings, including many Honda dealerships.

Spaceship Earth does not drip water: a 1-inch gap between each panel allows the triangles to expand and contract in the Florida heat and lets rainwater flow into two interior gutters that drain through the building's support legs into canals that run alongside the park.

Disney got the idea for the structure from the icons of the New York World's Fairs of 1939 and 1964, both held in Flushing Meadows, N.Y. The 1939 event featured the 180-foot-tall Perisphere, a sphere which held a slow-moving, educational ride (it portrayed Democracity, a "perfectly integrated garden city" from the year 2068). The icon of the 1964 fair was the Unisphere, a 140-foot open-grid Earth that symbolized global interdependence. It's still standing.

The attraction can also trace its parentage to the 1940s geodesic domes designed by engineer R. Buckminster Fuller. Billed as homes of tomorrow, his futuristic half-circles were composed of self-bracing triangles. The houses had no internal supports and could be built in one day. The "Bucky balls" caught on as weather stations and airport radar shelters, but never got beyond a cult following as private homes (one reason: they leaked water).

Fuller coined the phrase "Spaceship Earth." His 1963 treatise, "An Operating Manual for Spaceship Earth," argued that all the world's peoples must work together as a crew to guide our planet's future.

**Fun finds ❶** At the telephone switchboard, two out of three callers are told "I'm sorry, that line is busy." ❷ The radio station's call letters "WDI" refer to Walt Disney Imagineering. ❸ A desk placard on the right side of the computer room promotes "Think," the slogan of IBM founder Thomas J. Watson. It inspired the 1990s Apple slogan, "Think Different." ❹ Nearby: a manual for the System 360 Job Control Language used on 1964 IBM mainframes and ❺ a 1960s IBM Selectric typewriter. ❻ The garage-wall snapshot resembles a classic Microsoft photo.

**Fun facts ❶** Science-fiction author Ray Bradbury ("Fahrenheit 451") helped design the attraction, along with consultants from the Smithsonian Institution, the University of Southern California and the University of Chicago. ❷ The caveman is speaking a Cro-Magnon language. The cave drawings are based on images found in the Salon-Niaux cave in Ariège, France. ❸ The Egyptian hieroglyphics replicate actual Middle Eastern drawings. The pharaoh's words come from a real letter. ❹ The refocused script has changed the meaning of a few scenes. The former Greek thespians are now teaching math. The burning of Rome is now a fire at the Library of Alexandria. And though they were once "debating ideas," Disney's medieval scholars are now "watching over... books to save our dreams of the future." ❺ The family watching television originally appeared in the post-show at Space Mountain. ❻ Touchscreen "Work" futures always predict "a great big, beautiful tomorrow," the title of the theme song to Magic Kingdom's Carousel of Progress. ❼ Why is there a long pause after the questions? Because that's where Disney originally planned a pop quiz. "While we're creating your future," narrator Dench was to say, "let's see how much you remember about the past." ❽ The building weighs 16 million pounds. That's 158 million golf balls.

**Hidden Mickeys ❶** As blots made by the sleeping monk on the top right of a piece of parchment. ❷ As bottle rings on the table of the first Renaissance painter.

▶ Just want to play the games? You can enter the Project Tomorrow area through side doors.

**The Where's the Fire? exhibit** has guests search for home fire hazards at Innoventions West

# Innoventions

★★★★ ✔ Presentations avg 20 min. Allow 2–3 hrs for all exhibits. Wait times vary by exhibit. Open 9a–7p. Indoor queues. Fear factor: None. Access: Guests may stay in wheelchairs, ECVs. Assistive listening. *AuDe* Debuted: 1994, revised 2009.

These two large buildings house interactive presentations from outside sponsors. Many exhibits are new. Each building also has a Kim Possible World Showcase Adventure Recruitment Center.

### Innoventions East

Raytheon's math-based **Sum of All Thrills** is the first-ever Innoventions ride. You design a virtual roller coaster, jet plane or bobsled experience, then ride it atop a slow-moving robotic arm. Guests manage virtual trash at the Waste Management **Don't Waste It** game, pushing garbage-truck-like carts to a sorting station, incinerator and landfill. Children love to push the carts, which beep whenever they back up. The **House of Innoventions** tour includes an overhead descending oven, a dining table made of corrugated cardboard and a miniature talking robot. The Federal Alliance for Safe Homes' **StormStruck** combines a theatrical show with a display showing how two differently built Florida homes fared during Hurricane Charley in 2004. Underwriters Laboratories' **Test the Limits Lab** lets you swing a hammer at a TV, smash a 55-gallon drum onto a helmet and cause other havoc. An **Environmentality Corner** display gives you a chance to make rudimentary paper.

### Innoventions West

**Runtime** at the new IBM ThinkPlace records videos of you walking, jumping and dancing and then uses them in a game. T. Rowe Price's **The Great Piggy Bank Adventure** offers lessons on setting financial goals. The **Slap Stick Studios** theater hosts a wacky Velcro Cos. game show where contestants use Velcro to solve silly problems. In Liberty Mutual's **Where's the Fire?,** guests use flashlight-like devices to uncover home fire hazards. A companion tour teaches fire safety to children. **Segway Central** offers test drives on the Segway Human Transporter (1–7p, riders must be at least 16 years old. Those under 18 require legal consent). Also at Innoventions West is a no-charge **PlayStation arcade.**

| Average Wait | |
|---|---|
| 9am | 0 min |
| 10am | 0 |
| 11am | 0 |
| Noon | 0 |
| 1pm | 0 |
| 2pm | 0 |
| 3pm | 0 |
| 4pm | 0 |
| 5pm | 0 |
| 6pm | 0 |
| 7pm | closed |
| 8pm | closed |
| 9pm | closed |

▶ The Innoventions exhibits get crowded when the weather turns cold or rainy.

# Ellen's Energy Adventure

★ ★ ★ 45 min. (new shows begin every 17 min.)
Capacity: 582. Open 9a–7p. Outdoor, unshaded
queue. Fear factor: The Big Bang portrayal is loud.
Access: ECV guests must transfer. Assistive listening;
handheld captioning. *AuDe* Debuted: 1996.

This 45-minute multimedia presentation about the history and future of energy combines three theatrical films with a tram ride past Audio-Animatronics dinosaurs.

Watching a series of video screens, you meet star Ellen DeGeneres in her apartment as friend Bill Nye* stops by. Watching her old college roommate (Jamie Lee Curtis) compete on the game show "Jeopardy!" she soon falls asleep.

Dreaming she's a contestant, Ellen learns that all of her categories deal with one thing she knows nothing about: energy. When she asks Nye for help, he takes her back in time for a crash course in Energy 101.

Moving into a large theater, you watch as three

| Average Wait | |
| --- | --- |
| 9am | 0 min |
| 10am | 10 |
| 11am | 10 |
| Noon | 10 |
| 1pm | 10 |
| 2pm | 10 |
| 3pm | 10 |
| 4pm | 10 |
| 5pm | 10 |
| 6pm | 10 |
| 7pm | closed |
| 8pm | closed |
| 9pm | closed |

**Disney's Universe of Energy pavilion,** home to Ellen's Energy Adventure

huge screens dramatically display the Big Bang and the creation of the Earth: billions of years compressed into one stunning minute. Then the seating area breaks apart into ride vehicles and you travel to the Mesozoic Era—a swamp filled with dinosaurs—to get a close-up look at the beginning of fossil fuels. Arriving in a third theater, you're brought back to the present through a series of radio broadcasts, then watch as Ellen learns about man's energy use. Finally you return to the first theater, where you watch Ellen become a "Jeopardy" champion.

The show cries out for updating. Produced when the average price of a gallon of gasoline was $1.30, the show ignores the problems of fossil fuels. There's no mention of the Middle East, no talk of global warming or the need for fuel efficiency. The show was created in conjunction with Exxon-Mobil, its sponsor until 2004.

**Fun finds ❶** After Trebek says to Ellen, "Your first correct response!" her lips don't move when she yells "Freeze!" **❷** Nye's lips stay shut when, in front of a solar mirror, he says "all right."

* A one-time mechanical engineer, Nye hosted "Bill Nye the Science Guy," a 1992-1998 PBS preteen program which Disney later sold as a video series.

▶ Sit in the theater's back right corner. You'll spend more time with the dinosaurs.

# Mission Space

★★★★ ✓ 6 min. Capacity: 160. Open 9a–9p
*FastPass* Indoor, air-conditioned queue. Fear factor: Intense, can cause disorientation, headaches, nausea. Take warnings seriously: do not ride if you have serious health issues or head cold. Access: ECV, wheelchair guests must transfer. Activated video captioning. Height restriction: 44 in. Debuted: 2003.

So intense it includes motion-sickness bags, this flight simulator offers realistic sensations of space travel. Developed with NASA, it's Disney's most advanced attraction ever.

Why do riders get sick? Because you spin. You can't tell it when you're in your vehicle, but the ride is a centrifuge, a circular machine with a series of rapidly rotating containers on its spokes. As it spins, it applies centrifugal force to its contents (that's you) that mimic the G-forces of a rocket launch and then the weightlessness of space. The spinning creates forces up to 2 Gs, or twice that of the Earth's gravity. That may not sound like much—it's less than many roller coasters—but you feel it

| Average Wait | |
|---|---|
| 9am | 0 min |
| 10am | 30 |
| 11am | 30 |
| Noon | 30 |
| 1pm | 40 |
| 2pm | 25 |
| 3pm | 15 |
| 4pm | 20 |
| 5pm | 25 |
| 6pm | 10 |
| 7pm | 10 |
| 8pm | 15 |
| 9pm | 0 |

**Crowds are often light** at Mission Space late in the afternoon and after dark

throughout the ride. It's one of the ways NASA trained astronauts for decades.

Many adults have no problem with the ride, and children often fare better than their parents. Still, the side effects have landed some riders in the hospital. A few guests have died, though in each of those cases the rider had existing health problems and ignored the warning signs. The most common troubles are dizziness and a lingering headache. To avoid getting sick, continually stare straight at your monitor and do not close your eyes. Don't eat or drink alcohol before you go. If you do feel bad afterward, get lots of fresh air, take it easy and have some saltine crackers or a soda.

### A mission to Mars
The story begins as soon as you enter the building. You're in the year 2036 at the International Space Training Center. You're there to train for a mission to Mars.

After the voice of Mission Control ("CSI" actor Gary Sinise, also known for his roles in 1995's "Apollo 13" and "Mission to Mars") introduces you to your vehicle, you climb in your trainer and buckle in. Once a cast member seals the door, a control panel pivots into place. As you angle into launch position, you look out into a blue (video) sky

▶ Disney also offers a mild version of the ride in which the centrifuge does not spin.

**Guests wait in the Mission Space queue area** as a giant Gravity Wheel—a prop from Disney's year-2000 movie "Mission to Mars"—rotates in the background.

with birds passing overhead. Then the engines power up and the countdown begins.

"3... 2... 1... Zero!" The earth rumbles and, as the G-forces push your body back into the seat, it truly feels like you're on your way to Mars. Soon Mission Control breaks in with instructions. "Initiate first stage separation... now!" Sinise tells the mission commander. The others get similar orders.

You head past the space station, are slingshot around the moon and feel weightless for a moment. Some unexpected troubles complicate things, your team performs with flying colors, and you land on Mars safely.

**Postshow activities**

With entrances from both the exit area and the gift shop, the **Advanced Training Lab** is a series of calm experiences for all ages. Mission Space Race is a group video game. Space Base is a preschooler climbing area with a crawl-through rocket, some zany mirrors and a lookout tower. The Expedition: Mars video game tests your joystick skills as you rescue fellow astronauts. Everyone will get a kick out of Postcards from Space, a video booth which puts your animated face into an alien abduction, saucer invasion or other goofy space scenes and e-mails the results anywhere you choose.

**Fun finds ❶** Alongside the first queue room (the "Space Simulation Lab") is a 35-foot model of a Gravity Wheel. The slowly rotating prop from the 2000 film "Mission to Mars" has mock exercise rooms, offices, work areas and sleeping cubicles. **❷** Nearby is a Lunar Roving Vehicle display unit, on loan from the National Air and Space Museum in Washington, D.C.

**Fun facts ❶** The logo for Horizons, the previous attraction at this site, appears on the Gravity Wheel hub. **❷** Ride music was composed by Trevor Rabin. As a member of Yes, he wrote 1983's "Owner of a Lonely Heart." **❸** Centrifuges are used to separate fluids of different densities, such as cream from milk.

**Hidden Mickeys Courtyard: ❶** As overlapping craters on the moon sphere, above and to the left of the Luna 8 impact site. **❷** As tiny round blue and black tiles in the patio, 40 feet from the Fastpass entrance. **Queue: ❸** A notepad on a left desk reads "Mickey and Goofy are scheduled to launch at exactly 3 p.m." **❹** As Mars craters on the far left and **❺** right monitors above the desks. **Postshow: ❻** In a circuit board grid to the upper left and right of the Expedition Mars joystick consoles. **Gift shop: ❼** As black craters in the mural behind cash registers, under Minnie's foot. **❽** A profile of Mickey appears in the reddish dust in the photos of space on the ceiling, above a Spaceman Mickey statue. **❾** As three electrical boxes on the walls. One is a Mickey profile.

▶ **The Mission Space Cargo Bay gift shop sells freeze-dried astronaut food.**

© DISNEY

# Test Track

★★★★★ ✔ 5 min. Capacity: 192. Open 9a–9p. *FastPass* Indoor air-conditioned queue. Fear factor: Intense for those scared by speed. Closed during thunderstorms. Access: Must be ambulatory. Assistive listening; activated captioning. Height restriction: 40 in. Debuted: 1999.

Themed to be an automobile proving ground, Test Track is a big-bucks take on a classic dark ride, as a small vehicle speeds you around dark corners and through barriers. With 34 tight turns but no falls or loops, the mile-long course is perfect for those who like speed and thrills but hate roller coasters.

The queue includes displays of 22 testing demonstrations. It leads to a Briefing Room, where engineers Bill and Sherry appear on a video link. As Bill determines your test schedule, Sherry programs it into a computer. "And depending on how you and your vehicle hold up," Bill adds, "we'll even throw a few surprise tests in there."

"Surprise tests?" Sherry asks. "Yeah. Pick one."

**Average Wait**

| | |
|---|---|
| 9am | 0 min |
| 10am | 30 |
| 11am | 60 |
| Noon | 60 |
| 1pm | 110 |
| 2pm | 90 |
| 3pm | 95 |
| 4pm | 110 |
| 5pm | 95 |
| 6pm | 70 |
| 7pm | 70 |
| 8pm | 60 |
| 9pm | closed |

**The fastest ride at Walt Disney World,** Test Track reaches speeds up to 65 mph

With a grin, Sherry chooses the Barrier Test, which slams its car into a wall. Before you can protest, you board your vehicle and off you go. Heading to an (indoor) testing grounds, you rumble over some blocks, skid through some cones and twist up a hill.

Then things go wrong. Did Sherry forget to turn off those Environmental Test robots? Oh no! You get sprayed with acid! Miss that sign that said to turn on your headlights? Oh no! Here comes a truck! And remember that surprise test? Oh no! You're heading right into the…

At the last second a hidden door opens, and outside you go for the Handling Run. A series of elevated banked corners leads to a burst around the building at 65 mph.

**Fun finds ❶** The left anticorrosion robot is labeled "CRUS-T." **❷** The right one is "RUS-T." **❸** In the post show, a house of mirrors re-creates GM's truck plant in Shreveport, La. Can you spot the real walls?

**Hidden Mickeys ❶** As washers on the left side of a desk near queue area 7b. **❷** As fender stains on the left side of the Corrosion Chamber. **❸** As stains on a car door on that chamber's right side. **❹** As crash-test stickers on an open gas-tank filler door on a car to your left in the Barrier Test area. **❺** As a coil of hoses on that floor, just before the wall.

▶ The adjacent gift shop offers a unique souvenir: a remote-control Test Track car.

# The Seas with Nemo & Friends

★ ★ ★ ★ ✓ **Allow 60 min. Open 9a–9p. Indoor queue. Fear factor: None. Access: Guests may remain in wheelchairs, ECVs. Reflective captioning, assistive listening.** *AuDe* **Debuted: 1982, 2007.**

There's a lot to like in this revamped pavilion, which is themed to the 2003 Disney/Pixar film "Finding Nemo." Quality attractions combine with live marine-life aquariums, exhibits and demonstrations.

First, there's a ride. Once you enter the building, a long walkway takes you under the sea and eventually to a "clam-mobile," a vehicle similar to a Haunted Mansion Doom Buggy. It takes you past animated dioramas and synchronized, see-through video screens that re-create scenes from the movie. In the finale, the animated fish appear to swim with the real ones in the pavilion's huge aquarium.

You exit on the first floor of the two-story pavilion, which includes some interesting sea life exhibits, a

### Average Wait

| | |
|---|---|
| 9am | 0 min |
| 10am | 10 |
| 11am | 15 |
| Noon | 20 |
| 1pm | 20 |
| 2pm | 20 |
| 3pm | 10 |
| 4pm | 10 |
| 5pm | 5 |
| 6pm | 5 |
| 7pm | 0 |
| 8pm | 0 |
| 9pm | closed |

**The entrance sign** to The Seas with Nemo & Friends pavilion portrays waves crashing onto a rocky shoreline

stunning theatrical show and some fascinating demonstrations.

### Downstairs

"That was cool!" said the 60-year-old man to his wife, as the couple exited **Turtle Talk with Crush** (★ ★ ★ ★ ★ ✓ 12 min. Avg wait 15 min). He's right. The pavilion's headline attraction, this theatrical show amazes children, but also even the most worldly adult. Appearing on a huge video screen that looks as if it's a viewing window into the ocean, the sea-turtle star of the 2003 film "Finding Nemo" interacts with guests in real-time conversations.

Crush addresses guests individually ("Elizabeth, your polka-dot shell is totally cool!"), asks specific questions ("Is that your female parental unit in the fourth row? She's a total babe!") and reacts to their responses. His facial expressions are priceless. The reptile works in some turtle trivia and welcomes blue tang Dory, who can speak whale perhaps a little too well.

The sea turtle mostly talks to kids who sit down front, but sometimes seeks out guests along the theater's center aisle.

The queue area holds jellyfish, stingrays, and fish from the Great Barrier Reef.

▶ To have Crush talk with your child, have her sit down front and wear a funny hat.

Also downstairs, a **Nemo & Friends** room displays live versions of many of the movie's stars. Walk-around tubes hold clownfish (Nemo), regal blue tangs (Dory) and Moorish idols (Gill), as well as sea horses, eels, camouflaged frogfish and venomous lionfish and scorpionfish. In a re-creation of the film's sunken submarine, **Bruce's Shark World** has kid-friendly interactive displays and photo props.

### Upstairs

On the second floor, a huge **saltwater aquarium** simulates a Caribbean coral reef. It's filled with blacknose, brown and sand tiger sharks; some angelfish, cobia, snapper and tarpon; schools of lookdown; a Goliath grouper; sea turtles; and a few rays. An observation tunnel extends into it.

There are three daily **fish feedings,** at 10 a.m., 1 p.m. and 3:30 p.m. A diver unloads his food pouch in front of you while a narrator adds educational trivia.

A side area holds a bachelor herd of **dolphins**—Rainer (born in 1986), Calvin and Kyber (1997) and Malabar (2001). Stop by at 10:45 a.m., 2:15 p.m. or 4:15 p.m. to see a **dolphin training session,** which can include identity-matching, rhythm-identification or echolocation lessons. Huge bars keep the dolphins in their area; otherwise they would hassle the fish.

**A bottlenose dolphin** interacts with a young guest in the Seas pavilion's aquarium

A **manatee aquarium** holds two Florida sea cows. You can watch them munch on heads of lettuce from above the surface or through an underwater window on the first floor. Five-minute talks are given at 15 and 45 minutes after each hour.

A **mariculture room** displays how commercial farming can prevent overfishing of clownfish, queen conchs, bamboo sharks and giant clams. There's an exhibit on coral reef propagation.

**Fun finds ❶** The Audio-Animatronics gulls sitting on the rocks outside the pavilion squawk "Mine! Mine! Mine!" just as they do in "Finding Nemo." (The voice is "Finding Nemo" director Andrew Stanton.) ❷ Clinging to the aquarium glass, sea star Peach often begs "Hey wait! Take me with you!" as clam-mobiles pass her by. As the animated fish around her continue to sing "Big Blue World" she adds "It's a nice song but they just never stop! Never, never, ever, ever, ever!" ❸ Rub Bruce's sandpapery skin in Bruce's Shark World and he'll say "Ooooooo! That's good!"

**Fun facts ❶** The aquarium's 3,500 inhabitants represent 65 species. ❷ The observation area has 61 acrylic windows that are 4 to 8 inches thick. Each 24-foot central panel weighs 9,000 pounds. ❸ Since the parrotfish naturally eat coral, Disney plants synthetic coral (dental plaster) into the artificial reef.

▶ The pavilion's daily dolphin training sessions are at 10:45am, 2:15pm and 4:15pm.

**The animated sea turtle star
of "Finding Nemo" interacts
with guests in real-time at
Turtle Talk with Crush**

MICAELA NEAL

# Soarin'

★★★★★ ✔ 5 min. Capacity: 174. Open 9a–9p.
The Land pavilion. *FastPass* Indoor, air-conditioned
queue. Fear factor: Troubling for some who fear
heights. **Access:** ECV and wheelchair users must
transfer. Handheld captioning. Height restriction:
40 in. Debuted: 2005 (Disneyland 2001).

This one may take you by surprise, as it really does give you the feeling of flight. More than just a 5-minute film, Soarin' uses an innovative theater to immerse you in its experience. Exhilarating but not scary, it's a smooth, fun fantasy everyone will love.

After you board a multi-seat "hang glider," you lift up to 40 feet into an 80-foot projection dome. From all sides your vision is filled with the beauty of California. You get the impractical delight of gliding over the Golden Gate Bridge and El Capitan, an aircraft carrier and the evening traffic of Los Angeles. Your glider tilts as it travels, your legs dangling free underneath.

The seating device is equipped with hidden special effects. Fans put wind

| Average Wait | |
|---|---|
| 9am | 0 min |
| 10am | 30 |
| 11am | 60 |
| Noon | 65 |
| 1pm | 70 |
| 2pm | 80 |
| 3pm | 75 |
| 4pm | 80 |
| 5pm | 90 |
| 6pm | 80 |
| 7pm | 70 |
| 8pm | 60 |
| 9pm | closed |

**Soarin'** flies you high, virtually, over the Golden Gate bridge and many other California sights

in your hair, odorizers let you smell pines and oranges, surround-sound speakers recreate a crashing surf and waterfall.

The entranceway, waiting area and theater resemble an airport. Cast members dress as airline employees. The gift stand looks like a ticket counter; the ride's walkway is a concourse; its boarding areas gates. The theater has runway lights; the gliders navigation lights.

Along the standby queue, a combination of video screens and motion-detection technology encourages guests to virtually fly a bird through a river canyon and launch paint balls against a digital canvas.

**Fun facts** ❶ Cast members may name your flight "No. 5-5-0-5," a reference to the ride's opening date of May 5, 2005. ❷ Locations seen include Redwood Creek, Napa Valley, the Sierra Mountains, La Quinta's PGA West golf complex and the USS Stennis aircraft carrier off San Diego. ❸ A hang glider over Yosemite is computer generated. So is an errant golf ball.

**Hidden Mickeys** ❶ As a blue balloon at the beginning of the Palm Springs scene, held by a man behind a golf cart at the far lower left. ❷ As a small Mickey silhouette on that errant golf ball. Flinch and you'll miss it. ❸ In the second burst of Disneyland fireworks, in the center of the screen.

▶ The best Soarin' seats are top-row center. Ask the gate attendant for Row 1, Gate B.

The Living with the Land boat ride travels through greenhouses filled with exotic plants

# Living with the Land

★★★★ 14 min. Capacity: 20 per boat. Open 9a–9p. The Land pavilion. *FastPass AuDe* Indoor, air-conditioned queue. Fear factor: None. Access: ECV users must transfer. Handheld captioning. Debuted: 1982 (as Listen to the Land); revised 1993, 2009.

This indoor boat ride takes a subject usually thought of as dull as dirt—agricultural science—and presents it as entertainment. A trip through four working greenhouses, it's filled with plants most Americans never see, and some odd growing techniques. Your boat meanders so close to the plants that you can often smell the leaves and fruit. The ride was refurbished in 2009 to include more tropical species and some new displays.

Crops include coconuts, papayas, 2-foot jackfruit, 3-foot winter melons and 500-pound Atlantic giant pumpkins. Many plants hang from strings or trellises, roots in the air. Some grow on overhead conveyor belts. An aquaculture hut has catfish, sturgeon, shrimp, eels, even young alligators.

The ride begins with a journey through artificial rainforest, desert and farm habitats, some of which have Audio-Animatronics animals.

**Hidden Mickeys ❶** In the queue area mural (as bubbles under the word "nature," a Mickey profile). **❷** In the mural behind the loading area, an angled Mickey formed by green and blue circles (near the right wall, near the floor). **❸** In the quonset hut as algae behind the sturgeon. **❹** In the last greenhouse, as green test-tube caps behind lab windows.

# The Circle of Life: An Environmental Fable

★★★ 13 min. Capacity: 482. Open 9a–9p. The Land pavilion. Avg wait 7 min. Fear factor: None. Guests may stay in wheelchairs, ECVs. Handheld, reflective captioning; assistive listening. Debuted: 1995.

This movie uses the stars of 1994's "The Lion King" to teach environmental protection. When Timon and Pumbaa start to clear their savanna to build a resort, Simba tells them about a creature who first lived in harmony with nature, but now often forgets that everything is part of the circle of life. Live-action scenes show smokestacks, clogged highways and an oil-soaked bird, but also wind turbines, electric cars and recycling.

| Average Wait | |
| --- | --- |
| 9am | 0 min |
| 10am | 10 |
| 11am | 15 |
| Noon | 20 |
| 1pm | 25 |
| 2pm | 25 |
| 3pm | 20 |
| 4pm | 25 |
| 5pm | 30 |
| 6pm | 25 |
| 7pm | 20 |
| 8pm | 15 |
| 9pm | closed |

▶ A Behind The Seeds tour ($16, 45 min) offers an informative backstage view of the greenhouses.

© DISNEY

**A dog greets "shrunken" guests** during Honey I Shrunk the Audience. *Photo illustration.*

# Honey, I Shrunk the Audience

★★★ 15 min. Preshow: 5 min. Kodak slide show. Capacity: 570. Open 9a-7p. *FastPass* Air-conditioned indoor queue. Fear factor: Some children will be terrified by the 3-D animals and scurrying mice effects. Access: Guests may remain in wheelchairs, ECVs. Assistive listening; reflective captioning. *AuDe* Debuted: 1994.

"Everybody either hates the mice or hates the snake." That's what one cast member says about the 3-D movie Honey, I Shrunk the Audience. Featuring the realistic sensations of mice crawling at your ankles, wild cats in your face and a gigantic snake that tries to bite you, it's the only Epcot attraction that routinely reduces toddlers to shrieking, sobbing lumps. In fact, it seems to be created by someone who takes glee in scaring children. "Here dearie," we can hear some evil Imagineer cackling, "take a seat…"

The attraction has other problems, too. The movie is murky and a little out of focus from most seating locations, and its dialogue is hard to hear.

The story sounds innocent. You're in the auditorium of the Imagination Institute, on hand to watch Professor Wayne Szalinski (Rick Moranis, reprising his role from 1989's "Honey, I Shrunk the Kids") accept the Inventor of the Year Award.

But when the bumbling nerd gets lost in the wings, everything goes wrong. Before you know it the auditorium fills with scurrying rodents (actually prerecorded sounds coupled with some convincing special effects under your seat), a sharp-toothed lynx and ferocious lion pop out of the screen right at your face, then a snake slides into the theater and opens its fangs.

Soon Szalinski fixes things and everyone is safe. But wait—Szalinski blew up the dog, a curious canine who looks in at you, sniffs and sneezes. It's about the only effect where you don't hear crying afterward.

**Fun finds** ❶ An upside-down waterfall propels water up and into a pool in front of the Imagination pavilion. ❷ A single splash of water seems to hop from pad to pad at the Leap Frog Fountain, directly in front of the attraction. ❸ Jelly-like blobs of water hang in midair after they break off from the streams of the nearby Jellyfish Fountain.

### Average Wait

| | |
|---|---|
| 9am | 10 min |
| 10am | 10 |
| 11am | 10 |
| Noon | 10 |
| 1pm | 10 |
| 2pm | 10 |
| 3pm | 10 |
| 4pm | 10 |
| 5pm | 10 |
| 6pm | 10 |
| 7pm | closed |
| 8pm | closed |
| 9pm | closed |

▶ The screen has the best focus if you sit in the center rear of the theater.

# Journey into Imagination... with Figment

★★ 6 min. Capacity: 224. Open 9a-7p. Air-conditioned indoor queue. Fear factor: A dark room has the loud clamor of an oncoming train; a blast of air projects the odor of a skunk; the last room has a sudden flash. Access: Guests may remain in wheelchairs, ECVs. Handheld captioning. *AuDe* Debuted: 1983, revised 1998, 2002.

A tongue-in-cheek open-house tour of the stuffy—and, of course, fictional—Imagination Institute, this slow-moving dark ride is constantly interrupted by Figment, a mischievous dragon. The ride stops at various labs, where Institute director Dr. Nigel Channing (Eric Idle) attempts to demonstrate how his outfit is studying a particular human sense in order to "capture and control" imagination. Freethinking Figment, however, believes imagination works best when it's not controlled, but rather set free.

The trip includes stops at sight, sound and smell labs, as well as a tour of Figment's upside-down house.

Though the ride appeals to many young children, it's a long way from Disney's best and, ironically, one of the company's least imaginative attractions. There is, however, one great effect: in a cage past the Sight Lab, a huge butterfly appears to disappear as you go by. Post-show activities include a chance to conduct music by waving your arms.

And just who, you may ask, is Figment? In Disney's original Journey Into Imagination ride (1983–1999), he was the creation of Dreamfinder, a jolly wizard-like scientist. Composed of elements that Dreamfinder found in his travels—such as horns of a steer, the snout of a crocodile and the delight at a child's birthday party—he was voiced by Billy Barty. Today Figment's voice is Dave Goelz, the long-time voice of Muppets Gonzo and Dr. Bunsen Honeydew.

The theme song, "One Little Spark," was written by the Sherman Brothers, who also created the infamous "It's a Small World."

| Average Wait | |
|---|---|
| 9am | 0 min |
| 10am | 0 |
| 11am | 0 |
| Noon | 0 |
| 1pm | 0 |
| 2pm | 0 |
| 3pm | 0 |
| 4pm | 0 |
| 5pm | 0 |
| 6pm | 0 |
| 7pm | closed |
| 8pm | closed |
| 9pm | closed |

**Mischievous dragon Figment** takes a call during Journey into Imagination... with Figment

**Fun finds** Lining the entrance hall are office doors of ❶ Professor Wayne Szalinski, the subject of the attraction Honey, I Shrunk the Audience, ❷ 1997's "Flubber" inventor Dr. Phillip Brainard and ❸ Dean Higgins, the principal in 1969's "The Computer Wore Tennis Shoes." ❹ There's a page for Merlin Jones ("Your monkey is on the loose"), the chimp teacher in 1965's "The Monkey's Uncle." ❺ A look-through door lets you see into Dimension Hall, a corridor that seems much longer than it really is. To see the room's actual size look into it from the opposite window, an unmarked pane in the ImageWorks lab just left of the "Magic Photo Studio." ❻ Red tennis shoes sit outside the ride's computer room, a second reference to the 1969 film. ❼ As you enter Figment's upside-down house you pass under a real Chevrolet S-10 pickup.

**Hidden Mickeys** ❶ A Mickey Mouse-eared headphone sits in the ride's Sight Lab, on top of the left wheeled table. ❷ As two small circular carpets and ❸ a flowered toilet seat in Figment's bathroom. ❹ Between the letters "I" and "M" in the ImageWorks logo. ❺ In place of a letter in the eyechart in the Kodak demonstration area at the entrance to ImageWorks.

▶ A color chart hangs on a wall just past the Sight Lab. Reading it out loud is nearly impossible.

**Disney's Hotel du Canada** facade recalls Ottawa's Chateau Laurier

of rustic villages, ornate cities, the Scottish influence of the Maritimes and the ruggedness of the Canadian west.

It's dominated by a three-dimensional French Gothic "Hotel du Canada" facade. Based on Ottawa's Chateau Laurier, it sits behind a flower garden inspired by Victoria's Butchart Gardens. Alongside an entrance courtyard, a log cabin, trading post and 30-foot totems represent a Native village. Carved by a Tsimshian Indian in 1998, the leftmost totem (the only real one) shows the Raven folkbird releasing the sun, moon and stars from a carved cedar chest. Up the steps, a stone building reflects British styles of the east coast.

The back of the pavilion recalls the Canadian Rockies. A flowered path leads to a small canyon, where a 30-foot waterfall flows into a stream. Pine-studded slopes surround a shaft opening to what Disney calls Maple Leaf Mine (the entrance to the theater), which is trimmed with shoring and Klondike equipment.

# Canada

A funny film, an offbeat rock band and a good restaurant highlight this 3-acre salute to our northern neighbor. The first pavilion you come to if, like most folks, you tour World Showcase in a counterclockwise pattern, Disney's Canadian pavilion is not its most elaborate but often its most crowded.

Unfortunately, exploring this miniature Canada can seem almost as exhausting as hiking the real thing. It's a decent walk back to the theater, and there's no way to get off your feet unless you eat at the restaurant or sit on a sun-baked bench.

All ages will find the movie funny, but overall there's little for kids. A Kidcot table sits next to the restaurant's front door.

For many, the best part of the pavilion is its landscaping and architecture, a mixture

# O Canada!

★ ★ ★ 14 min. Capacity: 600. No seats. Covered outdoor queue. Fear factor: None. Access: Guests may remain in wheelchairs, ECVs. Assistive listening, reflective captioning. *AuDe* Debuted: 1982, revised 2007.

Projected on a wraparound screen in a stand-up theater, this travelogue surrounds you with the people and places of Canada. An update of a film that played here until 2007, it dumps its previous devotion to the outdoors for a joke-filled journey that equally focuses on urban centers. As explained by host Martin Short, the movie wants to

| Average Wait | |
|---|---|
| 9am | closed |
| 10am | closed |
| 11am | 10 min |
| Noon | 10 |
| 1pm | 10 |
| 2pm | 10 |
| 3pm | 10 |
| 4pm | 10 |
| 5pm | 10 |
| 6pm | 10 |
| 7pm | 10 |
| 8pm | 10 |

▶ Canadian sweet treat: Pure maple sugar candy ($10 per 15-piece box). It melts in your mouth .

**The U.K. pavilion's architecture** re-creates historic facades. The Sportsman's Shoppe (above right) mimics the white-stone Abbotsford on its left, Henry VIII's red-brick Hampton Court on its right.

correct the misconception that Canada is nothing more than a Great White North. Stand in the center of the theater for the best experience.

The film mixes scenes of mountains and redwoods with stops in Montreal, Quebec City, Toronto, Vancouver and Victoria. The old New Brunswick video is still present, but you no longer hear from that area's heavily accented locals. The Mounties that used to circle around you to start the show now kick off its conclusion. As for music, lumberjack ballads have been replaced by orchestral tracks. The theme song ("Canada, You're a Lifetime Journey") is now sung by 2006 "Canadian Idol" winner Eva Avila.

Unfortunately, whereas the old movie made it appear *you* were riding a dogsled or racing a toboggan, the new one makes Short the participant. None of the new footage wraps around you, the unique feature of these CircleVision 360 presentations. Instead, new segments simply encircle you with multiple versions of the same image.

Developed in the 1950s by Disney video engineer (and original Mickey Mouse animator) Ub Iwerks, the technique uses nine projectors to display synchronized video on screens that wrap around its audience. Filming is done by a nine-lens camera. (Why nine? Because the concept only works with an odd number. Each projector sits in a gap between two screens, yet lines up with one screen directly across from it.) Once a major type of Disney attraction, CircleVision 360 theaters now exist only at Epcot. The other one is in the China pavilion.

**Hidden Mickeys ❶** On both sides of the left totem underneath the top set of hands. **❷** As wine-rack bottles behind Le Cellier's check-in counter.

# United Kingdom

Though it doesn't have an attraction, this pavilion has so much to see and do you can spend hours here. You can stop in for a brew at a British pub, relax to a Beatles tribute band, or take in a rowdy street show. The area includes two nice gardens.

Getting around is easy. Buildings line both sides of the promenade, and most all of the stores are interconnected. Kids will enjoy watching the street performers, browsing at the toy shop, stopping in at the Kidcot table there, and meeting characters Winnie the Pooh, Tigger, Mary Poppins and Alice (from "Alice in Wonderland"). Cast members often chalk out a promenade hopscotch game at 11 a.m.

▶ **U.K. sweet treat:** Cadbury dairy milk caramel candy bar ($3), filled with flowing caramel.

**The France pavilion** recalls the Paris of a hundred years ago

# France

A good spot to get off your feet even if you're not hungry, this pavilion offers a nice film in a cozy theater, a tempting array of pastries and some good dining experiences. A couple of small shops stock fine perfume and wine. The perfume shop is worth walking in just for its aroma.

For children, Belle and the Beast, Princess Aurora and sometimes Marie (from 1970's "The AristoCats") pose for pictures and sign autographs. A Kidcot table sits in the Souvenirs de France gift shop.

You approach the pavilion on a replica of the Pont des Arts footbridge, then gaze upon the Paris of La Belle Époque, "the beautiful time" from 1870 to 1910. Three-story facades have copper and slate mansard roofs, many with chimney pots. A rear shop is based on the Les Halles fruit and vegetable market, an 1850 iron-and-glass-ceilinged Parisian structure. Towering behind it all is the Eiffel Tower, complete with its period-correct tawny finish. Disney built the one-tenth-scale replica using Gustave Eiffel's blueprints.

Each building represents a different historical period. The brick turrets and medieval crenulation of the Sportsman's Shoppe mimic Henry VIII's 16th-century Hampton Court. Its white-stone side is Abbotsford, the 19th-century Scottish estate where Sir Walter Scott wrote novels. Across a street is the 16th-century thatched-roofed cottage of Anne Hathaway, the wife of William Shakespeare. Further down the street sits a half-timbered 15th-century Tudor leaning with age, a plaster 17th-century pre-Georgian, a stone 18th-century Palladian and a home built of angled bricks. Bordering the World Showcase lagoon, the Rose & Crown Pub is divided vertically into three styles—a medieval rural cottage, a 15th-century Tudor tavern and an 1890s Victorian bar.

## Impressions de France

★★★★ 18 min. Capacity: 325. Air-conditioned indoor queue. Fear factor: None. Access: Guests may remain in wheelchairs, ECVs. Assistive listening, reflective captions. *AuDe* Debuted: 1982.

Set to an ethereal classical score, this movie fills your field of vision with the fairytale grandeur of the French landscape. The 200-degree screen packs 40 scenes in 18 minutes. Starting off over the cliffs of Normandy, your trip include stops at four chateaus, a church, market, vineyard, the gardens of Versailles, a rural bicycle

| Average Wait | |
|---|---|
| 9am | closed |
| 10am | closed |
| 11am | 10 min |
| Noon | 10 |
| 1pm | 10 |
| 2pm | 10 |
| 3pm | 10 |
| 4pm | 10 |
| 5pm | 10 |
| 6pm | 10 |
| 7pm | 10 |
| 8pm | 10 |

▶ French sweet treat: Strawberry tart ($4) with berries, creamy filling; Boulangerie Pàtisserie.

**A Moroccan cast member** plays a darbouka drum while waiting out a thunderstorm

tour and an antique Bugatti race through Cannes. And that's just the first five minutes. Still to come are hot-air balloons, fishing boats, a train, Notre Dame and a flight above the Alps.

The only sour note comes early, when the stuffy narrator intones "My Frahnce awakens with the early dawn." Well, duh!

Based on Napoleon III's elegant royal theater in Fontainebleau, the intimate auditorium has padded, if petite, seats.

## Morocco

This exotic pavilion features food, merchandise and music that is little-known in the West. It includes some small shops, table-service and fast-food restaurants and an exhibit. A smart layout makes the pavilion easy to visit. Alongside the promenade is a cafe with a tiny sweet shop; a handful of small stores connect to it from behind. The smell of incense in the air will remind some baby boomers of a head shop. Created by the Kingdom of Morocco, the pavilion is managed independently of Disney.

Kids can meet Aladdin, Princess Jasmine and Genie in a room behind the shops. A Kidcot table sits in an open-air market.

Meant to evoke a desert city, buildings are made of brick, tan plaster and reddish sandstone. Like most Moroccan cities, it's divided into two sections, the Ville Nouvelle (new city) and the medina (old town). The new city fronts the promenade. Anchored by two sandstone towers topped with fortress-like crenelation, a fountain courtyard and two buildings recall Casablanca and Marrakesh. Towering over the courtyard is a large prayer tower, a replica of the Koutoubia Minaret in Marrakesh.

The medina of Fez (Morocco's religious and cultural center) lies in back, behind the 8th-century Bab Boujouloud Gate. On the left is the Fez House, a replica of a central courtyard of a traditional Moroccan home, complete with the sounds of the family. On the right is an open-air market, its bamboo roof loosely lashed to thick beams. Restaurant Marrakesh is a Southern Moroccan fortress. Past the restaurant stands a reproduction of the Nejjarine Fountain in Fez. Rising above the old city is a replica of the Chellah Minaret, a 14th-century necropolis found in Morocco's capital city of Rabat.

Landscaping represents Morocco's agriculture—date, olive and sour orange trees; mint and ornamental cabbage plants. Along the shoreline is a working replica of an ancient waterwheel, an ingenious contraption that shuttles water from the lagoon to a grid of nearby desert gardens. The wheel lifts

▶ Moroccan sweet treat: Flakey, honey-drenched baklava ($3); Tangierine Cafe, Oasis snack stand.

**The rear of the Japan pavilion** resembles the country's historic Nijo and Shirasagijo castles

**Hidden Mickeys ❶** As brass plates on a green door of the Souk-Al-Magreb promenade shop. **❷** As a dome window in a minaret on the photo backdrop in Aladdin's meeting area. Mickey's in the upper right-hand segment, next to a small ladder.

# Japan

Though you can't tell it as you walk by, this pavilion includes a full-size department store, two restaurants and an exhibit gallery. No characters appear, but children will enjoy watching candy artist Miyuki and listening to a storyteller. Japan's Kidcot table is located in a small exhibit hall. The pavilion is run by the Mitsukoshi company, Japan's oldest retail business. It was founded in 1673.

Graceful architecture and landscaping symbolize aspects of Japanese culture.

Elements on the left side of the complex represent culture and religion. An 83-foot pagoda recalls the 8th-century Horyuji Temple in Nara. Its five stories represent the five elements of creation—earth, water, fire, wind and sky. A hill garden's evergreens symbolize eternal life, its rocks the long life of the earth and its koi-filled water the brief life of animals and man. In the garden, the rustic Yakitori House is modeled on Kyoto's 16th-century Katsura Imperial Villa.

Housing the store and two restaurants, the building on the right represents commerce. Though it may look bland to Western eyes, the structure recalls the ceremonial Shishinden Hall of the 8th-century Gosho Imperial Palace at Kyoto.

The rear of the complex symbolizes Japan's political history. Once you pass through a (very thin) 17th-century wood and stone Nijo castle with its sculptures of mounted samurai warriors, you cross a moat to enter what appears to be the Shirasagijo (White Heron) castle, a 14th-century feudal fortress which in real life still overlooks the city of Himeji. Its curved stone walls protect white-plaster buildings topped with blue-tile roofs.

water in compartments inside it, then releases it into a series of wooden troughs.

Moroccan artists created the pavilion's detailed tiles from nine tons of ceramic pieces. Deliberate imperfections in the work reflect the Muslim belief that only Allah creates perfection.

## Gallery of Arts and History

Used in possession rituals, a guitar-like gimbri is among the antique musical instruments and other artifacts on display in this small three-room hall. The gallery itself is a piece of art, heavily tiled and molded, with an intricate raised ceiling that's a work of art unto itself. Easy to overlook, it sits to the left of the front courtyard.

▶ Japanese sweet treat: Botan rice candy ($1). Each piece has a melt-in-your-mouth wrapper.

Robotic figures of Benjamin Franklin and Mark Twain host the American Adventure attraction

## 'Timeless Beauty' photo exhibit

Photography lovers will want to check out Timeless Beauty: World Heritage Sites of Japan. The touring exhibition features nearly 60 images by Kazuyoshi Miyoshi, an awardee of the prestigious Kimura Ihee Award in Japan. The photographs pay homage to places designated as World Heritage Sites, locations around the world adopted by a 1971 United Nations treaty to identify places that "belong to all people" around the globe. The exhibit is located at the left rear of the pavilion, in the Bijutsu-kan Gallery.

**Hidden Mickeys** ❶ In the metal tree grates in the courtyard. ❷ As the center of a koi-pond drain cover, near a bamboo fence.

# The American Adventure

The focus of this U.S. pavilion is its attraction, a theatrical history lesson that uses many Audio-Animatronics figures. Plan to spend up to an hour here—30 minutes for the show and up to another 30 in the worthwhile small exhibit of historical artifacts. A Kidcot table is outside, by the gift shop.

The colonial (English Georgian) building uses 110,000 hand-formed bricks, laid with an old-fashioned one-then-a-half technique. In a departure from typical Disney theme-park design, the structure uses *reversed* forced perspective to appear just three stories tall, though it rises more than 70 feet. The illusion only works from a distance; up close the second-story windows look huge.

## The American Adventure

★★★★★ ✓ 30 min. Capacity: 1,024. Air-conditioned indoor queue. Fear factor: None. Access: Guests may remain in wheelchairs, ECVs. Assistive listening, reflective captioning available. *AuDe* Debuted: 1982; revised 1993, 2007.

Combining film footage with Audio-Animatronics versions of dozens of historic figures, this theatrical attraction is on par with the best museum presentations found in Washington D.C. It's inspiring, thoughtful and educational.

The only World Showcase attraction that is critical of its country, the show embraces the triumphs of America and the optimism of its people, but doesn't

| Average Wait | |
| --- | --- |
| 9am | closed |
| 10am | closed |
| 11am | 20 min |
| Noon | 20 |
| 1pm | 20 |
| 2pm | 20 |
| 3pm | 20 |
| 4pm | 20 |
| 5pm | 20 |
| 6pm | 20 |
| 7pm | 20 |
| 8pm | 20 |

▶ **U.S. sweet treat:** Flat, sugary funnel cakes ($6, $8 with ice cream), at the Funnel Cake kiosk.

The Italy pavilion re-creates the Doge's Palace of Venice. Plaster columns resemble veined marble.

twitches and pulls of a real animal. The film, a combination of real and re-created images, pans across paintings and photos in a style later made famous by documentarian Ken Burns.

The show includes both proud and ugly episodes of the American story. Chatting with Franklin after the Revolutionary War, Twain says "You Founding Fathers gave us a pretty good start... [but then] a whole bunch of folks found out that 'We the People' didn't yet mean all the people." Subsequent scenes cover slavery and Native Americans.

A photomontage finale covers events of the past 50 years. Images added in 2007 include that of Apple founder Steve Jobs with the first Macintosh computer and Muhammad Ali lighting the torch at the 1996 Atlanta Olympics.

Twelve statues along the sides of the auditorium represent the Spirits of America.

Hidden from view, the staging system is a mechanical marvel. Just beneath the sight line of the audience is a mass of wiring and hydraulic cables which give movement to the figures. Underneath sits a 175-ton scene changer—a steel frame 65 feet long, 35 feet wide and 14 feet high. It wheels in 13 sets horizontally, raising them into view on telescoping hydraulic supports. Other devices bring in side elements. Behind all that is a 155-foot rear-projection screen that shows a 70mm film. The show uses 35 Audio-Animatronics characters, including three Ben Franklins and three Mark Twains.

shy away from our country's flaws and challenges. Ben Franklin and Mark Twain tell the American story, leading you from the time of the Pilgrims through World War II, with help from everyone from George Washington and Thomas Jefferson to Will Rogers and Rosie the Riveter.

At the end, Franklin quotes Thomas Wolfe: "So, then, to every man his chance... the right to live, to work, to be himself, and to become whatever thing his manhood and his vision can combine to make him."

The robots move convincingly. For a moment Franklin appears to walk; Frederick Douglas sways on a rocking raft. Some movements are subtle. Braving Valley Forge, Washington shifts his weight in his saddle, and his horse has the indistinct

## National Treasures

This small group of artifacts from famous Americans is worth wandering through. Pieces include one of Abraham Lincoln's stovepipe hats (with frayed edges), a kinetoscope, kinetophone and tinfoil phonograph of Thomas Edison, a microscope used by George Washington Carver, chairs from the homes of Benjamin Franklin and

▶ Best U.S. beer: Samuel Adams draft ($6), sold at the Fife & Drum Tavern promenade stand.

**The outdoor plaza** of the Germany pavilion

George Washington and a pool cue from the den of Mark Twain. The exhibit is in the American Heritage Gallery, off on the left side of the lobby.

# Italy

Except for watching its street performers, this pavilion offers little to do but spend money. The restaurant is expensive, and there's nothing for kids but a Kidcot table, located behind the La Bottega gift shop.

Ironically, the entrance area is one of the most attractive in the World Showcase. It's designed to look like Venice.

A town square resembles the Piazza San Marco. The two freestanding columns mimic the square's two 12th-century monuments, one topped by the city's guardian, the winged lion of St. Mark the Evangelist, the other crowned by St. Theodore, the city's former patron saint. He's shown killing the dragon that threatened the city of Euchaita, an act that gave him the courage to declare himself a Christian. The 10th-century Campanile (bell tower) dominates the skyline, though this version is just 100 feet tall, less than a third the height of the original. Gold-leafed ringlets decorate an angel on top.

On the left of the square is a replica of the 14th-century Doge's (leader's) Palace. Its facade replicates many details of the original. The first two stories rest on realistic marble columns that front leaded-glass windows. The third floor is tiled and topped by marble sculptures, statues, reliefs and filigree. Adjoining the palace, a stairway and portico reflect Verona.

With the World Showcase lagoon doubling as the Adriatic Sea, a waterfront area includes replicas of the city's bridges, gondolas and striped pilings.

On the right side of the pavilion, the La Bottega gift shop resembles a Tuscany homestead. A sculpture behind it of Neptune and his dolphins recalls Bernini's 1642 fountain in Florence.

# Germany

Like its Italian pavilion, Disney's miniature Germany is little more than shops and food. But in this case, it's worth a stop. Not only can you sample the foods at an outdoor cafe (with tables tucked into a recessed patio), the restaurant is the most fun place to eat in the World Showcase. Still, there's no entertainment except in the restaurant.

If you've got children, make sure you stop at the miniature outdoor train village, located to the right of the main pavilion. A walkway leads over track tunnels and alongside the little town, which has its own

▶ Italian sweet treat: A Baci Perugina hazelnut chocolate fortune ball (71¢), sold at La Bottega.

**An army of half-size reproductions** of ancient "tomb warriors" is displayed in the China pavilion

ond story recall the rule of the Hapsburg emperors. The rear facade combines the looks of two 12th-century castles, the Eltz and the Stahleck.

**Hidden Mickeys ❶** In the center of the crown of the left-most Hapsburg emperor statue on the second story of Das Kaufhaus. ❷ A three-dimensional Mickey Mouse is often hiding in the train village. Usually he's a plastic figure standing in a window of a hilltop castle.

# China

This pavilion has a good exhibit, Disney's best remaining CircleVision 360 movie, memorable entertainers, an interesting department store and some good food. For kids, Mulan and Mushu from Disney's 1998 film "Mulan" appear. A Kidcot table sits at the back of the store.

The China pavilion was refurbished in 2008. Its restaurant and counter-service cafe have new menus and decor.

A Suzhou-style garden and reflecting ponds symbolize the order and discipline of nature. Keeping with Chinese custom, it appears old and in a natural state. Alongside the lagoon, large pockmarked boulders demonstrate a tradition of designing surprising views in landscapes by creating holes in waterside rock formations.

The pavilion is anchored by a triple-arched gate. Behind it sits a miniature Hall of Prayer for Good Harvests, the circular main building of Beijing's 1420 Temple of Heaven, a summer retreat for emperors. Its rotunda alludes to the cycles of nature. Twelve outer columns represent the months of the year and the years in a cycle of the Chinese calendar. Four central columns denote the seasons, a central beam represents earth, a topping beam heaven. A floor stone is cut into nine pieces, reflecting the Chinese belief that nine is a lucky number.

Architecture also includes facades of an elegant home, a school house and shop fronts reflecting European influences. The gallery has a formal saddle-ridge roof line.

wee little live landscape. Four working trains roam out over the rivers and through the woods, each on its own track. Snow White and Dopey appear to the left of the pavilion. Germany's Kidcot table sits inside a teddy bear shop. The village was refurbished in 2008.

As for architecture, an outdoor plaza has some interesting detailing. Its centerpiece is a sculpture of the patron saint of soldiers, St. George, slaying a dragon during a trip to the Middle East. A clock comes to life at the top of each hour with a 3-minute animated display. On the right side of the plaza, the facade of the Das Kaufhaus shop was inspired by the Kaufhaus, a 16th-century merchants' hall in the Black Forest town of Freiburg. Three statues on its sec-

▶ German best beer: Spaten Oktoberfest draft ($8), medium-dark with a roasted nut flavor.

**Gift shop facades** recall coastal cottages at Disney's Norway pavilion

## Reflections of China

★★★★ 20 min. Capacity: 200. No seats. Air-conditioned indoor queue. Fear factor: None. Access: Guests may stay in wheelchairs, ECVs. Assistive listening; reflective captioning available. *AuDe* Debuted: 1982, updated 2003.

You stand up to watch this poetic travelogue. It includes 30 vistas that wrap around you, which provides a sense that you are actually at the various locations. Sights include everything from the Great Wall and the Forbidden City to the modern cityscapes of Hong Kong and Shanghai to rural areas that include Tibet and Inner Mongolia. One scene was filmed by a camera hanging from a banking helicopter. The host portrays 8th-century Chinese poet Li Bai. The movie's mages are crisp; its sound clear.

Developed in the 1950s by Disney video engineer Ub Iwerks (the original animator of Mickey Mouse), the movie uses nine projectors to synchronize video onto nine screens arranged above its audience. Dubbed CircleVision 360, it places projectors into the gaps between its screens so that everything lines up. Filming is done by a nine-lens camera. Originally a major type of Disney attraction, CircleVision 360 theaters now exist only here and at Epcot's Canada pavilion.

| Average Wait | |
|---|---|
| 9am | closed |
| 10am | closed |
| 11am | 15 min |
| Noon | 15 |
| 1pm | 15 |
| 2pm | 15 |
| 3pm | 15 |
| 4pm | 15 |
| 5pm | 15 |
| 6pm | 15 |
| 7pm | 15 |
| 8pm | 15 |

## Tomb Warriors — Guardian Spirits of Ancient China

The focus of this exhibit is the terra cotta "spirit army" found in the tomb of China's first emperor Qin Shi Huang (259–210 BC). The largest archeological find in the world, the 22-square-mile site contains 8,000 full-size statues arranged in military formations. None of those original figures are here, but an army of 200 half-size reproductions offers a sense of the real thing. A side display shows how the site is being excavated. The exhibit also includes two dozen tomb artifacts from the Han, Six, Sui and Tang Dynasties (through 906 AD). They're small, but real. The exhibit is in the Gallery of the Whispering Willow, in the rear center of the pavilion.

# Norway

Welcome to Norway, where men are menn and women are kvinner and meatballs are

▶ Chinese sweet treat: A tasty cup of ginger ice cream ($3) from the promenade snack stand.

kjottkakers and all in all there are just way too many consonants. Pronunciation differences aside, the beautiful country is the basis of one of Epcot's best pavilions.

The big attraction is the restaurant, where a gaggle of Disney princesses host every meal. It also has another bevy of beauties: a group of perfectly toned Norwegian natives that greet you at every cash register. The guys look good, too.

On the downside, there's no live entertainment, and if you don't want to dine with the dames no indoor place to eat.

A Kidcot table sits inside the shop.

The grounds combine a variety of architectural styles. Standing at the entrance is a replica of the 13th-century Gol Church of Hallingdal, one of Norway's stave churches that played a key role in the country's movement to Christianity. Next door, a bakery has a sod roof, a traditional way to insulate homes in Norway's mountains. Gift shop facades recall coastal cottages. The restaurant and rear facade re-create Akershus, a 14th-century Oslo fortress.

## Maelstrom

★★★ 15 min. (5 min ride, 5 min wait, 5 min film). Capacity: 192. *FastPass* Air-conditioned indoor queue. Fear factor: Often dark, with a few scary faces. In the film, two loud flashes will jolt those of any age. Access: Wheelchair, ECV users must transfer. Assistive listening; handheld and reflective captioning. Debuted: 1988.

Themed to Norway's rich seafaring heritage, this indoor boat ride has a quirky appeal. After you set sail in a dragon-headed longboat, you head up a dark chainlift, where a god above urges you to "seek the spirit of Norway." Your search starts off peacefully but becomes a confused chaos (a "maelstrom") after trolls commandeer your ship. Falling into the North Sea, you make landfall at a fishing village.

The second half of the attraction is optional. After you climb out of your boat, you head in to a small theater where you can stay for a short film. "The Spirit of Norway" portrays the daydreams of a young boy. As he examines an old Viking ship, he imagines many

| Average Wait | |
|---|---|
| 9am | closed |
| 10am | closed |
| 11am | 5 min |
| Noon | 10 |
| 1pm | 10 |
| 2pm | 20 |
| 3pm | 30 |
| 4pm | 35 |
| 5pm | 40 |
| 6pm | 30 |
| 7pm | 30 |
| 8pm | 30 |

types of successful Norwegians. The point? "The spirit of Norway… is in its people!" Cynics will note that, based on the gender of the actors, the spirit of Norway is apparently mostly in its men.

## Vikings: Conquerors of the Seas

Axe in hand, a lifesize Rögnvald the Raider stares you down in this five-case exhibit inside the Stave Church Gallery. The displays also include figures of Erik the Red and King Olaf, a detailed scale model of the 9th century Viking ship and authentic swords, arrows and axe blades, some of which date back more than 1,000 years.

**Hidden Mickeys** Mickey Mouse appears three times in the mural behind the Maelstrom loading area: ❶ As Mickey ears on a Viking in the middle of a ship toward the left, ❷ as shadows on a cruise-line worker's blouse (her right pocket is Mickey's head, her clipboard ring is his nose) and ❸ at the far right on the watch of a bearded construction worker wearing a hardhat. ❹ As black circles on King Olaf II's tunic embroidery in the Stave Church.

# Mexico

Great entertainment, good shopping and a mutant freak of an attraction make this pavilion an interesting diversion. Housed in what appears to be an ancient pyramid, its cool, dark marketplace, restaurant, new tequila bar and boat ride are all great ways to get out of the sun.

A Kidcot table sits just inside the entrance. Donald Duck signs autographs and poses for pictures in his garb from Disney's 1944 film "The Three Caballeros."

The pyramid facade is modeled on the Aztec temple of serpent god Quetzalcoatl in the ancient city of Teotihuacan. Traditionally the god of the morning and evening star, Quetzalcoatl later became known as the patron of priests, inventor of books and of the calendar, and as the symbol of death and resurrection. His worship involved human sacrifice. Quetzalcoatl himself is depicted by heads along Disney's priests' steps.

Inside the building, the entry portico to the "outdoor" market resembles a Mexican mayor's mansion. Surrounding facades represent the 16th-century silver mining town of Taxco. Back outside, the Cantina de San Angel cafe looks similar to the 17th-century San Angel Inn in Mexico City.

▶ Norwegian sweet treat: A Daim candy bar ($2), milk chocolate with an almond caramel center.

**The facade of the Mexico pavilion** is modeled on the Aztec temple of serpent god Quetzalcoatl

## Gran Fiesta Tour

★★★ 8 min. Capacity: 250. Air-conditioned indoor queue. Fear factor: None. Access: ECV users must transfer. Handheld captioning. *AuDe* Debuted: 1982, revised 2007.

An update of the old El Rio Del Tiempo attraction, this dark boat ride is still a tour through the cultural history of Mexico, but now its video screens tell a story based on Disney's 1945 movie "The Three Caballeros." After the three singing amigos—ladies man Donald Duck, suave Brazilian parrot José Carioca and hyper Mexican cowboy rooster Panchito—plan to reunite for a concert in Mexico City, Donald disappears to take in the sights and his feathered friends try to find him.

Like the film, the ride is a strange trip. In Acapulco, Donald's bathing suit falls off. At night, he heads to a bar to smooch live-action, human señoritas.

As for reliving the cultural history of Mexico, you start off in the country's 1st century, sailing through a rainforest before passing a Mayan pyramid and drifting into a temple. A Small World-style celebration includes the Day of the Dead. In modern Mexico you pass Acapulco's cliffs and grottos, then travel to Mexico City's Reforma Boulevard, where the Three Caballeros' concert takes place.

**'Come here, my little enchilada!'** The most bizarre movie in the Disney canon, 1945's "The Three Caballeros" combines psychedelic animation with a storyline that makes Donald Duck a libidinous wolf. Its point? The charms of Latin America. The film's plot is mirrored in the Gran Fiesta attraction. When Donald has a birthday, his presents are pop-up books that include Brazilian playboy parrot José Carioca and Mexican six-gun-shooting cowboy rooster Panchito. The rooster tosses sombreros to his friends, proclaims the trio "three gay caballeros" and takes them on a flying-serape tour of his country. On Acapulco Beach, Donald goes ga-ga for dozens of live-action bathing beauties ("Come to Papa! Come here, my little enchilada!") and keeps losing his swimming suit. At night the duck can't stay away from the clubs, where he dances with still more real-life señoritas. Bizarre animation includes illogical color changes and an overdose of morphing gags.

### Average Wait

| | |
|---|---|
| 9am | closed |
| 10am | closed |
| 11am | 0 min |
| Noon | 0 |
| 1pm | 0 |
| 2pm | 0 |
| 3pm | 0 |
| 4pm | 0 |
| 5pm | 0 |
| 6pm | 0 |
| 7pm | 0 |
| 8pm | 0 |

▶ Best Mexican drinks: The premium margaritas available only at the new tequila bar.

IllumiNations' lasers and fireworks light up the sky over the World Showcase Lagoon

# IllumiNations: Reflections of Earth

★ ★ ★ ★ ✔ 15 min. Preshow: 30 min of instrumental world music from Japan, South America, Scandinavia and Spain. Fear factor: Loud, bright explosions and fire can be intense for toddlers, some preschoolers. Cancelled during thunderstorms. World Showcase Lagoon. Access: Guests may remain in wheelchairs, ECVs. Debuted: 1988; revised 1997, 1999.

Synchronized to a symphonic world-music score, this nightly fireworks and special-effects extravaganza uses the entire World Showcase as its stage, as strobe lights flash on, and laser beams shoot from the various international pavilions. A rotating Earth moves across the water and shows moving images on its continents, eventually unfolding to reveal a giant torch. Though there's no narration, the show tells the history of the world in three acts: "Chaos," "Order" and "Celebration."

"Chaos" begins with the dawn of time—the Big Bang and the creation of Earth—symbolized by a lone shooting star that explodes into a fiery "ballet of chaos."

"Order" brings the planet under control. Scenes on the globe depict primal seas and forests; the development of cultural landmarks including the Sphinx, the Easter Island statues and Mount Rushmore; and historical figures such as the Dalai Lama, Martin Luther King Jr., Mother Teresa and, if you look closely, Walt Disney. The coolest image: a video of a running horse that transforms into a cave painting.

The third act, "Celebration," begins as the globe unfurls into a lotus flower and a 40-foot torch rises from its heart. Celebrating both human diversity and the unified spirit of mankind, a fireworks finale heralds a new age of man—the 21st century.

IllumiNations ends with a loud crackle, sending you off to embrace the future. As you leave, the exit song is "We Go On."

### Where to watch it

The symmetrical show is directed to the front of the park, toward Spaceship Earth. Therefore, the best viewing spot is World Showcase Plaza, where you'll see everything as the designers intended it. An added plus: the plaza is the closest viewing spot to Epcot's main exit, so you'll be ahead of the masses when the show ends.

The show can be viewed from throughout the World Showcase (soundtrack

▶ Pick out a viewing spot for IllumiNations at least 30 minutes early to get a good view.

**Loading the guns.** A cast member packs mortar tubes with fireworks for an IllumiNations show.

speakers line the lagoon), but watching IllumiNations from another location is like sitting at the side, or rear, of a theatrical stage: It's interesting, but you don't get the full experience.

**Fun facts ❶** 2,800 fireworks launch from 750 mortar tubes in 34 locations. Some ring the shore, just a few feet from unsuspecting guests. ❷ The four fountain barges pump 5,000 gallons of water per minute. ❸ The 150,000-pound "inferno barge" has 37 propane nozzles. ❹ The 28-foot steel globe rotates on a 350-ton barge that houses 258 strobes, six computers and an infrared guidance system. Wrapped in more than 180,000 light-emitting diodes, the globe was the world's first spherical video display. ❺ The performance uses 67 computers in 40 locations. ❻ The pavilions are outlined in 26,000 feet of lights. ❼ The Morocco pavilion does not participate in the show. ❽ The music supervisor was Hans Zimmer, the composer for the 1994 Disney movie "The Lion King." ❾ The songs "The Promise" and "We Go On" are performed by country singer Kellie Coffey. ❿ There are 19 torches around the lagoon, symbolizing the first 19 centuries of human history. The 20th torch, in the globe, represents the Millennium. ⓫ Disney occasionally tests some IllumiNations effects, or releases leftover fireworks or propane, after midnight.

# Kim Possible World Showcase Adventure

★★★★ ✔ **Allow 45–60 min. Recruitment Stations open 9a–7p; Field Stations open 11a–9p. Fear factor: None. Access: Guests may remain in wheelchairs and ECVs. Debuted: 2009.**

A cell-phone-like "Kimmunicator" helps you trigger hidden effects at the World Showcase pavilion in this secret-agent scavenger hunt. Your mission? To save the world, by helping Kim Possible and her friends vanquish a silly villain. You make a reservation to play it.

You get started at one of three Recruitment Stations, which are located in Future World's Innoventions buildings as well as on the bridge between Future World and World Showcase. Here, you swipe your park ticket to receive a Mission Pass, a Fastpass-style reservation ticket for use later in the day. One pass is good for up to three "Kimmunicator" handsets.

When your time comes, you report to your assigned Field Station (located at the International Gateway, Italy or Norway) to get your handset and receive your mission.

Then it's simple: Just follow the instructions on the device. Focused on one particular pavilion (the U.K., France, Japan, Germany, China, Norway or Mexico), you search for clues and eventually capture your bad guy. When you're done, you return the handset to a drop box.

The experience is fun even if you've never heard of Kim Possible. The best parts are the hidden effects. With the touch of a button you can make a jade monkey appear in China, a chimney smoke in Norway, a beer stein yodel in Germany, a waterfall emerge in Japan, a volcano erupt in Mexico. Ever get the urge to turn the tiny townsfolk in Germany's miniature train village into red-eyed zombies? This is your chance.

**ON THE ANIMATED TELEVISION SERIES** "Kim Possible," Kim is a redheaded high school cheerleader who saves the world from comic super villains in her spare time—an easier job that dealing with the everyday challenges of being a teenager. She's helped by best friend and crush Ron Stoppable and his pet naked mole rat Rufus, as well as computer genius Wade.

▶ The best IllumiNations viewing spot is World Showcase Plaza. The show plays to that direction.

# Disney's Hollywood Studios

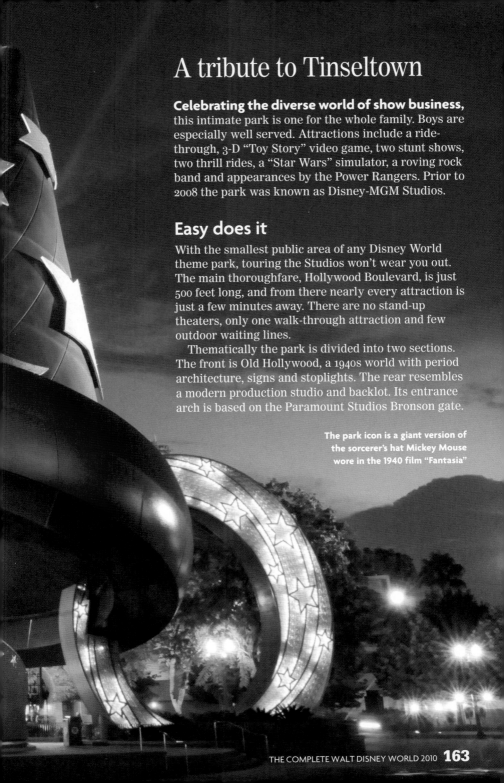

# A tribute to Tinseltown

**Celebrating the diverse world of show business,** this intimate park is one for the whole family. Boys are especially well served. Attractions include a ride-through, 3-D "Toy Story" video game, two stunt shows, two thrill rides, a "Star Wars" simulator, a roving rock band and appearances by the Power Rangers. Prior to 2008 the park was known as Disney-MGM Studios.

## Easy does it

With the smallest public area of any Disney World theme park, touring the Studios won't wear you out. The main thoroughfare, Hollywood Boulevard, is just 500 feet long, and from there nearly every attraction is just a few minutes away. There are no stand-up theaters, only one walk-through attraction and few outdoor waiting lines.

Thematically the park is divided into two sections. The front is Old Hollywood, a 1940s world with period architecture, signs and stoplights. The rear resembles a modern production studio and backlot. Its entrance arch is based on the Paramount Studios Bronson gate.

The park icon is a giant version of the sorcerer's hat Mickey Mouse wore in the 1940 film "Fantasia"

*i* Information

✚ First Aid

$ ATM Locations

☏ Pay Phones

**Block Party Bash Route**

N

Sunset
Ranch
Market

SUNSET BLVD

ENTRANCE

Starring
Rolls Cafe

ANIMATION COURTYARD

Hollywood
Brown Derby

HOLLYWOOD BLVD

Hollywood
& Vine

'50s Prime
Time Cafe

MICKEY AVE

Echo
Lake

PIXAR PLACE

COMMISSARY LANE

ABC
Commissary

Backlot
Express

Sci-Fi
Dine-In

Studio
Catering Co.

NEW YORK STREET

Toy Story
Pizza Planet
Arcade

S T R E E T S

Mama Melrose's
Ristorante Italiano

O F     A M E R I C A

## ATTRACTIONS

1 **American Idol Experience**

2 **Beauty and the Beast —
Live on Stage!**

3 **Disney's Block Party
Bash** (step-off)

4 **Fantasmic!**

5 **The Great Movie Ride**

6 **High School Musical 3:
Senior Year — Right
Here! Right Now!**

7 **"Honey, I Shrunk the
Kids" playground**

8 **Indiana Jones Epic Stunt
Spectacular!**

9 **Jim Henson's
MuppetVision 3-D**

10 **Journey into Narnia:
Prince Caspian**

11 **Lights, Motors, Action!
Extreme Stunt Show**

12 **The Magic of Disney
Animation**

13 **Playhouse Disney —
Live on Stage!**

14 **Rock 'n' Roller Coaster
Starring Aerosmith**

15 **Sounds Dangerous**

16 **Star Tours**

17 **Streets of America
New York Street**

18 **Studio Backlot Tour**

19 **Toy Story Mania!**

20 **The Twilight Zone Tower
of Terror**

21 **Voyage of Little Mermaid**

22 **Walt Disney: One Man's
Dream**

# Attractions at a glance

## EXHIBITS

**10** Journey Into Narnia: Prince Caspian ★ 15 min. Avg wait 15 min. Violent video. Mickey Ave. Glorified movie trailer. Some props.

**12** The Magic of Disney Animation ★★★★ ✔ Allow 45 min. Avg wait 15 min. Animation Courtyard. *AuDe* Short film, computer games, character meet-and-greet, exhibits, drawing lesson.

**17** New York Street ★ Unlimited; allow 15 min. No wait. Streets of America. Movie-set-style facades replicate New York City.

**22** Walt Disney: One Man's Dream ★★★ ✔ Allow 35 min. No wait. Mickey Ave. *AuDe* Walt Disney, Disney Co. memorabilia; short biographical film.

## PLAYGROUND

**7** 'Honey, I Shrunk the Kids' Movie Set Adventure ★★★ Unlimited; allow 15–30 min. No wait. Streets of America. Soft-floored play area has tunnels, oversized props.

## RIDES

**5** The Great Movie Ride ★★★★ ✔ 22 min. Avg wait 30 min. "Alien" creature moves toward you. Hollywood Blvd. Indoor tram tours classic film scenes.

**14** Rock 'n' Roller Coaster Starring Aerosmith ★★★★★ ✔ 1 min 22 sec. Avg wait 70 min. Height restriction 48 in. Very fast start. Sunset Blvd. *FastPass* Dark roller coaster loops, corkscrews, blares rock tunes.

**16** Star Tours ★★★ 7 min. Avg wait 25 min. Height restriction 40 in. Can cause motion sickness. Echo Lake. *FastPass* Wacky adventure aboard "Star Wars" motion simulator.

**19** Toy Story Mania! ★★★★★ ✔ 7 min. Avg wait 90 min. Pixar Place. *FastPass* Ride-through series of 3-D video games.

**20** The Twilight Zone Tower of Terror ★★★★★ ✔ 4 min. Avg wait 50 min. Height restriction 40 in. Sudden, swift drops, lifts in dark; creepy atmosphere. Sunset Blvd. *FastPass* Out-of-control elevator falls 13 stories.

## SOUND-EFFECTS PRESENTATION

**15** Sounds Dangerous ★ 12 min. Avg wait 7 min. Some scary sounds. Echo Lake. Dark sound-effects show uses headphones.

## SPECIAL EFFECTS TOUR

**18** Studio Backlot Tour ★★ 30–40 min. Avg wait 20 min. Water demo uses fire; canyon has disasters. Streets of America. Backlot-themed walking/ tram tour includes a stop in effects-filled Catastrophe Canyon.

## STREET PARTY

**3** Disney's Block Party Bash ★★★★★ ✔ 22 min. Hollywood Blvd, Echo Lake. Classic Pixar characters star in interactive show with dancers, acrobats.

## THEATRICAL SHOWS

**1** The American Idol Experience ★★★★ ✔ 20–25 min. Finale 45 min. Echo Lake. Talent contest stars amateur singers.

**2** Beauty and the Beast—Live on Stage ★★★★★ ✔ 25 min. Gaston stabs the Beast. Sunset Blvd. *AuDe* Musical tale old as time.

**4** Fantasmic! ★★★★ 25 min. Arrive 90 min early. Loud noises, bright flashes, fire, villains. Sunset Blvd. Evening outdoor extravaganza has lasers, dancing fountains, water screens, fireworks.

**6** High School Musical 3: Senior Year—Right Here! Right Now! ★★★ 20 min. In front of Sorcerer's Hat, Hollywood Blvd. Cast of 14 singers and dancers perform "High School Musical" routines. Children join in during select numbers.

**8** Indiana Jones Epic Stunt Spectacular! ★★★★ 30 min. Avg wait 10 min. Echo Lake. *FastPass* *AuDe* Performers re-enact scenes from 1981's "Raiders of the Lost Ark."

**11** Lights, Motors, Action! Extreme Stunt Show ★★★ 33 min. Avg wait 20 min. Streets of America. *FastPass* Outdoor show imagines action-movie chase scenes with jumping cars, motorcycles.

**13** Playhouse Disney—Live on Stage! ★★★★★ 22 min. Avg wait 20 min. Animation Courtyard. Preschooler puppet show.

**21** Voyage of the Little Mermaid ★★★★ 17 min. Avg wait 30 min. Ursula makes some toddlers cry. Animation Courtyard. *FastPass* Musical stage show tells Ariel's story with puppets, live singer, effects.

## 3-D MOVIE

**9** Jim Henson's MuppetVision 3-D ★★★★ ✔ 25 min. Avg wait 15 min. Streets of America. *AuDe* Muppet cast. Fun, very detailed queue.

**The Tune-In Lounge sits adjacent to the 50's Prime Time Cafe**

## Restaurants and food

Disney's Hollywood Studios has four table-service restaurants, one buffet and three indoor fast-food spots. Make **reservations** (available 180 days in advance; 190 days for Disney resort guests) as early as possible at 407-WDW-DINE (407-939-3463) or online at **disneyworld.disney.go.com/dining**. If you will be using the **Disney Dining Plan,** note that the Hollywood Brown Derby (at right) takes two credits.

### TABLE SERVICE

**50's Prime Time Cafe** ★★★★ ✔ *DP* American $$$ L: $11–17, 11a–4p. D: $12–21, 4p–park close. Seats 225, also 14 at bar. Echo Lake. Fried chicken, meatloaf, pot roast—it's all good, but expect trouble if you don't eat your vegetables (or put elbows on the table) at this surreal dining spot. Formica tables, sparkly vinyl chairs and period knickknacks re-create 1950s dinettes as your server plays the role of your fussy mom, aunt or uncle. Ask for a TV

table and you'll get a black-and-white set playing food-related vintage sitcom clips. Desserts include yummy s'mores and PB&J milkshakes. Adjacent Tune-In Lounge offers mixed drinks and the full restaurant menu.

**The Hollywood Brown Derby** ★★★★★ ✔ *DP2 Disney Signature* American $$$$ L: $15–32, 11:30a–2:50p. D: $22–36, 3:30p–park close. Seats 224. Hollywood Blvd. A sincere homage to the Tinseltown landmark, the Derby brings back the heyday of Old Hollywood. It is modeled from the 1929 second location of the famous restaurant, a legendary dining spot for hundreds of movie stars. Over 1,000 celebrity caricatures line the walls (the black frames hold original art; the gold frames show reproductions), which surround a narrow terrace and sunken dining room. Soft lighting, inlaid-wood tables. A favorite dining destination for Orlando locals. Heart-healthy dishes highlight a menu of meats, noodle bowls, pasta and seafood. Two classic Derby items also appear: the original chopped Cobb salad (tossed at your table) and tart grapefruit cake. California wines. The guestbook holds signatures of visiting celebrities. Another throwback: tableside phone service. Arrange it with the hostess and your child (of any age) will get a call from Goofy. Gawrsh!

**Mama Melrose's Ristorante Italiano**
★★★★ ✔ *DP* California Italian $$$ L: $12–20, Noon–3:30p. D: $12–$22, 3:30p–1 hr before park close. Seats 250. Streets of America. Offering the best value of Studios restaurants, Mama's has good flatbreads, eggplant, meats, pasta, salads and seafood at decent prices. Sauces and soups are made from scratch; smooth desserts are packed with flavor. Decor is that of a converted warehouse. Twinkly white Christmas lights hang from an open ceiling; walls are covered with Californian and Italian pop-culture memorabilia. Wood tables, chairs and floors. Friendly, unpretentious.

**Sci-Fi Dine-In Theater Restaurant** ★★★ *DP* American $$$ L: $12–22, 11a–4p. D: $12–23, 4p–park close. Seats 252. Commissary Lane. It's all about atmosphere at this dark, starlit dining room, which re-creates the look of a 1950s drive-in theater. You sit in a replica of a vintage GM convertible, facing a large screen showing trailers from kitschy sci-fi films such as "Catwomen of the Moon" and "Devil Girl From Mars," News of the Future newsreels, corny intermission bumpers and (non-Disney) space-age cartoons. Sound comes from drive-in speakers; some servers roller skate. Though the menu is varied, the best bet is the basic hamburger and Oreo cookie milkshake. Can be chilly. Ask for a car seat when you make your reservation; otherwise you may end up at a back patio table.

**BUFFET**

**Hollywood & Vine** ★★★★ ✔ *DP* Character buffet $$$$ "Little Einsteins" June, Leo; JoJo, Goliath from "JoJo's Circus." B: $27 (children $15), 8–10:20a. L: A $27 (children $15), 11a–2:25p. ★★ *DP* American buffet $$$$ D: $31 (children $16). 3:30p–30 min before park close. Seats 468. Echo Lake. Sparse crowds at these breakfast and lunch

buffets let you spend more time with characters than at any other Disney meal. Every 20 minutes human hosts lead kids and stars in singing and dancing. Breakfast has Mickey-shaped waffles and a build-your-own burrito station; lunch offers good salads, salmon and spoon bread. Character-free dinner buffet is overpriced.

**INDOOR FAST FOOD**

**ABC Commissary** ✔ *DPQ* Burgers, chicken, fish. L,D: 11a–park close. Seats 562 inside, 16 outside. Commissary Lane. Comfortable carpeted cafe. Cushioned booths, chairs. Thick crowds, slow service at peak periods. Promotional spots for ABC television shows play constantly.

**Backlot Express** *DPQ* Burgers, hot dogs, grilled sandwiches, salads. 11a–8p. Seats 600. Echo Lake. Themed as crafts shop, filled with real down-and-dirty clutter including the Toon Patrol truck and Bennie the Cab stunt car from 1988's "Who Framed Roger Rabbit."

**Toy Story Pizza Planet Arcade** *DPQ* Individual pizzas, salads. 11a–7:30p. Seats 584. Streets of America. Noisy arcade looks nothing like one in 1995's "Toy Story." Tables are upstairs. Open floor plan amplifies racket.

**OUTDOOR FAST FOOD**

**Min and Bill's Dockside Diner** Shakes, pretzels, beer, frozen lemonade. 10a–8p. Seats 140. Looks like a boat. Echo Lake.

**Starring Rolls Cafe** ✔ *DPQ* Pastries, sandwiches, coffee. B: 9–11:30a. L: 11:30a–4p. Seats 60. Uses Brown Derby kitchens. Sunset Blvd.

**Studio Catering Co.** *DPQ* Sandwiches, chili dogs, salads, desserts. 11:30a–7p. Seats 498, mostly in shade. Adjacent outdoor bar. Streets of America.

**Sunset Ranch Market** *DPQ* Food court. Breakfast bagels, burgers, fresh fruit, hot dogs, pizza, salads, sandwiches, turkey legs, hand-dipped ice cream. B: park open–10:30a. L,D: 10:30a–park close. Seats 400. Sunset Blvd.

**NOTABLE SNACK STANDS**

One of the park's best-kept secrets, The Writer's Stop (Echo Lake, next to Sci-Fi Dine-In) re-creates the atmosphere of a small bookstore cafe (once the one in the sitcom "Ellen"), offering baked goods, coffee and frozen drinks. Peevy's Polar Pipeline (Echo Lake, behind Keystone Clothiers) has flavorful frozen drinks.

# Shopping

## ENTRANCE AREA

**Movieland Memorabilia** General merchandise. Half outside turnstiles, half inside.

## ANIMATION COURTYARD

**Animation Gallery** Fine art. Lithographs, oils, porcelain, 2-ft. character figurines, Disney books. At exit to The Magic of Disney Animation.

**Animation Courtyard cart** Playhouse Disney items. Children's wear, toys. Across from Playhouse Disney—Live on Stage.

**In Character** Princess, Tinker Bell costumes. Toys.

**The Studio Store** Children's merchandise. Minnie Mouse costumes, toys.

## ECHO LAKE

**The American Idol Experience stand** "American Idol" merchandise. At show exit.

**Indiana Jones Adventure Outpost** "Indiana Jones" items. Toys, T-shirts. At show exit.

## HOLLYWOOD BOULEVARD

**Adrian & Edith's Head to Toe** Embroidered and monogrammed items. Custom Mickey ears. Name honors Adrian of Gowns by Adrian, who designed the ruby slippers of 1939's "The Wizard of Oz"; and legendary costume designer Edith Head. Facade recalls Chapman Park Market Bldg. in L.A.'s Koreatown. The tiny shop's foyer towers 30 feet.

**Celebrity 5 & 10** Housewares. Art Deco facade recalls J.J. Newberry on actual Hollywood Blvd.

**Cover Story** Photopass shop. Jedi Training Academy photo pickup. The ceiling's film-roll theme recalls Frank Lloyd Wright.

**Crossroads of the World** Sundries. Outdoor kiosk. Replica of Streamline Moderne stand at 1937 Crossroads of the World open-air shopping mall.

**The Darkroom** Photo shop. Photo accessories. Facade is clone of The Darkroom, a 1938 Hollywood photo shop known for camera-like window.

**Keystone Clothiers** Fashion apparel, jewelry. Five facades include replicas of Hollywood's Max Factor Building and Jullian Medical Building.

**L.A. Cinema Storage** Children's wear, toys.

**Mickey's of Hollywood** Main souvenir store. T-shirts, other apparel, toys. Caps, novelty hats. Housewares, books, costume jewelry, pet items, sandals. Facades modeled after 1926 Hollywood Blvd Baine Building, black-marble-and-gilt Security Pacific Bank on Wilshire Blvd. (itself a copy of L.A.'s Richfield Oil Building, with black and gold trim to represent the "Black Gold" of oil industry), L.A. vet clinic ("Pluto's Palace Gifts"), Santa Monica Blvd. Streamline Moderne building ("Disney & Co").

**Sid Cahuenga's One-Of-A-Kind** Show-biz memorabilia. Autographed posters, photos. A tribute to 1930s and 1940s Craftsman bungalows that later became Hollywood tourist shops.

**Sorcerer's Hat shop** Pin central.

## PIXAR PLACE

**Story Dept.** "Toy Story," Toy Story Mania items. Outdoor stand across from Toy Story Mania.

## STREETS OF AMERICA

**AFI Showcase Shop** Show-biz merchandise. At exit to Studio Backlot Tour.

**It's a Wonderful Shop** Christmas items.

**Stage 1 Co. Store** Children's, Muppets items. Housewares, toys. Next to MuppetVision 3-D.

**Studio Prop Shop** Toys. Geared to boys. Across from the "Honey I Shrunk the Kids" playground.

**Tatooine Traders** "Star Wars" merchandise. Star Tours souvenirs. At exit to Star Tours.

**The Writer's Stop** Books. Bestsellers. Coffee shop. Between Sci-Fi Dine-In, Streets of America.

**Youse Guys Moychendise** NYC-themed Disney merchandise. New York Street outdoor stand.

## SUNSET BLVD.

**Legends of Hollywood** Toys. Geared to boys. Streamline Moderne facade, corkscrew tower recall 1938 Academy Theater in Inglewood, Calif.

**Mouse About Town** Fine jewelry, watches. Exterior inspired by the Berman Bldg. on L.A.'s actual Sunset Blvd., which used to be home to talent agencies and a furrier.

**Once Upon a Time / Sunset Club Couture** Fashion apparel, T-shirts. Adjoining shops. Once Upon a Time exterior recalls 1926 Carthay Circle Theatre, which hosted the premiere of "Snow White and the Seven Dwarfs" in 1937.

**Planet Hollywood Super Store** Apparel.

**Rock Around the Shop** Rock 'n' Roller Coaster apparel, toys. At exit to Rock 'n' Roller Coaster.

**Sweet Spells** Candy store. Adjoins Villains in Vogue. Outside facade ("Beverly Sunset") is a replica of New York City's Colony Theatre as it appeared in 1928, when it premiered the first Mickey Mouse sound cartoon, "Steamboat Willie." After being renamed the Broadway Theatre in 1940, it premiered Disney's classic "Fantasia."

**Tower Gifts** Twilight Zone Tower of Terror, "Twilight Zone" items. At exit to Tower of Terror.

▶ **Leo** Little Einsteins plush. 12-inch. Animation Courtyard cart. $16

▼ **Starspeeder 3000** Star Tours toy with lights, sound. Tatooine Traders. $20

Elizabeth Taylor

▲ **Celebrity photos** from Hollywood's Golden Years. 8x10 inches, matted. AFI Showcase Shop. $19.95

◀ **Mr. Potato Head** 9-inch Toy Story Mania barker plush. Story Dept. stand. $13.95

▶ **Park music** Fantasmic soundtrack $18.98. The Lawn Boys (Mulch, Sweat and Shears) $12.95. Various stores.

▼ **The Twilight Zone Tower of Terror Clue** Classic detective game. With Disney characters. Tower Gifts. $40

◀ **Mighty Muggs** vinyl 6-inch Indiana Jones figure. Indiana Jones Adventure Outpost. $16.95

◀ **Rock 'n' Roller Coaster purse** Vinyl with metal studs. Rock Around the Shop. $24.95

▶ **Hollywood Tower Hotel door hanger** The Twilight Zone Tower of Terror. Plastic. Tower Gifts. $4.95

Do Not Disturb

▲ **Mickey Sorcerer's Hat** Lights up. Adult. Mickey's of Hollywood. $36.95

◀ **Kermit the Frog** 20-inch posable plush. Stage 1 Co. Store. $20

**Villains in Vogue** Disney Villain merchandise. Housewares, T-shirts, toys. Adjoins Sweet Spells. Central facade inspired by former Pasadena Winter Garden ice skating rink. Righthand facade recalls 35er bar in Pasadena's Old Town.

## Character locations

**Annie, June, Leo, Quincy** Stars of TV series "Little Einsteins" Animation Courtyard; June, Leo also at ✳ Play 'N Dine character meals, Echo Lake.

**Belle** Star of 1991's "Beauty and the Beast" Sorcerer's Hat, Hollywood Blvd.

**Chip 'n Dale** 1940s–50s cartoon chipmunks Sorcerer's Hat, Hollywood Blvd.

**Daisy Duck** Donald Duck's girlfriend Sorcerer's Hat, Hollywood Blvd.

**Donald Duck** Foul-tempered fowl Sorcerer's Hat, Hollywood Blvd.

**Friar Tuck, Little John** Merry men in 1973's "Robin Hood" Sorcerer's Hat, Hollywood Blvd.

**Geppetto** Woodcarver in 1940's "Pinocchio" Sorcerer's Hat, Hollywood Blvd.

**Green Army Men** From "Toy Story" films Pixar Place, roaming street.

**Goofy** Good-natured, dim-witted dog-man Sorcerer's Hat, Hollywood Blvd.

**Handy Manny** Star of TV series "Handy Manny" Animation Courtyard.

**Mr. and Mrs. Incredible, Frozone** Superheroes from 2004's "The Incredibles" ✳ The Magic of Disney Animation, Animation Courtyard.

**Jojo, Goliath** Girl clown, pet lion from "JoJo's Circus" Animation Courtyard; also at ✳ Play 'N Dine character meals, Echo Lake.

**Kim Possible, Ron Stoppable** Teenage secret agent, best friend in TV series "Kim Possible" New York Street, Streets of America.

**Lightning McQueen, 'Mater** NASCAR-like race car, tow truck in 2006 movie "Cars" Luigi's Garage, Streets of America.

**Lilo, Stitch** Stars of 2002's "Lilo & Stitch" Sorcerer's Hat, Hollywood Blvd.

**Luxo Jr.** Desk-lamp mascot of Pixar Animation Studios Across from Toy Story Mania, Pixar Place.

**Mary Poppins, Penguins** From 1964's "Mary Poppins" Sorcerer's Hat, Hollywood Blvd.

**Mickey, Minnie Mouse** Optimistic everyman, girlfriend Sorcerer's Hat, Hollywood Blvd. Mickey

**Top: The Power Rangers appear near Lights Motors Action. Above: Stars of Disney's latest animated film (at press time, "Up") appear at The Magic of Disney Animation.**

✳ Air-conditioned meeting area.

Appearance times vary. For weekly updated schedules of Walt Disney World characters and street performers log on to pages.prodigy.net/stevesoares.

also at ❊ The Magic of Disney Animation, Animation Courtyard (as Sorcerer's Apprentice).

**Mike, Sulley** Stars of 2001's "Monsters, Inc" Streets of America, at exit to Backlot Tour.

**Pinocchio** Star of 1940's "Pinocchio" Sorcerer's Hat, Hollywood Blvd.

**Pluto** Mickey's pet Sorcerer's Hat, Hollywood Blvd.

**Pocahontas, Gov. Ratcliffe** Star, corrupt Jamestown leader (and main villain) from 1995's "Pocahontas" Sorcerer's Hat, Hollywood Blvd.

**Power Rangers** From various TV series In front of Lights, Motors, Action; Streets of America.

**Prince Caspian** Star of 2008's "The Chronicles of Narnia: Prince Caspian" ❊ Journey Into Narnia: Prince Caspian, Mickey Ave.

**Queen of Hearts, Tweedledee, Tweedledum** Foul-tempered monarch, plump twin brothers in 1951's "Alice in Wonderland" Sorcerer's Hat, Hollywood Blvd.

**Snow White, Evil Queen** Star, stepmother from 1937's "Snow White and the Seven Dwarfs" Sorcerer's Hat, Hollywood Blvd.

**Woody, Buzz Lightyear** "Toy Story" stars ❊ Woody's Picture Shootin' Corral, Pixar Place.

# Street performers

### IMPROVISATIONAL TROUPE

**Citizens of Hollywood** 30 min. Various spots on Hollywood Blvd. and Sunset Blvd. Showtimes at Guest Relations. Residents of a 1940s Tinseltown— directors, divas, has-beens, wanna-bes, public works employees—roam the park's Old Hollywood section. Guest-participation skits include a dating game, celebrity spelling bee.

### MUSICAL REVUE

**High School Musical 3: Right Here! Right Now!** 20 min. In front of Sorcerer's Hat, Hollywood Blvd. Fourteen lively singers, dancers perform choreographed "High School Musical" routines. Children join in for select numbers.

### LIGHTSABER TRAINING

**Jedi Training Academy** 20 min. Left of Star Tours, Streets of America. Kids learn lightsaber techniques, duel Darth Vader. Arrive 15 min. early to give your child good chance at participating.

### MUSICIANS

**Mulch, Sweat and Shears** 25 min. Streets of America. Humorous landscape-crew-turned-rock-band invites audience participation.

Top: Script girl Paige Turner of the Citizens of Hollywood improvisational troupe. Above: A cheerleader in the street show "High School Musical 3: Right Here! Right Now!"

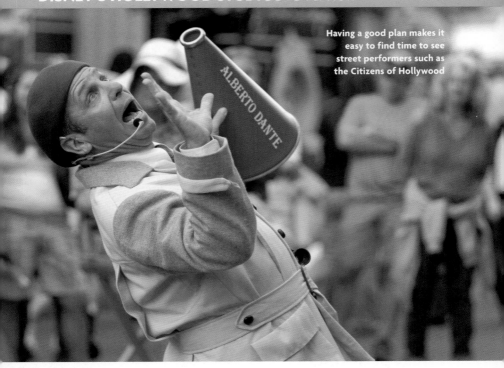

Having a good plan makes it easy to find time to see street performers such as the Citizens of Hollywood

# Planning Your Day

**With its many scheduled shows** and the most popular ride in all of Walt Disney World, it's important to have a good plan when you visit Disney's Hollywood Studios. The key to a great day is simple: Be through the turnstiles before 9 a.m., and get Fastpasses for the Toy Story Mania attraction within the first few minutes. Follow that rule and your whole day will fall into place.

## 1. Choose a day to go

Before deciding what day to visit Hollywood Studios, check what time the park closes on each day of your vacation. Choose a day with late hours, one that includes a performance of Fantasmic, a laser and fireworks spectacle. Performances are usually on Tuesday, Thursday, Friday and

Sunday. Operating hours are posted six months early at the "Calendar" link at **disneyworld.disney.go.com/parks/ hollywood-studios.**

▶ **'Extra Magic Hours'** The park usually opens an hour early on Wednesdays or Saturdays for guests staying at Disney resorts, and stays open late for these guests on Sundays or Mondays.

## 2. Decide what to do

Hollywood Studios has two of the most thrilling rides in Walt Disney World: The Twilight Zone Tower of Terror and Rock 'n' Roller Coaster Starring Aerosmith. Other quality attractions include Toy Story Mania, The American Idol Experience and, for preschoolers, Playhouse Disney—Live on Stage. You'll find an "Attractions At a Glance" summary of everything there is to do earlier in this chapter; further back are detailed descriptions. If you are traveling with children, give them this book and have them point out what they would like to see.

The small size of the park makes it relatively easy for guests in wheelchairs or ECVs to get around. Hearing-impaired guests can take advantage of sign-language interpreted performances on Sundays and Wednesdays: Block Party Bash (3 p.m.), Beauty and the Beast—Live on Stage (12:45 p.m.), Indiana Jones Epic Stunt Spectacular (4:15 p.m.), the High School Musical 3 street show (11 a.m.) and The American Idol Experience (6 p.m.).

## 3. Family matters

Hollywood Studios offers a lot for boys, with the most stunt shows and thrill rides of any Disney park. It also has the best attraction for preschoolers: Playhouse Disney—Live on Stage.

▶ **Height restrictions** exist at Rock 'n' Roller Coaster Starring Aerosmith (48 in), Star Tours (40 in) and Twilight Zone Tower of Terror (40 in).

▶ **Fear factors** All rides with height restrictions (see above) also have scary elements. Others that might frighten young children include Fantasmic (loud noises, bright flashes, fire, villains); Great Movie Ride ("Alien" creature moves toward you); Journey Into Narnia: Prince Caspian (violent movie clips); Voyage of the Little Mermaid (giant villain Ursula threatens); Studio Backlot Tour (a canyon scene simulates disasters).

▶ **Kids meals** Every restaurant offers a children's menu. Playhouse Disney characters appear at Hollywood & Vine for breakfast and lunch. Dining spots with kid-friendly extras include the 50's Prime Time Cafe; its desserts include s'mores and PB&J milk shakes.

▶ **Baby care** A Baby Care Center is at the park entrance, next to Guest Relations. It provides changing rooms, nursing areas, a microwave and a playroom. Diapers, formula, pacifiers

## PARK RESOURCES

**ATMs** Outside gate on right beside Package Pickup window; inside Toy Story Pizza Planet Arcade.

**First Aid center** Minor emergencies. Registered nurses. Next to Guest Relations at park entrance.

**Guest Relations** General questions, dining reservations, currency exchange. Maps, Times Guides for all WDW parks. Stores items found in park that day. Multilingual. Walk-up window outside gate, office inside.

**Lockers** $7 a day plus $5 deposit. Rent at Crossroads of the World kiosk, entrance plaza. Lockers are next to Oscar's Super Service.

**Mobile app** (Verizon) $10, at m.disneyworld.com. "Mobile Magic" covers all WDW theme parks.

**Package pickup** Up to 3 hours before you leave, anything you buy in the park can be sent to the front of the park free of charge. Packages can be delivered the next day to your Disney hotel or shipped to your home. Entrance plaza.

**Parking** $14 per day. Free for Disney resort guests, annual passholders.

**Strollers** Singles $15/day, $13/day length of stay. Doubles $31, $27. Oscar's Super Service, inside gate.

**Tip Board** Shows wait times for most attractions. Hollywood Blvd. at Sunset Blvd.

**Transportation** Boats, walkways lead to Epcot, BoardWalk, Yacht and Beach Club, Swan and Dolphin resorts. Buses to all other Disney resorts, Animal Kingdom, Blizzard Beach, Epcot and Wide World of Sports, Magic Kingdom (via TTC). No direct service to Downtown Disney, Typhoon Lagoon.

**Wheelchairs, Scooters** Wheelchairs $12/day, $10/day length of stay. Electric Convenience Vehicles (4-wheeled scooters) $50/day, $20 deposit. Oscar's Super Service, entrance plaza.

# HOUR-BY-HOUR WAIT TIMES

This table shows the average **wait time** (in min) for each ride or show in Disney's Hollywood Studios that has one. The Honey I Shrunk the Kids Playground, Jim Henson's MuppetVision 3-D, Sounds Dangerous and Walt Disney: One Man's Dream have no waits. *Live shows are shown with the early arrival time needed to get a good seat.

| ATTRACTION | 9A | 10A | 11A | Noon | 1P | 2P | 3P | 4P | 5P | 6P | 7P | 8P | 9P |
|---|---|---|---|---|---|---|---|---|---|---|---|---|---|
| American Idol* | N/A | N/A | 20 | 20 | 20 | 20 | 20 | 20 | 20 | 20 | 20 | N/A | N/A |
| Beauty and Beast* | N/A | 20 | 20 | 20 | 20 | 20 | 20 | 20 | 20 | N/A | N/A | N/A | N/A |
| Great Movie Ride | 0 | 20 | 35 | 35 | 35 | 40 | 35 | 30 | 35 | 40 | 30 | 20 | 30 |
| Indiana Jones* | N/A | 10 | 10 | 10 | 10 | 10 | 10 | 10 | 10 | 10 | 10 | N/A | N/A |
| Journey into Narnia | 0 | 15 | 15 | 15 | 15 | 15 | 15 | 15 | 15 | 15 | 15 | 15 | 15 |
| Lights Motors Action* | N/A | 20 | 20 | 20 | 20 | 20 | 20 | 20 | 20 | 20 | 20 | N/A | N/A |
| Little Mermaid | 0 | 20 | 20 | 20 | 20 | 30 | 30 | 30 | 20 | 10 | 30 | 10 | 10 |
| Magic of Animation | CLSD | 10 | 10 | 15 | 15 | 20 | 20 | 20 | 20 | 0 | 0 | 0 | 0 |
| Playhouse Disney* | N/A | 20 | 20 | 20 | 20 | 20 | 20 | 20 | 20 | N/A | N/A | N/A | N/A |
| R'n'R Coaster | 0 | 50 | 55 | 70 | 80 | 80 | 70 | 80 | 65 | 80 | 75 | 85 | 85 |
| Star Tours | 0 | 10 | 35 | 35 | 40 | 40 | 45 | 35 | 20 | 25 | 15 | 25 | 20 |
| Studio Backlot Tour | CLSD | 15 | 10 | 20 | 20 | 25 | 35 | 20 | 15 | CLSD | CLSD | CLSD | CLSD |
| Tower of Terror | 0 | 50 | 55 | 55 | 50 | 55 | 40 | 50 | 65 | 30 | 55 | 70 | 60 |
| Toy Story Mania | 35 | 65 | 55 | 70 | 85 | 130 | 135 | 130 | 90 | 110 | 100 | 80 | 70 |

Data based on surveys taken on random days during the summers of 2008 and 2009.

and over-the-counter medications are available for purchase. Moms can nurse their babies anywhere; good spots include corner seats at the ABC Commissary and Backlot Express and, if it happens to be open, the dark theater of Sounds Dangerous.

▶ **Lost children** Report them to Guest Relations or any cast member.

## A MAGICAL DAY

## 4. Decide where to eat

Flip back a few pages to find listings of every Hollywood Studios restaurant.

## 5. Make a plan

As you create your plan, note the average wait times and typical Fastpass return times for the rides and shows

| | |
|---|---|
| **8:30a** | Arrive at the park. As you wait for the gates to open (typically at 8:50 a.m.), pick up a Times Guide from the Guest Relations window at your left. |
| **9:00a** | Get Fastpasses for Toy Story Mania. |
| **9:05a** | Ride Toy Story Mania. |
| **9:35a** | Ride The Great Movie Ride. |
| **10:05a** | Go through the Animation Gallery shop to enter The Magic of Disney Animation to meet Mickey Mouse. Look at the exhibits. |

| | |
|---|---|
| **10:30a** | Draw a Disney character at the Animation Academy in The Magic of Disney Animation. |
| **11:00a** | Walk down Sunset Blvd. to get Rock 'n' Roller Coaster Fastpasses. |
| **11:25a** | Use your Fastpasses to ride Toy Story Mania a second time. |
| **Noon** | Lunch at the Hollywood Brown Derby. Check your Times Guide for Indiana Jones and Beauty and the Beast show times, then fine-tune the following schedule: |

# FASTPASS RETURN TIMES

Seven attractions at Disney's Hollywood Studios offer Disney's Fastpass system, a free service which reserves a time for you to return later in the day without standing in the regular line. The table below shows the average return times for Fastpasses dispensed at each participating Studios attraction for each hour of the park day. Note that an entire day's worth of Fastpasses for Toy Story Mania typically runs out by noon.

| ATTRACTION | 9A | 10A | 11A | Noon | 1P | 2P | 3P | 4P | 5P | 6P | 7P | 8P | 9P |
|---|---|---|---|---|---|---|---|---|---|---|---|---|---|
| Indiana Jones | * | * | * | * | * | * | * | * | * | * | N/A | N/A | N/A |
| Lights Motors Action | * | * | * | * | * | * | * | * | * | * | N/A | N/A | N/A |
| Little Mermaid | 10:05 | 11:05 | 12:05 | 1:15 | 2:15 | 3:50 | 4:50 | 6:15 | 7:05 | 8:10 | 8:50 | OUT | OUT |
| R'n'R Coaster | 10:30 | 12:30 | 2:20 | 4:30 | 6:20 | 8:10 | OUT | OUT | OUT | OUT | OUT | OUT | OUT |
| Star Tours | 10:00 | 11:00 | 12:00 | 1:00 | 1:45 | 2:50 | 3:55 | 5:00 | 5:50 | 6:25 | 7:25 | OUT | OUT |
| Tower of Terror | 10:15 | 11:55 | 12:50 | 2:20 | 3:30 | 5:45 | 7:30 | OUT | OUT | OUT | OUT | OUT | OUT |
| Toy Story Mania | 10:45 | 4:05 | 7:30 | OUT | OUT | OUT | OUT | OUT | OUT | OUT | OUT | OUT | OUT |

*During our survey period, Fastpasses for the Indiana Jones Stunt Spectacular and Lights Motors Action were always good for the next show. Data based on surveys taken on random days during the summers of 2008 and 2009.

you want to see. Assume you need to arrive 15 minutes early for a table-service reservation. Live entertainment and character-greeting schedules are online at **pages.prodigy.net/stevesoares**. For a road-tested ready-made plan, see our "A Magical Day" schedule below.

# 6. Weather issues

With its small size and focus on theatrical shows and indoor attractions, the Studios is easy to manage when it's hot or raining. At the Animation Courtyard, The Magic of Disney Animation is easy to duck into (just enter through the exit, at the Animation Gallery shop); you can spend as long as you like inside. Likewise, Walt Disney: One Man's Dream is a self-guided indoor tour, again with no time limit. As you move between attractions, a good way to stay out of the weather is to walk through stores instead of on streets and walkways. The Indiana Jones and Lights, Motors, Action stunt shows, the Studio Backlot Tour and "Honey I Shrunk the Kids" playground close due to rain, and the Block Party Bash street party can get cancelled. Fantasmic is cancelled when lightning is in the area.

| | | | |
|---|---|---|---|
| **1:15p** | See MuppetVision 3-D. | | Amphitheater for the 10 p.m. Fantasmic show (if scheduled). |
| **1:55p** | See the Indiana Jones stunt show. | | |
| **2:35p** | Stand along Hollywood Blvd. to see the Block Party Bash at 3 p.m. | **Bonus** | Something on our list you don't want to do? See a performance of Citizens of Hollywood instead (times are at Guest Relations). Those with young children may want to substitute Playhouse Disney—Live on Stage. Those with fans of the "High School Musical" movies should try to work in that street show. |
| **3:35p** | Arrive at Beauty and the Beast—Live on Stage; show is at 4 p.m. | | |
| **4:30p** | Ride Twilight Zone Tower of Terror. | | |
| **6:15p** | Arrive for the American Idol Experience finale show at 7 p.m. | | |
| **7:50p** | Dinner at '50s Prime Time Cafe. Share s'mores for dessert. | | |
| **9:00p** | Arrive at the Hollywood Hills | | |

**Off to see the Wizard,** Dorothy and her pals chat in a Great Movie Ride diorama

# The Great Movie Ride

★★★★ ✓ 22 min. Capacity: 560. Indoor, air-conditioned queue. Fear factor: Intense for preschoolers. The "Alien" creature moves toward you from the ceiling and then appears suddenly out of the right wall. The Wicked Witch looks real. Access: ECV users must transfer. Assistive listening, handheld captioning. Debuted: 1989.

The Studio's original showcase attraction creates a dreamlike tribute to the Golden Age of Hollywood. A guided indoor tram travels through 16 classic film scenes, each one brought to life on a soundstage set that features Audio-Animatronics characters.

You pass a robotic Gene Kelly "Singin' in the Rain" (1952) and "Public Enemy" James Cagney (1931), get stuck in gangster and Old West shootouts, encounter a stalking "Alien" (1979) with Sigourney Weaver on the Nostromo and travel to Munchkinland to confront the Wicked Witch of the West from "The Wizard of Oz" (1939). Other sets portray the Fountain of Beauty from "Footlight Parade" (1933), the jungle of "Tarzan and His Mate" (1934), the airport finale of "Casablanca" (1942), the rooftops of "Mary Poppins" (1964) and the Well of Souls of "Raiders of the Lost Ark" (1981). Robotic characters also depict Clint Eastwood and John Wayne. The best character is the witch, one of Disney's most realistic robots. The green-skinned villain flexes her backbone, swivels her hips and points her finger.

The ride showcases nearly every movie genre. Comedy comes from the tram operator, a self-absorbed projectionist who introduces herself by proclaiming "I love movies!" An homage to Buster Keaton's character in the 1923 comedy "Sherlock Jr.," she takes you into some of her favorite films. Soon a second performer (a gangster or Old West outlaw) steps out of a set and hijacks your vehicle. The ride concludes in a theater, with a three-minute montage of film clips.

For the best experience, ask a cast member to let you sit in the first seats in either the first or second row. Since you'll be next to the guide her spiel will make more sense, as you'll always be viewing the same scene. You'll also get an up-close view of the hijacker, who may direct a few lines your way.

The building's entrance facade and lobby are full-size re-creations of Grauman's Chinese Theatre, a 1927 Hollywood landmark.

| Average Wait | |
|---|---|
| 9am | 0 min |
| 10am | 20 |
| 11am | 35 |
| Noon | 35 |
| 1pm | 35 |
| 2pm | 40 |
| 3pm | 35 |
| 4pm | 30 |
| 5pm | 35 |
| 6pm | 40 |
| 7pm | 30 |
| 8pm | 20 |
| 9pm | 30 |

▶ Ask to sit up front. You can see better, and the narration will be in sync with the scenes.

Disney imagineers look back on their Great Movie Ride work with fondness. "It's really dear to my heart," says producer Eric Jacobson, "not only because of the effects, but also because of all the work we did. Getting the rights to those films was not a simple task."

### Celebrity handprints

More than 100 celebrities have placed their hands and feet into the theater's concrete courtyard. Front and center is the work of Warren Beatty, who stopped by as part of the premiere of the 1990 movie "Dick Tracy," held at Downtown Disney. Nearby are the marks of Bob Hope. Jim Henson brought Kermit; Dustin Hoffman and Robin Williams brought their kids. Others on hand: George Burns, Tony Curtis and George Lucas.

Most of the prints are from the early 1990s, made during the park's old "Star of the Day" events. All are authentic except the impressions of Judy Garland, which are replicas of those at the original theater.

**Fun finds ❶** During the 1995 handprint ceremony for Charlton Heston, a photographer yelled "Charlton!" just as the then-72-year-old star was drawing the "R" in his first name, causing him to look up. When Heston got back to work, he accidentally skipped the "L" in his name, creating a signature that reads "Charton" Heston. ❷ Window displays include photos from the actual Chinese Theatre premieres of "Mary Poppins" and "The Jungle Book." ❸ Lobby displays include Julie Andrews' "Mary Poppins" carousel horse, which also appears in a queue-line trailer. ❹ The actual Chinese Theatre is shown in the "Singin' in the Rain" trailer. ❺ The boarding area is lined with real soundstage equipment. ❻ Its lights, including those on a mural and marquee, synchronize to the ride's opening music. ❼ As you enter Gangster Alley, an argument takes place in a flat above Patrick J. Ryan's Bar. ❽ In the Western town, a Sheriff's Office sign swings when hit by an illusionary bullet. ❾ Along the Nostromo's left floor, inside jokes on the first video screen include the ride's "estimated time till next special effects failure" and ❿ a "welcome to all aliens visiting from the Glendale galaxy" (Glendale, Calif., is home to Walt Disney Imagineering). ⓫ The third video screen lists an astronaut as "still programming the witch." ⓬ Once it captures its victim, the eyes of the Anubis statue glow red. ⓭ Along the left wall of the skeleton room, a snake squirms out of a sarcophagus eye and ⓮ a pharaoh pets a mummified cat. ⓯ Just as in the movie, a Munchkin pops out of a yellow-brick-road manhole at the beginning of the song "Ding Dong the Witch is Dead." ⓰ After the Wicked Witch warns "Just try to stay out of my way, just try," a Munchkin hiding behind her peeks out for a moment.

**Fun facts ❶** Replicas of statues at the real Chinese Theatre (themselves replicas of real Forbidden City statues), two Fu Dogs guard the entrance doors. Fu Dogs were used in early China to ward off evil spirits. ❷ Filling 95,000 square feet, the ride has more than 60 Audio-Animatronics characters. ❸ The Cagney robot wears one of the star's actual tuxedos, donated by his family. ❹ Gangster Alley contains references to many classic films. Ryan's Bar, J.L. Altmeyer & Sons Novelty Manufacturing, the Red Oaks Social Club and Western Chemical Co. are settings in "The Public Enemy." The signs "Dead End" and "Society for Juvenile Delinquents" refer to the 1937 Bogart film "Dead End." ❺ In the Western town, a "Ransom Stoddard" placard alludes to the attorney Jimmy Stewart played in 1962's "The Man Who Shot Liberty Valence." ❻ Historical references include a "021-429" license plate on a gangsters' 1931 Chrysler (the Feb. 14, 1929, St. Valentine's Day massacre) and the Western town's Monarch Saloon (Leadville, Colo., home of outlaw gambler Doc Holliday) and Cochise County Courthouse (site of Tombstone, Ariz.'s gunfight at the O.K. Corral). ❼ The "No Help Wanted" and "Sheriff's Office" signs are real movie props from the old MGM backlot. ❽ The attraction was built to portray three "Wizard of Oz" scenes. The "Fantasia" room was to be the tornado (note its sepia-toned funnel). In the final theater, you were to be told to "pay no attention to that man behind the curtain." Copyright snags forced the cutback. ❾ Not all of Disney's handprints are on display. Among those backstage: Johnny Depp's.

**Hidden Mickeys ❶** As a silhouetted profile in the second-story windows of the Western Chemical Co. building, on your left as you enter Gangster Alley. ❷ Mickey's tail and one of his shoes appear on a poster under the one for "The Public Enemy" on the alley's left wall. ❸ As a left-facing, light-gray profile on a piece of broken dark-gray stone below the Ark of the Covenant in the Well of Souls. ❹ A full-figure Mickey pharoah appears on the Well's left wall, just past the second statue of Anubis. An Egyptian Donald Duck is serving him some cheese.

**Other hidden characters ❶** Minnie Mouse hides in the boarding-area mural. Facing left, her profile is just above and to the right of a central tile roof, tucked under palm fronds. ❷ On the left wall of the Well of Souls, a center carving two blocks up from the floor shows a pharaoh holding "Star Wars" character R2-D2 while C-3PO repairs him with a screwdriver. (As many "Raiders" fans know, the carving appears on the same wall in the movie).

▶ Want the outlaw hijacker? Tell the cast member at the entrance to the boarding area.

**Three contestants** sing in preliminary American Idol Experience shows. A daily finale has seven.

# The American Idol Experience

★★★★ ✔ 20–25 min, finale 45 min. Showtimes at 11a, Noon, 1p, 2p, 4p, 5p, 6p. Finale 7p. Capacity: 1040. Covered outdoor queue. Fear factor: None. Access: Guests may remain in wheelchairs, ECVs. Assistive listening. Debuted: 2009.

The famous pause is there: "This… is the American Idol Experience!" So is the music. So is Ryan Seacrest, at least on video. Close your eyes and you might think you're in the audience at the popular television program.

You don't have to be a fan of "American Idol" to enjoy this live amateur talent show. Music fans will like it, as will fans of the spontaneous. Anything can happen: Singers forget lyrics, sing off key, awkwardly try to add in dance moves. Sometimes someone belts out a performance that inspires cheers and standing ovations from the audience. Whatever happens, it's compelling.

Each day, seven competitions lead to a championship finale, which is almost

| Average Wait | |
|---|---|
| 9am | closed |
| 10am | closed |
| 11am | 20 min |
| Noon | 20 |
| 1pm | 20 |
| 2pm | 20 |
| 3pm | 20 |
| 4pm | 20 |
| 5pm | 20 |
| 6pm | 20 |
| 7pm | 20 |
| 8pm | closed |
| 9pm | closed |

always the best show of the day. Almost twice as long, it pits the seven earlier winners against each other. The finale is held nightly at 7 p.m.

Produced in the park's former ABC Theater, the show lets audience members select its winners. As selected park guests perform shortened versions of hit songs on an "American Idol"-like stage, the crowd votes for its favorite using electronic keypads on the side of each seat.

Much like the television series, the show features an entertaining host and a three-judge panel that critiques each singer. The judges, all "music industry insiders" (i.e. Disney actors) with distinct personalities, critique and give advice to each singer. The cynical judge can be almost as mean as Simon Cowell, which can be jarring. We've seen teenage contestants tear up, their parents sitting in the audience in shock.

Video montages highlight past "American Idol" winners and contestants.

Singers compete for a golden "Dream Ticket," which awards a front-of-the-line spot at a regional "American Idol" audition.

Anyone 14 or older can try out. Daily auditions are held from 9 a.m. to 2 p.m. Aspiring contestants first sing an a cappella song in front of a backstage screener, in an audi-

▶ For details on auditioning for The American Idol Experience log onto disneyworld.com

**Clockwise from above:** American Idol Experience contestant Tiffany Lovett. Judges react to a performance. The bust of comedian Harvey Korman in the ATAS Hall of Fame Showcase. The Sounds Dangerous sound-effects show is rarely open. American Idol Experience finale winner Meta Summer.

tion room that resembles its television counterpart. Those making the cut to Round Two audition again using their choice of over a hundred pre-selected tunes. Three contestants are chosen for each of seven preliminary shows. Before they go onstage, each meets with a professional coach and hair and makeup artists.

### ATAS Hall of Fame Showcase

Located in front of the American Idol theater, this small plaza has 15 bronze busts of television stars, all members of the Academy of Television Arts and Sciences Hall of Fame. Included are Lucille Ball, Andy Griffith and Mary Tyler Moore. Plaques on a back wall list all the inductees for each year. The plaza draws little attention, even from Disney. The company stopped adding busts and plaques in 1996.

**Hidden Mickeys ①** As a dark splotch on the right side of the onstage arch (hidden among other splotches) and **②** as a similar splotch on the left.

# Sounds Dangerous

★ 12 min. Capacity: 240. No wait. Outdoor covered queue. Fear factor: Some scary sounds. Access: Guests may stay in wheelchairs, ECVs. Assistive listening. Debuted: 1999. Often closed.

Love Drew Carey? Then you might enjoy this sound-effects show. Seated in a dark theater, you're part of a test audience for a TV pilot, which stars Carey as a klutzy television investigator. When he shorts out his spy cam, the theater goes completely dark. You're at the mercy of your imagination when he opens a jar of bees, gets a shave and bumps an elephant. With few visuals, the show's slapstick comedy often falls flat.

Better is the postshow, **SoundWorks,** which lets you dub your voice to cartoon and movie stars and create old-fashioned sound effects with help from the late sound wiz Jimmy MacDonald. Walls display gadgets he used for 20 films. You can enter SoundWorks from the Sounds Dangerous exit.

▶ The park's least popular attraction, Sounds Dangerous operates only during peak periods.

**Indiana Jones** punches a sword-wielding assassin in the Indiana Jones Epic Stunt Spectacular

# Indiana Jones Epic Stunt Spectacular

★★★★ 30 min. Capacity: 2,000. *FastPass* Covered outdoor theater. Fear factor: None unless kids think the action is real. Closed during rain. Access: Guests may remain in wheelchairs, ECVs. Assistive listening; handheld captioning. *AuDe* Debuted: 1989, revised 2000.

Seventeen live performers re-create physical stunts from 1981's "Raiders of the Lost Ark" in this outdoor stage show.

First you relive the opening scene, as an actor portraying Indiana Jones literally drops into a Mayan ruin to pursue a golden idol. Next, Indy and girlfriend Marion take on a village of Cairo villains. Indy fights 'em off with his bullwhip and gun, many folks fall off building facades and Marion makes a death-defying escape out of a flipping, flaming truck.

For the finale, our heroes are at a North African Nazi airfield. When a Flying Wing comes in for fuel, Indy and Marion try again to escape. They fight Nazis in, on and around the spinning plane, fleeing to safety just as leaking fuel sparks a huge explosion.

**Meat, with cheese**

Basically the same since 1989, the show hasn't lost its appeal. Most of its stunts look real, there's always something to watch and there's plenty of humor. Audience volunteers are ridiculed throughout the show, as are some of the cast. Cartoonish sound effects add to the fun. Between scenes you see how sets can be quickly dismantled, how heavy-looking props can be featherlight and see how to fake a punch.

For flavor, Disney pretends the show is a real film shoot. Mock cameramen peer through mock cameras; a pretend director barks out pretend directions. When the "Assistant Director of the Second Unit" decides "We're going to shoot 36 instead of 24 frames per second," his boss declares "I like it!"

The show's creation was overseen by George Lucas. "Raiders of the Lost Ark" stunt coordinator Glenn Randall personally designed the stunts.

The first performance of the day usually has the smallest crowd. The last show is often the best looking, as the darker sky makes the explosions more dramatic.

| Average Wait | |
| --- | --- |
| 9am | n/a |
| 10am | 10 min |
| 11am | 10 |
| Noon | 10 |
| 1pm | 10 |
| 2pm | 10 |
| 3pm | 10 |
| 4pm | 10 |
| 5pm | 10 |
| 6pm | 10 |
| 7pm | 10 |
| 8pm | n/a |
| 9pm | n/a |

▶ Arrive early to sit in the first few rows. You'll get a closer view and feel heat from the fires.

**Clockwise from top left:** A truck flips and explodes in a Cairo street. Indy and Marion escape a Nazi excavation camp. Volunteer extras practice being scared. An ax-wielding statue in a Mayan ruin.

**Fun finds Out front:** ❶ Just to the left of the Fastpass machines, a British archeologist has dug a hole and lowered himself down to the bottom of it. Pull on his rope and he'll become irritated and talk to you ("I say! Stop mucking about up there!").
**Preshow:** ❷ One of the audience volunteers is actually a professional stuntman. Can you spot him first? **Cairo scene:** ❸ Indy says the signature Lucas line "I have a bad feeling about this" during the street scene. ❹ In reality the truck of Marion's kidnappers stops behind its building. A second empty truck finishes the circle. Attached to the building by a pole, it "flips" by rotating over. Though Marion appears to run out of that truck, she actually returns through a small gray crate just to its right.
**Airfield scene:** ❺ The sidecar motorcycle is a duplicate of the one Harrison Ford commandeered in the 1989 movie "Indiana Jones and the Last Crusade." It even has the same front-fender license number: wh38475. ❻ In reality, the Flying Wing mechanic falls through an easily visible trapdoor.
**Left exit area:** ❼ Behind the Outpost gift shop sit three vehicles used in the filming of "Indiana Jones and the Last Crusade," in the scenes where Indy and the Nazis are racing to find the Holy Grail. Just off the sidewalk you'll find the Nazi staff car and truck, as well as the "Steel Beast" tank (its side gun barrel is still "exploded" from when Indy stuffed it with a rock). Each vehicle still displays the symbol of the film's version of the Republic of Hatay.

**1981'S "RAIDERS OF THE LOST ARK"** starts its story in 1936. Archaeology professor Dr. Henry "Indiana" Jones Jr. has just returned from Peru, where he has failed to recover an idol from the Temple of the Chachapoyan Warriors. But when the Army learns that Nazi Germany wants to find the Ark of the Covenant (a casket used by ancient Hebrews to hold the Ten Commandments; legends say its supernatural powers can wipe out entire armies) it sends Indy to find it first. First reuniting with gutsy old girlfriend Marion Ravenwood, Jones soon arrives in Cairo, where Nazis have recruited henchmen to kidnap Marion and steal her medallion, which can reveal the ark's location. As Indy fights off a gang of assassins, Marion knocks one out with a handy frying pan, but soon is taken away in a truck, which explodes. At first Indy thinks Marion is dead, but later finds her captive at an excavation camp where Nazis are about to fly the Ark to Germany on a Flying Wing. While the plane is fueling, the couple takes it over. Marion shoots Nazis from the cockpit while Indy's fight with a mechanic ends when the bad guy is shredded by a propeller. When leaking fuel catches fire, Indy and Marion run to safety just before everything blows up.

▶ To be in the show, jump and scream wildly when the casting director asks for volunteers.

# Star Tours

★ ★ ★ 7 min. Capacity: 240. *FastPass* Indoor, air-conditioned queue. Fear factor: The vehicle's unpredictable sways and dives can cause motion sickness in guests of any age. Access: ECV guests must transfer to wheelchairs. Guest-activated captioning. Height restriction: 40 in. Debuted: 1989 (Disneyland 1987).

You journey into space in this elaborate "Star Wars" motion simulator.* For a Lucas project it's surprisingly unrestored, but it does have the same mix of wit and action of the early "Star Wars" films. (Note: The ride is scheduled to close in October, 2010. A new 3-D version of the attraction will debut in 2011. The update will incorporate characters from the three "Star Wars" prequel films released between 1999 and 2005. One segment will re-create the podracing scene from "Star Wars Episode I: The Phantom Menace." New 3-D video and dialogue sequences are currently being produced at the Lucasfilm studio near San Francisco, Calif.)

The current story begins as you enter the building. You're in deep space, inside a spaceport during a time after the 1983 movie "Return of the Jedi." Darth Vader is dead and the Republic and its rebels (the good guys) have a tentative hold on the galaxy. R2-D2 and C-3PO are working for intergalactic airline Star Tours. You're there to board a tourist shuttle to the Ewoks' moon of Endor.

The queue weaves through a maintenance bay, where C-3PO and R2-D2 are repairing a Star Tours shuttle. Then you step into a Droidnostics Center, as a robotic mechanic assembles pilots and navigators.

Finally you board your shuttle, which is known as a StarSpeeder 3000. Veteran R2-D2 is its navigator but the ship's pilot is a rookie droid, RX-24. "Rex" is sitting in front of the passengers, at the controls. You watch him work.

| Average Wait | |
|---|---|
| 9am | 0 min |
| 10am | 10 |
| 11am | 35 |
| Noon | 35 |
| 1pm | 40 |
| 2pm | 40 |
| 3pm | 45 |
| 4pm | 35 |
| 5pm | 20 |
| 6pm | 25 |
| 7pm | 15 |
| 8pm | 25 |
| 9pm | 20 |

* Used by airlines and militaries to train pilots, these enclosed, garbage-truck-sized machines create a sensation of flight by synchronizing their tilts, dives and other movements to films that simulate the view out of windshields.

Unfamiliar with the controls, Rex starts making mistakes immediately. As you depart, he sends your ship off the side of its docking ledge and straight down into a repair bay, barely missing a swinging crane before flying out a side door. Once underway, he flies right past Endor—your supposed destination—and into a field of ice crystals. You tunnel through the biggest one.

It gets worse. Once that crisis is over, you learn that an enemy destroyer is nearby, and is pulling you toward it. "Oh no!" Rex yells. "We're caught in a tractor beam!"

A rebel fighter pilot breaks in on your video monitor. "Star Tours?!? What are you doing here? This is a combat zone!"

You pull free but then get hit, and fall toward a Death Star. Fortunately, R2-D2 repairs your ship just in time, and you escape.

Still, your adventure is not over.

"I've always wanted to do this!" Rex says as he dives toward the Death Star. "We're going in!" Just like in the finale of 1977's "Episode 4: A New Hope," you skim along the surface, zooming under bridges and into a trench, blasting bad guys along the way. You watch as the lead fighter drops two torpedoes down the Death Star's exhaust port, and rocket away just as it explodes.

Nearly skidding into a fuel tanker on the way in, you return shaken but sound.

Choose a middle row for a fun ride that won't make you queasy, or the back seats for lots of rock 'n' roll. The front row is the most calm. Perfect for photos, a climb-on replica of a Speeder Bike (the woods-weaving vehicle of "Return of the Jedi") sits across from the ride entrance.

**Fun finds** Landscape: ❶ The facade is a stage set of a village of Ewoks, the teddy-bear creatures that helped save the day in 1983's "Return of the Jedi." Redwood, sequoia and pine trunks are just tall enough for a film scene. Nearby is a 35-foot-tall Imperial Walker. ❷ At night Ewok sounds (talking and drumming) come from the tree huts. **First queue room:** ❸ Just inside are directors chairs for C-3PO and R2-D2. ❹ "Don't insult me, you overgrown scrap pile!" C-3PO snaps to R2-D2 in the maintenance bay. ❺ Pages call "Egroeg Sacul" ("George Lucas" backward), Dr. Tom Morrow (host of 1970s Disney attraction Flight to the Moon) and the owner of a vehicle with the ID THX-1138 (the title of George Lucas' first movie, from 1971). ❻ Little red men chase each other across the bottom of the large video screen. **Second queue room:** ❼ A watermelon-sized robot circles around the left floor of the Droidnostics

▶ For the calmest ride, sit in the front of the theater. The back row is the bumpiest.

Center. **8** The mechanic droid asks for your help ("Could you tell me where this goes?") and gets offended by your attention ("Take a picture, it will last longer"). **9** A wiggling hand and foot hide in a pile of robotic junk on your right. **10** "Excuse me but you'll have to check the excess baggage," the gate attendant tells you. "Oh, I'm sorry, I didn't realize that was your husband." **11** As you leave, two robotic hawks above you tend their nests. **Simulator: 12** A red plastic strip attached to Rex reads "Remove Before Flight." **13** "I have a bad feeling about this!" Rex yells as you fly into the crystals, repeating a signature Lucas line. **14** As you re-enter the maintenance bay Lucas himself appears as a control-room operator. He's standing in an office in front of you. **Exitway: 15** Just before the gift shop, a glass case on the right displays sketches and a page of the script from 1999's "Star Wars Episode 1: The Phantom Menace."

**Fun facts 1** Anthony Daniels provided the voice of C-3PO as well as the alien voice in the maintenance bay. **2** In the Droidnostics Center are two droid robot props (behind G2-9T) who appeared in 1977's "Star Wars Episode 4: A New Hope."

**Hidden Mickey** An Ewok child holds a Mickey doll in the pre-boarding video.

**Star Tours' first queue room** creates a life-size "Star Wars" Maintenance Bay. Attended by Audio-Animatronics versions of C-3PO and R2-D2, a StarSpeeder 3000 undergoes tests.

**A SPACE FANTASY** that takes place "a long time ago, far, far away," the "Star Wars" movies tell a tale of good versus evil. Combining a space-opera plot similar to those of Buck Rogers serials of the 1930s and '40s with special effects and modeling inspired by the 1968 film "2001—A Space Odyssey," the films' mix of wit, mythology and simulated reality has entranced audiences for more than three decades.

Some classic "Star Wars" vehicles and weapons play key roles in your Star Tours flight. You become caught in an Imperial Star Destroyer's tractor beam, an invisible force field that can capture and redirect rebel ships. Rebel forces fly the X-Wing starfighter. The symbol of the rebel fleet, its double-layered wings separate into an "X" formation during combat. Luke Skywalker flew one in the first "Star Wars" trilogy. The bad guys use the TIE starfighter, named for its twin ion engines. These bare-bolts machines lack hyperdrives and deflector shields. The Empire's most horrific weapons are its Death Stars. Powered by a fusion reactor in its center, each of these moon-sized space stations is staffed with over a million troops. Its main weapon is a superlaser housed in a crater-like cannon well.

There have been three Death Stars. The first fell victim to Luke Skywalker when he dropped a pair of proton torpedoes into its exhaust port. The second was never finished; the rebels destroyed it in 1983's "Return of the Jedi." The third appears during your flight. It's destroyed by the X-Wing in front of you.

▶ Perfect for photos, a climb-on replica of a Speeder Bike sits across from the ride entrance.

**A poster along the entranceway** shows the cast of Jim Henson's MuppetVision 3-D

# Jim Henson's MuppetVision 3-D

★★★★ ✔ 25 min inc preshow. Capacity: 584. Indoor, air-conditioned queue (also rarely used shaded outdoor queue). Fear factor: None. Access: Guests may remain in wheelchairs, ECVs. Assistive listening; reflective, activated video captioning. *AuDe* Debuted: 1991.

Built around a 3-D film, this inspired show mixes vaudeville humor with silly effects. As you sit in the red-velvet theater from the 1970s television series "The Muppet Show," you watch a typical Muppet misadventure. Nicki Napoleon and his Emperor Penguins perform in the orchestra pit, while cranky curmudgeons Statler and Waldorf watch with you from the balcony.

The Muppets have retrofitted the auditorium to debut a new film technology, with the Swedish Chef in charge of the equipment.

As the movie begins, you visit the lab of Dr. Bunsen Honeydew, creator of the devilish Waldo, a "living, breathing 3-D effect."

Everything goes wrong. Inept assistant Beaker gets caught in the machine, then nearly sucks up the audience with a Vacuu-Muppet. Miss Piggy storms off after her song's special effects are revealed as nothing more than plastic butterflies on sticks.

The finale nearly destroys the theater. When Sam Eagle is forced to condense his patriotic "three-hour extravaganza" into 90 seconds, all the performers end up onstage at once. The result is a chaos of falling, tripping, shooting and, in one case, stripping.

The effects look their age, but the show has a timeless wit and—despite Kermit's assurance that it won't—plenty of "cheap 3-D tricks." Don't miss the preshow, 12 minutes of inspired confusion that plays out over synchronized video monitors. The rarely-used outdoor queue area is also worth a look. Wrapping around the rear of the building, the covered walkway is lined with zany drawings and posters.

The attraction was the last major project of Muppet creator Jim Henson, who died just before it debuted. His touch is everywhere, from queue-line and theater details to plot points such as the title of Sam Eagle's presentation—"A Salute to All Nations But Mostly America." That's also him voicing Kermit and the Swedish Chef.

| Average Wait | |
|---|---|
| 9am | 0 min |
| 10am | 0 |
| 11am | 0 |
| Noon | 0 |
| 1pm | 0 |
| 2pm | 0 |
| 3pm | 0 |
| 4pm | 0 |
| 5pm | 0 |
| 6pm | 0 |
| 7pm | 0 |
| 8pm | 0 |
| 9pm | 0 |

▶ Head here in the afternoon. There's rarely a long wait, and the queue is air conditioned.

**Fun finds Courtyard:** ❶ In the fountain, Gonzo and Fozzie film Miss Piggy. Clad in a gown and sandals, she's re-creating her Statue of Liberty role in the film's finale. ❷ She stands on a half shell, an homage to William Bouguereau's 1879 painting "The Birth of Venus." ❸ Underneath, Rizzo and two friends snorkel for coins and fish for dollars. ❹ An exterior building staircase leads to the projection room, where the Swedish Chef runs an editing-and-catering business. Its slogan: "Frøöm Qüick Cüts tø Cöld Cüts." ❺ A grayscale Gonzo hangs from a clock tower in tribute to the 1923 Harold Lloyd black-and-white film "Safety Last!" ❻ An Acme anvil honors classic Warner Bros. cartoons. ❼ Atop a side wall, large planters hold ice cream sundaes. One is half-eaten. **Outdoor queue:** ❽ Posters promote faux films such as "Pirates of the Amphibian: At Wit's End" and, starring Dr. Teeth's rock band, "High School Mayhem." ❾ MuppetLabs placards help you get from "here" to "there," learn "How to Stick Out Your Tongue and Touch Your Ear" and understand the surprisingly complex 3-D glasses. **Entryway:** ❿ A Security Office "Key Under Mat" sign isn't lying. ⓫ Inside the office is a wanted poster for Fozzie (for impersonating a comic) and ⓬ a Piggy pinup calendar. ⓭ A directory case lists Statler and Waldorf's Institute of Heckling and Browbeating and Gonzo's Dept. of Poultry and Mold Cultivation. ⓮ A sign above the 8-foot entrance archway reads "You must be shorter than this to enter." A chipped top indicates someone didn't see it. ⓯ A door leading to the MuppetLabs' Dept. of Artificial Reality reads "This is not a door." **Queue room:** ⓰ Hanging from the ceiling is a net full of Jell-O, a reference to 1950s Mouseketeer Annette Funicello. ⓱ Next to it is a bird cage with a perch—a fish. ⓲ A box for the Swedish Chef from Oompah, Sweden's "Sven & Ingmar's Kooking Kollection" holds "Der Noodle Frooper." ⓳ Catwalks hold toy soldiers and frontiersmen from the film's finale and the "Pigs in Space" SwineTrek spaceship from "The Muppet Show." ⓴ Along the walls are large reprints of 1984's "Kermitage Collection" calendar portraits, including parodies of Henri Rousseau ("The Sleepy Zootsy") and Hans Holbein ("Jester at the Court of Henry VIII)"—a painting of Fozzie holding a banana to his ear which includes the Latin phrase Bananum In Avre Habeo ("I'm holding a banana in my ear."). ㉑ Hanging from

**A twirling brass fountain** features Miss Piggy as "Ms. Liberty." She's holding a box of chocolates.

the ceiling, a photo shows the banjo-playing Henson Muppet from a "Muppet Show" band. ㉒ Down front is a "2-D Fruities" box with flat cutouts of a banana, cherry and lemon; ㉓ a hydraulic tube from the film's MuppetVision machine; ㉔ a box of Gonzo's props with "mold, fungus, helmets, helmets covered with fungus and mold, helmets with mold—no fungus" and "fungus and mold—no helmets;" ㉕ and a crate of emergency tuxedos for the penguins stamped "Open in the event of an event." ㉖ The birds' food has arrived in a box from Long Island Sound and Seafood Supplies ("Everything from Hearing to Herring"). ㉗ A sarcophagus peers through a pair of 3-D glasses. **Theater:** ㉘ Manning the projector, the Swedish Chef reassures Kermit that "der machinen is goin' der floomy floomy." Later, when the penguin orchestra fires a cannon at it, he yells "Schtupid crazy birds!" ㉙ The penguins cackle at Statler and Waldorf's barbs (especially when Waldorf says the birds "probably took the job for the halibut") and cough when squirted by Fozzie's boutonniere. One

▶ Sit in the rear center of the theater to have the movie appear in the best focus.

gets sucked up by Beaker's VacuuMuppet. ㉚ Statler and Waldorf gape at the MuppetVision machine, nod as Waldo bounces off people's heads, duck from the VacuuMuppet and hide when the Chef brings out his cannon. ㉛ As you leave, cannonball holes in the wall disappear. Changes in lighting expose, then conceal, them. **Movie:** ㉜ A chicken wanders behind Kermit as he begins the MuppetLabs tour. Later, another flies off its perch. ㉝ A Beethoven bust wears a pair of 3-D glasses on its head. ㉞ Two goldfish eventually swim in a beaker above the Chinese takeout boxes. ㉟ When Kermit returns, Scooter and Janis bicycle behind him. ㊱ After Kermit says "This way, folks," a brass bald eagle wears the 3-D glasses. ㊲ Miss Piggy loses her head as she is pulled into the lake. It falls backward. ㊳ Some marching-band members aren't wearing pants. **Exitway:** ㊴ Posters include ads for penguin outfitter Frankie: "Large formalwear for the hard-to-fit. Small formalwear for the hard-to-find." **Stage 1 Company Store:** ㊵ The Muppet lockers and Happiness Hotel front desk from 1981's "The Great Muppet Caper" form a back corner. ㊶ Nearly two dozen silly signs include one over a doorway that reads "Absolutely no point beyond this point."

**Fun facts** ❶ The outdoor queue area and covered bus shelter are a salute to a closet Henson, Frank Oz and others decorated in 1963, when the Muppets were booked on "The Jack Paar Program" at the NBC Studios in New York. Mistakenly arriving six hours early, they killed time by decorating their dressing room's utility closet with some Muppet touch-up paint, covering the walls with loopy designs and faces and incorporating pipes as noses. ❷ When Sweetums walks on screen and for no apparent reason starts knocking a paddle ball into the audience, he's channeling a famously pointless scene from the 1953 Vincent Price film, "House of Wax."

**Hidden Mickeys** ❶ On Gonzo's ring float in the fountain. ❷ In a small sketch of a DNA model in the "5 Reasons" poster along the outdoor queue. ❸ As a test pattern in the early moments of the preshow video. ❹ In the film finale, park guests behind the fire truck hold Mickey balloons. ❺ Outside the Stage 1 Co. Store, as purple paint drips on a recessed light under a bronze lion head. ❻ As green drips on a wood bureau shelf along a side wall. ❼ Mickey's red shorts hang above the hotel desk.

**Top to bottom:** A hot-air balloon tops the MuppetVision 3-D building. A pipe above the outdoor waiting area recalls an NBC Studios closet Jim Henson, Frank Oz and others surreptitiously decorated in 1963. A poster along the outdoor queue promotes a (fictitious) new Muppet movie. Sam Eagle and Gonzo appear in a preshow video.

▶ The queue room is filled with real Muppet memorabilia. Plan time to look through it.

**Hot hatch.** An Opel Corsa leaps through fire in the finale of Lights, Motors, Action

# Lights, Motors, Action Extreme Stunt Show

★★★ 40 min. Arrive 30 min early for a good seat. Capacity: 5,000. *FastPass* Outdoor, shaded queue. Fear factor: None. Action is far from the seating area. Closed during rain. Access: Guests may remain in wheelchairs, ECVs. Assistive listening. Debuted: 2005.

Cars and motorcycles fly through the air— and barely miss each other—as they skid and spin on the ground in this outdooor stage show, as skilled stunt drivers demonstrate how chase scenes are created for modern action-adventure films. The premise is the filming of a European spy thriller, with a working crew on a live set. Unfortunately, most of the action takes place far from the viewing area, making the show one of Disney's least immersive experiences.

There are four scenes. First, six Opel Corsas race around in a choreographed chase. The cars return to jump over a blockade of produce stands and trucks.

| Average Wait | |
| --- | --- |
| 9am | n/a |
| 10am | 20 |
| 11am | 20 |
| Noon | 20 |
| 1pm | 20 |
| 2pm | 20 |
| 3pm | 20 |
| 4pm | 20 |
| 5pm | 20 |
| 6pm | 20 |
| 7pm | 20 |
| 8pm | n/a |
| 9pm | n/a |

Then three motorcycles arrive, one jumping through what appears to be a plate-glass window as the cars drive on two wheels and, for a moment, two guys end up on Jet Skis. This scene ends as a motorcyclist falls and, thanks to a special jumpsuit, catches fire. For the finale, a car jumps directly at the audience as 40-foot fireballs billow in the air. After each scene, an enthusiastic director ("That was awesome!") appears to combine the shots into a completed scene.

There's also a car that breaks in half.

The set resembles a seaside village marketplace in southern France (one shop is the Café Fracas, the "restaurant of the noisy rumpus"). The show debuted at Disneyland Paris, hence the French connection.

**Fun facts** ❶ Each car has a 2-stroke, 150-hp engine with four forward and four reverse gears, letting it reach the same speed in either direction. ❷ Each car weighs just 1,300 pounds, less than half that of a similar production vehicle. ❸ The "live" video was filmed before the show opened in 2005.

**Hidden Mickeys** ❶ A vintage full-figure Mickey appears in the window of the Antiquites Brocante ("Secondhand Antiques") shop. ❷ As a gear and two circular belts in the top right corner of the motorcycle shop window.

▶ Sit low in the stands for the most exciting view. Sit on the left to exit past a glimpse backstage.

**A tram appears to have crashed** through the entrance facade of the Studio Backlot Tour

# Studio Backlot Tour

★★ 30–40 min. Capacity: 1,000. Open 10a-6p. Outdoor, shaded queue. Fear factor: Simulated disasters. Cancelled during thunderstorms. Access: Guests may remain in wheelchairs, ECVs. Handheld and activated video captioning. Debuted: 1989, revised 2004.

The Disney company shut down its working Florida backlot years ago. What's left of this tour? A dated water-effects demo, a staged prop room, a stop at a fancy faux disaster set, and, one lone authentic moment: a peek into Disney's costume and set shops, which supply most of the clothing worn by cast members in attractions, shows and other public areas at theme parks around the world.

The tour begins with a demonstration of how water cannons and fire bursts can simulate torpedo and bombing attacks, as volunteers get splashed on a PT boat. A small prop room is a queue area for a tram tour. It heads to Catastrophe Canyon, a Mojave Desert effects area that simulates earthquake, fire and flood.

| Average Wait | |
|---|---|
| 9am | closed |
| 10am | 15 min |
| 11am | 10 |
| Noon | 20 |
| 1pm | 20 |
| 2pm | 25 |
| 3pm | 35 |
| 4pm | 20 |
| 5pm | 15 |
| 6pm | closed |
| 7pm | closed |
| 8pm | closed |
| 9pm | closed |

As you return you pass Walt Disney's 1960s jet, and some movie vehicles and props. New is the chicken coop from 2009's "Hannah Montana: The Movie."

You exit through a walk-through exhibit, an American Film Institute (AFI) Showcase of movie-villain costumes. A display case holds antique film cameras and projectors.

**Fun finds Queue:** ❶ The Black Pearl figurehead from 2003's "Pirates of the Caribbean: Curse of the Black Pearl," **Prop Warehouse:** ❷ Cans of eyeballs and glue from 1988's "Who Framed Roger Rabbit," ❸ the tiny Austin of England taxi from 1984's "The Muppets Take Manhattan," ❹ an 18-foot Holy Temple statue from 1989's "Indiana Jones and the Last Crusade" and ❺ furniture from the 1990s TV show "Dinosaurs." ❻ A hang glider and balloon basket (with pilot and chicken) is from Epcot's old World of Motion attraction.

**Hidden Mickeys** ❶ As a blue-sky cutout in the white clouds of the "Harbor Attack" backdrop. ❷ In the prop room, on the "Marvin's Room" refrigerator door and as hanging cannon balls. ❸ At Catastrophe Canyon, as gauges on your right on top of the third barrel from the exit. ❹ A full-figure Mickey hides in a mural to your right just as you enter the AFI exhibit. He stands on top of a gravestone about halfway up the right third of the scene.

▶ Want to volunteer for the Harbor Attack demonstration? Ask an entranceway cast member.

**Girls race around a giant can of Play-doh** at the 'Honey, I Shrunk the Kids' movie set playground

# 'Honey, I Shrunk the Kids' Movie Set Adventure Playground

★★★ Unlimited. Capacity: 240, including parents. Fear factor: None. Closed during thunderstorms. Access: Guests may remain in wheelchairs, ECVs. Located between Streets of America and the Studio Catering Co. fast-food restaurant. Debuted: 1990.

This soft-floored outdoor playground lets children pretend they're the size of bugs, lost in a suburban backyard. Topped by towering blades of grass, it's a small area but is filled with things to do. Many small nooks and crannies, including a series of dimly lit "ant tunnels," tempt kids to explore.

Oversized props include an Oreo cookie, a Super Soaker water gun, a climb-on ant, a large climb-on spider web and a slide that appears to be a huge roll of camera film (kids from the digital age may wonder about that last one). Cynics will note that the props' scale varies wildly. The ant is larger than the film roll. The Super Soaker is the same size as the cookie.

Children love every inch, of course, but parents can get cranky. Cramped into a small triangular area surrounded by tall walls, the playground is usually stuffy and sometimes very humid It's often crowded, but offers almost no place for adults to sit. Also, it's easy for parents to lose sight of their children, though there's only one exit—the entrance—and it's narrow and always monitored by a Disney cast member.

The playground is the most fun early in the day, when skies are cloudy, or very late in the afternoon.

The area is based on the 1989 movie "Honey, I Shrunk the Kids," in which an inventor mistakenly shrinks his children who then get lost in their own yard.

**Fun finds** The playground has three hidden interactive features: ❶ As you enter, look to your left for a leaky garden hose, which occasionally squirts water on unsuspecting heads. In-ground squirters are nearby. ❷ Walk up to the top of the back wall to find the nose of a huge dog. It sniffs you, then sneezes. ❸ Look behind the entranceway, to the right of the dried bubble gum, to discover the Sound Steps, three-inch-high cut grass stalks that make noise when you step on them.

| Average Wait | |
| --- | --- |
| 9am | 0 min |
| 10am | 0 |
| 11am | 0 |
| Noon | 0 |
| 1pm | 0 |
| 2pm | 0 |
| 3pm | 0 |
| 4pm | 0 |
| 5pm | 0 |
| 6pm | 0 |
| 7pm | 0 |
| 8pm | 0 |
| 9pm | 0 |

▶ Bring a camera. The oversized props make good photo backgrounds.

## The Magic of Disney Animation

★ ★ ★ ★ ✔ Unlimited (Film: 10 min. Animation Academy: 10 min. Rest self-guided.) Capacity: Theater: 150; Animation Academy: 50. Outdoor, shaded queue. Fear factor: None. Access: Guests may remain in wheelchairs, ECVs; lap boards available for drawing. Reflective, video captioning. *AuDe* Debuted: 1989, revised 2004.

This lightweight attraction consists of a short film, a hands-on drawing lesson, some computer games, an air-conditioned chance to meet characters and some exhibits.

A short film, **"Drawn to Animation,"** shows how Disney animators created Mushu, the dragon sidekick in 1998's "Mulan." An open area has preschooler-friendly computer games. Nearby, Mickey Mouse and characters from recent Disney movies greet guests and pose for pictures.

You learn how to draw a Disney character at the superb **Animation Academy.** A classroom setting has you sit at a drafting table

| Average Wait | |
|---|---|
| 9am | 0 min |
| 10am | 10 |
| 11am | 10 |
| Noon | 15 |
| 1pm | 15 |
| 2pm | 20 |
| 3pm | 20 |
| 4pm | 20 |
| 5pm | 20 |
| 6pm | 0 |
| 7pm | 0 |
| 8pm | 0 |
| 9pm | 0 |

**The Magic of Disney Animation** sits in a building that was once a working animation studio

and follow step-by-step instructions from a live instructor to create a Disney character. You keep your sketch.

The final area is the **Animation Gallery,** a few small rooms filled with conceptual models and drawings, including Tinker Bell as a redhead and Buzz Lightyear with a pompadour. A glass case holds a dozen Oscar statuettes (mostly authentic duplicates) won by the Disney company. The one for the 1969 short "It's Tough to be a Bird" is the actual award from the Oscar ceremony.

The attraction building is the former East Coast home of Disney Feature Animation. Working in the area that now holds video games and character greetings, artists here created the Roger Rabbit cartoons "Tummy Trouble" and "Roller Coaster Rabbit;" painted cels for "The Little Mermaid;" produced segments of "Beauty and the Beast," "Aladdin" and "The Lion King;" and created the films "Mulan," "Lilo & Stitch," "Brother Bear" and "Home on the Range" in their entireties. At its peak the studio had a staff of 350. Disney closed it in 2004.

**Fun find** Take too long to make choices at the Soundstage computer screens and Ursula, the sea witch from 1989's "Little Mermaid," will shout "Hurry and make a choice! I have fish sticks in the oven!"

▶ There's typically no wait after the characters leave, which is usually about 5:30 p.m.

She wants more. Gadgets and gizmos aplenty aren't enough for Ariel, the Little Mermaid.

# Voyage of the Little Mermaid

★ ★ ★ ★ 17 min. Capacity: 600.
*FastPass* Queue partially outdoors in shade, partially indoors and air-conditioned. Fear factor: Ursula scary appearance and threatening voice causes some toddlers to cry. Access: Guests may remain in wheelchairs, ECVs. Assistive listening, reflective captioning. Debuted: 1992.

Black-light puppets, live actors and imaginative effects retell the story of Ariel in this condensed version of the 1989 movie, "The Little Mermaid."

As a water curtain opens across the stage, the show begins with a rousing blacklight puppet version of "Under the Sea." Then you meet Ariel (she wants legs, and Prince Eric) who belts out "Part of Your World" like a Broadway star. The evil Ursula the Sea Witch—a parade-float-sized robotic octopus—slithers in to trick Ariel out of her voice, singing "Poor Unfortunate Soul." Video clips advance the plot to the finale, where the live actress grows her gams and hugs her honey.

The Howard Ashman lyrics alone make the show worthwhile. *"Out in the sun they slave away,"* Sebastian the crab sings, *"while we devotin' full time to floatin'."* The theater's high-backed cloth seats, dark ambiance and cool breezes make it a great place to relax.

**Fun find** Hanging over the theater's right entrance door is a Disney-fied replica of P.T. Barnum's 1842 FeJee Mermaid. On a tour of the United States, the infamous huckster displayed what he billed as a real mermaid caught off the Fiji Islands. In truth it was simply the shriveled body of a monkey stitched to the dried tail of a large fish.

| Average Wait | |
|---|---|
| 9am | 0 min |
| 10am | 20 |
| 11am | 20 |
| Noon | 20 |
| 1pm | 20 |
| 2pm | 30 |
| 3pm | 20 |
| 4pm | 30 |
| 5pm | 20 |
| 6pm | 10 |
| 7pm | 30 |
| 8pm | 20 |
| 9pm | 10 |

**REBEL REBEL** The 1989 film "The Little Mermaid" broke new ground for a Disney heroine: Ariel's dream comes true because she takes control. Her problem: She wants legs, and the human Prince Eric. Ursula the Sea Witch offers to make the girl human—if Ariel will give up her voice and agree to get it back only if she kisses Eric within three days. Ursula transforms herself into a rival beauty with Ariel's voice, and nearly marries the prince herself. A singing crab and a friendly fish help Ariel land her man. The movie leaves out some grim moments of Hans Christian Andersen's original 1836 fable. In that version, the Sea Witch takes the teen's voice by cutting out her tongue, and the prince dumps her for the girl next door.

▶ The best seats are in the middle of the theater. The front row sits too low to see on the stage.

# Playhouse Disney — Live on Stage

★★★★★ 22 min. Capacity: 600. Open 10a–5p. Outdoor shaded queue. Fear factor: None. Access: Guests may remain in wheelchairs and ECVs. Assistive listening, reflective and activated captions. Debuted: 2001, updated 2008.

Characters from the Playhouse Disney television programs "Mickey Mouse Clubhouse," "Handy Manny," "Little Einsteins" and "My Friends Tigger and Pooh" star in this puppet show. Four short stories include plenty of opportunities for kids to bounce, cheer, clap and move about. The audience sits on a carpeted floor.

| Average Wait | |
|---|---|
| 9am | n/a |
| 10am | 20 min |
| 11am | 20 |
| Noon | 20 |
| 1pm | 20 |
| 2pm | 20 |
| 3pm | 20 |
| 4pm | 20 |
| 5pm | 20 |
| 6pm | n/a |
| 7pm | n/a |
| 8pm | n/a |
| 9pm | n/a |

Life-like puppets blink their eyes and open their mouths. The sound is crisp, and nearly a hundred spotlights provide professional theatrical lighting.

The plot? Mickey Mouse wants to throw Minnie a surprise party, but none of his pals can figure out how to pull it off. The stories teach gentle lessons about working together.

**An elaborate puppet show,** Playhouse Disney Live on Stage features the stars of such television shows as (clockwise from top left) "Mickey Mouse Clubhouse," "My Friends Tigger and Pooh" and "Handy Manny"

**Fun finds** ❶ When Casey stands to the side of the stage, the live host sometimes "chats" with the puppets nearby. ❷ When Casey asks Goofy what he learned from the "Little Einsteins" story, for a moment the dippy dog can't think of anything.

**DESIGNED FOR PRESCHOOLERS,** Disney Channel Playhouse Disney programs include **"Mickey Mouse Clubhouse,"** in which Mickey and his pals help viewers solve problems (when they need help they shout "Oh Tootles!" which brings forth a magical flying machine equipped with mouse-ka-tools; a clubhouse appears when they call "Meeska, Mooska, Mickey Mouse!"), **"Handy Manny,"** featuring bilingual handyman Manny Garcia and his talking tools; **"Little Einsteins,"** which uses classical music to urge viewers to interact with four smart children who travel the world, and **"My Friends Tigger & Pooh,"** where, Winnie the Pooh characters solve mysteries. A new friend, 6-year-old Darby, often reminds impatient Tigger to "think, think, think."

▶ Have your children sit along an inner aisle to interact with Casey, the live host.

**Early bird.** A 1960s Audio-Animatronics parrot on display at Walt Disney: One Man's Dream.

# Walt Disney: One Man's Dream

★★★ ✓ Allow 35 min. Capacity: 200. Fear factor: None. Access: Guests may remain in wheelchairs, ECVs. Assistive listening, handheld and reflective captioning available. *AuDe* Located on the walkway between Pixar Place and the Animation Courtyard. Debuted: 2001.

A salute to the life of Walt Disney, this exhibit combines memorabilia exhibits with a short film. It includes the school desk Disney used as a Missouri second-grader, his studio desk from the 1930s and his (re-created) 1960s office.

| Average Wait | |
|---|---|
| 9am | 0 min |
| 10am | 0 |
| 11am | 0 |
| Noon | 0 |
| 1pm | 0 |
| 2pm | 0 |
| 3pm | 0 |
| 4pm | 0 |
| 5pm | 0 |
| 6pm | 0 |
| 7pm | 0 |
| 8pm | 0 |
| 9pm | 0 |

Walt Disney's role in theme-park history is well represented. Hand-built by Disney himself in 1949, a wooden diorama displays early ideas for dark rides such as Peter Pan's Flight. The "Dancing Man" electronic marionette tested techniques that led to Audio-Animatronics robots. A simulated TV studio shows Disney filming a video to interest investors in his ultimate dream: the Experimental Prototype Community of Tomorrow (EPCOT). The back room has two Audio-Animatronics figures you can control yourself: a robotic man and a Tiki bird.

A 200-seat theater shows a moving biographical film. Narrated by Walt Disney himself through vintage audio clips, the 16-minute film explores Disney's never-ending drive and the hardships he overcame.

# Journey Into Narnia: Prince Caspian

★ 15 min. Avg wait 10 min. Outdoor shaded queue. Capacity: 200. Fear factor: Video has violent scenes. Access: Guests may remain in wheelchairs, ECVs. Assistive listening; handheld, reflective captioning available. Next to One Man's Dream. Debuted: 2008.

This walk-through promotional display for the 2008 movie "The Chronicles of Narnia: Prince Caspian" consists of the viewing of a making-of video and a few props and costumes used in the film. The exhibit area resembles the movie's vault where the lion Aslan sacrificed himself. In front of the exhibit entrance, Prince Caspian himself poses for photos in front of a backdrop of the movie's Dancing Lawn.

▶ One Man's Dream is a great spot to duck out of a rainstorm. You can stay as long as you like.

HE TALKS & SINGS!

BOARDWALK
POTATO HEAD
BARKER

STEP RIGHT UP
and build your own
Mr. Potato Head
Boardwalk Barker!

Pieces store
inside

Fit pieces
anywhere on
potato body

USE THE
SILLY
PIECES
AND YOUR
IMAGINATION
TO CREATE
ALL SORTS OF
WACKY
LOOKS!

**Mr. Potato Head,** a talking Audio-Animatronics figure, interacts with guests at Toy Story Mania

# Toy Story Mania

★★★★★ ✔ 7 min. (game play 5 min.) Capacity: 108. *FastPass* Indoor, air-conditioned queue; overflows into outdoor area. Fear factor: None. Vehicles move from game to game in a jerky, funhouse fashion. Access: Offline loading area for disabled guests, into vehicles that have shooting guns with buttons as well as pull strings. ECV users must transfer. All ride vehicles offer closed captioning. Debuted: 2008.

This high-tech ride takes you alongside a series of 3-D video shooting galleries. Climbing into a vehicle that pairs you with a partner, you don 3-D glasses and travel five dark corridors lined with large video screens. At each one, you stop and play a virtual midway game, shooting virtual objects out of what appears to be an old-school, spring-action cannon. Each game is hosted by a different "Toy Story" character.

As you play, you actually see the objects you launch leave your gun and travel into the screens. Sprays of water let you "feel" some explosions, while blasts of air enhance the sensation

| Average Wait | |
|---|---|
| 9am | 30 min |
| 10am | 60 |
| 11am | 60 |
| Noon | 70 |
| 1pm | 70 |
| 2pm | 130 |
| 3pm | 150 |
| 4pm | 65 |
| 5pm | 80 |
| 6pm | 85 |
| 7pm | 80 |
| 8pm | 80 |
| 9pm | 70 |

that some targets pop off the screen and fly past you. Designed to appeal to all ages and skill levels, the games are easy to play but offer hidden challenges (see next page).

Unfortunately, the biggest challenge is avoiding a long line. On a typical day when the park opens at 9 a.m., the standby wait for Toy Story Mania will be 30 minutes by 9:05 a.m., at least an hour by 10 a.m., and up to two hours by noon. As for Fastpasses, the entire supply for a day is typically distributed before noon.

The ride takes its inspiration from the concept that Andy's toys spring to life whenever he is away. In this case, Andy has received a "Midway Games Play Set" for his latest birthday, and the toys have opened the box and set up the game booths and carnival trams in his absence.

The waiting area features a 5-foot 2-inch Audio-Animatronics Mr. Potato Head, who acts as the ride's carnival barker. Thanks to a library of audio clips recorded by comedian Don Rickles, the character says more lines of dialogue than any other Disney robot, and can chat with guests personally. His eyes can look at the guest he's speaking with, and his mouth moves to form vowel sounds and words. He occasionally takes off his ear; sometimes his hat.

▶ To avoid a long wait, get here within 5 minutes of the park opening or get a Fastpass.

# YOU'VE GOT A FRIEND IN... YOUR PARTNER!

BY MICAELA NEAL There are three keys to getting a high score on Toy Story Mania: Shoot constantly (your cannon can fire six objects per second), know where the high-value targets are, and... teamwork! To get a top score, you have to work together with the person sitting next to you. That way, the two of you can hit multiple targets simultaneously, which will reveal hidden levels of the game.

| GAME BOOTH | HIGH-VALUE INITIAL TARGETS | HOW TO REVEAL BONUS TARGETS |
|---|---|---|
| **HAMM AND EGGS** | ❶ In the doorway of the barn is a 500-point horse. ❷ The green ducks in the lake are also 500 points. ❸ A 500-point squirrel runs up both the left and right edges of the screen. ❹ Three gophers repeatedly pop up along the bottom. The brown gophers are worth 500 points; the gray ones 1000 points. ❺ The animals in the tree are 1000 points each. A 1000-point goat peers out of the barn window. A 1000-point mouse skitters along the barn's roof. | ❶ Hit the mouse (see Tip No. 5 at left) and the barn will rotate to reveal its interior, which is filled with 2000-point rats. Hit every barn rat and more rats appear in the grass as 1000-point targets. ❷ Hit the fox on top of the henhouse (in the bottom left corner of the screen) and three hens will scurry out. The first is worth 1000 points; the second is worth 2000 points; the third 1000 points. ❸ Hit the 500-point donkey that walks along the hills and the animal will turn and run the other way as a 2000-point target. |
| **BO PEEP'S BAAA-LOON POP** | ❶ Each of the recurring pink three-headed sheep balloons are worth 1000 points. ❷ The balloons on the clouds are worth 500 points each. ❸ 2000-point hot-air balloons occasionally float in the sky. ❹ Sheep balloons at the bottom of the screen are worth 500 points each. | ❶ Hit a pink flower balloon to have a 500-point bee balloon fly out and float toward you. ❷ Hit all the balloons on the left cloud to have blue 500-point balloons rain down. ❸ Hit all the balloons on the right cloud to make the sun shine, which releases yellow 500-point balloons. ❹ **Team up with your partner** to simultaneously hit all the balloons on both clouds to create a rainbow, which causes many 2000-point multicolored balloons to fall from the sky. Note: this only works if the two final balloons are popped within the same second. |
| **GREEN ARMY MEN SHOOT CAMP** | ❶ Helicopters hover with plates worth 1000 points. Other 1000-point plates appear within the mass of plates, while more are carried by trucks along the bottom. ❷ Airplanes tow plates worth 2000 points. Others are tossed up on either side of the mountain. | **Team up with your partner** to simultaneously hit the two 2000-point plates that are tossed up from the sides of the mountain (see note at left) at the same time. Doing so will open the mountain and reveal a tank that shoots plates toward you worth 5000 points each. |
| **BUZZ LIGHTYEAR'S FLYING TOSSERS** | ❶ Meteors near the sides of the screen are 500 points. ❷ Rockets are 1000 points. ❸ Aliens with jetpacks are worth 2000 points. ❹ Aliens at the top corners of the screen are 5000 points. | **Team up with your partner** to simultaneously hoop all of the aliens in the large central rocket to launch it and reveal a huge robot. When the robot's mouth opens, toss rings into it to score—if you reveal the robot early enough—up to 2000 points per toss. |
| **WOODY'S ROOTIN' TOOTIN' SHOOTIN' GALLERY** | All initial targets are worth 100 points each. | ❶ Each 100-point target triggers a series of bonus targets worth up to 1000 points each. ❷ As your vehicle moves from the first screen to the second (or from the second to the Woody's Bonus Roundup screen), hit two 100-point or 500-point targets close together to reveal a 2000-point target. |
| **WOODY'S BONUS ROUNDUP** | The second-to-last mine cart on each track is always worth 2000 points. | ❶ Hit the 1000-point targets by two bats above the carts to wake them up and reveal 5000-point targets. ❷ Hit all of the carts on a track and the last one will be worth 5000 points. ❸ The final target increases its point value up to 2000 if you hit it often enough. |

**Clockwise from top left:** Green Army Men hoist a Scrabble board across from the entrance to Toy Story Mania. The ride's Fastpasses are often fully distributed before noon. Woody dolls at a gift stand.

**Fun finds Exterior: ①** Across the Pixar Place walkway, some of Andy's toys are sending messages to Toy Story Mania riders. Across from the Fastpass machines, a Green Army Man has hung a Mr. Spell off the side of the building. Messages include "Toy Story Midway Mania... More fun than a barrel of monkeys... Sorry monkeys." Other Army Men have hung a Scrabble board across from the ride entrance. Spelling out the message "You've got a friend in me," it hints at the teamwork the ride requires to get a high score (see previous page). **②** Andy has left a note on the door of the back of the Pixar Place entrance gate that explains the setup: Mr. Spell is a "signal corps communicator;" the Scrabble board is a "top secret message decoder." **Queue room, first area: ③** A pink crayon is the only one in the room unused. Why? "It's Andy's room," an Imagineer tells us. "He's a boy." **Queue room, third area: ④** The Pixar star ball and Luxo Jr. lamp sit on either side of Mr. Potato Head. **⑤** Toy blocks under him show the letters "P" and "H." **⑥** Near the end of the standby queue, Andy has painted a rough version of Nemo from 2003's "Finding Nemo." **Loading area: ⑦** Books on wall murals that portray Andy's room are the same as those in his room in the "Toy Story" film. **Game: ⑧** At Bo Peep's Baaa-Loon Pop, pop a water balloon to be sprayed with water. **⑨** On the right cloud, pop the second balloon from the left to have it fly toward you. **⑩** At the Green Army Men Shoot Camp, hit either of the two yellow plates to have an adjacent

cannon fire a shot at you. **⑪** At Buzz Lightyear's Flying Tossers, hoop one of the aliens wearing a jetpack to have it fly over your head. **⑫** Hoop one of the rockets to have it shoot toward you. **⑬** As your vehicle moves to Woody's Rootin' Tootin' Shootin' Gallery, a wall mural of a carnival includes Toy Story Mania as one of its attractions. **⑭** At the Shootin' Gallery, a bank-robbing squirrel pops out of the bank when you hit the target next to it. **⑮** Hitting the target by the bird nest causes the bird sitting on it to pop up in the air. Sequential targets make baby birds fly away. **⑯** A beaver pops up when you hit the target on the dam. Sequential targets make the beaver squeak. **⑰** At the prize booth, confetti will pop out of your gun. **⑱** On some screens, Bo kisses Woody as the curtain closes. **Exit area: ⑲** Two blocks facing the exit walkway show the letters "C" and "U." **⑳** As you leave, you pass a "Tin Toy" Little Golden Book that has jammed Andy's bedroom door closed, so the toys can play with his new game indefinitely.

**Hidden Mickeys ①** Near the end of the standby queue, upside down, as a paint splotch under the tail of a Nemo-like clownfish. **②** In the boarding area mural, as frames around Bullseye, Mr. Potato Head and Slinky Dog on the Toy Story Midway Games Playset box. **③** Toward the end of the ride, on a mural to your right as you rotate into position for the screen that tallies your score, as the dot in the exclamation point of the phrase "Circus Fun!"

▶ All Toy Story Mania Fastpasses for a day are usually distributed before noon.

**Swaying dancers** are persuaded to "Kill the Beast!" during "The Mob Song"

# Beauty and the Beast — Live on Stage

★ ★ ★ ★ ★ ✔ 25 min. Capacity: 1,500. Outdoor queue. Fear factor: During "The Mob Song" Gaston stabs the Beast, but you don't see the wound. Cancelled during turbulent thunderstorms. Access: Guests may remain in wheelchairs and ECVs. Assistive listening. *AuDe* Debuted: 1991, revised 2001.

This uplifting show re-creates the spirit of Disney's 1991 animated film by focusing on the movie's music. "Belle," "Gaston," "Be Our Guest," "Something There," "The Mob Song," "Beauty and the Beast"—they're all here, and sound and look terrific. Most lead vocals are sung live.

The supporting cast is outstanding. When Gaston struts on stage the village girls fight over him with flirty passion; when he chooses Belle instead they stalk off in a huff. The "Be Our Guest" maids squeal in delight when Lumiere announces dinner. Two tickle Belle with their feather dusters; later two whisper to each other, leave the stage and return with a giant sundae that transforms into a warbling diva.

Colorful costumes and creative lighting effects add to the theatrical feel. In the first scene the supporting dancers wear six different hues. In the ballroom scene Belle's gold gown is offset by vivid pink dresses. The Hollywood Bowl-like stage arch flashes during "Be Our Guest;" dappled lights color "The Mob Song." The open-air theater is covered with a roof.

## Celebrity handprints

Thirty television stars have left impressions outside the theater, in a small plaza next to the rear bleachers. "Star Trek's" Scotty, James Doohon, added "Beam Me Up." "Jeopardy" host Alex Trebek wrote "Who is Alex Trebek?" Also here: Morey Amsterdam, Imogene Coca, Bob Denver, June Lockhart, George Wendt, even journeyman Martin Mull.

**Fun finds ❶** The show begins with a pun: a ringing bell. ❷ "The Mob Song" includes a quote from Shakespeare. "Screw your courage to the sticking place" Gaston says as he rallies the villagers to kill the Beast, the same phrase Lady Macbeth uses to urge her husband to kill Duncan. ❸ As Gaston incites the mob, a few villagers remain skeptical.

| Average Wait | |
| --- | --- |
| 9am | n/a |
| 10am | 20 min |
| 11am | 20 |
| Noon | 20 |
| 1pm | 20 |
| 2pm | 20 |
| 3pm | 20 |
| 4pm | 20 |
| 5pm | 20 |
| 6pm | 20 |
| 7pm | n/a |
| 8pm | n/a |
| 9pm | n/a |

▶ For a full experience, get in line 45 minutes before showtime and sit down front.

**Max axe.** A 40-foot guitar graces the entrance. Its neck transforms into a simulated coaster track.

# Rock 'n' Roller Coaster Starring Aerosmith

★★★★★ ✔ 1 min, 22 sec. **Capacity:** 120 (5 24-seat vehicles). *FastPass* **Indoor, air-conditioned queue. Fear factor: Anticipating the launch scares even adults. Access: ECV users must transfer. Height restriction: 48 in. Debuted: 1999.**

This popular roller coaster has a lot going for it—an indoor dark track, a powered launch that blasts you to 57 mph in 2.8 seconds, two loops, a tight corkscrew, rock music and a fun theme.

Aerosmith tunes blast from speakers surrounding your seat as you zoom through a half-mile of twists and turns that re-create a frantic Los Angeles freeway trip. You pass *through* both the famous HOLLYWOOD sign and a huge billboard doughnut. Baby-blue coaster cars resemble vintage Cadillacs.

Plenty thrilling for most Disney guests, the ride gets mixed reviews from hardcore coaster freaks. In fact, though the launch is truly exhilarating, every-

| Average Wait | |
|---|---|
| 9am | 0 min |
| 10am | 50 |
| 11am | 55 |
| Noon | 70 |
| 1pm | 80 |
| 2pm | 80 |
| 3pm | 70 |
| 4pm | 80 |
| 5pm | 65 |
| 6pm | 80 |
| 7pm | 75 |
| 8pm | 85 |
| 9pm | 85 |

thing after it is rather mild. You slow down dramatically after the first couple of turns, and average just 28 mph.

The smooth ride has no steep drops and you're not jerked around in your seat.

**"I got you a really fast car"**
The grins begin as you enter the building, which Disney has deemed to be the studios of "G-Force Records." Step through the lobby and you're off on a time-warp to the 1970s. Along the walls are displays of real vintage recording and playback gear.

**ALL-AMERICAN ROCK 'N' ROLL** Known for its driving riffs and suggestive lyrics, Aerosmith formed in Boston in 1970. Its raunchy swagger, highlighted by singer Steven Tyler's prancing stage antics, drew comparisons to the Rolling Stones. Tyler and Stones singer Mick Jagger even looked similar. Early hits included 1975's "Walk This Way," which, like the Stones' earlier "Satisfaction," used a groove so strong the words didn't matter. Aerosmith also created rock music's first power ballad, adding strings to 1973's piano-based "Dream On." Plagued by drug abuse in the late 1970s, the band got back on track in 1986, when Tyler and lead guitarist Joe Perry appeared on rap group Run D.M.C.'s cover of "Walk This Way." The video became an MTV staple.

▶ For the most tense launch, ask to sit in the front seat. You'll have little clue it's coming.

Soon you come to Studio C, where you find the rock band Aerosmith (courtesy of a video screen) mixing the rhythm tracks to their "new" number "Walk This Way." Suddenly the guys have to leave; they're late for a concert. But no worries: they offer you—and everyone else in line—backstage passes to the show. As the band's manager phones for a car she counts the crowd, then tells the limo company "We're going to need a stretch. In fact, make it a super stretch."

"The show is all the way across town," she tells you after she hangs up, "but I got you a really fast car."

You're then ushered into a grimy back alley, where up pulls your ride, a baby-blue Cadillac convertible. Your trip takes you to the backstage entrance of an L.A. arena, where a red carpet leads to (a video of) the band performing on stage.

**Built to look like** vintage Cadillac convertibles, Rock 'n' Roller Coaster vehicles loop, corkscrew and speed through a Hollywood night on their way to an Aerosmith concert

**Fun finds** ❶ Mimicking guitar necks, lobby columns have fret boards and strings. ❷ The first display case holds a 1958 Gibson Les Paul Standard guitar as well as a disc cutter, a device that "cut records" by etching sounds from a mixing console onto a master disc. ❸ Record players in the second case range from a 1904 external-horn Edison Fireside to a 1970s Disc-O-Kid. ❹ Put your ear to doors marked "Studio A" or "Studio B" to hear Aerosmith rehearsing. ❺ Concert posters in the next room include one for a 1973 show from Aerosmith's first national tour, as the opening act for the New York Dolls. It's midway down on the right. ❻ An MC5 poster includes a still-visible marijuana leaf that Disney has covered with a small American flag. As you stand in the alley, signs on the rear of the G-Force building indicate that ❼ repair work has been done by Sam Andreas and Sons Structural Restoration, ❽ the garage is run by Lock 'n' Roll Parking Systems ❾ and that its dumpster is owned by the Rock 'n' Rollaway Disposal Co. ❿ A glass case displays rates for Wash This Way Auto Detail. ❿ Each limo license plate sports a message such as 2FAST4U or H8TRFFC. ⓫ The concert video loop occasionally shows Tyler screaming "Rock 'n' Roller Coaster!!!"

**Fun facts** ❶ Aerosmith's manager is played by actress Illeana Douglas. ❷ The disc jockey heard on the car radio is longtime Los Angeles rock jock Uncle Joe Benson. ❸ The squeal heard as each limo peels out is prerecorded. It comes from barely visible speakers under the driveway. ❹ Most of the ride takes place in "Stage 15," the structure behind the G-Force building. ❺ When Disney chose Aerosmith to partner with for the attraction, initially the company couldn't reach frontmen Steven Tyler and Joe Perry—the two were vacationing with their families at Walt Disney World.

**Hidden Mickeys** Twice on the building's sign: ❶ Tyler's shirt has Mickey silhouettes; ❷ the boy wears mouse ears. ❸ As tile pieces in a beige section of the foyer's floor mosaic, just before you leave the room. ❹ As a distorted carpet pattern in the first display room. ❺ As cables on the recording studio floor. ❻ On the registration sticker on each of the limos' rear license plates. ❼ As the "O" in the phrase "Box #15" on a trunk along the ride's exit walkway.

▶ **Long legs? Ask for an odd-numbered row. Those seats have far more legroom.**

THE TWILIGHT ZONE® IS A REGISTERED TRADEMARK OF CBS INC. AND IS USED PURSUANT TO A LICENSE FROM CBS INC.

**The side of Disney's Hollywood Tower Hotel** shows its ornate Mission Revival architecture

# The Twilight Zone Tower of Terror

★★★★★ ✔ 4 min. Capacity: 84. *FastPass* Indoor, air-conditioned queue; overflows into shaded outdoor queue. Fear factor: Drops are smooth, but mind games are intense. Access: ECV guests must transfer. Activated captioning. Height restriction: 40 in. Debuted: 1994; revised 1996, 1999, 2002.

Loaded with special effects and superb detailing, this drop-tower-like thrill ride appeals to nearly everyone except those with an intense fear of falling. The ride takes place in what appears to be an old Los Angeles hotel. As you arrive to "check in," you learn the regular elevators are broken, and take a back-room freight elevator to get to your room. But once the doors close, you soon join the souls of earlier guests in a supernatural "dimension of time and space," where you fall up to 130 feet.

The queue area includes a detailed hotel lobby, library and boiler room. Perhaps best of all, it's never the same ride twice.

| Average Wait | |
|---|---|
| 9am | 0 min |
| 10am | 40 |
| 11am | 40 |
| Noon | 45 |
| 1pm | 50 |
| 2pm | 80 |
| 3pm | 40 |
| 4pm | 60 |
| 5pm | 80 |
| 6pm | 20 |
| 7pm | 60 |
| 8pm | 80 |
| 9pm | 60 |

## A 'somewhat unique' story

Meant to recall the peculiar style of the television series "The Twilight Zone," the experience is even more fun if you know its story. According to Disney lore, the luxurious 12-story Hollywood Tower Hotel opened in 1917. Known for its old-world opulence, it was a gathering place for Tinseltown elite.

On Oct. 31, 1939, the hotel hosted a Halloween party in its rooftop lounge, and many guests checked in for the night. But at precisely 8:05 p.m. a huge lightning bolt hit the hotel. Its force dematerialized two wings of the building, including two elevator shafts. Among the victims were five people who were in one of the elevators—a child actress with her nanny, a young Hollywood couple and a hotel bellhop. The remaining guests ran out of the hotel in horror, leaving their luggage and other belongings behind.

The hotel stood deserted for decades, but now has mysteriously reopened. In fact, the staff from that fateful 1939 night is still on hand, unaged, with no memory of the disaster or the time that has passed. The oblivious workers haven't done any maintenance, cared for landscaping, or even dusted.

As you arrive to check in, the passenger elevators still aren't working, so a bellhop asks you to wait in the library.

▶ Hang onto your stuff! Anything loose will go flying during your fall.

Then things get freaky. As the library power goes out, its black-and-white television set comes on, just in time for an episode of the 1960s series, "The Twilight Zone." Host Rod Serling describes a "somewhat unique" fable about a maintenance service elevator. His preview shows those five guests boarding their elevator car just before the flash. *"We invite you if you dare to step aboard,"* Serling says, *"because in tonight's episode, you are the star."*

Next you're directed into a back boiler room, where you board a rusty service elevator to get to your room. But as the doors close, you discover that this elevator clearly has a mind of its own.

First its lights go out, and it whisks you to the fourth floor, where its doors open to reveal a rooming hall. At first things are normal—Do Not Disturb signs hang on most room doors, with shoes and wine bottles in front of them. But then lightning flashes in the window, and those five elevator guests flicker into view. They beckon you to follow them down the hall, until, wrapped in a crackling net of electricity, they again become invisible. The back wall of the corridor disappears, revealing a night sky. The hall window floats, and shatters.

The doors close and up you go again, this time to the 13th floor, a level that doesn't exist. The doors open. You hear Serling speak: *"One stormy night long ago, five people stepped through the door of an elevator and into a nightmare. That door is opening once again, and this time it's opening for you."*

Your car moves forward in the dark, next to moving silhouettes of that spooky quintet. Ahead of you is a star field. It too moves, forming a line which separates to become the edge of another pair of doors, which open into one of those lost elevator shafts.

You move into the space. The doors slam shut. It's completely dark. Silent. Tense.

Then your entire elevator car is tossed—violently— up, down—down, up—up, up, down. Occasionally doors in front of you open, revealing the open sky. You may see those five figures again, or hear rain fall, or smell something odd. After about a minute the madness stops. Your car arrives calmly in the basement.

*"The next time you check into a deserted hotel,"* Serling says, *"make sure you know just what kind of vacancy you're filling. Or you may find yourself a permanent resident of… 'The Twilight Zone.'"*

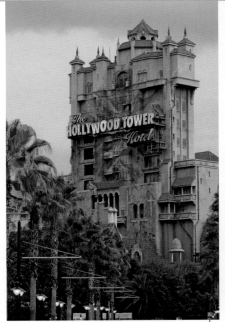

**The front of the hotel** appears to have been severely damaged from a lightning strike

### The science of spooky

Hidden behind all the theming is a unique mix of innovative engineering, classic special effects and modern math. Combining three distinct ride systems, the attraction's mechanics represent a novel example of applied science. Its elevators go up, move forward, then plummet down and soar up a second shaft, all in a seamless experience.

The first system is obvious: an elevator. When you leave the boiler room, you're in a standard, 50-foot elevator shaft, with sliding doors and two stops.

The second system kicks in at the top of the shaft. As your elevator car (an independent vehicle, which rode up the shaft in a cage) moves forward, it's using the technology of a self-guided pallete driver, an automated machine used by companies such as Anheuser-Busch to move inventory through large warehouses. Controlled by an unseen computer, it rolls on wheels and gets its power from an on-board battery.

The third system is Disney's own. Once your cabin enters the drop shaft, it's silently locked into a second cage that is tightly suspended on a looped steel cable. Pulled by high-speed winches and motors, the

▶ Your fall is over when you see the turning spiral from "The Twilight Zone."

**A decaying Cupid statue** stands in an entrance garden of the Twilight Zone Tower of Terror

The attraction has a reprogrammable ride system, which Disney has used to keep the ride fresh. At first the experience was one plummet of about 100 feet. A 1996 revision added a half drop and a false fall. Three years later Disney debuted a seven-fall experience that brought faster acceleration, more weightlessness and more shaking. Finally, on New Year's Eve 2002, the company introduced "Tower of Terror 4," the current mix of random drops and special effects.

**Fun finds** Lobby: ❶ Right of the reception desk, an American Automobile Association plaque honors the hotel's 13-diamond status. It was presented when the ride opened. ❷ Desk items include a fedora, topcoat, newspaper, open registration book, alligator-skin luggage and mail-slot mail and messages. ❸ A bag, cane and white fedora lean against the concierge desk. ❹ A concierge desk poster promotes a show by "Anthony Freemont," a 6-year-old boy who used telepathic powers to terrorize his neighbors in the 1961 "Twilight Zone" episode "It's a Good Life." ❺ A diamond ring, white glove and two glasses rest on a left table. A champagne bucket is adjacent. ❻ A mah-jongg game is in progress on a nearby table. The pieces are properly positioned. ❼ Tea has been served to the players; a cart holds cups, roses and a newspaper. ❽ Another teacup rests on the end table in front of a fireplace; a goblet and small plate sit on a table to the right. **Library:** ❾ The Serling footage has been altered to remove a cigarette from his right hand. ❿ The little girl sings the nursery rhyme "It's Raining, It's Pouring" in the video (and on the fourth floor). Bookcases hold such items as ⓫ the devil-headed, "Ask Me a Yes or No Question" fortune-telling machine from the 1960 episode "Nick of Time," a story of a man unable to make decisions for himself, and ⓬ the tiny silver robot featured in the 1961 episode "The Invaders," a tale of a farm woman who kills what appear to be small invading aliens. **Boiler room:** ⓭ Though the dials of the service elevators go to "12," their arrows go to an unmarked "13." **Elevator:** ⓮ As your doors close, a hint at your destination—a "1" on the left door and a "3" on the right—disguises itself as a "B," the elevator's letter. ⓯ The small inspection certificate on the interior wall of the elevator is signed by "Cadwallader," a jovial character in the 1959 episode "Escape Clause" who secretly is the devil. Dated Oct. 31, 1939, the certificate has the number 10259, a reference to the date the TV program premiered: Oct. 2, 1959. When your ride is over, you sit next to a basement "storage area" that includes ⓰ a "Special Jackpot $10,000" slot machine from the 1960 episode "The Fever" (a talking slot drives a tightwad crazy) and ⓱ two ventriloquist dummies used in 1962's "The Dummy"(a dummy

cage "falls" faster than the pull of gravity (you reach 37 mph in 1.5 seconds, about a quarter of a second faster than a free fall) and shoots up with similar speed. The result: though you never are free of the ride's grasp, you feel completely out of control.

Most of the elevator effects are created by simple, time-tested methods. At your first stop, a long corridor filled with translucent and disappearing objects is really a shallow area filled with see-through screens showing images from hidden projectors. Though it looks far away and 8 feet tall, the end of the hall is actually just a few feet in front of you, and only 4 feet high. Once your elevator moves forward, mirrors on the floor and ceiling make it seem like those planes have disappeared. The characters to your side are simply moving plastic cutouts, split down the middle to make them look warped. In front of you, the changing star field comes from synchronized fiber-optic lights built into the doors to the final drop zone.

Each ride is different, as a computer system chooses the particulars of your fall using a random-number generator based on modulo functions—calculations that search for two numbers that, when divided by a third number, have the same remainder.

▶ Glance around at the library detail quickly. The lights go out almost immediately.

switches places with his human owner) and 1964's "Caesar and Me" (a ventriloquist uses a cigar-smoking dummy to commit crimes). **Basement:** ⓘ The clock in the basement office (the "Picture If You Will" souvenir-photo area) is stuck on 8:05, the time of the lightning strike. ⓘ In the far top left corner of that office is a small silver spaceship, the home to the library's "Invaders" robot. ⓘ The bulletin-board notes to the right seek finders of items such as "Pocket watch, sentimental value, broken crystal" a reference to the 1963 episode "A Kind of Stopwatch" (in which a bank robber stops time forever when he breaks an unusual timepiece). **Gift shop:** ⓘ The display windows are decorated for 1939's Halloween.

**Fun facts** ❶ The footage of Serling is from the introduction of the 1961 "Twilight Zone" episode, "It's a Good Life." Though he originally said "This, as you may recognize, is a map of the United States," on the video the clip cuts away as he pronounces the word "map" and instead you hear him say "maintenance service elevator." Serling's lines are voiced by impersonator Mark Silverman. ❷ The lobby in the video is not the one at the attraction. Disney filmed it in California with a similar set. ❸ The elevators have four loading areas but only two exits. The tracks merge on the top floor. ❹ The cast members' break room is between the drop shafts. When you scream, they hear you. ❺ The ride's engines are at the top and bottom of the shafts. Each develops 110,000 foot-pounds of torque and uses regeneration for deceleration control. ❻ The Tower is 199 feet high, just short enough to not need aircraft warning lights. ❼ Landscaping resembles the chaparral-covered hills of L.A.'s Griffith and Elysian Parks. ❽ While planning the attraction Disney considered housing it in a real resort, the Haunted Hollywood Hotel. Madman owner Mel Brooks would chase guests into an elevator. Another idea had actors filming a horror movie, with a walk-through segment narrated by Vincent Price. ❾ The attraction was struck by lightning as it was being built in 1993.

**Hidden Mickeys** ❶ As a pair of folded wire-rim glasses on the concierge desk (the temples form Mickey's face, the eye rims make his ears). ❷ 1932's "What! No Mickey Mouse?" is the song featured on some sheet music in the left library, on a bookcase directly in front of the entrance door. ❸ The little girl in the TV video is holding a 1930s Mickey Mouse doll. ❹ As large, round ash doors beneath a fire box on a brick furnace in the boiler room (on your right just after you've entered the basement). ❺ As water stains just to the left of a fuse box on the boiler room's left wall, just past the spot where the queue divides. ❻ On the 13th floor, in the center of the star field as it comes together in a pinpoint.

MICAELA NEAL

**Reputedly untouched since 1939,** the Hollywood Tower Hotel lobby (the Twilight Zone Tower of Terror entrance) is covered in dust and cobwebs

**TRANSCENDENTAL TV** "There is a fifth dimension beyond that which is known to man... a middle ground between light and shadow, between science and superstition... it is an area which we call The Twilight Zone." Along with a four-note theme song ("do-do-do-do, do-do-do-do..."), those words welcomed viewers to "The Twilight Zone," an imaginative television anthology that aired from 1959 to 1964. Placing ordinary people into extraordinary situations, the episodes often had mind-bending twists, with confused characters in unfamiliar, sometimes supernatural surroundings. Host Rod Serling created the show after getting fed up with censorship hassles at his job as a writer of the dramatic series "Playhouse 90." Though the CBS program was as popular as today's "American Idol" (each episode was watched by about one in 10 Americans) Serling had to fight to keep it on the air. In the 1960s, a rating that size was considered pitiful. Though the show made him a giant in the TV industry, Serling stood only 5-foot-5 and weighed just 137 pounds. A chronic smoker, he died from complications of heart surgery in 1975, at age 50.

▶ Some of the park's few air-conditioned benches line the walls just past the elevator exit.

**Sheriff Woody and Bo Peep** "get down and get funky" during Disney's Block Party Bash

# Block Party Bash

★ ★ ★ ★ ★ ✓ 22 min (5-min staged, scored setup; 12-min show (reduced during summer); 5-min departure. Arrive 15 min early for good spot, 30 min for best spots. 1st show on Hollywood Blvd, 2nd in front of American Idol Experience and Sounds Dangerous. Cancelled during rain. Fear factor: None. Access: Special areas for ECV and wheelchair guests. Debuted: 2008 (Disneyland 2005).

Unlike a parade, the Pixar-themed Block Party Bash is not a continuously moving procession. It's a staged street performance that rolls out and stops. Twice. The first show is on Hollywood Boulevard. That's followed by an identical second show along the walkway that connects the Sorcerer's Hat to Sounds Dangerous.

Dressed as everything from cowgirls to ladybugs, cheerleaders dance to disco, Motown and rock classics. Joining them are acrobats and jumping stilt-walkers, as well as characters from the "Toy Story" films, "A Bug's Life" (1998), "Monsters, Inc." (2001) and "The Incredibles" (2004). Park guests dance in the street, toss beach balls with the performers and compete in a mock scream contest. The show has 114 live performers and a support crew of 30.

The **best viewing areas** for the first show are in front of the Hot and Fresh popcorn stand for "Toy Story" characters, at the corner of Hollywood and Vine for "Monsters, Inc." stars and at the Cover Story shop for those of "A Bug's Life." For the second show, stand at the ATAS Showcase for "Toy Story," in front of The American Idol Experience for "Monsters, Inc." and between there and the Sorcerer's Hat for "A Bug's Life." Shady spots are grabbed 30 minutes early; Hollywood Blvd. benches even earlier.

**Fun finds** "Toy Story" float: ❶ The brand name of Mike the tape recorder is "Oldskool." ❷ The crayon brand is "Pixola." ❸ The eyes of Lenny (the pair of binoculars) move as they watch guests. **"Monsters, Inc." float:** ❹ From his vantage point, Sulley's control panel reads "071555," a reference to the July 15, 1955, opening of California's Disneyland. ❺ A sign indicates the float has had "4 Accident-Free Days." ❻ Its rear license plate expires in May 2005, the month the Bash debuted at Disneyland. **"A Bug's Life" float:** ❼ The Nutrition Facts on the back of the box of animal crackers indicate it has 15,000 calories, including "Calories from fat: 14,999." ❽ It has zero percent of vitamin "A113," a reference to a CalArts classroom that appears in every Pixar film. ❾ Cracker ingredients include "natural vanilla, minimally natural vanilla, I-can't-believe-it's-not-vanilla, you-could-call-it-vanilla-if-you-wanted-to vanilla," "lions, tigers and bears, oh my!" and "vita-veta-vegamins."

▶ Souvenir rubber balls are often tossed out to the crowd at the end of Block Party Bash.

*Mickey Mouse uses a magical sword in Fantasmic*

# Fantasmic!

★★★★ 25 min. Capacity: 9,900 (6,900 seats).
Arrive 90 min early for the best seats. Snack bar.
Outdoor queue. Cancelled during rain. Fear factor:
Loud noises, bright flashes, villains may frighten
small children. Access: Guests may remain in
wheelchairs, ECVs. Assistive listening; reflective
captioning. Debuted: 1998 (Disneyland 1992).

The kitchen sink of Disney's evening extravaganzas, this outdoor theatrical show includes seemingly every entertainment device the company could muster—boats, cannons, characters, fireworks, flames, fountains, lasers, music, smoke, even video projected onto water screens. It tells a story of good versus evil, as a dreaming Mickey Mouse imagines colorful animals and princesses and vanquishes Disney villains.

Most of the action takes place on a 60-foot-tall island mountain, which sits about 100 feet in front of a semicircular amphitheater. In between is a narrow lagoon that's filled with fountains and hidden special effects.

Fantasmic plays only a few times a week, but sometimes twice a night. If there are two shows, the second one is less crowded. Seating begins 90 minutes before showtime.

For reserved seating for the first show, a **Fantasmic dinner package** offers meals at The Hollywood Brown Derby, Hollywood &

Vine buffet or Mama Melrose's Ristarante Italiano and seats on the side of the theater. The package price is the same as dinner separately, but must be guaranteed with a credit card when you make your reservation.

**Dream weaver**
The show begins as Mickey, dressed as the Sorcerer's Apprentice, conducts water fountains like instruments in an orchestra, conjuring water screens that show clips from Disney films. As his powers increase, he imagines live-action flowers and animals.

After Monstro the whale (from 1940's "Pinocchio") lunges at the audience the theater turns dark—Mickey's dream has become a nightmare. A series of villains threaten, including Gov. Ratcliffe (1995's "Pocahontas") the Evil Queen (1937's "Snow White and the Seven Dwarfs") Jafar (1992's "Aladdin") and Maleficent (1959's "Sleeping Beauty"), who transforms into a dragon and ignites the lagoon with her breath.

A brief boat parade features Ariel (1989's "The Little Mermaid"), Belle (1991's "Beauty and the Beast") and Snow White. The finale has a delightful now-you-see-Mickey, now-you-don't, now-you-do farewell.

**Hidden Mickey** Pinocchio's water-screen bubble forms Mickey's head; two others form his ears.

▶ Fantasmic often plays to standing-room-only crowds. Most seats fill at least an hour early.

# Disney's
# Animal
# Kingdom

## Creativity gone wild

**Though it's not as famous** as Magic Kingdom, in many ways Disney's Animal Kingdom is much more magical. Set in 500 acres of lush landscape, Disney's largest theme park features a real safari through a 110-acre African wilderness, two Broadway-style shows, a thrilling roller coaster and up-close encounters with live animals. The park's mission: to make it easy—and fun—to appreciate the beauty, magnificence and importance of the animal world.

## The intrinsic value of nature

Though the park's zoological operations are respected worldwide, they are fully hidden from guests—secretly taking place behind man-made hills, rivers and rocks. Scientists are breeding endangered species at the park, and on-site researchers are studying animal behaviors, but guests barely hear about it.

Why? Because Disney wants you to see the real world of animals, not the artificial world of zoos. "Disney is all about storytelling, and here real live animals help tell them," executive designer Joe Rohde says. The park's stories "tend to propose conflicts—mostly conflicts with no full resolution—that get you to think about the intrinsic value of nature. You are free to engage in our stories at any level you want, including saying 'I'm not really interested, I'm just here to have fun.'"

"We want to tug people's heartstrings," adds park vice president Dr. Beth Stevens, "and get them to care about animals."

Laid out in a classic hub-and-spoke style, this park welcomes you with an entranceway through the aptly named Oasis, a tropical jungle, which leads to centrally located Discovery Island. From there five lands radiate outward.

A lion surveys the re-created
African savanna of Disney's
Animal Kingdom theme park

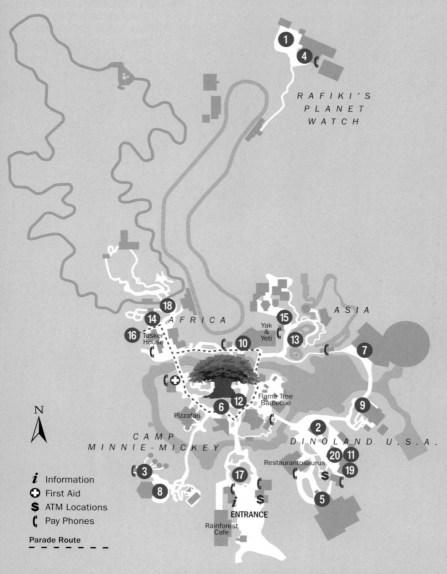

RAFIKI'S
PLANET
WATCH

AFRICA

ASIA

Yak & Yeti

Tusker House

N

Flame Tree Barbecue

Pizzafari

Discovery Island Trails

CAMP
MINNIE-MICKEY

DINOLAND U.S.A.

Restaurantosaurus

*i* Information
✛ First Aid
$ ATM Locations
☎ Pay Phones

**Parade Route**
– – – – –

ENTRANCE

Rainforest Cafe

## ATTRACTIONS

1. Affection Section
2. The Boneyard
3. Character Greeting Trails
4. Conservation Station
5. Dinosaur!
6. Discovery Island Trails
7. Expedition Everest
8. Festival of the Lion King
9. Finding Nemo
   — The Musical
10. Flights of Wonder
11. Fossil Fun Games
12. It's Tough To Be a Bug!
13. Kali River Rapids
14. Kilimanjaro Safaris
15. Maharajah Jungle Trek
16. Mickey's Jammin' Jungle
    Parade (step-off)
17. Oasis exhibits
18. Pangani Forest
    Exploration Trail
19. Primeval Whirl
20. TriceraTop Spin

# Attractions at a glance

## ANIMAL EXHIBITS

**1 Affection Section** ★★★ ✓ Allow 15 min. No wait. Rafiki's Planet Watch. Petting zoo.

**4 Conservation Station** ★★★★ ✓ Allow 30 min. No wait. Rafiki's Planet Watch. Actual research, vet facility has viewable procedures, exhibits, presentations.

**6 Discovery Island Trails** ★★★★ ✓ Allow 20 min. No wait. Discovery Island. Walkways wind through tropical garden, massive Tree of Life roots; pass exotic wildlife habitats.

**14 Kilimanjaro Safaris** ★★★★★ ✓ 22 min. Avg wait 25 min. Preshow video shows killed animals. Africa. *FastPass* Bouncy open-air truck ride roams 100 acres; encounters elephants, giraffes, lions, rhinos, more.

**15 Maharajah Jungle Trek** ★★★★★ ✓ Allow 30 min. No wait. Asia. *AuDe* Walking trail around crumbling palace passes exotic Asian animals. Nice aviary.

**17 Oasis exhibits** ★★★★ ✓ Allow 15 min. No wait. Oasis. Lush garden hosts unusual animals such as a giant anteater, spoonbills and wild pigs.

**18 Pangani Forest Exploration Trail** ★★★★★ ✓ Allow 30 min. No wait. Africa. *AuDe* Walkway past African animals; through aviary, gorilla habitat.

## BIRD SHOW

**10 Flights of Wonder** ★★★★ ✓ 25 min. Avg wait 15 min. Asia. Free-flying natural behaviors. Conservation themed.

## CARNIVAL GAMES

**11 Fossil Fun Games** ★★★ ✓ Allow 15 min. No wait. $2.50. DinoLand U.S.A. Midway games.

## CHARACTER-GREETING ATTRACTION

**3 Character Greeting Trails** ★★★ Avg wait 15 min. Camp Minnie-Mickey. Stars can include Chip 'n Dale, Donald Duck, Daisy Duck, Goofy, Koda and Kenai, Mickey and Minnie Mouse, Pocahontas.

## PARADE

**16 Mickey's Jammin' Jungle Parade** ★★★★★ ✓ 15 min. Arrive 30 min early. Huge mechanical puppets and humorous character SUVs highlight safari-themed procession. Circles Discovery Island; starts, and ends, in Africa.

## PLAYGROUND

**2 The Boneyard** ★★★★ ✓ Allow 15–30 min. No wait. DinoLand U.S.A. Dig-site play area has climbing zone, slides, tunnels.

## RIDES

**5 Dinosaur!** ★★★★ ✓ 3 min, 30 sec. Avg wait 20 min. Height restriction 40 in. Dark, intense. DinoLand U.S.A. *FastPass* Jerky open-top vehicle searches for dinosaurs.

**7 Expedition Everest** ★★★★★ ✓ 3 min. Avg wait 40 min. Height restriction 44 in. High lift, dark travel, one steep drop. Asia. *FastPass* Smooth roller coaster speeds into, out of mountain, goes backward, finds Yeti.

**13 Kali River Rapids** ★★★★ ✓ 6 min. Avg wait 40 min. Height restriction 38 in. Jerky, wet. Asia. *FastPass* Whitewater raft floats down threatened rainforest river.

**19 Primeval Whirl** ★★★★ ✓ 2 min, 30 sec. Avg wait 20 min. Height restriction 48 in. One steep drop. DinoLand U.S.A. *FastPass* Kitschy spinning coaster has time-travel theme.

**20 TriceraTop Spin** ★★★ 90 sec. Avg wait 9 min. DinoLand U.S.A. Four-seat hub-and-spoke ride; cartoon-dinosaur vehicles.

## THEATRICAL SHOWS

**8 Festival of the Lion King** ★★★★★ ✓ 28 min. Avg wait 25 min. Camp Minnie-Mickey. In-the-round revue includes stilt walkers, acrobats, fire-baton twirler. Based on 1994 film "The Lion King."

**9 Finding Nemo—The Musical** ★★★★★ ✓ 35 min. Avg wait 45 min. DinoLand U.S.A. Spectacle retells 2003's "Finding Nemo" with huge puppets, live singers.

## 3-D MOVIE

**12 It's Tough To Be a Bug!** ★★★★ 8 min. Avg wait 8 min. Intense for preschoolers. Discovery Island. *FastPass AuDe* Funny show displays insect survival skills. Stars characters from 1998's "A Bug's Life."

# Restaurants and food

Animal Kingdom has two table-service restaurants, a buffet (with a character breakfast) and four fast-food spots.

The Asian Yak & Yeti restaurant resembles a Himalayan guest house

Make **reservations** (available 180 days in advance; 190 days for Disney resort guests) as early as possible at 407-WDW-DINE (407-939-3463) or online at disneyworld.disney.go.com/dining. If you are using the **Disney Dining Plan,** note that both table-service spots only take the Premium and Platinum plans.

### TABLE SERVICE

**Rainforest Cafe** ★ ★ ★ **American $$$$** (Premium, Platinum plans only). B: $9–$14, 8:30–10a. L,D: $11–$40, 10a–park close. Annual passholders, DVC members save 10% on up to four entrees. Seats 985 plus 72 at bar. Entrance plaza. Run by outside company; direct reservations: 407-938-9100. *DP* Kids love this dark, themed dining spot. Every 20 minutes, robotic elephants and gorillas come to life in a realistic jungle of plants, trees and waterfalls. Expect a long wait except at breakfast, which offers the best value.

**Yak & Yeti** ★ ★ ★ ★ ✔ **Pan-Asian $$$$** (Premium, Platinum plans only). L,D: $17–25. 11a–park close. Annual passholders, DVC members save 10% on up to four entrees. Same management as Rainforest

Cafe. Direct reservations: 407-824-YETI. Seats 250 plus 8 at bar. Asia. *DP* Tasty sauces over slightly exotic foods distinguish this two-story "guest home." Best bets include egg rolls, fried mahi mahi and a delicious cheesecake-like mango pie. Dining areas are lined with Asian artifacts.

### BUFFET

**Tusker House** ★ ★ ★ ★ ✔ **Character meal $$$** Donald Duck, Daisy Duck, Mickey Mouse, Goofy. B ("Donald's Safari Breakfast"): $19 (children $11), opt. photo package. 8–10:30a. ★ ★ ★ ★ ✔ **African-flavored buffet $$$$** L: $20 (children $11), 11:30a–3:30p. D: $27 (children $13), 4p–park close. Seats 1,206. Bar seats 256. Africa. *DP* At breakfast, characters visit tables and dance with guests. For lunch and dinner, unlimited couscous, hummus, tabbouleh and samosas (topped with mango chutney!) make a great veggie plate. Meats are good, desserts better. Ambient African music is pleasant, though concrete floors and plaster ceilings make things noisy. The "Safari Orientation Centre"

of Disney's mythical Harambe village, the dining area is lined with real African artifacts; faux maps and notices. The serving room resembles an outdoor market.

### INDOOR FAST FOOD

Pizzafari ✓ Individual pizzas, salads, sandwiches. B: 9–10:30a. L,D: 10:30a–park close. Seats 680. Discovery Island. Vivid murals, floor mosaics, ceiling art add to clean, cool, relaxing feel. *DPQ*

Restaurantosaurus Burgers, chicken, hot dogs L,D: 11a–park close. Seats 750. DinoLand U.S.A. Lavishly wacko theme (excavation-student dorm was original Dino Institute). Right-corner "rec room" stays peaceful, cool. *DPQ*

### OUTDOOR FAST FOOD

Flame Tree BBQ ✓ BBQ meats, baked beans, corn on the cob. Seats 500. Discovery Island. Shady pavilions in garden setting, some waterside. Each has predator-and-prey motif. *DPQ*

Yak & Yeti Local Food Cafes Pork, lo mein, egg rolls. Seats 350. Asia. The mango pie is not that served in the Yak & Yeti restaurant. Bar walk-up window (Quality Beverages) around corner. *DPQ*

### FOOD TO GO

Picnic in the Park Prepackaged picnic L,D $8–10 pp for 3–6 people. Sandwich or rotisserie meats, sides, desserts, bottled water, plates, utensils. Order at park entrance or Tusker House. Pickup meal 2 hrs. 15 designated park picnic areas. *DPQ*

Beastly Bazaar Store sells prepackaged salads, sandwiches, desserts. Discovery Island, near Asia.

### BARS AND DRINK WINDOWS

Rainforest Cafe Specialty drinks, smoothies. Indoor. Full menu. Seats 72. Entrance plaza.

Dawa Bar ✓ African beer, specialty drinks. Shaded outdoor patio. Seats 256. Africa.

Yak & Yeti ✓ Specialty drinks, unique daiquiris. Full menu. Indoor. Seats 8. Asia.

Quality Beverages Specialty drinks, Asian beers. Window at Local Food Cafes. Asia.

### NOTABLE SNACK STANDS

Hand-dipped treats are offered at Safari Ice Cream (Discovery Island, Africa walkway) and Dino-Bite (DinoLand U.S.A., at Restaurantosaurus; indoor seating available). Asia's Royal Anandapur Tea Co. (across from Yak & Yeti) brews unusual teas. Africa's Harambe Fruit Market (in front of Kilimanjaro

Safaris) and Asia's Drinkwalla (across from Yak & Yeti) have fresh fruit. Coffee, hot dog and ice-cream-bar stands are throughout the park.

## Shopping

### ENTRANCE AREA

Outpost General merchandise. At entrance, near bus and tram drop offs.

Rainforest Cafe gift shop General merchandise. Children's wear, T-shirts, wildlife-themed books, sandals, toys. No Disney items.

### ASIA

Bhaktapur Market Asian merchandise. Books, decorative items, sandals, silk wraps, sundries, teapots, Yak & Yeti merchandise. Small shop run by adjacent Yak & Yeti management.

Expedition Everest cart Expedition Everest T-shirts, toys. Entrance to Expedition Everest.

Kali cart Kali River Rapids T-shirts, sandals, toys. At Kali River Rapids exit.

Mandala Gifts Jewelry, Asian sundries. Small shop in front of Yak & Yeti restaurant.

Serka Zong Bazaar Expedition Everest, Mt. Everest, Yeti merchandise. Hindu prayer flags. Expedition Everest exit. Decor has hundreds of Asian mountain artifacts. Wall photos, maps show actual Everest and expeditions.

Serka Zong cart Winnie-the-Pooh T-shirts, toys. Entrance to Serka Zong.

### AFRICA

Mombasa Marketplace / Ziwani Traders African merchandise. Handmade African pottery, woodcarvings, musical instruments; books, Disney caps, novelty hats; children's, fashion apparel; wildlife, Kilimanjaro Safaris T-shirts; jewelry; pins; toys. Ziwani Traders replicates an African safari outfitter. Authentic gear, supplies line the ceiling.

### DINOLAND U.S.A.

Chester and Hester's Dinosaur Treasures Disney toys. Candy, caps, hats. In front of Dino-Rama. Themed building is amateur fossil hunter's rural gas-station-turned-tacky-souvenir-stand.

Dino Institute gift shop Dinosaur items. Toys, T-shirts, books. Dinosaur exit.

### DISCOVERY ISLAND

Beastly Bazaar Candy, Christmas. Housewares, pet goods. Walkway to Asia. Decorated with crabs, fish, other sea life; animals that catch them.

**Creature Comforts** Children's wear. Books, Minnie Mouse children's costumes. Walkway to Africa. Decor has striped and spotted animals. **Disney Outfitters** Fashion apparel, fine jewelry. Menswear, children's wear, watches. **Art of Disney** boutique: lithographs, oils, porcelain, 2-ft. character figurines. Between entranceway, DinoLand U.S.A. Woodsy decor is embellished with animals from cardinal compass headings; art boutique has animals of ground; left room has those of air, with mural of animal constellations. **Island Mercantile** Main souvenir store. T-shirts, Disney souvenirs, toys. Pin Central. Between entranceway, Camp Minnie-Mickey. Colorful decor features migrating and working animals.

**RAFIKI'S PLANET WATCH**
**Out of the Wild** Wildlife-themed items. Books, T-shirts, plushies. Pocahontas costumes, snacks. Outdoor stand. Conservation Station.

# Character locations

**Baloo, King Louie** Bear, orangutan from 1967's "Jungle Book" On trail off Asia–Africa walkway.
**Chip 'n Dale** Chipmunks in 1940s–50s cartoons Character greeting trails, Camp Minnie-Mickey.
**Donald Duck, Daisy Duck** Foul-tempered fowl, girlfriend Character greeting trails, Camp Minnie-Mickey. Also at ✳ Donald's Safari Breakfast, Tusker House, Africa.
**Flik** Ant star of 1998's "A Bug's Life" River overlook off Asia–Africa walkway.
**Goofy** Good-natured, dim-witted dog-man Character greeting trails, Camp Minnie-Mickey; DinoLand U.S.A. Also at ✳ Donald's Safari Breakfast, Tusker House, Africa.
**Jiminy Cricket** From 1940's "Pinocchio" ✳ Conservation Station, Rafiki's Planet Watch.
**Koda, Kenai** Stars of 2003's "Brother Bear" Character greeting trails, Camp Minnie-Mickey.
**Lilo, Stitch** Stars of 2002's "Lilo & Stitch" Outside Island Mercantile shop, Discovery Island.
**Mickey Mouse** Optimistic everyman Character greeting trails, Camp Minnie-Mickey. Also at ✳ Donald's Safari Breakfast, Tusker House, Africa.
**Minnie Mouse** Mickey's girlfriend Character greeting trails, Camp Minnie-Mickey.
**Pluto** Mickey's pet DinoLand U.S.A.

✳ Air-conditioned meeting area.
Appearance times vary. For weekly updated schedules of Walt Disney World characters and street performers log on to pages.prodigy.net/stevesoares.

**Characters at Animal Kingdom include Lilo (top) from the 2002 movie "Lilo & Stitch" and cartoon chipmunk Chip (above)**

▲ **Coffee mug** Handmade in Zimbabwe. Mombasa Marketplace. $28

▶ **Carnotaurus** "Dinosaur" ride souvenir, latex. Dino Institute gift shop. $11.95

▲ **Cheetah plush** 15-inch, with park logo. Beastly Bazaar. $16.95

▶ **'Tigger, is that you?' T-shirt** Tie dye, kid's sizes. Various stores. $26.95

▼ **Chip 'n Dale Conservation T-shirt** Juniors. Disney Organic Collection. Disney Outfitters. $24.95

▼ **'Peace' Buddha bank** Bhaktapur Market. $21.29

▲ **Baby Simba** Disney's Babies plush. Various stores. $19.95

▲ **Park music** Ambient instrumentals $19.98. Attraction soundtracks $12.98. Various stores.

◀ **Safari Minnie Mouse bean bag** Various stores. $13.95

◀ **Beadworx glass parrot** Glass beads with galvanized metal. Island Mercantile. $50

▶ **Ceremonial mask** Handmade in Indonesia. Mombasa Marketplace. $22

"I'm having fish tonight!" Bruce the shark sings in Finding Nemo— The Musical

**Pocahontas** Star of 1995's "Pocahontas"
✳ Conservation Station, Rafiki's Planet Watch;
Character greeting trails, Camp Minnie-Mickey.
**Rafiki** Baboon from 1994's "The Lion King"
✳ Conservation Station, Rafiki's Planet Watch.
**Terk** Girl gorilla from 1999's "Tarzan" Across from
Pizzafari, Discovery Island.
**Winnie the Pooh, Eeyore, Piglet, Tigger**
From 1977's "The Many Adventures of Winnie the Pooh"
Boat landing across from Flame Tree BBQ,
Discovery Island.

# Street performers

## MUSICIANS
**Gi-Tar Dan** 20 min, courtyard, Camp Minnie-Mickey.
Funnyman sings about animals, invites children to
join in.
**Mor Thiam** 20 min, various locations, Africa. 5 days wk.
Djembe drum master. Often invites audience to
join in. Unaffected living legend, has been called
Africa's greatest percussionist; has played with B.B.
King. (Father of R&B artist Akon.)
**Tam Tams of Congo** 20 min, in front of the Tusker
House restaurant, Africa. Rousing native percussion
quintet brings guests of all ages on stage for quick
lessons in West African dances.
**Tropicals** 20 min, various locations, DinoLand U.S.A.
Steel-drum band often plays Disney tunes.
**Village Beatniks** 20 min, in front of Flame Tree BBQ,
Discovery Island. Percussion group uses five drum
sets, zendrum, cow bell to create syncopated
cadences. Guests shake rhythm tubes.

## ACROBATS
**Smear, Splat & Dip** 20 min, DinoLand U.S.A. Three
dippy painters balance, juggle.

## PERFORMANCE ARTISTS
**DiVine** 20 min, on walkway between Africa and Asia.
Covered in foliage, slow-moving stilt-walker
blends into landscape.
**Pipa the Talking Recycling Bin** 20 min,
Conservation Station, Rafiki's Planet Watch. Roving trash
can jokes with guests.

## CULTURAL REPRESENTATIVES
**Asian cultural representatives** Pavilion next
to Yak & Yeti, Asia. Natives from Thailand, Bali and
other countries talk about homelands.
**Harambe School** 20 min, Harambe Village, Africa.
Botswanans, Namibians, South Africans discuss
homelands at tiny open-air spot.

**Top: Acclaimed African drummer Mor Thiam appears in Disney's Harambe Village. Above: Performance artist DiVine appears in Asia.**

A light rain is an ideal time for a Kilimanjaro Safaris ride. The covered truck keeps you dry, and the animals are usually more active.

# Planning Your Day

**Unlike Walt Disney World's** other theme parks, Disney's Animal Kingdom does not require creating a convoluted plan in order to fully enjoy it. Except for the most crowded days, only a few rides have long lines. And though it's usually most rewarding to see them early in the day, the park's exotic animals can be viewed any time.

## 1. Choose a day to go

The best days to visit Animal Kingdom are those with cloudy skies and cooler temperatures. Not only will the animals will be more active on these days and, therefore, easier to see, but you'll be more comfortable as you roam the park's many expansive outdoor areas.

▶ **'Extra Magic Hours'** The park usually opens an hour early on Mondays for guests staying at Disney resorts, and stays open late for these guests on Wednesdays or Fridays. Schedules are posted six months early at the "Calendar" link at **disneyworld.disney. go.com/parks/animal-kingdom**. The extra morning hour makes it easier to view animals when they are active. Nights are pretty—twinkly white bulbs line most walkways; DinoLand U.S.A. is lit like a roadside carnival.

## 2. Decide what to do

The park has four "must" things to do—ride its roller coaster, see its two theatrical shows, and see its wildlife. Zoological exhibits include Kilimanjaro Safaris, an open-air truck ride through an African setting. Lesser attractions are worthwhile, too. In fact, there's barely a dud in the bunch. You'll find an "Attractions At a Glance" summary earlier in this chapter; further back are detailed descriptions and animal guides. Traveling with children? Give them this book and have them point out what they would like to see.

As for lines, there are only two attractions where the wait gets really long: the Expedition Everest roller coaster and Kali River Rapids raft ride. Get Fastpasses for them, and, if you can, Kilimanjaro Safaris. Its lines can get long during the middle of the day.

The self-guided nature of the animal exhibits makes them ideal for guests who want to take things at a slow pace. On Saturdays, hearing-impaired guests can see sign-language interpreted performances of Festival of the Lion King (usually the 1:30 p.m. show) and Mickey's Jammin' Jungle Parade.

# 3. Family matters

Animal Kingdom is one of Walt Disney World's most family-friendly theme parks, since it has so many animal exhibits and live shows. Three attractions are geared specifically to young children: TriceraTop Spin, the Boneyard playground and the Affection Section petting zoo.

▶ **Height restrictions** exist at the Dinosaur (40 in), Expedition Everest (44 in), Kali River Rapids (38 in), and Primeval Whirl (48 in) rides.

▶ **Fear factors** All rides with height restrictions (see above) also have scary elements. The 3-D movie It's Tough to be a Bug has frightening in-theater effects and threatening robotic insects.

▶ **Kids meals** Every restaurant offers a children's menu. The park has one character meal: Donald's Safari Breakfast at Africa's Tusker House. Most kids also love Rainforest Cafe at the very front of Animal Kingdom.

▶ **Baby care** A Baby Care Center sits behind the Creature Comforts store on Discovery Island. It provides changing rooms, nursing areas, a microwave and a playroom free of charge, and sells diapers, formula, pacifiers and over-the-counter medications. Moms can

## PARK RESOURCES

**ATMs** Entrance plaza, on the right; outside Dinosaur Treasures, DinoLand U.S.A.

**First Aid center** For minor emergencies. Registered nurses. Behind Creature Comforts, Discovery Island.

**Guest Relations** Multilingual cast members answer questions, make dining reservations, solve problems. Has maps, Times Guides for all WDW theme parks, exchanges foreign currency, stores items found in the park that day. Entrance plaza.

**Lockers** $7 a day plus $5 deposit. Next to Guest Relations.

**Mobile app** (Verizon) $10, at m.disneyworld.com. "Mobile Magic" covers all WDW theme parks.

**Package pickup** Up to 3 hours before you leave, anything you buy in the park can be sent to Package Pickup for you to pick up on your way out free of charge. Packages can also be delivered the next day to your Disney hotel or shipped to your home. Entrance plaza.

**Parking** $14 a day per car. Those staying at a Disney resort, and annual passholders, get free parking.

**Strollers** Singles $15/day, $13/day length of stay. Doubles $31, $27. Replacements at Africa's Mombasa Marketplace. Entrance plaza.

**Tip Board** Displays waiting times for most attractions. Discovery Island.

**Transportation** Disney buses run to Animal Kingdom from all WDW resorts, Epcot, Disney's Hollywood Studios and Blizzard Beach. Magic Kingdom guests take a monorail to the Transportation and Ticket Center, then a bus. No direct service to Downtown Disney, Typhoon Lagoon.

**Wheelchairs, Scooters** Wheelchairs $12/day, $10/day length of stay. Electric Convenience Vehicles (4-wheeled scooters) $50/day, $20 deposit. Entrance plaza.

## HOUR-BY-HOUR WAIT TIMES

This table shows the average **wait time** (in min.) for each park attraction that has one. Zoological exhibits and DinoLand U.S.A. playground and carnival games have no waits. *Live shows listings indicate the average early arrival time needed to get a good seat.

| ATTRACTION | 9A | 10A | 11A | Noon | 1P | 2P | 3P | 4P | 5P | 6P | 7P | 8P |
|---|---|---|---|---|---|---|---|---|---|---|---|---|
| Dinosaur | 0 | 25 | 35 | 20 | 40 | 35 | 25 | 20 | 20 | 15 | 10 | 5 |
| Expedition Everest | 15 | 40 | 50 | 45 | 55 | 45 | 45 | 35 | 30 | 45 | 40 | 20 |
| Festival of the Lion King* | 10 | 20 | 20 | 20 | 30 | 30 | 30 | 30 | 30 | 30 | N/A | N/A |
| Finding Nemo—The Musical* | N/A | 30 | 30 | 30 | 30 | 30 | 30 | 30 | 30 | N/A | N/A | N/A |
| Flights of Wonder* | N/A | 15 | 15 | 15 | 15 | 15 | 15 | 15 | 15 | 15 | N/A | N/A |
| It's Tough To Be a Bug | 0 | 5 | 10 | 15 | 10 | 10 | 5 | 5 | 5 | 5 | 5 | 5 |
| Kali River Rapids | 10 | 20 | 35 | 60 | 80 | 45 | 50 | 60 | 30 | 30 | 10 | CLSD |
| Kilimanjaro Safaris | 15 | 35 | 25 | 25 | 30 | 45 | 20 | 20 | 20 | 20 | 10 | CLSD |
| Primeval Whirl | 10 | 35 | 25 | 20 | 30 | 20 | 20 | 15 | 20 | 10 | 20 | 10 |
| TriceraTop Spin | 0 | 5 | 5 | 5 | 20 | 20 | 10 | 10 | 10 | 10 | 5 | 5 |

Data based on surveys taken on random days during the summers of 2008 and 2009.

nurse anywhere at Animal Kingdom; good spots include the back rooms at Pizzafari and Restaurantosaurus restaurants during non-meal hours, and the Song of the Rainforest exhibit at Conservation Station. Its cool, dimly-lit, family-sized audio booths are often ignored by guests.

▶ **Lost children** Report them to Guest Relations or any cast member.

## 4. Decide where to eat

Flip back a few pages to find listings of every Animal Kingdom restaurant.

## 5. Make a plan

As you create your plan, keep in mind the average wait times and typical Fastpass return times for the rides and shows you want to see. You can find weekly schedules for parades and fireworks at the "Calendar" link at **disneyworld.disney.go.com/parks/animal-kingdom**. Schedules of characters and street performers are at **pages.prodigy.net/stevesoares**. Assume you need to arrive 15 minutes early for a table-service reservation. For a road-tested ready-made plan, see our "A Magical Day" schedule below.

## A MAGICAL DAY

**8:30a** Arrive at the park. As you wait for the gates to open (typically 8:50 a.m.), pick up a Times Guide from the Guest Relations window at your left.

**9:05a** Get Fastpasses for the Expedition Everest roller coaster.

**9:10a** See the Asian animal exhibits along the Maharajah Jungle Trek walkway. The giant bats will be at their most lively.

**9:45a** Ride Kilimanjaro Safaris.

**10:30a** See the African animals along the Pangani Forest Trail. Gorillas and meerkats should be active.

**11:30a** Ride the Expedition Everest roller coaster. Ask for the front row for the best views, the back seat for the biggest thrill.

**12:00p** Get Fastpasses for the Kali River Rapids raft ride. (Don't want to get wet? Make plans to see Mickey's Jammin' Jungle Parade.)

**12:15p** Lunch. While you eat, check

## FASTPASS RETURN TIMES

Six Animal Kingdom attractions offer Disney's Fastpass system, a free service which reserves a time for you to return later in the day to experience that ride or show without standing in the regular line. This table shows the average **return times** for Fastpasses dispensed at those attractions for each hour of a typical park day. Note that all of these attractions typically have Fastpasses available until at least 4 p.m.

| ATTRACTION | 9A | 10A | 11A | Noon | 1P | 2P | 3P | 4P | 5P | 6P | 7P | 8P |
|---|---|---|---|---|---|---|---|---|---|---|---|---|
| Dinosaur | 10:10 | 10:45 | 11:45 | 12:45 | 1:45 | 2:45 | 3:45 | 4:45 | OUT | OUT | OUT | CLSD |
| Expedition Everest | 10:10 | 11:45 | 12:50 | 2:30 | 4:00 | 5:00 | 6:00 | 6:30 | 7:00 | OUT | OUT | CLSD |
| Kali River Rapids | 10:10 | 11:20 | 11:50 | 1:20 | 2:40 | 4:00 | 5:15 | 6:30 | OUT | OUT | OUT | CLSD |
| Kilimanjaro Safaris | 10:10 | 11:10 | 12:20 | 1:20 | 2:20 | 3:20 | 4:20 | 5:20 | 6:20 | OUT | OUT | CLSD |
| Primeval Whirl | 10:10 | 10:45 | 11:45 | 12:45 | 1:45 | 2:45 | 3:45 | 4:45 | OUT | OUT | OUT | CLSD |
| It's Tough To Be a Bug | 10:10 | 11:15 | 11:35 | 12:35 | 1:35 | 2:45 | 3:45 | 4:45 | 5:45 | OUT | OUT | CLSD |

Data based on surveys taken on random days during the summers of 2008 and 2009.

## 6. Beating the heat

Because of its abundance of trees, plants and shade, Animal Kingdom stays cooler than Disney World's other theme parks, though its walkways are so long the heat can still get to you. Fountains in Asia and water sprays in Africa offer some relief. The Conservation Station and Dinosaur buildings and the theaters for Festival of the Lion King, Finding Nemo—The Musical and It's Tough To Be a Bug are air-conditioned, as are all indoor shops and restaurants. Fast-food spots Pizzafari and Restaurantosaurus almost always have open tables that make it easy to take a break.

## 7. What if it rains?

It can be tough to ignore the weather at Animal Kingdom, since it has the fewest indoor attractions of any Disney World theme park. Kilimanjaro Safaris rides are actually *better* during a rain, as the animals are usually more active. No park attraction closes due to rain, but Mickey's Jammin' Jungle Parade can get cancelled. Roller coasters Expedition Everest and Primeval Whirl temporarily close when lightning is in the area, as does The Boneyard, Kali River Rapids and TriceraTop Spin. A good spot to duck out of the rain is the centrally located Pizzafari fast-food restaurant.

your Times Guide for the afternoon start times of Festival of the Lion King, Finding Nemo—The Musical and Mickey's Jammin' Jungle Parade, and adjust the plan below accordingly.

**1:30p** Get in line to see the 2 p.m. performance of Festival of the Lion King. You'll get a great seat.

**3:00p** Ride Kali River Rapids or see Mickey's Jammin' Jungle Parade.

**4:15p** Get in line to see Finding

Nemo—The Musical. The least crowded show of the day usually starts at 4:45 p.m.

**5:00p** Choose from any of the attractions in DinoLand U.S.A. (waiting lines will be short).

**Bonus** This schedule has extra time built into it, to account for bathroom breaks, snack stops, etc. As time allows, check out the live performers in Africa or the animals in the Oasis.

# The Oasis

★ ★ ★ ★ ✓ Allow 15 min. No wait. 3 trails (1200 ft), 13 viewing areas, 17 species. Fear factor: None. Access: Wheelchair, ECV accessible. Debuted: 1998.

The thematic entrance to the park, this zoological area connects Animal Kingdom's turnstiles and guest services area with its Discovery Island hub. Lush tropical and subtropical plants from throughout the world — flowering trees, vines and shrubs such as jacarandas, tabebuias, orchids as well as bamboo, eucalyptus, palms and broad-canopied evergreens—combine to create a unique natural entranceway.

Tucked under that canopy, a man-made haven of pools, streams and waterfalls is, in essence, its own small zoo. Displayed in natural habitats, exotic animals include a babirusa, swamp wallaby, spoonbills and black swans. College interns greet early-morning guests with terrariums, antlers and other hand-held wildlife exhibits.

**Fun finds** ❶ Can't find the anteater? It likes to rest in the gully directly in front of the guest overlook rail. ❷ Where's the wallaby? Try the shady spot to the far left of its viewing area. ❸ A swaying footbridge runs alongside the top of the left walkway. Water bubbles from rocks underneath. ❹ The footbridge leads to a small cave-like area where you can touch the back of

**Like Main Street U.S.A.** at Magic Kingdom, the Oasis serves as the Animal Kingdom entranceway and sets the tone and feel of the park

the waterfall. A bench is rarely occupied. ❺ The park dedication plaque sits in front of the black swans.

**Fun fact** Used for bathing, feeding and, yes, pooping by the many birds, the water in the ponds and streams is continually cleaned and recirculated through pipes that run under the walkways.

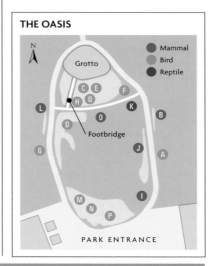

**THE OASIS**

Mammal
Bird
Reptile

▶ Park animals are most active first thing in the morning and late in the day.

# Animals of the Oasis

**A** **Admin's stork** Will defecate on its legs to maintain body temperature by evaporative cooling.

**B** **Babirusa** Up to a foot long, males' upper tusks extend through the snout and curve back toward the face. Legend says the babirusa hangs from trees at night by its tusks. Eats clay to cleanse system. "Babirusa" means "pig deer" in Malay language.

**Ducks** **C** **Chiloe wigeon** Small dabbling duck. Metallic green head, white cheeks; female quacks. **D** **Indian spotted duck** Gets name from orange and yellow spots on bill. **E** **Rosybill pochard** Dark plumage offset by bright pink-red bill.

**Macaws** **F** **Hyacinth macaw** World's largest parrot. Cobalt blue, though has no blue pigment in plumage; feather structure produces a blue cast. **G** **Military macaw** Olive-green feathers make it look as if it is dressed in army fatigues. **H** **Scarlet macaw** Has brilliant multicolored plumage. Longest tail feathers of any macaw.

**I** **Patagonian cavy** One of the world's largest rodents; just under 3 ft long. Related to a guinea pig, but resembles a small deer with a rabbit-like head. Long legs let it run up to 28 mph and leap to 6 ft.

**J** **Reeve's muntjac** Called "barking deer" due to call it makes when alarmed. Male has short antlers to throw rivals off-balance and large canine teeth that curl from lips like tusks, used to injure enemies.

**K** **Rhinoceros iguana** Large lizard has pointed snout scales that resemble rhinoceros horns.

**L** **Southern giant anteater** Can be up to 9 ft long. Sucks up 30,000 ants, termites a day by flicking 2-ft-long tongue 160 times a minute. To protect claws, walks on front knuckles. Largest claws of any mammal, longest tongue of any mammal of its size. Uses tail as a blanket when sleeping.

**Spoonbills** Wading birds. Feed by swinging open spoon-shaped bills in water. In mating ritual, males offer female sticks for her nest; when she accepts one she has chosen her mate. Lines nest with leaves. Disney's spoonbills hatch eggs, raise young in spring. **M** **African spoonbill** is white. **N** **Roseate spoonbill** has pink, red and orange plumage; some crustaceans it eats feed on algae that give bird its rosy color.

**O** **Swamp wallaby** Small kangaroo cousin. Survives dry habitats by drinking sea water when fresh not available. Also known as the black wallaby or, due to its musky odor, "the stinker."

**Swans** **P** **Black swan** Only swan with all black plumage. Longest swan neck. **Q** **Black-necked swan** White body; large red bill knob. Parents piggy-back young to protect them from cold water, predators.

**From top:** Disney's roseate spoonbills hatch eggs and raise young each spring. The Southern giant anteater walks on its front knuckles. The rhinoceros iguana has pointed snout scales that resemble rhinoceros horns.

© DISNEY

**Bugs seems to join the audience** in the 3-D movie It's Tough To Be a Bug (photo illustration)

# It's Tough To Be a Bug

★★★★ 8 min. Capacity: 430. *FastPass* Mostly shaded outdoor queue. Fear factor: Intense for preschoolers, with darkness, fog, cartoonish menacing bugs. Access: Guests may remain in wheelchairs, ECVs. Assistive listening, reflective captioning. *AuDe* Debuted: 1999.

Housed inside the trunk of the Tree of Life, this show combines a 3-D movie with startling theater effects. Hosted by Flik, the mild-mannered ant of 1998's "A Bug's Life," it has a cute charm and some wicked wit.

To show how bugs have "developed some amazing survival techniques," Flik brings out a tarantula who shoots poison quills, a soldier termite who sprays acid and a stink bug who, well, stinks. A robotic Hopper, the grasshopper villain of "A Bug's Life," crashes the show. What bugs him? People.

"You guys only see us as monsters!" he roars. Maybe it's time you got a taste of your own medicine!" A 3-D attack on the audience includes a giant fly swatter, a can of bug spray and some angry spiders and hornets.

| Average Wait | |
| --- | --- |
| 9am | 0 min |
| 10am | 5 |
| 11am | 10 |
| Noon | 20 |
| 1pm | 10 |
| 2pm | 5 |
| 3pm | 5 |
| 4pm | 5 |
| 5pm | 5 |
| 6pm | 5 |
| 7pm | 5 |
| 8pm | 5 |
| 9pm | 5 |

All ends well, of course. A musical finale recalls grand Busby Berkeley production numbers. Singing honeybees proclaim "We're Pollinators!" then a circling bug chorus exclaims *"If it weren't for the fact that we liked the taste, you'd be out there wallowing in shoulder-high waste!"*

**Fun finds** ❶ Just outside the lobby, a wall plaque honors Dr. Jane Goodall's work with chimpanzees. It's next to a carving of David Graybeard, one of her subjects. ❷ Lobby posters promote previous shows "A Stinkbug Named Desire," "Barefoot in the Bark," "Beauty and the Bees" "Little Shop of Hoppers" and "Web Side Story." ❸ The lobby displays a giant dung ball from "The Dung and I." ❹ Lobby music features instrumentals from those shows. ❺ The auditorium looks like it's inside an anthill. ❻ The projection booth is a wasp nest. ❼ The pre-show announcer reports that "the stinkbug will be played by Claire DeRoom." ❽ After Claire performs, Flik tells her "Hey, lay off the churros!" ❾ As the performance ends, fireflies swarm to the exit signs.

**Fun fact** Character voices include those of actors Dave Foley (Flik), Cheech Marin (Chili the tarantula) and Kevin Spacey (Hopper).

**Hidden Mickeys** As spots on a root in the lobby, left of the theater's handicapped entrance.

LYRICS © DISNEY

▶ The best seats are in the center of the back rows. Lean back in your seat to feel all the effects.

## Discovery Island Trails

★ ★ ★ ★ ✓ Allow 20 min. 2 trails (1680 ft), 9 viewing areas, 15 species. Fear factor: None. Access: Guests may stay in wheelchairs, ECVs. Debuted: 1998.

Live animals, including flamingos, kangaroos and small primates, surround the Tree of Life in the park's largest tropical habitat. The lush area is filled with pools, waterfalls—and some hidden winding walkways. The trails aren't marked, so they're tough to find but never crowded. Most of the area is shady, a blessing on a hot day.

Crested cranes, exotic deer, lemurs and tamarins roam within the Tree of Life Garden, a lush area directly in front of the tree. To its left, a series of connected ponds holds flamingos, otters and whistling ducks. The otter pond has an underwater viewing area.

To the left of the ponds, a small trail often has its entrance partially blocked by a gift cart or character greeting line. It leads to a gray- and red-kangaroo exhibit and eventually to a ring-tailed-lemur habitat that's behind the Fastpass machines for the attraction It's Tough to be a Bug.

A second trail runs behind the tree along the Discovery River, from the gate to the park's Africa section to the gate for Asia. This path is home to macaws, crested porcupines, storks and Galapagos tortoises.

**Hidden walkways** wind through wildlife habitats that surround Discovery Island's Tree of Life

### The Tree of Life

Rising 145 feet, the man-made Tree of Life is one of only a handful of artificial trees among the 4 million living plants at Animal Kingdom. It's leafy canopy spreads 160 feet.

Carved into the tree's gnarled roots, mighty trunk and sturdy branches is a tapestry of more than 300 animals. Its leaves—of many colors and four shapes and sizes, all attached by hand to more than 8,000 of the tree's end branches—number more than 103,000. Its trunk is 50 feet wide and spreads to 170 feet in diameter at its sprawling base. A giant expansion joint encircles the tree at each branch unit. Inside it all is a support structure similar to an offshore oil rig.

"The Tree of Life is a technological marvel, but it's also a symbol of the diversity and grandeur of our animal life," says Disney Imagineer Joe Rohde. "We want you to regard it with awe and wonder and to translate those feelings to the real animal world."

The tree took 18 months to build. Its trunk was first assembled outside of the Animal Kingdom site, so that the animal sculptures could be created in a fluid fashion. The trunk was then cut into a dozen segments and flown to a construction site near the theme park, put back together, and transported by crane to its final location.

▶ The Discovery Island trails are not marked. They can be tough to find, but are rarely crowded.

# Discovery Island animals

**Ⓐ African crested porcupine** Largest, heaviest African rodent; up to 60 lbs. Covered with long, barbed quills. Shoulder quills stand erect to form crest. Quill length varies from 1 to 12 in. Usually quills lie flat against body, but when alarmed the animal raises its quills as if getting goosebumps. Does not shoot quills. Quills easily fall out, and can get imbedded in a predator's skin. Scales on tips lodge in the skin like fishhooks and are difficult to pull out. New quills grow in to replace lost ones. Newborns have soft spines that later harden.

**Ⓑ Asian catfish** World's largest scaleless freshwater fish. Up to 10 ft, 650 lbs. Travels yearly up to 600 miles, from South China Sea up Mekong River.

**Ⓒ Asian small-clawed otter** World's smallest otter at 2 to 11 lbs. Playful; chases other otters on land and in water at speeds to 18 mph. Unique (for otters) non-webbed front paws look like hands.

**Ⓓ Axis deer** Females fight like boxing kangaroos, pawing at each other while standing on hind legs. Male has branched antlers, ruts almost constantly, makes loud, bugle-like bellow.

**Ducks Ⓔ Eyton tree duck** Spends most of its time on land, not on water. Has long tan plumes on wings. **Ⓕ White-faced whistling duck** Sounds like a squeak toy, with a high-pitched three-note whistle.

**Ⓖ Galapagos tortoise** World's largest tortoise at 5-ft long. Herbivore. Lives only in Galapagos archipelago (named for animal, in Spanish "galapagos" means tortoise), 600 miles west of Ecuador. Can live up to 150 yrs (documented), but it's a slow life; top speed is only 0.16 mph. Peaceful, lazy life centers on grazing and wallowing in puddles. At night, sleeps partially submerged in mud, water or brush. Can retain so much water can go without eating or drinking for a year. Males fight by facing each other, opening their mouths, and stretching their heads as high as they can. Whoever stretches the highest wins.

**Ⓗ Helmeted guinea fowl** Common in southern, western Kenya. Call is a grating, rasping, staccato "kek-kek-kek." Nest is shared among females, can have 50 eggs.

**Ⓘ Kangaroos** Only large mammal that hops, can jump 9 ft in air, leap 40 ft, run 30 mph. Black-leg tendons act as giant springs. At speed can outpace racehorse. At rest, weight supported by tripod of hind legs, tail. Licks forearms to stay cool. Cannot walk backward. Inch-long hairless newborn resembles jellybean: still-developing joey has no back legs, crawls into mother's pouch, stays 9 mo. Mother produces different milk for different joeys; controls progress of pregnancy so each newborn has open teat. Gestation typically takes 35 days, can be delayed nearly a year. Males box to

## DISCOVERY ISLAND

Kids Discovery Club activities

Tree of Life

Mammal
Bird
Reptile
Fish

Underwater viewing area

Entrance to It's Tough To Be a Bug

N

gain dominance. **Red kangaroo** World's largest marsupial. Can stand nearly 7 ft, weigh 200 lbs. Color matches soil of Australian outback. Can go without drinking if green grass is available. **Western gray kangaroo** Least common large kangaroo in U.S. zoos. Ⓙ **Lappet-faced vulture** Unlike other vultures, sometimes eats live prey. Folds of skin (lappets) hang off bare, pink head. Wingspan 9 ft. **Lemurs** Ⓚ **Collared lemur** In wild, will salivate on poisonous millipedes and roll them between hands before eating, possibly to remove toxins. Reddish-blond beard, long furry tail. Ⓛ **Ring-tailed lemur** Uses long tail as flag to signal location or warn of danger. Females dominant. Male competes for female by rubbing tail with wrist-gland odor, arching tail over back and shaking it at other males while baring teeth. Golden eyes. Long tail; black and white tail rings. Ⓜ **Lesser flamingo** Smallest, brightest pink flamingo; also most numerous. Pink color comes from diet, which includes algae, aquatic insects, crustaceans. Stands on one leg to rest. Social, lives in groups from a few birds to tens of thousands. Ritualized displays include head-flagging (stretching neck with head high and rhythmically turning from side to side), wing salute (with tail cocked, neck outstretched) and marching together before switching direction abruptly. In East Africa, up to a million lesser flamingos gather together, forming the largest flock of birds in the world. Ⓝ **Red-fronted macaw** Smallest standard-sized macaw. Mostly green with brilliant red forehead, crown and ear patches; turquoise flight and tail feathers; and neon orange under the wings. **Storks** Ⓞ **Painted stork** When young, can make loud call to attract attention; by 18 months practically voiceless like adult. Has bright pink patch on its back during breeding season. Ⓟ **Saddle-billed stork** Builds a large stick nest in tops of tall trees that will hold one egg. Has colorful black, red and yellow bill. Ⓠ **White stork** Lives in African grasslands. German legend of bird bringing babies comes from centuries of migration from Africa to northern Germany to nest on chimneys, roofs in spring, a time of many human births. Lifelong mates share incubating, feeding young. Chicks mew, do not cheep or squawk. Ⓡ **Tambaqui** Freshwater fish; looks similar to the smaller piranha and is sometimes confused with the carnivorous fish; it mostly eats plants. Ⓢ **West African crowned crane** Golden, halo-like crown; red face patch. Mostly gray and white with some golden tail feathers.

**From top:** The West African crowned crane has a golden, halo-like crown. The ring-tailed lemur uses its long tail as a flag, to signal its location or warn of danger. The red-fronted macaw is the smallest standard-sized macaw.
**Opposite page:** The western gray kangaroo is rarely seen in American zoos. The Galapagos tortoise is the world's largest tortoise.

MACAWS, CROWNED CRANE: MICAELA NEAL

# Festival of the Lion King

★★★★★ ✓ 28 min. Capacity: 1,375. Partially shaded outdoor queue. Fear factor: None. Access: ECV, wheelchair accessible. Assistive listening, handheld captioning. Debuted: 1998.

A spectacular revue of the best songs from the 1994 film, "The Lion King," this in-the-round show combines the pageantry of a parade with the excitement of a tribal festival. Live singers, dancers, acrobats, stilt walkers and giant puppets fill your field of vision as they celebrate the joy of life.

The show opens as the dancers interpret a sunrise, accompanied by the dramatic African chant from "The Circle of Life." A chorus of "I Just Can't Wait to be King" brings in nearly 50 more performers, including wisecracking emcee Timon. A 12-foot animated Simba stands atop Pride Rock, a parade float. Another float has Pumbaa.

The performance is filled with memorable moments. Silly Tumble Monkey acrobats use still rings, bars and a flying trapeze. A dramatic fire-baton twirler performs

| Average Wait | |
|---|---|
| 9am | 10 min |
| 10am | 20 |
| 11am | 20 |
| Noon | 20 |
| 1pm | 30 |
| 2pm | 30 |
| 3pm | 30 |
| 4pm | 30 |
| 5pm | 30 |
| 6pm | n/a |
| 7pm | n/a |
| 8pm | n/a |
| 9pm | n/a |

**Each dancer and stiltwalker costume** in the Festival of the Lion King uses cuffs, a headpiece, leotard, leggings, skirt, yoke and makeup to transform its wearer into an abstract animal

to "Be Prepared." A ballet dancer soars in the air during a touching "Can You Feel the Love Tonight" duet. There's an audience sing-along to "The Lion Sleeps Tonight," while a gospel-like finale synchronizes dancers, singers, kites and lighting effects into a kaleidoscopic circle of life.

Where to sit? As you enter the theater you'll find four seating areas. To see the show the way it's intended, sit in the quadrant at the back right. This way Timon will face you during his "Hakuna Matata" number and you'll sit between the Pumbaa and Simba float puppets, which will make those characters easy to hear.

Though the most spirited shows are those with a full house, the first show of the day is the easiest to get into. Typically held at 9:40 a.m., it's often less than half full.

**Fun finds ❶** As Timon's float enters and heads to a corner, he looks at the dancer holding the float's remote control and says "Slow down! I'm supposed to be center stage!" **❷** The Tumble Monkeys "pick bugs" off guests and each other. **❸** Their musical cues include a Tarzan yell, a cow moo, a train whistle, a *gargled* version of Duke Ellington's 1937 "Caravan" and a snippet of the 1923 ditty "Yes, We

▶ Get to the theater 40 minutes before showtime to have a choice of the best seats.

**Clockwise from top:** Meerkat Timon hosts the show. Children briefly join the performers on stage. A Tumble Monkey acrobat. A stilt walker in a dramatic stance. A ballet bird boogies during the finale.

Have No Bananas." ❹ Timon is a show all by himself. Able to blink his eyes and move his mouth, he cracks up watching the monkeys, trembles during "Be Prepared" and swoons throughout "Can You Feel the Love Tonight?" ❺ The giraffe often mouths the words to the songs. ❻ As you exit, you hear Timon say "Could somebody hose down those Tumble Monkeys? They're starting to smell a little gamey." ❼ Puppeteers hide inside the floats, and can see out. If the floats are still present as you leave, stand in front of one of the puppets and wave or say "Hi." You may get a response.

**LION CUB SIMBA** finds his place in nature's circle of life in Disney's acclaimed 1994 movie "The Lion King." After his father is killed by his uncle Scar, Simba thinks he caused it and flees into exile. Befriended by freewheeling meerkat Timon and warmhearted (and often pungent) warthog Pumbaa, Simba adopts the duo's "hakuna matata" (no worries) attitude as he grows up. After childhood sweetheart Nala re-enters his life, however, the adult Simba returns and takes his place as king.

▶ Watch the movie first. The show's more fun after you refresh your memory of the film.

# Kilimanjaro Safaris

★★★★★ ✓ 22 min. Capacity: Apx 36 per truck, max 4,320 guests per hr. Open 9a–dusk. *FastPass* Covered outdoor queue. Fear factor: Video shows slaughtered animals, finale has audible gunshots. Access: ECV users must transfer. Assistive listening; handheld and activated captioning. Debuted: 1998.

One of the best zoological attractions in the United States, this jerky open-air truck ride takes you through a near-perfect re-creation of African jungles and savannas. You'll splash through rivers, cross bridges, climb hills, and encounter dozens of free-roaming rare and exotic animals. Though the most dangerous animals are kept away from your vehicle by unseen barriers, others can come right up to it.

No matter how many times you ride you never know what you'll see. Bongos, cheetahs, elephants, giraffes, lions, mandrills, okapi, warthogs… they're all here. The 100-acre habitat can't be completely authentic—if it was many of the animals would be eating each other—but it sure seems to be.

**Top:** A safari truck approaches a giraffe. **Above:** A cheetah surveys the savanna.

## 'Poachers may be involved'

Supposedly an effort by Disney's nearby village of Harambe to replace its timbering economy with eco-tourism, Kilimanjaro Safaris takes you on a "two-week" trip through the "800-square-mile Harambe Wildlife Preserve." The story begins in the queue, as videos introduce you to the refuge and show its main problem: poachers. Soon you board your ride, a flatbed logging vehicle retrofitted with bench seats and a canvas top.

Once underway, your driver establishes radio contact with warden Wilson Matuah. He flies above you in his spotter plane, occasionally giving directions to herds.

Eventually Matuah radios with an urgent plea: he has spotted poachers with a baby elephant, and he needs your help to rescue it. Cutting short your trip, your driver leaves

| Average Wait | |
|---|---|
| 9am | 0 min |
| 10am | 35 |
| 11am | 25 |
| Noon | 25 |
| 1pm | 30 |
| 2pm | 45 |
| 3pm | 20 |
| 4pm | 20 |
| 5pm | 20 |
| 6pm | 20 |
| 7pm | 10 |
| 8pm | closed |
| 9pm | closed |

▶ The best trips are early in the day or during a light rain, when the animals are lively.

the preserve and chases the poachers through a hot springs gorge and into a clearing. The poachers escape, but the warden recovers the baby.

Redone in 2007, the radio transmissions are a condensed version of a previous storyline ("They've shot Big Red!") that played a much larger role in the experience.

**Fun finds** ❶ At the start of the standby queue, an answering machine in the safari office answers a ringing phone with "Harambe Wildlife Preserve... When it comes to safaris, we go wild!" ❷ A poster just past the office shows "Big Red" and "Little Red," two elephants featured in the ride's original poacher-focused theme. ❸ The deflated hot-air balloon of the Kinga balloon-safari business (advertised on Harambe posters) is stored in the rafters above the queue. ❹ Faux prehistoric tribal drawings appear on the gate just past the flamingos and on rocks to your right as you pass the lions.

**Fun facts** ❶ Disney created the rutted road by coloring concrete to look like soil, then rolling truck tires through it and tossing in dirt, stones and twigs. ❷ Not everything is real. There's a reason your driver says the termite mounds are "as hard as concrete." A pile of ostrich eggs is equally tough to crack. All of the baobab trees are artificial. The first one the truck passes is actually a storage shed, used to hold extra feed and lawn mowers. ❸ The acacia trees are actually Southern live oaks with their lower branches removed. ❹ The "rickety" bridge will only act up if a truck crosses it at exactly 4 mph. ❺ The safari has the largest collections of Nile hippos and African elephants in North America. ❻ The first hippo pool contains all males; the second females. ❼ The animals respond to sound cues to come in at night. Elephants hear drums, hippos a triangle, crocodiles a metal bar banging in water. ❽ You no longer see zebras except far in the distance. They were moved after some skirmished with a baby sable antelope. A greater kudu was moved to Animal Kingdom Lodge after it jumped a fence. ❾ The trucks run on propane. ❿ Each truck cost $100,000. ⓫ Kilimanjaro Safaris is the largest Disney attraction in the world. The entire Magic Kingdom would fit inside it.

**Hidden Mickeys** ❶ Just beyond clay pits past a baobob tree, as a puffy spot between a split branch. ❷ As the flamingo island. ❸ Just past the island before the gate, as an indentation in a right boulder.

**Circle of life:** Animals from Disney's 1994 film "The Lion King" represented in Kilimanjaro Safaris include (from top) the mandrill (Rafiki), lion (Simba, et al) and warthog (Puumba). **Right:** Baby elephants are common on the savanna.

▶ As you leave the exit pavilion, a short walkway to your right leads to a gorilla viewing area.

# Animals of Kilimanjaro Safaris

**① African elephant** Largest land animal, at 20 ft long, up to 14,000 lbs. Trunk alone holds 3 gal of water and has more muscles (40,000) than human body, combines long nose with upper lip; 2 finger-like projections at tip can pluck grasses, manipulate small objects. Communicates by trumpets, grunts, low-frequency rumbles inaudible to people but heard by other elephants 5 mi away. Sensitive skin; can feel a fly. Few natural enemies but hunted to near extinction for tusks, which are made of same material as human teeth, ivory dentine. Both sexes have tusks. Females can breed only 3–6 days every 4 yrs, gestation 21 mo. Bulls find mates by listening for female rumbles that bulls can hear for miles. When mating takes place, entire herd often takes part in noisy "mating pandemonium"— females, calves mill, circle, wave trunks, trumpet for up to hour. Four babies born at Disney; 2 males (2003, 2008), 2 females (2004, 2005). When program began Disney babyproofed habitat by increasing shade, closing gaps between boulders, installing shallow backstage pool that allows calves to safely learn to swim.

**② Ankole cattle** Huge whitish horns are hollow, full of blood vessels, which cool cow on hot days. World's largest horn circumference: up to 28 in. Also known as Watusi cattle, Cattle of Kings.

**③ Bontebok** World's rarest antelope. Extinct in wild. Chocolate-brown coat has purplish sheen. Both sexes have backswept, ringed horns.

**④ Cheetah** Fastest land animal; accelerates 0–70 mph in 3 secs, but can outrun prey only for short distance. Non-retractable claws help traction, only slightly curved. Balances using long tail. Hunts by day using sight. Pale golden coat with black spots. Naturally hunts in daylight, so Disney's safari guests often see cheetahs alert, eyeing intended prey.

**⑤ Egyptian goose** Sacred in ancient Egypt. Tan, chestnut eye mask; pink legs. Alongside queue.

**⑥ Eland** World's largest antelope, up to 2,200 lbs, stands up to 6 ft tall. Can jump over each other from standing start. Can survive for a month with no water, getting liquid from plants. Both sexes have spiraled horns. Farmed in S. Africa.

**⑦ Greater flamingo** Largest, palest flamingo. Bent bill held upside down in water to filter-feed.

**⑧ Greater kudu** Antelope. Can leap over 8-ft fence. Reddish-tan coat has 6-10 white stripes. Males have spiraling horns up to 5 ft long.

**⑨ Helmeted guineafowl** Calls with a grating, rasping, staccato "kek-kek-kek."

**⑩ Impala** The most agile antelope; can jump 8 ft straight up, run 40 mph, bound up to 40 ft, and change direction in midair. A male attracts a female and scares off other males by repeatedly sticking out tongue. Males have curving, ridged horns.

**⑪ Lion** Largest African predator, up to 550 lbs. Most social big cat, forming prides of 5–10. Female hunts; male defends pride, bushy mane protects neck in battle. Can run 37 mph, leap 40 ft. Sleeps up to 20 hrs a day. Roar can be heard 5 mi away.

**⑫ Mandrill** World's largest and most colorful monkey, up to 85 lbs. Non-aggressive, social; bares massive canine teeth as greeting, with corners of mouth wide open. Ground-dwelling; energetically beats on ground when upset. Bright red and blue markings on muzzle, rump. Most colorful mandrills are males who have mated with many females. Inspiration for Rafiki, a wise mandrill with a baboon tail, in Disney's 1994 film "The Lion King."

**⑬ Nile crocodile** Larger, more aggressive than American alligator, up to 20 ft long. Hatchlings call to mother from inside eggs before hatching; both parents roll eggs in mouths to crack shells. Mother carries newborns in jaws to water; guards for up to 6 mo. Disney's crocs trained to come in at night. Keepers ring bell, dangle food in front of enclosure.

**⑭ Nile hippopotamus** Most aggressive African animal. Can outrun man over short distance. Largest mouth of any land mammal. Spends day in water, grazes on land at night on up to 150 lbs of vegetation. Ears, eyes, nose on top of head; can keep track of its surroundings while hiding bulk under water. Webbed feet. Can hold breath 12 min. Up to 15 ft long, 8,000 lbs. Closest relatives: whales, dolphins. Said to sweat blood due to oozing of pinkish oil that moisturizes skin. Disney's hippo herd is largest in United States.

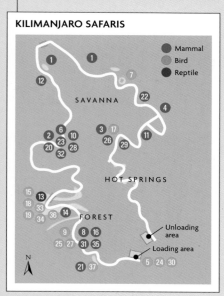

## KILIMANJARO SAFARIS

● Mammal
● Bird
● Reptile

SAVANNA

HOT SPRINGS

FOREST

Unloading area

Loading area

N

⑮ **Northern pintail duck** Brown and gray body; white breast.

⑯ **Okapi** Only mammal that grooms its ears, eyelids with tongue, which is 14 in long. Solitary, lives in Congo's dense Ituri Forest. Sleeps 5 min daily. Not identified as species until 1900. Giraffe relative; appearance combines giraffe's body, face, walk (simultaneously stepping with front, hind leg on same side of body) with zebra's black-and-white rear. Male has giraffe-like knobs on head.

⑰ **Ostrich** World's fastest two-legged animal; top speed 45 mph. World's largest bird, 8 ft tall. Widest eyes (2 in) of any land creature. Largest eggs (2.5 lbs) of any land animal. Too heavy to fly. Fans body with wings to stay cool. Contrary to myth, does not stick head in sand, rather "hides" by laying head on ground.

⑱ **Pink-backed pelican** Gray and white. Feeds in groups by herding fish then scooping up.

⑲ **Red-billed teal** Mallard-like duck. Brown-gray plumage, brown cap.

⑳ **Reticulated giraffe** World's tallest animal, at up to 20 ft. On avg 6-ft legs support 6-ft torso topped by 6-ft neck, ft-high head. Balances with longest tail (8 ft) of any land mammal, feet 1-ft wide. Generally quiet, though adults can grunt, hiss, moo, snort. Calves bleat. Stride 15 ft, can run 45 mph. Tongue up to 20 in long. Heart 2 ft wide. Neck has only 7 vertebrae, same as human. Unlike most grazing animals, cannot lower head to ground without splaying legs. Females give birth standing up. Newborns drop head-first, avg 6 ft tall, grow 1 inch a day. Knobby skin-covered "horns" called ossicones.

**Rhinoceros** Has existed 60 million years but today only 10,000 left (less than 15% of 1970 population), as poached for its two muzzle horns, an alleged aphrodisiac in Asian folk medicine. Actually, horns are made of the same material, keratin, as human nails and would grow back if simply cut. Often wallows in mud for protection from sunburn, insects; sensitive hide appears armored. Can charge at 40 mph. ㉑ **Black rhinoceros** Up to 3,200 lbs. Solitary herbivore; uses hooked upper lip like a finger to select leaves, twigs. Horns can reach 4 ft.

㉒ **White rhinoceros** Largest rhino at up to 5,000 lbs. Sociable herbivore. Not white, hide is slate gray to yellow-brown. Name is mistranslation of Afrikaans word "wijt" ("wide"), for broad mouth.

㉓ **Sable antelope** Aggressive. Males fight by dropping to knees to clash stout, heavily ringed horns. At rest, adults lie in ring around young, horns out. Symbol of Disney's "Harambe Wildlife Preserve."

㉔ **Sacred (royal) ibis** Worshipped as the god Thoth in ancient Egypt, supposedly protected

**From top:** The eland is the world's largest antelope. Extinct in the wild, the bontebok is the world's rarest antelope. The misnamed white rhino is actually slate or yellow-brown. Ankole cattle have the world's thickest horns, with a circumference of up to 28 in.

country from plagues, serpents. Often mummified and placed in pharaohs' tombs. Alongside queue.

**㉕ Saddle-billed stork** Builds a large stick nest that will hold one egg in tops of tall trees. Colorful black, red, yellow bill looks like a horse saddle.

**㉖ Scimitar-horned oryx** Extinct in wild due to poaching of its long, smooth horns shaped like scimitar swords. Specialized for desert living, sweats only when body temperature exceeds 116°F.

**㉗ Stanley crane** Blue-gray, black tail, white cap. When courting, a pair simultaneously picks up grass clumps and tosses in air. South Africa's national bird.

**㉘ Thompson's gazelle** One of smallest antelopes at 2–4 ft tall. Can run 50 mph, bounds (stots) into air. Most common E African gazelle; favorite prey of cheetahs. Pointed horns.

**㉙ Warthog** Only grassland pig; pads on knees for grazing, tough snout for rooting underground stems. Like other pigs, keeps cool by taking mud baths. Male face covered in wart-like skin growths, has 2 6-in lower tusks, 2 curved upper tusks that can grow to 2 ft. Male performs courtship chant of rhythmic grunts. Most famous warthog is Pumbaa, comedic stinker in 1994 Disney film "The Lion King."

**㉚ West African crowned crane** Golden, halo-like crown; red face patch. Mostly black and white with some golden tail feathers.

**㉛ Western bongo** Largest forest antelope. Up to 8 ft tall, 900 lbs. Shy; known as Ghost of (Kenyan) Forest. Chesnut coat usually has 13 white stripes ("Bongo" is Swahili for 13). Long backswept horns.

**㉜ White-bearded wildebeest** Called "gnu" for grunting call. Gregarious, sleeps in rows, births in groups. Migrates annually in herd up to 1.5 million, world's largest wildlife movement. Newborn can run day born. Cow-like horns. Partial inspiration for face of Beast in 1991 Disney film "Beauty and the Beast."

**㉝ White-breasted cormorant** Diver, catches fish with hooked bill. Intertwines necks to court.

**㉞ White-faced whistling duck** With a high-pitched three-note whistle, sounds like a squeak toy.

**㉟ Yellow-backed duiker** World's largest duiker, up to 175 lbs. Brown coat has yellow patch on rounded back. Duikers are named for their habit of diving into underbrush when startled ("duiker" means "diver" in Afrikaans).

**㊱ Yellow-billed duck** Only African duck with yellow bill. Has dark gray plumage.

**㊲ Yellow-billed stork** White; red face and legs, large yellow bill. Stirs up water and mud with foot to flush out prey.

**From top:** To protect their young, adult sable antelopes lie in a ring around them, horns out. The most agile antelope, an impala can leap 40 feet and change direction in midair. The white-bearded wildebeest helped inspire the face of the Beast in Disney's 1991 "Beauty and the Beast." The aggressive Nile crocodile can reach up to 20 feet in length.

A **male gorilla** watches guests photograph him alongside the Pangani Forest Exploration Trail

# Pangani Forest Exploration Trail

★ ★ ★ ★ ★ ✔ Allow 30 min. 1 trail (2100 ft), 9 viewing areas, 10 species plus aviary birds, indoor exhibits. Fear factor: None. Access: Guests may stay in wheelchairs, ECVs. *AuDe* Debuted: 1998.

Streams and waterfalls weave through the grounds of this self-guided tour of African animals, including an okapi, meerkats and gorillas. The entire area is shady, and benches are scattered throughout.

Presented as a series of research areas in a natural environment, the trail has a scientific theme.

An outdoor hut (the "Endangered Animal Rehabilitation Centre") offers a good view of Angola black-and-white colobus monkeys and a yellow-backed duiker. Live displays inside a replica research station include a huge one dedicated to the naked mole rat.

You won't notice it when you enter the large aviary, a screened-in area with a waterfall, pond and over two dozen species of exotic birds. Don't miss the gigantic nest of the hammerkop stork or the hanging homes of taveta golden weavers. Kids love watching the fish on display, which often suck up small pebbles and spit them out.

A 40-foot glass wall lets you view hippos underwater. It's best early, when the 100,000-gallon tank is clear. Stay quiet and the hippos may come up to the window.

A suspension bridge and viewing island divide two large gorilla habitats. One has a family (a silverback, two moms and three kids); the other a bachelor troupe.

The word "pangani" is Swahili for "place of enchantment."

**Fun finds** ❶ Eight cabinet drawers in the research station open to show collections of preserved giant beetles, butterflies, claws, feathers, seashells, scorpions, small skulls (including those of bush pigs and dwarf crocodiles) and tarantulas. ❷ At the hippo area, a small monitor displays short, narrated videos of wild hippos and elephants.

**Hidden Mickeys** In the research station, as ❶ a small shape on a backpack to the left of the naked mole rat exhibit, and ❷ as an "O" in the word "Asepco" on a box of antiseptic soap on a small ledge behind the desk lamp. Two ears are created by white notebook-paper reinforcement rings.

| Average Wait | |
| --- | --- |
| 9am | 0 min |
| 10am | 0 |
| 11am | 0 |
| Noon | 0 |
| 1pm | 0 |
| 2pm | 0 |
| 3pm | 0 |
| 4pm | 0 |
| 5pm | 0 |
| 6pm | 0 |
| 7pm | 0 |
| 8pm | 0 |
| 9pm | 0 |

▶ The gorillas are most active early each morning, when they eat, drink and often play together.

# Animals of the Pangani Forest Exploration Trail

**A** **African cichlid** Small, striped fish. Protects young by hiding them in mouth. Hundreds of species evolved in Africa's large lakes.

**B** **African lungfish** Eel-like; has retained ability to breathe air, has two developed lungs. Lives in small pools that often evaporate; can use long, fleshy fins to plod along in mud. Ancestors developed true limbs, evolved into early 4-legged land animals. Also called salamanderfish.

**C** **Angolan black and white colobus monkey** Rarely descends to ground. Uses branches as trampolines, jumps to get leverage for leaps up to 50 ft. Named "colobus" (derived from Greek word for "mutilated") because it has no thumbs.

**D** **Gerenuk** Antelope, stands to eat tree leaves. Hip joints swivel so backbone aligns with hind legs.

**E** **Nile hippopotamus** See Kilimanjaro Safaris.

**F** **Okapi** See Kilimanjaro Safaris.

**G** **Slender-tailed meerkat** Lives in burrows in organized multifamily communities of up to 30 individuals. Group divides jobs among members, such as babysitting and food finding. Sentry duty is shared by rotating guards. Often stands on hind legs and gazes at surroundings. Females nurse by standing upright. Can kill snakes, including striking cobras. The most famous meerkat is Timon, from 1994 Disney film "The Lion King."

**H** **Stanley crane** See Kilimanjaro Safaris.

**I** **Western lowland gorilla** Largest (up to 450 lbs), most powerful primate, but also least aggressive. Iconic chest beating is just display. Most populous gorilla, with about 94,000 wild animals. Shared traits with humans include 32 teeth, presence of fingerprints, ability to stand upright, ability to use tools, ability to learn sign language, same female menstruation cycle of apx 28 days, same 9 month gestation, same general age for juveniles to hit puberty (at around 11 or 12 years). Mature males have silver back. Adult male twice weight of female.

**J** **Yellow-backed duiker** See Kilimanjaro Safaris listing.

## Research station exhibits

**African bullfrog** Nearly 5 lbs. Resembles "Star Wars" character Jabba the Hut.

**African mud turtle** Aquatic. Folds head into shell sideways instead of straight in.

**African pygmy mouse** World's smallest mammal. Stacks pebbles in front of burrow; overnight pebbles gather dew; in morning mouse drinks dew.

**Dung beetle** Feeds on feces. Rolls dung into balls.

**Dwarf African dormouse** Resembles tiny squirrel. Long brush-like tail can detach if attacked, does not re-grow.

**Emperor scorpion** Black. 9 in long. Glows in dark under black lights.

**Hedgehog tenrec** Like hedgehog will roll itself into ball when threatened. Long white-tipped spines on body. Active in daytime.

**Kenyan sand boa** Small, orange and black. Kills prey by constriction. Likes to burrow.

**King baboon spider** Velvety. Active burrower.

**Madagascar hissing cockroach** Hisses by forcing air through abdomen's breathing pores.

**Naked mole rat** Not a mole or a rat, but plenty naked, pink and virtually hairless. Related to guinea pig. Lives underground in total darkness. Giant queen keeps a male harem and rules with brute force, shoving her soldiers and workers around to prod them into action. Everyone's naked, and blind, but all individuals have their own identity: a custom odor achieved by carefully rolling around in the community toilet. Only mammal that organizes itself into ant-like colonies. Digs with four buck teeth but doesn't swallow dirt; the teeth are outside of its mouth in front of hairy lips and side skin folds that close completely.

**Pancake tortoise** Flat, pliable shell lets it squeeze into tight openings.

**Spider tortoise** Has spider-web pattern on shell.

**Spiny mouse** Coarse, spiny hairs on back, tail. Tail can detach if attacked.

**Spiny-tailed lizard** Gets all liquid from food. Excess salts excreted through salt gland.

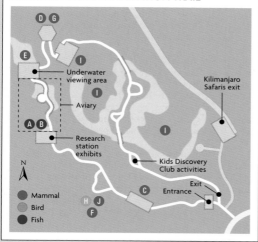

**PANGANI FOREST EXPLORATION TRAIL**

D  G
E
I
Underwater viewing area
Kilimanjaro Safaris exit
Aviary
A  B
Research station exhibits
Kids Discovery Club activities
N
Exit
C  Entrance
● Mammal
● Bird      H  J
● Fish      F

# Aviary birds

**African green pigeon** Yellow-green; purplish markings. Gizzard adapted for grinding fig seeds.

**African jacana** Chestnut. Oversized blue-gray feet for walking on vegetation in water.

**African pygmy goose** Actually a duck. Chestnut underparts; green wings, ear patches.

**Amethyst starling** Purplish plumage can look blue or red depending on light.

**Bearded barbet** Black on top, red underneath. Prominent tufted "beard" under bill.

**Black crake** Sturdy yellow bill, pink legs. Perches on hippos, warthogs and pecks parasites.

**Blue-bellied roller** Blue plumage, dark green back. Snaps up escaping insects at grass fires.

**Blue-breasted kingfisher** Large bill red on top, black on bottom. White lining under wings.

**Blue turaco** Largest turaco. Blue-black crest, hooked yellow red-tipped bill, rusty underparts.

**Brown-necked parrot** Bright green, tangerine-colored crown. Beak shape makes it appear to smile.

**Golden-breasted starling** Brilliant plumage of blue, green, purple, yellow.

**Green woodhoopoe** Downturned orange bill, large white spots on long tail. Related to kingfisher.

**Hammerkop stork** Dull brown; large, dense crest. German "hammerkopf" meaning hammerhead. Builds one of world's largest, most intricate nests.

**Hottentot teal** Smallest African duck. Blue bill.

**Madagascar crested ibis** Mostly brown with white plumes on neck, along wings; partially bare head; dense green crest.

**Olive pigeon** Courtship display of deep bows then flight with wing-clapping, glide to ground.

**Pink pigeon** One of world's rarest birds. Only 20 wild birds in 1980s; since has slowly recovered.

**Racquet-tailed roller** Pale-blue undersides, rusty back. Long double tail streamer with teardrop shapes on tips.

**Red and yellow barbet** Red bill, head. Covered with pattern of black, red, white, yellow.

**Snowy-crowned robin-chat** Gold, red body; black wings, head. White stripe on crown.

**Superb starling** Bright orange breast; blue-black wings, head, back. Common in Kenya.

**Taveta golden weaver** Small, bright yellow. Builds spherical green-grass nest over water.

**White-bellied go-away turaco** Gray. Call sounds like "go-away."

**White-headed buffalo weaver** Gray wings, orange feathers under tail. Builds large, messy nest of twigs, grasses; short tubular entrance on bottom.

**From top:** The western lowland gorilla is the largest and most powerful primate. The slender-tailed meerkat lives in multifamily communities. The African green pigeon is specially adapted for grinding fig seeds. The Nile hippopotamus is the most aggressive African animal.

MICAELA NEAL

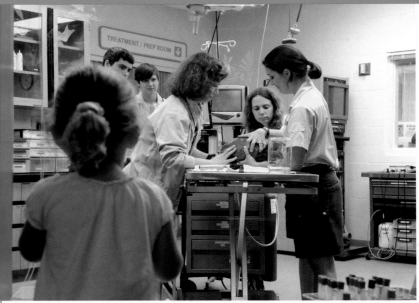

**A young girl** peers through a window to watch a gopher tortoise exam at Conservation Station

# Conservation Station

★★★★ ✓ **Allow 45 min. 49 species. Open 9:30a–dusk. Fear factor: None. Access: Guests may stay in wheelchairs, ECVs. Debuted: 1998.**

Visiting this animal-care area can be exhausting if you are out of shape. To see it means walking to a train station, catching a train, then walking down a long path. Once you reach the building, you stay on your feet. Still, it's one of the few places at Disney that presents a world that's totally real.

Named after the shaman mandrill in the 1994 film "The Lion King," the area features **Conservation Station,** an indoor exhibit center with a lot of fascinating science to see. In the mornings, observation windows let you look in on a real veterinary clinic, with medical procedures on animals that can weigh up to 500 pounds. Expect to see anything from a bandage change on a goat to a root canal on a gorilla. Vets explain what's going on, and overhead cameras give you an up-close view. Usually about three animals are brought in each morning.

| Average Wait | |
|---|---|
| 9am | closed |
| 10am | 0 min |
| 11am | 5 |
| Noon | 5 |
| 1pm | 5 |
| 2pm | 5 |
| 3pm | 5 |
| 4pm | 5 |
| 5pm | 5 |
| 6pm | closed |
| 7pm | closed |
| 8pm | closed |
| 9pm | closed |

Other windows peer in on researchers studying elephant vocalizations and tracking a sea turtle off the Florida coast. Adjacent exhibits include a food preparation area and arachnid, insect and reptile displays.

You can zoom in on the park's primates, elephants, giraffes and other animals with remote-control Animal Cams. You'll hear rain, booming thunder and buzzing insects in the Song of the Rainforest exhibit, a group of cool, dark, family-sized audio booths.

Eco Hero kiosks let you "speak" with Dr. Jane Goodall or George Schaller of the Tibet Wildlife Reserve. A Caring for the Wild exhibit has a telescope used by Dr. Goodall and notebooks of Dian Fossey. A short film offers a look at endangered creatures.

Disney cast members bring out lizards, owls, parrots and snakes. Meet-and-greet characters include Pocahontas, Rafiki and Jiminy Cricket.

An adjacent petting zoo, **Affection Section** has domestic animals. Roaming free are African pygmy, San Clemente and Nigerian dwarf goats and Gulf Coast native and Tunis sheep. Behind a fence is a Dexter cow, a llama, two rare Guinea hogs and two Sicilian miniature donkeys. The largest goat, a brownish-gray fella named Luke, will steal stuff right out of your pockets.

▶ Take the first train of the day and you'll probably see an exam-room procedure.

**Pleased to meet you.** A goat nuzzles the authors' daughter at Affection Section.

To get to the area, you take the **Wildlife Express** train from the Harambe Village station in the park's Africa section, which runs past Disney's "Jurassic Park"-style animal-care facilities. Then you walk down a path, called **Habitat Habit,** that is highlighted by a display of cotton-top tamarins.

**Fun finds** Harambe railroad station ❶ Plastered with posters, station walls are stenciled "Affixing of Advertisements is Forbidden." **Trains** ❷ Ankole cattle skulls are strapped to the fronts of the locomotives. **Landscape** ❸ Individual impressions of animals and the Tree of Life in the walkway under the Habitat Habit pavilions appear again in a Circle of Life impression at Conservation Station. **Conservation Station** ❹ Restroom placards give you The Scoop on Poop and offer a Whiz Quiz.

**Fun facts** ❶ Why such a fancy train? Because its track was originally meant to be a safari of its own, before the care facilities grew larger than planned. ❷ The thatched-roof huts along the return train track were handmade in Indonesia.

**Hidden Mickeys** Planet Watch railroad station ❶ As blue circles in the rafter's cross beams. **Landscape** ❷ As overlapping circles in the grates of Affection Section trees and in the Conservation Station lobby. **Conservation Station** On the left wall of the inside entrance mural, left to right: ❸ As a squirrel's pupil, ❹ wrinkles on a hippo chin (a profile),

❺ a scale behind the eye of a crocodile, ❻ a shadow on a walrus neck to the right of its tusks, ❼ an owl's pupils, ❽ a spot on a yellow fish (obscured by an octopus), ❾ black spots on a butterfly's left wing (above a bat). On the right wall, right to left: ❿ As a pink spot on a spider abdomen (above a white owl chick), ⓫ in a opossum pupil, ⓬ as black spots on the yellow wings of a butterfly (above a praying mantis arm). Middle wall, right to left: ⓭ As an ostrich pupil, ⓮ green snake scales, ⓯ a sucker on a starfish (a profile), ⓰ on the top of a butterfly body (a detailed, smiling Mickey face), ⓱ as spots on butterfly wings (under a monkey) and ⓲ as a silver frog's left pupil (a profile). In the Song of the Rainforest area, left to right: ⓳ As yellow flower petals, ⓴ as a white spot on a fly (above a flower), ㉑ as a tree shadow in front of the rainforest doors (a profile), ㉒ as a white spot on a tree to the left of "The Accidental Florist" sign, ㉓ as a spot on the tree bark (across from a fly) about 4 feet off the ground, ㉔ as a bark impression in the "Song of the Rainforest" sign to the lower right of Grandmother Willow's face (a profile), ㉕ as a nearby painted hole in a leaf, ㉖ as spots on a wooden cockroach inside a tree in the front of the area, ㉗ as three dark green spots on a chameleon side above the "Giant Cockroach" sign and ㉘ as and petri dishes in the far left window of the reptile display room. **Affection Section** ❶ As a pattern on a sheared sheep. ❷ As orange spots on a stage wall, right of a lizard door.

▶ **Have questions? Cast members will cheerfully discuss animal nutrition and health care.**

# Animals of Rafiki's Planet Watch

## Habitat Habit

**Cotton-top tamarin** Squirrel-size monkey. Very rare; more in captivity than wild. Named for puffy crest of fur on head. Mate for life; live as family. Older siblings help care for infants. Black face; mottled gray-brown shoulders, back and rump; white stomach and limbs. Long dark tail.

## Conservation Station

**American alligator** True prehistoric beast; basically unchanged for more than 100 million years. Among last surviving members of the Archosauria, the Super Order which included most dinosaurs. Back has rows of embedded bony plates; feet are webbed. Thick, wrinkled, blackish-gray hide lined with rows of horny scales. Eats only once or twice a week; hunts at night. Usually drowns prey, then swallows whole. Adult males snack on young alligators, mother will eat own offspring if they compete with her for food. Became endangered in 1950s; after legal protection has rebounded. Up to 16 ft; 1,300 lb.

**Asian giant centipede** Aggressive; poisonous bite. Large, to 8 in. Also in Maharajah Jungle Trek.

**Beetles** These insects have modified forewings that have evolved into hard wing cases to cover and protect their abdomens and hind wings. **Black stag beetle** Has long, antler-like jaws for combat. **Madagascar hissing cockroach** Hisses by forcing air through abdomen breathing pores. Large, wingless.

**European fire salamander** At 11 in, one of the largest salamanders. Comes in a variety of bright colors and patterns; has poison glands on each side of head behind eyes. (A newt-like amphibian with bright markings, the salamander was once thought to be able to endure fire.)

**Frogs Hourglass tree frog** Rusty brown skin looks like cream or yellow paint dripped on it. Also known as Bereis' tree frog. **Poison dart frog** Sports some of the most brilliant colors on earth; variety includes black, blue, copper, gold, green, red and yellow. Some wild species are among the world's most toxic animals; in captivity the frog never develops venom.

**Giant katydid** Bright green, camouflaged to look like a leaf.

**Lizards Asian water monitor** World's third longest lizard, can reach length of 9 ft. **Blue-tongued skink** Has bright blue, curled tongue. Mostly drab, tan. **Prehensile-tailed skink** Herbivore. Female shows fierce protective behavior toward young; will sometimes "adopt" orphaned juveniles. **Spiny-tailed lizard** Lives in desert. Rarely needs to drink as gets all liquid from food. Excretes excessive salts through salt gland. Also on Pangani Forest Exploration Trail.

**Newts** Small, slim amphibian with lungs. Typically lives on land as an adult; returns to water to breed. **Axolotl** Exhibits phenomenon known as neoteny, the retention of immature features in adult. Remains in larval form throughout life, with visible feathery gill stalks surrounding head. Also called the Mexican walking fish. **Emperor newt** Colorful; bumpy orange head, orange warty ridge down brown back. Warts are venom glands, ooze toxin when newt is grabbed.

**Scorpions** Terrestrial arachnids have pincers, poisonous stingers at ends of tail, which animal holds curved over back. **Desert hairy scorpion** Largest N American scorpion. Can reach length over 6 in. Brown. **Whip scorpion** Has long, whiplike tail, or telson; can squirt acid when attacked. Flat body. **Tanzanian tailless whip scorpion** Can be 8 in wide with legs extended.

**Snakes Burmese python** Among the world's largest snakes, can reach 23 ft. Girth can be thick as a telephone pole. **Everglades rat snake** Bright orange; orange eyes, red tongue. **Puerto Rican boa** Endangered. Will often hang down in front of a cave to catch flying bats. **Rosy boa** Vertically striped. Native to SW US.

**Spiders** These eight-legged predatory arachnids have fangs that inject poison into prey; most spin webs to capture insects. **Brazilian salmon pink tarantula** Gets name from long pink hairs on abdomen, legs. Third largest tarantula species. **Golden starburst baboon tarantula** Tan, with striking starburst pattern on back of thorax. **Indian ornamental tarantula** Intricately patterned; bright yellow patches on front legs. **Malaysian earth tiger tarantula** Rare. Yellow-tan thorax; long, gray legs.

**Toads** These tailless amphibians have short, sturdy bodies and short legs, typically with dry, warty skin. **Colorado river toad** Largest US native toad. Olive green; smooth, shiny skin. **Puerto Rican crested toad** Endangered. Bumpy skin; crest on nose. **Surinam toad** Aquatic. Almost completely flat. Also called a star-fingered toad. Young develop in pockets on mother's back.

**Turtles Chinese box tortoise** Small, with high domed shell. During courtship male extends, sways, undulates neck while drooling, vocalizing with lip-smacking hiss. Terrestrial. **Egyptian tortoise** Tiny, males max 4 in long, females 5 in. Shell combines pale yellow, black. Endangered. Terrestrial. **Gopher tortoise** Digs deep burrows that it shares with other animals. Endangered. Terrestrial.

**Velvet ant** Despite name is not an ant, but rather a parasitic wasp. Lays eggs inside larva of other wasps. Female covered with soft, velvety hair.

**Wheel bug** Resembles gray grasshopper. Predator of caterpillars, other soft-bodied insects. Name comes from wheel-shaped structure on body.

## Affection Section

**Dexter cow** Smallest N American cow; 3 ft tall. Can produce more milk for its size daily than any other cow; avg 1.5–2.5 gal. Originally from S Ireland. Most are black; some red. Both sexes have horns.

**Goats** It's the devil! Well actually it's a goat, but people have associated the animal with Beelzebub since it was domesticated 10,000 years ago. For centuries Satan was thought able to transform into a goat at will, and is still often portrayed with the creature's hooves and horns. Farmers once believed owning a goat would protect them from the devil, or that when a goat could not be found it must be meeting with him. Sailors once thought a goat on board would ensure a calm sea, which helped it become common in N America. **African pygmy goat** Natural barrel shape makes it appear perpetually pregnant. Silver-gray coat with black on head and legs; white on face. Male has larger horns. Both sexes have beard. **Nigerian dwarf goat** Slimmer, rarer than African pygmy goat. Raises hackles (hair along spine) when alarmed. Coat color varies, some solid, some patterned. Fleshy wattles. **San Clemente goat** Rare; descended from wild goats living on San Clemente Island, Calif. Spanish seafarers in 1500s placed it on the island as food source for crews. Coat red or tan with black markings.

**Guinea hog** Unique to N America. Very rare; fewer than 200 left. Exceptional mothering skills. Medium to long coarse black hair. Tail has single curl.

**Llama** S American member of camel family. Domesticated in 16th century in Andes mountains. Pack animal, can carry up to 100 lbs. Brought to US in 1920s by William Randolph Hearst for his private zoo. Coat ranges from red, black, beige or rust; may be spotted, solid, patterned. In 2000 Disney film "The Emperor's New Groove," Emperor Kuzco (David Spade) was turned into llama by power-hungry advisor Yzma (Eartha Kitt).

**Sheep** **Gulf coast native sheep** Brought to SE US by Spanish in 1500s. Oldest known breed in N America. Indigenous to portions of all Gulf Coast states. White coat; rarely tan or brown. Wool-free face, legs and belly. Both sexes horned. **Tunis sheep** One of the oldest indigenous US breeds. Introduced in 1799 as gift to Pennsylvania man from ruler of Tunisia. Cream-colored wool, reddish face and legs, pendulous ears, chubby tail.

**Sicilian miniature donkey** Known for dark cross-shaped stripe along back, shoulders. Legend says Mary rode one the night Jesus was born, and thereafter the animals have mark of the cross. Gray body; light nose, belly, inner legs.

**From top:** The Gulf Coast native sheep is the oldest known breed in North America. The cotton-top tamarin is a rare squirrel-size monkey. A type of newt, the axolotl remains in larval form throughout its life.

© ITHACA COLLEGE

**A parrot** appears to answer math problems in a demonstration of natural learning behaviors

# Flights of Wonder

★★★★ ✓ 25 min. Capacity: 1,150. Covered seating. Fear factor: None. Access: ECV, wheelchair accessible. Assistive listening. Debuted: 1998.

The birds fly just inches above the audience in this live presentation, which demonstrates natural bird behaviors in an entertaining, conservation-themed show. Altogether you'll see about 20 birds, including a Harris hawk, East African crowned crane and bald eagle. (The eagle, alas, doesn't fly.)

One bird lands on the wrist of an adult volunteer. Another flies directly at two audience members chosen to sit onstage.

The show has many fun moments. After the host tosses a grape for a hornbill to catch, he asks for a child to come down and try it. "I'll toss the grape," he says, "you fly up and get it."

Often a parrot sings a song or two. Sometimes a child gets to challenge a parrot in math. (Want your child to be picked? You'll increase the odds if you sit front row center and have her wave wildly when the trainer asks for volunteers.)

| Average Wait | |
|---|---|
| 9am | n/a |
| 10am | 5 min |
| 11am | 5 |
| Noon | 5 |
| 1pm | 5 |
| 2pm | 5 |
| 3pm | 5 |
| 4pm | 5 |
| 5pm | 5 |
| 6pm | n/a |
| 7pm | n/a |
| 8pm | n/a |
| 9pm | n/a |

Though the subject is serious—the need to understand wildlife on its own terms, and to value the survival of endangered and threatened species—the presentation is anything but. Just as the show gets started, it's interrupted by a loony lost tour guide ("Guano Joe," or sometimes "Guano Jane"), who wanders up on stage, tour flag in hand, in search of his group. You soon learn that he suffers from FOB—"fear of birds." As he faces his fears, you witness various up-close-and-personal flight demonstrations.

Arrive 15 minutes early to see a brief preshow in front of the theater with a great horned owl. When the main show is over, handlers also bring out a bird or two for a brief meet-and-greet session.

Shows take place in a shaded outdoor theater, and are held rain or shine. During a significant shower the regular show is scrapped, and trainers simply walk through the audience with birds on their wrists.

The grassy natural stage features a backdrop of a crumbling stone building set in a shady grove. According to Disney lore, the area was the gathering place of long-gone, animal-loving maharajahs, and is being used now by the natives of Anandapur, Disney's fictional Asian country, to acquaint others with the birds of their area.

▶ To have birds fly over you during Flights of Wonder, sit front and center or along an aisle.

**Tigers appear to roam freely** through Disney's realistic Maharajah Jungle Trek habitats

# Maharajah Jungle Trek

★ ★ ★ ★ ★ ✓ Allow 30 min. 1 trail (1500 ft), 7 viewing areas, 14 species plus aviary. Fear factor: None. Access: Guests may stay in wheelchairs, ECVs. *AuDe* Debuted: 1998.

Set in an elaborate re-creation of a decaying hunting lodge, this sequence of outdoor animal exhibits combines exotic Asian creatures with the architecture and natural beauty of India and Nepal. Among the sights are tigers, bats, a komodo dragon and a lush aviary filled with bizarre birds.

Most areas are shady. Benches are scattered throughout. Large overhead fans help keep you cool in the bat pavilion, the only indoor area.

Intricate facades and artifacts tell a Disney-crafted story of a great king and his three sons. As shown in four murals at the second tiger viewing area, one son built the structures, the second son planted the gardens and the third hunted tigers. Later, as the story goes, the lodge and its surrounding forest were given to local villagers, who use it today as a wildlife refuge.

| Average Wait | |
| --- | --- |
| 9am | 0 min |
| 10am | 0 |
| 11am | 0 |
| Noon | 0 |
| 1pm | 0 |
| 2pm | 0 |
| 3pm | 0 |
| 4pm | 0 |
| 5pm | 0 |
| 6pm | 0 |
| 7pm | 0 |
| 8pm | 0 |
| 9pm | 0 |

**Fun finds** ❶ Just past the footbridge, an environmental history of man is shown in a sequence of carvings on a wall to your right. Man emerges out of the water; comes to a paradise rich with wildlife; chops down its tree; faces floods, death and chaos; and finally gains happiness when he learns to respect nature. ❷ You enter the aviary via the tomb of Anantah, the first ruler of Disney's mythical Anandapur kingdom. His ashes are said to be in the fertility urn in the middle of the room.

**Fun facts** ❶ The tiger pool is kept at 70 degrees, and includes fish for the cats to catch. ❷ The bridge over the tiger habitat is actually a wall separating the cats from an area of barred geese. ❸ The aviary weeds are frayed by hand for a consistent look.

**Hidden Mickeys** ❶ At the second tiger viewing area, in the first mural on your right as swirls of water under a tiger. ❷ As a golden earring in the first mural on your left. ❸ As three small bushes in that same mural. ❹ As rocks in a mountain range above a flying dove in the second mural on your left. ❺ As swirls in a cloud formation in the second mural on your right. ❻ Past the tigers, as a leaf in a mural to your left, about 9 feet off the ground. ❼ In the top right of a mural left of the Elds deer habitat, an orange flower and two leaves form a detailed Mickey face and waving arm. ❽ As necklace beads in the middle stone carving, just before the aviary.

▶ Disney's bats are most active first thing in the morning. The tigers are liveliest around 5 p.m.

# Animals of the Maharajah Jungle Trek

**A** **Asian giant centipede** Aggressive; has poisonous bite. Also in Conservation Station.

**B** **Banteng** Shy ox. Grazes in swamp forests; bamboo jungles. Shoulder hump. Both sexes have horns. First endangered species to be successfully cloned.

**C** **Bar-headed goose** One of world's highest-flying birds, migrates seasonally over Himalayas from Nepal to India. Body pale gray; head has black bars.

**D** **Bats** Only flying mammal. Hands formed into wings; skin membrane stretched between fingers, body, hind legs. Roosts, feeds hanging by hind feet. Circulatory valves keep blood from rushing to head. Uses echolocation to navigate in darkness. Groom, lick each other to express affection, often nuzzle snouts. More closely related to humans than rodents. **Malayan flying fox** World's largest bat. 6 ft wingspan so massive can't take off from ground. Vegetarian; can eat up to body weight daily. **Rodriquez fruit bat**

**Below:** The rare Rodriquez fruit bat only eats fruit. **Bottom:** The world's largest lizard, the Komodo dragon can weigh 250 lbs.

Can hover over ground. Wingspan 3 ft. Only eats fruit; spits out hard pulp, seeds, skin, often in a tidy mouth-shaped pellet. Only few hundred left in wild; only found on Rodriguez Island in Indian Ocean.

**E** **Blackbuck** In Hindu mythology, transports moon goddess Chandrama, bestows prosperity to areas it lives. Most hunted animal in India during 18th, 19th, 1st half of 20th century. Females tan, males dark brown. Males have ringed, spiraling horns.

**F** **Blood python** Up to 50 lbs; up to 8 ft long.

**G** **Elds deer** Most endangered deer. Lives only in eastern India, in 15-sq-mi Loktak Lake marsh. Wide spreadable hooves. Antlers sport at least six points.

**H** **Java green peafowl** Most vividly colored green peafowl. Noted ventriloquists. Found in Java, on Malay Peninsula. Only 1,000 exist in wild.

**I** **Komodo dragon** World's largest lizard; up to 250 lbs. Can reach 10 ft long. Prehistoric. Saliva contains lethal bacteria. Juveniles roll in feces to avoid being eaten by adults. When fleeing attacker, will vomit up to 200 lbs of food to increase speed.

**J** **Malayan tapir** World's largest tapir, up to 1,200 lbs. Resembles fat black pig with white saddle and elephant's trunk. Related to both horse, rhino.

**K** **Sarus crane** Tallest flying bird at 6 ft; 8 ft wingspan. During courtship, pair will bow; hop, strut, flap wings as it circles; performs coordinated honks.

**L** **Tiger** World's largest cat at up to 660 lbs. Can leap 30 ft, drag up to 3,000 lbs. No two have same black stripe pattern, which is on both fur and skin. Ears turn individually, can rotate 180 degrees.

**M** **White-lipped tree frog** World's largest tree frog, meows when disturbed.

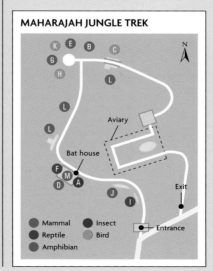

**MAHARAJAH JUNGLE TREK**

Mammal — Insect
Reptile — Bird
Amphibian

Aviary
Bat house
Exit
Entrance

# Aviary birds

**Argus pheasant** One of world's largest pheasants. Brown plumage, egg-shaped "eyes" on flight feathers.

**Black-browed barbet** Known as "bird of five colors" due to black, blue, green, red, yellow feathers around face.

**Black-collared starling** White; bright yellow eye patch. Feeds by blindly probing dense vegetation with open bill.

**Black-naped fruit dove** Only male has black nape; female solid bright green.

**Bleeding-heart dove** Named for crimson patch on breast, which looks like bleeding wound.

**Crested wood partridge** Builds large domed nest by tossing plants over back, partially covering itself.

**Fairy bluebird** Male is vibrant turquoise; female dull blue-green. Eyes are bright red.

**Fire-tufted barbet** Bright green; red crown tuft.

**Golden-crested mynah** Builds nest in tree cavity; "mynah" means "bubbling with joy."

**Golden pheasant** Kept by George Washington at Mt. Vernon; males among most colorful birds, with blue, black, gold, green, red, rust feathers.

**Green-winged dove** Pale gray; iridescent green wings, back feathers. Bobs head during courtship.

**Hooded pitta** Twig path leads to entrance of dome-shaped ground nest.

**Indian pygmy goose** Mostly white; dark gray markings.

**Jambu fruit dove** Pale pink patch on white breast. Female builds flimsy nest of grasses, roots and twigs collected by her mate.

**Mandarin duck** Has prominent crest, orange-gold "sails" in its wings.

**Masked plover** Characteristic yellow mask, long pink legs. Call is loud, penetrating rattle.

**Nicobar pigeon** Iridescent dark green. Hunted for its gizzard stone, used in jewelry.

**Pied imperial pigeon** Builds messy nest of sticks in a coconut palm.

**Pink-necked green pigeon** Pink throat, orange breast. Builds nest so flimsy contents can be seen from below.

**Stella's lorikeet** Sometimes sleeps on back, with feet straight up in the air. Mostly green; head, breast, underparts scarlet.

**White-headed duck** Black neck, tan body, distinctive blue bill that appears swollen.

**White-throated kingfisher** Turquoise wings, tail, back; large red bill. Eats poisonous scorpions after beating prey against perch to remove stingers.

**Wompoo fruit dove** Soft green above, vivid yellow and purple underneath. Eats large fruit whole.

**From top:** The Malayan tapir is the world's largest tapir. The banteng grazes in swamp forests and bamboo jungles. The male blackbuck has ringed, spiraling horns. In Asia, the mandarin duck symbolizes happiness and fidelity.

MICAELA NEAL

# Kali River Rapids

★★★★ ✓ 6 min. Capacity: 240 (20 12-person rafts). *FastPass* Outdoor queue mostly shaded. Fear factor: Bumpy, splashy; one steep drop. Closed during thunderstorms. Access: ECV users must transfer. Height restriction: 38 in. Debuted: 1999.

Hot? Don't mind getting wet? Then you'll love this raft ride, which continually finds ways to cool you off and spray—or perhaps soak— you with water. Set within realistic scenes of a pristine jungle in the midst of being clear-cut and burned, the twisty trip is so much fun you'll hardly remember its none-too-subtle lesson. The splashy river is filled with geysers, an abrupt waterfall, overhead water jugs and mischievous elephant statues.

Don't, however, wait in a long line for this one; standing in the heat for 30 minutes or more isn't worth it. Instead, use a Fastpass.

**Fun finds** ❶ In the queue, Mr. Panika's Shop sells "Antiks Made to Order." ❷ The late Michael Jackson and a Nike logo appear on the murals in the last queue room. The King of Pop rides a

**Top:** Kali River Rapids guests ride in a round, 12-person raft. **Above:** Guests watching the river can spray water on unsuspecting riders.

raft named the Sherpa Surfer; the Nike swoosh icon appears on a girl's white shirt on the raft Khatmandoozy. The murals were created in Nepal, India, by a fan of Jackson and the shoe company.

**Fun facts** ❶ Raft names include Baloo Me Away, Delhi Donut, Khatmandoozy, Papa-Do-Ron-Rani and So Sari. ❷ The river is the Chakranadi, Sanskrit for "the river that runs in circles." ❸ Kali is the Hindu goddess of destruction.

### Average Wait

| | |
|---|---|
| 9am | 0 min |
| 10am | 20 |
| 11am | 35 |
| Noon | 70 |
| 1pm | 80 |
| 2pm | 45 |
| 3pm | 55 |
| 4pm | 60 |
| 5pm | 40 |
| 6pm | 30 |
| 7pm | 10 |
| 8pm | closed |
| 9pm | closed |

▶ Take your river trip at the end of the day. If you get soaked, it won't matter.

The **Expedition Everest roller coaster** climbs into, and falls out of, a snowy mountain range

# Expedition Everest

★★★★★ ✓ **3 min. Capacity: 170.** *FastPass* **Indoor, outdoor queue is mostly covered. Fear factor: The lift rises high over the ground, you travel backwards in darkness 10 sec; one turning drop. Closed during thunderstorms. Access: ECV and wheelchair users must transfer. Height restriction: 44 in. Debuted: 2006.**

A modern Disney megaride, Expedition Everest combines sly Disney mind games with coaster-like thrills. Aboard an out-of-control railcar that races forward and backward through a mountain, you swoop into the mysterious world of the Yeti.

| Average Wait | |
|---|---|
| 9am | 0 min |
| 10am | 40 |
| 11am | 50 |
| Noon | 45 |
| 1pm | 55 |
| 2pm | 45 |
| 3pm | 45 |
| 4pm | 40 |
| 5pm | 30 |
| 6pm | 45 |
| 7pm | 40 |
| 8pm | 20 |
| 9pm | 0 |

What begins as a peaceful trip through a forest soon turns into a tense chase around a mountain and through its dark caves. Though it doesn't go up-side-down, your 4,000-foot journey climbs 200 feet, stops twice, goes backward, takes an 80-foot drop and hits a top speed of 50 mph.

It's the mental tricks that psych you out. As one 8-year-old girl put it, "That monster was like 100 feet tall!" Actually, he's only 18.

## A monster myth

The ride's back story is a tale of a mythical creature, weird accidents, wise villagers and clueless entrepreneurs.

"The Legend of the Forbidden Mountain" begins in the 1920s, a time when tea plantations flourished in the mountains of the imaginary Asian kingdom of Anandapur. Private rail lines carried the tea to villages, where it was shipped to distant markets. The Royal Anandapur Tea Co. used one such route through the early 1930s, sending steam-donkey trains through the mysterious mountains to the village of Serka Zong.

Starting in 1933, however, the railroad was plagued with accidents. Some residents drew a connection between the mishaps and increasing British expeditionary attempts to reach the summit of nearby Mt. Everest, invoking the spirit of the Yeti, the fabled, monstrous creature that guards the sacred area. By 1934, equipment breakdowns and strange track snaps caused the tea company to pull up stakes.

The legend of a guardian beast continued to circulate among locals. It came to a head in 1982, with the tragic disappearance of the Forbidden Mountain Expedition.

Cut to today. Bob, a bohemian American, grooves to the village's Hare Krishna vibe

▶ **Sit in the back for the wildest ride. You'll get whipped harder and fall faster.**

**Nine out of ten riders agree... Expedition Everest's 80-foot drop is a highlight of their Animal Kingdom day**

but doesn't believe in the Yeti. To earn a living, he's teamed up with local entrepreneur Norbu, and restored the railroad to create Himalayan Escapes Tours and Expeditions, a business that makes it easy for trekkers to get to Everest quickly. Instead of hiking for two weeks through foothills and smaller ranges, now climbers can arrive at the foot of Everest in just a few hours, riding safely on a quaint old steam train.

**Fun finds** ❶ Plaster on the Fastpass building and gift shop simulates the Himalayan building material of dried yak dung. ❷ A bulletin-board note on the wall of Gupta's Gear (left of the main village) reads "Billy—It's a small world after all! Met your brother on the trail... Mikey." ❸ Steam escapes from each train's boiler after it pulls back into the boarding area. ❹ It pulls out with a "toot-toot!" ❺ The Yeti's claw marks and footprints appear in snow to your right at your first stop. ❻ When you stop in the cave, watch the track in front of you. It flips over.

**Fun facts** ❶ The mountain range combines three freestanding structures. The ride itself is a dynamic system with framing that extends to the foundation. The building has its own beams and columns, as does the Yeti. Though intertwined like spaghetti, the three structures don't touch. If they did, the mountain's plaster and stucco would shake off. Some building beams run down the middle of A-frame ride columns. ❷ The mountains use 1,800 tons of steel, 18.7 million pounds of concrete, 2,000 gallons of stain and paint and 200,000 square feet of rock work. ❸ The Yeti has a potential thrust of 260,000 pounds of force, more than a 747 airliner. It's Disney's most advanced Audio-Animatronics creature. ❹ Much of the queue-line woodwork, including the entire Yeti temple, was handcrafted by Himalayan artists. ❺ Buddha statues, Nepalese Coke bottles, the desk phone and potbellied stoves are among 8,000 items Disney imported from Asia. ❻ The 6-acre area has 900 bamboo plants and 100 types of bushes. ❼ The buildings were aged with blowtorches, chainsaws and hammers. ❽ "Serka Zong" is Tibetan for "fortress of the chasm."

**Hidden Mickeys** ❶ In the queue, as a tiny Mickey hat worn by a Yeti doll in Tashi's Trek and Tongba Shop, on the top shelf of a cupboard to the right. ❷ As black water bottle caps in a display of patches in the same shop. ❸ As a dent and two holes in a tea kettle that's part of the wreckage of a camp in the Yeti museum. ❹ On the left wall after the museum, a Mickey with eyes, a nose, and a Sorcerer's hat appears as wood stains in a photo that shows a woman with a walkie-talkie.

**The Yeti legend** Yetis are not real. Scientists worldwide agree there is no credible evidence of an animal roaming the Himalayas that is not already an identified mammal. Some scholars say people who claim to see a Yeti are probably spotting a golden monkey, a Himalayan primate that shares the mythical creature's face, hairy body, blue skin and ability to live in cold climates. The legend, however, is quite real. For hundreds of years, Himalayan natives have told stories about a humanoid monster that fiercely guards the area around Mt. Everest. The reports increased in the early 20th century, when Westerners began to climb the mountains and reported seeing an "Abominable Snowman."

One of the most famous Western reports appeared in 1925. Traveling with a British geological expedition at about 15,000 feet, Greek photographer N.A. Tombazi saw a large creature moving among some lower slopes. He reported its movement was "exactly like a human being, walking upright and stopping occasionally to uproot or pull at some dwarf rhododendron bushes." A thousand feet away from the creature, Tombazi didn't take its picture, but two hours later reached the area and found 15 footprints. He described them as "similar in shape to those of a man, but only six to seven inches long by four inches wide. The marks of five distinct toes and the instep were perfectly clear... undoubtedly those of a biped."

Western interest in the Yeti peaked decades later. Sir Edmund Hillary, who climbed Everest in 1953, led a 1960 trip attempting to prove, or disprove, the Yeti's existence. Sponsored by the World Book Encyclopedia, the expedition was outfitted with infrared film and trip-wire and time-lapse cameras. It found nothing.

But the myth lived on. The villain-turned-good-guy of 1964's stop-motion classic "Rudolph the Red-Nosed Reindeer" is a Yeti named Bumbles. Disney added the creatures to Disneyland's Matterhorn ride in 1978, and the 2001 Disney/Pixar film "Monsters Inc." includes a disgruntled Abominable Snowman voiced by John Ratzenberger. "'Abominable!'" he complains. "Why can't they call me the 'Adorable Snowman,' or the 'Agreeable Snowman,' for crying out loud? I'm a nice guy!" The legend still lives on in Nepal, where the Yeti has a religious meaning to some and is a tourist money maker.

The term "Abominable Snowman" was coined by mistake. While exploring the Himalayas in 1921, British Lt. Col. C.K. Howard-Bury spotted what he thought were gray wolves. When his Sherpa guides told him their prints were those of a "met-teh," or "man-sized wild creature," he misheard them to say "metoh-kangmi," or "snow creature." Reporting this incident, British newspaper editor Henry Newman quoted the words as "metch kangmi," which he said meant "abominable or filthy man of the snow."

▶ If you can, ride it at night. The mountain is lit in orange and purple, but the track stays dark.

© DISNEY

**Too close for comfort.** An angry carnotaurus threatens guests riding a Dinosaur Time Rover.

# Dinosaur!

★★★★ ✔ **3 min, 30 sec. Capacity: 144.** *FastPass* Indoor, air-conditioned queue. Fear factor: Dark, loud, threatening, intense. Can be terrifying for young children. Access: ECV and wheelchair users must transfer. Assisted listening, video captioning. Height restriction: 40 in. Debuted: 1998 (as "Countdown to Extinction").

You'll remember the end of this dark indoor thrill ride for days: a dinosaur gets right in your face and lets loose with an unearthly roar. The rest of the trip is almost as tense, which can make it terrifying for little kids, but extra fun for dinosaur fans, teenagers, or others who enjoy a brief, controlled adventure.

You start off in the Dino Institute Discovery Center, a thinly disguised parody of the Smithsonian's National Museum of Natural History in Washington, D.C. As you pass earnest murals and displays, a multimedia show explains how an asteroid wiped out the dinosaurs long ago.

The Institute has a special exhibit on its new high-tech vehicle, called the Time Rover. In an Orientation Room, director Helen Marsh (actress Phylicia Rashad, via video) explains that the vehicle is designed to take you peacefully back to the Age of the Dinosaurs.

But her assistant has a different plan. Once Marsh leaves the room, Dr. Grant Seeker (Wallace Langham, of television's "CSI") reprograms her computer to send you to a time just before the asteroid strikes, to bring an iguanodon to the present.

Soon a flashing, smoky tunnel sends you 65 million years back in time, to a dark forest. As you career forward you see many dinosaurs, including an alioramus swallowing its dinner. Suddenly a huge carnotaurus starts chasing your Time Rover. Then it gets worse—your power starts to fail. As a massive meteor destroys your trail, it appears that you, too, are about to become extinct.

In a final burst of speed, you find your iguanodon, narrowly miss the last lunge of the carnotaurus and crash back to the present. Security monitors show you did indeed pick up the iguanodon.

### Dino-Sue

A cast of the largest, most complete Tyrannosaurus rex fossil ever found (Sue, uncovered in South Dakota in 1990) stands in

| Average Wait | |
|---|---|
| 9am | 0 min |
| 10am | 25 |
| 11am | 35 |
| Noon | 30 |
| 1pm | 35 |
| 2pm | 35 |
| 3pm | 25 |
| 4pm | 20 |
| 5pm | 20 |
| 6pm | 15 |
| 7pm | 10 |
| 8pm | 5 |
| 9pm | 0 |

▶ Sit on the far right side of your Time Rover for the closest encounter with the carnotaurus.

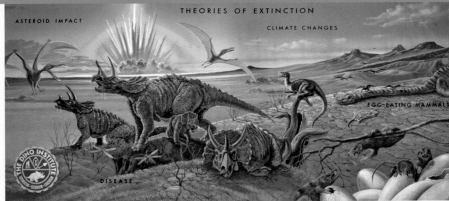

THEORIES OF EXTINCTION

ASTEROID IMPACT

CLIMATE CHANGES

EGG-EATING MAMMALS

THE DINO INSTITUTE

DISEASE

**Top:** A mural parodies a stuffy museum. **Above left:** A statue of Aladar from Disney's year-2000 film "Dinosaur" greets guests out front. **Above right:** A cast of the skull from Sue, a South Dakota T-Rex.

front of the Dinosaur attraction. Named after paleontologist Sue Hendrickson, the 67-million-year-old creature is estimated to have been 45 feet long and 14 feet tall. Much of the real fossil's bonework (now at Chicago's Field Museum) was done in the late 1990s in front of Disney guests, where today's Dino-Rama carnival sits.

### Cretaceous Trail

This shady path meanders through a garden that uses ancient plant species to replicate a dinosaur-era jungle. The greenery includes conifers, ferns, mosses, more than 20 magnolia species and the third largest cycad collection in North America. Dinosaur sounds and statues add a lightweight touch. The trail is wheelchair and ECV accessible.

**Fun finds** ❶ Trees that appear to be growing behind the Dino Institute building are actually on its roof. They serve to help create the illusion that the building is simply a small museum, not a huge indoor ride. ❷ An entrance dedication plaque is dated April 22, 1978—exactly 20 years before the attraction opened. ❸ Smithsonian allusions include

a cheap lobby diorama with a plastic rat glued to a plastic tree, beneath which swim plastic fish in a plastic pond. ❹ Dr. Seeker claims flash photography "interferes with the homing signal and that's not good." ❺ Actually an above-ground warehouse, the "underground research facility" where the ride begins creates a convincing illusion of being under ground. It's cooler than the earlier rooms, and has flickering lights. ❻ In the loading area, three red, yellow and white pipes are discreetly labeled with the chemical makeup of, respectively, ketchup, mustard and mayonnaise, a reference to the ride's original sponsor, McDonald's. ❼ Gift-shop monitors show the iguanodon continuing to wander the building. ❽ A cast of an ancient sea turtle hangs over the gift shop.

**Fun facts** ❶ The Triceratops skeleton in the lobby is a cast of the only articulated Triceratops ever found. It was discovered in North Dakota in 1994. ❷ An "enhanced motion vehicle," your Time Rover gets its movements from 3,000 PSI of hydraulic pressure. On-board tanks hold 100 gallons of fluid.

**Hidden Mickey** The three-circle shape appears as marks on a tree trunk in a lobby mural.

▶ A climb-on dinosaur on the Cretaceous Trail makes a good photo prop.

**Out for a spin. Primeval Whirl riders start to spin as they head down the ride's big drop.**

**Dúmbo XL.** Unlike its famous cousin, TriceraTop Spin has room for four.

# Primeval Whirl

★★★★ 2 min, 30 sec. Capacity: 52 on each of two tracks. *FastPass* Covered outdoor queue. Fear factor: One steep drop. Jerky. Spinning can affect those with inner-ear issues. Closed during thunderstorms. Access: ECV and wheelchair users must transfer. Height restriction: 48 in. Debuted: 2002.

A spoof of the nearby Dinosaur attraction, this spinning roller coaster also takes you back to the age of hitchhiking dinosaurs, but here in a tongue-in-cheek "time machine" equipped with a kitchen timer, clock radio and alarm clock, candy-colored and stylistically cued like a 1950s automobile. Comic dinosaur and meteor cutouts line the track, as do animated cartoon clocks and vortexes. A queue-area time portal is decorated with egg beaters and hubcaps.

An updated take on an old Wild Mouse coaster, the ride has cars that speed up slowly as they head down a switchback track. Once the meteors hit, the cars start to spin.

**Hidden Mickeys** As craters that appear throughout the ride.

| Average Wait | |
| --- | --- |
| 9am | 0 min |
| 10am | 35 |
| 11am | 30 |
| Noon | 20 |
| 1pm | 30 |
| 2pm | 30 |
| 3pm | 20 |
| 4pm | 20 |
| 5pm | 20 |
| 6pm | 10 |
| 7pm | 20 |
| 8pm | 10 |
| 9pm | 0 |

# TriceraTop Spin

★★★ 1 min, 30 sec. Capacity: 64. Covered outdoor queue. Fear factor: None. Closed during thunderstorms. Access: ECV users must transfer. Debuted: 2001.

This carnival attraction is Disney's most elaborate hub-and-spoke ride. Circling around a colorful spinning top that has playful dinosaurs popping out of its rim, you ride in a chubby triceratops that climbs, dips and dives at your command. The vehicles circle the top once every 13 seconds, the same speed as Magic Kingdom's similar Dumbo the Flying Elephant.

Though the ride doesn't have the charm of Dumbo, it is easier to enjoy. There's rarely a long line, and a large covered queue area has huge fans to keep you cool. Each vehicle seats four, so small families can ride together.

Manic banjo and fiddle music adds a cute cornpone touch. Extra eye candy includes flying cartoon comets on the hub and, at night, white light bulbs lining the hub and spokes.

| Average Wait | |
| --- | --- |
| 9am | 0 min |
| 10am | 5 |
| 11am | 5 |
| Noon | 5 |
| 1pm | 20 |
| 2pm | 20 |
| 3pm | 10 |
| 4pm | 10 |
| 5pm | 10 |
| 6pm | 5 |
| 7pm | 5 |
| 8pm | 5 |
| 9pm | 0 |

▶ To avoid getting dizzy on Primeval Whirl, stare at the orange radio in front of you.

**A dino double!** The authors' daughter with some Fossil Fun Games winnings.

# Fossil Fun Games

★★★ ✓ Allow 15 min. Capacity: 1–10 per game. Fear factor: None. Access: Guests may remain in wheelchairs and ECVs. Debuted: 2002.

The centerpiece of Disney's tongue-in-cheek roadside carnival (the purposely tacky Chester and Hester's Dino-Rama, which also includes funhouse mirrors, a photo booth and a snack stand), these six colorful midway games have silly dinosaur themes. Three are designed for children, three for adults. Each costs $2.50 to play; you buy vouchers at a nearby cart, which accepts credit cards. Each game awards cartoonish stuffed dinosaurs and other creatures to its winners. Unlike some carnivals, the games aren't rigged and their prizes, though small, are often easy to win.

For children, the midway offers an easy water-squirt game (Fossil Fueler), a ball-rolling racing derby (Mammoth Marathon) and a mallet-strike game (Whac-A-Pachycephalosaur). Each requires only two players and always awards a prize. (In other words, if one has no one waiting to play it—a common situation, especially in the early morning—you and a child can spend $5 and one of you will absolutely win a small stuffed dinosaur worth at least that much.)

Our daughter, who has played the games for years, offers these tips on how to win:

**Fossil Fueler:** For the most accurate shooting, use your free hand to cradle the front of your gun.

**Mammoth Marathon:** Roll the balls gently. If you use too much force a ball will go into a hole with a lesser value, which will make your mammoth move slowly. Ask for a practice ball before your race starts.

**Whacky Packy:** Wait until you see a head pop up before you swing. Don't anticipate.

Three other games require serious skill to win anything, and some luck—a ball toss (Comet Crasher), basketball throw (Bronto Score) and a classic strongman mallet strike that sends a weight up a pole to ring a bell (Dino-Whamma, which these days is rarely open). Prizes for these latter three games are not guaranteed, regardless of how many people compete.

For all games, smaller prizes can be saved up and traded in for larger ones. Prizes can be sent to package pickup free of charge, so you don't have to carry them with you.

| Average Wait | |
|---|---|
| 9am | 0 min |
| 10am | 0 |
| 11am | 0 |
| Noon | 0 |
| 1pm | 0 |
| 2pm | 0 |
| 3pm | 0 |
| 4pm | 0 |
| 5pm | 0 |
| 6pm | 0 |
| 7pm | 0 |
| 8pm | 0 |
| 9pm | 0 |

▶ Whac-A-Pachycephalosaur ("Whacky Packy") is the easiest game for kids.

MICAELA NEAL

# The Boneyard

★ ★ ★ ★ ✓ **Allow 15–30 min. Capacity: 500. Fear factor: None. Closed during thunderstorms. Access: Guests may remain in wheelchairs, ECVs. Debuted 1998.**

Geared for toddlers through elementary-age kids, this large outdoor playground is filled with opportunities for kids to burn off energy. Themed to be a dinosaur-bone dig site, two distinct areas are connected by an overhead footbridge. Highlights include a three-story tower of nets and slides (parents can lead kids up to the slide entrances) and a sandy pit where kids can look for woolly mammoth bones.

| Average Wait | |
|---|---|
| 9am | 0 min |
| 10am | 0 |
| 11am | 0 |
| Noon | 0 |
| 1pm | 0 |
| 2pm | 0 |
| 3pm | 0 |
| 4pm | 0 |
| 5pm | 0 |
| 6pm | 0 |
| 7pm | 0 |
| 8pm | 0 |
| 9pm | 0 |

Extras include a maze of walk-through tunnels, walls embedded with dinosaur skeletons; climb-on bones, rocks and a Jeep; steep net and rope-climbing ramps; and waterfalls sized just right to drench a young head. Mesh overhead canopies filter the sun. An abundance of hidden nooks and crannies makes it easy to lose sight of your child, but there's only one exit, and its shut gate is monitored.

**A 1970s Jeep** sits "stuck in the mud" of The Boneyard playground

**Fun finds** ❶ Though it looks like a Stegosaurus shoulder bone, the Boneyard marquee is in the shape of the original Animal Kingdom, before the addition of Asia. An "N" points north. ❷ Notes sound when kids bang a "xylobone" embedded in a wall near the Jeep. ❸ Nearby, dinosaur tracks trigger loud roars when kids step on them. ❹ On a whiteboard along the top back wall, the dig's three fictional grad students and their professors have posted their findings and work schedules. ❺ The students' notes to each other and personal possessions are scattered throughout the playground, on the bulletin board at the DinoLand U.S.A. entrance and in the nearby Restaurantosaurus, where they supposedly live in the rafters. ❻ Scientific debates about dinosaurs appear on signs throughout the playground. ❼ Ambient music (via "pirate radio station" W-DINO) includes "Brontosaurus," a 1970 U.K. hit for the Move, a band that would later become the Electric Light Orchestra.

**Fun fact** The woolly mammoth was not a dinosaur. It lived just 10,000 years ago. Dinosaurs died off 65 million years earlier.

**Hidden Mickeys** ❶ As a water stain under the drinking fountain near the entrance. ❷ As a quarter and two pennies on a table behind a fenced-in area, on the second level by the slides in the back. ❸ As a fan and two hardhats in a fenced-off area at the back of the woolly mammoth excavation.

▶ The Boneyard offers plenty of shady spots for parents to get off their feet.

**'Haven't you seen Jaws?'** Marlin (right) confronts his son in Finding Nemo—The Musical.

# Finding Nemo — The Musical

★ ★ ★ ★ ★ ✔ 35 min. Capacity: 1,700. Outdoor queue is not shaded. Indoor, air-conditioned theater. Fear factor: None. Access: ECV, wheelchair accessible. Reflective captioning. Debuted: 2007.

Singers who somersault as they "swim" above the stage... giant jellyfish that billow through the theater... a chorus line of shimmying sharks. The creativity never ends in this musical version of the 2003 film, "Finding Nemo." A spectacle of color, movement and imagination, it redefines the meaning of the term "puppet show."

Costumed live singers act out the roles of Nemo, Dory and other characters as they simultaneously operate larger-than-life puppet versions. Peripheral characters are brought to life by the Japanese style of puppetry called *bunraku*, in which one huge puppet is operated by multiple puppeteers. The puppets were created by Michael Curry, who also did the park's parade floats as well

| Average Wait | |
|---|---|
| 9am | n/a |
| 10am | 30 min |
| 11am | 30 |
| Noon | 30 |
| 1pm | 30 |
| 2pm | 30 |
| 3pm | 30 |
| 4pm | 30 |
| 5pm | n/a |
| 6pm | n/a |
| 7pm | n/a |
| 8pm | n/a |
| 9pm | n/a |

as the puppets for the Broadway production of Disney's "The Lion King."

The songs are accessible and seamlessly fit into the story. The show also includes acrobats, dancers, animated backdrops and terrifically abstract props, like a fish net comprised simply of six bowed ladders.

The production takes place in the Theater in the Wild, located along the walkway between DinoLand U.S.A. and Asia. Sit in the middle to see the full spectacle, or along the center catwalk to be immersed in it.

As you leave, the movie's "Mine! Mine!" sea gulls bid you "Bye! Bye!" They're voiced by Andrew Stanton, the film's director.

**Hidden Mickey** As three blue bubbles, two lit and one drawn, at the bottom left of the stage wall.

A curious clownfish defies his overprotective father in 2003's "Finding Nemo," swimming out to a boat only to be captured by an aquarium diver. Searching for his son, dad Marlin encounters Dory, an absentminded blue tang, as well as sharks, jellyfish and sea turtles. Meanwhile, son Nemo makes new friends in a fish tank in Sydney. They teach Nemo that he's stronger than he thinks, and help him reunite with his dad.

▶ The last show of the day is usually the least crowded.

**The view from one of the guest floats** in Mickey's Jammin' Jungle Parade

# Mickey's Jammin' Jungle Parade

★★★★★ ✔ 15 min. Circles around Discovery Island. Starts, and exits, in Africa. Arrive 15 min early for good spot, 30 min for best spots. Cancelled during rain. Fear factor: None. Access: Special viewing locations for those in wheelchairs, ECVs. Assistive listening. Debuted: 2001.

Towering mechanical animal puppets, whimsical stilt-walkers, colorful Jeeps and Land Rovers, dozens of dancers and infectious music combine to celebrate the harmony between man and animals in this lively procession, which winds along shady pathways that are often just 12 feet wide.

Handcrafted in a leafy motif from what appears to be natural materials, the abstract puppets move like real creatures: a chameleon sticks out its tongue; a frog jumps.

Dancing alongside are safari guides, creature-costumed stilt-walkers and Disney characters including Pluto, Chip 'n Dale, Timon from Disney's 1994 "The Lion King," Terk from 1999's "Tarzan," Baloo and King Louie from 1967's "The Jungle Book" and Brer Bear and Brer Rabbit from the 1946 "Song of the South."

A whimsical back story adds to the fun. The parade portrays Mickey Mouse and Rafiki, the mandrill from "The Lion King," taking the other characters on a camping trip. Minnie Mouse, Donald Duck and Goofy have their own safari trucks, though none appear to know how to pack. Donald totes a leaky boat. Minnie brings a bathtub. Goofy's the worst: he's brought everything from his bowling trophy to, literally, his kitchen sink.

A catchy soundtrack ties everything together. It features Disney versions of three great party songs—the 1954 New Orleans standard "Iko Iko," South African legend Miriam Makeba's 1960s dance tune "Pata Pata" and "Mas Que Nada," the 1966 signature tune of Brazil's Sergio Mendes.

Selected at random each day, up to 25 park guests ride in the parade.

**Fun finds ❶** Minnie's bathtub blows bubbles and **❷** has a Donald Duck rubber ducky. **❸** Goofy's hood ornament, a bowling trophy, topples over as his engine overheats. **❹** Strapped onto Goofy's hood is Aladdin's lamp and carpet. **❺** His vehicle carries a Donald Duck life preserver. **❻** Timon's backpack is full of bugs. **❼** The driver of the hippo rickshaw is the animal's pic-pic bird. **❽** The kangaroo float has a spring for a tail. Its drummer sits in the mechanical marsupial's pouch. **❾** Brooms create the mane and tail of the zebra stilt-walker.

▶ The parade passes through Africa on its way out and back. Crowds are light for the return trip.

A teenager soaks up the sun at Disney's Blizzard Beach water park

# Water Parks

Giggles, laughs and squeals fill the air. Close your eyes at either of these two water parks and you'll hear more happy people than anywhere else at Disney World. Why? Because it's just so much fun to ride a water slide, float down a lazy river or splash in a pool, especially when you're in such a fully realized fantasy atmosphere.

The U.S. has more than 1,000 water parks, but few offer the immersive theming of these two from Disney. Instead of plastic culverts and support columns, you see mountain streams and palms. Instead of rap and pop songs, you hear reggae tunes and Christmas ditties. And since these are Disney parks, everyone greets you with a smile, and everywhere you look is spic-and-span.

How do the two parks compare? Typhoon Lagoon offers more shade, unique snorkeling, face-first rides, bigger waves and more preschooler activities, while Blizzard Beach has more sun, longer and faster slides and the most for preteens and teens. The parks share a number of policies. Swimwear can't have rivets, buckles, or exposed metal. You can bring in small toys, towels, picnic coolers, food, strollers and wheelchairs, but not boogie boards, water toys, tubes (all tube rides have complimentary ones), glass containers or alcohol.

If bought separately, 2010 water park tickets are $45 for adults, $39 for children 3–9. When the water parks close for inclement weather, guests who have been inside less than three hours get complimentary rain checks (conditions apply).

To get the most of your day, arrive before a park opens. Do the slides before noon, the lazy rivers and playgrounds after lunch.

## Blizzard Beach

It's a zany combination: a water park that looks like a ski resort. Disguised as ski slopes, water slides extend down the sides of Mt. Gushmore, a 90-foot snow-capped peak. Around it is a beach, wave pool, lazy river and children's areas. The 66-acre park sits east of Animal Kingdom.

Meals at three outdoor counter cafes feature hamburgers, hot dogs, sandwiches, salads and individual pizzas ($4–$9, at Lottawatta Lodge in the Alpine Village, the Warming Hut on the left side of Melt-Away Bay and Avalunch near the Ski Patrol Training Camp). Snack stands sell funnel cakes and cotton candy (Melt-Away Bay), ice cream treats ($4–$8, Sled Dog Expeditions, Ski Patrol Training Camp), hot mini donuts (Alpine Village), nachos (Cooling Hut, Alpine Village) and snow cones (Snow Balls, near Ski Patrol Training Camp). Other stands offer coffee, tea and pastries (Frosty the Joe Man, Melt-Away Bay) and beer and specialty rum drinks (Frostbite Freddies at Alpine Village, Polar Pub at Melt-Away Bay).

As for shops, the Beach Haus (Alpine Village) has beachwear and swimming suits from Quiksilver, Roxy and Element. Across from

**AS DISNEY TELLS IT,** in early 1995 Central Florida experienced a freak winter snowstorm. Gazing at the flakes falling outside of their Disney World offices, the company's Imagineers had a brainstorm: "Let's build a ski resort!" Immediately they built a mountain, a ski jump, slalom courses, a chairlift and lodge. But just as they finished, the warm weather returned and the snow turned to slush. Reluctantly, the workers began to board things up. But then they spotted a lone alligator, blue from the cold but full of energy. Strapping on skis, he careened down the jump, flew through the air, landed on the women's restrooms, crashed into the gift shop... and emerged with a smile. Watching this "Ice Gator," as they named him, the Imagineers realized that their failed ski resort would make a great water park. The jump could be a body slide. The slalom, bobsled and sledding runs could be mat and tube rides. The slushy creek? A perfect lazy river. Basking in their genius, the Imagineers named their creation **Blizzard Beach** and proudly opened it to the public—on April Fools Day, 1995.

**Though her boyfriend** chickened out moments earlier, a teen girl still prepares to brave Summit Plummet

the changing rooms, the Shade Shack has sunglasses, sandals, beach towels and disposable cameras. A branch of Hawaii-based Pearl Factory, North Pearl has farm-raised Japanese akoya pearls in oysters (6–9 mm, $15), settings ($10–$900) and pearl jewelry.

You enter the park through a re-creation of an alpine village, with buildings that include changing rooms, lockers, food stands and shops. There's an ATM at the ticket and Guest Relations booth, which also serves as Lost and Found. Inside the turnstiles is the Beach Haus shop, which rents lockers and towels and sells sunscreen. Around the corner, Snowless Joe's stand offers the same services and has complimentary lifejackets. The lockers themselves are in three places. Most are centrally located at Snowless Joe's. Other sit along the right side of the park near the Ski Patrol Training Camp preteen area, and along the left side next to the Downhill Double Dipper tube slide.

A First Aid station is to the right of the Beach Haus. Cast members take lost children to Snowless Joe's. Blizzard Beach parking is free. The Bizzard Beach telephone number is 407-560-3400.

## Lazy river

**Cross Country Creek** Circling the park, this 3,000-foot stream has seven entry points, each with a stack of complimentary tubes. Lined with palms and evergreens, the river flows under bridges, over springs and through a cave with ice-cold dripping water. A round-trip journey takes about 25 minutes. The water is 2.5 feet deep.

## Children's area

**Tikes Peak** Gentle slides, rideable baby alligators and an ankle-deep squirting "ice" pond highlight this preschool playground. There's a fountain play area, a little waterfall, sand boxes, lawn chairs, chaise lounges and picnic tables. Kids should wear water shoes: the pavement can get hot. **Height restriction: Must be under 48 in.**

## Preteen area

**Ski Patrol Training Camp** This inventive spot features Fahrenheit Drop, cabled T-bars that drop kids into an 8-foot pool; and the Thin Ice Training Course, slippery walks on floating "icebergs" with overhead rope grids for support. Also here: wide Snow Falls slides designed for a parent and child to ride together; Cool Runners, two short, bumpy tube slides; and Frozen Pipe Springs, a short, steep, covered body slide.

## Body slides

**Slush Gusher** This 90-foot slide starts off slow, gradually gaining speed over the first drop. You get some airtime off the second drop, however, thanks to some playful Disney designers who followed the second lip with a steep drop. Heavier riders fly higher. The trip takes about 10 seconds; top speeds can reach 50 mph. The 250-foot flume has the look of a melting snow-banked gully. *Height restriction: 48 in.*

**Summit Plummet** One of the tallest, fastest water slides in the United States, this 350-foot chute has a 66-degree, 120-foot fall. A mock ski jump, the launch tower looms 30 feet above Mt. Gushmore. Lying down at the top of the ramp, you cross your arms, cross your feet and push yourself off this real Tower of Terror. There's a blur of sky and scenery as you fall, then a roar of water when you splash down. The impact can send much of your swimsuit where the sun never shines. Speeds can reach 60 mph. If you don't wear a T-shirt, the trip can sting your skin. In fact, the fall is so scary even some of its designers don't care for it. "I made the mistake when we were building it of going up the stairs and looking down," says Disney Imagineer Kathy Rogers. "I thought, 'There's no way I'd put my body in there!' I did it once and said, 'Done!'"

Summit Plummet has no exit stairs. Those who chicken out at the loading area squeeze back down the entrance steps doing what cast members call "the walk of shame." There's an observation deck as well as a viewing area at the end of the ride with a rider-speed display. *Height restriction: 48 in.*

## Wave pool

**Melt-Away Bay** A one-acre spot nestled against the base of Mt. Gushmore, this swimming pool appears to be created by streams

**Blizzard Beach tubers take it easy** on the Cross Country Creek lazy river

of melting snow that wash down into it. Bobbing waves wash through the water for 45 minutes of every hour. Perfect for sunbathing, a sandy beach lines the shore.

## Mat slides

**Toboggan Racers** Based on an amusement park gunnysack slide, this 8-lane, 250-foot mat slide has you race down its series of dips face first. Great for families, it's more fun than scary. To go fast, push off quickly then lift up the front of your mat slightly so it doesn't dig in the water. Regardless of technique, heavier riders usually win.

**Snow Stormers** When you were a kid, did you have a sled? If so, these three racing slides will bring back those memories. Lying face-first on a mat, you weave down a hill of S-curves dug into the ground like

high-banked gullies. The 350-foot track is plenty fast, even a little scary — as you careen up the corners the splashing water makes it tough to see. A horizontal line on the wall gives you a point of reference.

Want to win the race? Keep your elbows on the mat and your feet up. To be fair to your lighter-weight kids, give them a second or two head start.

## Tube slides

**Downhill Double Dipper** This side-by-side racing run takes you through a tunnel with two steep drops before shooting you through a curtain of water at 25 mph. Your time is shown at the finish line. The 230-foot ride stands 50 feet high. Pull up on your tube handles just before the catch pool to fly across the water. *Height restriction: 48 in.*

**Runoff Rapids** You climb 127 steps to ride these three 600-foot flumes, but they're worth every huff and puff. Two allow two-person tubes, so friends or family members ride together. A third is like a watery Space Mountain, enclosed in darkness except for some pinlights. All three make you feel like a bobsledder, sliding you up on banked curves before shooting you into a catch pool.

**Teamboat Springs** All ages smile on this, the world's longest family raft ride. Sitting in a raft the size of a kiddie pool, you slide down a high-banked 1,200-foot-long course, spinning on tight curves which may toss

**Top:** Riders are timed as they race each other on Downhill Double Dipper, Disney World's scariest tube ride. **Above:** A three-person chair lift allows easy access to the Slush Gusher and Summit Plummet body slides as well as the Teamboat Springs family raft ride. A separate Single Rider line saves time during busy periods for those who don't mind riding with strangers. Stairways also lead up the mountain.

**Braced for impact,** a crowd at the Typhoon Lagoon surf pool awaits a breaking wave

you up on their steep walls. One thing's for sure: your rear end will get soaked. Thirty holes line each raft's bottom edge. A 200-foot ride-out area takes you under a collapsing roof that's dripping with cool water. *There's often a minimum of four riders per tube, when smaller groups ride together.*

**Fun facts ❶** An eclectic Blizzard Beach soundtrack mixes summertime tunes with Christmas ditties. **❷** Equipment from the "Sunshine State Snow Making Co." sits along the Toboggan Racers queue and on the Cross Country Creek bank past Reindeer Landing. **❸** Barrels of equipment and "Instant Snow" from the "Joe Blow Snow Co." sit along the walkways to Slush Gusher, Summit Plummet and Teamboat Springs. **❹** Snow is melting off a roof of a small building across from the Downhill Double Dipper entrance marked "Safe to Approach Unless Melting." **❺** Just after you enter the park, Ice Gator's ski tracks appear on the roof of the women's dressing room, behind a sign reading "Caution: Low Flying Gator." Directly across that walkway, his silhouette forms a hole in the side of the Beach Haus shop. **❻** "Ancient" drawings on the walls of the Cross Country Creek cave include a beach chair with umbrella, Ice Gator, a Yeti, people in tubes, people on skis and a skier with a leg cast. **❼** The Northern Lights shine through the cave's ceiling. **❽** "B-r-r-r-occoli" and "Sleet Corn" are planted in Ice Gator's garden alongside the creek, just past Manatee Landing. **❾** As you float by Ice Gator's house he often sneezes and says "Anybody got a hanky?"

# Typhoon Lagoon

With an atmosphere that's one part Hawaii and two parts Gilligan's Island, this tropical park is an unsung Disney masterpiece. Like Magic Kingdom, its fun theme, passionate design and variety of things to do make it easy to have fun. Lushly landscaped, Typhoon Lagoon consists of four areas: a Harbor Village entrance, a central surf pool and lazy river, and two attraction zones that border the river. Across the street from Downtown Disney, the park covers 61 acres.

Three outdoor counter cafes offer hamburgers, hot dogs, sandwiches, salads and individual pizzas ($4–$9, at Leaning Palms, Harbor Village; Typhoon Tilly's, North Shore; and Lowtide Lou's, South Shore). Snack stands sell hot mini donuts (Harbor Village), funnel cakes and fried ice cream (Water Works), ice cream treats (Snack Shack, North Shore; Happy Landings, Harbor Village; Dippin' Dots cart, South Shore) and hot dogs and pretzels (Surf Doggies, surf pool). Other stands sell coffee, tea, pastries (Coffee Cappucino, surf pool) and beer and rum drinks (Let's Go Slurpin', surf pool).

For shopping, Singapore Sal's (Harbor Village) has beach and swimwear from Quiksilver, Roxy and Element, Disney beach towels and sundries. The Pearl Factory (Shark Reef, North Shore) sells farm-raised Japanese

**Family float.** Orlando's Rathbun family relaxes under the lush landscaping of Castaway Creek.

akoya pearls in their oysters (6–9 mm, $15), settings ($10–$900) and pearl jewelry.

Singapore Sal's rents lockers and towels, sells sunscreen and has an ATM. Most lockers are nearby; some are at Shark Reef. A photo stand offers complimentary lifejacket use. A First Aid station sits behind the Leaning Palms restaurant. Lost children are taken to High 'N Dry Towels. Lost and Found is at the Guest Relations kiosk. Parking is free. The park phone number is 407-560-7223.

## Surf pool

It's not everyone's cup of chowder, but this giant wave pool is a perfect playground to many. Surf's up all day. Waves vary between bobbing 2-foot swells and body-surfable 6-foot breakers. Emerging with a "whoomph!" from two underwater doors, 80,000 gallons of water sweep down the pool every 90 seconds. Each wave is met by hundreds of people who swim into it, swim with it or get knocked down by it. A sign in front shows the wave schedule. Twice the size of a football field, the mushroom-shaped lagoon includes wading pools with kid-sized slides, infant-friendly bubbling tide pools with climb-on boats and a white sandy beach.

## Lazy river

**Castaway Creek** This shady, palm-lined stream takes you on a tropical journey around the park. Along the way you'll be sprayed a few times by misters along the shore, drizzled on by the tank and pipes of a broken-down waterworks, and, as you're forced through a waterfall at a cave entrance, completely soaked. There's a lot to look at. You pass three crashed boats, travel along the kiddie playground and go under a suspension bridge. Once the river splits in two. The 2,100-foot waterway is 15 feet wide and 3 feet deep. It moseys along at 2 feet per second; a round trip takes about 25 minutes. There's never a wait, though the river can get crowded in the afternoon.

## Children's area

**Ketchakiddee Creek** What was once, according to Disney, a no-man's land of volcanoes and geysers has become an elaborate tyke-sized water park with 18 activity spots. Your toddler will likely break into a huge grin as he or she splashes through the tube slide's three little dips toward the end of this palm-lined, 100-foot course. The surrounding area is filled with ankle-deep pools and creeks and low bubbly fountains. A 12-foot Blow Me Down boiler is topped with hoses that shake, shimmy and squirt. More adventurous kids will hurl themselves down the two slip 'n' slides—cushy 20-foot mats with 20-degree drops. Everyone has a blast at the S.S. Squirt. Using swiveling water cannons, you'll spray each other with multiple streams of water as you take sides in a battle of oversized sand sculptures. To keep you soaked, a whistle shoots a continuous spray in the air. Many families build sandcastles. There are shady chairs and picnic tables. *Height restriction: must be under 48 in. for slides.*

## Body slides

**Humunga Kowabunga** Like Splash Mountain without the boat, these zippity speed slides drop you 51 feet in just a couple of seconds. Three identical dark tubes sit at 60-degree angles and extend 214 feet. Speeds can reach 30 mph. Don't want to go? A waiting bench overlooks the catch pool. *Height restriction: 48 in.* **Storm Slides** High-banked walls hug these three swooping flumes, which take you through rocky gulches on the shady side of Mount Mayday. Each slide is different: Rudder Buster (on the left as you stand at the boarding area) has a small tunnel; Stern Burner (in the middle) has a longer dark tunnel; Jib Jammer (on the right) has no tunnel. Top speed is 20 mph. The slides' average length is 300 feet. **Bay Slides** Located in the calm left corner of the surf pool (an area called Blustery Bay), these two 35-foot slides are for kids too old for Ketchakiddee Creek but too young for the Storm Slides or Humunga Kowabunga. One is uncovered with a few gentle bumps; the other has a 4-foot tunnel. The walkway wanders out of your sight, but it's just 10 steps and leads only to the slides. Many parents wait in the water to catch their kids. *Must be under 60 in.*

## Saltwater snorkeling

**Shark Reef** Darth Vader lives! You hear nothing but your own breathing as you snorkel past "smiling" rainbow parrotfish and other tropical beauties as well as passive rays and leopard and bonnethead sharks in

**Dads join in the water-cannon fun** at Typhoon Lagoon's Ketchakiddee Creek children's area

crystal-clear, cold saltwater. The fish usually swim away from you, but if you're very still one may come close. You can take as long as you want in the water, and even can take a break on a small center island. Use of masks, snorkels and vests is complimentary. You rinse off (beforehand and afterward) in an outdoor shower. Changing areas, lockers, showers and a picnic area are nearby.

Don't want to go? Portholes in an overturned, walk-through tanker let you watch your family as they swim by.

An optional Supplied Air Snorkeling adventure ($25) introduces guests to the basics of scuba diving. Run by the National Association of Underwater Instructors (NAUI), the 30-minute session includes use of an air tank, regulator, flippers and instruction. You can't dive deep, but you get plenty of time in the pool. *Ages 5 and older. Summer only.*

## Tube slides

**Keelhaul Falls** A big "C" curve, this gentle 400-foot slide slowly builds up speed. The ride ends just after you slide up on a bank.

**Mayday Falls** This swervy, rippled flume simulates white-water rafting. A relatively long, fast course (460 feet at about 15 feet per second, lean back to go faster), it features a triple vortex that can turn you around. There's one small waterfall.

**Gangplank Falls** The three- to five-passenger rafts on this short family adventure are plenty of fun. You brave waterfalls, dripping caves and squirting pipes as you twist past crates of fireworks on the banks. The 300-foot ride is over in about 30 seconds.

**Crush 'n' Gusher** With both lifts and dips, this water-jet-powered ride gives you the experience of a roller coaster. Riding in either a two- or three-person tube, you're dropped by a conveyor belt into a flume, then thrust up a few lift hills. Lean back and a lip before each drop may get you airborne. Push your feet down to stay in control. Riders choose from three slides, each of which offers a slightly different experience. **Pineapple Plunger** provides the most air time, with two peaks and three medium-length tunnels. **Coconut Crusher** has one peak and a long, short and medium tunnel. **Banana Blaster** has

**Left:** New Jersey's Amanda Mathus, 14, braces for the splash on the Stern Burner Storm Slide, which goes through a tunnel. **Below:** Shark Reef snorkelers swim past a (real) overturned tanker.

**The Gangplank Falls** tube slide has rafts that hold up to five people

one peak, one long tunnel and two medium tunnels. It's the longest ride by a few seconds, but doesn't take three-person rafts. Each ride lasts about 30 seconds. The slides average 420 feet. Waiting lines are covered. The attraction is meant to be the remains of the Tropical Amity (say it slowly) fruit-packing plant. The flumes are, supposedly, old wash spillways that were used to clean the fruit before it was shipped. *Height requirement for slides: 48 in.*

Aptly named Out of the Way Cay, Crush 'n' Gusher's remote 5-acre setting is hidden from the rest of the park, tucked behind the dressing rooms. Besides the tube ride, it includes a small gradual-entry pool and many beach chairs and chaise lounges.

**Fun facts** ❶ To the right of the turnstiles, hanging nautical flags spell out "Piranha in pool." ❷ The surf pool wall resembles a levee ready to burst. Water spits out between plank seams. ❸ An alligator totem stands under the clock tower, by Lagoona Gator's shack. ❹ Inside the shack are posters and flyers for The Beach Gators ("So cold blooded, they're hot!") and the film "Bikini Beach Blanket Muscle Party Bingo." A Surfin' Reptile magazine includes the article "How to Get a Golden Tan Without Being Turned into a Suitcase." ❺ In front of the Happy Landings snack bar, a rack of outboard motors lets you squirt water through their props at lazy river riders. ❻ Ripped open by a Great White, a "shark-proof" cage sits along the Shark Reef walkway, past the showers.

**ONCE UPON A TIME** there was a bayside village called the Placid Palms Resort, tucked into a valley next to a volcanic mountain in Florida (apparently, one of the few). Over the years the Placid Palms had been subject to earthquakes as well as geothermal rumblings, but overall the place remained tranquil. Even when cruise ships arrived, the resort stayed a quiet, thatch-roofed haven. That all changed in 1955, when Hurricane Connie slowly passed through the area, pounding it for a full hour. A boat blew through a building. A surfboard sliced through a tree. Crates of fireworks blew in from the nearby island warehouses of Mr. Merriweather Pleasure. A next-door fruit processing plant lost its walls but gained a tractor, which teetered on the roof. A small adjacent harbor had been cut off from the sea, trapping an overturned boat, thousands of fish and even a few sharks. Suffering the worst fate: a shrimp boat named Miss Tilly. Blown in from Safen Sound, Fla., it became impaled on the peak of Mt. Mayday. "No worries!" said the laid-back villagers. Sign paint in hand, they renamed the Placid Palms the Leaning Palms, the center of a new topsy-turvy tropical playground of pools, rapids, rivers and streams. They christened the spot **Typhoon Lagoon.**

A lonely Titan marches through the world of the Downtown Disney Cirque du Soleil spectacle La Nouba

# Downtown Disney

Located near the eastern edge of the Disney property on the 43-acre Village Lake, this 120-acre commercial district is divided into three sections. The largest area, the 66-acre West Side, is a nightlife district. Located between Marketplace and West Side, Pleasure Island was, until 2008, a nightclub area. The area's shops and restaurants are still open. At the east end of Downtown Disney, the Downtown Disney Marketplace is a 1970s-vintage open-air mall. Originally known as the Walt Disney World Shopping Village, it has 25 shops and restaurants and various outdoor stands. Water taxis shuttle guests between West Side and Marketplace.

## Resources

Marketplace has three **ATMs:** near Tren-D, next to the Ghirardelli Chocolate Shop and inside the World of Disney store. West Side has two: at the House of Blues Company Store and Wetzel's Pretzels. Aspirin, Band-Aids and other **first-aid supplies** are available at World of Disney, Tren-D, the Marketplace marina, Mickey's Groove, DisneyQuest and the Cirque du Soleil box office. Downtown Disney has two **Guest Relations** offices, at the Marketplace (between Team Mickey's and Arribas Brothers, 8:30a–11p Sun–Thurs, to 11:30p Fri–Sat) and at the West Side (across from Wetzel's Pretzels, 9a–11:45p). Rental **lockers** are located at the Marketplace marina near Cap'n Jack's Restaurant. **Strollers** ($15 day, $100 deposit) and **wheelchairs** ($12 day, $100 deposit) rent at the West Side DisneyQuest Emporium; in the Marketplace at Disney's Design-A-Tee Shop. A **mailbox** sits next to the World of Disney fountain. Downtown Disney **parking** is free.

## Entertainment

### Pleasure Island

**Raglan Road** ★ ★ ★ ★ ★ ✓ Live band, dancer No cover. Band plays 7p–1:30a Mon–Sat, Irish table dancer every half hour. All ages. Seats 600. Reservations: 407-938-0300. A cheerful crowd sings along to an Irish band, with occasional breaks for an Irish step-dancer at this gem of a spot, a favorite hangout of Disney cast members. Brought over from the Emerald Isle, house band Creel starts off with acoustic Irish tunes. Later the 3-piece band plugs in; its Irish rock sets get rowdy. The dancer performs on a small table (an old parson's pulpit) in the middle of the room. Guests seated at her feet get a uniquely memorable show.

## West Side

**AMC Theater** ★ ★ ★ ★ Movie theater A $10, C 2–12 $7, Sr. 60+ $9. Digital 3-D movies $2 addl. Hours vary. 24 theaters, 18 with stadium seating, 2 3-story auditoriums with balconies. Audio: THX Surround Sound, Sony Dynamic Digital Sound. Listening devices available. Guests may remain in wheelchairs, ECVs. 110,000-sq-ft complex. Seats 5,390. Only public movie theater on Disney property. AMC movie listings: 888-262-4386. Local box office: 407-827-1308.

**Bongos Cuban Cafe** ★ ★ ★ ★ Live band, dancing No cover. Live Latin traditional and pop music, dance floor, dancing starting at 10p Fri, Sat. All ages. Created by pop star Gloria Estefan and her husband, Emilio. Seats 560. 407-828-0999.

**Characters in Flight** ★ ★ ★ ★ Tethered helium balloon rides. A $16, C $10. Hours Sun–Thur 10:30a–11p; Fri–Sat 10:30a–mid. 9-min rides (2 min ascent, 5 min at 400 ft, 2 min descent.) Flights and times subject to change due to weather. Capacity: Up to 30 (Winds 0–3 mph: up to 30; 3–12 mph up to 20; 12–22 mph up to 10; over 22 mph does not fly). Access: Guests may stay in wheelchairs, ECV users must transfer to a wheelchair. Children under 12 must be accompanied by adult. Refunds due to weather given on day of purchase only. Debuted: 2009. Riders see up to 10 miles on this tethered-balloon ride. Attached to a 19-foot-wide open-air gondola that holds up to 30 riders, the world's largest tethered gas balloon lifts 400 feet in the air. The circular gondola's walls are waist-high; holes in the netting above are large enough to fit a camera lens through. Since the balloon uses helium instead of heated air, the ride is silent. An FAA-certified hot-air balloon pilot rides along on each trip. The balloon glows

**The five-story DisneyQuest building** is one of the anchors of Downtown Disney West Side

at night. Wind speed determines the ride's capacity: the stronger the wind, the fewer the riders.

**DisneyQuest** ★ ★ ★ **Electronic games** A $41, C $35. Admission included in Water Park Fun & More ticket upgrade, Premium Annual Pass. Sun–Thurs 11:30a–10p, Fri–Sat to 11p. Height restrict: 51 in. for CyberSpace Mountain virtual roller coaster, Buzz Lightyear's AstroBlaster; 48 in. Mighty Ducks Pinball Slam life-size pinball game; 35 in. Pirates of the Caribbean. Children under 10 must be accompanied by an adult. No strollers. Gift shop; 2 counter cafes. 407-828-4600. Virtual reality experiences highlight this five-story arcade, which was state-of-the-art about a decade ago. Evening crowds can create 30-minute waits for the most popular games. Those include **Pirates of the Caribbean: Battle for Buccaneer Gold** (the best game here), which takes a crew of four into a 3-D world as they search for gold and battle pirate ships; **Aladdin's Magic Carpet Ride,** a virtual-reality hunt for a magic lamp; and **Buzz Lightyear's AstroBlaster,** where you battle other guests in cannon-firing bumper cars. Creative types will love the **Animation Academy.** Its 30-minute classes teach you how to draw a Disney character. Other rooms offer classic arcade games such as Donkey Kong, Frogger, Mario Bros., Pac-Man and Space Invaders. Like a ticket to a Walt Disney World theme park, the admission price includes unlimited experiences. DisneyQuest is least crowded on fair-weather weekdays from 4 to 6:30 p.m.

**House of Blues** ★ ★ ★ ★ **Music hall / restaurant** $8–$95. Showtimes typ 7–9:30p. General adm (restaurant diners get priority). Doors open 1 hr before showtime weekdays, 90 min early weekends. All ages. Capacity 2,000. 407-934-BLUE or hob.com. One of a handful of restaurant and music halls created by Hard Rock Cafe founder Isaac Tigrett and entertainer Dan Aykroyd, this two-story performance venue books a wide range of acts, but blues and rock dominate. First-come first-serve tables and stools seat 150; there's standing room for 1,850. Folk art, hardwood floors and quality sound and lighting add to the experience. (Tucked underneath the stage: a metal box of Mississippi mud.) The outside looks like a rusty, funky shack. The adjacent restaurant (no cover) has acoustic live entertainment on its Front Porch bar from 6 p.m. to 11 p.m., and a plugged-in show Thursdays–Saturdays from 10:30 p.m. to 2 a.m.

**La Nouba** ★ ★ ★ ★ ★ ✓ **Musical European circus** A $69–$120, C $56–$97. Showtimes Tues–Sat 6p, 9p. Arrive 30 min early. 90-min shows, no intermission. Best ages 4 and up. Gift shop; snack stand. Seats 1,671. Tickets available 6 mos in advance. Info, tickets: 407-939-7600, www.cirquedusoleil.com or at the box office. With costumes, choreography, music and stagecraft that befit a Broadway extravaganza, this invigorating Cirque du Soleil spectacle fills you with delight. It blends the traditions of a European circus with mod-

**Cirque du Soleil's La Nouba begins** with an invasion by the lock-step Urbanites

ern acrobatics, dance and street entertainment. There are no animals, just humans—acrobats, dancers, clowns, gymnasts and others—putting on a show filled with action, color, whimsy and a quirky sense of humor. Designed for a Disney audience, it's performed on an Elizabethan stage.

Up high are tightrope walkers, trapeze artists and, in the show's most beautiful moment, hanging aerialists wrapped in huge red-silk ribbons. Onstage, performers cavort and somersault inside a pair of giant open wheels and jump, spin and twist on two BMX bikes. Four ever-smiling Asian girls dance, flip and climb on each other as they play Diabolo. A finale gymnastic ballet features power-track and trampoline performers. Their surreal diving into, and out of, windows looks like a film running backwards.

But there's so much more.

Sideshow characters—including a quartet of all-white simpletons and a flightless, envious Green Bird—participate sometimes as performers, sometimes as spectators. Each scene is presented as a figment of the imagination of a cleaning woman, a character who eventually becomes a princess. Childish clowns Balto and Serguei entertain between acts.

There's no master of ceremonies; instead the whole show is scored live. Hidden in towers alongside the stage, the band's zesty mix of classical, jazz, hip hop, klezmer, techno and bluegrass adds an emotional ac-

cent to every performer. Some songs have vocalists—an androgynous male who performs at high alto registers and a spirited female who adds some Gospel soul. Both sing exclusively in words that sound vaguely French, but are nonsensical. Acoustics are crystal clear.

Though it doesn't tell a tale, La Nouba does have story elements. The opening is a meeting of two worlds, a modern urban society and an early 20th-century circus. Determined, de-personal and de-saturated, the Urbans march in lock step as they toe society's line. By contrast, the neon circus folk each march to their own beat. Movie buffs will find references to 1997's "The Fifth Element" (the odd music and warbling diva) and 1998's "Dark City" (the looming cityscapes and unexpectedly moving floors). Art lovers will sense Calder and Matisse.

The show's purpose, its producers say, is to "wake up the innocence in your heart." You'll be surprised how much it succeeds.

Every seat is good, but spending the money to sit down front does pay off—you'll see every costume and makeup detail, every smile and grimace, every tensed muscle. You'll hear the clowns squeak and grunt and the acrobats shout verbal cues. Catch the eye of a performer and he or she might wink back. Front-row center is Row 1, Section 103. Tickets go on sale six months in advance.

© SCHUSSLER CREATIVE

**Popular themed restaurant T-REX** features dinosaur skeletons outside, robotic dinos inside

# Dining

## Marketplace

**Cap'n Jack's** ★ ★ ★ *DP* **Seafood/American $$$$** L,D: $13–$24, 11:30a–10:30p. Seats 113, including 15 at bar. Direct reservations: 407-828-3971. Though its worn wood decor is due for a makeover, this unpretentious 1970s throwback has good food. The pot roast falls apart in your mouth.

**Earl of Sandwich** ★ ★ ★ ★ ★ ✓ **American/British $** B: $2–$5, 8:30a–10:30a. L,D: $5–$6, 10:30a–11p. Seats 190 including 65 outside. 407-938-1762. Tasty hot sandwiches make this counter-service restaurant a favorite of Disney locals. The crusty bread is baked all day; beef is roasted every morning. A good side dish: chunky cole slaw with touches of garlic and sour cream. The best deal: the $1.95 cup of steaming hot, creamy-orange tomato soup. Morning sandwiches include a breakfast BLT. Owned by the ancestors of John Montagu, the fourth Earl of Sandwich.

**Ghirardelli Soda Fountain** ★ ★ ★ **Ice cream $$** $3–$30, 10:30a–11p Sun–Thurs, 10:30a–mid Fri–Sat. Booths, tables, bar. Seats 88, including 22 outside. Info: 407-934-8855. Cones, waffle cones, banana splits, chocolate drinks, floats, milkshakes, specialty sundaes. Hot fudge sauce made daily.

**McDonald's** ★ ★ **Fast food $** B: $2–$6, 8–10:30a. L,D: $3–$9, 10:30a–mid Sun–Thurs, till 1a Fri, Sat. Seats 254, including 114 outside. 407-938-1762. Coffee, dessert bar.

**Rainforest Cafe** ★ ★ ★ **American $$$$** L,D: $13–$37, 11a–11p Sun–Thurs, till mid Fri, Sat. Accepts Disney Dining Premium, Platinum plans only. Annual passholders save 10% off up to four entrees. Seats 575. Reservations: 407-827-8500. No same-day reservations. A robotic rainforest filled with elephants, gorillas and other animated creatures comes to life every 20 minutes at this highly themed restaurant. A huge menu has many generous choices. See our Rainforest Cafe review in the Animal Kingdom theme-park chapter.

**T-REX** ★ ★ ★ ★ ✓ **American $$$$** L,D: $12–$30, 11a–11p Sun–Thurs, till mid Fri, Sat. Accepts Disney Dining Premium, Platinum plans only. Annual passholders save 10% off up to four entrees. Small playground adjacent. Seats 626, including 26 at the bar. Reservations: 407-828-TREX (8739). A dinosaur take on Rainforest Cafe, this big, brash, very loud restaurant surrounds you with life-sized animated dinosaurs and other prehistoric creatures who "live" in different dining environments. The loudest is the geothermal room, where a meteor shower hits every 21 minutes. Nearby is a glowing blue ice cave, where diners sit by a woolly mammoth mom and her infants. Dotted with large aquariums filled with live fish, a sea-life area is topped by swaying octopus tentacles that reach out 45 feet. Walls are embedded with real fossils.

The huge menu has a little of everything—chicken, hamburgers, pasta, sandwiches, salads, seafood, steak. The food is good and portions are generous. Our favorite item is the blackened mahi-mahi Tribal

Tacos, dry and spiced just right in soft corn tortillas. Sized for a family to share, desserts include the ridiculous Ice Age Indulgence, a slowly melting stack of whipped cream layered between ice cream sandwiches. Mixed drinks are highlighted by "Cotton-Tinis"—spirits served over cotton candy.

Reservations are a must for dinner, when standby waits can exceed 90 minutes. Parties of 7–9 should ask for the giant jellyfish booth; the owner's favorite spot.

**Wolfgang Puck Express** ★ ★ ★ ★ ✓ Calif. Fusion $
B: $9–$11, 9a–11a. L,D: $10–$16, 11a–11p. Seats 184, including 96 outside. 407-828-0107. This indoor counter-service restaurant blares rock music down on its diners, an irritation that makes it tough to enjoy the first-rate food, an imaginative mix of pasta, pizza, salads, sandwiches and soups. Signature items include Crispy Cornflake French Toast and delicious butternut squash soup for lunch and dinner. Hardwood tables, concrete floors.

## Pleasure Island

**Fulton's Crab House** ★ ★ Seafood $$$$$ L: $11–$17, 11:30a–3:30p. D: $20–$74, 4–11p. Seats 660, including 24 outside. Direct reservations: 407-934-BOAT (2628). OK for lunch, expensive for dinner, this white-tablecloth spot offers lots of crab dishes. Best bets include the filling crab-and-lobster bisque and Lobster Narragansett. You'd never guess this 20,000-square-foot replica paddlewheeler isn't the real thing. It looks just like an old riverboat from the outside, and inside its narrow halls, creaky floors and wooden ceilings suggest a long life on the water. Actually, it was built by Disney as a restaurant and, despite appearances, is not floating. Ask to sit on the lake side of the semicircular Constellation Room on the second deck. Its ceiling glows blue at night.

**Paradiso 37** ★ ★ ★ ★ ✓ Americas street cuisine $$$ L,D: $9–27, Sun–Wed 11:30a–mid, Thr–Sat 11:30a–1a. Seats 250, 100 outside, 20 stools at bar. Live entertainment nightly: 6–11:30 p.m. Sunday–Thursday, 6–12:30 a.m. Friday and Saturday. Direct reservations: 407-934-3700. This classy little lakefront eatery is an interesting alternative to the more touristy restaurants nearby. The menu represents the 37 countries of the Americas. An eclectic mix of dishes focuses on "street" food, from hot dogs and hamburgers to Peruvian beef skewers and Chilean-style salmon. The

**From top:** Lobster Narragansett at Fulton's Crab House. Ribs, Steak & Shrimp Trio at Rainforest Cafe. Chicken and rib Boneyard Buffet at T-REX. Sushi assortment, signature smoked salmon pizza at Wolfgang Puck Cafe.

concept works especially well with appetizers, such as Central American "crazy corn" (roasted on the cob, covered in cheese) or a Mexican dipping trio of fresh guacamole, chunky chili con carne and thick white queso fundido. Thirty-seven tequilas ($8–$50 a glass) are displayed in a two-story lighted wall bar with thousands of color-changing LEDs. At night the place positively glows. Loud world music thumps day and night. Friendly servers wear pastel collared shirts and khaki shorts.

**Portobello** ★ ★ ★ ★ Italian $$$$$ L: $10–$24, 11:30a–3:45p. D: $9–$40, 4–11p. Seats 414, including 86 outside. Direct reservations: 407-934-8888. A 2008 refurbishment shifted the theme of the former Portobello Yacht Club to that of a Tuscan country trattoria. A variety of antipasti and entrees are inspired by dishes of Milan, Rome and Tuscany. Other changes include a nicer third outdoor dining space.

**Raglan Road** ★ ★ ★ ★ ★ ✓ Irish pub, restaurant $$$$ L: $10–$16, 11a–3p. D: $12–$29, 3–11p. "Pub Grub" 11p–1:30a. Live band, table step-dancer evenings Mon–Sat. 2 outdoor bars. Merchandise shop. Children welcome. Seats 600, including 300 outside. Direct reservations: 407-938-0300. Run by Irish proprietors and an Irish chef, this pretension-free bar and restaurant is the real thing. The food is a step beyond tradition—pub classics that have gone to cooking class. Tender meats are topped with subtle glazes, smooth mashed potatoes are covered in crispy braised cabbage. The creamy Rustic Chicken soup will warm your soul. Our daughter will vouch for the rich bread pudding, served with creamers of warm butterscotch and creme anglaise. There's a full selection of ales, stouts, lagers and whiskeys. Raglan Road was built using raw and recycled materials from Ireland, including antiques from Irish homes and two 130-year-old bars with traditional leaded-glass dividers. The restaurant is named after a street on the south side of Dublin immortalized in a 1960s folk song. The adjacent **Cooke's of Dublin** offers counter-service fish and chips, with fried candy bars for dessert.

# West Side

**Bongos Cuban Cafe** ★ ★ ★ Cuban $$$$ L: $8–$17, 11a–4p. D: $14–$33, 4–11p Sun–Thurs, 4p–mid Fri–Sat. Seats 560, including 60 outside and 87 at the bar. No reservations. Direct line for information: 407-828-0999. Housed in a whimsical building dominated by a three-story adobe pineapple, this festive eatery disappoints those who know Cuban food. Decent sides include yuca (a boiled root, similar in taste to a potato) and plan-

tains. Bamboo bars and beautiful mosaic murals recall the B.C. (Before Castro) Cuba of the 1940s and 1950s. Ask to sit in the pineapple, where each booth is a different bold color, or on the second-story patio. An outside bar serves sandwiches, snacks, desserts and drinks. Bongos was created by pop-star Gloria Estefan and her husband Emilio.

**House of Blues** ★ ★ ★ ★ ★ ✓ Southern $$$ L,D: $11–$27, 11:30a–11p Sun–Mon, 11:30a–mid Tue–Wed, 11:30a–1:30a Thurs–Sat. Seats 578, including 158 at outside tables and 36 at outdoor bar. No reservations. Gospel brunch with live music Sun. 10:30a, 1p, in Music Hall, 250 seats. A: $34, C: $17. Direct line for information: 407-934-BLUE. With good food and a comfy atmosphere, House of Blues is an ideal spot to refresh from too much Mickey. The tried-and-true Southern menu includes tender pork ribs and a soothing cornbread that melts in your mouth. Folk art covers the walls, ceilings, railings, window frames, lamps, even bathroom stalls. Kids will love the art and picking through the lobby's bucket of crayons to make their own.

**Planet Hollywood** ★ American $$$ L,D: $12–$27, 11a–1a; bar only until 2a. Seats 800. Direct line for information: 407-827-7827. Shaped like a planet, this three-story cafe is filled with celebrity and movie memorabilia, including a blue gingham dress Judy Garland wore in 1939's "The Wizard of Oz." Other than good hamburgers, the menu is uninspired, the atmosphere loud, the service irritating.

**Wetzel's Pretzels** ★ ★ ★ ✓ Snacks $ $4–$7, 10:30a–11p Sun–Thr, to mid Fri, Sat. 36 outdoor seats. This indoor counter stand serves hot hand-rolled soft pretzels with a variety of coatings. There's also fresh-squeezed lemonade as well as Haagen-Dazs ice cream treats.

**Wolfgang Puck Cafe** ★ ★ ★ ★ ✓ Calif. Fusion $$$$ L: $11–$25, 11:30a–4p. D: $13–$29, 4–10:30p, Tue–Thurs till 11p, Fri, Sat till 11:30p. Weekend lunch serves dinner menu. Disney Annual Passholders save 20% at lunch, 10% at dinner. Takeout window. Private room for groups. Seats 586, including 30 at sushi bar. Direct reservations: 407-938-WOLF. Imaginative dishes make up for the noisy atmosphere at this lakeside dining room. Dinner includes Puck's famous veal weinerschnitzel. We love the butternut squash soup and creamy mashed potatoes. The sushi is good, too.

**Wolfgang Puck Dining Room** ★ ★ ★ ★ Calif. Fusion $$$$$ D: $25–$60, 6–9p Sun–Thurs, 6–10p Fri–Sat. Seats 120. Direct reservations: 407-938-WOLF. This white-tablecloth eatery blends flavors into entrees that feature chicken, fish, steak and veal. Located on the second floor of the Puck building, the room's orange walls are dominated by a gigantic ornamental hookah.

# Shopping

## Marketplace

**Arribas Brothers** Hand-cut crystal, hand-blown glass Artisans work before your eyes. Engraving.

**The Art of Disney** Fine art Disney-themed oil paintings, animation cels, lithographs, theme-park attraction posters, Lenox china figurines, plates, vases and other quality art pieces fill the walls.

**Basin** All-natural toiletries Massage and shampoo bars, bath bombs, body butters, lotions, salt and sea scrubs. Make-your-own candle station. Intoxicating aroma.

**Design-A-Tee Shop** Personalized Hanes T-shirts Replaced Disney's Wonderful World of Memories in 2008.

**Disney's Days of Christmas** Holiday shop Ornaments, collectibles, figurines, Mickey-eared Santa hats. Embroidery, engraving. Disney's largest holiday shop.

**Disney's Pin Traders** Pin central Open-air shop.

**Disney Tails** Pet items Within Pooh Corner.

**Ghirardelli chocolate shop** Sweets Candy, fudge sauce, baking cocoa, hot-chocolate mix. Free samples.

**Goofy's Candy Co.** Sweets Custom apples, cookies, marshmallow treats. Jellybeans, lollipops, coffees.

**LEGO Imagination Center** LEGO World's largest Pick-A-Brick wall has 320 bins. Giant display creations. Outdoor area lets children create masterpieces.

**McDonald's** McDonald's souvenirs Caps, coffee mugs, pins, puzzles, salt and pepper shakers, ties.

**Mickey's Mart** Disney items under $10.

**Mickey's Pantry** Housewares Mickey Mouse-styled small appliances, kitchen items. Non-Disney cookware, food, tableware, wine.

**Once Upon a Toy** Toys 16,000-sq-ft. Theme-park items, Hasbro items. Build-Your-Own Mr. Potato Head station. Huge Game of Life spinner rotates on ceiling.

**Pooh Corner** Winnie The Pooh merchandise Apparel, backpacks, pillows, plushies, toys. Adorable infantwear.

**Rainforest Cafe store** Various. Rainforest Cafe and animal-themed apparel, plushies, toys. Animated decor.

**T-REX Dino-Store** Dinosaur children's apparel, toys. Build-A-Bear Workshop "Build-A-Dino" area. Kids search for faux fossils in outdoor "sand" pit and sluice.

**Team Mickey's Athletic Club** Disney, ESPN sportswear, sporting goods. Custom Louisville Slugger bats.

**Trend-D** Stylish Junior apparel Disney, Billabong, Hurley, Roxy brands. Half the stock exclusive to this shop.

**World of Disney** Department store Separate rooms for girls ("Princesses"), Ladies and Juniors, Boys, Men, Infants, Hats and T-shirts, Housewares, Home Accessories, Jewelry and Pins, Candy and Snacks, Souvenirs. Bibbidi Bobbidi Boutique (10 chairs, 407-WDW-STYLE, reservations book quickly) is makeover salon for young girls; Fairy Godmothers apply cosmetics, style hair.

## Pleasure Island

**Curl by Sammy Duvall** Beachwear Youth fashion apparel, purses, hats, jewelry, sunglasses, surf boards, skate boards. Owned by legendary water-skier.

**Fuego By Sosa Cigars** Hand-rolled cigars 100 smokes. Cocktail lounge. Must be 18 to smoke, 21 to drink.

**Orlando Harley-Davidson** Harley-Davidson items. Apparel for men, women, kids. Collectibles, pet items. No motorcycles for sale. One or two display bikes.

**Shop for Ireland** Irish merchandise. Fashion apparel, infantwear, mugs, cookbooks. At Raglan Road.

## West Side

**Bongos shop** Cuban items Apparel, mugs, margarita glasses, maracas, coffee. At Bongos Cuban Cafe.

**Candy Cauldron** Sweets Jellybeans. Candied apples, chocolate-covered strawberries made in front of guests. Shop recalls Evil Queen's dungeon in 1937's "Snow White and the Seven Dwarfs."

**Cirque du Soleil Boutique** Apparel, accessories Stunning Cirque-branded scarves, purses, fashion apparel, masks, figurines, circus caps. La Nouba souvenirs.

**DisneyQuest Emporium** General Disney items

**House of Blues Company Store** Blues CDs, cornbread mix, folk art, hot sauce, incense.

**Hoypoloi** Home-accent gallery Unusual clocks, figurines, fountains, lamps, paintings, pottery, windchimes.

**Magic Masters** Magic tricks Pick a trick, a magician performs it, you can buy it. Replicates Harry Houdini's private library, has a "secret" door. Books, DVDs.

**Magnetron Magnetz** Magnets Tiny shop has 50,000 quirky refrigerator magnets, knickknacks.

**Mickey's Groove** General Disney shop

**Planet Hollywood on Location** Apparel

**Pop Gallery** Art gallery Pop art includes signed paintings, three-dimensional wall hangings, wild glass sculptures. Small champagne bar.

**Sosa Family Cigars** Cigars Hand-rolling demonstrations. Adults can smoke on the premises.

**Starabilias** Closed in 2009.

**Sunglass Icon** Sunglasses Ray-Ban, Maui Jim, Oakley.

**Virgin Megastore** Closed in 2009.

### Downtown Disney Hidden Mickeys

**Marketplace landscape:** ❶ As a 20x20-foot arrangement of pavement squirters at the original Marketplace entrance, to the right of the Earl of Sandwich restaurant. ❷ The squirters themselves are small Mickeys. **Once Upon a Toy:** ❸ As robotic claws that hold toys, suspended from a hanging track. ❹ As blue support bars under stands that hold plushies. **World of Disney:** ❺ In a mural in the Women and Juniors room, as a red and white design on a blue flag to the left of the Queen of Hearts and as a gold design on Tweedledee's sumo cloth. ❻ As a design in a mural in the facing room, above the Chinese Theatre doors behind the floating Three Little Pigs. **DisneyQuest:** ❼ As ancient symbols in the carpets of Adventureport and the 5th-floor cafe. **Cirque du Soleil:** ❽ Outside the box office as black floor tiles inside both restroom doors.

A snowy version of Cinderella Castle highlights a hole at Disney's Winter Summerland miniature golf course

# Sports and Rec

## Bicycle and surrey rentals

Ten resorts rent **bicycles** ($9 hr, $22 day) and/or multi-seat **surreys** ($20–$22, 30 min): the BoardWalk, Caribbean Beach, Coronado Springs, Fort Wilderness, Old Key West, Polynesian (surreys only), Port Orleans, Saratoga Springs, Wilderness Lodge and Yacht and Beach Club (bikes only).

## Boat charters

The **Pirates and Pals Fireworks Voyage** (Nightly. $54 A, $31 C 3–9. Contemporary Resort marina. 407-WDW-PLAY) includes an onboard pirate storyteller and onshore character greetings as you float out to watch Wishes. You can view Wishes or IllumiNations with up to 9 friends on a standard **pontoon boat** ($275–$325. 1 hr. Guide, snacks. Wishes boats: Contemporary, Grand Fla., Polynesian, Wilderness Lodge marinas. Illuminations: Yacht Club dock. 407-WDW-PLAY). The **Breathless II** (Ages 3 and up; up to 7 people. 30 min ride: $95 per group. 90 min IllumiNations cruise: $275. Yacht Club marina. 407-WDW-PLAY) is a 26-foot mahogany replica of a 1930s Chris-Craft inboard. The 52-foot Sea Ray **Grand 1** ($480 per hr, up to 18 people. Inc captain, deckhand. Food, butler opt. Grand Floridian marina. 407-824-2682). cruises Seven Seas Lagoon and Bay Lake.

## Boat rentals

With the world's largest rental-boat fleet and many lakes, lagoons and canals, Disney World offers nearly every way imaginable to get on the water. Boats vary by resort marina; call 407-WDW-PLAY (939-7529) for details. Choices include two-seat **Sea Raycers** ($32 per 30 min, $45 per hr. Ages 12–15 may drive with licensed driver. Min height 60 in. Max weight 320 lbs per boat), **17-foot Boston Whaler Montauk** ($45 per 30 min), **21-foot SunTracker pontoon boats** ($45 per 30 min), **12-foot Sunfish sailboats** ($20 per hr), **13-foot Hobie Cats** ($25 per hr), **canoes and kayaks** ($7 per 30 min) and **pedal boats** ($6.50 per 30 min). The Walt Disney World Swan and Dolphin has **swan pedal boats** ($12–$14 per 30 min).

Sammy Duvall's Watersports Centre has three-seat **Sea-Doo personal watercraft** (non-guided rides $80 per 30 min, $135 per hr. 1-hr morning group rides into Seven Seas Lagoon $135. Max 3 riders per vehicle, max combined weight 400 lbs. Operator must be 16 with valid driver's lic; renters must be 18. 407-939-0754. Contemporary Resort marina).

## Campfire

Held at a small outdoor amphitheater, **Chip 'n Dale's Campfire Sing-a-Long** (Free. Fort Wilderness. Schedule: 407-824-2727.) includes a fire-pit marshmallow roast, 30-minute sing-a-long with the chipmunks (sit on the benches to interact) and a Disney movie on a large outdoor screen. A snack bar sells s'mores kits and packs of marshmallows and sticks. Outdoor movie programs without characters are offered seasonally at the Beach Club, Contemporary, Grand Floridian, Old Key West, Saratoga Springs, Wilderness Lodge and Walt Disney World Swan and Dolphin resorts. Port Orleans Riverside has a campfire sing-a-long (with no movie) seasonally.

## Carriage and wagon rides

Available at the Fort Wilderness, Port Orleans Riverside and Saratoga Springs resorts, **horse-drawn carriage rides** ($45. 25 min. 5:30–10p. Those under 18 must ride with adult. Reservations accepted 90 days in adv at 407-939-PLAY (7529). Same-day availability info at 407-824-2832.) hold up to four adults or a small family. Fort Wilderness trips travel through natural areas. Fort Wilderness offers **wagon rides** ($8 A, $5 C 3–9. Under 3 free. 45 min. 7p, 9:30p. Fireworks rides often avail. Departs from Pioneer Hall. Children under 11 must ride with adult. No reservations. Group rides with 24 hrs notice: 407-824-2734.) down its trails. You ride with up to 32 other guests.

## Diving and snorkeling

Spend 40 minutes inside a 5.7-million-gallon saltwater aquarium at **Epcot DiveQuest** ($175, 40 min in water, 3 hr experience. Inc gear, lockers,

**The authors' daughter** holds one of many bass she caught on a morning Disney fishing trip

showers. Park adm not req. Ages 10 and up. Ages 10, 11 must dive with adult. 3 hrs. Open-water cert req. 407-WDW-TOUR), a guided tour at The Seas with Nemo & Friends pavilion. You'll swim with more than 65 species, including non-aggressive sharks, rays and sea turtles. You explore with up to 12 others. Includes a presentation on marine life and an overview of the pavilion. The **Epcot Seas Aqua Tour** ($140, 30 min in water, 2.5 hr total. Inc instruction. Park adm not req. Ages 10 and up (under 18 must dive with adult). 407-WDW-TOUR) puts you in the tank with scuba-assisted snorkel (SAS) equipment. Proceeds from both experiences go to the Disney Worldwide Conservation Fund.

## Dolphin encounter

You'll spend 30 minutes in knee-deep water with bottlenose dolphins, learn about the anatomy and behavior of these mammals and watch biologists do research during **Dolphins in Depth** ($175, 3 hrs. Inc T-shirt, photo of guest with dolphin, refreshments, use of wetsuit. No swimming. Park adm not req. Ages 13 and up. Those under 18 must be with adult. 407-WDW-TOUR). No interaction is guaranteed, but then again

you may get to feel a heartbeat. Trainers work with guests individually. Proceeds go to the Disney Wildlife Conservation Fund.

## ESPN Wide World of Sports

This 220-acre compound includes a 9,500-seat baseball stadium, two large fieldhouses, a tennis compound with a stadium court, a 400-meter track and field center and many outdoor baseball, softball and soccer fields.

The complex is the leading venue for amateur and professional sports in the United States. It hosts more than 11,000 events each year—an average of 30 per day—in 50 sports with athletes from more than 70 countries. Events include various AAU tournaments and National Championships. New hi-definition video screens and Jumbotrons make it easier for parents and friends to follow the action.

Held in February and March, Atlanta Braves Spring Training includes 15 exhibition games during its six-week season. During the summer, the Tampa Bay Buccaneers NFL team holds its training camp.

A 100-lane bowling center is scheduled to open in 2010. The United States Bowling Congress will stage 13 events there, with tournaments beginning in 2011.

The center draws 250,000 athletes and 1.2 million spectators a year. Spectators can attend amateur events for a nominal fee. Tickets for professional events are available through Ticketmaster outlets or at the ESPN Wide World of Sports box office. For prerecorded information call 407-828-FANS (3267); to speak with someone call 407-939-1500. Parking is free.

## Fishing

Since all Disney fishing is catch-and-release and only a handful of anglers are on the water at any time, catching a largemouth bass is almost guaranteed when you take a pontoon-boat **guided fishing excursion** ($230–$260, 2 hrs for up to 5 guests; $445 for 4 hrs, each add'l hr $110. Inc bait (shiners addl), guide, equipment, refreshments, digital camera. No license req. Trips on Bay Lake, Seven Seas Lagoon, Crescent Lake, Village Lake and Lago Dorado at Disney's Coronado Resort. Leaves early am, mid am, early pm. 407-WDW-BASS (939-2277). Reservations taken 2 wks in adv.). Guests routinely catch bass weighing

2 to 8 lbs. Most trips catch five to 10 fish; guests average 2.5 fish per hour. Bay Lake and Seven Seas Lagoon are teeming with bass; the largest fish (up to 14 lbs.) are in Crescent and Village lakes. The Bass Anglers Sportsman Society (BASS) runs the programs. You can **fish from the shore** (Cane poles $4.25 30 min, $9 day, 4–6 pole pkg $14 30 min, $28 day. Rods $5.50 30 min, $9.50 day. Bait inc. No lic required. No reservations) at Fort Wilderness (407-824-2900) and Port Orleans Riverside (407-934-6000).

## Golf

(Greens fees $39–$180 for 18-hole courses (req cart rental inc); $38 for Oak Trail ($20 for under 18). Club, shoe rental avail. Proper golf attire req. 18-holes have putting greens, driving ranges. Free transportation from Disney-owned resorts. Reservations 90 days in advance for Disney resort guests, 60 days other players. Cancellations require 48 hrs notice. Fla resident Annual Golf Membership ($50) saves up to 60% (based on time of year) on greens fees after 10a for member, up to three guests; 20% on instruction. Add'l summer savings. 407-WDW-GOLF, disneyworldgolf.com.)

Grouped into three facilities, Disney's five golf courses each offer a different experience. There's the long course, the short course, the flat course, the water course. And the kid-friendly 9-hole.

Home to deer, egrets, herons, otters, alligators and an occasional bald eagle, each course is designated as a wildlife sanctuary by the Audubon Cooperative Sanctuary System. All but the Lake Buena Vista course roam far from civilization. Best months to play are September, April and May, when the weather's nice and good tee times are easy to book. Build extra time into your round, as the pace may be slower than you expect.

How's that shoulder turn? It needs to be efficient on the long-game **Magnolia course** (Yardage: 5,232–7,516. Par: 72. Course rating: 69.4–76.5. Slope rating: 125–140. Designer: Joe Lee. Year open: 1971. Next to Shades of Green, across from Polynesian Resort), a rolling terrain that sits amid more than 1,500 magnolia trees. The Magnolia has elevated tees and greens and 97 bunkers, the most of any Disney course. And the greens are quick. Host to the final round of Disney's PGA Tour tournament stop since 1971, the course has tested pros from Jack Nicklaus to Tiger Woods.

Pretty palms. Ugly hazards. The **Palm course** (Yardage: 5,311–6,957. Par: 72. Course rating:

**The 'mouse trap.'** A bunker at the Magnolia golf course's No. 6 green resembles Mickey Mouse.

69.5–73.9. Slope rating: 126–138. Designer: Joe Lee. Year open: 1971. Next to Shades of Green, across from the Polynesian Resort) has them both. Water hazards line seven holes and cross six. The Palm is shorter and tighter than the Magnolia. Rated one of Golf Digest's Top 25 Resort Courses, it has a few long par 4s and a couple of par 5s that can be reached in two using a fairway wood. The large, elevated greens can be maneuvered with good lag putting. Save a sprinkle of pixie dust for hole No. 18. A long par 4, it has been rated as high as fourth toughest on the PGA Tour.

A 9-hole walking course, **Oak Trail** (Yardage: 2,532–2,913. Par: 36. Course rating: 64.6–68.2. Slope rating: 107–123. Designer: Ron Garl. Year open: 1980. Next to Shades of Green, across from Polynesian Resort) is nice for a quick nine, practice, or letting a developing golfer practice. With small greens and two good par 5s, the course requires accuracy with short irons. The longest hole, the 517-yard No. 5, features a double dogleg. Water hazards cross three fairways. Most greens and tees are elevated. The scorecard lists separate pars for children 11 and under and 12 and over. Golf shoes must be spikeless; tennis shoes are permitted.

Set within rolling Florida terrain, the beautiful **Osprey Ridge course** (Yardage: 5,402–7,101. Par: 72. Course rating: 69.5–74.4. Slope rating: 123–131. Designer: Tom Fazio. Year open: 1992. Just east of Fort Wilderness Resort) winds through challenging dense vegetation, oak forests and moss hammocks. More than 70 bunkers, mounds and a meandering ridge provide obstacles, banking and elevation changes. Some tees and greens are 20 feet above their fairways. The course often has swirling winds. One bit of relief: fairway waste bunkers have hard sand, so you can play a shot out of one with a more-normal swing.

The least forgiving Disney course, the **Lake Buena Vista course** (Yardage: 5,204–6,802. Par: 72. Course rating: 68.6–73.0. Slope rating: 122–133. Designer: Joe Lee. Year open: 1972. Saratoga Springs) has narrow, tree-lined fairways and small greens. You tee off at the Saratoga Springs Resort, then weave through Old Key West. Play demands accuracy on the tee shot as well as the approach. Errant shots can hit windows. Signature hole No. 7 has an island green; No. 18 is a 438-yard dogleg to the right. Ten holes have water hazards.

All greens have ultra-dwarf TifEagle Bermuda grass. It offers a truer, fast roll.

PGA pros offer year-round **golf lessons** ($50–$150, 45 min lesson for single golfer $75, $50 ages 17 and under. Shades of Green center. All ages, skills. Individual lessons, clinics: 407-WDW-GOLF (4653). Group lessons: 407-938-3870). Choose from one-on-one instruction focused on a specific skill, video swing analysis or on-course lessons that include course management and strategy, club selection and short-game skills.

## Horseback riding

You ride on shady pine and palmetto trails inside Fort Wilderness on one of Disney's **guided horseback rides** ($46, 45 min. Daily starting at 8:30a. Ages 9 and up. Height min 48 in. Max weight 250 lbs. Closed-toe shoes req; no sandals, flip-flops. No trotting. Req reservations can be made 30 days in advance at 407-WDW-PLAY). Rides start at the Tri-Circle D Livery. Go early and you'll likely see wildlife such as snakes and deer. Smaller kids can take a short **pony ride** ($4, cash only. Ages 2–8. Max height 48 in. Max weight 80 lbs. 10a–5p daily. 407-824-2788) at the petting farm. A parent walks the pony.

## Jogging

A wooded 1.5-mile trail threads through the Fort Wilderness Resort. There's a bike path to it from Wilderness Lodge. Guests can take a 1-mile stroll on the Epcot Resorts promenade (connecting the Boardwalk and Yacht and Beach Club resorts) and continue along the BoardWalk side to Disney's Hollywood Studios. A 1.4-mile walkway leads around a lake at Caribbean Beach. Two paved guest walkways weave through the Port Orleans resorts (1-mile and .7-mile), while a mile trek circles Lago Dorado at Coronado Springs. Shorter walkway loops exist at the Contemporary, Polynesian and Grand Floridian resorts.

## Miniature golf

($12.50 A, $10.50 C. 10a–11p. Gardens course at Fantasia Gardens closes 10:30p. Last tee time 30 min before close. 2nd rounds 1/2 price if same day or next day. In-person same-day reservations accepted. 407-WDW-PLAY) Across the street from the Walt Disney World Swan and Dolphin, the two-course **Fantasia Gardens** (407-560-4753) is busy at night, when tee-time waits can be an hour. Splashing brooms and dancing-ostrich topiaries line the Gardens course, which is themed to Disney's 1940 movie, while the adjacent Fairways course replicates real links with bunkers, roughs, undulating hills and holes up to 103 feet long. Adjacent to Blizzard Beach, **Winter Summerland** (407-560-7161) is often deserted at night. Two whimsical courses are themed to the activities of elves who, as the story goes, vacation here (see Fun Facts). Their tiny trailers dot the landscape. Getting a hole-in-one is easy, as greens often funnel into their cups.

## Spas

Treatments at the **Grand Floridian Spa** (407-824-2332, at the Grand Floridian Resort. Parking at Disney's Wedding Pavilion) include an aromatherapy massage and body wrap and signature citrus-zest facials. Couples can get massages together in a candle-lit room. The Asian-inspired **Mandara Spa** (407-934-4772, at the Walt Disney World Dolphin resort) includes couples suites, a steam room and two indoor gardens. It offers baking-soda micro-therapy, cellulite reductions, Glycolic facials, seaweed wraps, stone therapies and tooth-whitening programs. Popular treatments at the **Saratoga Springs Spa** (407-827-4455, at Saratoga Springs Resort) include a maple sugar body polish, Adirondack stone therapy massage, mineral springs hydrotherapy and signature Mystical Forest treatments. A French whirlpool has 72 jets. All three spas offer mother-daughter packages,

**The Richard Petty Driving Experience** puts you behind the wheel of a 630-horsepower stock car

## Stock car driving

(Rides $115. Drives $420–$1380 (8–30 laps). Hrs: 9 a–4p. Duration: 30 min–1 hr for rides (3 min in car); 3–4 hrs for drives (10–15 min driving car). Gift cards available. Drives require reservations, include training. Cars reach speeds of 145 mph on ridealongs, which don't require reservations. Adj to Magic Kingdom parking lot. Must be 14 or older to ride, 18 or older to drive. One-day Safe Driving Program (June, Dec) for drivers 15 to 25: $329–$399. Spectators welcome. 1-800-BE-PETTY, 1800bepetty.com.)

The engine rumbles. You tremble. Then you tear down a race track at over 100 mph, by yourself, driving a 630-horsepower stock car.

Held at the Walt Disney World Speedway, lessons at the Richard Petty Driving Experience start off with a training session that includes time out on the track. Then, wearing a fire cap, driving suit and helmet, you climb through the window, pop on the steering wheel and strap in.

Almost always in a turn, you tail your instructor who's in a car of his own. He watches you in a mirror, and drives as fast as you can handle. I (Julie) averaged 122 mph (fastest in my class!) and even passed a guy on Lap 7. The NASCAR-style vehicles have tube frames, huge V-8s, 4-speed manual transmissions and product logos plastered everywhere. The doors don't open; you climb in through the hole for the window.

## Surfing lessons

Know how to swim? In decent shape? If so, then you are almost guaranteed to learn how to ride the crest of a wave at the **Craig Carroll Surfing School** ($150. Must be 8 yrs or older, strong swimmer. Most students have never surfed. Days, hrs vary with season. 2.5-hr lesson has 30 min on land, 2 hrs in water. Surfboards provided. Spectators OK. Max 12 students a day; classes sell out quickly. Reservations accepted 90 days early at 407-WDW-SURF.), held before park hours at the Typhoon Lagoon surf pool. Conducted on dry land, a step-by-step introductory lesson is easy to follow, then instructors hop in the water to demonstrate the technique. You get plenty of personal attention. After each attempt Carroll critiques you from the lifeguard stand, then an instructor in the water adds more tips. Waves average about 5 feet for adults; half that for kids.

About 70 percent of students succeed. Females do best. "Girls don't think as hard about it, and try to do exactly what you say," Carroll explains. "Boys tend to think it's a macho thing."

A pro surfer since the 1970s, Carroll coached world-champion Kelly Slater. While not at Disney, he runs the Ron Jon Surf School in nearby Cocoa Beach.

**A mom and daughter** take off on a parasailing flight behind the Contemporary Resort

## Tennis

Walt Disney World has 34 **lighted courts.** All general court use is complimentary except at the Grand Floridian ($10.65 hr, same-day reservations at 407-621-1991; parking at Disney's Wedding Pavilion). Some resorts reserve their courts for their own guests, though the BoardWalk, Contemporary, Fort Wilderness Campground and Yacht Club welcome guests from any Disney-owned resort. Organized programs for all ages and abilities are offered on the two Grand Floridian courts. These include **private lessons** ($80 hr), **hitting lessons** ("Play the Pro," $80 hr) and **convention-style group tournaments** ($25 hr). An adjacent **pro shop** (407-WDW-PLAY) rents rackets and ball machines and re-strings and re-grips guest rackets.

## Tours

(No backstage photography. Photo IDs req. To book any tour but a VIP outing call 407-WDW-TOUR).

**Around the World at Epcot** ($95, Epcot admission req. 2 hrs. Daily. Ages 16 and up. Max weight 250 lbs.) Group trip takes Segway through Epcot.

**Backstage Magic** ($219, Whispering Canyon lunch inc, theme park admission not req. 7 hrs. Mon–Fri. Ages 16 and up.) Takes you behind the scenes at Magic Kingdom, Epcot and Disney's Hollywood Studios. The longest Disney World tour.

**Backstage Safari** ($70, Animal Kingdom admission req 3 hrs Mon, Wed, Thr, Fri. Ages 16 and up.) Tours the vet hospital, elephant barn and other facilities of Disney's Animal Kingdom.

**Behind the Seeds** ($16, Epcot admission req. 45 min. Daily. All ages.) An inside look at the four greenhouses and fish farm at The Land pavilion.

**Disney's Family Magic Tour** ($30, Magic Kingdom adm req. 2 hrs. Daily. All ages.) A Magic Kingdom primer for first-time visitors with children; a skip (literally) through the park.

**ESPN Wide World of Sports Guided Tour** (Complimentary. 1 hr. All ages.) An inside look at the complex on selected days when sporting events are scheduled.

**Holiday DeLites** ($179, No park adm req. 3 hrs. Mon, Wed. 5p. Late Nov–Dec. Ages 16 and up.) Includes stops at backstage decorations shop, Main Street U.S.A., Osborne Dancing Lights, and seats for the Candlelight Processional.

**Keys to the Kingdom** ($65, inc lunch at Columbia Harbour House. Magic Kingdom adm req. 4 hrs. Goes backstage, underground. Daily. Ages 16 and up.) Guides discuss Magic Kingdom's history and philosophies.

**The Magic Behind Our Steam Trains** ($45, Magic Kingdom adm req. No cameras. 3 hrs. Mon, Tue, Wed, Thr, Sat. Ages 10 and up.) An inside look at Magic Kingdom's Walt Disney World Railroad shows how trains are prepared for operation. Also discusses Walt Disney's love of steam trains.

**Mickey's Magical Milestones** ($25, Magic Kingdom adm req. 2 hrs. Mon, Wed, Fri. Ages 16 and under must be with adult.) Visits Magic Kingdom attractions and locations that trace the career of Mickey Mouse.

**Nature–Inspired Design** ($124, Epcot adm req. 3 hrs. Inc stops at Soarin', The Land greenhouses, Seas pavilion and off-road backstage Segway tour. Tue, Sat. 8:15a. Ages 16 and up.) Besides getting to ride a Segway backstage, guests learn how Epcot design uses the concepts of air, land, sea.

**Undiscovered Future World** ($55, Epcot adm req. 4 hrs. Mon, Wed, Fri. Ages 16 and up.) Learn about Walt Disney's planned Experimental Prototype Community of Tomorrow, visit all Future World pavilions and glimpse backstage areas.

**Learning to surf.** Danielle Finke, 20, gets off her knees on her second attempt.

**VIP Tours** ($175–$315 per hr, min 6 hrs. Daily. All ages. 407-560-4033.) Guided custom tours based on your custom itinerary.

**Wild by Design** ($60, inc light breakfast. Animal Kingdom adm req. 3 hrs. Mon, Wed, Thr, Fri. Ages 14 and up. Guests under 16 must be with adult.) Covers the art, architecture, storytelling and animal care at Disney's Animal Kingdom.

**Wilderness Back Trail Adventure** ($85. 2 hrs. Tue–Sat; 8:30, 11:30a. Ages 16 and up. Max weight 250 lbs. Starts from Mickey's Backyard BBQ pavilion. Same-day walk-up reservations at Fort Wilderness marina.) Ride a Segway X2 through shady off-road trails of the Fort Wilderness Campground.

**Yuletide Fantasy** ($79, Late Nov–Dec. No theme park adm req. 3 hrs. Mon–Sat. Ages 16 and up.) Tours the holiday decorations of the Magic Kingdom, Epcot and a few resorts.

## Water sports

Working out of the Contemporary Resort, Sammy Duvall's Watersports Centre (407-939-0754) will take you parasailing, water-skiing or tube riding.

**Parasailing** (Single riders $95 for 8–10 min at 450 ft. or $130 for 10–12 min at 600 ft. Tandem riders $170 for 8–10 min at 450 ft. or $195 for 10–12 min at 600 ft. Min weight per flight 130 lbs. Max weight 330 lbs.) will give you a birds-eye view of Walt Disney World. Hundreds of feet above the 450-acre Bay Lake, you can see everything from Ani-mal Kingdom's Tree of Life to Typhoon Lagoon's Miss Tilly. Attached to an open parachute, you're pulled by a powerboat down below. You never get wet, as you take off and land on the back of the boat.

You can also **water-ski, tube, wakeboard or kneeboard** (Per boat: $85 30 min, 165 1 hr, $135 per addl hr. Up to 5 skiers. Inc equipment, driver, instruction. Extra charge if picked up from Fort Wilderness, Grand Floridian, Polynesian or Wilderness Lodge) behind a MasterCraft inboard. Instructors are friendly and patient, especially with kids.

A legendary water skier himself, Duvall has won more than 80 pro championships.

**Fun facts ❶** Here is Disney's story regarding the creation of Winter Summerland: Late one Christmas Eve as Santa Claus was flying over Central Florida, he glanced down and was shocked to see snow on the ground! Landing immediately, Santa purchased the spot as a vacation retreat for his elves. The little people built two golf courses: one for elves who enjoyed snow, a second for those who loved sun. ❷ Once worn down, the foot-wide tires used on the Richard Petty cars are sold for $5. ❸ Nicknamed the "Mickyard," the one-mile tri-oval was built in 1995 by the Indy Racing League. Many pro races were held here, including five Indy 200s and some Craftsman Truck Series events. A large grandstand held over 51,000 fans. Racing stopped in 2000.

Disney's All-Star Movies Resort is dominated by gigantic Disney characters, such as Pongo from 1961's "101 Dalmatians"

# Accommodations

The Walt Disney company runs 19 resorts on its Florida property, which it divides into five categories. Motel-style **Value Resorts** have food courts, pizza delivery, pools, playgrounds and hourly luggage service. Most rooms sleep four. Disney's **Moderate Resorts** are, for the most part, large complexes with at least one restaurant, limited room service, a swimming pool with a slide and some on-site recreation. One, the Fort Wilderness Resort, is a campground with cabins, as well as spots for RVs and tents. Most Moderate Resort rooms sleep four. **Deluxe Resorts** are luxurious complexes, with big lobbies, fine restaurants and beautifully landscaped grounds. They also add full room service, club levels, fitness centers, many children's activities, child care and valet parking. Most rooms sleep five. Often available for nightly rentals, **Disney Vacation Club** (DVC) timeshare units have kitchens and sleep up to 12. All Disney resorts have shops, arcades, laundry services and free transportation to Disney theme parks, water parks and Downtown Disney. For reservations call 407-WDW-MAGIC (939-6244).

## Benefits of Disney resorts

The themed architecture and decor, lush landscaping and, in most cases, quality restaurants at a Disney-owned resort immerse you in a vacation experience. Disney's reputation as a clean, family environment is well-deserved: grounds crews, maintenance workers and security guards seem to be everywhere. The convenient location makes it easy to take a midday break from theme-park or other adventures.

**Complimentary DIsney transportation** (boats, buses and monorails) takes you to all theme and water parks, golf courses and Downtown Disney. In some cases, it takes just a few minutes to get from your hotel room to a theme park.

Each day one of the four theme parks opens one hour early, or stays open up to three hours late for Disney resort guests with theme-park tickets. Water parks also participate. These **Extra Magic Hours** offer you uncrowded time in the parks and make it easier to plan out your vacation.

A Disney resort I.D. (your **"Key to the World"**) lets you charge park food, merchandise and other services to your room. Disney's free package pickup and delivery service will take anything you buy from Disney and deliver it to your room.

**Other savings** include discounts on dining and golf. Resort guests save up to 30 percent on Disney restaurant dining by buying a Disney Dining Plan when they purchase their theme park tickets. They also get preferred tee times at Disney's five golf courses, as well as free golf-club rental with the purchase of an 18-hole greens fee.

Disney's innovative **Magical Express** service offers complimentary shuttle and luggage delivery from the Orlando International Airport (OIA) to your Disney resort. In other words, you don't have to rent a car, you completely bypass baggage claim and your bags are automatically placed in your room. When it's time to return home, you check your luggage at your hotel (domestic flights only) and then hop on a bus back to the airport. If your flight departs late in the day, you can check out of the hotel, check your luggage at the desk nearby, then go off and still fully enjoy your last day at Disney.

You have to book the Magical Express service at least 10 days in advance. Participating airlines for return luggage check-in include American, Continental, Delta, JetBlue, Northwest and United. The service is extraordinarily popular. On some days more than 10,000 people use it, and that's just on the incoming buses. The Walt Disney World Swan and Dolphin, Shades of Green and the Downtown Disney resorts are not included in the program. For details call Magical Express Guest Services at 866-599-0951.

*Note: All Disney resort addresses in the following listings are in the city of Lake Buena Vista, Fla., ZIP code 32830. All phone numbers go to a central telephone bank.*

# Disney's All-Star Resorts

★ ★ $ **Rack Rates** $82–$160. Suites $190–$355.
**Location** SW WDW, near Animal Kingdom. **Distance to** Magic Kingdom: 5 mi. Epcot: 5 mi. Hollywood Studios: 3 mi. Animal Kingdom: 1 mi. Blizzard Beach: 1 mi. Typhoon Lagoon: 4 mi. Downtown Disney: 4 mi. Wide World of Sports: 3 mi. **Size** 5,740 rooms, 298 suites, 246 acres. **Built** 1994 (All-Star Movies 1999). **Last renovation** 2007–2009. **Restaurants** None. Food courts 6:30a–mid, each seats 550. Room service (including pizza) 4p–mid. **Swimming pools** Two per resort, one kiddie pool. Located behind each resort's central hall, the main pools have fountains that shoot water over swimmers' heads. Open 8a–mid. **Children's programs** Pool activities. **Other amenities** At each resort: Arcade, laundromat, laundry service, playground, small shop with groceries. **Complimentary transportation** Buses: Disney theme parks, water parks, Downtown Disney. **Check In** 3p. **Check Out** 11a. **Telephone** Movies: 407-939-7000. Music: 407-939-6000. Sports: 407-939-5000. **Fax** All-Star Movies: 407-939-7111. All-Star Music: 407-939-7222. All-Star Sports: 407-939-7333. **Address** All-Star Movies: 1901 W Buena Vista Dr. All-Star Music: 1801 W Buena Vista Dr. All-Star Sports: 1701 W Buena Vista Dr. Zip Code 32830.

**If all you want is a clean room,** comfy bed and good swimming pool, these three resorts are right up your alley. Classified by Disney as Value Resorts because of their low rates and relatively few amenities, these side-by-side complexes are the first choice for hundreds of youth groups, as well as many families who want to stay on Disney property but save most of their money for theme parks and other fun. (Disney's Pop Century Resort has a similar appeal.)

Built to compete with the rash of discount motels on nearby U.S. 192, each All-Star Resort is laid out like a typical budget complex, but on a giant scale. A central building holds the food court and bus station, and fronts the main swimming pool. Three-story lodging buildings spread out from there, with parking lots nearby.

**Standard rooms** (260 sq ft, sleep 4, 2 double beds with 1 king optional) are spread out among detached, three-story buildings. All-Star Music has **family suites** (520 sq ft, sleep 6, 1 king bed, 1 sleeper-sofa double bed, 2 single beds convert from chair and ottoman, kitchenette, 2 full baths). All rooms open to outdoor walkways.

Rooms are fairly plain, but the buildings that hold them are boldly decorated. Structurally little different from those at a Holiday Inn Express, each lodging building is coated with bright paint, and its stairwells and elevator entrances are hidden by way-larger-than-life icons—either Disney film characters (All-Star Movies), musical instruments (Music) or sports gear (Sports).

None of the All-Star Resorts has a table-service **restaurant**. Instead, each has a food court serving all three meals (each accepts Disney Dining Plan Quick Service credits), as well as a bakery, convenience store and small bar open to its main swimming pool.

When full the three resorts can hold an astounding 23,556 guests, so food courts and bus stations often have long lines, especially in the mornings. Heat is a factor too. Unlike most other Disney resorts, lodging elevators are not air-conditioned, and bus waiting areas are not shaded. Landscaping is often sparse, though native pine trees cover much of the grounds.

Besides decor, differences among the resorts include food courts (All-Star Movies has the best one; others are weak), pool ambience and waiting times for the Disney buses (All-Star Sports is the first stop for buses, All-Star Music second, All-Star Movies last).

**Fun finds All-Star Movies:** ❶ Photographs on the back lobby wall include shots of Walt Disney and his team posing with Academy Awards. A 1938 panoramic image shows the entire Biltmore Bowl banquet hall as Shirley Temple and Frank Capra present Disney with an eight-Oscar honor for 1937's "Snow White and the Seven Dwarfs." ❷ A 1940s theater projector sits in the food court. **All-Star Music:** ❸ Between the two Jazz Inn buildings, a 10-foot weathered fountain is surrounded by benches, cobblestones and a wrought-iron fence with climbing roses. **All-Star Sports:** ❹ In the courtyard of the basketball buildings, palms are arranged to resemble a basketball team at a tip-off.

**Hidden Mickeys All-Star Music:** ❶ Around the Jazz Inn, the three-circle shape appears as a screw top on top of a cymbal. ❷ As beige designs on the front and back of the cowboy boots of the County Fair buildings. **All-Star Sports:** ❸ Between the lodging buildings, as a large round platform and two gray pavement ovals. ❹ As a pattern of a baseball and two white circles in the gift shop carpet.

▶ **Average guest ratings** (0–5): Expedia 4.2. Hotels.com 4.3. Orbitz 4.0. TripAdvisor 4.1. Travelocity 2.5.

**Opposite page:** Bright paint and trim pieces such as a megaphone staircase wrap add life to an otherwise ordinary lodging building at All-Star Sports. **At right, from top:** Giant cowboy boots mark the elevator entrance to an All-Star Music lodging building. Statues of the stars of Disney's 1944 "The Three Caballeros" (shown, Panchito and Donald Duck) squirt water into an All-Star Music pool. Unlike guests at other Disney resorts, All-Star guests wait in the sun for Disney buses. Furnished with two double beds, All-Star rooms are modestly decorated.

© DISNEY

# Disney's Animal Kingdom Lodge

★★★★★ ✓ **$$$ Rack rates** $240–$580, suites $760–$2990, villas $275–$2260. **Location** SW corner of WDW, near Animal Kingdom. **Distance to** Magic Kingdom: 6 mi. Epcot: 5 mi. Hollywood Studios: 3 mi. Animal Kingdom: <1 mi. Blizzard Beach: <1 mi. Typhoon Lagoon: 5 mi. Downtown Disney: 5 mi. Wide World of Sports: 9 mi. **Size** 762 rooms, 19 suites, 708 villas, 74 acres. **Built** Jambo House: 2001 (last renovation 2007). Kidani Village: 2009. **Restaurants** Jambo House: 2:1 buffet (B, D); 1 table service (D). Fast food. Kidani Village: 1 (L, D). **Recreation** Each section: Swimming pool with slide, hot tubs, kiddie pool, play area; animal viewing (24 hrs); playground; arcade. Sunrise truck ride through Animal Kingdom habitat; sunset ride into resort savannas (both extra charge). Kidani Village: BBQ pavilion; basketball; shuffleboard, tennis courts. **Children's programs** African crafts, activities (some extra charge). Night-vision animal spotting. Poolside crafts. Kidani Village Community Hall has games, activities. **Other amenities** Both sections: Laundromat, laundry services, massage services, shops. **Complimentary transportation** Buses: Theme parks, water parks, Downtown Disney. **Check In** 3p. **Check Out** 11a. **Telephone** 407-938-3000. **Fax** 407-938-4799. **Address** 2901 Osceola Parkway, 32830.

**Wildlife lovers will appreciate this** African-themed resort, where giraffes, zebras and other exotic animals roam freely behind most guest rooms, and viewing walkways extend into the habitats.

The Disney Deluxe Resort is so family-friendly that parents and children alike could spend their entire vacation here and never get bored. Animals are always on display. The swimming and water-play areas are some of Disney's best. The staff includes young adults from Botswana, Namibia and South Africa, who host small family activities nearly every hour of the day—most of which are complimentary. To top it off, restaurants include three of Walt Disney World's best, including its No. 1 buffet spot. A bona fide African theme dominates the stunning architecture and decor, which also incorporate many subtle allusions to Disney's 1994 movie, "The Lion King."

The only downer: bus service. Unless you have a car, it's the only realistic way to get to a theme park, or, for that matter, from the new timeshare side of Animal Kingdom Lodge to the older side. (Why Animal Kingdom Lodge is not connected to its namesake, Disney's Animal Kingdom theme park, is one of Disney's more baffling frustrations.)

The original lodge, now called **Jambo House**, consists of 19 interconnected lodging buildings. They arc into a 33-acre savanna, home to giraffes, flamingos, zebras, os-

**Top:** Wildlife savannas wrap around the sides and back of Disney's Animal Kingdom Lodge

triches, gazelles and other non-aggressive species. An interpretative walkway leads into the area as well.

Topped by what appears to be a thatched roof, the main lobby's four-story atrium has a look all its own. Chandeliers look like spears and shields; an indoor suspension bridge fronts a large window that overlooks a savanna. Glass cases hold real African artifacts, from ancient Sahara stone axes to modern Ghanaian gold-dust containers and Burkinan marriage baskets. A 16-foot Nigerian ceremonial mask stands in the corner.

Doubling the size of Animal Kingdom Lodge, **Kidani Village** is a new Disney Vacation Club (timeshare) complex that often offers nighty rentals. It's surrounded on three sides by its own 13-acre savanna. Animals include giraffes, zebras, rare okapi and red river hogs. Finished in 2009, Kidani Village has its own swimming pool area, restaurant, and, alas, pedestrian parking garage. Though common areas are less elaborate than the original Jambo House, Kidani's studios and suites are the most stunning on Disney property. (One hundred and nine rooms in the Jambo House buildings have also been converted to DVC properties.)

**Standard rooms** (340 sq ft. Sleep 4. 2 queen beds or 1 queen plus bunk beds, small refrigerator, flat-screen TV, Internet service optional. Club level.) have multicolored fabrics and dark wood furniture handcrafted in Africa. Rooms above the first floor have balconies which extend about 4 feet; the few on the ground level have patios. Most overlook wildlife savannas, though some face the pool or parking lot.

Jambo House **suites** (1-, 2- and 3-bedroom units sleep up to 9, kitchens or kitchenettes) are at prime locations at the end of animal trails. There are five one-bedroom suites, 12 two-bedroom parlor suites and Vice Presidential and Presidential suites. Some have pool tables. Opened in 2009, Kidani Village has 492 **villas** (studio, 1-, 2- and 3-bedroom units sleep up to 12). There are 216 villas at Jambo House.

Refurbished for 2010, the Jambo House **swimming pool** is the largest at any Disney World resort. Open 24 hours a day, it has a 67-foot water slide as well as a "zero-entry" gradual ramp. A kiddie pool, two isolated

**Top to bottom:** The Animal Kingdom Lodge Presidential suite features a curved couch, remote-control fireplace and domed thatched roof in the living room. Its large wood-carved bed was built within the room. Giraffes roam the grounds. Some standard rooms have bunk beds. Typical guest rooms include hand-carved furniture and colorful African-print bedspreads.

SUITE PHOTOS © DISNEY

hot tubs and a shady playground are nearby. The Kidani Village swimming complex has those features as well as a 4,200-square-foot interactive water-play area.

Complimentary **children's and family activities** (9:30a–11p) range from African cultural lessons to after-dark animal spotting with night-vision goggles. Children play games and experience African culture at **Camp Kidani** ($30; $27 for DVC members, ages 5–12, 6–8p nightly, at Kidani Village, 407-WDW-DINE). The **Wanyama Sunset Safari** ($170 adults and children ages 8 and older, 407-938-4755) takes guests out into the animal savannas in a truck, then to a meal at Jiko. For club-level guests only, a **Sunrise Safari Breakfast Adventure** ($65 A, $32.50 C, includes meal; tickets to Disney's Animal Kingdom theme park required; 407-938-4755) is an extended trip through the Kilimanjaro Safaris habitat at the Animal Kingdom theme park.

Among shops, **Zawadi Marketplace** at Jambo House includes an African art boutique with drawings, paintings and sculptures by Nigerian artist Timothy Adebule.

# Dining

**Boma–Flavors of Africa** ★★★★★ ✓ African/American buffet $$$ B: $19 (children $11), 7:30–11a. D: $31 (children $15), 4:30–9:30p. Seats 400. Jambo House. *DP*
Outstanding food, ambience and value come together at this, the authors' favorite Disney restaurant. Though all the standard American selections are present, breakfast is highlighted by a creamy sausage and biscuit skillet, pap (a white-cornmeal take on cream of wheat, great with brown sugar), roasted meats and grilled tomatoes. Dinner appetizers include mulligatawny and seafood chowder, lavosh bread with three types of hummus and numerous salads. Entrees include roasted meats and salmon. There's a standard-fare children's station at both meals, though many kids will prefer dishes like falafel (mashed chickpeas) and fufu (mashed white and sweet potatoes). Some foods are spiced with coriander and cumin, but none are very hot. Boma's decor outshines anything in its class. Hanging light fixtures mix hand-cut tin with hand-blown glass. Many of the wood tables have fabric inlays. Dining chairs have hand-carved, distressed or leather seatbacks. A colored concrete floor looks like dirt; stone walkways wind through it. Several seating areas sit under abstract thatched huts. The buffet area resembles an outdoor market, with each serving station appearing to be in its own hut or makeshift stand.

**Jiko—The Cooking Place** ★★★★★ ✓ African fusion $$$$ D: $26–$39, 5:30–10p. Seats 300. Jambo House. *DP2 Disney Signature* Nervous about trying African food? With the sophisticated selections at this Disney jewel, there's no need to be. The beef, chicken, fish, lamb, pork, shellfish and vegetarian dishes here are hearty and comforting, tasty but not too spicy. Jiko specializes in unusual flavor combinations: cherries with goat cheese, roasted sweet potatoes with spiced yogurt, even filet mignon with macaroni and cheese. If you want something unique, Jiko does not disappoint. The South African wine selection is the largest in the U.S. Representing a sunset, the back wall of the dining room slowly changes color every 20 minutes. Another wall is a translucent piece of orange, green and yellow curved glass. Hanging from the ceiling are stylized kanu birds, flying over diners to bring them good luck.

**Sanaa** ★★★★★ ✓ Indian-inspired East African $$–$$$$ L: $11–$19, 11:30a–3p. Bar only: 3–5p, desserts, beverages. D: $14–$28, 5–9p. Seats 124, 24 in lounge. Kidani Village. *DP* Wildlife lovers will enjoy Sanaa, the only Disney restaurant where you watch land animals roam outside your window. It's also a find for sophisticated palettes. With beef, chicken, fish, lamb, pork, shellfish and vegetarian/vegan options, the balanced menu offers many dishes that are neither hot nor spicy. Lunch has both a burger and club sandwich; dinner adds a New York strip steak. Popular dishes include tandoori chicken and shrimp and a combo meal of meats slow-cooked in gravy. The bread service is a must. Addictive chai cream and mango pudding are featured desserts.

Outside arched, floor-to-ceiling windows are African animals such as giraffes, ostriches, storks, wildebeest and zebras. Able to get within 15 feet of the building, the creatures are always in a relaxed, natural state. A feeding truck arrives between 1 and 4 p.m.

Sanaa's decor is a stylized version of a African marketplace, complete with acacia trees hung with lights that resemble ripe fruit. Display cases contain necklaces, tapestries and other African market goods. Tables and chairs are carved dark wood; the floor is textured concrete and stone. Lighting is colorful, yet subtle.

The Kidani Village parking garage makes Sanaa easy to visit even for those not staying at the resort. Just park in the Timon section and take the elevator to the lobby. Sanaa is just down the steps. Ask for a window table.

**The Mara** ✓ American/African fast food. 7a–11:30p. Bakery 6a–11:30p. Small food store has fruit, snacks, S. African wines. Seats 250. Spacious, relaxed. Cartoons play on televisions. Jambo House. *DPQ*

**Victoria Falls Lounge** 4p–mid. Seats 48. Tucked in above the Boma buffet. Noisy when Boma is bustling. Jambo House.

**Capetown Lounge and Wine Bar** Noon–mid; appetizers 4–10p. Same African wines as adjacent Jiko restaurant. Jambo House.

**Sanaa Lounge** 4p–mid. African wines, beer and spirits. Adjacent to Sanaa. Kidani Village.

**Room service** 6a–mid. *DP2*

**Fun finds** ❶ Five abstract animal heads hang from the lobby's upper-level walkways. ❷ Metal antelopes leap along the fourth-floor railing. ❸ Lion and giraffe faces hide in the stair railing that leads to the rear savanna. ❹ At the bottom of those steps a lion face hides in plain sight. Ventilation vents form its eyes, a primitive ladder its nose, wall indentations its mouth.

**Hidden Mickeys** Jambo House: ❶ Outside, as a design above the lower roof in the mouth of the second tall figure left of the motor lobby. ❷ As a yellow spot on the back of the right spotted creature just inside the entrance. ❸ As a design on the right middle lobby chandelier, facing the check-in counter. ❹ In the back of the lobby, as a leaf about two-thirds of the way up the left vine staircase. ❺ To the left of the pelican viewing area, as spots on the tallest giraffe in the stone carving. ❻ As dents in rock along that overlook's walkway, 4 feet off the ground. ❼ Behind the pool slide as three dents in a brown rock wall, 3 feet off the ground. ❽ As a small green shape to the right of a wall above the Mara snack bar. ❾ Inside Mara, as a hole in a painted leaf on a wall in front and above the wine selection and ❿ on the third leaf from the left tree on the upper left wall. ⓫ As circles in the Jiko ceiling, formed by the tops of a column and two ovens along the show kitchen. **Kidani Village:** ⓬ In the lobby, as an impression in the rock wall just inside the door to the animal overlook. At the Sanaa restaurant ⓭ as white spots in the dark center of round tabletops, ⓮ as three woven disks on the wall behind the reception desk and ⓯ as a basket with two extensions on the side wall with the label "Tanzanian Cooking Utensils."

**Average guest ratings (0–5):** Expedia 4.6. Hotels.com 4.4. Orbitz 4.6. TripAdvisor 4.1. Travelocity 4.2.

**At Kidani Village, from top:** Wildlife roams behind the timeshare property, opened in 2009. The intimate lobby overlooks a wildlife savanna. The decor of the Sanaa ("sah-NAH") restaurant was inspired by African market places. A two-story living room anchors a three-bedroom villa.

EXTERIOR, LOBBY, SANAA PHOTOS © DISNEY

# Disney's BoardWalk Inn and Villas

★★★★★ ✓ **$$$$$ Rack rates** $340–$860, suites $645–$2780, villas $340–$2260. **Location** Centrally located on Disney property, between Epcot and Disney's Hollywood Studios. **Distance to** Magic Kingdom: 4 mi. Epcot: <1 mi. Hollywood Studios: <1 mi. Animal Kingdom: 4 mi. Blizzard Beach: 2 mi. Typhoon Lagoon: 2 mi. Downtown Disney: 2 mi. Wide World of Sports: 4 mi. **Size** 378 rooms, 20 suites, 533 villas, 45 acres. **Built** 1996. **Last renovation** 2009. **Restaurants** 4. Pizza window, lounge, snack shops. **Recreation** Three pools, each with hot tub. Main pool has slide. Kiddie pool. BBQ grill. Arcade, fitness center, lighted tennis courts, playground. Bicycle, surrey rentals. Two nightclubs. **Children's programs** Pontoon-boat adventure. Comp. activities at pool, Villas Community Hall. **Business amenities** Conference center. Business center. **Other amenities** Laundromat, laundry service. Shops sell groceries, upscale and ESPN apparel, fine art, Disney goods. **Complimentary transportation** Boats: Epcot, Hollywood Studios. Buses: Magic Kingdom, Animal Kingdom, water parks, Downtown Disney. **Check In** 3p (Villas 4p). **Check Out** 11a. **Telephone** 407-939-5100. **Fax** 407-939-5150. **Address** 2101 N Epcot Resorts Blvd, 32830.

**Fans of the big-band era** should like this nostalgic resort, where tunes such as "Rhapsody in Blue" waft through the air and all of the buildings look as if they were built before 1940. A waterfront boardwalk has nightly performers and midway games.

Surrounded by water on three sides, the Disney Deluxe complex includes a hotel, timeshare villas and a conference center.

Most rooms and suites spread out among two semicircular arcs of interconnected buildings. Some overlook the lake, though most face landscaped areas or pools. **Standard rooms** (385 sq ft. Sleep 5. 2 queen beds, sleeper sofa, small refrigerator, flat-screen TV, work desk with pull-out table. Balcony or patio. Club level.) got a nice makeover in 2009. New furnishings include plush mattresses on wood-framed beds. There's also new carpet, marble sinks and wall treatments with scenes of a vintage Disney World that never was.

**Suites** (sleep 4–9) have been redone as well. Two-story garden suites each have an individual front lawn with a white picket fence. Inside is a master bedroom upstairs with a king bed and a bathroom with a whirlpool tub. Downstairs is a sleeper sofa and standard bath. Often available for nightly rentals, **timeshare villas** (sleep 4–12; studio, 1-, 2- and 3-bedroom units, balconies or patios, some 2-story) line the main swimming pool and surrounding area.

Meant to resemble a 1940s Atlantic City, N.J. oceanside resort, the BoardWalk has the look of a community that has grown over time. "Newer" structures appear unrelated to their neighbors; mom-and-pop shops have

tucked themselves into residential buildings. Noted for his renovation of New York City's Times Square, postmodern architect Robert A.M. Stern restricted his palette to American looks common before World War II. He used the same approach at the nearby Disney-developed village of Celebration.

The Luna Park **swimming pool** area features a 200-foot Keister Coaster slide that looks like a 1920s roller coaster, with small dips and sweeping turns. Nearby is a kiddie pool, playground and sunny hot tub. Two quiet pools are somewhat shady. The Villas one is nicely landscaped with a large grill. The Inn has a lesser version of the same thing: smaller pool, fewer trees, no grill.

Nightlife at the resort includes boardwalk **midway games** and street performers as well as the **Atlantic Dance Hall** (adults only) and dueling-piano bar **Jellyrolls** ($10 cover, adults only).

Notable children's activities include the **Albatross Treasure Cruise** ($34, includes lunch, ages 4–12, reservations at 407-WDW-PLAY), a pontoonboat treasure hunt that sails to Epcot.

Among shops, **Wyland Galleries** offers fine art from marine-life artist Robert Wyland. Also represented is former Disney animation background artist James Coleman.

A **conference center** (9,600 sq ft ballroom, 14 breakout rooms) rivals the Grand Floridian's for luxury, with cushy carpets, floral wallpaper.

## Dining

### Big River Grille & Brewing Works ★★★★
✓ **American $$$** L,D: $9–$29, 11:30a–11p. Seats 190, including 50 outside. Direct reservations: 407-560-0253. *DP* Sporting Disney World's only micro brewery, this classy little bar and grill offers down-to-earth food and six handcrafted beers—light lagers to ales. Gunmetal tables make it noisy when crowded. With a pair of flat-screen televisions, the small bar can be a less-crowded alternative to the nearby ESPN Club (see below).

**ESPN Club** ★★★ **Sports Bar $$** L,D: $10–$15, 11:30a–11p. Seats 450. *DP* Two restaurants in one, this spot combines a sports bar with a second room that hosts radio talk shows. It has 123 television monitors. Weekends can be packed. During fall football games competing fans mix in a face-to-face ruckus.

**Opposite page:** A family pedals a bicycle surrey down the resort's restaurant-lined boardwalk.
**Top to bottom:** The motor lobby. Many guest rooms overlook a central green; villas overlook waterways. Cooks prepare appetizers at the new Kouzzina by Cat Cora restaurant. Street performers and midway games liven the nightlife.

**Flying Fish Cafe** ★★★ Seafood $$$$$ D: $27–$42, 5:30–10p. Seats 193. *DP2 Disney Signature* Cramped, crowded and loud, the atmosphere at this pricey nightspot interferes with enjoyment of its food. Sit in back for the best experience. Fish is better at Kouzzina (below).

**Kouzzina by Cat Cora** ★★★★★ ✔ Greek/American $$$$ B: $10–$12, 7:30–11a. D: $16–$28, 5–10p. Seats 232. DVC members save 10% on up to 4 breakfast entrees. *DP* Opa! People who like bold flavors—especially Greek ones—will raise their glasses to Kouzzina (*"koo-ZEE-nah"*). The first restaurant of Cat Cora, the only female winner of the television series "Iron Chef," it mixes Greek cuisine with southern staples such as greens and sweet potatoes. Entrees, none of which are bland, include fish, meats, pasta and a vegetarian option. The moist whole fish can be filleted at the table; green olives and braised greens add taste. Dessert features freshly made doughnuts drizzled with warm honey. A plaster ceiling and wood floors, tables and chairs create a bustling noise that adds a sense of camaraderie; a private room is available. The Disney-operated restaurant replaces Spoodles.

**BoardWalk Bakery** Baked goods, sandwiches. *DPQ*
**Seashore Sweets** Ice cream, snacks.
**Pizza window** Pizza by the slice or pie. *DPQ*
**Belle Vue Room** ✔ Pastries, coffee 8–11a. Mixed drinks 4–12p. Intimate lounge with sofas, chairs and small tables. Complimentary board games. *DPQ*
**Room service** 24 hours at Inn; 6a–mid at Villas. *DP2*

**Fun finds** ❶ In the lobby, an antique miniature carousel animates every half hour. ❷ Mutoscopes in the hall play "Cat in the Bag" with Felix the Cat and W.C. Fields in "The Golfer." ❸ Miss America memorabilia decorates Seashore Sweets. ❹ A trumpeting elephant hides in the Luna Park grounds.

**Fun fact** The Luna Park complex is named after an early amusement park in Atlantic City, N.J.

**Hidden Mickeys** ❶ In the foyer, as a spot on the neck of a white carousel horse. ❷ As a second spot on its rump. ❸ On the sign for Seashore Sweets, as a cloud to the top right of the left woman.

▶ **Average guest ratings** (0–5): Expedia 4.7. Hotels.com 4.8. Orbitz 4.5. TripAdvisor 4.0. Travelocity 5.0.

**Top to bottom:** The BoardWalk Resort's intimate lobby includes period antiques. Shutters connect a bedroom to its bath in a BoardWalk villa. A birdhouse-like marker identifies one of the resort's two-story garden suites, which have small front yards lined with trees and picket fences. Refurbished in 2008, guest rooms are trimmed in soft whites, yellows and greens.

A dad awaits his daughter at the
'Keister Coaster' water slide

# Disney's Caribbean Beach Resort

★★★★ ✓ **$$ Rack rates** $149–$304. **Location** Centrally located within Walt Disney World, near Disney's Hollywood Studios. **Distance to** Magic Kingdom: 5 mi. Epcot: 4 mi. Hollywood Studios: 3 mi. Animal Kingdom: 5 mi. Blizzard Beach: 3 mi. Typhoon Lagoon: 1 mi. Downtown Disney: 2 mi. Wide World of Sports: 3 mi. **Size** 2,112 rooms, 200 acres. **Built** 1988. **Last renovation** 2008. **Restaurants** One (dinner only), food court. **Recreation** Central swimming pool with slide. Nearby large kiddie pool, hot tub. Each lodging area has small basic pool. Four playgrounds (at Barbados, Jamaica, Trinidad, Old Port Royale lodging areas). Arcade. Bicycle, surrey; boat (canoe, pedal, power, sail) rentals. Guided fishing trips. Hammocks. Picnic area. Volleyball court, 1.4-mi walking trail. **Children's programs** Pontoon-boat adventure. Complimentary arts and crafts, beach and pool activities. **Other amenities** Laundromat, laundry service, shop with groceries. **Complimentary transportation** Buses: Disney theme parks, water parks, Downtown Disney. A separate shuttle circles within resort. **Check In** 3p. **Check Out** 11a. **Telephone** 407-934-3400. **Fax** 407-934-3288. **Address** 900 Cayman Way, 32830.

**Here's a resort that appeals to those** who would rather spend money on outdoor recreation options than the frills of a deluxe room. For the same cost as staying at a Disney Deluxe resort, families can stay at Caribbean Beach—with its Disney Moder-

ate rates—and add in a daily activity like renting a boat or going on a fishing trip. Now that sounds like a vacation.

Lodging buildings cluster into self-contained villages, which wrap around a 42-acre lake. In the middle is Old Port Royale, a dining, shopping and recreation center. A registration building sits near the entrance.

It's easy to remember which village you are in, because each is painted its own pastel color. Each is named after a different Caribbean island, and has its own beach, small pool and parking area.

**Rooms** (314 sq ft. Sleep 4. 2 queen beds, small refrigerator, Internet service optional. Accessed by outdoor walkways.) have a subtle "Finding Nemo" decor, with tropical fabrics. In 2009 384 rooms within the Trinidad South area were remodeled with a pirate theme. Molded-plastic beds resemble ships, dressers look like old crates and drapes that close off bathroom sinks from view are printed with skulls and crossed swords. Kids may love it.

A central **swimming pool** appears to sit within a stone fort. Cannons spray swimmers; a small slide has a 90° turn. Nearby is a kiddie pool and hot tub. Less crowded quiet pools sit within each lodging area.

**Top:** Caribbean Beach lodging areas sit within a palm-and-pine landscape

A new water playground for young children looks like a wrecked pirate boat, with mini-slides, fountains and a big barrel that dumps water from above. Wading water is ankle deep. Parents can recline in shady chaise lounges just a few feet away.

**Children's activities** include the Islands of the Caribbean Pirate Adventure Cruise ($34, ages 4–12, 2 hours, reservations at 407-WDW-PLAY), a pontoon-boat treasure hunt. Street dances: Daily 15-minute "street dances" at the food court include a limbo party at 12:15 and 5 p.m. and an electric slide/macarena at 6:30 p.m.

If you stay here, consider renting a car. Many rooms are a long walk from a bus stop or the central complex. The Martinique and Trinidad North villages are next to Old Port Royale; Trinidad South is farthest away.

Another negative: Though the resort can hold over 8,000 guests, the food court can seat only a few hundred at a time. At 9 a.m. it can take up to 45 minutes to stand in line for your food, stand in line to pay, stand in line for coffee, and then find an open table. Our advice: Eat breakfast somewhere else, or during non-peak hours.

## Dining

**Shutters** ★ ★ ★ Caribbean American $$$$ D: $16–$28, 5–10p. Seats 132. *DP* Carved out of a corner of the food court, three small dining rooms offer meat and pasta entrees that have a dose of Caribbean flavors. Though cursed with Disney's most generic decor (the walls are dotted with stamped metal pieces straight from a Pier One sidewalk sale) Shutters is comfortable, with fat chairs and big tables.

**Centertown Food Court** American B: $2–$8, 6:30–11:30a. L,D: $6–$15, 11:30a–11p. Seats 500. Small food store sells fruit, snacks. *DPQ*

**Room service** Pizza, salads, dessert. 4–11:30p. *DP2*

**Fun finds ❶** The food court looks like an outdoor market. Two-story interior walls are building facades with balconies, shuttered windows and thatched roofs. The blue ceiling is a sky. ❷ Concrete alligators and turtles hide in the beach sand and on the island.

**Average guest ratings (0–5):** Expedia 4.1. Hotels.com 3.8. Orbitz 4.1. TripAdvisor 3.8. Travelocity 4.0.

**Top to bottom:** The main swimming pool appears to wind through a stone fort. Hammocks and playground pieces line a central lake. Some guest rooms have a Pirates of the Caribbean theme, with furnishings inspired by old ships and a skull-and-swords drape in front of bathroom sinks. Most rooms have a bright decor accented with "Finding Nemo" characters.

# Disney's Contemporary Resort

★ ★ ★ ★ ✓ **$$$$ Rack rates** Rooms: $285–$880, suites $930–$2950, villas $385–$2475. **Location** NW corner of WDW, near Magic Kingdom. **Distance to** Magic Kingdom: <1 mi. Epcot: 4 mi. Hollywood Studios: 4 mi. Animal Kingdom: 7 mi. Blizzard Beach: 5 mi. Typhoon Lagoon: 6 mi. Downtown Disney: 7 mi. Wide World of Sports: 7 mi. **Size** 632 rooms, 23 suites, 295 villas, 55 acres. **Built** 1971. Last renovation 2008–2009. **Restaurants** Three. Fast food, lounges, snack shops. **Recreation** 2 pools (1 w/slide), kiddie pool, 2 hot tubs. Tennis, beach volleyball crts. Guided fishing trips. Powerboat, personal watercraft rntls. Water sports. Also private Bay Lake Tower complex. **Children's programs** Arts and crafts; beach, pool games; evening beach campfire with movie. Bay Lake Tower Community Center has video, board games. **Business amenities** Convention center. Business center. **Other amenities** Arcade, laundromat, laundry service, fitness center, massage services, salon, shops. **Complimentary transportation** Monorail: Magic Kingdom, Epcot; Grand Floridian, Polynesian resorts. Boats: Wilderness Lodge, Fort Wilderness resorts. Buses: Hollywood Studios, Animal Kingdom, water parks, Downtown Disney. **Check In** 3p (Bay Lake Tower 4p). **Check Out** 11a. **Telephone** 407-824-1000. **Fax** 407-824-3539. **Address** 4600 N World Dr, 32830.

**There's nothing warm and cuddly** about the Contemporary Resort. Its modern, stark architecture and decor stand in sharp contrast with most other Walt Disney World resorts, which emphasize nostalgia. But for those who want minimal theming—or want to be close to Magic Kingdom—this Disney Deluxe complex can be ideal.

In fact, there is no resort more convenient to the world's most popular theme park. The Contemporary is the only resort where guests can walk to the park, and the only one with direct monorail service from an indoor train station.

Grounds include a distinctive 15-story A-frame, a garden-wing annex, and Bay Lake Tower, a new crescent-shaped timeshare tower. The lakefront resort also has the most extensive water recreation of any Disney hotel complex and a large convention center.

**Rooms** (394 sq ft. Sleep 5. 2 queen beds, daybed, desk, sm refrigerator. Flat-screen TV, PC. Internet service optional. Small balcony or patio. Club level.) have Asian-inspired decor, with white lighting fixtures offset against tan fabrics and dark woods. A small desk holds a flat-screen monitor connected to a PC. Rooms on higher A-frame floors have memorable views.

Sitting above the atrium, 14th-floor **suites** (sleep up to 8, Club services) serve as convention hospitality rooms. The size of three standard rooms, one-bedroom suites (1182 sq ft. 6-

**Top:** The authors' daughter jumps backward into the Contemporary Resort's main swimming pool.

seat living area, 2 baths, 3 balconies) have Scandinavian decors with abstract lithographs.

The main **swimming pool** has a 17-foot-high spiraling slide, a large central fountain and a row of smaller sprays. A second pool sits next to the lake. It's round, and gets deeper in its center. Cabana tents are available for rent (407-WDW-PLAY; 407-824-2464 same-day). Nearby are a kiddie pool, two hot tubs and a beach volleyball court. A Bay Lake Tower pool includes a "zero-entry" side and a 20-foot-high spiraling slide wrapped in a glass block. A hot tub, Mickey Mouse-shaped kids fountain, shuffleboard and bocce ball courts and a barbecue pavilion with shaded picnic tables are nearby. The **Sammy Duvall Watersports Centre** (407-939-0754, details in Sports and Rec chapter) offers parasailing, water-skiing and tubing trips and rents personal watercraft. The **Electrical Water Pageant** passes the resort nightly at 10:05 p.m.

Opened in the fall of 2009, Bay Lake Tower has 295 modern **villas** (studio, 1-, 2- and 3-bedrm units sleep up to 12). A restricted Disney Vacation Club complex, the tower has its own lakeside recreation area and private rooftop lounge with a fireworks viewing deck.

A 120,000-square-foot **convention center** (4 ballrooms, 33 breakout rooms, 1,600 sq ft stage) includes space in the A-frame as well as an adjacent dedicated building.

## Dining

**California Grill** ★★★★★ ✓ New American $$$$$
D: $26–$44, 5:30–10p. Seats 156. *DP2 Disney Signature*
Superb fare is matched by an entertaining view at this Disney landmark, which is perched atop the resort's A-frame tower. Signature items include grilled pork tenderloin and an oak-fired beef filet that's so tender you don't get a steak knife. Sushi is prepared by Okinawa native Yoshie Cabral, famous for her imaginative sauces and use of fruit.

The view is better than you'd expect, since the surrounding land is so flat. Sit along the west windows before sundown and you'll see the steam of the Liberty Square Riverboat; diners along the south wall look down at Epcot's Spaceship Earth.

You can watch Magic Kingdom's Wishes fireworks show from inside or from rooftop

CHEF MICKEY'S PHOTO © DISNEY

**Top to bottom:** Monorail trains run through the Contemporary's A-frame atrium. With angled brick dividers, the South Wing mimics the look of the A-frame. Mickey Mouse greets diners at Chef Mickey's, a buffet restaurant. Standard guest rooms have a modern Asian decor of browns, greens and yellows.

**The new Bay Lake Tower** timeshare building connects to the rest of the Contemporary Resort via an elevated covered walkway. Studios and suites are often available for nightly rentals.

walkways. To beat the crowd head to the northwest terrace 10 minutes early. Book a table three months in advance for prime dining times; six months for large parties.

**Chef Mickey's** ★★★★ **Character buffets $$$$** Mickey, Minnie Mouse; Donald Duck; Goofy; Pluto. B: $23 (children $13), 7–11:30am. D: $30 (children $15), 5–9:30pm. Seats 405. *DP Disney Signature* This cute character experience is worth it if you dine at an uncrowded time, such as 11 a.m. Disney's only "Fab 5" character meal, it features Mickey Mouse as a chef and his pals as cooks. Each dining room, however, often has only one character, who during busy periods has to divide time among 100 diners. Huge buffets include PB&J pizzas for breakfast, good meats and salmon for dinner. Expect to be asked to pose for an optional photo package. Reserve a table at least a month early.

**The Wave** ★★★★ ✓ **American $$$$** B: $7–$18, 7:30–11a. L: $12–$21, noon–2p. D: $18–$26, 5:30–10p. Lounge: noon–mid. Buffet, private rooms avail. Opened 2008. Seats 222 plus 100 in lounge. *DP* Interesting taste blends distinguish this upscale dining spot. Pricey menus make it a bargain for Disney

Dining Plan guests, a luxury for others. Breakfast has smoked salmon, egg and griddle dishes. Lunch offers salads, sandwiches, stews, fish; dinner adds steak and pasta. Intense dessert flights. Wavy decor includes cylindrical salt-and-pepper shakers that look like stainless steel hockey pucks. Southern hemisphere Stelvin wines. Beer and wine flights, organic draft beer, press pot and organic coffee, specialty teas.

**Contempo Cafe Fast food.** 6a–10p. Light fare 10p–mid. Seats 112. New as of 2009. Food quality has been uneven. Confusing electronic ordering. *DPQ*

**California Grill Lounge** 5–11:30p. Adjoins the 15th-floor restaurant; shares its view. No reservations.

**Outer Rim Lounge** Noon–mid. 30 seats, 7 bar stools. Appetizers 4–10p. 4th-floor concourse.

**Top of the World Lounge** 5p–mid. Seats 100. Appetizers. Large outdoor patio has room for 400. Bay Lake Tower. (Bay Lake Tower guests only.)

**The Wave Lounge** Noon–mid. Wine, cocktails. Adjoins 1st-floor restaurant. Seats 100.

**Contemporary Grounds Coffee bar.** 6:30a–5p. Cartoons on TV. Lobby, near Convention Center.

**Room service** 24 hours. *DP2*

**Fun facts** ❶ Reflecting the American Southwest, the eight-story atrium mural was designed by Mary Blair, known for her abstract sets used in Disney's It's A Small World attraction and the vivid backgrounds of the films "Cinderella" (1950) and "Alice in Wonderland" (1951). ❷ Built between 1969 and 1971 by U.S. Steel, the hotel was an experiment in modular construction. While its steel skeleton was assembled at the site, rooms were built on an assembly line three miles away. Workers created a steel room shell, then added in electrical, plumbing and air conditioning systems; ceiling, floor and wall coverings; bathroom fixtures; even furniture. An average of 15 rooms were finished a day, then the nine-ton units were trucked to the resort, lifted by crane and slid into the A-frame, much like a huge set of dresser drawers. The result was a financial disaster. Though each room had been forecast to cost $17,000, the final amount was close to $100,000. ❸ The California Grill was originally a supper club. Performers included crooners Lou Rawls and Mel Torme. ❹ On Nov. 17, 1973, in an hour-long, televised Q&A session with 400 Associated Press editors in one of the Contemporary Resort's ballrooms, President Richard Nixon proclaimed his innocence in the Watergate cover-up, declaring "I am not a crook."

**Fun find** One of the goats in the atrium mural has five legs. It's facing the monorail tracks at the height of the seventh floor.

**Average guest ratings** (0–5): Expedia 4.5. Hotels.com 4.4. Orbitz 4.5. TripAdvisor 3.7. Travelocity 4.0.

PHOTOS © DISNEY

# Disney's Coronado Springs Resort

★★★★ ✔ \$\$ \$154–\$310, suites \$350–\$1320. **Location** Next to WDW's Western Way entrance, between Hollywood Studios and Animal Kingdom. **Distance to** Magic Kingdom: 4 mi. Epcot: 3 mi. Hollywood Studios: <1 mi. Animal Kingdom: 2 mi. Blizzard Beach: <1 mi. Typhoon Lagoon: 3 mi. Downtown Disney: 4 mi. Wide World of Sports: 5 mi. **Size** 1,877 rooms, 44 suites, 125 acres. **Built** 1997. **Last renovation** 2009. **Restaurants** One (B, D). Also food court (B, L, D), fast-food cafe. Room service 7a–11p. **Recreation complex** Swimming pool with slide, children's programs, playground with swings, sand play area, kiddie fountain pool, sand volleyball court; 22-person hot tub, arcade. **Other recreation** Three lodging-area swimming pools. Fitness center. Bike, surrey, boat (kayak, pedal, power) rentals. Guided fishing trips. Hammocks. **Convention center** 220,000 sq ft of flexible, functional space; 60,000-sq ft ballroom; 86,000-sq ft exhibition hall; 45 breakout rooms. Business center. **Other amenities** Second arcade, hair salon, laundromat, laundry service, shop with groceries. **Complimentary transportation** Buses: Disney theme parks, water parks, Downtown Disney. **Check In** 3p. **Check Out** 11a. **Telephone** 407-939-1000. **Fax** 407-939-1001. **Address** 1000 W Buena Vista Drive, 32830.

**With old-fashioned swing sets,** treasures buried in the sand and a sneaky spitting jaguar next to a winding water slide, children may never realize they're at a convention complex if they hang out at the first-rate rec

complex at this Disney Moderate Resort. An expense-account restaurant philosophy kills off some of the family fun, but if you're planning to eat mainly at the theme parks, Coronado Springs is worth considering.

Laid out in a circle, the resort is anchored by its dining, shopping and convention center. Three lodging areas arc outward around a 15-acre lake. Next to the convention center are apartment-like Casitas. Halfway around the lake, a more spacious Ranchos area is landscaped with sagebrush, cactus and gravel. Finally comes the Cabanas, a quaint, slightly tropical area dotted with queen palms, many with swaying hammocks underneath.

Refurbished in 2009, **rooms** (314 sq ft. Sleep 4. 2 queen beds, small refrigerator. Flat-screen TV. DVD players in Club Level rooms. Accessed by outdoor walkways.) have modern blue, green and yellow color schemes.

Adjacent to the Ranchos area, the recreation center also includes a large **swimming pool** (a waterfall flows into it off a four-story pyramid, while a statue blows a stream of water), a kiddie fountain pool, a 22-person hot tub, a sand **volleyball court** and an indoor arcade. Set amid dense tropical

**Disney's Coronado Springs Resort** is anchored by a dining, shopping and convention complex

landscaping, the area imagines Francisco Vasquez de Coronado's discovery of a lost Mayan kingdom. Smaller **quiet pools** are located in each lodging area. Organized **children's activities** (daily, some have a small fee) include arts and crafts and pool games.

The Spanish Colonial complex has architectural details such as arched doorways and windows, tile roofs and mosaic accents. The Ranchos area recalls rural regions of the American Southwest. The Cabanas section suggests Mexico's Gulf Coast resorts.

Unless their meeting planner has arranged for Pargo taxi service, business guests staying in the Ranchos and Cabanas have a long walk to the convention center.

## Dining

The Disney touch is absent at Coronado Springs restaurants, which are run by the same company that operates the San Angel Inn at Epcot's Mexico pavilion.

**Maya Grill** ★ ★ ★ American/Latin $$$$ B: $17 (children $11), 7–11a. D: $22–$34, 5–10p. Seats 220. *DP* Served in a comfortable if dated atmosphere, these uninspired dinner entrees have just a touch of Latin flavor. Wines come from Argentina, Chile and Spain. Breakfast is an American buffet. The room has a three-story open ceiling, wood tables with metal tops and wide, nicely upholstered chairs.

**Pepper Market Food Court** American/Mexican B: $3–$11, 6–10:30a. L,D: $10–$22, 11a–11p. Seats 420. A waiter gets your drinks, which means an automatic 10 percent tip. Mall quality. *DPQ*

**Cafe Rix Fast food** B: $5–$7, 6:30–11a. L,D: $7–$11, 11a–mid. Seats 50. Pastries, sandwiches, gelato. *DPQ*

**Rix Lounge** 5p–2a Wed–Sun. Seats 220. $15 cover, VIP tables (seat up to 12) have $500 min. Appetizers. Nightly DJ, live band some evenings. Private rooms.

**Room service** 7a–11p. *DP2*

**Hidden Mickeys** ❶ Jutting out from a bolt, a detailed Mickey face is on the top left of the left entrance door. ❷ As sidewalk impressions near the lamppost closest to the boat and bike rental.

▶ **Average guest ratings** (0–5): Expedia 4.0. Hotels.com 4.2. Orbitz 3.7. TripAdvisor 3.7. Travelocity 3.6.

**This page, top to bottom:** Themed to Francisco Vasquez de Coronado's discovery of a lost Mayan kingdom, the Dig Site recreation center is anchored by a 4-story pyramid. Lodging areas include apartment-like Casitas, a Ranchos area landscaped with cactus and gravel and slightly tropical Cabanas. Refurbished in 2009, Coronado Springs guest rooms have a modern Mexican decor and flat-screen televisions.

# Disney's Fort Wilderness Resort

★ ★ ★ ★ ✔ $–$$$$$ **Rack Rates** Campsites $43–$116, cabins $265–$410. **Location** NW corner of WDW, SE of Magic Kingdom. **Distance to** Magic Kingdom: 2 mi. Epcot: 4 mi. Hollywood Studios: 4 mi. Animal Kingdom: 6 mi. Blizzard Beach: 4 mi. Typhoon Lagoon: 6 mi. Downtown Disney: 6 mi. Wide World of Sports: 6 mi. **Size** 784 campsites, 409 cabins, 740 acres. **Built** 1971. **Last renovation** 2009. **Restaurants** Buffet. Two dinner shows (1 seasonal). **Recreation** Central pool with slide. Nearby kiddie pool, splash zone, hot tub. Basic pool at cabins. Arcade. Archery instruction. Beach. Bicycle, surrey rentals. Basketball, horseshoes, tennis, tetherball, volleyball courts. Cane-pole fishing, guided fishing trips. Picnic areas. Playgrounds. Carriage, wagon, trail, pony rides. Segway tour. Stable. .75-mi walking trail, 1-mi exercise trail. Watercraft rentals. **Children's programs** Nightly campfire with Chip 'n Dale, movie. Complimentary arts and crafts, pool activities. **Other amenities** Dog park, golf cart rentals, laundromat, general store. **Complimentary transportation** Boats: Magic Kingdom. Buses: Disney theme parks, water parks, Downtown Disney. A separate shuttle circles within resort. **Check In** 3p. **Check Out** 11a. **Telephone** 407-824-2900. **Fax** 407-824-3508. **Address** 3520 N Ft. Wilderness Trail, 32830.

**A heapin' helpin' of outdoor activities** makes it easy to get back to nature at this Old West-themed cabin-and-campsite complex. A Disney Moderate Resort, Fort Wilderness is tucked into a thick pine forest

and, in some cases, the remains of a drained cypress wetland. Lined with creek-like canals, it sits on a 450-acre natural lake.

The registration building and riding stables are at the entrance. From there, three roads branch off into 28 loops, each of which is lined with either cabins or campsites. In back, a commercial "Settlement" area includes a restaurant, general store, music hall and marina, from which boats ferry guests to Magic Kingdom. Like all the resort's other public areas, the Settlement has no parking lot. Many guests rent golf carts ($62.84/day, 407-824-2742) to get around.

Though still a little worn, **cabins** (504 sq ft. Sleep 6. Living room with Murphy bed, kitchen, bath, bedroom with one double bed and two bunk beds, deck, picnic table, outdoor grill. A/C, vaulted ceilings, daily housekeeping) got new furniture, carpeting, fixtures and paint in 2008–2009. Cabins are located in the front of the resort. Some sit in the old swamp. Wheelchair-accessible versions are available.

Designed for recreational vehicles, the center of Fort Wilderness is filled with **campsites** (picnic table, outdoor grill; concrete pad) with **full hook-up** (water, electric and sewer). Usually the choice of large RV owners, Preferred

**Above:** Most Fort Wilderness cabins sit in a pine forest. Some are in a drained cypress swamp.

sites sit closest to the Settlement and include cable-television and Internet service. All are close to air-conditioned comfort stations with private showers, ice dispensers, laundromats and vending machines.

**Partial hook-up tent sites** (water, electric, level pads) line the sides of the property. Groups of 20 or more can reserve the tents-only Creekside Meadow. If you don't have a tent, Disney will rent you one for $31.95 a night.

Fort Wilderness is the only Walt Disney World resort that takes pets ($5/day). They're allowed at select campsites, but not in cabins. Leashed dogs are allowed on golf carts; dogs can run free at a new **dog park**.

Refurbished in 2009, the main **swimming pool** now has a water slide, hot tub and children's splash zone. A smaller **quiet pool** sits in the cabins area. Scattered throughout the camping loops are **playgrounds** as well as **basketball, horseshoes, tetherball** and **volleyball courts.** Hammocks line a lakeside beach.

Horse lovers can get their fill with **guided horseback rides** ($46. 45 min. Daily starting at 8:30a. Ages 9 and up, max weight 250 lbs, min height 48 in. Closed-toe shoes. No trotting. Reservations 407-WDW-PLAY.) through the woods and **pony rides** ($4, cash only. Ages 2–8, max weight 80 lbs, max height 48 in, a parent walks the pony. 10a–5p daily, 407-824-2788). Walk through a **stable** to see Magic Kingdom's draft horses or catch a blacksmith fitting shoes. Ride a Segway X2 on the **Wilderness Back Trail Adventure Tour** ($90, 2 hr. Tues, Fri, Sat at 8:30a, 11:30a. Ages 16 and up. Weight 100–250lbs. Starts from Mickey's Backyard BBQ pavilion. Reservations 407-WDW-TOUR. Same-day walk-up reservations at the marina.) **The Archery Experience** ($25, 90 min. Thurs, Fri, Sat, 2:45–4:15p. Ages 6 up. At the Bike Barn. Reservations 407-WDW-PLAY up to 90 days in advance) includes instruction.

The nightly **Chip 'n Dale's Campfire Sing-a-Long** is a 30-minute songfest with the mischievous chipmunks followed by a Disney movie shown on an outdoor screen. There's a different film each night. Guests roast marshmallows over a fire pit and make s'mores. A snack bar sells supplies including roasting sticks, and hot dogs and beer.

Two stores—**Meadow Trading Post** and **Settlement Trading Post**—stock camping supplies, groceries and souvenirs.

Disney's **Electrical Water Pageant** passes Ft. Wilderness nightly at 9:45 p.m.

**Top to bottom:** Guests roast marshmallows at Chip 'n' Dale's Campfire Sing-a-Long. RV sites include concrete pads, picnic tables and barbecue grills. Some take pets. Cabins have a small living room with Murphy bed, kitchen and dining area; bedrooms include bunk beds.

# Dining

**Trail's End Restaurant** ★ ★ ★ American buffet $$$$
B: $14 (children $9), 7:30–11:30a. L: $15 (children $10),
11:30a–2p. D: $21 (children $12), 4:30–9:30p Sun–Thurs,
4:30–10p Fri–Sat. Take-out service noon–2p daily, 4:30–
9:30p Sun–Thurs, 4:30–10p Fri–Sat. Seats 192, 6 at bar.
Settlement. *DP* Simple, hearty food includes
the same famous fried chicken as the Hoop-
Dee-Doo Revue next door. You eat off metal
plates and drink from jelly jars. With trophy heads on the walls and wagon-wheel
chandeliers hanging from acoustical tile,
the dining room looks like a Route 66 tourist trap. A take-out menu includes pizza.

**Hoop-Dee-Doo Musical Revue** ★ ★ ★ ★ Dinner show $$$$$ D: $53–$62 (children $27–$32), 2-hr shows
at 5, 7:15, 9:30p. Tues–Sat. Seats 360. Pioneer Hall. *DP2*
The food is nothing special, yet everyone
swears by it. The songs and skits are never
that funny, yet the whole room keeps laughing. Why? Because the spirit of this thing is
just so dang contagious. Kids in particular
love the six rootin'-tootin' Wild West performers and their frequent forays into the
audience. The food is all-you-can-eat fried
chicken, ribs, mashed potatoes and, if you
want, unlimited draft beer. As for the show,
the handsome heartthrob, the dumb blonde,
"Call me butter! I'm on a roll!"—nothing's
changed in decades. And why should it?

**Mickey's Backyard Barbecue** ★ ★ ★ Character
country show, buffet $$$$$ Mickey Mouse, Minnie Mouse,
Goofy, Chip 'n Dale. D: $45 (children $27). 2-hr shows at
6:30p, 9:30p. Thurs, Sat except Jan, Feb. Seats 300.
Settlement. *DP2* Hosted by live performers
Tumbleweed and Sarsaparilla Sal, this corny
country show is especially fun for those who
have a cotton for line dancing. Held in an
outdoor pavilion, it includes a live band and
dance instruction. A buffet offers pork ribs,
chicken, corn on the cob, watermelon and
beer. You share a long table with others. Arrive early for a good seat. The characters
dance, but do not visit every table.

**Crockett's Tavern** Lounge. Nachos, pizza, chicken
wings. Pioneer Hall. *DP*

**Room service** None.

**Fun fact** The resort's tree-trunk trash cans are
recycled props from the 1955–1971 Indian Village
attraction at Frontierland in California's Disneyland.

▶ **Average guest ratings** (0–5): Expedia 4.5. Hotels.com
4.3. Orbitz 4.2. TripAdvisor 4.4. Travelocity 5.0.

**Top to bottom:** Recreation includes horseback
and wagon rides and kayak rentals. Many guests
get around the resort on rental carts.

WAGON, HORSEBACK, KAYAK PHOTOS © DISNEY

# Disney's Grand Floridian Resort & Spa

★★★★★ **$$$$$ Rack Rates** Rooms $410–$1070, suites $1080–$2965. **Location** Northwest corner of Disney property, near Magic Kingdom. **Distance to** Magic Kingdom: <1 mi. Epcot: 4 mi. Hollywood Studios: 5 mi. Animal Kingdom: 7 mi. Blizzard Beach: 5 mi. Typhoon Lagoon: 7 mi. Downtown Disney: 7 mi. Wide World of Sports: 7 mi. **Size** 842 rooms, 25 suites, 40 acres. **Built** 1988. **Last renovation** 2009. **Restaurants** Six. Character meals, signature restaurants, snack bar, tea room. **Recreation** Two swimming pools, hot tub. Main pool has long slide, waterfall. Kiddie pool, splash zone. Arcade. Beach. Boat rentals. Guided fishing trips. Tennis courts. Walking trail. **Children's programs** Campfire, movie at night. Pontoon-boat adventure. Tea parties. Tennis clinics. Complimentary activities at pool. **Business amenities** Convention center (40,000 sq ft, 2 ballrooms, 16 breakout rooms). Business center. **Other amenities** Child-care center, laundromat, laundry service, salon, spa. Six shops sell bath items, groceries, Disney merchandise, upscale apparel, fine art. **Complimentary transportation** Monorail: Magic Kingdom, Epcot, Contemporary, Polynesian resorts. Boats: Magic Kingdom. Buses: Hollywood Studios, Animal Kingdom, water parks, Downtown Disney. **Check In** 3p. **Check Out** 11a. **Telephone** 407-824-3000. **Fax** 407-824-3186. **Address** 4401 Grand Floridian Way, 32830.

**If you want the best**—and can pay for it—this most indulgent of all the Disney Deluxe resorts may be the best choice for you. It recalls a time when a fabulous resort *was* the destination, not simply a place to stay while visiting a separate destination. Expensive and elegant, Disney World's flagship resort reflects old-money affluence—specifically, the spare cash of Yankee tycoons of a hundred years ago, a time when a young Walt Disney was shoveling snow on a cold Missouri farm. With its gabled roofs, clapboard siding and miles of moldings, scrolls and turnposts, the Grand Floridian brings that Victorian era back to life.

The luxe amenities include direct monorail access, a full spa, a lovely little conference center and many dining options, including three high-roller restaurants and two relative bargains—Disney World's best character-meal breakfast and dinner.

A five-story atrium, the lobby is topped with three large illuminated stained-glass domes. An afternoon grand pianist and retro orchestra entertain.

**Standard rooms** (440 sq ft. Sleep 5. 2 queen beds with 1 king optional, small refrigerator, daybed, Internet service optional. Terraces. Club level) are situated in four detached buildings. Victorian decor includes light woods and fabrics, ceiling fans and marble-topped sinks. Each room has live plants and special touches such as iPod docks in clock radios. **Suites** (sleep 2–8) come in a variety of configurations.

New for 2010: Italian marble flooring on the outskirts of the main lobby and mezzanine floors. Silhouettes of Disney characters have been set into the marble. You can find Tinker Bell in front of the second floor elevator bay.

A calm **swimming pool** sits in a central courtyard, surrounded by a kiddie pool and hot tub. A second **beachside pool**, however, is the family favorite. It has a swerving 181-foot slide that takes 12 seconds to travel, as well as a 20-foot waterfall. A fountain play area keeps little ones entertained; a "zero-entry" side welcomes wheelchair guests. (Cabanas available for rent; deluxe accoutrements and attendant among options: Call 407-WDW-PLAY in advance or 407-824-2464 for same-day reservations.)

Princess Aurora attends **My Disney Girl's Perfectly Princess Tea Party** (Garden View Lounge, $264.28 for 1 A, 1 C ages 3–11. Addl A $89.54, C $174.74, 407-WDW-DINE) a formal morning affair with operatic storyteller. Each girl receives an elaborate doll, other merchandise. Tea concludes with the Grand Princess Parade through the lobby. An afternoon **Wonderland Tea Party** (1900 Park Fare, $42.60 ages 4–10, 407-WDW-DINE) is hosted by "Alice in Wonderland" characters. A pontoon boat takes children on a treasure hunt in the **Pirate Adventure** ($34 ages 4–12, 407-WDW-PLAY). A complimentary **campfire and movie** happens on the beach on select nights. Reservations are required at the **tennis courts** (2 clay, $10.65 per person/per hour. Lessons available. 407-621-1991).

Disney's **Electrical Water Pageant** passes Grand Floridian nightly at 9:15 p.m.

Among shops, **Commander Porter's** offers men's designer clothing, golf apparel; **Summer Lace** has upscale women's resortwear.

## Dining

**1900 Park Fare** ★★★★★ ✓ Character buffets $$$$$
Breakfast characters: Mary Poppins, Winnie the Pooh and Tigger, Alice and Mad Hatter. Dinner characters: Cinderella, Prince Charming, others such as stepsisters Anastasia and Drizella, Lady Tremaine, Gus, Jacques. B ("Supercalifragilistic Breakfast"): $25 (children $14), 8–11:30a. D ("Cinderella's Gala Feast"): $36 (children $18), 4:30–8:30p. Seats 270. *DP* A variety of face characters make these meals truly entertaining. At breakfast, Alice romps up to greet children even if they're not quite sure who she

**Opposite page:** The Grand Floridian recalls Sunshine State seaside resorts of 100 years ago.
**Top to bottom:** The resort's quiet pool is lined with palms. The family pool includes a waterfall. Guest rooms feature pastel decors; upper-level rooms (as shown here) have vaulted ceilings.

**Beach bond.** A father plays with his son on the beach behind Disney's Grand Floridian Resort.

is ("They call me Alison," she confides). At dinner, Cinderella chats with adorable little clones of herself while Prince Charming makes the moms blush as he proposes table by table. The 40-item buffets include lobster Benedict for breakfast, good meats for dinner. Reservations can be hard to come by, but breakfast often has no-shows.

**Cìtricos** ★★★★★ ✔ **Mediterranean $$$$** D: $22–$46, 5:30–10p. Seats 190. *DP2 Disney Signature* Lit with a soft yellow glow, Cìtricos is lined with windows that overlook the main pool and marina. Imaginative takes on chicken, pork and seafood. White tablecloths. Noisy.

**Grand Floridian Cafe** ★★★ **American $$$$** B: $9–$18, 7–11:30a. L: $10–$25, 11:30a–2p. D: $17–$28, 5–9p. Seats 326. *DP* Relaxed sunroom with good food, varied menus. The signature Boursin club sandwich is too rich. Terrazzo tables, tall ceilings and windows; sunlight can be blinding at breakfast.

**Narcoossee's** ★★★★★ ✔ **Seafood $$$$$** D: $26–$59, 5:30–10p. Seats 270. *DP2 Disney Signature* This cozy place knows how to make fish fancy. It's Disney's best seafood spot. Equally great: the tartare appetizers. Wood floors and ceilings look nice but keep the noise level high. The circular building sits over the Seven Seas Lagoon; its view of Magic Kingdom's Wishes fireworks show includes beautiful reflections in the water.

**Victoria & Albert's** ★★★★★ **Gourmet $$$$$** D: $125, $185 w/wine pairings (Chef's Table $175, $245 w/pairings). Two seatings. Formal dress. Harpist. Women

receive roses. Private restroom. No children. Seats 90, inc. 10 at Chef's Table. This formal restaurant tries to provide the best meal you've ever had, and even hip foodies concede it knows what it's doing. A six-course dinner is created to match your personal tastes. A Chef's Table option includes more courses, a kitchen tour and a chat with the cooks. Victoria & Albert's does not participate in the Disney Dining Plan.

**Gasparilla Grill and Games Fast food.** 24 hrs. Seats 150. Good food, though diners sit in an arcade. *DPQ*
**Garden View Tea Room** 2–4:30p L: $14–$25. 2–6p English-style delicate tea sandwiches, scones, tarts on flowery china. Many choices have three courses. Hot teas, specialty coffees, champagne. Elegant cozy lounge overlooking gardens.

**Mizner's Lounge** 5p–mid Wed–Sun. Carved marble bar.
**Room service** 24 hrs. *DP2*

**Fun find** ❶ Housekeepers twirl their way to work in a Courtyard Parasol Parade at 8 a.m.

**Fun fact** Each lobby chandelier weighs one ton.

**Hidden Mickeys** ❶ As tan border designs on the lobby staircase carpet. ❷ As a white pattern on the tan wallpaper. ❸ As a painted hot-air balloon on the ceiling of the convention center rotunda.

▶ **Average guest ratings** (0–5): Expedia 4.3. Hotels.com 4.0. Orbitz 4.8. TripAdvisor 4.2. Travelocity 4.2.

# Disney's Old Key West Resort

★ ★ ★ ★ $$$$$ **Rack Rates** Villas $295–$1725. **Location** Between Downtown Disney and Port Orleans French Quarter, in the eastern part of Disney property. **Distance to** Magic Kingdom: 4 mi. Epcot: 2 mi. Hollywood Studios: 3 mi. Animal Kingdom: 5 mi. Blizzard Beach: 4 mi. Typhoon Lagoon: 2 mi. Downtown Disney: 2 mi. Wide World of Sports: 3 mi. **Size** 761 villas, 74 acres. **Built** 1991. **Last renovation** 2006. **Restaurants** One. Fast food counter, lounge. **Recreation** 4 swimming pools, each with hot tub. Main pool has giant sandcastle slide, nearby kiddie pool. Arcades. Bicycle, surrey rentals. Boat rentals. Basketball, shuffleboard, volleyball courts; 3 tennis courts, 2 lighted. DVD rentals. Guided fishing trips. Fitness center. Marina. Playground. **Children's programs** Disney Movie Under the Stars campfire, movie some nights. Complimentary activities at pool, Community Hall, including sandcastle building. **Other amenities** Laundromat, laundry services. General Store sells groceries, Disney merchandise, resort apparel. **Complimentary transportation** Boats: Downtown Disney, Port Orleans French Quarter, Port Orleans Riverside, Saratoga Springs. Buses: Disney theme parks, water parks, Downtown Disney. A separate shuttle circles within resort. **Check In** 4p. **Check Out** 11a. **Telephone** 407-827-7700. **Fax** 407-827-7710. **Address** 1510 N Cove Rd, 32830.

**Staying at Old Key West** reminds this author of home—literally. Just like my neighborhood on Sanibel Island, Fla., the streets are lined with palms and pines, the restaurants serve mostly Midwestern comfort food, and the spacious homes—or, in this case, the spacious suites—are distinguished by their scratched wood floors, worn wicker chairs and a general sense of whoever takes care of this place must have their priorities elsewhere.

On Sanibel, islanders wouldn't have it any other way. But when you're paying a few hundred dollars a night—or more—for it, you may feel differently.

Fortunately, the resort is scheduled for a complete refurbishment in 2010. And once these places get fixed up, they'll be terrific.

Disney's first timeshare property, Old Key West is notable not just for its roomy accommodations (bedrooms are so big that, even with two queen beds, they still look empty), but also its tropical theme.

Inspired by Florida's Tropical Victorian architecture, building exteriors combine tin roofs with clapboard siding and gingerbread accents. Like other Disney Vacation Club resorts, it offers nightly rentals as owner bookings permit.

Two- and three-story lodging buildings—many of which back up to Disney's

**Above:** The Old Key West marina rents a variety of watercraft

Lake Buena Vista golf course—cluster into small groups along three roads. A central Hospitality House contains a registration area, restaurant, gift shop, community hall, fitness center and marina.

**Villas** (Studios 376 sq ft, sleep 4. 1-bedroom 942 sq ft, sleep 4. 2-bedroom 1,333 sq ft, sleep 8. 2-story 3-bedroom 2,202 sq ft, sleep 12. Internet opt.) are accessed from outdoor walkways.

The main **swimming pool** has a slide that looks like a giant sandcastle. Nearby is a kiddie pool, playground and hot tub. Three **quiet pools** are scattered among the villages.

Complimentary **children's and family activities** at the Community Hall include arts and crafts, pool parties and sandcastle building. The Hall also has board games, DVD rentals and table tennis. A **campfire** or **movie** takes place near the main pool on select nights (Campfire 8p Mon, Fri. Movie 8p Tues, Thurs, Sat.).

# Dining

**Olivia's Cafe** ★★★ American $$$ B: $9–$13 7:30–10:30a. L: $10–$17, 11:30a–5p. D: $15–$28, 5–10p. Seats 156, inc. 22 outside. *DP* Though it looks tropical, this restaurant knows that when it comes to food, most tourists like to stick to the stuff they know. Steak and prime rib highlight dinner. Want something different? Try the key lime tart. Supposedly "Olivia's" home before being converted to a restaurant; the place is decorated with family memorabilia and photos.

**Good's Food To Go** Fast food B: 7–10:30a. L,D: 11:30a–10p. Outdoor counter. Burgers, hot dogs, salads, sandwiches. *DPQ*

**The Gurgling Suitcase** 11:30a–mid. Tiny bar next to Good's has a few seats indoors, more outside. The lounge got its name from the days of Prohibition, when travelers coming to the United States from Cuba carried alcohol in the fake bottoms of valises. **Room service** Pizza, salads, sandwiches, wings, desserts, beer, wine from 4p–mid.

**Fun Finds** Authentic old Key West postcards, photos and memorabilia line the walls of Olivia's.

**Hidden Mickey** As three seashell imprints in a walkway from Building 36 to its parking spaces.

▶ **Average guest ratings** (0–5): Expedia 4.3. Hotels.com 3.8. Orbitz 4.5. TripAdvisor 4.1. Travelocity 4.2.

**Top to bottom:** A lighthouse sits near the main Old Key West swimming pool. A dolphin fountain near the pool. Lodging buildings have Tropical Victorian tin roofs and pastel clapboard siding. Grand Villas have the largest living areas of any Walt Disney World timeshare unit.

# Disney's Polynesian Resort

★★★★★ ✔ $$$$$ **Rack Rates** Rooms: $365–$930, suites $630–$3005. **Location** NW corner of Disney property, near Magic Kingdom. **Distance to** Magic Kingdom: 1 mi. Epcot: 4 mi. Hollywood Studios: 4 mi. Animal Kingdom: 6 mi. Blizzard Beach: 5 mi. Typhoon Lagoon: 6 mi. Downtown Disney: 6 mi. Wide World of Sports: 7 mi. **Size** 853 rooms, 5 suites, 39 acres. **Built** 1971. **Last renovation** 2006. **Restaurants** Four. Character meal, dinner show, lounge, snack shop. **Recreation** Two swimming pools, hot tubs. Main pool has 2-story slide, waterfall. Kiddie splash zone. Arcade. Beach. Boat rentals. Campfire. Guided fishing trips. Hula dancing, lessons. Playground. Surrey rentals. 1.5-mile-long walking trail. **Children's programs** Complimentary activities at pool, lobby. **Other amenities** Child-care center, laundromat, laundry service. Three shops. **Complimentary transportation** Monorail: Magic Kingdom, Epcot, Contemporary, Grand Floridian resorts. Boats: Magic Kingdom. Buses: Hollywood Studios, Animal Kingdom, water parks, Downtown Disney. **Check In** 3p. **Check Out** 11a. **Telephone** 407-824-2000. **Fax** 407-824-3174. **Address** 600 Seven Seas Drive, 32830.

**Families will enjoy this** tropical Disney Deluxe resort. It offers large rooms, two nice pools, four child-friendly dining options and a location that's just a seven-minute monorail ride from Magic Kingdom. High in quality but not overtly luxurious, the resort has a distinctive laid-back attitude.

Walt Disney World's original hotel, the Polynesian consists of standard 1970s-style lodging buildings, but they're disguised by lots of wood trim and sit within a spacious and lush landscape. Torch-lit walkways wander through the grounds, which are anchored by a central building with restaurants, shops and monorail station. A 40-foot-tall atrium lobby includes a rocky waterfall.

Refurbished in 2006 and 2007, **standard rooms** (415 sq ft. Sleep 5. 2 queen beds, small refrigerator, daybed. Flat-screen TV. Balcony or patio. Internet service optional. Club level.) feature hand-carved furnishings and batik-print fabrics. **Suites** (sleep up to 9) are also available.

One drawback: if you're not familiar with the grounds, it can be easy to get lost at night. The lodging buildings look similar, and the walkways, while charming, don't provide much light. There are few directional signs except near the main building.

Nestled against a simulated volcano, the Nanea **swimming pool** is centrally located behind the lobby. Kids love standing underneath its waterfall and taking repeat trips down its slide—a slippery two-story tunnel with squirting water and eerie colored lights. Listen closely to hear the pool's un-

**Top:** A marina lantern fronts a waterside lodging area at Disney's Polynesian Resort.

derwater music. One end is a "zero-entry" gradual ramp for disabled users. Nearby is a kiddie sprinkler area and hot tub. Tucked in to a lodging area, the smaller **East pool** is less crowded. Hidden behind its lounge chairs are six shady open huts, each with its own table and ceiling fan.

Guests can join in **hula dancing** (lobby, Tues–Sat, 3:45p, no charge) or get a lesson with friendly resort icon Auntie Kaui (lobby, Sat, 11a, no charge). Guests can be picked up for Sammy Duvall **watersports**—parasailing, water-skiing, tubing, personal watercraft rental—behind the Contemporary Resort for an extra charge (407-939-0754).

Evening activities feature a torch-lighting ceremony with a fire-baton twirler. It's held just outside the front doors. Later, a musician entertains in the lobby.

Disney's **Electrical Water Pageant** passes the Polynesian Resort nightly at 9 p.m.

Three shops line the lobby. **Wyland Galleries** features bronzes, giclees, Lucite pieces and other pricey fine art. Most are from marine-life artist Robert Wyland.

## Dining

**Kona Cafe** ★★★ Pan-Pacific American $$$$ B: $9–$14, 7:30–11:30a. L: $11–$19, noon–3p. D: $17–$26, 5–10p. Seats 163. *DP* Originally a coffee shop, this high-ceilinged, carpeted room is open to the lobby atrium. Dotted with wood tables and a few half-booths, it's been upgraded over the years to a full-service restaurant. It serves a Pan-Pacific-flavored breakfast, lunch and dinner and offers 100-percent Kona coffee as well as a full bar. The best meal is breakfast. With nuts in the batter and a topping made of crushed pineapple, brown sugar and butter, the Macadamia-Pineapple Pancakes are so flavorful you don't need syrup. Though it has its fans, we say skip the Cafe's Tonga Toast. Two slices of battered, deep-fried, sugar-coated sourdough bread stuffed with a banana, it's basically just a huge doughnut. Prepared in a small show kitchen, desserts include a pecan-pie-like Chocolate-Macadamia Nut Tart, a Kilauea Torte "brownie volcano" that's filled with warm liquid chocolate and the Kona Kone, a vanilla-and-chocolate ice

**Top to bottom:** Monorail routes connect the Polynesian to Magic Kingdom and Epcot. The main swimming pool nestles against a simulated volcano. Tiki statues dot the resort. A volcanic stream appears to flow into the pool. Spacious standard guest rooms feature dark woods, tall headboards and exotic-print fabrics.

© DISNEY

**Get your hands up.** Girls get a quick hula lesson during the Spirit of Aloha dinner show

cream waffle cone that's surrounded by a base of cotton candy and topped with a chocolate Mickey stick.

**'Ohana** ★★★★ **Character breakfast $$$** Lilo, Stitch, Mickey Mouse, Pluto. B ("Mickey and Friends Character Breakfast"): $19 (children $11), 7–11a. ★★★★ **Buffet $$$$** D: $31 (children $15), 5–10p. Seats 300. *DP* One of Disney's most popular character meals, this breakfast is a memorable time for kids who love Lilo and Stitch. Mickey and Pluto are just as friendly, but they're definitely second fiddle. Every hour the characters lead a maraca-shaking parade around the room. The fixed "family-style" menu (all-you-can-eat but brought to your table) includes fresh coconut-pineapple bread, scrambled eggs, sausage and bacon. After you check in, a cast member will direct you to stand in a line to pose for an optional photo package. You can skip it if you like. Carnivores, come hungry for dinner. Skewers of Polynesian-flavored meats and seafood are grilled over an open fire pit and then continually brought to your table at this all-you-can-eat dinner. They're served with Hawaiian-style appetizers, good bread, salads and vegetables. Overlooking the pool and marina, some tables offer a distant view of Cinderella Castle.

**Spirit of Aloha** ★★★ **Dinner show $$$$$** D: $51–60 (children $26–$31), 2-hr shows at 5:15, 8p. Tues–Sat. Seats 420. Luau Cove. *DP2* A dancing, drumming and musical tour of Hawaii, New Zealand, Samoa, Tahiti and Togo, this venerable dinner show features skimpy costumes and lots of booty shaking. An odd first half has corny jokes and sitcom-style skits. Kids learn the hula. The meal is an all-you-can-eat feast of pork ribs, chicken and rice. If you go, splurge for the front-of-the-house seats. Folks who sit in back have a hard time hearing.

**Captain Cook's Snack Company Fast food.** 6:30a–11p. Seats 150. Standard choices plus flatbread, stir-fry dishes, sushi. Pineapple Dole Whip dessert. *DPQ*

**Kona Island Cafe Coffee Bar** 6:30a–4p. Pastries, coffee. Transforms into the **Kona Island Cafe Sushi Bar** 5–10p. Alcoholic drinks.

**Tambu Lounge** 1p–Mid., at 'Ohana. Large-screen TV. **Room service** 6:30a–12p. *DP2*

**Fun Finds ❶** A volcanic stream behind the Grand Ceremonial House appears to flow into the main swimming pool. **❷** Known affectionately as Auntie Kaui, the diminutive Hawaiian woman stringing leis in the lobby has been at her job since the resort's opening day in 1971. Before that she worked at Disneyland. She's really friendly.

**Fun Fact** John Lennon signed the paperwork to officially disband the Beatles while staying at the Polynesian Resort with 11-year-old son Julian (and 23-year-old mistress May Pang) over the 1974 Christmas holiday. His was the last signature on the agreement.

▶ **Average guest ratings** (0–5): Expedia 4.4. Hotels.com 4.2. Orbitz 4.8. TripAdvisor 4.0. Travelocity 4.2.

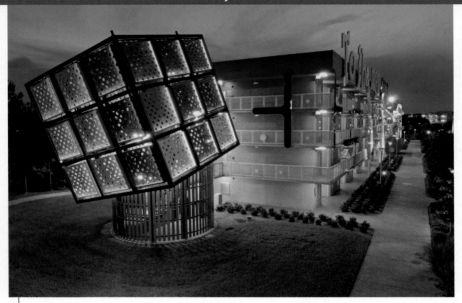

# Disney's Pop Century Resort

★★★ ✔ **$ Rack Rates** $82–$174. **Location** Close to Interstate 4, near Disney's Hollywood Studios and ESPN Wide World of Sports. **Distance to** Magic Kingdom: 6 mi. Epcot: 5 mi. Hollywood Studios: 3 mi. Animal Kingdom: 4 mi. Blizzard Beach: 4 mi. Typhoon Lagoon: 2 mi. Downtown Disney: 3 mi. Wide World of Sports: 2 mi. **Size** 2,880 rooms, 177 acres. **Built** 2003. **Last renovation** 2007. **Restaurants** None. Food court 6:30a–mid. Room service (including pizza) 4p–mid. **Swimming pools** Three themed pools, 3 adjacent kiddie pools. 1960s Hippy Dippy pool has 4 giant metal flowers that spray swimmers; kiddie pool with flower shower. 1950s pool is shaped like a bowling pin. 1990s computer pool (a rectangle) has spongy keyboard deck. Open 7a–mid, lifeguards, water features 10a–10p. Goofy water-jet playground fountain located between 1960s, 1970s areas. **Other amenities** Per resort: Arcade, laundromat, laundry service, playground, shop with groceries, Memory Lane walking trail IDs yearly events 1950 to 1999. **Complimentary transportation** Buses: Disney theme parks, water parks, Downtown Disney. **Check In** 3p. **Check Out** 11a. **Telephone** 407-938-4000. **Fax** 407-938-4040. **Address** 1050 Century Drive, 32830.

**Your children will know** they are someplace special if you stay at this Disney Value Resort. Though meant to appeal to nostalgic adults, it looks—at least to young eyes—like a child designed it. Bright buildings are the colors of poster paint. Towering props, for the most part, are of toys and cartoon characters. And everywhere you turn is a spirit of playfulness, silliness and yes, garish tackiness that may not be your cup of tea, but your children will love.

With room rates comparable to many off-property motels, Pop Century is an obvious choice for thrifty families who want the convenience of a Disney resort without the high cost. On the downside, the resort gets knocked for its huge size, small rooms and lack of a full-service restaurant.

Compared to most of its non-Disney competition, Pop Century is cleaner, better maintained, much better landscaped and. of course, more convenient to Walt Disney World. Compared to the similar All-Star Resorts, it's newer, with a better food court and shop, less wooded but overall more nicely landscaped, and the bus stop has a covered waiting area. Like the All-Star Resorts, Pop Century is popular with youth groups. It's the closest place to stay to the ESPN Wide World of Sports complex.

Grouped into five areas, the lodging area is a collection of four-story motel buildings, each decorated to illustrate a particular decade of American popular culture, from the 1950s to the 1990s. The buildings are adorned with gigantic props such as 41-foot Rubik's Cubes, 65-foot bowling pins and

iconic Disney characters, and topped with huge words and phrases such as "Flower Power" and "Do the Funky Chicken."

A central complex holds a food court (which accepts Disney Dining Plan Quick Service credits), arcade and gift shop; out front is the bus station, in back the main swimming pool. The food court's carpeted dining area has many comfortable booths, and features a soundtrack that includes chestnuts from Van McCoy's "Do The Hustle" to "Fire" by Jimi Hendrix.

**Rooms** (260 sq ft. Sleep 4. 2 double beds, Internet access optional. Accessed by outdoor walkways) are identical except for their location. Room decor is plain, with white walls trimmed by a small strip of wallpaper and a single poster on one wall. Bedspreads have Disney images. Rooms in the 1960s section ($10 surcharge) are closest to the bus stand, food court and lobby. 1950s rooms (no extra charge) are almost as close.

Pop Century has the best Disney bus service of any Disney World resort, with nonstop routes to nearly all Disney theme and water parks. On peak mornings, however, lines for the theme-park buses can be long. Checkout lines can be long, too.

**Fun finds ❶** The registration area features 51 display cases filled with cultural artifacts, everything from a 1955 Lionel accessories catalog to a 1998 Spice Girls videotape. **❷** A sticker on a 3-story Big Wheel states the trike can accommodate a rider who weighs up to 877 pounds. **❸** "Bowling lanes" line the bowling-pin pool. **❹** The adjacent laundry building looks like a bowling-shoe bin. **❺** A 1990s service building appears to be a stack of floppy disks. **❻** Food court (sometimes front desk) cast members do the Twist every day at 8 a.m. and the Hustle at 6 p.m. Guests can join in. **❼** A sign along the Memory Lane walking trail has its fact wrong. The St. Louis Gateway Arch opened in 1966, not 1961.

**Fun fact** Only half of Pop Century is finished. Opposite 33-acre Hourglass Lake are a few half-completed buildings of the 1900s–1940s "Legendary Years" section, which has been put on hold.

▶ **Average guest ratings** (0–5): Expedia 4.3. Hotels.com 4.2. Orbitz 4.2. TripAdvisor 4.4. Travelocity 4.2.

**Opposite page:** A Rubik's Cube facade disguises a Pop Century stairway. **At right, from top:** Lodging buildings are topped with decade-specific words and catchphrases. A huge 1970s Mickey Mouse telephone faces foosball props. Goofy overlooks a play fountain. A juke box fronts a 1950s swimming pool. Guests room are modestly decorated, with two double beds.

# Disney's Port Orleans Resorts

## Port Orleans Riverside

★ ★ ★ ✓ **$$ Rack Rates** $149–$264. **Location** NE WDW, near Downtown Disney. **Distance to** Magic Kingdom: 4 mi. Epcot: 2 mi. Hollywood Studios: 4 mi. Animal Kingdom: 6 mi. Blizzard Beach: 4 mi. Typhoon Lagoon: 2 mi. Downtown Disney: 2 mi. Wide World of Sports: 4 mi. **Size** 2,048 rooms, 235 acres. **Built** 1992. **Last renovation** 2001. **Restaurants** One (dinner only); food court (B,L,D). **Recreation** Central pool with slide, kiddie pool. Five basic pools in lodging areas. Bicycle, surrey, boat (power, kayak) rentals. Guided fishing trips, cane-pole fishing, carriage rides (same-day reservations available at 407-824-2832). **Children's programs** Pontoon-boat adventure. **Other amenities** Arcade, laundromat, laundry service, playground, shop with groceries. **Complimentary transportation** Buses: Theme parks, water parks, Downtown Disney. Boats: Downtown Disney, Old Key West, Port Orleans French Quarter, Saratoga Springs. **Check In** 3p. **Check Out** 11a. **Telephone** 407-934-6000. **Fax** 407-934-5777. **Address** 1251 Riverside Drive, 32830.

**The only Disney Moderate resort** with rooms that sleep five, this southern-themed complex has a lot of appeal for active families. It has a large kid-friendly swimming complex and recreation options including cane-pole fishing and carriage rides.

The resort has two lodging areas. Set within shady live oaks and other hardwoods, the Magnolia Bend area has four distinct sections, each with a trimmed green lawn and adjacent parking lot. Buildings recall Southern plantations, with white columns and sweeping entrance facades. The smaller Alligator Bayou area has a completely different feel. Walkways meander through an unkempt landscape of palmettos, pines and lots of pine needles, leading to rustic lodging buildings that look more like the homes of plantation workers than owners.

**Rooms** (314 sq ft. 2 queen beds, small refrigerator, Internet service optional. Accessed by outdoor walkways.) vary between the two areas. Magnolia Bend rooms sleep four, with cherry woods and tapestries. They sleep four. Alligator Bayou rooms have a backwoods feel, with hickory furnishings and quilted bedspreads. These rooms sleep five, thanks to the addition of trundle beds.

On the downside, as of 2009 the Riverside restaurant only serves dinner. A food court offers all three meals.

The resort's name comes from a river that curves through it. Though actually a man–made canal, it looks natural in many places, with grasses and water plants lining the banks. A central registration and dining

**Top:** Pontoon boats await renters at the Port Orleans Riverside marina.

complex resembles a riverboat landing. An adjacent Ol' Man Island recreation area includes a **swimming pool** with the most waterfalls of any Disney pool. A swerving slide dribbles water on those who go down it. A small nearby dock rents cane fishing poles and sells bait. Peaceful **quiet pools** sit between the lodging sections.

Notable children's activities include the **Bayou Pirate Adventure** ($34, ages 4–12, reservations at 407-WDW-PLAY), a pontoon-boat scavenger hunt that tells the tale of John Lafitte.

**Boatwright's Dining Hall** ★ ★ ★ ★ ✓ Southern **American** $$$$ D: $16–$27, 5–10pm. Seats 206. *DP* This underrated spot has the look of a 19th-century boat shop, where unseen workers have just taken a break from building a 46-foot cotton lugger. Shipbuilding tools line the walls, and some tables sit underneath the boat's wooden frame. The menu includes choices Yankees rarely see. The menu features jambalaya and a terrific blackened snapper served on grilled grits. Pecan pie is homemade. Wood tables sit on tile floors. **River Roost Lounge** 4p–mid. Large-screen TVs. Next to Boatwright's. Live entertainment Wed–Sat. Looks like a cotton exchange. Seats 100; 14 barstools. **Room service** Pizza, salad, dessert. 4p–mid. *DP2*

**Hidden Mickey** As a design on a Native American's sandal in the food court.

▶ **Average guest ratings** (0–5): Expedia 4.3. Hotels.com 4.3. Orbitz 4.2. TripAdvisor 4.2. Travelocity 4.5.

# Port Orleans French Quarter

★ $$ $149–$264. **Location** NE WDW, near Downtown Disney. **Distance to** Magic Kingdom: 4 mi. Epcot: 2 mi. Hollywood Studios: 4 mi. Animal Kingdom: 6 mi. Blizzard Beach: 4 mi. Typhoon Lagoon: 2 mi. Downtown Disney: 2 mi. Wide World of Sports: 4 mi. **Size** 1,008 rooms, 90 acres. **Built** 1991. **Last renovation** 2004. **Restaurants** None. Food court (B,L,D). Room service (pizza, salad, dessert). **Recreation** Central swimming pool with slide, hot tub, kiddie pool. **Other amenities** Arcade, laundromat, laundry service, playground, shop with groceries. **Complimentary transportation** Buses: Theme parks, water parks, Downtown Disney. Boats:

**Top to bottom:** Water splashes on a boy at the Ol' Man Island swimming pool. Parking is up close at the Parterre Place complex in the Magnolia Bend area. A still morning at a Magnolia Bend swimming pool. Alligator Bayou lodging buildings tuck in to a natural woodland. Carved trunk bedposts and an exposed pine frame lend a primitive feel to Alligator Bayou rooms.

Downtown Disney, Old Key West, Port Orleans Riverside, Saratoga Springs. **Check In** 3p. **Check Out** 11a. **Telephone** 407-934-5000. **Fax** 407-934-5353. **Address** 2201 Orleans Dr, 32830.

**Want to stay at a Disney Moderate resort** and all the others are full? Here's your only option. You get a decent room, a pool with a slide, and a food court that, for breakfast, serves beignets—those squares of fried dough doused with powdered sugar made famous at New Orleans' Café du Monde. But fried dough will only take you so far.

Themed to the Big Easy's French Quarter and Garden District, the resort has narrow, tree-lined walkways, lots of wrought-iron railings and some intimate gardens. The pool area is themed to a Mardi Gras parade; the food court looks like it's a warehouse for Mardi Gras parade props.

With such a rich source, you'd think the resort would have lots of personality. Instead, it comes off as a cheap Disney clone. The architecture cuts corners with fake shutters that are obviously too small. The **swimming pool's** plastic icons are charm-free, with a shallow slide only preschoolers will enjoy. Landscaping is often sparse, landscape maintenance even sparser. And except for those beignets, the food court—even though this place is priced as a Disney Moderate resort, there is no restaurant—is poor, even by the standards of a shopping mall.

As for recreation, there isn't much except for the pool area. Port Orleans French Quarter guests are supposed to use the amenities of the adjacent Port Orleans Riverside Resort, but in reality these are two separate areas. Getting from one to the other requires either a 10- to 20-minute walk or waiting for a pontoon-boat water taxi, which usually takes longer.

**Standard rooms** (314 sq ft. Sleep 4. 2 double beds, small refrigerator, Internet service optional. Accessed from outdoor walkways) have cherry woods, pastel bedspreads and dark blue carpet.

**Scat Cat's Club** 4p–mid. Live entertainment Wed–Sat. Hurricane drinks. Seats 40 inside, 15 in lobby by small stage; 6 barstools.
**Room service** Pizza, salad, dessert. 4p–mid. *DP2*

▶ **Average guest ratings** (0–5): Expedia 4.3. Hotels.com 4.3. Orbitz 4.3. TripAdvisor 4.3. Travelocity 4.5.

**Top to bottom:** Mansard roofs and wrought-iron railings trim lodging buildings at the Port Orleans French Quarter Resort. A huge parade serpent "swims" through the pool area. Walkways have puns for names. A standard guest room.

# Disney's Saratoga Springs Resort

★ ★ ★ ✓ $$$$$ **Rack Rates** Villas $295–$1725.
**Location** North of Downtown Disney, in the eastern part of Disney property. **Distance to** Magic Kingdom: 5 mi. Epcot: 3 mi. Hollywood Studios: 4 mi. Animal Kingdom: 6 mi. Blizzard Beach: 4 mi. Typhoon Lagoon: 2 mi. Downtown Disney: 2 mi. WW of Sports: 4 mi. **Size** 828 villas, 65 acres. **Built** 2004. **Last renovation** 2009. **Restaurants** One (B,L,D). Also food court (B,L,D). 7:30a–11p, seats 112. **Recreation** 4 swimming pools, each with hot tub. Main pool has short slide, kiddie pool. Arcade. Bicycle, surrey rentals. Basketball, shuffleboard, volleyball courts; 2 lighted tennis courts. DVD rentals. Lake Buena Vista 18-hole golf course. Guided fishing trips. Fitness center. 2 playgrounds. Full-service spa. 2 walking trails. **Children's programs** Complimentary activities at pool, Community Center, including arts and crafts, ice-cream-making. **Other amenities** Laundromat, laundry services. Shop sells groceries. **Complimentary transportation** Boats: Downtown Disney, Port Orleans French Quarter, Port Orleans Riverside, Old Key West. Buses: Disney theme parks, water parks, Downtown Disney. Internal shuttle bus. Internal shuttle carries Treehouse Villas guests to bus stops in either The Springs or The Grandstand parking lots. **Check In** 4p. **Check Out** 11a. **Telephone** 407-827-1100. Fax 407-827-1151. **Address** 1960 Broadway, 32830.

**Unlike Disney's many** child-focused resorts, Saratoga Springs caters to adults. The spacious, equestrian-themed condo complex includes an 18-hole golf course, clubhouse restaurant with a pool table and bar and a full-service spa. Though actually quite spread out, the resort has many small gathering spots that give it a cozy feel.

Children have plenty to keep them occupied, of course. The main swimming pool has a short, dark slide and an interactive fountain. A water play area has hand-held squirters that look like stick ponies. A Community Hall features children's activities each day, including bingo, board games and arts and crafts projects. At night, the resort often shows complimentary Disney movies.

Lodging buildings cluster into five sections that horseshoe around a recreation center. **Timeshare villas** (Studios 365 sq ft. Sleep 4. 1-bedroom 714 sq ft. Sleep 4. 2-bedroom 1,075 sq ft. Sleep 8. 3-bedroom 2,113 sq ft. Sleep 9–12. All units furnished with table and chairs, kitchen facilities. Internet service optional. Accessed by outdoor walkways) feature large, masculine furniture. Larger units have whirlpool tubs.

The property sits on the grounds of the former Disney Institute.

A thematically unrelated **Treehouse Villas** area opened in 2009. Nestled into a separate wooded area, 60 stand-alone octagons

**Top:** Spacious grounds and nice landscaping lend a relaxed feel to the Saratoga Springs resort.

(Sleep 9. 3 bedrooms, 2 bath. Cathedral ceilings, granite countertops, flat-screen TV) are elevated 10 feet off the ground.

Although Saratoga Springs is a Disney Vacation Club timeshare property, nightly rentals are often available.

The main **swimming pool** has a 126-foot slide between cascading waterfalls, an interactive fountain area and a "zero-entry" gradual ramp. It often shows Disney movies at night; guests float while they watch. Nearby is a kiddie pool, playground and two hot tubs. Three **quiet pools** are scattered in the lodging areas, each with a hot tub and barbecue area.

The **Saratoga Springs Spa** (407-827-4455) offers facials, manicures, massages, pedicures and many relaxing treatments. Its French whirlpool has 72 jets. Complimentary **children's and family activities** at the Community Hall include arts and crafts, pool parties and sandcastle building. The Hall also has board games, DVD rentals, table tennis and a large-screen TV.

## Dining

**Turf Club Bar and Grill** ★ ★ ★ ★ ✓ **American** $$$ L: $10–$19, Noon–5p. D: $12–$29, 5–9p. Seats 146, inc. 52 outside. *DP* Great food at decent prices makes this cozy country-club retreat worth seeking out. Lunch attracts golfers; the restaurant sits above the pro shop of the Lake Buena Vista course. Dinner has steaks that are worth the money. The waiting area includes a walk-up bar, (B pastries, coffee. Comp. board games), large-screen TV and a billiards table. An outdoor balcony overlooks the golf course, a small lake and Downtown Disney.
**The Artist's Palette Food court** B: 7–11a. L,D: 11a–11p. Seats 112. Menu includes flatbreads for all meals. Nice dining area has padded booths, drawing easels for children. Store has fruit, snacks. *DPQ*
**Room service** None. Opt. grocery delivery service.

**Fun find** Frames of Disney horse stars line the wall of an alcove adjacent to the registration area.

**Hidden Mickey** As a white design at the bottom of the signs outside of the spa.

▶ **Average guest ratings** (0–5): Expedia 4.4. Hotels.com 4.6. Orbitz 4.8. TripAdvisor 4.3. Travelocity 4.1.

**Top to bottom:** Elevated 10 feet off the ground, Disney's Treehouse Villas blend into their pine environment. Octagon-shaped interiors are decorated in a "cabin casual" style. Saratoga Springs' three-bedroom Grand Villas feature two-story living rooms.

# Disney's Wilderness Lodge Resort

★★★★★ ✔ $$$$ **Rack Rates** Rooms: $240–$815, suites $850–$1455, villas $330–$1205. **Location** NW corner of Disney property, SE of Magic Kingdom. **Distance to** Magic Kingdom: 1 mi. Epcot: 3 mi. Hollywood Studios: 4 mi. Animal Kingdom: 6 mi. Blizzard Beach: 5 mi. Typhoon Lagoon: 5 mi. Downtown Disney: 5 mi. Wide World of Sports: 7 mi. **Size** 701 rooms, 27 suites, 136 villas, 65 acres. **Built** 1994. **Last renovation** 2006. **Restaurants** Three. Snack bar, lounge. **Recreation** Two swimming pools, 3 hot tubs. Main pool has slide. Kiddie pool. Arcade. Beach. Bicycle, surrey rentals. Guided fishing trips. Fitness center. Lobby tour. **Children's programs** Organized child-care center activities (2:30–4p, free). Campfire, movie at night. Villas: Community Center activities, board games, DVD rentals. **Other amenities** Child-care center, laundromat, laundry service. Shop. Meeting room. **Complimentary transportation** Boats: Magic Kingdom; Contemporary, Fort Wilderness resorts. Buses: Theme parks, water parks, Downtown Disney. **Check In** 3p (Villas 4p). **Check Out** 11a. **Telephone** Lodge: 407-824-3200, Villas: 407-938-4300. **Fax** 407-824-3232. **Address** 901 Timberland Dr, 32830.

**Do the words "rustic" and "woodsy"** appeal to you? If so, you'll appreciate Wilderness Lodge. Isolated yet convenient, a child favorite yet romantic, this Disney Deluxe resort recalls the Lincoln-Log retreats of the American West, in particular the Old Faithful Inn at Yellowstone National Park.

Nestled in a forest along the shores of 450-acre Bay Lake, the four-building complex consists of a central eight-story lodge and three guest wings, one of which is a Disney Vacation Club timeshare property.

A towering lobby atrium is dominated by four 60-foot bundled log columns which appear to support a wood truss.

**Standard rooms** (344 sq ft. Sleep 4. 2 queen beds with 1 king optional, small refrigerator, daybed, flat-screen TV, PC, Internet service optional. Balcony or patio. Club level.) and **suites** (Sleep 4) are decorated with Native American and wildlife motifs. A five-story wing houses **timeshare villas** (studio, 1- and 2-bedroom units sleep 4–8) that are often available for nightly rentals.

Portrayed as part of a mountain stream, a large **swimming pool** features a curving slide that sprays riders with mist. Nearby are two hot tubs (1 hot, 1 cold), a kiddie pool, and a geyser that erupts hourly. The Villas area has a smaller **quiet pool** with four bubbling "springs" and a 15-person whirlpool. A wooded .75-mile **walking trail** leads to Fort Wilderness. Guests can learn the history and architecture of the resort on the **Wonders of the Lodge** tour (select days, 9a).

Cast members hold complimentary children's and family **craft activities** from

**Top:** The main swimming area at Wilderness Lodge.

**Clockwise from top left:** A simulated hot spring in the Wilderness Lodge lobby creates a stream that flows outside, over a waterfall and eventually, it appears, into the swimming pool. The lobby is highlighted by a three-sided stone fireplace, the layers of which illustrate the geological history of the Grand Canyon. Standard guest rooms at Wilderness Lodge have a Northwestern style, with padded headboards topped with carved upper panels.

2:30–4 p.m. at the Cub's Den child-care center. Disney's **Electrical Water Pageant** passes the resort nightly at 9:35 p.m.

# Dining

**Artist Point** ★ ★ ★ ★ ✔ Pacific Northwest $$$$ D: $20–$43, 5:30–9:30p. Seats 225. *DP2 Disney Signature* This pretension-free dining room serves creative offerings that never get too trendy. Entrees are seriously Northwestern, but so well-prepared that anyone will find something to love. The L-shaped dining room mixes landscape murals with blond and cherry woods. Chairs are upholstered. Washington State, Oregon wines.

**Whispering Canyon Cafe** ★ ★ ★ ★ ✔ American barbecue $$$ B: $10–$15, 7:30–11:30a. L: $12–$18, 11:30a–2:30p. D: $17–$27, 5–10p. Seats 281. *DP* All-you-can-eat skillets are a specialty at this rowdy family favorite. During busy times staff hijinks become a free floor show. When my husband once scarfed one of our daughter's french fries, our cowgirl server yelled "Everyone! Repeat after me: 'Hey dad! Eat your own stinkin' food!'"

**Roaring Fork Snacks Fast food.** B: 6–11a. L,D: 11–mid. Seats 250. Grill, pizza, salads, sandwiches. *DPQ*

**Territory Lounge** 4:30–mid.; micro-brewed beers, Pacific Northwest wine. Appetizers. At Artist Point.
**Room service** 7–11a; 4p–mid. *DP2*

**Fun finds ❶** In the lobby is a convincing illusion of a bubbling hot spring. Water from it streams under a window wall to become an outdoor geothermal area, spills over a 15-foot waterfall and appears to flow into the swimming pool. ❷ The fourth-floor indoor balcony has cozy sitting areas and front and back porches. The fifth floor has a small back balcony. ❸ Hoofprints are embedded into sidewalks. Buffalo prints lead to the front lawn's buffalo topiaries. Raccoon prints are scattered in front of the pool bar.

**Hidden Mickeys ❶** As three stones above and to the right of the lobby fireplace. ❷ Behind the main building, as lumps of earth about a third of the way up a stream that flows from the geyser by the pool. ❸ As nuts in a small bulletin board at the entrance to Roaring Fork Snacks. ❹ As dents in the wood on a beam to the right of the exit to the Boat and Bike Rental. ❺ As dents in the wood on the second closest post to room 4035 and ❻ on the post closest to room 5066.

▶ **Average guest ratings** (0–5): Expedia 4.5. Hotels.com 4.6. Orbitz 3.9. TripAdvisor 4.3. Travelocity 4.2.

# Disney's Yacht and Beach Club Resort

★★★★★ ✓ $$$$$ **Rack rates** Rooms $340–$815, suites $580–$2610, villas $340–$1210. **Location** Centrally located at WDW, next to Epcot. **Distance to Magic Kingdom:** 5 mi. Epcot (by car): 4 mi. Hollywood Studios: 2 mi. Animal Kingdom: 5 mi. Blizzard Beach: 3 mi. Typhoon Lagoon: 3 mi. Downtown Disney: 3 mi. Wide World of Sports: 5 mi. **Size** 1,197 rooms, 112 suites, 208 villas, 30 acres. **Built** 1990. **Last renovation** 2003. **Restaurants** Five. Character meal, steakhouse, soda shop. **Recreation** 3-acre swimming complex. Arcade. Boat rentals. Boat rides. Guided fishing trips. Beach volleyball, croquet, tennis courts. Walking trail. **Children's programs** Pontoon-boat adventure. Complimentary activities at pool, Community Center. **Business amenities** Conference, business centers. **Other amenities** Child-care center, laundromat, laundry service, hair salon, massage services. Shops. **Complimentary transportation** Boats: Epcot, Hollywood Studios. Buses: Magic Kingdom, Animal Kingdom, water parks, Downtown Disney. **Check In** 3p. **Check Out** 11a. **Telephone** Beach Club: 407-934-8000. Villas: 407-934-2175. Yacht Club: 407-934-7000. **Fax** Beach Club: 407-934-3850. Yacht Club: 407-934-3450. **Address** Beach Club: 1800 Epcot Resorts Blvd. Yacht Club: 1700 Epcot Resorts Blvd, 32830.

**Families will have a ball** at the sister resorts of the Yacht and Beach Club. The Disney Deluxe complex's kid-friendly benefits include an uncrowded character meal, a soda shop that offers what might be the world's largest ice cream sundae and Disney World's best swimming complex.

The resorts are adjacent to Epcot via that theme park's back-entrance walkway. The Beach Club is literally next door.

Five-story, nautical-themed compounds with clapboard trim, both resorts evoke the look of 1870s summer homes on Martha's Vineyard and Nantucket. Inside, the stately Yacht Club is trimmed with statues, gold-fringed drapes and a red-white-and-blue carpet that seems straight from the The Hall of Presidents. The Beach Club, by contrast, is cool and relaxed. Its interior looks like the cover of a Coastal Living magazine.

The two resorts' only flaw: Breakfast. The Yacht Club's buffet is uninspired, and the Beach Club character buffet grows old after a visit or two. A good alternative is Kouzzina, at the nearby BoardWalk Resort.

Refurbished in 2009, **standard rooms** (381 sq ft. Sleep 5. 2 queen beds, small refrigerator, some daybeds. Internet service optional. Club level.) have nautical motifs, with ceiling fans and white furniture. **Suites** (sleep 4–8) share the theme, as do Beach Club **timeshare villas** (studio, 1-, 2- and 3-bedroom units sleep 4–8).

The best **swimming area** at any Disney World resort, Stormalong Bay is a miniature

**Top:** The rear lawn of the Yacht Club.

water park. Situated between the Yacht and Beach Clubs, it includes a meandering central pool, lazy river, shallow inlet with a real sandbar, a shady hot tub and an assortment of fountains, waterfalls and bridges. A spiral staircase on a life-sized simulated shipwreck leads to a 300-foot slide. Starting off in a dark tunnel (the inside of a fallen mast) it plummets into daylight at a rocky outcropping. Riders get showered by two waterfalls before splashing into the central pool. A kiddie pool with overhead sprinklers has an adjacent sandy play spot, while back on the pirate ship is a second kiddie pool with its own tiny slide. Designed so it appears to flow into the lake behind it, the 3-acre complex is themed to be a Nantucket lagoon. It continuously filters 750,000 gallons of water.

The Yacht Club marina offers rides in the **Breathless II** (30-min ride $95 per group. 90-min IllumiNations cruise $275. Ages 3 and up, 407-WDW-PLAY), a 26-foot Hacker Craft inboard that's a replica of a 1930s mahogany Chris-Craft. For children, the **Albatross Treasure Cruise** ($34 inc lunch, 2 hrs, ages 4–12, 407-WDW-PLAY) pontoon-boat scavenger hunt travels to the Swan and Dolphin and BoardWalk resorts and Epcot's Canada and Mexico pavilions. The resort has a small **conference center** (73,000 sq ft, 2 ballrooms, 21 breakout rooms, banquet space for 3,000).

Epcot's **IllumiNations** fireworks are visible nightly at 9 p.m.

## Dining

**Beaches & Cream** ★★★★ ✔ Soda shop $$ L,D: $6–$22, 11a–11p. Take-out counter. Seats 48. *DP* Next to Stormalong Bay. Gigantic sundaes are the draw at this tiny spot (three booths, six small tables) which also serves good burgers and sandwiches. The claim-to-fame is the ridiculous Kitchen Sink sundae that's served, literally, in a kitchen sink. A tin ceiling has a tray center with elaborate moldings.

**Cape May Cafe** ★★★★ ✔ Character breakfast buffet $$$ Goofy, Minnie Mouse, Donald Duck. B ("Goofy's Beach Club Breakfast"): $20 (children $12), 7:30-11a. ★★★★ Dinner buffet $$$$ D: $27 (children $13), 5:30–9:30p. Seats 235. Beach Club. *DP* The only Disney-operated character meal not in a theme park or on the monorail loop, this breakfast buffet is calm and relaxed. Small parties can often get in without a reservation. Children are a mix of ages. Narrow aisles continually

**Top to bottom:** The Yacht and Beach Club sit next to Epcot. The view from the Yacht Club dock. The Stormalong Bay lazy river. A Wurlitzer juke box at the Beaches and Cream soda shop. A standard Yacht Club guest room.

put characters right up next to your table. Five buffet lines are well tended. Background music is a mix of Disney and beach tunes. Listen closely and you'll hear Annette Funicello's 1965 duet with the Beach Boys, "The Monkey's Uncle." Though billed as a clambake, the dinner buffet devotes less than 10 percent of its buffet line to clams, mussels, corn-on-the-cob and potatoes. The standout item is a carved-to-order top sirloin. Subdued lighting and background music with sounds of sea gulls make it a nice place to recover at the end of a day.

**Captain's Grille** ★ ★ ★ American $$$$ B: $9–$16, 7–11a. L: $10–$18, 11:30a–2p. D: $15–$28, 5:30–9:30p. Seats 280. Yacht Club. *DP* Captain's Grille serves fine food in a setting so generic you'll hardly know you're at Disney. Breakfast is a heat-lamp buffet. Lunch offers salads and sandwiches; dinner steaks, chicken, fish, seafood.

**Yachtsman Steakhouse** ★ ★ ★ ★ ★ ✓ Steaks $$$$$ D: $27–$44, 5:30–10p. Seats 286. Yacht Club. *DP2* **Disney Signature** This white-tablecloth restaurant serves the same top cuts found in any fine steakhouse, but here they're more than just plated pieces of meat. The New York strip is brushed in a peppercorn brandy sauce. Prime rib comes with a savory bread pudding. Custom cuts of meat are available. Half of the restaurant is on a wood floor, the other half is carpeted.

**Beach Club Marketplace Fast food.** B: 7–11a. L,D: 11a–10p. Seats 16 outside. Pastries, salads, sandwiches, soups. Sm. food store sells fruit, snacks. *DPQ*

**Ale and Compass Lounge** 5p–2a. B: pastries, coffee. Yacht Club lobby.

**Crew's Cup Lounge** 12p–mid. Yachtsman Steakhouse.

**Martha's Vineyard** 5p–mid. Lounge. At Cape May Cafe.

**Room service** 24 hr. *DP2*

**Hidden Mickeys** ❶ In the entrance hall to the Solarium, as wheels of trunk-mounted tires of the far left yellow car and ❷ the far right blue car in the first painting to the left (Mickey faces). ❸ In that same painting, as the hood ornament on the right red car and right blue car. ❹ As a cloud in the second painting to the left (a detailed face). ❺ As a red balloon held by a girl at the right of the third painting on the left wall. ❻ As a yellow balloon held by the girl next to her.

▶ Average guest ratings (0–5): Expedia 4.5. Hotels.com 4.1. Orbitz 4.7. TripAdvisor 4.1. Travelocity

**At the Beach Club, top to bottom:** Beach chairs on the white sand lakefront beach. A sand volleyball court near a lodging building. A hot tub near a quiet pool. The kitchen of a Beach Club Villa. A standard Beach Club guest room.

# Non-Disney resorts

**Walt Disney World Swan and Dolphin**
★ ★ ★ ★ $$$$ $279–$555, suites $785–$3500. Location: Centrally located on Disney property, just north of Disney's Hollywood Studios. 2,265 rooms, 191 suites, 87 acres. Check In: 3p. Check Out: 11a. Swan: 407-934-4499, fax 407-934-4710, 1300 Epcot Resorts Blvd, 32830. Dolphin: 407-934-4000, fax 407-934-4884, 1500 Epcot Resorts Blvd, 32830. Self-parking $9 per day; valet parking $12 per day, $16 overnight.

These adjacent convention resorts are the signature properties of Starwood Hotels, a company that includes the Sheraton and Westin chains. In fact, more Starwood Preferred Guests use their points to stay at these two hotels than at any of the other 925 Starwood properties in 95 countries worldwide. The Swan is quiet and intimate. The Dolphin, with twice as many rooms and a large convention center, is boisterous and impersonal.

Designed by Michael Graves—perhaps best known for his line of housewares sold at Target stores—the Swan and Dolphin feature playful "entertainment" architecture with details such as enormous statues and fountains. The tallest structure at Walt Disney World, the Dolphin's 27-story-tall triangular tower sits between two wings topped with 20-foot tulip fountains and 56-foot statues of dolphinfish, or mahi mahi. In back, a nine-story waterfall cascades down giant clamshells. The 12-story Swan has two seven-story wings crowned with 47-foot swan statues. Its wings have 20-foot clamshell spouts. The buildings are connected by a palm-lined promenade that splits a lagoon.

Seen together, abstract designs on the buildings define the Dolphin as a tropical mountain surrounded by huge banana palms. Its waterfall splashes into the lagoon and onto the Swan, a huge sand dune.

**Rooms** Standard rooms (360 sq ft. Sleep 5. Dolphin rooms have 2 double beds, Swan 2 queens. Flat-panel TV, desk. Internet optional. Club level.) feature pale woods, muted floral carpeting and pastel drapes. Maple bureaus have frosted glass accents. "Heavenly" beds have pillow-top mattresses, white goose-down comforters. Rooms are especially well-lit. Suites sleep 5–10.
**Swimming pools** An elaborate swimming area (5 pools, 5 hot tubs, kiddie pool) arcs between the resorts. A meandering Grotto pool has a waterfall and a decent slide. Tiny waterfalls splash near a volleyball net that extends over a narrow area. During the summer, the pool shows a Disney movie every Saturday night, and hands out tubes for guests to float on as they watch it. The area also includes a spring pool, kiddie pool and two lap pools. A circus-themed beach area has two volleyball nets, a basketball court and a boat-like playground piece

**From top:** The Walt Disney World Swan, a standard Swan guest room, The Walt Disney World Dolphin, a standard Dolphin guest room, convention space at the Dolphin.

with covered slides. Children will enjoy finding the statue of a seal that sprays water out of its nose.

**Sports and Recreation** Basketball courts, beach, beach volleyball, pedal-boat rentals, full-service spa, 4 tennis courts. Disney's Fantasia Gardens miniature golf across street. Dolphin's Asian-inspired Mandara Spa specializes in Balinese massage and includes a hair and nail salon.

**Convention center** 254,000 sq-ft convention/exhibit space includes 4 ballrooms, 84 breakout rooms, 9,600 sq-ft ballroom. Business center. Disney's largest.

**Other amenities** Two arcades, child-care center, 2 fitness centers, hair salon, laundromat, laundry service, massage services, playground. Shops at the Dolphin include an art gallery, candy store.

**Distance to Disney theme parks** Magic Kingdom: 4 mi. Epcot: 3 mi. Hollywood Studios: 2 mi. Animal Kingdom: 4 mi. Blizzard Beach: 2 mi. Typhoon Lagoon: 2 mi. Downtown Disney: 3 mi. Wide World of Sports: 4 mi.

**Complimentary Disney transportation** Boats: Epcot, Hollywood Studios. Buses: Magic Kingdom, Animal Kingdom, water parks, Downtown Disney.

### DINING

**Fresh Mediterranean Market** ★ ★ ★ American/Mediterranean. B: $18 A, $11 C, 7:30–11a. L: $12–$24, 11a–3p. Seats 264. Dolphin. A breakfast buffet has a good fresh juice bar (try the Wheatgrass), roasted meats, griddle items, pastries and hot cereals. Lunch is a la carte, with Mediterranean salads, sandwiches, chicken, fish and pasta. The back verandah is a peaceful dining spot.

**Garden Grove Cafe** ★ American/Character meal. B weekdays: $17 A, $11 C, 6:30–11a. B weekends with characters: $19 A, $12 C, 6:30–11a (characters arrive 8a; Sat Goofy, Pluto; Sun also Chip 'n Dale). L: $11–$18, 11a–3p. D with characters: $29 A, $13 C, 5:30–10p (characters leave at 8:30p; Rafiki, Timon Mon, Fri; Goofy, Pluto other nights). Seats 150. Swan. Though it is pretty, this circular dining room is the worst table-service restaurant on Disney property. Many items leave an aftertaste.

**Il Mulino New York Trattoria** ★ ★ ★ ★ Italian. D: $16–$45, 5–10p. Seats 224. Swan. A variety of Abruzzi entrees are highlighted by creamy risottos and good seafood. Unlike the New York original, this Il Mulino has a relaxing atmosphere and attentive service. Lounge.

**Kimonos** ★ ★ ★ ★ ✓ Sushi bar. $5–$16, 5p–mid. Seats 105. Swan. More bar than restaurant, this friendly little spot combines karaoke sing-a-longs with sake, wine, beer and over 50 sushi creations. Red-bean, green-tea ice cream. Additional options for children.

**Shula's Steak House** ★ ★ Steakhouse. D: $24–$85, 5–10p. $10 split-plate charge. No child's menu. Seats 215. Direct reservations 407-934-1362. Dolphin. Big steaks for big bucks. Steaks are not at the level of the less expensive Yachtsman Steakhouse next door at Disney's Yacht Club Resort. The clubby decor commemorates Shula's 1972 undefeated season as coach of the Miami Dolphins. Young babes in a short black dresses greet you, and try to sell you an autographed Don Shula football for $295. Nice lounge with full menu.

**Todd English's bluezoo** ★ ★ ★ ★ Seafood. D: $27–$60, 5–10p. Seats 400. Dolphin. This high-style nightspot is all about the show. Designed to look as if it's underwater, a beautiful dining room has glass "bubbles" hanging overhead, animated ambient blue lights and throbbing techno music. Buried under it all is a coastal cuisine that suffers from a style-over-substance mindset. Good appetizers, predictable desserts. Lounge.

**Cabana Bar and Beach Club** Daytime grill, nighttime bar. Dolphin. Featuring an illuminated bar, this sophisticated spot next to the lap pool offers everything from seared tuna to hot dogs. Exotic woods and billowing wall coverings frame intimate seating areas.

**The Fountain** Soda shop. L,D: $7–$15, 11a–11p. Seats 58. Dolphin. Slow service. Uninspired menu.

**Picabu** ✓ Cafeteria. B: $4–$11. 6:30–11a (noon Sun). L,D: $7–$18. 11p–1:30a. 24 hrs. Seats 140. Dolphin. Hidden behind Fresh Mediterranean Market, this nice spot serves honest food in a clean, comfortable atmosphere that's surprisingly artistic. Back walls portray a trail of tail feathers left by a bird who flew down from the ceiling.

**Lobby Lounge** Full bar. AM coffee, pastries. Dolphin.

**Room service** 24 hours.

**Shades of Green** ★ ★ ★ ★ $ Exclusively for use by active, retired members of U.S. military, accompanying families, friends. Rates based on rank. This relaxed resort is the only Armed Forces Recreation Center in the continental United States. Comparable in scope to a Disney Deluxe Resort, it has large rooms, full-service restaurants and a great location, though it lacks Disney's signature themed architecture or decor. Not far from Magic Kingdom, Shades of Green sits directly across from the Polynesian Resort and next to Disney's Palm, Magnolia and Oak Trail golf courses. Each year an estimated 750,000 military guests stay here.

**Rooms** (455 sq ft. Sleep 5. 2 queen beds; 1 king optional. Daybed, small refrigerator, balcony or patio. Internet optional. Light oak woods.) are the best bargains at Disney. Rates are adjusted on a sliding scale; prices increase with rank and pay grade. Eligible guests and dependent spouses can each "sponsor" up to three rooms at a time, which allows nonmilitary friends and family members to stay here, too. Suites sleep 6–8.

The resort's ticket office (8a–9p) offers discounted Disney park tickets to eligible military members, including those who don't stay at Shades of Green. A special $55 golf rate is available for tee times after 10 a.m. that are booked at least 24 hours in advance.

Originally, Shades of Green was the Disney Golf Resort, a country club with no guest rooms. In 1993 Disney added a lodging area and renamed it the Disney Inn. In 1996 Disney sold the complex to the government, which enlarged it in 2004. In 2009 the Raytheon Co. donated a Family Technology Center game room with couches, computers, plasma TVs and Nintendo Wii and Microsoft Xbox game systems. The resort's name refers to the fact that, regardless of branch, all U.S. military standard uniforms include some shade of green.

# Downtown Disney area

Located near the Downtown Disney shopping and entertainment complex at the far eastern end of Walt Disney World, these hotels are run by outside companies. Though they lack the ambience of the Disney properties they offer better rack rates, and most often have rooms available when the Disney resorts are full. A complimentary shuttle service stops at each resort then heads to the Disney theme parks. Developed in the 1970s as Disney's Hotel Plaza, the area was extensively renovated after the 2004 hurricane season.

**Best Western Lake Buena Vista** $$ **$89–$111, suites $199–$210.** $9/night resort fee added. 321 rooms, 4 suites, 18 stories, 12 acres. Rooms, suites: sleep 4–5, 2 queen beds (1 king opt), balconies or patios. Wireless Internet. Cherry-walnut furniture, granite counter tops, Italian tile bathrooms. Amenities: Two restaurants, snack bar, Pizza Hut Express. Swimming pool, kiddie pool. Arcade, child-care service, fitness center, playground, tennis courts. Business center, car-rental counter, cyber cafe, laundromat. Garden gazebo. Check in 3p. Check out 11a. Valet parking $10/day. Lakefront. 407-828-2424; fax 407-827-6390. 2000 Hotel Plaza Blvd, 32830.

**Buena Vista Palace** $$ **$179–$344, suites $249–$1515.** 890 rooms, 124 suites, 27 stories, 27 acres. Rooms: sleep 4, 2 queen beds (1 king opt), balconies or patios. Refrigerator, wireless Internet. Suites sleep 4–8. 32-inch HD TV, ergonomic Herman Miller chairs. Amenities: Two restaurants including Disney character breakfast on Sundays, mini-mart. Three swimming pools (one partially covered), hot tub. Arcade; fitness center; playground; spa (407-827-3200); sauna; basketball, tennis, volleyball courts. Business center, car-rental counter, concierge, convention center, cyber cafe, laundromat, laundry services, salon. Check in 4p. Check out 11a. 407-827-2727. Fax: 407-827-3136. 1900 Buena Vista Dr, 32830.

**Doubletree Guest Suites** $$ **Suites $125–$424.** 229 suites, 7 stories, 7 acres. Suites: Sleep 6. 1 or 2 bedrooms. Sweet Dreams bedding. Microwave; refrigerator; 2 flat-screen TVs, B&W bathroom TV-radio. Wireless Internet. No balconies, though ground floor suites have patios. Amenities: One restaurant, mini-mart. Swimming pool, kiddie pool, hot tub. Fitness center, playground, pool table, tennis courts. Business center, car-rental counter, child-care service, laundromat, laundry services, meeting rooms. Check in: 4p Check out: 11a. Parking: $8/day; valet $16/day. The only all-suite hotel on Disney property. Chocolate chip cookies freshly baked throughout day. Renovated in 2006, 2007. A Florida Green Lodging hotel. 407-934-1000. Fax: 407-934-1015. 2305 Hotel Plaza Blvd, 32830.

**Hilton** $$ **$129–$239, suites $219–$319.** 704 rooms, 110 suites, 10 stories, 23 acres. Rooms: sleep 4, 2 double beds

**From top:** Downtown Disney hotels Best Western Lake Buena Vista, Buena Vista Palace, Doubletree Guest Suites, Regal Sun, Royal Plaza

(1 king opt), flat-screen TV, mini-bar, MP3 clock-radio. Wireless Internet opt. Suites sleep 4–6. Club level. Amenities: Seven restaurants including Benihana; Disney character breakfast buffet Sun (no reservations); mini-mart. Two swimming pools, kiddie pool with spray area. Arcade, fitness center, golf pro shop, pool table. Business center, car-rental counter, child-care services, concierge, cyber cafe, laundromat, salon. Check in 3p. Check out 11a. Parking: $10/day; valet $16/day. Most upscale Downtown Disney hotel; only one that offers Disney's Extra Magic Hours benefit. Renovated in 2008. A Florida Green Lodging hotel. 407-827-4000. Fax: 407-827-3890. 1751 Hotel Plaza Blvd, 32830.

**Holiday Inn** $–$$ **$79–$119.** 323 rooms, 14 stories, 10 acres. Rooms: sleep 4–5, 2 queen beds, sleeper sofa, 32-inch HDTV, pillow-top mattresses, refrigerator, work desk. Wireless, wired Internet service. Amenities: Restaurant, Kids Eat Free program (2–12 yrs). "Zero-entry" swimming pool with whirlpool. Business center, concierge, health club, laundromat, meeting rooms. Check in: 3p. Check out: 11a. Promoted to open in Feb. 2010 as this book went to press; the Holiday Inn has announced, then delayed, its rebirth every year since it was severely damaged by Hurricane Charley in 2004. Its makeover cost $25 million. 407-828-8888. Fax: 407-827-4623. 1805 Hotel Plaza Blvd, 32830.

**Regal Sun** $–$$ **$71–$127, suites $399–$487.** $15/night resort fee added. 619 rooms, 7 suites, 19 stories, 13 acres. Rooms: sleep 4, 2 queen beds (1 king opt), flat-screen TV, MP3 clock-radio, wireless Internet. Suites sleep 4–6. Amenities: Restaurant; English pub; Disney character breakfast Tue, Thur, Sat. Two swimming pools, kiddie pool, water playground for children. Fitness center; playground; basketball, shuffleboard, tennis, volleyball courts. Business center, car-rental counter, currency exchange, laundromat, laundry services, meeting rooms. Check in: 3p. Check out: 11a. Valet parking $15/day. Renovated in 2007. A Florida Green Lodging hotel. A favorite of British guests. Formerly The Grosvenor. 407-828-4444. Fax: 407-828-8192. 1850 Hotel Plaza Blvd, 32830.

**Royal Plaza** $$$ **$149–$199, suites $209–$219.** $8/night resort fee added. 394 rooms, 17 stories, 23 acres. Rooms: sleep 5, 2 double beds (1 king opt) with pillowtop mattresses, sleeper sofa, wireless Internet. Some kitchenettes, wet bars, whirlpool tubs. Suites sleep 4–5. Standard rooms are largest of any Downtown Disney hotel. Garden and (larger) tower rooms are available. Amenities: Restaurant (children 10 and under eat dinner free with paying adult at Giraffe Cafe), mini-mart. Swimming pool. Arcade, fitness center, tennis courts. Business center, laundromat, meeting rooms. Check in: 4p. Check out: 11a. Parking: $8/day, valet $16/day. A Florida Green Lodging hotel. 407-828-2828. Fax: 407-827-6338. 1905 Hotel Plaza Blvd, 32830.

**From top:** The Downtown Disney Hilton; sketches for the Holiday Inn entrance and atrium, a prototype Holiday Inn guest room

# Hotels within 10 miles

The following hotels are outside of Walt Disney World but within 10 miles of the property:

**Buena Vista Suites** ★ ★ ★ $$ **World Center Dr:** Restaurant. Free b'fast buffet. 8203 World Center Dr, 32821. 800-537-7737. Free WDW shuttle. WDW 2 mi.

**Caribe Royale All-Suite Resort** ★ ★ ★ ★ $$$ **World Center Dr:** Three-story atrium dotted with palms, floor-to-ceiling windows. Suites: Sleep 5–8. 2 queen beds (1 king opt), sleeper sofa, kitchen. Wireless Internet opt. Each suite has 2 flat-screen TVs; villas have 3. Lakeside 2-bedroom suites have screened patios, whirlpool tubs in master. Amenities: Arcades; business center; car-rental counter; concierge; lighted basketball, tennis courts; fitness center; laundromat; laundry services; massage services; 250,000-gal swimming pool w/ waterfalls, 75-ft slide; villas have own pool. Kiddie pool. Dining: 4 restaurants, 3 lounges. 150,000 sq ft meeting space. Many packages. Renovated 2009. A Fla. Green Lodging hotel. 8101 World Center Dr, 32821. 800-823-8300. Free shuttle. WDW 2 mi.

**Celebration Hotel** ★ ★ ★ ★ $$$ **Celebration:** Restaurants. 700 Bloom St, 34747. 888-499-3800. Free shuttle. WDW 4 mi.

**Comfort Inn** ★ ★ ★ $ Restaurant, Kids Eat Free program. Playground. Some suites. **Int'l. Dr. area:** 8134 Int'l. Dr, 32819. 407-313-4000. Shuttle $8 roundtrip. WDW 8 mi. **Lake Buena Vista:** 8442 Palm Parkway, 32836. 800-999-7300. Free shuttle. WDW 1 mi. **Universal Studios area:** 6101 Sand Lake Rd, 32819. 407-363-7886. Free shuttle. WDW 9 mi.

**Country Inn & Suites** ★ ★ ★ $ Kitchenettes. Free cont. b'fast. **Lake Buena Vista:** 12191 S. Apopka-Vineland Rd, 32830. 407-239-1115. Free shuttle. WDW 1 mi. **Int'l. Dr. area:** 7701 Universal Blvd, 32819. 407-313-4200. Free shuttle. WDW 8 mi. **U.S. 192 area:** 5001 Calypso Cay Way, 34746. 407-997-1400. Pet fee. Free shuttle. WDW 5 mi.

**Courtyard By Marriott** ★ ★ ★ $ Breakfast restaurant. **Lake Buena Vista:** 8501 Palm Pkwy, 32836. 407-239-6900. Free shuttle to outlet mall, WDW. WDW 1 mi. **Little Lake Bryan area:** 8623 Vineland Ave (Marriott Village), 32821. 877-682-8552. Shuttle $5 roundtrip. WDW 1 mi.

**Embassy Suites** ★ ★ ★ $$ 2-room suites with 2 TVs, refrigerator, microwave, work table. Restaurant(s). Free cooked-to-order breakfast. Evening Mgrs Reception. Business services. **Int'l. Dr:** 8978 Int'l. Dr, 32819. 407-352-1400. Free shuttle. WDW 5 mi. Also: 8250 Jamaican Ct, 32819. 407-345-8250. WDW 6 mi. **Lake Buena Vista:** 8100 Lake Ave, 32836. 407-239-1144. Free shuttle. WDW 3 mi.

**Floridays Orlando** ★ ★ ★ ★ $$$ **SeaWorld area:** All suites. Restaurant, kitchens, balconies. 2-person

**Water, water everywhere.** From top: Swimming areas at the Caribe Royale All-Suite Hotel and Gaylord Palms; a water bike behind the Hyatt Regency Grand Cypress.

jetted tubs. 12550 Floridays Resort Dr, 32821. 866-797-0022. Free shuttle to Epcot. WDW 3 mi.

**Gaylord Palms** ★★★★ $$$ **Adjacent to WDW:** $15/night resort fee. Opulent convention resort themed to signature Florida destinations such as Everglades, Key West and St. Augustine. Stunning glass-enclosed 5-acre atrium has alligators, koi, snakes, other live animals among lagoons and streams. Nightly live entertainment. Rooms: Sleep 4. 2 double or queen beds (1 king opt), refrigerator, stereo with CD player. Free wireless Internet. Suites: Sleep 4–8. Amenities: Arcade; business center; car-rental counter; concierge; convention center; bocce, croquet courts; fitness center; golf putting course; laundromat; laundry services; salon; sand volleyball court; adult swimming pool, kid's pool and water play area w/ squirting octopus; spa. Dining: 7 restaurants, including sushi bar. 400,000 sq ft of convention space. Parking: $12/day; valet $20/day. Many packages. A Fla. Green Lodging hotel. 6000 W. Osceola Pkwy, 34746. 407-586-0000. Free shuttle. WDW 1 mi.

**Grand Beach** ★★★ $$$ **Little Lake Bryan area:** 1- to 3-bedroom condos. Kitchens, lakefront, water sports. Whirlpool jet tubs. 8317 Lake Bryan Beach Blvd, 32821. 407-238-2500. WDW 2 mi.

**Hawthorn Suites** ★★★ $ **Lake Buena Vista:** Kitchens. Free breakfast. 8303 Palm Pkwy, 32836. 407-597-5000. Free shuttle to Epcot. WDW 1 mi.

**Hilton Garden Inn** ★★★ $$ Refrigerator, microwave. Garden Sleep System, HDTV. Restaurant. **SeaWorld area:** 6850 Westwood Blvd, 32821. 407-354-1500. WDW 4 mi. **Universal Studios area:** 5877 American Way, 32819. 407-363-9332. WDW 9 mi.

**Hilton Orlando Bonnet Creek** ★★★★ $$$$ **Adjacent to WDW:** Located between Disney's Caribbean Beach Resort and the Typhoon Lagoon water park on a strip of land surrounded by Disney property, this is the largest Hilton in mainland U.S. It opened in Nov. 2009. Sister hotel is adjacent Waldorf Astoria; shares amenities. A lagoon-style 2-acre pool has a zero-entry side. Rooms: Sleep 4. 2 queen beds (1 king opt), 42-inch flat-screen TV, MP3 clock radio. Wireless Internet opt. Suites: Sleep 4–6. Amenities: Arcade; complimentary bicycles; business cntr; child-care srvcs; children's programs; concierge; tennis, volleyball crts; fitness cntr; florist; golf course; jogging trails; laundromat; laundry srvcs; nature preserve; 2 swimming pools, water slide; spa. 122,000 sq ft of convention space. Dining: 6 restaurants, mini-mart. Parking: $13/day; valet $20/day. 14100 Bonnet Creek Resort Ln, 32831. 407-597-3600. WDW 1 mi.

**Homewood Suites** ★★★ $$ Studio, 1-, 2-bedroom suites. Kitchens, microwave, dishwasher. Free hot b'fast; light dinner, beverages Mon–Thur. Business services. **Int'l. Dr.:** 8745 Int'l. Dr, 32819. 407-248-2232. WDW 5 mi. Free shuttle. **Universal Studios area:** 5893 American Way, 32819. 407-226-0669. WDW 9 mi.

**Hyatt Regency Grand Cypress** ★★★★ $$$$ **Lake Buena Vista:** $18/night resort fee. Situated on 1,500 acres with a private 21-acre lake, this resort's extensive recreation facilities include four Jack Nicklaus signature golf courses: nine-hole North, nine-hole South, nine-hole East, and 18-hole New Course. Racquet club has 12 tennis courts (5 lighted), 2 racquetball courts and a basketball court. 800,000-gallon tropical pool features 2 slides, 12 waterfalls, suspension bridge. Trails for biking, hiking, horses. Rooms: Sleep 4. 2 dbl beds (1 king opt). balcony, minibar, clock radio with iPod dock. Wireless Internet opt. Suites: Sleep 6–8. Other amenities: Arcade; bike, boat, canoe, surrey rentals; business center; car-rental counter; child-care center; children's programs; concierge; convention center; equestrian center; fitness center; florist; Academy of Golf; laundromat; laundry services; massage services; salon; spa; water sports. Dining: 6 restaurants including sushi bar. Four lounges, nightly entertainment. 65,000 sq ft of meeting space. Renovated 2009. Valet parking $20/day. A Fla. Green Lodging hotel. One Grand Cypress Blvd, 32836. 407-239-1234. Free shuttle. WDW 1 mi.

**Marriott** ★★★★ $$$ **Lake Buena Vista:** Marriott Cypress Harbor: Pools, sauna, kitchens, washer/dryers, lake, water sports. 2 bed./2 ba. villas. 11251 Harbour Villa Rd, 32821. 800-845-5279. WDW 4 mi. **SeaWorld area:** Marriott Grande Vista: Lake, some kitchens and kitchenettes, sauna. 5925 Avenida Vista, 32821. 407-238-7676. WDW 5 mi. **World Center Dr. area:** Orlando World Center Marriott. Restaurants, pools (waterfalls, slides), spa, sauna, golf course, meeting rooms. 8701 World Center Dr, 32821. 800-228-9290. WDW 2 mi.

**JW Marriott Grande Lakes** ★★★★★ $$$$ **SeaWorld area:** Luxurious resort shares amenities, including Greg Norman-designed golf course, with adjacent sister hotel Ritz-Carlton Grande Lakes. Rooms: Sleep 4. 2 double beds (1 king opt), 32-inch flat-screen TV, minibar, some private balconies. Wireless Internet opt. Suites: Sleep 4. Amenities: Arcade; surrey bike rentals; business center; car-rental counter; life-size chess board; child-care services; children's programs; concierge; bocce ball, 3 lighted tennis, sand volleyball courts; eco-tours onsite; fitness center; fly-fishing school, fly-fishing onsite; golf course; jogging trails; laundromat; laundry services; meeting space; ropes course with zip line, giant swing; salon; swimming pool w/lazy river, kiddie pool; spa. Dining: 6 restaurants. 100,000 sq ft of meeting space. A Fla. Green Lodging hotel. Parking: $15/day; valet $20/day. 4040 Central Florida Pkwy, 32837. 407-206-2300. WDW 7 mi.

**Mona Lisa** ★★★★ $$ **Celebration:** 1-, 2-bed suites. Kitchens, washers/dryers. Restaurant. 225 Celebration Pl, 34747. 888-783-3408. Free WDW shuttle. WDW 2 mi.

**Monumental Hotel** ★★★ $ **Int'l. Dr. area:** Restaurant. 12000 Int'l Dr, 32821. 407-239-1222. Formerly Crown Plaza. WDW 4 mi.

**Nickelodeon Family Suites** ★★★ $$ **World Center Dr. area:** $25/night resort fee. Run by Holiday Inn, this family-focused resort offers wacky fun including a daily mass sliming and Nick shows starring guests. Suites: Sleep 4–7. Some bunk beds. Bright walls are decorated with cartoon characters. Family room has a 32-inch flat-screen TV with DVD player; bedroom has

25-inch TV. Refrigerator, kitchen. Wired Internet. Amenities: Arcade, arts & crafts, bsktball crt, business center, children's poolside activities, fitness center; laundromat, miniature golf, kid's play area, pool table, salon, 2 interactive water parks w/ 13 slides, 2 hot tubs, kid's spa. Dining: 6 restaurants, Nickelodeon character breakfast buffet daily (reservations req); mini-mart. A Fla. Green Lodging hotel. 14500 Continental Gateway, 32821. 877-387-5437. Free shuttle. WDW 1 mi.

**Omni Championsgate** ★ ★ ★ ★ $$$ **West of WDW:** Restaurants, pool w/lazy river, slides. 2 golf courses, golf academy, spa, steam room. 1500 Masters Blvd, 33896. 407-390-6664. Free shuttle. WDW 7 mi.

**Peabody Orlando** ★ ★ ★ ★ $$$ **Across from Orlando Convention Cntr:** Restaurants, beauty salon, spa, convention space. Mallard march at fountain twice daily. 9801 Int'l. Dr, 32819. 800-732-2639. WDW 6 mi.

**Radisson** ★ ★ ★ $ Restaurant. **U.S. 192 area:** 3011 Maingate Ln. 34747. 407-396-1400. Free shuttle. WDW 1 mi. Also: 2900 Parkway Blvd, 34747. 800-634-4774. Free shuttle. WDW 2 mi.

**Renaissance Orlando** ★ ★ ★ ★ $$ **SeaWorld area:** Restaurants, sushi bar, convention space, spa. Across street from SeaWorld. 6677 Sea Harbor Dr, 32821. 800-327-6677. WDW 4 mi.

**Residence Inn By Marriott** ★ ★ ★ $$$ Studios, suites. Kitchens. Free breakfast. Fee for pets. **Int'l. Dr. area:** 8800 Universal Blvd, 32819. 407-226-0288. Free shuttle. WDW 7 mi. **Lake Buena Vista:** 11450 Marbella Palm Ct, 32836. 407-465-0075. Free shuttle to Epcot. WDW 1 mi. **SeaWorld area:** 11000 Westwood Blvd, 32821. 800-889-9728. Free shuttle. WDW 4 mi.

**Ritz-Carlton Grande Lakes** ★ ★ ★ ★ ★ $$$$ **SeaWorld area:** This luxurious resort shares amenities, including a Greg Norman-designed golf course, with its adjacent sister hotel, the JW Marriott Grande Lakes. Rooms: Sleep 4. 2 dbl beds (1 king opt), hand-painted Italian furniture, 32-inch flat-screen TV, five-fixture bathroom, private balcony, iPod dock, twice-daily housekeeping service. Wireless Internet opt. Club Level. Suites: Sleep 4. Amenities: Arcade; surrey bike rentals; business center; car-rental counter; life-size chess board; child-care services; children's programs; club level; concierge; bocce ball, 3 lighted tennis, sand volleyball courts; eco-tours onsite; fitness center; fly-fishing school, fly-fishing onsite; golf course; jogging trails; laundromat; laundry services; meeting space; ropes course with zip line, giant swing; salon; spa; swimming pool w/zero entry, kiddie pool. Dining: 5 restaurants. 47,000 sq ft of meeting space. A Fla. Green Lodging hotel. Parking: Valet $17/day, $21/overnight. 4012 Central Florida Pkwy, 32837. 800-576-5760. WDW 7 mi.

**Rosen Centre** ★ ★ ★ $$$$ **Orlando Convention Cntr:** Restaurants, spa, salon, convention space, Club Level. 9840 Int'l. Dr, 32819. 800-204-7234. WDW 6 mi.

**Different strokes, different folks.** From top: Swimming areas at the Orlando World Center Marriott, JW Marriott Grande Lakes, Nickelodeon Family Suites, Ritz-Carlton Grande Lakes.

**Rosen Plaza** ★ ★ ★ $$ **Orlando Convention Cntr:** Restaurants, meeting space. Nightclub. 9700 Int'l. Dr, 32819. 800-627-8258. WDW 6 mi.

**Rosen Shingle Creek** ★ ★ ★ $$$ **Orlando Convention Cntr:** Restaurants, outdoor pools, spa, salon, convention space, golf course. 9939 Universal Blvd, 32819. 866-996-9939. WDW 7 mi.

**Sheraton** ★ ★ ★ $$ **Lake Buena Vista:** Sheraton Safari. Restaurants, meeting space. African theme. 12205 S. Apopka-Vineland Rd, 32836. 407-239-0444. Free shuttle. WDW 1 mi. **SeaWorld area:** Sheraton Vistana Villages. Suites w/kitchens. Restaurants. 8800 Vistana Centre Dr, 32821. 407-239-3100. Free shuttle. WDW 4 mi.

**SpringHill Suites** ★ ★ ★ $$ **Convention Center:** Sauna. Free continental breakfast. 8623 Universal Blvd, 32819. 407-938-9001. WDW 7 mi.

**Staybridge Suites** ★ ★ ★ $$$ Kitchens. Free cont'l b'fast. **Int'l. Dr. area:** 8480 Int'l. Dr, 32819. 800-238-8000. WDW 7 mi. **Lake Buena Vista:** 8751 Suiteside Dr, 32836. 800-238-8000. Free shuttle. WDW 1 mi.

**Villas of Grand Cypress** ★ ★ ★ ★ $$$$ **Lake Buena Vista:** Restaurants, convention space, lake with beach, 2 golf courses, spa, equestrian cntr, nature trails, complimentary boat, canoe use. 1 N. Jacaranda St, 32836. 800-835-7377. Free shuttle. WDW 4 mi.

**Waldorf Astoria Orlando** ★ ★ ★ ★ ★ $$$$ **Adjacent to WDW:** Located between Disney's Caribbean Beach Resort and the Typhoon Lagoon water park on a strip of land surrounded by Disney property, this elegant resort is the first Waldorf Astoria built outside of New York City. It opened in Nov. 2009. The centerpiece is a Rees Jones-designed 18-hole golf course. A formal signature pool is encircled by private cabanas with personalized poolside service. Like at the New York Waldorf, the lobby features a hand-crafted clock. Sister hotel is adjacent Hilton Orlando Bonnet Creek; shares amenities. Rooms: Sleep 5. 2 queen beds (1 king opt), 42-inch flat-screen TV, MP3 clock-radio. Wireless Internet opt. Suites: Sleep 5–8. Amenities: Arcade; complimentary bicycle use; business center; child-care services; children's programs; concierge; tennis; volleyball courts; fitness center; florist; golf course; jogging trails; laundromat; laundry services; nature preserve; 2 swimming pools, water slide, private cabanas; spa; wedding salon. 28,000 sq ft meeting space. Dining: 4 restaurants. Parking: $20/day (valet only). 14200 Bonnet Creek Resort Ln, 32831. 407-597-5500. WDW 1 mi.

**Worldquest** ★ ★ ★ ★ $$$ **World Center Dr. area:** All suites. Condo rentals. Free breakfast. 8849 Worldquest Blvd, 32821. 877-987-8378. WDW 2 mi.

**Wyndham Orlando** ★ ★ ★ $$ **Int'l. Dr.:** Family suites have bunk beds, play areas. Restaurants, sauna. Pet fee. 8001 Int'l. Dr, 32819. 407-351-2420. WDW 8 mi.

**Top three photos:** The Hilton Orlando Bonnet Creek exterior, pool area and standard guest room. **Lower two photos:** The Waldorf Astoria Orlando exterior and a deluxe guest room. Located next to Walt Disney World, the two hotels opened in 2009.

Bounty hunter Aurra Sing roams the
Backlot of Disney's Hollywood
Studios during Star Wars Weekends

# Special Events

## Winter

### Marathon Weekend
Jan 7–10. Entry fees: $125 (26.2), $120 (13.1), $40 (5K). Disabled runners welcome. Advance registration required; entry deadline is typically early Nov. but events can reach capacity much earlier. Details at 407-939-7810 or disneysports.com.

A pair of running events—a 26.2-mile full marathon and a 13.1-mile half marathon—highlight this January weekend. Typically more than 30,000 athletes compete. The route goes through theme parks. There's also a 5K run for families and children and a health and fitness expo at the host complex, the ESPN Wide World of Sports center. Note: Disney's Princess Half Marathon is March 7; a Minnie Marathon Weekend women's endurance event (15K, 5K and kids' races) follows in early May.

### Spring Training
Feb–March. Training sessions $12, games $15–$42. Tickets on sale Jan 9. Info, tickets: 407-939-4263, 407-839-3900 (Ticketmaster) or disneysports.com.

The Atlanta Braves Major League Baseball club holds its Spring Training at ESPN Wide World of Sports. Workouts start in February. More than a dozen Grapefruit League exhibition games follow in March.

## Spring

### ESPN: The Weekend
Early March

Legendary athletes join popular ESPN broadcasters during this no-extra-charge fan-fest at Disney's Hollywood Studios. The events include Q&A sessions, celebrity motorcades, interactive sports activities and live telecasts. Many fathers visit with their sons. Coincides with Atlanta Braves Spring Training.

### St. Patrick's Day
Wednesday, March 17

Two Disney World locations mark the Irish holiday with special events: The Raglan Road restaurant at Downtown Disney's Pleasure Island, and the U.K. pavilion at Epcot's World Showcase.

### Epcot International Flower and Garden Festival
March 3–May 16. No extra charge. Info: 407-W-DISNEY (934-7639).

Disney's most elaborate one-park promotion, this 75-day garden party includes hands-on seminars, demonstrations and celebrity guest speakers, as well as character topiaries, floating water gardens and 30 million flowers. Minnie's Magnificent Butterfly Garden often includes a live caterpillar/chrysalis exhibit. Themed weekends celebrate art, bugs and Mother's Day. Nightly concerts feature "Flower Power" acts from the 1960s and 1970s, such as Monkees singer Davy Jones. Vendor booths line the main walkways.

### Easter
Sunday, April 14

Outfitted in colorful homemade dresses, the Azalea Trail Maids from Mobile, Ala., greet guests at the entrance to Magic Kingdom and at that park's Town Square. Leashed (live) dogs appear with some Citizens of Main Street. The Magic Kingdom Easter Day parade includes the Maids, as well as the Easter Bunny and his wife.

### Star Wars Weekends
May–June. No extra charge. Info: 407-W-DISNEY (934-7639).

This fan-fest includes autograph booths featuring actors who have appeared in the "Star Wars" film series. Other highlights: roving characters such as bounty hunters Bobba Fett and Aurra Sing, special motorcades, Q-and-A sessions, trivia games and children's activities. Merchandise includes an incredibly popular Darth Mickey plushie. Many guests wear costumes. Get there when the park opens to take advantage of all of the activities, and be greeted at the entrance by humorous rooftop stormtroopers.

**Mobile, Alabama's Azalea Trail Maids** greet guests at Magic Kingdom every Easter

## Gay Days
First week in June. Info: 407-896-8431, gaydays.com.
Tens of thousands of gay adults come to Walt Disney World (especially Magic Kingdom) during the first week in June, most wearing red shirts in a sign of solidarity. Straight parents can be uncomfortable (a very few guests are flamboyant), but the experience does show children that even some old folks and yes, parents, are gay. There is, naturally, less demand for strollers as well as shorter lines at Fantasyland attractions. Disney does not sponsor the event but doesn't interfere with it.

# Summer

## Sounds Like Summer Concert Series
June–Aug
Cover bands perform timeless tunes from crowd favorites such as U2, Elton John and The Supremes. The complimentary (with park admission) shows take place three times nightly at the America Gardens amphitheater.

## Independence Day
July 4
Usually the most crowded day of the year at Walt Disney World, Independence Day features a Magic Kingdom fireworks show that surrounds guests watching from Main Street U.S.A. Historic characters visit Epcot's American Adventure pavilion to share their stories. Disney's Hollywood Studios presents a special fireworks show at 9 p.m., with skyrockets and patriotic music.

## Pirate & Princess Party
Aug–Sept. $46 adults; $40 children 3-9. Apx. a dozen evenings. Info and tickets: 407-W-DISNEY (934-7639).
Popular with young singles as well as families, these nighttime events feature a unique parade and one of Disney's most spectacular fireworks shows. Interactive events for children include a treasure hunt for a bibbidi-bobbidi-booty of beads and candy. Most major attractions are open, and lines are generally short. Many guests dress up. Though the parties officially run from 7 p.m. to midnight, partygoers can arrive as early as 4 p.m., which makes the price a bargain.

## Disney Step Classic
Sept 4, 5. Adv. tickets $25, $45 for two nights. ESPN Wide World of Sports
High school and collegiate step teams battle in a two-day competition and show. Portions of the 2009 event were aired on ESPN2.

## Disney's Royal Quinceañera Weekend
Late Aug–early Sept. $283. Info at 321-939-4555.
Epcot hosts this celebration of the passage of young Latinas into womanhood as they turn 15. A private viewing of IllumiNations follows a ball. Packages include stays at the Coronado Springs Resort and park tickets.

## Night of Joy
Early Sept. Adv. tickets $45, $76 for two nights. Day of event $5 more. Info and tickets: 407-827-7200.
Concerts by at least a dozen Contemporary Christian artists highlight this perennial

event, now again held at Magic Kingdom. Most of the park's major attractions are open.

# Fall

### Mickey's Not-So-Scary Halloween Party

Sept–Oct. $56 adults; $50 children 3–9. Many dates offer $7 advance savings. Friday events near Halloween, and the holiday itself, often sell out. Info and tickets: 407-827-7200.

There's nothing but fun during these charming Magic Kingdom evenings, which include a terrific parade—it starts with a galloping headless horseman—a spectacular fireworks show and many free-candy stations. Most attractions are not crowded. Many families wear homemade costumes.

### Epcot International Food and Wine Festival

Sept–Nov. Info: 407-WDW-FEST (939-3378). Demonstrations, seminars and entertainment included in Epcot admission.

Dozens of booths lining Epcot's World Showcase feature food and drink samples from Spain, India, Italy, Turkey, Ireland, Poland and other locales during this popular six-week festival. Special events include cooking demonstrations and pricey gourmet dinners and wine seminars. Nightly free concerts feature classic pop acts such as Kool & The Gang and David Cassidy.

### Wine & Dine Half Marathon Weekend

Oct 1–2. Entry fees TBA. Details at 407-938-3398 or disneywinedinerun.com.

Races for adults and children—and a family 5K through Magic Kingdom—culminate in an evening half marathon through multiple Disney theme parks, finishing inside Epcot for an exclusive after hours Food & Wine Festival experience for runners, friends and family.

### Children's Miracle Network Golf Classic presented by Wal-Mart

Oct.–Nov. $20 for any one day, $30 for a weekly badge. Proceeds benefit local Children's Miracle Network hospitals. Food packages avail. Info and tickets: 407-824-2250.

**Tweedledum appears in costume** as part of the parade at Mickey's Not-So-Scary Halloween Party

You'll be just a few feet away from the top names in men's golf with a pass to this PGA Tour tournament, held on Disney's Magnolia and Palm golf courses. Tiger Woods often participates.

### Festival of the Masters

Nov. No charge. Info: 407-824-4321.

One of the top art festivals in the United States, this Downtown Disney festival features over 150 artists, each of whom has won a primary award at a juried art show within the past three years. Works include paintings, photographs, sculptures and jewelry. Even more interesting are the pieces at the adjacent House of Blues folkart festival (on the lawn next to House of Blues), which features self-taught creators. Most of the artwork is for sale. Cirque du Soleil artists perform in front of their theater each afternoon. Chalk artists cover 6,000 square feet at the Marketplace. The festival has been held annually since 1975.

© DISNEY

**Cinderella Castle glows** for the Christmas season with 200,000 tiny Castle Dreamlights

# Christmas

Even the most determined Scrooge will warm up to Walt Disney World in the weeks between Thanksgiving and Christmas. The mood is most contagious at Magic Kingdom, which salutes the spirit of the American secular holiday with festive decorations, special shows, a Santa Claus parade (hands-down Disney's best procession) and a great fireworks display. Here's a guide to everything Disney World has to offer:

## Christmas decorations

### Magic Kingdom

Disney World's signature park focuses its decor on **Main Street U.S.A.** Thick garlands hang over the street, adorned with fruit, pine cones, poinsettias, giant plaid bows, bells and candles. Poinsettias hang from lampposts. Some second-story windows display Menorahs. The trolley has bows along its roof, and another bow on its horse's bridle. Inside the stores, garland embellishments often match the nearby merchandise. A 65-foot Christmas tree stands in the center of Town Square. The spruce is so thoroughly decorated most guests don't notice that it's artificial. A toy train circles its base.

**Cinderella Castle** looks draped in icicles thanks to a transparent net of 200,000 tiny white Castle Dreamlights. A nightly twilight ceremony (Cinderella's Holiday Wish, next spread) turns them on. Elsewhere, 18-inch bulbs trim Mickey's and Minnie's Country Houses at **Mickey's Toontown Fair.**

### Epcot

At World Showcase Plaza, Epcot's signature **holiday tree** is decorated in a world motif. Lovely at night, the **Germany** pavilion courtyard has trees, wreaths and garlands. The nearby miniature train village has its own decorations and a tiny tree lot. Inside American Adventure's **Liberty Inn** fast-food restaurant, a life-size gingerbread house sells cider and hot chocolate.

### Disney's Hollywood Studios

Straight out of a 1940s holiday musical, silver strands form garlands above **Hollywood Boulevard** while red and silver stars hang from **Sunset Boulevard** lampposts. Out front is a period-perfect 65-foot-tall tree.

Each storefront window, balcony and brownstone along the **Streets of America** is decorated to reflect the life of its tenant. One celebrates Hanukkah. Oversized bulbs and a giant Santa decorate other buildings. At night thousands of lights cover the facades in the **Osborne Family Spectacle of Dancing Lights.** Hanging from the rooftops in huge nets, they flash rhythmically to holiday tunes. Displays above include a spinning car-

**Toy soldiers from 1961's "Babes in Toyland"** march in the Magic Kingdom Christmas parade

ousel and rotating globe. Rope-light angels fly over a town square; others pray to a creche. Snow-like soap bubbles spray from overhead spouts. The spectacle was created by Little Rock, Ark., businessman Jennings Osborne in the 1980s for his 6-year-old daughter. To the dismay of many of his less-festive neighbors, it covered his home and yard, drawing throngs of traffic. The display uses 12 miles of extension cords.

### Disney's Animal Kingdom
**Entrance areas and hub walkways** display natural decorations. A 65-foot-tall Christmas tree is adorned with primitive metal and wood animals; gift-shop garlands are filled with berries, flowers, grain stalks and straw. At **Dinoland U.S.A.,** the tongue-in-cheek Dino-Rama carnival is trimmed with shredded-plastic trees, candy canes and a huge cheesy snowman. The Dinosaur Treasures gift shop has plastic Santas, Santa heads and a tree with pink flamingos and Styrofoam snowmen. Each tree at **Camp Minnie-Mickey** belongs, on close inspection, to a Disney character. The ornaments on Lilo's tree include her handmade doll and Elvis records.

The park's **ambient music** features nice flute-and-drum renditions of traditionals such as "Silent Night" in the entrance area, and obscure ditties such as Spike Jones' 1956 "My Birthday Comes on Christmas" and Augie Rios' 1958 "¿Donde Esta Santa Claus?" at Dinoland U.S.A.

### Disney resort hotels
All Disney-owned lodging complexes are decorated for the holidays. The largest **Christmas trees** are at the Contemporary (75 feet tall, with 77,000 lights), Wilderness Lodge (50 feet, 52,000 lights) and Grand Floridian (45 feet, 45,000 lights). Many resorts have **confectionery displays.** A 16-foot-tall gingerbread house sits in the Grand Floridian lobby; a concoction of honey, sugar, egg whites and apricot glaze covers its wood frame. There are miniature villages at Animal Kingdom Lodge and the Contemporary Resort, a complete Santa's workshop at the BoardWalk Resort and a sugary mountain at the Yacht Club. A life-size carousel spins in the lobby of Disney's Beach Club, with giant candy cane poles and ponies made of chocolate and fondant.

## Christmas attractions
### Magic Kingdom
**Belle's Enchanted Christmas ★ ★ ★ ★**
**Outdoor stage show** 16 min. Fairytale Garden, Fantasyland. Arrive 30 min early.
The princess uses audience members to retell the tale of her first Christmas in the Beast's castle (the story of the 1997 video "Beauty and the Beast: The Enchanted Christmas"). Sit by the stage steps and your child may be chosen to be in the show.

© DISNEY

**Celebrate the Season** ★★★★ ✓ **Outdoor stage show** Mickey Mouse, Minnie Mouse, Donald Duck, Chip 'n Dale, Pluto, Santa Goofy. 20 min. Cinderella Castle forecourt.

Remember when your neighbors got together for holiday sing-a-longs? When carolers came to your door? When your town held its Santa Claus parade? No? Well Disney does, and brings that holiday spirit back with this campy revue of hoofing horses, dancing reindeer and very merry elves who appear to have had just a little too much eggnog. When reindeer act out "Rudolph the Red-Nosed Reindeer," at first they don't let poor Rudolph (Pluto) join in their reindeer games. Nighttime shows are best, as spotlights add a theatrical flair.

**Cinderella's Holiday Wish** ★★★ **Outdoor stage show** Cinderella, Fairy Godmother, Mickey Mouse. 20 min. Cinderella Castle forecourt. 5:45p.

When Cinderella wants her home to sparkle for the holidays, her Fairy Godmother waves her wand, and suddenly the castle is covered with 200,000 twinkling lights.

**Holiday Wishes** ★★★★★ ✓ **Fireworks show** 15 min. Arrive 15 min early.

Fireworks form Christmas shapes while projected images decorate Cinderella Castle in this synchronized pyrotechnic presentation. During "O Christmas Tree" the castle becomes a Christmas tree: a star explodes above it while flood lights turn it green. The best viewing spot for the symmetrical show is on Main Street U.S.A., in front of the castle hub.

**Mickey's Once Upon a Christmastime Parade** ★★★★★ ✓ **Santa Claus parade** 15 min. Starts in Frontierland, to Liberty Square, down Main Street U.S.A. Find seats 45 min early.

This lively procession includes horse-drawn sleighs; marching toy soldiers; dancing reindeer, snowflakes and gingerbread men; elves; plenty of Disney characters; and, of course, Mr. Santa.

**A Totally Tomorrowland Christmas!** ★★★★ **Outdoor stage show** Stitch, Buzz Lightyear, Mike Wazowski. Tomorrowland Stage.

This comedic musical revue features pop versions of classic holiday songs. A fer-sure live singer hosts as the characters discover the true meaning of the season during their annual Christmas party. Playing the role of Rudolph: giant-eyeball Mike Wazowski.

## Epcot

**Holidays Around the World Storytellers** ★★★★★ **Cultural storytellers** 20 min. World Showcase pavilions. Hourly noon–dusk.

Sharing the seasonal legends and traditions of cultures from throughout the world, these actors perform to small crowds outside each World Showcase pavilion. **Canada:** Comic lumberjack Nowell describes Boxing Day, the Inuit's impish Nalyuks and the legend

**The Osborne Family Spectacle of Dancing Lights** lights up Disney's Hollywood Studios

of "people who come to homes dressed in strange outfits. We call them… relatives!" **United Kingdom:** Father Christmas tells how holiday cards and decorating with holly and mistletoe began in his countries. **France:** Pére Noél comically explains how children leave shoes on their doorsteps for him to put presents in. **Morocco:** A drummer describes the Festival of Ashura, which

gives presents to children who behave well. **Japan:** A vendor explains Daruma dolls, pupil-free charms that children paint eyes on as they make wishes. **The American Adventure:** One storyteller explains Hanukkah, another describes the principles of Kwanzaa. **Italy:** Good witch La Befana, who slides down chimneys to leave treats, explains why she travels on the anniversary of the day the Three Kings came to Bethlehem. **Germany:** St. Nicholas fills you in about the first Christmas tree and Nutcracker as well as the Christmas pickle, a hidden tree ornament that rewards its finder with an extra present. **China:** The Monkey King spins a tale of how he defeated a monster and found a magic stick. **Norway:** Farm girl Sigrid is sure Gnome Julenissen doesn't exist, though you can see him easily. The strangest, and most fun, Holiday Storyteller skit. **Mexico:** The Three Kings explain the customs of Posada.

**Candlelight Processional** ★★★★★ ✓
Religious Christmas pageant 60 min. Three times nightly at the America Gardens amphitheater, American Adventure pavilion.

This inspirational show recounts the birth of Jesus Christ with a 50-piece orchestra, 400 singers and a celebrity narrator (which in 2009 included Whoopi Goldberg, Isabella Rossellini and Vanessa Williams). Though free with park admission, the show is so popular that on peak evenings the only guaranteed way to see it is to buy a Candlelight Processional Dinner Package (407-939-3463, uses two Disney Dining Plan credits), which includes dinner at an Epcot restaurant. Otherwise you wait in a line for up to two hours.

## Backstage at Disney's Holiday Crafts shop

Decking the halls of Walt Disney World is a full-time job for 26 employees, who toil backstage at a 70,000-square-foot Holiday Services warehouse 12 months of the year. When I stop by one fall afternoon, each cast member is hard at work. Some scurry past me pushing shrink-wrapped wardrobe carts, each tagged with its ID number ("MK 035"), contents ("Checked and Fluffed Garland") and destination ("Main Street Train Station 2nd Floor"). Others drive forklifts loaded with crates of ornaments, or use long poles to remove giant 3-D stars from the building's rafters.

Outside, electricians test out what appears to be a utility pole. "This is the guts of the Main Street unit," one says, explaining that the contraption is the electrical transformer of Magic Kingdom's signature Christmas tree. Nearby sit six circular sections of greenery, some more than 10 feet tall. In a few days everything will be trucked over to the park, where crane operators will stack it together like a giant ring-toss game. The six-hour job will be done overnight so guests don't see it. Similar operations take place at the other theme parks. Each tree is used up to five years.

And yes, managing Walt Disney World's holiday trimmings is a 12-month job. In the spring the staff cleans and repairs the decorations. In the summer it designs new ones. In the fall the group prepares for installation; after Christmas it puts everything away.

The **Totally Tomorrowland Christmas** show is a new addition at Magic Kingdom

### Disney's Hollywood Studios

**Citizens of Hollywood** ★★★★★ ✔ **Street performers** 20 min. Hollywood Blvd, Sunset Blvd. Show times at Guest Relations.

Portraying directors, starlets, script girls and wanna-bes, these improvisational actors perform holiday street skits with audience participation. Appearing as a Hollywood Glee Club, they sing the lyrics to "Jingle Bells" to the music of "Joy to the World."

### Disney's Animal Kingdom

**Mickey's Jingle Jungle Parade** ★★★★★ ✔ **Character parade** 15 min. Circles Discovery Island. Starts, exits in Africa, at gate between Tusker House and Kilimanjaro Safaris. Choose a viewing spot 30 min early to get a shady seat.

A reworking of the theme park's regular safari-themed Mickey's Jammin' Jungle Parade, this 12-minute procession finds Mickey Mouse and Rafiki (the mandrill in 1994's "The Lion King") leading Minnie Mouse, Donald Duck and Goofy in an SUV parade that's headed out for a rustic holiday adventure. You can smell the chocolate when candy-making Minnie passes by in her truck; Donald's vehicle will spray you with artificial snow. Giant mechanical puppets include a partridge in a pear tree. Selected at random each day, up to 25 guests ride in the parade in giant rickshaws and open-top trailers.

**Campfire Carolers** ★★★★ ✔ **A cappella singing group.** 20 min. Camp Minnie-Mickey.

These youthful performers aren't above cracking a few jokes as they belt out holiday pop tunes. When one sings that she wants an "opotamus" for Christmas, the others correct her. "You must mean a hippopotamus!" "No, he doesn't have to be very cool." Crowds are small; you'll sit, or stand, just a few feet from the performers.

## On tape with Regis and Kelly

Though ABC-TV implies that it airs the Walt Disney World Christmas parade live on Christmas Day, the event is actually taped during the first weekend in December. Hosted by Regis Philbin and Kelly Ripa, the production fills Magic Kingdom's Main Street U.S.A. and Cinderella Castle forecourt stage with cameras, crews and celebrities. The work moves at a snail's pace. Hang out for awhile and you'll see stars painstakingly perform take after take of the same few-second sequence. Want to be on camera? Come early, look happy and wear festive clothes without advertising slogans. Special early-morning access may be available at www.lightshiptv.com.

# Avoiding the holiday crush

The week between Christmas and New Year's is Walt Disney World's most crowded time of the year, and not, frankly, the best time to visit. Not only does the Magic Kingdom theme park often close around lunchtime (after reaching its 80,000-person capacity), the throng includes many people who appear to have IQs somewhere south of Goofy's. Slowly wandering the park in an aimless fashion, they fill the walkways, clog the rides and crowd the restaurants and stores. We've even seen guests drunk, a rare sight at Walt Disney World.

The other parks can be almost as bad.

If you must visit Magic Kingdom during this week, arrive at the park by 7:30 a.m. Use the morning for attractions and to collect Fastpasses for later use. See the noon parade, then use your Fastpasses to ride the most popular attractions. After dark see the castle show and Holiday Wishes.

The week *before* Christmas is, overall, a much better time to visit. All the holiday events are happening but the monster crowd isn't here yet.

An easy way to enjoy the Magic Kingdom holiday fun is **Mickey's Very Merry Christmas Party** (7p–mid. $52 A, $46 C 3–9 adv; $7 more day of show). Held every few nights from early November through just before Christmas, these events have crowds of only 10,000 to 25,000 but give you all the park's holiday events, plus complimentary cookies and hot chocolate. It even "snows" on Main Street U.S.A. All major rides are open, and lines are short. For the best time arrive before 6:30 p.m. and see the less-crowded second parade. The least crowded parties are those before Thanksgiving; those on December Fridays and Saturday nights sell out early.

**Fun facts** ❶ Walt Disney World displays more than 1,500 Christmas trees during the holiday season, as well as 15 miles of garland and over 300,000 yards of ribbon. ❷ Each of Disney World's signature theme-park trees weighs at least 28,000 pounds each.

**Holiday hits** Walt Disney World's holiday celebration is filled with the vintage pop songs of the American Christmas experience: ❶ A hit for The Carpenters in 1978, **"The Christmas Waltz"** was written in 1954 for Frank Sinatra. Its music comes from a finger-exercising routine for piano players. ❷ **"Deck the Halls"** sets American lyrics to a 17th-century Welsh tune. ❸ Gene Autry was billed as the main draw of a 1946 Hollywood, Calif., Christmas parade, but during it noticed that children in the

**Dancers 'Celebrate the Season'** in front of the Magic Kingdom's Cinderella Castle

crowd were far more focused on the guy behind him, and kept yelling **"Here Comes Santa Claus"** instead of looking at him. The cowboy star responded by writing that 1947 classic. ❹ 1963's **"It's the Most Wonderful Time of the Year"** was penned by George Wyle, who later wrote the theme to the television series "Gilligan's Island." ❺ First published in 1840 as "One Horse Open Sleigh," **"Jingle Bells"** is a tribute to sleigh races that once took place down the streets of Medford, Mass. ❻ 1955's **"Mr. Santa"** novelty is a knockoff of the 1954 Chordettes hit, "Mr. Sandman." ❼ **"Must Be Santa"** debuted on the "Sing Along with Mitch [Miller]" television show in 1961. ❽ **"The Nutcracker Suite"** is a medley the Russian composer Tchaikovsky created from his own Nutcracker ballet. First performed in 1892, it includes the tale of a family whose Christmas presents include two life-sized dolls, each of which takes a turn to dance. ❾ **"O Christmas Tree"** is an English take of the 16th-century German carol, "Oh Tannenbaum" (literally, "Oh fir tree"). ❿ Based on a character that appeared in a 1939 Montgomery Ward newspaper ad, Autry's 1949 **"Rudolph the Red-Nosed Reindeer"** is the best-selling single in the history of Columbia Records. ⓫ **"We Wish You A Merry Christmas"** is a 16th-century English Christmas carol. ⓬ Published in 1934, **"Winter Wonderland"** was released in 1946 by both Perry Como and the Andrews Sisters. Each version sold a million copies.

© NASA

**Walt Disney** (left) poses with famed rocket pioneer Dr. Wernher von Braun, 1954

# Walt Disney

A tycoon with the mind of a farm boy. A storyteller who didn't finish high school. An artist who thought like an engineer. A visionary who loved the past. A mix of contradictory characters, Walt Disney was the personification of the American dream. He received hundreds of accolades, including 32 Academy Awards. But just as he started his grandest dream... he died.

The namesake of Walt Disney World was born in Chicago on Dec. 5, 1901. He had three older brothers and a younger sister.

Between the ages of 4 and 10, from 1905 to 1911, Disney was raised on a 45-acre farm near Marceline, Mo. Clad in overalls, the young boy spent much of his time playing with animals, swimming in a pond, picking apples, or daydreaming under a tree. He often ignored his homework to doodle animal pictures. While still in grade school, Disney sold cigars, gum and soda pop to passengers at the town's railroad depot. His uncle was a train engineer. Free to roam, the boy came to know an elderly Civil War veteran who told him dramatic old stories.

After his family moved to Kansas City, Disney impersonated Charlie Chaplin in skits with other neighborhood kids. When the family moved back to Chicago, Disney attended high school for just one year, contributing cartoons and photos to the school paper. He took night courses at Chicago's Academy of Fine Arts.

At 16 Disney dropped out of high school and left home. Germany had just signed an armistice ending World War I, but he still tried to enlist in the Army. Rejected because of his age, Disney instead snuck into the Red Cross, which sent him to France to drive an ambulance. He took up smoking.

Returning to Kansas City at age 20, Disney formed his first business. Using a borrowed camera and working in a shed, he made "Laugh-O-Gram" cartoons of a live little girl in an animated world. When his distributor went under, Disney paid the bills by producing a dental-health film ("Tommy Tucker's Tooth"), but soon he had to close shop, too. Raising train fare by photographing babies door-to-door, Disney soon headed to Hollywood. His brother Roy was already there.

Carrying a print of his last Kansas City cartoon, an unfinished extravaganza called "Alice's Wonderland," Disney applied at every major studio. Finally, a New York distributor agreed to market his work. He was in business again. Forming the Disney Bros. Studio, Walt and Roy set up shop in the rear of a real estate office. Running the money side of the operation, Roy insisted its name be changed to the Walt Disney Studio, today's Walt Disney Co.

The new business prospered. Disney celebrated by buying a Moon roadster, growing a mustache and, in 1925, marrying Lillian Bounds, a woman who inked and painted his celluloids. The couple later raised two daughters, Diane and the adopted Sharon.

In 1927 Disney created a new character: Oswald the Lucky Rabbit. Distributed by Universal, his 26 Oswald cartoons spawned an Oswald candy bar and some merchandise. But a year later, on a trip to New York to renew his contract, Disney learned of a clause in the deal that gave Universal ownership of the character. (The Disney company regained the rights to Oswald in 2006. Universal gave the bunny back in exchange for sportscaster Al Michaels.)

Devastated, on the train ride back to California Disney realized he needed a star he owned outright. Remembering a mouse that used to climb up on his desk in Kansas City, he told Lillian "I think it will be a mouse, and I think I'll call him Mortimer."

"Mortimer?" she asked. "I don't like it. What about Mickey?"

Using the general look of Oswald, Disney and partner Ub Iwerks designed a mouse, then cranked out two cartoons. Inspired by the fame of Charles Lindbergh, the first was the gag-filled "Plane Crazy." The second, "The Gallopin' Gaucho," cast Mickey as an Argentine outlaw. Neither sold.

Walt's solution? Make a talkie. With the recent success of "The Jazz Singer," he figured that distributors would want a cartoon with sound, too. To raise cash, he sold his roadster.

He was wrong. Again and again, distributors still said no. When a New York promoter offered to run the cartoon for free just for the publicity value, Disney, with no other options, reluctantly agreed. The first synchronized sound cartoon, "Steamboat Willie" premiered at New York's Colony Theatre on Nov. 18, 1928. The public loved it, but only one distributor showed interest: Universal. Walt said no.

Finally, Disney did strike a distribution deal. With a sound-machine salesman.

As his Mickey cartoons took the country by storm, Disney put his profits back into his company. To ensure his artists were skilled, he paid for them to attend art school and later set up an in-house training center. Disney introduced Technicolor to animation with the 1932 Silly Symphonies cartoon "Flowers and Trees." In 1937 he released "The Old Mill," which used a multiplane camera to add realistic depth to animation.

All of that, however, was a warm-up for Disney's next idea: an animated feature film. The idea had been tried in Europe (with "Lotte Reiniger's Adventures of Prince Achmed") but never in the States. Disney knew he had the story, a dramatic, romantic, sympathetic fairy tale he had seen as a kid as a silent film: "Snow White." Though Hollywood scoffed at the idea, dubbing it "Walt's Folly," Disney mortgaged his home to help cover expenses.

The gamble paid off. Premiering December 21, 1937, "Snow White and the Seven Dwarfs" was such a smash that within six months the Disney company had millions in the bank. The film went on to gross $8 million, at a time when a child's movie ticket was just 10 cents.

Not interested in making a sequel, Disney instead created 1940's imaginative "Fantasia" and "Pinocchio," 1941's "Dumbo" and 1942's "Bambi." All lost money. None could break even without the European market, which had disappeared with the outbreak of World War II.

There was more trouble. Rumors spread through the studio that major salary cuts and layoffs were coming. Soon union organizers appeared, and on May 29, 1941, many of the company's animators went on strike. The walkout ended in just a few weeks, but Disney firmly believed the strike was inspired by communists. In 1947 he testified before the House Un-American Activities Committee that there was a threat of Communism in the motion-picture industry, though he added "I don't think they have gotten very far, and I think the industry is made up of good Americans, just like in my plant—good, solid Americans."

For awhile Disney couldn't catch a break. "Dumbo" was scheduled to appear on the cover of Time magazine the first week of December, 1941, until Japan bombed Pearl Harbor. During the war the U.S. military took over the studio in an effort to protect a nearby Lockheed aircraft plant, an act which essentially shut down Disney's commercial business for years.

By now Disney was a chain smoker. Studio workers could tell if he was coming down the hall by listening for his cough.

Disney's golden touch returned in the 1950s. Animated films included 1950's "Cinderella," 1951's "Alice in Wonderland" and 1953's "Peter Pan." The 1954 movie "20,000 Leagues Under the Sea" was the company's first live-action film. Walt Disney embraced television, and found success with shows such as "The Mickey Mouse Club" and "Zorro."

During the decade Disney created a series of shorts on science and technology. Broadcasts of the "Disneyland" television show included three films produced with rocket designer Dr. Wernher von Braun. A 1957 episode of the show featured "Our Friend the Atom," a collaboration with the U.S. government designed to enhance the image of nuclear energy.

Back during the war, Disney would take his daughters to the carousel at Hollywood's Griffith Park, 10 miles from his home. "As I'd sit there," he later recalled, "I felt there should be something built where the parents and the children could have fun together." In 1951 he visited Copenhagen's Tivoli Gardens, a lushly landscaped park with fireworks, parades, a railroad and exotic buildings outlined with little white lights. "Now this is what an amusement place should be," Disney told his wife.

Two years later Disney bought 160 acres near Anaheim. Gathering some of his best motion-picture talent, he set about building Disneyland, the world's first theme park. Disney decided its central attraction would be a castle, and that its entrance would be a re-creation of a turn-of-the-century small town. As budgets increased Disney hocked his life insurance to get more cash. Construction began in July of 1954, and the park opened just one year later. It was a huge hit.

Success continued in the 1960s. The No. 1 movie of 1961 was "One Hundred and One Dalmatians." "Wonderful World of Color" was among the first color television programs.

Walt and Roy even entered the field of education, providing the funds to merge the Los Angeles Conservatory of Music with the Chouinard Art Institute (where Disney had earlier sent his animators) to create the California Institute of the Arts, the nation's first art institute to grant undergraduate and graduate degrees. Of Cal Arts, Walt said, "It's the principal thing I hope to leave when I move on to greener pastures. If I can help provide a place to develop the talent of the future, I think I will have accomplished something." The campus is located in the city of Valencia, 32 miles northeast of downtown Los Angeles.

Everything clicked in 1964. Disney's contributions to the New York World's Fair, including Carousel of Progress, Great Moments with Mr. Lincoln and It's a Small World, became its top attractions. In August "Mary Poppins" premiered at Grauman's Chinese Theatre, and became the studio's biggest hit to date.

In September President Johnson invited Disney to the White House to receive the Presidential Medal of Freedom, the nation's highest civilian honor. The man who 40 years earlier was bankrupt was now not only rich, but also a national hero.

Then 62 years old, in 1965 Disney had one dream left: to fix America's urban areas. His idea: Combine corporate sponsorships with the money he had just made from "Mary Poppins" and then—using 43 square miles of land he had secretly purchased in Florida—build an experimental city. Filled with technological advancements, it would demonstrate how communities could solve their housing, pollution and transportation problems. Disney called the project the Experimental Prototype Community of Tomorrow. "EPCOT" for short.

"I don't believe there is a challenge anywhere in the world that is more important than finding the solution to the problems of our cities," he said. "We think the need is for starting from scratch on virgin land and building a community that will become a prototype for the future. EPCOT will be a community of tomorrow that will never be completed, but will always be introducing and testing and demonstrating new materials and new systems."

The design called for a 50-acre town center enclosed in a dome, an internationally themed shopping area, a 30-story hotel and convention complex, office space, apartments, single-family homes, monorail and PeopleMover systems, an airport, underground roads for cars and trucks, even a nuclear power plant.

To make money he'd have a theme park, too, a larger version of Disneyland.

Disney planned to finish EPCOT by 1985.

On Nov. 15, 1965, Walt and Roy held a press conference in Orlando to announce the project. "I'm very excited about it," Walt said of his new dream, "because I've been storing these things up over the years. I like to create new things."

He began lining up sponsors. Monsanto was interested. General Electric, too.

But less than a year later, Disney got sick. The smoking had caught up with him.

In November 1966 doctors found a tumor the size of a walnut in Disney's left lung. When they operated, they discovered the cancer had spread through the lung, and the entire organ had to be removed. Afterward Disney went back to work, but returned to the hospital just two weeks later. His body wasn't recovering.

On the night of December 14, Disney lay in his hospital bed and discussed his Florida project with Roy. Using the acoustical tiles on the ceiling above, Walt showed Roy his detailed, if imaginary, vision of his ultimate dream—the roads, airport, everything.

The next morning, Walt Disney died.

Some called Walt Disney too naive, a boy who never became an adult. But, to him, that was the point. "The American child is sensitive, humorous, open-minded, eager to learn, and has a strong sense of excitement, energy, and curiosity about the world in which he lives," he wrote in 1963. "Lucky indeed is the grown-up who manages to carry these same characteristics into adult life. That's the real trouble with the world. Too many people grow up."

## Disney's Fab Five

Since his debut in 1928's "Steamboat Willie," **Mickey Mouse** has been an American pop-culture icon. Modeled in part on silent-film star Charlie Chaplin, Mickey was an underdog who dreamed big, a character everyone could root for. In the 1930s his optimistic attitude was the perfect antidote to the Great Depression. During World War II he become symbolic of the can-do attitude of the United States. During the 1960s Mickey was embraced by the counterculture, a symbol of mischievous rebellion.

Today Mickey Mouse is still enormously popular, the most recognized and celebrated cartoon character in history. Sure he's a corporate symbol, but he's also an honest, pure piece of Americana.

When Mickey Mouse cartoons debuted in the late 1920s, an opening short had been a common feature at movie theaters for more than a decade. But Mickey cartoons were different. Not only did they have sound, a novelty at the time, but Mickey had a strong personality, a happy-go-lucky approach to life that was said to be Walt Disney's alter ego. At many theaters, the name "Mickey Mouse" would be the largest on the marquee. In 1933 Mickey received 800,000 fan letters, the most of any Hollywood star. "Mickey Mouse is an international hero," Fortune magazine wrote in 1934, "better known than Roosevelt." The president himself began showing Mickey cartoons at the White House.

During World War II, the password of the Allied forces on D-Day was "Mickey Mouse." Mickey was banned in Nazi Germany in 1933, the Soviet Union in 1936, Yugoslavia in 1937, Italy in 1938 and East Germany in 1954.

After World War II Mickey became so popular with children artists found it difficult to give him interesting behaviors. If he misbehaved, parents would complain.

**Minnie Mouse** is Mickey's girlfriend. She's always around to flatter, giggle at and swoon over her main squeeze. Still, she does have her own life. Quick-witted and energetic, she loves animals, cooking and gardening, and can play the harmonica, guitar and piano.

She also gets mad. After Mickey forces her to kiss him in 1928's "Plane Crazy," Minnie slaps him, then jumps out of their open-cockpit airplane. She smashes a lamp on Mickey's head when he pulls her nose in 1930's "The Cactus Kid." And when she mistakenly thinks Mickey

SOURCES FOR THIS ARTICLE INCLUDE "WALT DISNEY: AN AMERICAN ORIGINAL" BY BOB THOMAS AND "WALT DISNEY AND THE QUEST FOR COMMUNITY" BY STEVE MANNHEIM

has given her a bone for a present in 1933's "Puppy Love," she kicks him out of her house and sobs "I hate him! I hate all men!"

As portrayed in the 1928 cartoon "The Gallopin' Gaucho," the couple first met in a bar in Argentina. When Minnie, a flirty dancer, bats her eyes at Mickey, a cigarette-smoking outlaw, he watches her perform, chugs a beer, then grabs her for a tango. Minnie has an old flame (suave, tap-dancing Mortimer) in the 1936 cartoon "Mickey's Rival." In 1933's "Mickey's Steam Roller," she has kids.

Walt Disney originally did the voices for both Mickey and Minnie.

He's rude, he's crude, he doesn't wear pants. He shouts, pouts and loses his temper at the drop of a pin. He often just likes to be mean. Yet who doesn't love **Donald Duck,** who responds to life the way we are tempted to, but rarely dare.

Created in 1934 as a foil for the then-gentlemanly Mickey, Donald soon emerged as Disney's most popular star. Besides his personality, Donald is famous for his nearly unintelligible voice, originally done by bird impressionist Clarence "Ducky" Nash. The "duck with all the bad luck" is also known for his "hopping mad" boxing stance, a leaning, jumping posture with one arm straight and the other twirling like a windmill.

A good-hearted simpleton, **Goofy** appeals to your inner idiot. Clumsy and gullible, he has a hard time concentrating and seldom finishes what he starts (just like many husbands). He has bad posture, his clothes don't fit, his stomach is too big, yet he always mugs for a camera. First known as Dippy Dog, Goofy made his debut in 1930. He later hosted a series of "How To" sports parodies. In the 1950s Disney transformed Goofy into George Geef, a suburban everyman often drawn without ears. As for the eternal question—man or dog?—the answer is... both. Though he has physical characteristics of a dog, including floppy ears and a snout, Goofy is an upright talking character.

One of the greatest dogs in Hollywood history, gangly yellow hounddog **Pluto** is the only Five Fab character who doesn't speak or walk upright (except at theme parks). Instead, Mickey's pet licks, sniffs, romps and runs in a fashion instantly recognizable to dog lovers everywhere. Always thinking, Pluto is known for his vivid expressions. (Pluto once spoke. In the 1931 short "The Moose Hunt," Pluto got down on his knees and, doing his best impersonation of Al Jolson, proclaimed "Mammy!" Moments later, he looked into Mickey's eyes and whispered "Kiss me!")

# 'Cinderella'

The classic rags-to-riches tale, "Cinderella" began as a Chinese fable. In the 9th-century "Yeh-Shen," a stepmother and two daughters humiliate a hard-working girl. But when a 10-foot fish gives her food, a beautiful dress and tiny slippers, she gains confidence.

Often sweeping the fireplace, the girl gets so covered in ash her stepsisters call her Cinderella ("cinder girl") in Charles Perrault's French version, written to entertain the 17th-century court of Louis XIV. When a king wants his son to wed, he has the prince invite all the land's maidens to a two-night ball. Cinderella's stepmom won't let her go, but then her fairy godmother (the spirit of her real mom) appears. Waving a magic wand, she turns a pumpkin into a coach, mice into horses, rats and lizards to footmen, and the girl's ragged dress into a ball gown, with glass slippers. Cinderella can go to the ball, the godmother says, but the magic wears off at midnight. The first night the girl mesmerizes the prince and leaves on time, but the next night she stays until the moment the clock strikes twelve. Rushing out, she loses a slipper, which the prince recovers. Determined to find her, he orders his Grand Duke (chief of staff) to test the shoe on every girl in the kingdom. On Cinderella's foot it slides on perfectly.

The story got bloody with Germany's Brothers Grimm version, "Aschenputtel," in 1812. When the slipper won't fit the stepsisters, their mom has them slice off their heels and toes and try again. During Cinderella's wedding, birds peck out the sisters' eyes.

Disney's 1950 film gave Perrault's tale new life. It cleaned up the plot, added a supporting animal cast and catchy songs, and beefed up the finale. Disney's stepmother locks Cinderella in her room when the Grand Duke arrives. The girl's mice pals unlock it, but then the stepmom trips the Duke, causing him to drop the slipper and break it. Cinderella, however, reaches into her pocket and pulls out the mate.

Walt Disney produced the first animated Cinderella in 1922, when his Laugh-O-Grams Co. produced an "Alice" silent cartoon based on the tale. Betty Boop danced her way through 1934's "Poor Cinderella." Rodgers and Hammerstein's 1957 musical "Cinderella" is still the most popular television special ever. Starring Julie Andrews, it drew 71 percent of all Americans with a TV set. The production was remade with Lesley Ann Warren in 1965, and with Brandy in 1997. Jerry Lewis learns geeks, too, have charms in 1960's "Cinderfella" when a Disney-like Cinderella pops out of the past to flirt with him: "If I weren't a married woman," she purrs, "Grrrr!"

Hollywood ignored the fable for decades, but in the '90s Cindy was back. In 1998's "Ever After," the princess-to-be (Drew Barrymore) enlightens her prince about social policy. In the 2004 musical "Ella Enchanted, a feisty "Ella" (Anne Hathaway) breaks out into Queen's "Somebody to Love."

# 'Beauty and the Beast'

The "Beauty and the Beast" fairy tale got its start in Roman mythology. In "Cupid and Psyche," philosopher Lucius Apuleius told the tale of Psyche, the youngest of three mortal sisters. Incredibly pretty, Psyche earns the envy of Venus, the goddess of beauty. But when Venus orders her son, Cupid, to make the girl fall in love with a castle-dwelling snake, Cupid himself falls in love with her, and secretly turns himself into the snake. In Cupid's castle invisible servants prepare Psyche's meals. Cupid eventually turns himself back to a man.

The story spreads over time. Eventually over 200 Eurasian folk tales have a similar plot: a beautiful girl with two mean sisters finds herself living with a beast, who becomes human once she cares for him. A Chinese version makes a few changes, adds a "golden shoe" and becomes the first "Cinderella."

The love of a good woman turns a pig into a prince in the first published beauty-and-beast fable. Produced soon after printing presses became widespread in 1553, "The Pig King" was one of many folk tales transcribed by Italian novelist Giovanni Straparola. This beast marries all three sisters, one at a time. He kills the oldest two because they don't like him "climbing into bed stinking with filthy paws and snout."

The Beast is a snake again in 1650, when the story becomes a popular parlor tale with French aristocrats. In this, the first story actually named "Beauty and the Beast," a king leaves home to get presents for his three daughters. When he comes upon a deserted castle he plucks a rose for his youngest, named Beauty. "Who said you could take my flower?" a voice asks. "I will kill you for that, unless you bring me one of your girls." Beauty volunteers. When she arrives the castle again seems empty, but the next morning she wakes up to find a serpent in her lap. "You must marry me," it hisses. Beauty says no, but the snake persists. Each day the reptile repeats its demand. Finally, Beauty gives in. "I won't marry a serpent," she says, "but I will marry a man." The snake, therefore, turns itself into a handsome prince.

Oodles of oo-lá-lá come into the story once French blueblood Gabrielle de Villeneuve gets hold of it in 1740. Writing for the pleasure of her salon friends, she turns her prince into a beast after he refuses a promiscuous fairy. When Beauty arrives, he doesn't ask "Will you marry me?" but "Will you go to bed with me?" He stays a beast until after the wedding night.

The story first becomes a child's fable 16 years later. In 1756, French tutor Jeanne-Marie Leprince de Beaumont publishes her version, a tale she wrote to prepare her young charges (girls ages 5–13) for arranged marriages. She bases her story on the earlier serpent tale, but makes the Beast a humble, gentle mammal.

Wanting her girls to believe love can make any man princely, Beaumont contrasted Beauty's beastly fate with that of her two sisters. The first marries a handsome man who thinks only of himself. The second weds a smart man who belittles his bride. "Many women," this Beauty observes, "are made to marry men far more beastly than mine." The author's own arranged marriage had been annulled when her philandering husband contracted a venereal disease. To encourage girls to read, Beaumont makes Beauty a book lover. Her story becomes the definitive "Beauty and the Beast" fairy tale.

The love of a beauty rescues the soul of a bloodthirsty beast in the first "Beauty and the Beast" movie, a 1947 French film by avant-garde artist Jean Cocteau. Though the adult melodrama's second act is little more than the Beast bellowing "Belle!" its surreal images (living busts and candelabras, a disembodied arm that pours wine) make it an art-house favorite. Its Beauty is no role model. She faints when she first sees the Beast and shudders ecstatically when she sees him again. A remake of the film appears in 1983 as an episode of the Showtime television series "Faerie Tale Theatre." Directed by French auteur Roger Vadim, it stars a blonde Susan Sarandon.

Can a man sleep in a sewer and still hook up with a society gal? That's the premise of the 1987–1990 CBS television series "Beauty and the Beast." Linda Hamilton plays Catherine Chandler, a wealthy New Yorker who wants more out of life. Ron Perlman is Vincent, her beasty boy beneath the streets.

It's no wonder that Disney's 1991 animated version was nominated for a Best Picture Oscar. Packed with life, humor and music, it also has a great message: A girl can be herself, speak her mind and still end up with a prince of a hubby. She ignores villagers who say she's a "most peculiar mademoiselle;" while street tarts swoon for the town hunk she pushes him off. When the Beast yells at her, she yells back.

Disney keeps the meat of Beaumont's tale but cuts the fat, eliminating the sisters and downplaying the dad. And it adds a villain: the handsome Gaston, who grows beastly as the Beast grows human.

On a different note, Disney's production is an homage to Broadway and Hollywood. The song "Belle" gets its bickering villagers and throwaway jokes from "Tradition," the rousing introductory number to 1964's "Fiddler on the Roof." Its "Bonjour! Bonjour!" refrain comes from the "Good Morning! Good Day!" opener to the 1963 stage play "She Loves Me." "Be Our Guest" is a tableware take on Busby Berkeley's "By a Waterfall" sequence in 1933's "Footlight Parade." Candelabrum Lumiere blends dashing Maurice Chevalier from 1958's "Gigi" with Pepé Le Pew, Warner Brothers' Looney Tunes scentimental skunk created in 1945.

## BOOKS

Anderson, Philip Longfellow. "The Gospel in Disney: Christian Values in the Early Animated Classics." Augsburg Books, 2004.

"The Annotated Classic Fairy Tales" edited by Marie Tatar. W.W. Norton & Company Ltd., 2002.

Appelbaum, Stanley. "The New York World's Fair 1939/1940." Dover Publications, 1977.

Bacher, Hans. "Dream Worlds: Production Design for Animation." Focal Press, 2007.

Barrie, J. M. "Peter Pan." Charles Scribner's Sons, 1911, 1985.

Barrier, Michael. "The Animated Man: A Life of Walt Disney." University of California Press, 2008.

Borgenicht, David. "The Classic Tales of Brer Rabbit." Running Press, 1995.

Brode, Douglas. "From Walt to Woodstock: How Disney Created the Counterculture." University of Texas Press, 2004.

Canemaker, John. "The Art and Flair of Mary Blair: An Appreciation." Disney Editions, 2003.

Canemaker, John. "Walt Disney's Nine Old Men and the Art of Animation." Disney Editions, 2001.

Capodagli, Bill. "The Disney Way, Revised Edition." McGraw-Hill, 2006.

Connellan, Tom. "Inside the Magic Kingdom." Bard Press, 1997.

Corey, Melinda and Ochoa, George. "The American Film Institute Desk Reference." Stonesong Press, 2002.

Davis, Stephen. "Walk This Way: The Autobiography of Aerosmith." Harper Paperbacks, 2003.

Dunlop, Beth. "Building a Dream: The Art of Disney Architecture." Harry N. Abrams, 1996.

"E.Encyclopedia Animal." DK, 2005.

Eisner, Michael. "Work in Progress." Random House, 1998.

Finch, Christopher. "The Art of Walt Disney." Harry N. Abrams, 2004.

Finch, Christopher. "Jim Henson: The Works: The Art, the Magic, the Imagination." Random House, 1993.

Finch, Christopher. "Walt Disney's America." Abbeville Press, 1978.

Fjellman, Stephen M. "Vinyl Leaves: Walt Disney World and America." Westview Press, 1992.

Gabler, Neal. "Walt Disney: The Triumph of the American Imagination" Vintage, 2007.

Griswold, Jerry. "The Meanings of 'Beauty and the Beast,' a Handbook." Broadview Press, 2004.

Grover, Ron. "The Disney Touch: Disney, ABC and The Quest for the World's Greatest Media Empire."

McGraw-Hill Trade, 1996.

Harris, Joel Chandler. "The Complete Tales of Uncle Remus." Houghton Mifflin Company, 1955.

Heide, Robert and Gilman, John. "Mickey Mouse: The Evolution, the Legend, the Phenomenon!" Disney Editions, 2001.

Hench, John. "Designing Disney: Imagineering and the Art of the Show." Disney Editions, 2003.

Kinney, Jack. "Walt Disney and Assorted Other Characters." Harmony, 1988.

Koenig, David. "Realityland: True-Life Adventures at Walt Disney World." Bonaventure Press, 2007.

Kurtti, Jeff. "Since the World Began: Walt Disney World's First 25 Years." Hyperion, 1996.

Kurtti, Jeff. "Walt Disney's Legends of Imagineering… Genesis of the Disney Theme Park." Disney Editions, 2008.

Lambert, Pierre. "Mickey Mouse." Hyperion, 1998.

Lane, Jack. "A Gallery of Stars: The Story of the Hollywood Brown Derby Wall of Fame." Luminary Press, 2005.

Lester, Julius. "Tales of Uncle Remus: The Adventures of Brer Rabbit." Puffin, 2006.

Malmberg, Melody. "The Making of Disney's Animal Kingdom Theme Park." Hyperion 1998.

Maltin, Leonard. "The Disney Films." Disney Editions, 1995, 2000.

Maltin, Leonard. "Of Mice and Magic: A History of American Animated Cartoons." Penguin Books, 1987.

Mannheim, Steve. "Walt Disney and the Quest for Community." Ashgate Publishing, 2002.

Marling, Karal Ann. "Designing Disney's Theme Parks: The Architecture of Reassurance." Hyperion, 1997.

Milne, A.A. "Winnie-the-Pooh." Puffin Books, 1926, 1992.

Neary, Kevin and Smith, Dave. "The Ultimate Disney Trivia Book Vols. 1–3." Hyperion, 1992, 1994, 1997.

"Official Guide: New York World's Fair 1964/1965." Time Inc., 1964.

Paik, Karen. "To Infinity and Beyond!: The Story of Pixar Animation Studios." Chronicle Books, 2007.

Philip, Neil. "The Complete Fairy Tales of Charles Perrault." Albion, 1993.

Philip, Neil. "The Illustrated Book of Myths: Tales and Legends of the World." DK, 1995.

Pinsky, Mark I. "The Gospel According to Disney: Faith, Trust, and Pixie Dust." Westminster John Knox Press, 2004.

Price, David A. "The Pixar Touch: The Making of a Company," Knopf, 2008.

Price, Harrison "Buzz." "Walt's Revolution! By the Numbers." Ripley

Entertainment, 2004.

Rafferty, Kevin. "Walt Disney Imagineering." Disney Editions, 1996.

Ridgway, Charles. "Spinning Disney's World: Memories of a Magic Kingdom Press Agent." Intrepid Traveler, 2007.

Samuelson, Dale. "The American Amusement Park." MBI, 2001.

Schickel, Richard. "The Disney Version: The Life, Times, Art and Commerce of Walt Disney." Simon & Schuster, 1968, 1985, 1997.

Schroeder, Russell K. "Disney: The Ultimate Visual Guide." Dorling Kindersley Ltd., 2002.

Schroeder, Russell. "Walt Disney: His Life in Pictures." Disney Press, 1996.

Smith, Dave. "Disney A to Z: The Official Encyclopedia." Hyperion, 1998, 2006.

Smith, Dave. "The Quotable Walt Disney." Disney Editions, 2001.

Smith, Dave and Clark, Steven. "Disney: The First 100 Years." Hyperion, 1999.

Surrell, Jason. "The Disney Mountains: Imagineering At Its Peak." Disney Editions, 2007.

Surrell, Jason. "The Haunted Mansion: From the Magic Kingdom to the Movies." Disney Editions, 2003.

Surrell, Jason. "Pirates of the Caribbean: From the Magic Kingdom to the Movies." Disney Editions, 2005.

Taylor, John. "Storming the Magic Kingdom." Knopf, 1987.

Telotte, J.P. "The Mouse Machine: Disney and Technology." University of Illinois Press, 2008.

Thomas, Bob. "Building a Company: Roy O. Disney and the Creation of an Entertainment Empire." Hyperion, 1998.

Thomas, Bob. "Walt Disney: An American Original." Hyperion, 1994.

Thomas, Frank and Johnston, Ollie. "The Illusion of Life: Disney Animation." Disney Editions, 1995.

Tieman, Robert. "The Disney Keepsakes." Disney Editions, 2005.

Tieman, Robert. "The Disney Treasures." Disney Editions, 2003.

Tieman, Robert. "The Mickey Mouse Treasures." Disney Editions, 2007.

Tieman, Robert. "Quintessential Disney." Disney Editions, 2007.

Twain, Mark. "The Adventures of Tom Sawyer." Fine Creative Media, 2003.

"25 Years of Walt Disney World." Disney's Kingdom Editions, 1996.

"Walt Disney Imagineering: A Behind the Scenes Look at Making the Magic Real." Hyperion, 1996.

Watts, Steven. "The Magic Kingdom: Walt Disney and the American Way of Life." Houghton Mifflin, 1997.

Zipes, Jack. "The Complete Fairy Tales of the Brothers Grimm." Bantam, 1992.

# Walt Disney World telephone directory

## GENERAL

**Bibbidi Bobbidi Boutique** Reservations 939-7895
**Birthday parties** ............................................. 939-2329
**Carriage rides** ............................................... 939-7529
**Childcare** All About Kids ............................. 812-9300
   Kid's Nite Out ............................................. 828-0920
**Convention information** ......................... 828-3200
**Disability special requests** ................ 939-7807
**Disney Institute** ...................................... 566-2620
**Disney live operator** General WDW info 824-2222
**Disney resort reservations** ................ 934-7639

**Tweedledum** takes a call at Magic Kingdom

**Disney Security** ......................................... 560-7959
   Urgent ........................................................... 560-1990
**Disney Vacation Club** .................... 800 800-9100
**Florist** General Disney florist ................... 827-3505
   Convention orders ..................................... 827-1266
   Wedding orders ........................................... 827-1277
**Foreign language assistance** ............ 824-2222
**Hearing Impaired (TTY)** Information ..... 827-5141
   Reservations ................................................ 939-7670
**Kennels** Disney's Animal Kingdom ......... 938-2100
   Disney's Fort Wilderness Resort ............ 824-2735
   Disney's Hollywood Studios ..................... 560-4282
   Epcot ............................................................. 560-6229
   Magic Kingdom .......................................... 824-6568
   After 24 hours ............................................. 824-4245
**Lost and Found** Disney's Animal Kingdom 938-2785
   Disney's Blizzard Beach ............................ 560-5408
   Disney's Hollywood Studios ..................... 560-3720
   Disney's Typhoon Lagoon .......................... 560-6296
   Downtown Disney ....................................... 828-3150
   Epcot ............................................................. 560-6646
   Magic Kingdom .......................................... 824-4521
   After 24 hours ............................................. 824-4245
**Merchandise** ............................................... 363-6200
**Post office** Celebration ............................. 566-1145
   Lake Buena Vista ........................................ 238-0223
**Restaurant** Reservations ........................... 939-3463
   Tables in Wonderland discount card ....... 566-5858
**Special-occasion cakes** Ordering ....... 827-2253
**SunTrust Bank** Downtown Disney ............ 828-6103

**Theme park ticket inquiries** ................ 566-4985
**Tours** ............................................................. 939-8687
   VIP Tours ...................................................... 560-4033
**Weather** ....................................................... 824-4104
**Wedding and honeymoons** ........... 877 566-0969
**Western Union** Goodings Supermarket .... 827-1200

## MEDICAL CARE

**Centra Care** In-Room Care ...................... 238-2000
   Walk-In Clinic ............................................. 239-6463
**Dental emergencies** Celebration Dental 566-2222
**Equipment rentals** Apria Health Care ..... 291-2229
   Care Medical Equipment ........................... 856-2273
   Walker Mobility .......................................... 518-6000
**Florida Hospital** Emergency Dept ............ 303-4034
**Turner Pharmacy** ...................................... 828-8125

## RECREATION

**AMC** Downtown Disney box office ............... 827-1308
   Movie listings ................................. 888 262-4386
**Atlanta Braves** Spring Training tickets ..... 939-4263
**Boat rentals** ............................................... 939-7529
**Cirque du Soleil** Box office ..................... 939-7600
**Disney Cruise Line** ................................. 566-7000
**DisneyQuest** Downtown Disney ................ 828-4600
**ESPN Wide World of Sports** ................. 828-3267
   Live operator ............................................... 939-1500
**Fishing excursions** ................................. 939-2277
**Golf reservations** .................................... 939-4653
**Horseback riding** Fort Wilderness ......... 824-2900
**House of Blues** Box office ....................... 934-2583
**Miniature golf** Fantasia Gardens ............ 560-4753
   Winter Summerland .................................... 560-7161
**Pony rides** Fort Wilderness ...................... 824-2788
**Reservations** General recreation ............. 939-7529
**Richard Petty Driving Exprnc** ....... 800 237-3889
**Spas** Grand Floridian Spa ......................... 824-2332
   Mandara Spa, WDW Dolphin ...................... 934-4772
   Saratoga Springs Spa ................................. 827-4455
**Surfing lessons** Typhoon Lagoon ........... 939-7873
**Tennis** ........................................................... 939-7529
**Water Sports** Sammy Duvall's .................. 939-0754

## TRANSPORTATION

**AAA** Emergency Road Service .............. 800 222-4357
**AAA Car Care Center** ............................. 824-0976
   After hours ................................................... 824-4777
**Alamo/National Rent A Car** .................. 824-3470
**Disney's Magical Express** ............ 866 599-0951
**Hess Express** Magic Kingdom .................. 938-0143
   Epcot Resort Area (Hollywood Studios) ...... 938-0151
   Downtown Disney ....................................... 938-0160
**Mears** Taxi cabs, limousines, etc. .............. 423-5566
**Orlando International Airport** ............. 825-2001
   Paging .......................................................... 825-2000
**Wrecker service** ....................................... 824-0976
**Yellow Cab** .................................................. 699-9999

**Area code 407 unless indicated**